IAIN PROVAN, Ph.D. (1986) in Old Testament, University of Cambridge, is Marshall Sheppard Professor of Biblical Studies at Regent College, Vancouver, British Columbia (Canada). His publications have focused on Old Testament historiography, narrative and theology, with particular attention to the books of Kings, Lamentations and Song of Songs/Ecclesiastes.

MARK J. BODA, Ph.D. (1996) in Old Testament, University of Cambridge, is Professor of Old Testament at McMaster Divinity College and Professor in the Faculty of Theology at McMaster University, Hamilton, Ontario. His publications have focused on the study of the Old Testament with emphasis on the Penitential Prayer and theological traditions, Persian period prophecy and historiography, and Old Testament Theology.

# Let us Go up to Zion

# Supplements

to

# Vetus Testamentum



VOLUME 153

*The titles published in this series are listed at brill.nl/vts*

# Let us Go up to Zion

## Essays in Honour of H. G. M. Williamson on the Occasion of his Sixty-Fifth Birthday

*Edited by*

Iain Provan and Mark J. Boda

BRILL

LEIDEN · BOSTON
2012

This book is printed on acid-free paper.

This publication has been typeset in the multilingual "Brill" typeface. With over 5,100 characters covering Latin, IPA, Greek, and Cyrillic, this typeface is especially suitable for use in the humanities. For more information, please see www.brill.nl/brill-typeface.

ISSN 0083-5889
ISBN 978 90 04 21598 6 (hardback)
ISBN 978 90 04 22658 6 (e-book)



FSC www.fsc.org MIX Paper from responsible sources FSC® C004472

PRINTED BY DRUKKERIJ WILCO B.V. - AMERSFOORT, THE NETHERLANDS

H. G. M. Williamson

CONTENTS

## PART V

## MISCELLANY

# PREFACE

It has been a great honour to work on this volume, cooperating with each other and with colleagues from all over the world to produce what we hope is a worthy tribute to Hugh Williamson as he reaches a milestone birthday. We found early on in the project that many were delighted to join us in this venture. This is testimony to the great respect Hugh has gained throughout the Old Testament guild from his mentors, colleagues, peers, students, and beyond.

The contributors to the volume have of course been crucial to its production, and to each of them we extend our thanks for their involvement in the process, from timely submission to quick revision of essays. There are, however, various other people who have been working behind the scenes, and they must not go unmentioned here. Alex Breitkopf, Iain Provan's teaching assistant at Regent College in the academic year 2010–2011, completed an enormous amount of work editing the essays, chasing down bibliography, and collating lists of abbreviations. He knows a lot more about Unicode font than he used to. Mark Boda's research assistant at McMaster Divinity College, Shannon Baines, spent considerable time poring over the essays with a watchful eye for any and all deviations from the chosen publishing style. In addition, Dustin Boreland and Suk-il Ahn, two Old Testament doctoral students at McMaster Divinity College, volunteered considerable time and energy for the volume. The editors are most grateful to all four editorial assistants for their work, without which this volume would never have reached the publisher with such speed. Their attention to detail and patient endurance in bringing a superb set of essays into line with the designated style is testimony to the readiness of now a third generation of young scholars to take up the baton first passed to the editors by Hugh Williamson.

Finally, we extend our thanks to the editorial board of Supplements to Vetus Testamentum and to Brill Academic Publishers for agreeing to accept the volume into the series. Hugh has been greatly involved in the series over many years, and has read hundreds of submitted manuscripts. It seems fitting that his own Festschrift should now find its home there.

Iain Provan and Mark Boda
June 2011

# THE ACHIEVEMENTS OF HUGH WILLIAMSON

*John A. Emerton*

Classical Hebrew is taught in two Faculties at the Universities of Oxford and Cambridge: the Faculty of Oriental Studies (recently renamed in Cambridge as the Faculty of Asian and Middle Eastern Studies) and the Faculty of Theology (Oxford) or Divinity (Cambridge). Although at Cambridge the Regius Professorship of Hebrew is assigned to the former Faculty, the holder is normally also a member of the Faculty Board of Divinity, and the Ordinances of the University state that the holder's duties include 'the interpretation of the Old Testament.' The natural implication is that some teaching in the Faculty of Divinity is expected in addition to the obligation to teach in the other Faculty.

So it was that, when the time came for me to take up my appointment in Cambridge in 1968, one of my duties in the first year was to lecture on the Hebrew text of Isaiah to candidates for the Theological Tripos Part II in 1969. One of those attending my lectures was a Trinity College undergraduate named Hugh Williamson. He was able and was specially interested in the Old Testament, and it was no surprise when he was placed in the First Class in the final examination. As a graduate, he wished to continue his study of the Old Testament, and he decided to work for the appropriate section of Part III of the Theological Tripos. Part III was an examination to be sat after, preferably, two years of further study in one branch of Theology, and Hugh chose the section devoted to the Old Testament. Much time in this course involved the study of the Hebrew language and many chapters of the Hebrew Bible; there was a stress on the subject-matter of the text as well as its language, and there was an examination paper on the Theology of the Old Testament. Hugh was awarded a graduate studentship at St John's College, and began the course in 1970. His work continued to be very good, and he was accepted by the Faculty of Divinity in 1972 as a research student; and I was appointed his supervisor. The subject that he chose for research was the books of Chronicles.

After his first academic year of research in Cambridge he was permitted to spend his second year at the Hebrew University of Jerusalem. This gave him (and his wife Jay) the opportunity to get to know the country in which most of the events of the Old Testament took place. He also had the chance to acquire fluency in Modern Hebrew, and to learn from the teachers at the Hebrew University and from others working in the Department of Bible. Among those whom he met was Sara Japhet, of whose work he had learned from an article in *Vetus Testamentum* for 1968. She argued against the widely-held view that the books of Chronicles, Ezra and Nehemiah were all parts of the same work. Hugh agreed with her, and he argues the case in the first part of his dissertation, which discusses the composition of Chronicles and its date (at some point within the fourth century). The second part examines the Chronicler's understanding of the nature of the people of Israel. He argues that, in the Chronicler's view, the nation included both returned exiles and inhabitants of the land of Judah in the former southern kingdom and also the descendants of inhabitants of the former northern kingdom who had remained loyal to the God of Israel. The Chronicler's work was thus an attempt to counter the exclusiveness of those who had returned from Babylon by granting some status to those who had never been exiled.

Hugh's dissertation was submitted in May 1975 during his ninth term of research—much earlier than many candidates manage. That fact is evidence of his ability to organise his time efficiently despite other commitments (see below). The examiners' reports were favourable, and Hugh proceeded to take his Ph.D.

The dissertation was then prepared for publication. Hugh decided to remove two sections which were not necessary parts of his argument and which could be published as articles. Thus, for example, an article on the relevant works of the Jewish historian Josephus appeared in *Vetus Testamentum* in 1977. The revised dissertation was accepted by the Cambridge University Press and was published in 1977 as *Israel in the Books of Chronicles.*

It is now necessary for us to move back to the autumn of 1974, shortly before the beginning of Hugh's last academic year as a research student. There was a crisis in the teaching of Hebrew in the Faculty of Oriental Studies. Sebastian Brock, one of the two Lecturers in Hebrew and Aramaic in the Faculty, had just moved to Oxford to a post in Aramaic and Syriac, in which he was specially interested, where he would not be expected to lecture on Hebrew; but a successor had not yet been appointed in Cambridge. Further, John Snaith, who held the other Lectureship in Cambridge, had a serious road accident shortly before the beginning of the Michaelmas Term and was granted sick leave, which was eventually to last for a year. There was thus a major problem in arranging the teaching of two languages. Several people offered help in the emergency. In particular, Brock generously offered to visit Cambridge once a fortnight to lecture on Syriac. My own teaching load became very heavy, and there were limits to what I could manage. The major problem was the teaching of elementary Hebrew. It occurred to me that Hugh Williamson had the necessary knowledge and was the kind of person who seemed likely to be able to teach well. The difficulty was that Hugh needed to finish writing his dissertation; but he was someone capable of organising his time well, and he seemed more likely than most people to be able to undertake the task in the circumstances. He kindly agreed, and proved to be a very good teacher, and was able both to undertake the teaching and to complete his dissertation; and, as I have said, he submitted the dissertation in unusually good time.

The University gave permission for the vacant post in Hebrew and Aramaic to be filled, though not at the full level of University Lecturer but at that of University Assistant Lecturer. However, the Faculty Appointments Committee did not succeed in finding someone suitable for appointment at that level who would be able to teach the subjects in the way we wished, that is, as a good teacher with an interest in the subject matter of the texts studied as well as with the expertise in the languages in which they were written.

As the academic year progressed, it became clear that someone to be taken seriously for appointment was Hugh Williamson. He had shown himself to be a capable teacher, and his dissertation had been completed and was soon shown to be worthy of a Ph.D. He also had a good earlier academic record. He had not had experience in studying Syriac, but he had shown his ability in other linguistic areas. Moreover, I was willing to undertake the teaching of Syriac, and it was hoped that Snaith would recover sufficiently well to resume teaching Syriac. Hugh was encouraged to apply for the post, was interviewed by the Appointments Committee, and was appointed.

At Cambridge, an Assistant Lecturer could hold office for no more than five years, after which either he was appointed to a full Lectureship or he ceased to hold an appointment. Hugh was appointed to a Lectureship well before the end of five years. Clare Hall elected him to a Fellowship in 1985. He served the Faculty well, and also the undergraduates (and, in due course, graduates). He was a good lecturer, teacher and examiner, and he dealt efficiently with any parts of the Faculty administration that came his way. His growing number of publications made a substantial contribution to the Faculty as a place of research.

Of course, I too benefited from having so able and agreeable a colleague. I was the editor of the scholarly quarterly journal *Vetus Testamentum*, and Hugh was very helpful to me in my editorial work: he wrote book reviews, and advised me about articles that had been submitted; and for several volumes he prepared the substantial indexes, which increased their value for scholars. In later years, he was to become a member of the journal's Editorial Board.

Among British biblical scholars, and indeed among scholars from many countries, the Society for Old Testament Study is an important scholarly body for encouragement of the study of this part of the Scriptures. Hugh has long been an active member, and he was honoured by being elected as its President for 2004. He has also been the Chairman of the Anglo-Israel Archaeological Society. He has himself had experience of Biblical Archaeology, for example sharing in the work of Tel Aviv University under David Ussishkin in excavating the site of Lachish, where Hugh helped to excavate the Assyrian siege ramp. When it was decided to close the British School of Archaeology in Jerusalem, he worked with Graham Davies and others in seeking to continue its work and the availability of its valuable library in what is now the Kenyon Institute. Articles on archaeological subjects are among Hugh's numerous publications.

It is, indeed, as the author of many books, articles, and book reviews that Hugh is best known among scholars, and a full list of these is to be found elsewhere in the present volume (pp. xvii–xxviii). Two comments in particular may be made on his published writings. First, they are regularly written clearly, and his arguments are presented lucidly. Second, they cover a wide range of topics. In his earlier years as a scholar, there were many books and articles relevant to the study of the books of Chronicles and related works; and the publication of his dissertation was followed by commentaries on Chronicles and also on the books of Ezra and Nehemiah (although he does not recognise them as the work of the Chronicler). More recently he has written two monographs and a number of articles on the book of Isaiah and he is now in the process of writing the International Critical Commentary volumes on Isaiah 1–27. The first volume, on chs. 1–5, appeared in 2006. In addition he has published many essays and articles on aspects of the text and language of other parts of the Hebrew Bible. He has also played a valuable role as the editor (or one of the editors) of no fewer than eight volumes.

British universities, in addition to the Ph.D. for people near the beginning of their careers, award doctorates at a higher level for well-established scholars in a variety of scholarly areas (such as Law, Letters, and Science). Except when they are conferred as Honorary Degrees, they are obtained by scholars who submit a substantial number of their publications for examination. Hugh thus became a Doctor of Divinity in 1986.

In 1993, the British Academy elected him to a Fellowship and he has since then played an active part in its affairs.

In Cambridge he was promoted from a Lectureship to a Readership in Hebrew and Aramaic in 1989. It can scarcely be doubted that, if he had stayed longer at Cambridge, he would have been promoted to an *ad hominem* Professorship. However, in 1992 he was appointed to the Regius Professorship of Hebrew in Oxford, which was accompanied by a Studentship (not to be understood in its more usual sense, but as corresponding to what would be called a Fellowship in any other College) at Christ Church. I am sorry that Cambridge lost such a distinguished scholar, but I cannot regret that he was appointed to one of the senior chairs at the University at which I myself began my work as a Hebrew scholar.

# ACADEMIC ACCOMPLISHMENTS OF H. G. M. WILLIAMSON

## Posts

Assistant Lecturer in Hebrew and Aramaic (1975–79), Lecturer (1979–89), Reader (1989–92), University of Cambridge
Fellow, Clare Hall (1985–92)
Regius Professor of Hebrew, University of Oxford (1992–present)
Student of Christ Church (1992–present)

## Editorial Boards, Research Project Leadership, Academic Societies and Honours

Member of Editorial Board, *Vetus Testamentum*
Member of Editorial Board, Supplements to Vetus Testamentum
Member of Editorial Board, *Oudtestamentische Studiën*
Secretary, Semantics of Ancient Hebrew Database project (2000–)
Fellow for Biblical Research, Tyndale House, Cambridge (1970)
Member, Tyndale Fellowship for Biblical Research (1970–)
Member (1975–), President (2004), Society for Old Testament Study
Member, Society of Biblical Literature (1985–)
Member, Institute of Biblical Research
Chairman of the Standing Committee for the British School of Archaeology in Jerusalem (1999–2001)
Member, Palestine Exploration Fund
Chairman, Anglo-Israel Archaeological Society (1991–2010)
Biblical Archaeology Society Award (1985)
Corresponding member, Göttingen Academy of Sciences (2008)
Fellow, (1993–), Vice-President (Chairman of the Humanities Group) (2009–11), British Academy

## Authored Books

*Israel in the Books of Chronicles*. Cambridge: Cambridge University Press, 1977.
*1 and 2 Chronicles*. New Century Bible Commentary. Grand Rapids: Eerdmans, 1982.

*Ezra, Nehemiah*. Word Biblical Commentary. Waco, Tex: Word, 1985.

*Ezra and Nehemiah*. Old Testament Guides. Sheffield: JSOT Press, 1987.

*Annotated Key to Lambdin's* Introduction to Biblical Hebrew. Journal for the Study of Old Testament Manuals. Sheffield: JSOT Press, 1989.

*The Book Called Isaiah: Deutero-Isaiah's Role in Composition and Redaction*. Oxford: Clarendon, 1994.

*Variations on a Theme: King, Messiah and Servant in the Book of Isaiah*. Didsbury Lectures. Carlisle, England: Paternoster, 1998.

*Studies in Persian Period History and Historiography*. Forschungen zum Alten Testament 38. Tübingen: Mohr Siebeck, 2004.

*Confirmation or Contradiction? Archaeology and Biblical History*. St. George's Cathedral Lecture 12. Perth: St. George's Cathedral, 2004.

*Commentary on Isaiah 1–5*. Vol. 1 of *A Critical and Exegetical Commentary on Isaiah 1–27*. International Critical Commentary. London: T&T Clark, 2006.

*Holy, Holy, Holy: The Story of a Liturgical Formula*. Julius-Wellhausen-Vorlesung 1. Berlin: de Gruyter, 2008.

## Edited Books

With Richard E. Friedman. *The Future of Biblical Studies: The Hebrew Scriptures*. Society of Biblical Literature Semeia Studies 16. Atlanta: Scholars Press, 1987.

With Donald A. Carson. *It Is Written: Scripture Citing Scripture: Essays in Honour of Barnabas Lindars, SSF*. Cambridge: Cambridge University Press, 1988.

With John Day and Robert P. Gordon *Wisdom in Ancient Israel: Essays in Honour of J. A. Emerton*. Cambridge: Cambridge University Press, 1995.

With Irmtraud Fischer and Konrad Schmid. *Prophetie in Israel: Beiträge des Symposiums "Das Alte Testament und die Kultur der Moderne" Anlässlich des 100. Geburtstags Gerhard Von Rads (1901–1971) Heidelberg, 18.–21. Oktober 2001*. Altes Testament und Moderne 11. Münster: LIT Verlag, 2003.

With J. Cheryl Exum. *Reading from Right to Left: Essays on the Hebrew Bible in Honor of David J. A. Clines*. Journal for the Study of the Old Testament: Supplement Series 373. London: Sheffield Academic Press, 2003.

With Bill T. Arnold. *Dictionary of the Old Testament: Historical Books*. Downers Grove, Ill.: InterVarsity, 2005.

*Understanding the History of Ancient Israel*. Proceedings of the British Academy. Oxford: Oxford University Press for the British Academy, 2007.

With David G. Firth. *Interpreting Isaiah: Issues and Approaches*. Leicester/ Downers Grove, Ill.: IVP Academic; Nottingham: Apollos, 2009.

## Translated Book

Noth, Martin. *The Chronicler's History*. Journal for the Study of the Old Testament: Supplement Series 50. Sheffield: JSOT Press, 1987.

## Journal Articles

"A Note on 1 Chr. vii 12." *Vetus Testamentum* 23 (1973): 376–79.

"The Accession of Solomon in the Books of Chronicles." *Vetus Testamentum* 26 (1976): 351–61.

"Eschatology in Chronicles." *Tyndale Bulletin* 28 (1977): 115–54.

"The Historical Value of Josephus' Jewish Antiquities xi.297–301." *Journal of Theological Studies* ns28 (1977): 49–66.

"The Translation of *IQpHab*. V, 10." *Revue de Qumran* 9 (1977): 263–65.

"*Da'at* in Isaiah liii 11." *Vetus Testamentum* 28 (1978): 118–22.

"'The Sure Mercies of David': Subjective or Objective Genitive?" *Journal of Semitic Studies* 23 (1978): 31–49.

"Sources and Redaction in the Chronicler's Genealogy of Judah." *Journal of Biblical Literature* 98 (1979): 351–59.

"Word Order in Isaiah xliii. 12." *Journal of Theological Studies* ns30 (1979): 499–502.

"The Death of Josiah and the Continuing Development of the Deuteronomic History." *Vetus Testamentum* 32 (1982): 242–48.

"The Composition of Ezra 1–6." *Journal of Theological Studies* ns34 (1983): 1–30.

"A Response to A. G. Auld." *Journal for the Study of the Old Testament* 27 (1983): 33–39.

"Nehemiah's Walls Revisited." *Palestine Exploration Quarterly* 116 (1984): 81–88.

"The Old Testament and the Material World." *Evangelical Quarterly* 57 (1985): 5–22.

"A Reconsideration of *'zb* II in Biblical Hebrew." *Zeitschrift für die alttestamentliche Wissenschaft* 97 (1985): 74–85.

"Isaiah 40,20—A Case of Not Seeing the Wood for the Trees." *Biblica* 67 (1986): 1–20.
"Reliving the Death of Josiah: A Reply to C. T. Begg." *Vetus Testamentum* 37 (1987): 9–15.
"Clutching at Catchlines." *Bible Review* 3 (1987): 56–9.
"The Governors of Judah under the Persians." *Tyndale Bulletin* 39 (1988): 59–82.
"Laments at the Destroyed Temple: Excavating the Biblical Text Reveals Ancient Jewish Prayers." *Bible Review* 6 (1990): 12–17.
"Isaiah 63,7–64,11: Exilic Lament or Post-Exilic Protest?" *Zeitschrift für die alttestamentliche Wissenschaft* 102 (1990): 48–58.
"'Eben Gĕlāl (Ezra 5:8, 6:4) Again." *Bulletin of the American Schools of Oriental Research* 280 (1990): 83–88.
"Ezra and Nehemiah in the Light of the Texts from Persepolis." *Bulletin for Biblical Research* 1 (1991): 41–61.
"Jezreel in the Biblical Texts." *Tel Aviv* 18 (1991): 72–92.
With Kenneth D. Tollefson. "Nehemiah as Cultural Revitalization: An Anthropological Perspective." *Journal for the Study of the Old Testament* 56 (1992): 41–68.
"Ancient Hebrew in a Modern University." *Journal of Jewish Studies* 44 (1993): 167–75.
"Sound, Sense and Language in Isaiah 24–27." *Journal of Jewish Studies* 46 (1995): 1–9.
"Tel Jezreel: The Rediscovery of a Biblical City." *Bulletin of the Anglo-Israel Archaeological Society* 15 (1996): 106–08.
"Tel Jezreel and the Dynasty of Omri." *Palestine Exploration Quarterly* 128 (1996): 41–51.
"Marginalia in Micah." *Vetus Testamentum* 47 (1997): 360–72.
"The Role of Biblical Studies in the Church Today: From the View of Academics." *Jian Dao* (1997): 235–41.
"Promises, Promises! Some Exegetical Reflections on Isaiah 58." *Word & World* 19 (1999): 153–60.
"Isaiah 62:4 and the Problem of Inner-Biblical Allusions." *Journal of Biblical Literature* 119 (2000): 734–39.
"Isaiah 8:21 and a New Inscription from Ekron." *Bulletin of the Anglo-Israel Archaeological Society* 18 (2000): 51–55.
"Hope under Judgement: The Prophets of the Eighth Century BCE." *Evangelical Quarterly* 72 (2000): 291–306.
"Mirror Images." *Expository Times* 117 (2005): 19–21.
"The History of Israel—Or: Twos into One Won't Go." *Expository Times* 119 (2007): 22–26.

"Comments on Oded Lipschits, the Fall and Rise of Jerusalem." Pp. 34–39 in "In Conversation with Oded Lipschits, *The Fall and Rise of Jerusalem*," edited by David Vanderhooft. *Journal of Hebrew Scriptures* 7 (2007): article 2.

"William McKane 1921–2004." *Proceedings of the British Academy* 150 (2007): 127–46.

"The Aramaic Documents in Ezra Revisited." *Journal of Theological Studies* 59 (2008): 41–62.

"Do We Need a New Bible? Reflections on the Proposed Oxford Hebrew Bible." *Biblica* 90 (2009): 153–75.

"When did the History of Israel Begin?" *Report of the Oxford Centre for Hebrew and Jewish Studies* (2009–10): 59–66.

## Articles in Volumes

"The Origins of the Twenty-Four Priestly Courses: A Study of 1 Chronicles 23–27." Pp. 251–68 in *Studies in the Historical Books of the Old Testament*, 251–68. Edited by John A. Emerton. Supplements to Vetus Testamentum 30. Leiden: Brill, 1979.

""We Are Yours, O David": The Setting and Purpose of 1 Chronicles 12:1–23." Pp. 164–76 in *Remembering All the Way: A Collection of Old Testament Studies*. Edited by Adam S. van der Woude. Oudtestamentische Studiën 21. Leiden: Brill, 1981.

"The Dynastic Oracle in the Book of Chronicles." Pp. 305–18 in *Isaac Leo Seeligman Volume: Essays on the Bible and Ancient World*. Edited by Alexander Rofé and Yair Zakovitch. Jerusalem: Rubinstein, 1983.

"Introduction." Pp. 11–26 in *The Chronicler's History*. Martin Noth. Translator H. G. M. Williamson. Journal for the Study of the Old Testament: Supplement Series 50. Sheffield: JSOT Press, 1987.

"Post-Exilic Historiography." Pp. 189–207 in *The Future of Biblical Studies: The Hebrew Scriptures*. Edited by Richard E. Friedman and H. G. M. Williamson. Society of Biblical Literature Semeia Studies 16. Atlanta: Scholars Press, 1987.

"Structure and Historiography in Nehemiah 9." Pp. 117–31 in *Proceedings of the Ninth World Congress of Jewish Studies (Panel Sessions: Bible Studies and Ancient Near East, Jerusalem 1988)*. Edited by M. Goshen-Gottstein. Jerusalem: Magnes Press, 1988.

"History." Pp. 25–38 in *It Is Written: Scripture Citing Scripture: Essays in Honour of Barnabas Lindars, SSF*. Edited by Donald A. Carson and H. G. M. Williamson. Cambridge: Cambridge University Press, 1988.

"The Concept of Israel in Transition." Pp. 141–61 in *The World of Ancient Israel: Sociological, Anthropological, and Political Perspectives: Essays by Members of the Society for Old Testament Study*. Edited by Ronald E. Clements. Cambridge: Cambridge University Press, 1989.

"The Prophet and the Plumb-Line: A Redaction-Critical Study of Amos vii." Pp. 101–21 in *In Quest of the Past: Studies in Israelite Religion, Literature and Prophetism. Papers read at the Joint British-Dutch Old Testament Conference, held at Elspeet, 1988*. Edited by Adam S. Van der Woude. Oudtestamentische studiën 26. Leiden: E. J. Brill, 1990. Repr. As "The Prophet and the Plumb-Line: A Redaction–Critical Study of Amos 7." Pp. 453–77 in *'The Place Is Too Small for Us': The Israelite Prophets in Recent Scholarship*. Sources for Biblical and Theological Study 5. Winona Lake, Ind: Eisenbrauns, 1995.

"The Temple in the Books of Chronicles." Pp. 15–31 in *Templum Amicitiae: Essays on the Second Temple Presented to Ernst Bammel*. Edited by William Horbury. Journal for the Study of the New Testament: Supplement Series 48. Sheffield: JSOT Press, 1991.

"What Shall I Cry?" Pp. 70–78 in *Best Sermons*. Volume 5. Edited by James W. Cox. San Francisco: Harper Collins, 1992.

"Isaiah 1.11 and the Septuagint of Isaiah." Pp. 401–12 in *Understanding Poets and Prophets: Essays in Honour of George Wishart Anderson*. Edited by A. Graeme Auld. Journal for the Study of the Old Testament: Supplement Series 152. Sheffield: JSOT Press, 1993.

"First and Last in Isaiah." Pp. 95–108 in *Of Prophets' Visions and the Wisdom of Sages: Essays in Honour of R. Norman Whybray on his 70th Birthday*. Edited by David J. A. Clines and Heather A. McKay. Journal for the Study of the Old Testament: Supplement Series 162. Sheffield: JSOT Press, 1993.

"The Role of Biblical and Theological Research in the Church Today: A View from the Academy." Pp. 189–97 in *Pathway into the Holy Scripture*. Edited by Philip E. Satterthwaite and David F. Wright. Grand Rapids: Eerdmans, 1994.

"Synchronic and Diachronic in Isaian Perspective." Pp. 211–26 in *Synchronic or Diachronic: A Debate on Method in Old Testament Exegesis. Papers Read at the Ninth Joint Meeting of the Oudtestamentisch Werkgezelschap in Nederland en België and the Society for Old Testament Study*. Edited by Johannes C. de Moor. Oudtestamentische Studiën 34. Leiden: E. J. Brill, 1995.

"Isaiah xi 11–16 and the Redaction of Isaiah i–xiii." Pp. 343–57 in *Congress Volume: Paris 1992*. Edited by John A. Emerton. Supplements to Vetus Testamentum 61. Leiden: E. J. Brill, 1995.

"Isaiah and the Wise." Pp. 133–41 in *Wisdom in Ancient Israel: Essays in Honour of J. A. Emerton.* Edited by John Day, Robert P. Gordon, and H. G. M. Williamson. Cambridge: Cambridge University Press, 1995.

"Hezekiah and the Temple." Pp. 47–52 in *Texts, Temples and Traditions: A Tribute to Menahem Haran.* Edited by Michael V. Fox, Victor Hurowitz, and Avi Hurvitz. Winona Lake, Ind: Eisenbrauns, 1996.

"The Problem with 1 Esdras." Pp. 201–16 in *After the Exile: Essays in Honour of Rex Mason.* Edited by John Barton and David J. Reimer. Macon: Mercer University, 1996.

"Relocating Isaiah 1:2–9." Pp. 263–77 in *Writing and Reading the Scroll of Isaiah: Studies of an Interpretive Tradition.* Volume 1. Edited by Craig C. Broyles and Craig A. Evans. Supplements to Vetus Testamentum 70/1. Formation and Interpretation of Old Testament Literature 1/1. Leiden: E. J. Brill, 1997.

"Isaiah 6,13 and 1,29–31." Pp. 119–28 in *Studies in the Book of Isaiah: Festschrift Willem A. M. Beuken.* Edited by Jacques T. A. G. M. van Ruiten and Marc Vervenne. Bibliotheca Ephemeridum Theologicarum Lovaniensium 132. Louvain: Leuven University Press, 1997.

"The Origins of Israel: Can We Safely Ignore the Bible?" Pp. 141–51 in *Origin of Early Israel—Current Debate: Biblical, Historical and Archaeological Perspectives: Irene Levi-Sala Seminar, 1997.* Edited by Shmuel Ahituv and Eliezer D. Oren. Beer-Sheva: Studies by the Department of Bible and Ancient Near East 12. Beer-Sheva: Ben-Gurion University of the Negev Press, 1998.

"The Messianic Texts in Isaiah 1–39." Pp. 238–70 in *King and Messiah in Israel and the Ancient Near East: Proceedings of the Oxford Old Testament Seminar.* Edited by John Day. Journal for the Study of the Old Testament: Supplement Series 270. Sheffield: Sheffield Academic Press, 1998.

"From Scholar to Student: Supervising Old Testament Phd Students." Pp. 122–30 in *Make the Old Testament Live: From Curriculum to Classroom.* Edited by Richard S. Hess and Gordon J. Wenham. Grand Rapids: Eerdmans, 1998.

"Judah and the Jews." Pp. 145–63 in *Studies in Persian History: Essays in Memory of David M. Lewis.* Edited by Maria Brosius and Amelie Kuhrt. Achaemenid History 11. Leiden: Nederlands Instituut Voor Het Nabije Oosten, 1998.

"The Belief System of the Book of Nehemiah." Pp. 276–87 in The Crisis of Israelite Religion: Transformation of Religious Tradition in Exilic and Post-Exilic Times. Edited by Bob Becking and Marjo C. A. Korpel. Oudtestamentische Studiën 42. Leiden: E. J. Brill, 1999.

"Gnats, Glosses and Eternity: Isaiah 51:6 Reconsidered." Pp. 101–11 in *New Heaven and New Earth—Prophecy and the Millennium: Essays in Honour of Anthony Gelston*. Edited by Peter J. Harland and Robert Hayward. Supplements to Vetus Testamentum 77. Leiden: E. J. Brill, 1999.

"'From One Degree of Glory to Another'": Themes and Theology in Isaiah." Pp. 174–95 in *In Search of True Wisdom: Essays in Old Testament Interpretation in Honour of Ronald E. Clements*. Edited by Edward Ball. Journal for the Study of the Old Testament: Supplement Series 300. Sheffield: Sheffield Academic Press, 1999.

"Exile and After: Historical Study." Pp. 236–65 in *The Face of Old Testament Studies. A Survey of Contemporary Approaches*. Edited by David W. Baker and Bill T. Arnold. Grand Rapids, Mich: Baker Books, 1999.

"Isaiah and the Holy One of Israel." Pp. 22–38 in *Biblical Hebrews, Biblical Texts: Essays in Memory of Michael P. Weitzman*. Edited by A. Rapoport-Albert and G. Greenberg. Journal for the Study of the Old Testament Supplement Series 333. Sheffield: Sheffield Academic Press, 2001.

"Biblical Criticism and Hermeneutics in Isaiah 1:10–17." Pp. 82–96 in *Vergegenwärtigung des Alten Testaments: Beiträge zur biblischen Hermeneutik. Festschrift für Rudolf Smend zum 70. Geburtstag*. Edited by Christoph Bultmann, Walter Dietrich and Christoph Levin. Göttingen: Vandenhoeck & Ruprecht, 2002.

"Reading the Lament Psalms Backwards." Pp. 3–15 in *A God So Near: Essays on Old Testament Theology in Honor of Patrick D. Miller*. Edited by Brent A. Strawn and Nancy R. Bowen. Winona Lake, Ind: Eisenbrauns, 2003.

"The Family in Persian Period Judah: Some Textual Reflections." Pp. 469–85 in *Symbiosis, Symbolism, and the Power of the Past: Canaan, Ancient Israel, and Their Neighbors from the Late Bronze Age through Roman Palaestina*. Edited by William G. Dever and Seymour Gitin. Winona Lake, IN: Eisenbrauns, 2003.

"Isaiah 1 and the Covenant Lawsuit." Pp. 393–406 in *Covenant as Context: Essays in Honour of E. W. Nicholson*. Edited by A. D. H. Mayes and Robert B. Salters. Oxford: Oxford University Press, 2003.

"Judgment and Hope in Isaiah 1.21–26." Pp. 423–34 In *Reading from Right to Left: Essays on the Hebrew Bible in Honor of David J. A. Clines*. Edited by J. Cheryl Exum and H. G. M. Williamson. Journal for the Study of the Old Testament: Supplement Series 373. London: Sheffield Academic Press, 2003.

"In Search of the Pre-Exilic Isaiah." Pp. 181–206 in *In Search of Pre-Exilic Israel: Proceedings of the Oxford Old Testament Seminar*. Edited by John Day. Journal for the Study of the Old Testament: Supplement Series 406. London: T&T Clark International, 2004.

"The Formation of Isaiah 2.6–22." Pp. 57–67 in *Biblical and Near Eastern Essays: Studies in Honour of Kevin J. Cathcart.* Edited by Carmel McCarthy and John F. Healey. Journal for the Study of the Old Testament: Supplement Series 375. London: T&T Clark International, 2004.
"Temple and Worship in Isaiah 6." Pp. 123–44 in *Temple and Worship in Biblical Israel: Proceedings of the Oxford Old Testament Seminar.* Edited by John Day. Library of Hebrew Bible/Old Testament Studies 422. London: T&T Clark International, 2005.
"Isaiah, Micah and Qumran." Pp. 203–11 in *Semitic Studies in Honour of Edward Ullendorff.* Edited by Geoffrey Khan. Studies in Semitic Languages and Linguistics 47. Leiden: E. J. Brill, 2005.
"A Productive Textual Error in Isaiah 2:18–19." Pp. 377–88 in *Essays on Ancient Israel in Its Near Eastern Context: A Tribute to Nadav Na'aman.* Edited by Yairah Amit, Ehud Ben Zvi, Israel Finkelstein, and Oded Lipschits. Winona Lake, Ind: Eisenbrauns, 2006.
"Once Upon a Time…?" Pp. 517–28 in *Reflection and Refraction: Studies in Biblical Historiography in Honour of A. Graeme Auld.* Edited by Robert Rezetko, Timothy H. Lim and W. Brian Aucker. Supplements to Vetus Testamentum 113. Leiden: Brill, 2006.
"On Getting Carried Away with the Infinitive Construct of נשא." Pp. 357*–367* in *Shai Le-Sarah Japhet: Studies in the Bible, Its Exegesis and Its Languages.* Edited by Mosheh Bar-Asher, Dalit Rom-Shiloni, Emanuel Tov, and Nili Waazana. Jerusalem: Bialik Institute, 2007.
"The Fortified City of Isaiah 25,2 and 27,10." Pp. 419–26 in *"Sieben Augen auf einem Stein" (Sach 3,9): Studien zur Literatur des Zweiten Tempels: Festschrift für Ina Willi-Plein zum 65. Geburtstag.* Edited by Friedhelm Hartenstein and Michael Pietsch. Neukirchen-Vluyn: Neukirchener Verlag, 2007.
"The Torah and History in Presentations of Restoration in Ezra-Nehemiah." Pp. 156–70 in *Reading the Law: Studies in Honour of Gordon J. Wenham.* Edited by J. Gordon McConville and Karl Möller. Library of Hebrew Bible/Old Testament Studies 461. London: T&T Clark International, 2007.
"Swords into Plowshares: The Development and Implementation of a Vision." Pp. 139–49 in *Isaiah's Vision of Peace in Biblical and Modern International Relations: Swords into Plowshares.* Edited by Raymond Cohen and Raymond Westbrook. Culture and Religion in International Relations. New York: Palgrave Macmillan, 2008.
"More Unity Than Diversity: Redaction, Rhetoric, and Reader." Pp. 331–45 in *Unity and Disunity in Ezra-Nehemiah.* Edited by Mark J. Boda and Paul Redditt. Sheffield: Sheffield Phoenix, 2008.

"Place-Names as Superlatives in Classical Hebrew." Pp. 73–79 in *Sacred History, Sacred Literature: Essays on Ancient Israel, the Bible, and Religion in Honor of R. E. Friedman on his Sixtieth Birthday.* Edited by Shawna Dolansky. Winona Lake, Ind.: Eisenbrauns, 2008.

"How did the Deuteronomists Envisage the Past?" Pp. 133–52 in *The Past in the Past: Concepts of Past Reality in Ancient Near Eastern and Early Greek Thought.* Edited by Hans M. Barstad and Pierre Briant. The Institute for Comparative Research in Human Culture, Oslo, Serie B: Skrifter 130. Oslo: Novus Press, 2009.

"Recent Issues in the Study of Isaiah." Pp. 21–39 in *Interpreting Isaiah: Issues and Approaches.* Edited by David G. Firth and H. G. M. Williamson. Leicester: Apollos; Downers Grove, Ill.: IVP Academic, 2009.

"Poetic Vision in Isaiah 7:18–25." Pp. 77–89 in *The Desert Will Bloom: Poetic Visions in Isaiah.* Edited by A. Joseph Everson and Hyun Chul Paul Kim. SBL Ancient Israel and Its Literature 4. Atlanta: SBL, 2009.

"Isaiah 30:1." Pp. 185–96 in *Isaiah in Context: Studies in Honour of Arie van der Kooij on the Occasion of His Sixty-fifth Birthday.* Edited by Michaël N. van der Meer, Percy S. F. van Keulen, Wido van Peursen, and R. Bas ter Haar Romeny. Supplements to Vetus Testamentum 138. Leiden: E. J. Brill, 2010.

"Prophetesses in the Hebrew Bible." Pp. 65–80 in *Prophecy and the Prophets in Ancient Israel: Proceedings of the Oxford Old Testament Seminar.* Edited by John Day. Library of Hebrew Bible/Old Testament Studies 531. London: T&T Clark International, 2010.

"Preaching from Isaiah." Pp. 141–56 in *'He Began with Moses . . .' Preaching the Old Testament Today.* Edited by Grenville J. R. Kent, Paul J. Kissling, and Laurence A. Turner. Nottingham: InterVarsity Press, 2010.

"Reflections on Redaction." Pp. 79–91 in *The Centre and Periphery: A European Tribure to Walter Brueggemann.* Edited by J. Middlemas, D. J. A. Clines and E. K. Holt. Hebrew Bible Monographs 27. Sheffield: Sheffield Phoenix Press, 2010.

"Welcome Home." Pp. 113–23 in *The Historian and the Bible: Essays in Honour of Lester L. Grabbe.* Edited by P. R. Davies and D. V. Edelman. Library of Hebrew Bible/Old Testameht Studies 530. London: T&T Clark, 2010.

"1 Esdras as Rewritten Bible?" Pp. 237–49 in *Was 1 Esdras First? An Investigation into the Priority and Nature of 1 Esdras.* Edited by L. S. Fried. Society of Biblical Literature Ancient Israel and its Literature 7. Atlanta: Society of Biblical Literature, 2011.

"Judah as Israel in Eighth-Century Prophecy." Pp. 81–95 in *A God of Faithfulness: Essays in Honour of J. Gordon McConville on his 60th Birthday.* Edited by Jamie A. Grant, Alison Lo and Gordon J. Wenham. Library of Hebrew Bible/Old Testament Studies 538. London: T&T Clark International, 2011.

"The Practicalities of Prophetic Writing in Isaiah 8:1." Pp. 357–69 in *On Stone and Scroll: Essays in Honour of Graham Ivor Davies.* Edited by Brian A. Mastin, Katharine J. Dell, and James K. Aitken. Beihefte zur Zeitschrift für die altestamentliche Wissenschaft 420. Berlin: de Gruyter, 2011.

"The Waters of Shiloah (Isaiah 8:5–8)." Pp. 331–43 in The Fire Signals of Lachish: Studies in the Archaeology and History of Israel in the Late Bronze Age, Iron Age, and Persian Period in Honor of David Ussishkin. Edited by Israel Finkelstein and Nadav Na'aman. Winona Lake, Ind.: Eisenbrauns, 2011.

"Isaiah—Prophet of Weal or Woe?" Forthcoming in *"Thus Speaks Ishtar of Arbela": Prophecy in Israel, Assyria and Egypt in the Neo-Assyrian Period.* Edited by Robert P. Gordon and Hans M. Barstad. Winona Lake, Ind.: Eisenbrauns.

"An Overlooked Suggestion at Proverbs 1.10." Forthcoming in *Leshon Limmudim: Essays on the Language and Literature of the Hebrew Bible in Honour of A. A. Macintosh.* Edited by David A. Baer and Robert P. Gordon. London: Continuum.

## Dictionary Articles

"Ahaziah," "Amaziah," and "Samaritans." Pp. 1:25–26, 1:39–40, 3:1378–81 in *The Illustrated Bible Dictionary.* Edited by James D. Douglas. Leicester: IVPress, 1980.

"Joel" and "Zerubbabel." Pp. 2:1076–80 and 4:1193–4 in *The International Standard Bible Encyclopedia.* Edited by Geoffrey W. Bromiley. Grand Rapids: Eerdmans, 1988.

"Samaritans." Pp. 724–8 in *Dictionary of Jesus and the Gospels.* Edited by Joel B. Green, Scot McKnight and I. Howard Marshall. Downers Grove/Leicester: IVPress, 1992.

"Palestine, Persian Administration of" and "Sanballat." Pp. 81–86 and 973–5 in *Anchor Bible Dictionary.* Volume 5.

"Ezra and Nehemiah." Pp. 420–41 in *New Bible Commentary: 21st Century Edition.* Edited by Don A. Carson *et al.* Leicester: IVPress, 1994.

"Chronicles, 1, 2: Theology of," "Nehemiah: Theology of," "Persia." Pp. 466–74, 977–82, 1046–48 in *The New International Dictionary of Old Testament Theology and Exegesis.* Volume 4. Edited by Willem A. Van Gemeren. Carlisle: Paternoster; Grand Rapids: Zondervan, 1996.

"Ezra and Nehemiah, Books of" and "Welch, Adam Cleghorn (1864–1943)." Pp. 1:375–82 and 2:629 in *Dictionary of Biblical Interpretation.* Edited by John H. Hayes. Nashville: Abingdon, 1999.

"Micah." Pp. 595–99 in *The Oxford Bible Commentary.* Edited by John Barton and John Muddiman. Oxford: Oxford University Press, 2001.

"1 Esdras." Pp. 851–58 in *Eerdmans Commentary on the Bible.* Edited by James D. G. Dunn and John W. Rogerson. Grand Rapids: Eerdmans, 2003.

"Jezreel," "Lachish," "Non-Israelite Written Sources: Egyptian Aramaic Papyri," and "Non-Israelite Written Sources: Old Persian and Elamite." Pp. 556–9, 635–8, 735–9, 739–43 in *A Dictionary of the Old Testament: Historical Books.* Edited by Bill T. Arnold and H. G. M. Williamson. Downers Grove: IVPress, 2005.

"Anglo-Israel Archaeological Society." Pp. 161–62 in *Encyclopaedia Judaica.* Volume 2. Edited by Michael Berenbaum and Fred Skolnik. 2nd edition. Detroit: Macmillan Reference, 2007.

"Isaiah, Book of." Forthcoming in *A Dictionary of the Old Testament: Prophetic Books.* Edited by Mark J. Boda and J. Gordon McConville. Downers Grove: IVPress, forthcoming.

* Not included in this list are Hugh's many book reviews and short notices (numbering over 450) in *Journal of Theological Studies, Interpretation, Vetus Testamentum, Journal of Egyptian Archaeology, Bibliotheca Orientalis, Evangelical Quarterly, The International Journal of Nautical Archaeology and Underwater Exploration, Trinity Journal, Biblical Archaeologist, Journal of Semitic Studies, Biblical Interpretation, Catholic Herald, Harvester, Society of Old Testament Studies Booklist, Theological Students Fellowship Bulletin, The Christian Graduate, Themelios, Epworth Review, Bulletin of the School of Oriental and African Studies, Church Times, Journal of Jewish Studies, Edebiyât, Journal of Biblical Literature, Journal for the Study of the New Testament, Ashland Theological Review, Palestine Exploration Quarterly, Expository Times, Theologische Literaturzeitung, Review of Biblical Literature.* Also not included are his more popular materials.

## LIST OF CONTRIBUTORS

Bill T. Arnold is Paul S. Amos Professor of Old Testament Interpretation, Asbury Theological Seminary.

Hans M. Barstad is Professor of Hebrew Bible and Old Testament Studies, School of Divinity, The University of Edinburgh.

John Barton is Oriel & Laing Professor of the Interpretation of Holy Scripture, University of Oxford.

Mark J. Boda is Professor of Old Testament, McMaster Divinity College and Professor in the Faculty of Theology, McMaster University.

Kevin J. Cathcart is Emeritus Professor of Near Eastern Languages, University College Dublin and Fellow of Campion Hall, Oxford.

David J. A. Clines is Emeritus Professor of Biblical Studies, University of Sheffield.

Graham Davies, Fellow of Fitzwilliam College, was formerly Professor of Old Testament Studies, University of Cambridge.

John Day is Professor of Old Testament Studies, the University of Oxford, and Fellow and Tutor of Lady Margaret Hall, Oxford.

Iain Duguid is Professor of Old Testament and Hebrew, Grove City College.

John Emerton is Emeritus Regius Professor of Hebrew, University of Cambridge, Fellow of St. John's College, Cambridge, and Honorary Canon of St. George's Cathedral, Jerusalem.

Richard Elliott Friedman is Ann & Jay Davis Professor of Jewish Studies, University of Georgia, and Katzin Professor of Jewish Civilization Emeritus, University of California, San Diego.

Susan Gillingham is Reader in Old Testament, University of Oxford, and Fellow and Tutor in Theology at Worcester College, Oxford.

Robert P. Gordon is Regius Professor of Hebrew, University of Cambridge, and Fellow of St. Catharine's College, Cambridge.

Judith M. Hadley is Associate Professor of Hebrew Bible and Archaeology, Villanova University.

Anselm C. Hagedorn is Privatdozent in Hebrew Bible/Old Testament at the Humboldt-Universität zu Berlin.

Elizabeth Hayes is Affiliate Professor of Old Testament, Fuller Seminary Northwest, Seattle.

Sara Japhet is Yehezkel Kaufmann Professor Emerita of Bible at the Hebrew University of Jerusalem.

John Jarick is Departmental Lecturer in Old Testament Studies, University of Oxford, and Tutor in Old Testament, Regent's Park College, Oxford.

Gary N. Knoppers is Edwin Erle Sparks Professor of Classics and Ancient Mediterranean Studies, Religious Studies, and Jewish Studies, Pennsylvania State University.

Arie van der Kooij is Professor Emeritus of Old Testament Studies, Leiden University.

Reinhard G. Kratz is Professor of Old Testament, University of Göttingen.

André Lemaire is Directeur d'études émérite, Philologie et épigraphie hébraïques et araméennes, École Pratique des Hautes Études (Sorbonne, Paris).

A. A. Macintosh is a Fellow, Emeritus Dean and sometimes President of St. John's College, University of Cambridge.

J. G. McConville is Professor of Old Testament Theology, University of Gloucestershire.

Jill Middlemas is Research Associate, Department of Old Testament, Theology Faculty, University of Zurich.

Alan Millard is Emeritus Rankin Professor of Hebrew & Ancient Semitic Languages, The University of Liverpool.

Patrick D. Miller is Charles T. Haley Professor of Old Testament Theology Emeritus, Princeton Theological Seminary.

Nadav Na'aman is Professor of Biblical History, Department of Jewish History, Tel Aviv University.

Iain Provan is Marshall Sheppard Professor of Biblical Studies, Regent College.

David J. Reimer is Senior Lecturer, Biblical Studies, The University of Edinburgh.

Wolter Rose is Senior Lecturer of Semitic Languages and History and Culture of the ancient Near East at Kampen Theological University

Alison G. Salvesen is Polonsky Fellow in Jewish Bible Versions, Oxford Centre for Hebrew and Jewish Studies.

Kevin L. Spawn is Associate Professor of Old Testament, Regent University School of Divinity.

Lena-Sofia Tiemeyer is Senior Lecturer in Hebrew Bible, University of Aberdeen.

Thomas Willi is Professor Emeritus, Theologische Fakultät der Ernst-Moritz-Arndt-Universität Greifswald.

## ABBREVIATIONS

| | |
|---|---|
| AB | Anchor Bible |
| *ABD* | *Anchor Bible Dictionary*. Edited by D. N. Freedman. 6 vols. New York, 1992 |
| *ABL* | *Assyrian and Babylonian Letters Belonging to the Kouyunjik Collections of the British Museum*. Edited by R. F. Harper. 14 vols. Chicago, 1892–1914 |
| ABRL | Anchor Bible Reference Library |
| *ADAJ* | *Annual of the Department of Antiquities of Jordan* |
| *AfO* | *Archiv für Orientforschung* |
| *AHw* | *Akkadisches Handwörterbuch*. W. von Soden. 3 vols. Wiesbaden, 1965–1981 |
| *AJA* | *American Journal of Archaeology* |
| ALASP | Abhandlungen zur Literatur Alt-Syrien-Palästinas und Mesopotamiens |
| AnBib | Analecta biblica |
| *ANET* | *Ancient Near Eastern Texts Relating to the Old Testament*. Edited by J. B. Pritchard. 3rd ed. Princeton, 1969 |
| AOAT | Alter Orient und Altes Testament |
| AOTC | Apollos Old Testament Commentary |
| Aq. | Aquila |
| ArBib | The Aramaic Bible |
| ATA | Alttestamentliche Abhandlungen |
| ATANT | Abhandlungen zur Theologie des Alten und Neuen Testaments |
| ATD | Das Alte Testament Deutsch |
| ATDan | Acta theological danica |
| AV | Authorized Version |
| *BA* | *Biblical Archaeologist* |
| *BAR* | *Biblical Archaeology Review* |
| *BASOR* | *Bulletin of the American Schools of Oriental Research* |
| BDB | *A Hebrew and English Lexicon of the Old Testament*. F. Brown, S. R. Driver, and C. A. Briggs. Oxford, 1907 |
| BEATAJ | Beiträge zur Erforschung des Alten Testaments und des antiken Judentum |
| *BeO* | *Bibbia e oriente* |
| BETL | Bibliotheca ephemeridum theologicarum lovaniensium |

| | |
|---|---|
| BEvT | Beiträge zur evangelischen Theologie |
| *BHQ* | *Biblia Hebraica Quinta* |
| *BHS* | *Biblia Hebraica Stuttgartensia*. Edited by K. Elliger and W. Rudolph. Stuttgart, 1983 |
| BHT | Beiträge zur historischen Theologie |
| *Bib* | *Biblica* |
| BibOr | Biblica et orientalia |
| *BIOSCS* | *Bulletin of the International Organization for Septuagint and Cognate Studies* |
| *BJRL* | *Bulletin of the John Rylands University Library of Manchester* |
| *BK* | *Bibel und Kirche* |
| BKAT | Biblischer Kommentar, Altes Testament. Edited by M. Noth and H. W. Wolff |
| *BN* | *Biblische Notizen* |
| BOT | Boeken van het Oude Testament |
| BSHT | Breslauer Studien zur historischen Theologie |
| BThSt | Biblisch-Theologische Studien |
| BWANT | Beiträge zur Wissenschaft vom Alten und Neuen Testament |
| *BZ* | *Biblische Zeitschrift* |
| BZAW | Beihefte zur Zeitschrift für die alttestamentliche Wissenschaft |
| *CAD* | *The Assyrian Dictionary of the Oriental Institute of the University of Chicago*. Chicago, 1956– |
| CAH | Cambridge Ancient History |
| CBET | Contributions to Biblical Exegesis and Theology |
| *CBQ* | *Catholic Biblical Quarterly* |
| CBQMS | Catholic Biblical Quarterly Monograph Series |
| CC | Continental Commentaries |
| CCSL | Corpus Christianorum: Series latina. Turnhout, 1953– |
| ConBOT | Coniectanea biblica: Old Testament Series |
| *COS* | *The Context of Scripture*. Edited by W. W. Hallo. 3 vols. Leiden: 1997– |
| CSA | Copenhagen Studies in Assyriology |
| CSCO | Corpus scriptorium christianorum orientalium. Edited by I. B. Chabot et al. Paris, 1903– |
| CSF | Collezione di studi fenici |
| *CTA* | *Corpus des tablettes en cuneiforms alphabétiques découvertes à Ras Shamra-Ugarit de 1929 à 1939*. Edited by A. Herdner. Mission de Ras Shamra 10. Paris, 1963 |
| D | Deuteronomic Source |

| | |
|---|---|
| *DCH* | *Dictionary of Classical Hebrew*. Edited by D. J. A. Clines. Sheffield, 1993– |
| *DSD* | *Dead Sea Discoveries* |
| EBib | Études bibliques |
| EEF | Egypt Exploration Fund |
| *EncJud* | *Encyclopaedia Judaica*. 16 vols. Jerusalem, 1972 |
| *Epist.* | *Epistulae* |
| *ErIsr* | *Eretz-Israel* |
| ETANA | Electronic Tools and Ancient Near East Archives (http://www.etana.org) |
| *ETL* | *Ephemerides theologicae lovanienses* |
| *ExAud* | *Ex auditu* |
| *ExpTim* | *Expository Times* |
| FAT | Forschungen zum Alten Testament |
| *FGH* | *Die Fragmente der griechischen Historiker*. Edited by F. Jacoby. Leiden, 1954–1964 |
| FOTL | Forms of the Old Testament Literature |
| FRLANT | Forschungen zur Religion und Literatur des Alten und Neuen Testaments |
| GCS | Die griechische christliche Schriftsteller der ersten [drei] Jahrhunderte |
| *GJPA* | *Grammatik des jüdisch-palästinischen Aramäisch.* Gustaf H. Dalman. Leipzig: $^{1}$1894, $^{2}$ amplified 1905 = 1960, 1978, 1981, 1989 |
| GKC | *Gesenius' Hebrew Grammar.* Edited by E. Kautzsch. Translated by A. E. Cowley. 2nd ed. Oxford, 1910 |
| H | Holiness Code |
| *HALOT* | *The Hebrew and Aramaic Lexicon of the Old Testament.* L. Koehler, W. Baumgartner, and J. J. Stamm. Translated and edited under the supervision of M. E. J. Richardson. 4 vols. Leiden, 1994–1999 |
| *HAR* | *Hebrew Annual Review* |
| HAT | Handbuch zum Alten Testament |
| HKAT | Handkommentar zum Alten Testament |
| HO | Handbuch der Orientalistik |
| HSM | Harvard Semitic Monographs |
| HSS | Harvard Semitic Studies |
| HTKAT | Herders theologischer Kommentar zum Alten Testament |
| *HUCA* | *Hebrew Union College Annual* |
| *IB* | *Interpreter's Bible.* Edited by G. A. Buttrick et al. 12 vols. New York, 1951–1957 |

| | |
|---|---|
| IBC | Interpretation: A Bible Commentary for Teaching and Preaching |
| ICC | International Critical Commentary |
| *IDB* | *The Interpreter's Dictionary of the Bible.* Edited by G. A. Buttrick. 4 vols. Nashville: Abingdon, 1962 |
| *IEJ* | *Israel Exploration Journal* |
| *Int* | *Interpretation* |
| *ISBE* | *International Standard Bible Encyclopedia.* Edited by G. W. Bromiley. 4 vols. Grand Rapids, 1979–1988 |
| *JAOS* | *Journal of the American Oriental Society* |
| *JBL* | *Journal of Biblical Literature* |
| *JCS* | *Journal of Cuneiform Studies* |
| *JEA* | *Journal of Egyptian Archaeology* |
| *JESHO* | *Journal of the Economic and Social History of the Orient* |
| *JHS* | *Journal of Hellenic Studies* |
| *JNES* | *Journal of Near Eastern Studies* |
| *JNSL* | *Journal of Northwest Semitic Languages* |
| Joüon | *A Grammar of Biblical Hebrew.* P. Joüon. Translated and revised by T. Muraoka. 2 vols. Subsidia biblica 14/1–2. Rome, 1991 |
| *JQR* | *Jewish Quarterly Review* |
| *JRAS* | *Journal of the Royal Asiatic Society* |
| JSJSup | Journal for the Study of Judaism in the Persian, Hellenistic, and Roman Periods: Supplement Series |
| *JSOT* | *Journal for the Study of the Old Testament* |
| JSOTSup | Journal for the Study of the Old Testament: Supplement Series |
| JSNTSup | Journal for the Study of the New Testament: Supplement Series |
| *JSS* | *Journal of Semitic Studies* |
| *JTS* | *Journal of Theological Studies* |
| *KAI* | *Kanaanäische und aramäische Inschriften.* H. Donner and W. Röllig. 2nd ed. Wiesbaden, 1966–1969 |
| KAT | Kommentar zum Alten Testament |
| $KBL^3$ | *Hebräisches und aramäisches Lexikon zum Alten Testament.* L. Koehler and W. Baumgartner. 3rd ed. Leiden, 1967–96. |
| KEHAT | Kurzgefasstes exegetisches Handbuch zum Alten Testament |
| KHC | Kurzer Hand-Commentar zum Alten Testament |
| KJV | King James Version |
| LCL | Loeb Classical Library |
| LHBOTS | Library of Hebrew Bible/Old Testament Studies |
| LXX | Septuagint |
| *MARI* | *Mari: Annales de recherché interdisciplinaires* |

| | |
|---|---|
| *Meg. Ta'an.* | *Megillah Ta'anit* |
| MnS | Mnemosyne Supplementum |
| MT | Masoretic Text |
| NAB | New American Bible |
| NAC | New American Commentary |
| NASB | New American Standard Bible |
| NCB | New Century Bible |
| NCBC | New Cambridge Bible Commentary |
| NEAEHL | *The New Encyclopedia of Archaeological Excavations in the Holy Land.* Edited by E. Stern. 4 vols. Jerusalem, 1993 |
| NEB | New English Bible |
| NEchtB | Neue Echter Bibel |
| NICOT | New International Commentary on the Old Testament |
| *NIDB* | *New International Dictionary of the Bible.* Edited by J. D. Douglas and M. C. Tenney. Grand Rapids, 1987 |
| NIV | New International Version |
| NIVAC | New International Version Application Commentary |
| NJB | New Jerusalem Bible |
| NJPS | Tanakh: The New JPS Translation |
| NKJV | New King James Version |
| NRSV | New Revised Standard Version |
| *NTS* | *New Testament Studies* |
| OBO | Orbis biblicus et orientalis |
| ÖBS | Österreichische biblische Studien |
| OBT | Overtures to Biblical Theology |
| *ODNB* | *Oxford Dictionary of National Biography.* Edited by H. C. G. Matthew and B. H. Harrison. 60 vols. Oxford-New York, 2004 |
| *OEANE* | *The Oxford Encyclopedia of Archaeology in the Near East.* Edited by E. M. Meyers. New York, 1997 |
| OG | Old Greek |
| OL | Old Latin |
| OLA | Orientalia lovaniensia analecta |
| OLP | Orientalia lovaniensia periodica |
| *Or* | *Orientalia* |
| OTG | Old Testament Guides |
| OTL | Old Testament Library |
| OTM | Old Testament Message |
| *OtSt* | *Oudtestamentische Studiën* |
| P | Priestly Source |

| | |
|---|---|
| *PAAJR* | *Proceedings of the American Academy for Jewish Research* |
| PEFQS | Palestine Exploration Fund Quarterly Statement |
| *PEQ* | *Palestine Exploration Quarterly* |
| *PSBA* | *Proceedings of the Society of Biblical Archaeology* |
| PTMS | Pittsburgh Theological Monograph Series |
| RAS | Royal Asiatic Society |
| *RB* | *Revue biblique* |
| *RBL* | *Review of Biblical Literature* |
| REB | Revised English Bible |
| *RevExp* | *Review and Expositor* |
| RIMA | The Royal Inscriptions of Mesopotamia, Assyrian Periods |
| *RQ* | *Römische Quartal schrift für christliche Altertumskunde und Kirchengeschichte* |
| RSV | Revised Standard Version |
| *RTP* | *Revue de théologie et de philosophie* |
| RV | Revised Version |
| SAA | State Archives of Assyria |
| SAACT | State Archives of Assyria Cuneiform Texts |
| SAAS | State Archives of Assyria Studies |
| SBA | Society of Biblical Archaeology |
| SBL | Society of Biblical Literature |
| SBLDS | Society of Biblical Literature Dissertation Series |
| SBLEJL | Society of Biblical Literature Early Judaism and Its Literature |
| SBLMS | Society of Biblical Literature Monograph Series. |
| SBL SemeiaSt | Society of Biblical Literature Semeia Studies |
| SBLSCS | Society of Biblical Literature Septuagint and Cognate Studies |
| SBLSymS | Society of Biblical Literature Symposium Series |
| SBLWAW | Society of Biblical Literature Writings from the Ancient World |
| SBS | Stuttgarter Bibelstudien |
| *ScrHier* | *Scripta hierosolymitana* |
| SCS | Septuagint Commentary Series |
| *Sem* | *Semitica* |
| SGKAO | Schriften zur Geschichte und Kultur des Alten Orients |
| *SJOT* | *Scandinavian Journal of the Old Testament* |
| SOTSMS | Society for Old Testament Studies Monograph Series |
| *SR* | *Studies in Religion* |
| *ST* | *Studia theologica* |

STDJ Studies on the Texts of the Desert of Judah
StPB Studia post-biblica
Sym. Symmachus
*TA* *Tel Aviv*
TAVO Tübinger Atlas des Vorderen Orients
TCS Texts from Cuneiform Sources
*TDNT* *Theological Dictionary of the New Testament*. Edited by G. Kittel and G. Friedrich. Translated by G. W. Bromiley. 10 vols. Grand Rapids: Eerdmans, 1964–1976.
*TDOT* *Theological Dictionary of the Old Testament*. Edited by G. J. Botterweck and H. Ringgren. Translated by J. T. Willis, G. W. Bromiley, and D. E. Green. 8 vols. Grand Rapids, 1974–
TEG Traditio Exegetica Graeca
Theod. Theodotion
*Transeu* *Transeuphratène*
*TRE* *Theologische Realenzyklopädie*. Edited by G. Krause and G. Müller. Berlin, 1977–
TS Texts and Studies
TSAJ Texte und Studien zum antiken Judentum
*TSBA* *Transactions of the Society of Biblical Archaeology*
*TynBul* *Tyndale Bulletin*
*UF* *Ugarit-Forschungen*
UTB Uni-Taschenbücher
UUA Uppsala universitetsårsskrift
Vulg. Vulgate
VL *Vetus Latina: Die Reste der altlateinischen Bibel*. Edited by E. Beuron, 1949–
*VT* *Vetus Testamentum*
VTSup Supplements to Vetus Testamentum
WBC Word Biblical Commentary
WMANT Wissenschaftliche Monographien zum Alten und Neuen Testament
*WO* *Die Welt des Orients*
*WTJ* *Westminster Theological Journal.*
WUNT Wissenschaftliche Untersuchungen zum Neuen Testament
*ZA* *Zeitschrift für Assyriologie*
*ZAH* *Zeitschrift für Althebraistik*
*ZAW* *Zeitschrift für die alttestamentliche Wissenschaft*
ZBK Zürcher Bibelkommentare
*ZDPV* *Zeitschrift des deutschen Palästina-Vereins*

# PART I

# HISTORY OF RESEARCH

# THE BEGINNINGS OF 'BIBLICAL ARCHAEOLOGY'

Graham Davies

At the beginning of his masterly account of "A Century of Biblical Archaeology" Roger Moorey understandably gave a prominent place to the foundation of The Society of Biblical Archaeology in 1870 and its chief instigator and first President, Samuel Birch.[1] He cites there the judgement of an eminent scholar of an earlier generation that the choice of the name for the Society was "a stroke of genius, for it appealed not only to philologists, but to theologians of all shades of thought."[2] In view of the origins and declared purpose of the Society, which will be examined further below, it was not the most obvious name to choose, and one might be forgiven for thinking that the decision had an ulterior motive. This is certainly what A. H. Sayce, a later President of the Society, recalled being told: "Birch insisted on the word 'Biblical' being introduced into the title of the Society in order, as he said, 'to attract subscriptions'."[3] What has not, I think, previously been observed is that it may have been just at this time that the expression 'Biblical Archaeology' was beginning to be used. Even if it was not, the activities and publications of the Society over the almost fifty years of its existence will have served in many ways to determine the meaning of an expression which has in more recent times been the focus of much controversy.[4] That in itself would make the history of the Society a worthwhile topic for study, but it did also play a quite central role in its time in the advancement and dissemination of research in Near Eastern and biblical studies. It is the more surprising that (as far as I have been able to discover) only brief accounts of it have previously been published.[5]

---

[1] P. R. S. Moorey, *A Century of Biblical Archaeology* (Cambridge: Lutterworth, 1991), 3–5.

[2] Ernest A. Wallis Budge, *The Rise and Progress of Assyriology* (London: Martin Hopkinson, 1925), 262.

[3] Archibald H. Sayce, *Reminiscences* (London: Macmillan, 1923), 55.

[4] See William G. Dever, "Biblical Archaeology Today: Death and Rebirth," in *Biblical Archaeology Today, 1990* (ed. Avraham Biran and Joseph Aviram; Jerusalem: Israel Exploration Society, 1993), 706–22; and my *The Schweich Lectures and Biblical Archaeology* (Oxford: Oxford University Press for the British Academy, 2011), ch. 3.

[5] See Francis Legge, "The Society of Biblical Archaeology," *JRAS* 1919: 25–36; Budge, *Rise and Progress*, 261–65; Charles F. Beckingham, "Appendix: The Society of Biblical Archaeology

## I. The Founding of the Society

Unlike the Palestine Exploration Fund and the Egypt Exploration Fund, which were founded in 1865 and 1882, the Society of Biblical Archaeology (hereafter SBA) was not formed to encourage exploration and excavation, but to hold meetings in London for the reading and discussion of scholarly papers which were then published in its journals.[6] There are two published accounts of its foundation. One, whose author was evidently the first Secretary of the Society, William Cooper, is dated January 1872 and traces its origin to a meeting convened by Samuel Birch, who was by this time Keeper of Oriental Antiquities at the British Museum and a distinguished Egyptologist, and Mr. Joseph Bonomi of the Soane Museum, at the latter's rooms in Lincoln's Inn Fields on 18 November 1870. Those invited were "gentlemen interested in the Antiquities and Philology of Egypt, Palestine and Western Asia."[7] The second account, in E. A. Wallis Budge's memoir of Birch, gives more details of the background to this meeting and confirms that the initiative came very much from the side of Oriental scholarship rather than from biblical scholars. It speaks of the lack of any journal or society dedicated specifically to the archaeology of the ancient Near East, and of both scepticism and apathy on the part of the general public towards the new discoveries of texts and their decipherment. Birch and Bonomi had "often talked over these difficulties" and it was the latter who one day suggested: "Why not establish a new Society, whose only aim and object shall be to publish and explain Egyptian and Assyrian texts. We will print the text in one line and the transliteration and translation beneath it."[8] Negotiations were also undertaken with the leading members of four older societies, who agreed to wind them up if they were made life members of the new one.[9]

1870–1919," in *The Royal Asiatic Society: Its History and Treasures* (ed. Stuart Simmonds and Simon Digby; Leiden: E. J. Brill, 1979), 155–58.

6 The "Objects" printed in *TSBA* 2 (1873): xxv–xxvi and the revised "Rules and Regulations" published in *TSBA* 4 (1876): 396 did provide for the possible establishment of a fund to support excavations, but apparently this was never put into practice.

7 William R. Cooper, "Introduction," *TSBA* 1 (1872): i–iv (i).

8 Ernest A. Wallis Budge, "Memoir of Samuel Birch, LL.D., D.C.L., F.S.A., & c.," *TSBA* 9/1 (1886): 1–41 (16).

9 Budge, "Memoir of Samuel Birch," 15–16. The other societies were the Syro-Egyptian Society, the Palestine Archaeological Association, the Chronological Institute and the Anglo-Biblical Institute. A particular benefit of this arrangement was that the libraries of these societies were added to the new library of the SBA: see *Catalogue of the Library of the*

The proposals of Birch and Bonomi having been accepted, a public meeting was held at the Royal Society of Literature on 9 December 1870, at which Birch took the chair. Those present resolved that:

> A Society be initiated, having for its objects the investigation of the Archaeology, Chronology, Geography, and History, of Ancient and Modern Assyria, Arabia, Egypt, Palestine, and other Biblical Lands, the promotion of the study of the Antiquities of these countries, and the preservation of a continuous record of discoveries, now or hereafter to be in progress.

The name of the Society was also agreed, together with the names of those who would form a "Provisional Council" to prepare "Laws" and conduct the preliminary business of the Society. It included Birch, Bonomi, the Assyriologists Sir Henry Rawlinson and W. H. Fox Talbot, and thirteen others.[10]

The inaugural meeting was held on 21 March 1871, when Birch gave an address on "The Progress of Biblical Archaeology," which also set the course for the new Society.[11] It was a carefully balanced essay, designed to win support from the widest possible audience. Its opening words were of "the study of Oriental literature, philology and history" and "the progress of the interpretation of inscriptions hitherto unknown." It surveyed the progress of archaeological discovery in Egypt, "Assyria" (i.e. Mesopotamia), Phoenicia, Cyprus, Palestine and other lands. But Birch mentioned the connection with the Bible five times in the first paragraph, even to the extent of being ready "to test the information [the new discoveries] afford by what is known from the pages of the sacred Volume, and the Greek and Roman historians." This theme was continued, with specific examples, in his summary of the findings of Egyptian and Mesopotamian archaeology. All in all, "They ought to rally round the Society all who take an interest in the comparative study of Biblical history";[12] "Its scope is Archaeology, not Theology; but to Theology it will prove an important aid."[13]

It was an impressive appeal, and the new Society quickly established itself with a growing and distinguished following. Further papers were read in May, June, November and December and published in the first Part of the Society's *Transactions* in January 1872. By the end of 1872 it

---

*Society of Biblical Archaeology* (London: Society of Biblical Archaeology, 1876), v–vi, where some details of the other societies are given.

10 Cooper, "Introduction," ii–iii. Six of the Council were clergy.

11 Samuel Birch, "The Progress of Biblical Archaeology," *TSBA* 1 (1872): 1–12.

12 Ibid., 5.

13 Ibid., 12.

had 165 members (including 13 lady members who paid half the normal subscription) and an impressive list of 24 Honorary Foreign Members, who included many of the great names of the day: H. Brugsch, F. Chabas, G. Ebers, H. Ewald, C. Clermont-Ganneau, F. Lenormant, R. K. Lepsius, G. Maspero, F. de Saulcy and E. Schrader. But Ewald was the only biblical scholar among them. Over the following years the membership steadily grew, reaching 500 ordinary members in 1879 and a peak of 619 in 1886. Foreign libraries subscribed to the journal(s) and in 1882 70 of the subscribing members lived outside the United Kingdom.[14]

The "Objects" of the SBA were first printed in 1873. In addition to matters already mentioned, they provided for the collection of sketches, photographs and other material and for regular monthly meetings from November to June. "Theological and Political Papers" were banned and the subscription was set at one guinea per annum, a large sum at the time. In 1876 a much fuller set of "Rules and Regulations" were agreed, with 49 paragraphs, which added to the Objects specific provisions about the President, Council, Members, Librarian and Secretary, Anniversary Meeting (in January, for reports and elections), Special Meetings, Ordinary Meetings (at which papers were read) and Papers. The topics banned were now described as "polemical and political": perhaps "theological" had created problems of definition.[15]

The Society's first premises were at 9 Conduit St., Hanover Square, London, and meetings continued to be held there until 1893. In 1876 larger rooms for the office and library were rented at 33 Bloomsbury St., near the British Museum, but by 1880 these were too small and the Society moved to 11 Hart St. (now Bloomsbury Way), where it remained until 1892. A still larger building being then required to house the library and other resources of the Society, a lease was taken on 37 Great Russell St., and from March 1893 the regular meetings were held there too. This remained the Society's home until its demise in 1919.[16]

[14] In the early years exact figures were not noted: for those given above see Arthur Cates, *Secretary's Report for the Year 1878* (London: Society of Biblical Archaeology, 1879), 4; *PSBA* 8 (1885–86): 65; *TSBA* 7 (1882): 476–77.

[15] "Objects," xxv–xxvi; "Rules and Regulations," 396–402.

[16] *TSBA* 6 (1878): 574; *PSBA* 3 (1880–81): 33; 14 (1891–92): 489–90; 15 (1892–93): 94–95.

## II. Presidents and Secretaries

Such an organisation could not have developed and flourished without the guidance of skilful and committed Officers, particularly its Presidents and Secretaries.[17] The Presidents deserve special mention. There were only three who held office for substantial periods: Samuel Birch (1870–1885), Peter le Page Renouf (1887–1897) and Archibald Henry Sayce (1898–1919). The first two died in office, while Sayce's tenure was ended by the winding-up of the Society. Walter Morrison (1836–1921), a Vice-President since (at least) 1872, stood in while a successor was found in 1886 and 1897.[18]

Birch (1813–1885) has already come to our attention for his leading role in the foundation of the SBA.[19] His contributions to Egyptology before 1870 included, along with many shorter pieces, the publication of the Sallier papyri (1841), the Anastasi papyri (1842, 1844), the Abbott and D'Orbiney papyri (1860) and an Egyptian grammar and dictionary (1867), the latter being "the first Hieroglyphic Dictionary ever published."[20] He had come to the study of Egyptian at a crucial time in its development and his eminence in it in England was compared to that of Richard Lepsius in Germany.[21] As President he was constant in his attendance at the Society's meetings, and it was remembered that he had "by his varied scholarship, unfailing industry and watchful care, done all that was in his power to carry forward the work for which the Society was founded."[22]

---

[17] The following served in other capacities: Hon. Secretary—1878–82: A. Cates; Foreign Secretary—1870–77: T. L. Donaldson; 1877–88: A. H. Sayce; 1888–1901: R. Gwynne; 1902–19: F. Legge; Treasurer—1870–77: J. W. Bosanquet; 1878–1910: B. T. Bosanquet (Hon.); 1911–19: W. H. Rylands; Librarian—1875–99: W. Simpson (Hon. from 1879); 1900–02: W. H. Rylands; 1903–19: W. L. Nash.

[18] Sir A. H. Layard was in fact elected President for 1886 (*PSBA* 8 [1885–6]: 71) and Morrison was described as "Vice-President" when he took the chair on 2 February (ibid., 81). But by 6 April he was "President" and he was subsequently regarded as President for the whole year (ibid., 109; *PSBA* 9 [1886–7]: 60). Evidently Layard withdrew early in the year for an unknown reason.

[19] See on him the extended Memoir by Budge referred to in note 8.

[20] Budge, "Memoir," 14–15.

[21] By Budge, "Memoir," 5–6.

[22] W. H. Rylands, "Secretary's Report for the Year 1886," *PSBA* 9 (1886–87): 56–61. According to T. G. H. James, Birch regarded the foundation of the Egypt Exploration Fund (EEF; later the Egypt Exploration Society) in 1882 as regrettable competition (*ODNB* 5:798–99), and James thought that it was the popularity of the latter that in the end killed the SBA. Birch certainly would not support the Fund (cf. Margaret S. Drower, "The Early Years," in *Excavating in Egypt: The Egypt Exploration Society 1882–1982* [ed. T. G. H. James; London: British Museum Publications, 1982], 14, 24), but after his death relations improved and the EEF rented accommodation in the Society's house (Drower, "The Early Years," 34:

Like Birch, it was chiefly Egyptology that brought Renouf (1822–1897) to the Presidency of the SBA.[23] He had been Professor of Ancient History and Geography at the new Catholic University in Dublin.[24] For this role he taught himself Egyptian, and so well that he was able to publish two significant articles on the debate about Champollion's decipherment of hieroglyphics. But he and his family were not happy in Dublin, and in 1864 he moved to London to become a Chief Inspector of Schools. After Birch's death he was appointed in 1886 to succeed him as Keeper of Egyptian and Assyrian Antiquities at the British Museum, but his tenure there was brief, and it ended in acrimony in 1891.[25]

Sayce (1845–1933) was in several ways the antithesis to both Birch and Renouf.[26] He was primarily an Assyriologist, not an Egyptologist. He lacked institutional ties to the British Museum, though he had often worked there. He was not only the son of an Anglican clergyman, but one himself. And, perhaps connected with this, though it was by no means inevitable, he had (and made very public) a strong interest in the apologetic value of ancient Near Eastern literature for the defence of the truth of the Bible against 'higher criticism.' Unlike the others and especially in his later years, he was a great traveller, explorer and excavator—his poor health made the English winters unwelcome—and in 1890 he moved his extensive library to Egypt. His election as President represented a change, and it is an interesting question how much, if any, impact it had on the ethos of the Society and, perhaps, its decline and eventual demise. We shall return briefly to these issues at the end.

The first of the Secretaries—again there were only three—was William Cooper (1843–1878), a young man who had been introduced to Egyptology

the address there should be "37 Great Russell St."). In view of the difference in aims James's view about the demise of the SBA may be questioned (for other explanations see below).

[23] Renouf's letters have recently been published in a splendidly annotated edition by Kevin J. Cathcart: *The Letters of Peter le Page Renouf* (4 vols.; Dublin: University College Dublin, 2002–04). There is a biographical "Introduction" in vol. 4, xi–xxix, which adds much to the "Biographical Record" by W. H. Rylands in *PSBA* 19 (1897): 271–79 (with list of publications on pp. 317–41). A much fuller "Biography" by Edith Renouf (his daughter) appeared in *The Life-Work of Sir Peter le Page Renouf* (ed. Gaston Maspero et al.; 4 vols.; Paris: Ernest Leroux, 1902–1907), 4:v–cxxxiii.

[24] Cathcart, *Letters*, 4:xviii.

[25] See the correspondence in Cathcart, *Letters*, 4:273–340: the disputes continued for some years.

[26] His *Reminiscences* contain a wealth of personal detail and entertaining anecdotes; the essential biographical facts and a more objective evaluation of his strengths and weaknesses are more readily gained from his entry in *ODNB* 49:158–60 (see also Budge, *Rise and Progress*, esp. 185–88).

by Bonomi and published a book on Egyptian religion in 1873.[27] He was energetic in the early years of the Society: the series of *Records of the Past* was his idea, and he was responsible for collecting and arranging the contributions. But he became seriously ill in 1876 and had to move away from London, which limited what he could do in the last two years of his short life. It was also alleged that he lacked the necessary business sense.[28] Arthur Cates acted in his place as "Joint Secretary" in 1877 and remained as Honorary Secretary until 1882. From 1878 to 1902 the Secretary was W. H. (Harry) Rylands, who was not only an efficient and far-sighted administrator but a contributor to the Society's scholarly publications. He saw the Society through a number of changes and difficulties and was made a Vice-President on his retirement from his post. In the last years of the Society he became Honorary Treasurer.[29] He was succeeded by Walter Nash, who had already undertaken a number of administrative tasks for the Society, and he continued in this role (and also as Honorary Librarian) until the end of its independent existence.[30]

## III. Publications and Classes

The fact that the SBA sponsored two distinct journals, both of which were published simultaneously in its middle years, requires some clarification. The *Transactions* contained almost exclusively papers that had been read at the Society's meetings. From 1874 each volume also included a "Condensed Report" of the previous year's meetings, with summaries of the papers and details of other business. In 1878 it was decided to circulate these reports as monthly pamphlets, entitled *Proceedings of the Society of Biblical Archaeology*, "not only to place in the hands of the Members, a fuller account of the proceedings at the ordinary meetings than has hitherto been possible but also by the co-operation of the Members, to establish a

---

[27] William R. Cooper, *Serpent Myths of Ancient Egypt* (London: Robert Hardwicke, 1873). He has a brief entry in *ODNB* 13:292–93.

[28] By Budge, "Memoir," 17. Cates and Birch were more generous in their appreciation of Cooper's services: Cates, *Secretary's Report*, 1–2; *Records of the Past*, 11 (ed. S. Birch; London: Samuel Bagster, 1878), ii.

[29] To judge from his response to a vote of thanks, he found the lack of support from the wider membership very trying (*PSBA* 25 [1903]: 8–9).

[30] His name is immortalised in the naming of the Nash Papyrus, which belonged to him at the time of its publication (Stanley A. Cook, "A Pre-Massoretic Biblical Papyrus," *PSBA* 25 [1903]: 34–56 (34, 56).

medium of communication on subjects interesting to the Society."[31] The first of these pamphlets appeared in November 1878. It was soon being envisaged that they might become a "Journal of Biblical Archaeology."[32] At first only short notes were included in addition to the summaries of meetings, but gradually longer papers began to appear and eventually even papers that had been read at meetings.[33] By 1887 this was becoming established as the rule.[34] Almost two years had elapsed between the publication of the last Part of *Transactions* 8 and the first Part of *Transactions* 9 in 1886, but the inclusion of the Memoir of Birch in the latter suggests that it was still regarded as the Society's premier publication. By January 1889 it had become clear that the rationale for continuing the series of *Transactions* had been eroded by the success of the *Proceedings* as what the Secretary could now call "an important monthly Journal of Biblical Archaeology," and a year later it had been decided that the *Transactions* would not continue beyond the completion of the ninth volume and the "possible" production of an index volume.[35] As a result of financial difficulties the second and final Part of *Transactions* 9, containing papers read between 1884 and 1887, was not published until 1893 (and it left the Society in debt until 1899) and the Index did not appear until 1903.

The contents of the journals, which included as indicated the papers read at the monthly meetings of the Society, are an important criterion for assessing the sense in which it understood itself as a "Society of Biblical Archaeology." The impression gained from even a cursory examination of the material that was published must be that 'Biblical Archaeology' was only occasionally understood as implying the comparison of the new discoveries with specific biblical passages or books. There were articles of this kind, particularly about the story of the Exodus of the Israelites from

---

[31] Cates, *Secretary's Report*, 4.

[32] *PSBA* 2 (1879–80): 24. The original intention had been that they should be bound in with the *Transactions*, but this idea was quickly abandoned. It did mean, however, that for the first five years the *Proceedings* were printed without volume numbers and were headed "Session 1878–9" or, from the following year, "Tenth Session, 1879–80" etc. The *Proceedings* for 1883–84 were titled "Volume VI. Fourteenth Session" and this then became the regular format. As a result it has become customary to refer to the preceding issues as "Volumes 1–5" and I have followed that practice in this essay.

[33] The first of the latter seems to have been the President's paper: S. Birch, "Four Fragments of Papyrus belonging to the Edinburgh Museum of Science and Art," *PSBA* 7 (1884–85): 79–89.

[34] *PSBA* 9 (1886–87): 59; cf. *PSBA* 10 (1887–88): 4–59, 80–81, 135.

[35] *PSBA* 11 (1888–89): 59–60; *PSBA* 12 (1889–90): 130.

Egypt.[36] But they were in a minority. By far the majority of the articles and papers were publications or re-editions of Egyptian or Mesopotamian texts which made little or no reference to the Bible, or discussions of detailed points of interpretation in such texts. There was relatively little interest in the results of excavation other than inscribed material: these were left to the Palestine Exploration Fund and the Egypt Exploration Fund, it seems.[37]

Among the other publications of the SBA pride of place belonged to *Records of the Past*, a series of twelve volumes published between 1873 and 1881 under the editorship of Birch. They contained translations of a large number of ancient Near Eastern texts, with the volumes alternating between Mesopotamian and Egyptian literature (with a few West Semitic inscriptions also included).[38] The introductions and notes for each text were sparse until the final volumes. The series gave the general reader access to the actual words (so far as they were then understood) of the literatures of ancient peoples that were beginning to stand alongside those of the Greeks and Romans and the Old Testament.[39]

Another early project of the Society was what came to be called "the Archaic Classes." These were public classes in Ancient Egyptian and Akkadian ("Assyrian" as it was then called), and they took place for the first time in 1875, with Renouf and Sayce as the main teachers. They helped to introduce some students to the languages who would later become specialists themselves, and they led to the publication of two pioneering teaching grammars. But there were difficulties in keeping them running.[40]

---

36 E.g. August Eisenlohr, "On the Political Condition of Egypt before the reign of Ramses III; probably in connection with the Establishment of the Jewish Religion. From the Great Harris Papyrus," *TSBA* 1 (1872): 355–84.

37 Two highlights for biblical scholarship among the articles published were George Smith, "The Chaldean Account of the Deluge," *TSBA* 2 (1873): 213–34; and Cook, "A Pre-Massoretic Biblical Papyrus" (the text subsequently known as the "Nash Papyrus"), *PSBA* 25 (1903): 34–56.

38 For a full list of the contents (by W. H. Rylands) see *Records of the Past*, 12 (ed. S. Birch; London: Samuel Bagster, 1881), 145–61.

39 A. H. Sayce edited a second series of *Records of the Past*, in six volumes (London: Samuel Bagster, 1888–92), which contained partly new texts and partly revisions of those published earlier: for a list of the contents see vol. 6 (1892), 153–55. This was not so successful: in the preface to the final volume Sayce lamented that "the public seems to prefer books about the ancient inscriptions of the Oriental world rather than translations of the inscriptions themselves" (ibid., vi). The volumes were in the same format as the earlier ones (though with much fuller introductions and notes), but for some reason did not bear any explicit association with the SBA.

40 Cates, *Secretary's Report*, 5.

The contents of the journals and other publications, and the classes it provided, thus confirm what one could deduce from the original aims of the Society and the research focus of its Presidents, namely that it was in reality more what would today be called a 'Society for Near Eastern Studies' than a 'Society of Biblical Archaeology.' It was 'biblical' in a geographical and historical sense, in that the texts which were its primary interest came from what in the later nineteenth century was still thought of above all as 'the world of the Bible,' the world of which the Bible had for centuries been the centre. Perhaps it is one measure of the success of the Society that its name increasingly came to seem inappropriate for what it was doing and expressions like 'ancient Near Eastern literature' came to be used instead. More and more the study of the ancient civilisations came quite rightly to be valued for its own sake, and 'Biblical Archaeology' came to mean something different, in which comparisons with, and for many confirmation of, the Bible were the central concerns.

## IV. The Demise of the Society

These considerations are important as we come, finally, to seek for the reasons for the Society's demise. Was it perhaps due to its having a name that had too many resonances of a bygone age? Hardly so: if the name had been felt to be a problem, it could surely have been changed. We should instead look, first, at the final years of the Society to see whether there are signs of a gradual decline or a sudden crisis. Then we may consider whether there were internal weaknesses in the Society and factors external to it which made it unable to continue as an independent body.

In the years leading up to the first World War the Society was flourishing. It had about 400 members and a distinguished Council, meetings were regular, the journal had many foreign subscriptions and the annual accounts reported a comfortable if not a large surplus each year. Legacies had even made it possible to establish a reserve fund.[41] But, as what might be called an 'obituary' of the Society by its Foreign Secretary makes especially clear, the war brought increasingly severe challenges which the Society was unable to handle.[42] Between 1913 and 1916 the membership

[41] The Council's Report for 1913 could still state that, despite growing economic pressures in the country as a whole and an increase in rent, the Society's situation was "so far satisfactory" (*PSBA* 36 [1914]: 5).

[42] See Legge, "Society," 25–36. Some but not all of the problems were also noted in the Annual Reports for 1914 to 1917 printed in *PSBA*.

fell by over a third to around 250, mainly due to the loss of foreign subscriptions. This inevitably affected the Society's finances, which were only (just) kept in credit by donations of £50 from Walter Morrison in 1915 and 1916 and from A. H. Gardiner and others in 1917. It also became increasingly difficult to find speakers and contributors to the journal because of the demands of war service of various kinds. Yet the *Proceedings* continued to appear until 1918, and the Council's Report in January of that year gave no hint that drastic action was soon to take place. But informal discussions with members of the Royal Asiatic Society (RAS) had already begun and a joint committee was set up to explore possible terms for what was euphemistically called an "amalgamation" of the two Societies. The RAS had actually proposed such a move long ago and it had been explored again in 1901 at the SBA's request. The last meeting of the SBA was held in March, and in July its members were informed of the terms of an agreement which would be discussed at a forthcoming General Meeting. The Offices and Library were closed at the end of August.[43] On 8 October a General Meeting of the RAS "ratified and confirmed" a provisional agreement between the two Societies to amalgamate. This provided for the transfer of membership from the SBA to the RAS without any formal re-election and at a reduced subscription; the delivery of the property (including the Library) of the SBA and "a very acceptable and considerable sum in invested funds" to the RAS; and the inclusion of the words "with which are incorporated the Proceedings of the Society of Biblical Archaeology" on the cover of the RAS's journal. The sum transferred to the RAS amounted to some £850, including the proceeds of the sale of the lease on the SBA's house and other items. Legal formalities meant that the amalgamation became official only in mid-1919. Sayce was made an Honorary Vice-President of the RAS.[44]

Whatever the appearances, the effective result of these arrangements was the disappearance of a Society which had continued to its end to

[43] W. L. Nash, printed letter attached to the "November-December 1918" issue of *PSBA*, which was evidently published in advance, probably in August. I have not been able to trace any records such as minute books of the SBA which might provide further details of the discussions that took place. Beckingham ("Appendix," 158) was also unable to locate them. The terms agreed by the joint committee (which met on 13 April) and the wording of the formal agreement which gradually took shape can, however, be found in the Minute Book of the RAS Council for 1905–1922. The decisive meetings of the RAS Council took place on 14 May, 11 June and 16 September: some residual matters were resolved at a Special Meeting on 25 January 1919.

[44] "Notes of the Quarter," *JRAS* 1919: 129, 458, 468; *JRAS* 1920: 430; Legge, "Society," 36. The wording agreed remained on the cover of the journal until 1940; in 1941 it was replaced (until 1990) by "with which is incorporated the Society of Biblical Archaeology."

provide a valuable setting for the discussion and publication of ancient Near Eastern literature.[45] The RAS, as before, devoted most of its energies to regions further to the East. Although other societies and Schools were able to sustain the study of different parts of the ancient Near East, the absence of a Society which brought them together has been, it may be argued, a regrettable weakness of British scholarship until very recently.[46]

The demise of the SBA was evidently regarded at the time as an unavoidable consequence of the first World War and, in the RAS, as something to be welcomed. But was its collapse unavoidable? It is ironic that it took place just as the War was ending at last, and it is perhaps surprising that there was no move to keep the Society afloat, on a leaner scale if necessary, in the hope of better times ahead. Legge's 'obituary' while not addressing this issue directly, does perceptively provide some clues to internal weaknesses in the Society which made it more vulnerable to the crisis of the War than other societies which came through it relatively unscathed.[47] He writes, first, of changes in the disciplines which the SBA had fostered. The age of great discoveries was apparently past, and the professionalisation of Near Eastern archaeology had made it more difficult to present its work to a general audience. This suggests that the Society had not faced the question of whether it was to be a meeting-place for scholars or a means of providing information to the wider public–or how it could continue to be both.[48] Secondly, he mentions the financial impact of the withdrawal of the Egypt Exploration Fund from its tenancy of two-thirds of the Society's house in Great Russell St. Perhaps in smaller accommodation, sufficient for its own purposes, the Society would have been more secure. Thirdly, he cites the ill-health of the Secretary, Walter Nash, significantly adding that he "had kept the Society together since Mr. Rylands' retirement in 1902." In fact by 1918 the three chief Officers of the Society (Sayce, Nash and Rylands) were probably all in their mid to late seventies, and Sayce had been out of the country in the winter and spring

[45] Budge put it well: "During that period it did more to promote and stimulate the interest of the general public in the archaeology and history of 'Bible Lands' than any other Learned Society in the country…Its decease is to be regretted, especially by Assyriologists…" (*Rise and Progress*, 265).

[46] The British Association for Near Eastern Archaeology (BANEA) has come to provide such a meeting-place, but its focus is more on fieldwork than texts and on Western Asia than Egypt.

[47] Legge, "Society," 33–35.

[48] A scholarly emphasis would have been appropriate, as the Schweich Lectures of the British Academy had since 1908 become a very effective mode of public education: see my *The Schweich Lectures and Biblical Archaeology*.

for many years: between 1916 and 1919, the crucial time for the Society's survival, he was on a prolonged world tour which took in extended stays in the United States, Japan and Egypt.[49] It would surely have been better for the Society if one or more of its younger members had been at the helm by this time. As it was, exhaustion and a consequent inability to adapt to changing circumstances were probably at least as much the causes of the Society's end as the effects of the War itself.[50]

---

[49] *Reminiscences*, 420–60. Remarkably Sayce never mentions his Presidency of the SBA in these memoirs, nor the Society itself after 1898.

[50] It is a special pleasure for me to contribute this study to a volume in honour of a valued friend and colleague of many years, who has in the field, in administrative roles and in his writings shown a sustained concern for archaeology and its relationship to biblical studies. I am grateful to Kathy Lazenbatt, the Librarian of the RAS, for making it possible for me to see the records of its meetings held in 1901–1902 and 1918–1919 and for drawing my attention to C. F. Beckingham's account of the SBA. My researches were also made simpler and more productive by the fact that the Divinity Faculty Library in Cambridge possesses almost complete sets of both *TSBA* and *PSBA*, presented by Professor William Horbury, as well as an unbound sequence of *PSBA* from 1880 to 1889 which must once have belonged to J. B. Lightfoot, successively Hulsean and Lady Margaret's Professor at Cambridge and (from 1879) Bishop of Durham.

# MISSION AMONG THE JEWS, HOLY LAND AND ARAMAIC STUDIES: THE CASE OF GUSTAF DALMAN

Thomas Willi

The Theological faculty of Greifswald's university has a special reputation for Old Testament studies. One may think about personalities like Julius Wellhausen in the 19th century, and Leonhard Rost and Alfred Jepsen among others in the 20th century. The faculty also houses an institute of its own, that has occupied a prominent place since its founding in February 1922,[1] and since 1925 has borne the name of *Gustaf Hermann Dalman* who on June 9th of that same year celebrated his 70th birthday. This anniversary was celebrated by him not in Greifswald, but in Jerusalem, surrounded not only by representatives of the German consulate and of the American and the British Archaeological Institutes, as well as by an Austrian prelate and by the vicar of the Latin Patriarchate, but also by scholars like Samuel Klein (1886–1940) and Joseph Klausner (1874–1958).[2] It seems, therefore, quite appropriate to honour Hugh Williamson, not only one of the leading exegetes of the Old Testament, but also a specialist on land *and* literature of the Persian period with Jerusalem as its focus, with the following brief portrait of a quite unusual and—in spite of his conservative position—pioneering personality.

## I. Mission among the Jews and Holy Land Studies

Dalman's *vita* has been described quite exhaustively by Julia Männchen.[3] We will concentrate on the inner motives of his life and work and their

[1] See Julia Männchen, *Das Herz zieht nach Jerusalem. Gustaf Dalman zum 150. Geburtstag* (Greifswald/Putbus: Rügendruck, 2005), 16–18.

[2] Gustaf H. Dalman, "Gustaf Hermann Dalman," in *Die Religionswissenschaft der Gegenwart in Selbstdarstellungen* (ed. Erich Stange; Leipzig: Meiner, 1928), 1–29 (8).

[3] Julia Männchen, *Gustaf Dalmans Leben und Wirken in der Brüdergemeine, für die Judenmission und an der Universität Leipzig 1855–1902* (Abhandlungen des Deutschen Palästinavereins 9/1; Wiesbaden: Harassowitz 1987); idem, *Gustaf Dalman als Palästinawissenschaftler in Jerusalem und Greifswald: 1902–1941* (Abhandlungen des Deutschen Palästinavereins 9/2; Wiesbaden: Harassowitz, 1993); idem, *"Gustaf Dalman—auf der Grenze: Leben und Forschen zwischen Kirche und Wissenschaft,"* in *Greifswalder theologische Profile*

interrelation. The two factors that determined Dalman's path, and to which he reacted in his own unique way, made him a personality with a high profile. On the one side lies the fact that he is, by birth and education, related to the *Herrnhuter Brüdergemeine*; while on the other side, lie his exchanges with Franz Delitzsch (1813–1890), head and inspiring teacher of a widespread conservative school of biblical exegetes. Both factors play a key role for Dalman, although not in the sense of simple "influence," but also as challenges to which Dalman responded with a distinctive independence.

The influence of the Herrnhut pietistic community is obvious at first glance when perusing Dalman's biography.[4] Born June 9th, 1855, in the Herrnhut center Niesky, educated at the local Pædagogium and having pursued his formation at the theological seminary in Gnadenfeld, he immediately was engaged there as lecturer from 1881 until 1887. He increasingly freed himself from the particular restrictions of his surroundings and at last left Gnadenfeld for Leipzig. Nonetheless his affiliation with the Herrnhuter Brüdergemeine gave him an access to Jews and Judaism quite different from that which was typical within Germany in those days—an access that was characterized by self-critical affinity as well as by critical distance.

With respect to Franz Delitzsch, already as a grammar school pupil Dalman had sought contact with him by trying to translate the Gospel into Hebrew. Delitzsch, the conservative Lutheran, not only became for Dalman in his Hebrew studies "my best counsellor,"[5] but also accompanied him as early as in his Gnadenfeld period and paved his way to the mission among the Jews and to academic life at Leipzig University when Dalman left the Brüdergemeine. After intensive contact by way of letters and personal encounters Delitzsch installed in 1887 the then 32 year-old Dalman as lecturer at the seminary of the Institutum Judaicum in Leipzig, founded some seven years earlier. Delitzsch had already introduced him to the academic world of Leipzig University, where in 1883 he submitted his study entitled "Traditio rabbinorum veterrima de librorum Veteris Testamenti

(ed. Tilman Beyrich, Irmfried Garbe, and Thomas Willi; Greifswalder theologische Forschungen 12; Frankfurt: Peter Lang, 2006), 109–26.

[4] Männchen, *Dalmans Leben*, 5–40; Christoph Levin, "*Gustaf Dalman und die Brüdergemeine*," in *Festakt Prof. Gustaf Dalman "Zum 150. Geburtstag,"* (ed. Christfried Böttrich; Greifswalder Universitätsreden [N.F.] 117; Greifswald: Ernst-Moritz-Arndt-Universität Greifswald, 2005), 10–26.

[5] Dalman, *Religionswissenschaft der Gegenwart*, 26.

ordine atque origine illustrata" that provided him the degree "Licentiatus Theologiae." On September 16th 1887 he received the "Dr. phil." with an enquiry on "Der leidende Messias nach der Lehre der Synagoge."[6] On November 6th 1891, the year after Delitzsch's death, he reached the level of "Privatdocent" by completing his Habilitationsschrift "Die richterliche Gerechtigkeit im Alten Testament."[7] Already in 1889 his renowned study about *Der Gottesname Adonaj und seine Geschichte* had appeared,[8] and in 1890, *Jesaja 53: Das Prophetenwort vom Sühneleiden des Heilsmittlers, mit besonderer Berücksichtigung der synagogalen Litteratur.*[9]

The latter study is of particular interest and provides a key for understanding Dalman's role as the collector of his famous library, the core of the Gustaf-Dalman-Institute,[10] as well as for understanding his life story and his engagement in the Leipzig Institutum Judaicum. It was Dalman, not Delitzsch, who was responsible for the teaching and training at the seminary. He could rely on such outstanding personalities as R. Jechiel Zwi Lichtenstein (1831–1912), a Hungarian Rabbi, and above all, R. Jisrael Isser Kahan (Cohn, 1858–1924) whom Delitzsch had installed in the Institutum Judaicum that he had founded in 1886, and whom Rudolf Kittel assigned to teach Jewish studies at the university in 1911, in which position he became the predecessor of Lazar Gulkowitsch (1898–1941).

[6] Gustaf H. Dalman, "Der leidende Messias nach der Lehre der Synagoge im ersten nachchristlichen Jahrtausend" (Ph.D. diss., Leipzig University [Karlsruhe: Reiff] 1887); published in completed form as Gustaf H. Dalman, *Der leidende und der sterbende Messias der Synagoge im ersten nachchristlichen Jahrtausend* (Schriften des Institum Judaicum in Berlin 4; Berlin: Reuther, 1888).

[7] This appeared in 1897 as *Die richterliche Gerechtigkeit im Alten Testament* (Studien zur biblische Theologie 2; Kartell-Zeitung akademisch theologischer Vereine auf deutschen Hochschulen; Berlin: Nauck, 1897).

[8] Gustaf H. Dalman, *Der Gottesname Adonaj und seine Geschichte* (Berlin: Reuther, 1889).

[9] Gustaf H. Dalman, *Jesaja 53: Das Prophetenwort vom Sühneleiden des Heilsmittlers, mit besonderer Berücksichtigung der synagogalen Litteratur* (Schriften des Institutum Judaicum in Leipzig 25; Leipzig: Faber, 1890); a second edition, but textually identical, was published as *Jesaja 53: Das Prophetenwort vom Sühneleiden des Heilsmittlers, mit besonderer Berücksichtigung der synagogalen Litteratur* (Schriften of the Institutum Judaicum in Berlin 13; Berlin: Evangelische Vereins-Buchhandlung, 1891).

[10] Ibid., 16 n. 2, cites ed. princ. of the Jerusalem Talmud (Venice 1524) i.e., the vol. of the Dalman library with the actual sign. J VI 1; ibid., 17 n. 4, refers to the ed. Pesaro of the Aruch, i.e., J XXI 50; ibid., 17 n. 5 cites Midrash Tanchuma in the ed. Mantua 1563, i.e., J VI 67; ibid., 19 nn. 1 and 2, cite Zohar vol. II and III of the ed. princ. Mantova 1559, p. 212[a], respectively its Vorlage ed. Cremona 1560 p. 95[c], i.e., J XII 11b and 11c; ibid., 29 n. 1, refers to Midrash Rabba, ed. Venice 1545, i.e., to J VII 3; ibid., 31 n. 1, uses ch. 55 of BerR in the ed. pr. Constantinople, i.e., J VI 1. Dalman must have had all these volumes in his disposition as early as 1890.

Whoever wants to appreciate Dalman's academic work has to take into account both affinities as well as differences between Dalman and Delitzsch, undoubtedly the most excellent 19th century Bible exegete who took account of Jewish studies in his biblical interpretation. Delitzsch, and Dalman with him, stands as a signal against an isolated 'critical' view of the Old and of the New Testament that totally neglected the Jewish aspects and perspectives.

Delitzsch saw the key to his biblical-theological attitude towards Judaism in "that love for Israel that has love for Jesus as its root."[11] On this point Dalman joined his mentor. Nevertheless Dalman was anything but Delitzsch's epigone. By his very nature he was exactly the opposite, and there could be no bigger difference than that between the charismatic Delitzsch who "could take (his hearers) to the third heavens"[12] and Dalman whose "performance" has been described as "very quiet, lacking in verve, but functional and sensitive."[13] He brought education and literary production of the seminary of the Institutum Judaicum down to earth, introducing a touch of self-examination. Dalman had entered Leipzig at a time when Delitzsch's life was coming to its end and when the mission among the Jews had, also for this reason, yet to find its future way. Dalman was responsible not only for the institution alone, but beginning with 1888, also for the editing of the widespread mission periodical *Saat auf Hoffnung*.[14]

How was Dalman supposed to establish a 'mission' among the Jews? In his utterings he above all pleads against a collective oblivion and suppression of Jews by church and society: "Es ist seltsam, das die dem Christentum am nächsten stehende Religion zu den Religionen gehört, welchen am wenigsten Beachtung geschenkt wird."[15] A programmatic lecture, held

[11] Franz Delitzsch, "Christentum und jüdische Presse. Selbsterlebtes," *Saat auf Hoffnung* 19 (1882): 83–146 (85–6); separately published as *Christentum und jüdische Presse. Selbsterlebtes* (Erlangen: Andreas Deichert, 1882); cf. Siegfried Wagner, *Franz Delitzsch: Leben und Werk* (TVG Monografien; Giessen: Brunnen, 1978), 409.

[12] Samuel I. Curtiss, *Franz Delitzsch: A Memorial Tribute* (Edinburgh: T&T Clark, 1891), 45; see Wagner, *Franz Delitzsch*, 100.

[13] Allgemeines Verwaltungsarchiv [Wien], Unterricht 22/II, Zl. 17764/1897, cited by Georg Sauer, "*Ernst Sellin in Wien," Jahrbuch für die Geschichte des Protestantismus in Österreich* (FS für Wilhelm Kühnert) 96 (1980): 138–46, cf. Männchen, *Dalmans Leben*, 58 with n. 235 (translation by present author).

[14] Journal of the Centralverein für Mission unter Israel, founded in 1870/71; issues 1–72 in 1863–1935, ended (after the moratorium induced by the national-socialist ban) with issue 73 in 1950.

[15] Gustaf H. Dalman, *Christentum und Judentum* (Schriften des Institutum Judaicum zu Berlin 24; Leipzig: Faber, 1898), 6.

at Berlin on March 14th 1898, on "Christianity and Judaism" sees one, if not *the* decisive reason for the Christian misjudgment of the "importance of the Jewish religion," in the behaviour of growing Zionism. The Zionist would, starting from the "peculiarity of the Jewish race," treat religion as irrelevant and by doing so lay the groundwork for the "feeling of the broad mass of our people," as Dalman quite obliquely paraphrases German antisemitism.[16] He agrees with Zionism only insofar as he is personally convinced that the "vitality of the Jewish race does *not* depend on its religious practice."[17] When he, though, denied any religious meaning to Jewishness in the sense of being born as a Jew and adhering to a Jewish way of life, he certainly was inspired by his individualistic-pietistic religiousness. "Der *persönliche* Heiland als der Mittelpunkt des Christentums, wie ihn die Brüdergemeine verkündigt, seine Sprache, seine Bibel, sein Land, sein Volk sollten erfasst werden"—in such a way did Dalman conceive of his life's work and did he explain the goal of mission among Jews *and* Holy Land studies as he understood them.[18] For Dalman it was about the—Jewish—people, it was about the—biblical—land, it was about the—Aramaic—linguistic culture. Time and time again his words bear an *apologetic undertone*, as Abraham Berliner rightly observed and complained early on. He acknowledges Dalman was a "Trachten und Streben nach Wahrheit," but that this was disturbed by "apologetics" resulting from "eine nicht ganz ungetrübte Anschauung."[19] Dalman was anxious about Paul Billerbeck's rabbinical commentary on the New Testament with its whole host of parallels in the Jewish literature; he wants to assure "dass *Jesu Person* nicht in ihrer Umwelt verschwindet, sondern *aus ihr herausgehoben* wird als derjenige, den Gott nicht nur seinem Volke, sondern der Menschheit zum Erlöser geschaffen hat."[20]

These words, written shortly after his 70th birthday, shows the problem of Dalman as a missionary to the Jews. It is, for sure, not the Christian witness, "die Vertretung der Botschaft vom Weltheiland vor den Juden"—that is "bei einem in der Brüdergemeine Aufgewachsenen

---

16 Ibid., 5.

17 Ibid., 12 n. *.

18 Dalman, *Religionswissenschaft der Gegenwart*, 26. Cf. also Männchen, *Dalmans Leben*, 142.

19 Abraham Berliner, "Marx," *Literarisches Centralblatt für Deutschland* 38/27 (1887): 727; cf. Christian Wiese, *Wissenschaft des Judentums und protestantische Theologie im wilhelminischen Deutschland—Ein Schrei ins Leere?* (Schriftenreihe des Leo Baeck-Instituts 61; Tübingen: Mohr Siebeck 1999), 99.

20 Dalman, *Religionswissenschaft der Gegenwart*, 26.

selbstverständlich"—but it is the constant *reservatio mentalis* that leads to a certain ambivalence against Judaism and its tradition, not even exempting the Old Testament. Dalman even tries to legitimate the traditional Christian *enseignement de mépris* against Judaism by a spiritualistically motivated protestant abrogation of the Old Testament itself: "Mose's Gesetz galt einer bestimmten Kulturepoche, welche nie wiederkehren wird; ausserdem hat Gott selbst es durch seine vollendete Offenbarung in Christo antiquiert."[21] He does not even refrain from caricaturing Zionism and its goals for a Jewish community in Palestine by using what appears to be outdated biblical notions:

> Aber selbst wenn die kühnsten Hoffnungen der Zionisten sich erfüllen und Palästina von den Juden Russlands, Rumäniens, Persiens und Nordafrikas neu bevölkert wird, so wird dieses Neujudäa doch niemals zu dem Mittelpunkt des jüdischen Volkes werden, nach welchem alle sich sehnen... Weder das *Gesetz* Mose's noch seine talmudische Fortbildung kann jemals in einem jüdischen Gemeinwesen zur allseitigen Ein- und Durchführung gelangen.... Vollends gilt von dem Bau des *Tempels* und der Wiederherstellung des *Opferdienstes*, dass keine Partei im Judentum ihn wünschen kann... Grössere Aussicht auf Verwirklichung hat der Plan einer jüdischen Universität in Jerusalem.

These utterings arose between the 1st Zionist Congress in Basel and the visit of Wilhelm II to Jerusalem. It is not at all bold to assume that the views expressed here influenced Dalman's second period, when he worked in Jerusalem and studied in the Holy Land, as much as they did in his Leipzig years.[22] At any rate he never revised them. With such a perspective his engagement, described in a short telegram formula by the sentence "Das Herz zieht nach Jerusalem,"[23] shows to a certain degree the character of competition or corrective, for Dalman was convinced that the Zionist construction work lacked a decisive religious motif. Dalman and his 'Palästinawissenschaft' must certainly be asked whether Palestine merely becomes a cabinet or museum of a 'biblical' world while dissipating the Jewish presence. Dalman warns of a development that "in der Jerusalemer Börse Kurse für die Weltmacht des Geldes notiert werden,... jedes Dorf sich in eine europäische Villenkolonie verwandelt, wenn statt der melancholischen Weise der Hirtenflöte die Modemelodien Europas auf

[21] Dalman, *Christentum und Judentum*, 8.

[22] Against Albrecht Alt, "Gustaf Dalman†," *Palästina-Jahrbuch* 37 (1941): 5–18 (7).

[23] January 1915 replying to Otto Procksch who had asked him if he would consider to teach as Professor at Greifswald.

den Feldern getrillert werden, . . . dann hat das Heilige Land aufgehört, der Welt etwas zu sein."[24] Dalman's missionary goals, positively understood, represent an effort to stop the Jewish emancipation from becoming totally secularized and to give it a religious foundation and a Christian meaning. Dalman's strong point was not to present 'solutions' for the so-called 'Jewish question'—there were enough 'solutions' in his times, some of them unfortunately 'final.'

Dalman again and again stressed the danger emanating from the Jews, although, as he put it, "a Jewish mission among Christians" had no chance at all.[25] But he envisages the "influence of Judaism" as negative insofar it does not contribute to deepening, but to leveling out Christian belief by opposing against all, "was die unterscheidenden Eigentümlichkeiten des Christentums ausmacht."[26] To respond "muss man das Judentum in seinem Verhältnis zum Christentum kennen lernen."[27] The quality and significance of Judaism have to be measured not exclusively, but essentially by the whole of what is transmitted to Christianity and what Christianity has received and retained from it. At the final count the balance looks quite positive for Judaism:

> Die Kirche verdankt den Juden das griechische und das lateinische Testament, das erstere unmittelbar, das letztere durch die Vermittlung der jüdischen Lehrer des Hieronymus. Ebenfalls durch jüdische Lehrer ist die Kenntnis des Hebräischen im Reformationszeitalter zu uns gekommen. Von der Synagoge erhielten wir damals den bis dahin von ihr gehüteten Grundtext des Alten Testaments.[28]

What, then, has Christianity "in advantage of the Jews"? Dalman's answer is as simple as problematic: "Durch den Auferstandenen besitzt das Christentum eine Macht über Diesseits und Tod, welche dem Judentum fehlt. Denkt man seine lebendige Person hinweg, so wüsste ich nicht, worin hier die Überlegenheit des Christentums bestünde."[29] Seen against this background it is not astonishing that Dalman, when the concrete tasks for the seminary of the Institutum Judaicum are in view, always brings in a single task: the training and instruction of the students in *Judaicis*. It is not

24 Gustaf H. Dalman, "Die Juden im heutigen Palästina, was sie wollen und sollen," *Saat auf Hoffnung* 54 (1917): 30–31.

25 Dalman, *Christentum und Judentum*, 10.

26 Ibid., 10.

27 Ibid., 11.

28 Ibid., 13.

29 Ibid., 18–19.

enough to be good preachers and theologians: they must understand the Jews, speak their language and think through Christianity as to its relation to Judaism. Once Dalman, looking back on his life, formulated what for him personally was the ideal and his—never fulfilled—wish: "Ein theologischer Lehrstuhl für die Beziehungen von Christentum und Judentum, so nötig er wäre, weil die ihr Studium voraussetzende umfassende Arbeit von niemandem nebenher geleistet werden kann, war in der ganzen Welt nirgends vorhanden."[30]

## II. Aramaic versus Hebrew Studies

In spite of all his devotion to his *mentor* Delitzsch, Dalman behaved wholly independently not only in missionary questions but also in linguistic matters. He accepts the lines of his master *generally*, but *in concreto* he handles them in such a way that they go in quite a new direction, in a certain sense in the opposite direction. Pithily expressed: Dalman matured into a pioneering Aramaist because, or even *although*, Delitzsch had handed over to him the heart of his work, the translation of the New Testament into Hebrew.

Delitzsch's enterprise, along with its missionary goals, has a long prehistory that goes back as far as Sebastian Münster's *Evangelium secundum Matthæum in lingua Hebraica*, published 1531 in Basel under the title *Torat ha-mashiach*.[31] He recommended it expressly as *nativa sua hoc est Hebraica lingua*. The double claim remained fundamentally the same as that of Delitzsch's most renowned Hebrew translation that was published in 1877 by the *British and Foreign Bible Society*. From 1885 onward Delitzsch had to compete with the new translation of Isaac Edward Salkinson (1822–1883) that now was looked after by such an outstanding expert as Christian David Ginsburg (1831–1914).

In February 1890 Delitzsch, already on his deathbed, trusted his work to Gustaf Dalman who took care of the 11th edition in 1892 and the 12th in 1901, although he was very critical of Delitzsch's method, writing: "nach eigenem Ermessen aus dem Hebräisch aller Perioden ... bis zum Abschluss

30 Dalman, *Religionswissenschaft der Gegenwart*, 15.

31 For bibliography for this edition and for the later Basel editions of 1557 and 1582 see Joseph Prijs and Bernhard Prijs, *Die Basler hebräischen Drucke* (Olten: Urs Graf, 1964), 82–3 (no. 48), 143–4 (no. 99), 228 (no. 135), for the text's provenience, see ibid., 500 (Beilage 19).

der Mischna einen Dialekt zu bilden, welcher sich eigne, das Gefäss der neutestamentlichen Gedankenwelt zu werden."[32] On July 3th, 1934, Dalman noticed "dass er, seit 1901 die 12. Auflage von Delitzschs Hebräischem Neuen Testament erschien, nichts mehr mit diesem Werk zu tun hatte."[33]

So it remains true that Dalman, the one to whom Delitzsch entrusted his Hebrew translation of the New Testament, turned out to be one of the most outspoken critics of the enterprise, whereas specialists like Emil Kautzsch, Hermann Leberecht Strack, Samuel Rolles Driver and Carl Siegfried loudly praised it. Meanwhile Dalman had, in his typical manner, adopted a different approach to the language and culture of Jesus and the New Testament: the investigation of Aramaic. It is time to reevaluate a widespread verdict formulated by Karl Heinrich Rengstorf—himself a student *in rabbinicis* and some time assistant to Dalman—, namely, that Dalman's Aramaic studies should be qualified "als überholt."[34]

For Franz Rosenthal in his "Die Aramaistische Forschung seit Th. Nöldekes Veröffentlichungen,"[35] Dalman is credited with opening the door for understanding the regional variations in Aramaic during the transition period from middle (300 BCE–200 CE) to late Aramaic (200–700 CE). His "Grammatik des jüdisch-palästinischen Aramäisch"[36] with the complementary "Aramäischen Dialektproben"[37] and in the semantic field the "Aramäisch-neuhebräisches [Hand-] Wörterbuch zu Targum, Talmud und Midrasch, mit Vokalisation der targumischen Wörter nach südarabischen Handschriften und besonderer Bezeichnung des Wortschatzes des Onkelostargums, Teil I–II"[38]—an extract of the large dictionaries of Jacob Levy

[32] Gustaf H. Dalman, "Das hebräische Neue Testament von Franz Delitzsch," *Saat auf Hoffnung* 39 (1902): 154; cf. Männchen, *Dalmans Leben*, 54.

[33] Julius Böhmer, *Das Geheimnis um die Geburt von Franz Delitzsch* (Kassel/Leipzig: König, 1934), 22 n. 47.

[34] Karl H. Rengstorf, "Gustaf Dalmans Bedeutung für die Wissenschaft vom Judentum," *Wissenschaftlich Zeitschrift der Ernst Moritz Arndt-Universität Greifswald: Gesellschafts- und sprachwissenschaftliche Reihe* 4.4/5 (1954/55): 373–76 (376): "Dennoch wird es dabei bleiben müssen, dass DALMANs Theorie über die sprachlichen Grundlagen einer Rückübertragung der Worte Jesu in ihre Ursprache als solche als überholt zu gelten hat..." Cf. too Karl-Heinz Bernhardt, "Dalman, Gustaf," in *TRE* 8 (ed. Gerhard Müller; Berlin: de Gruyter, 1981), 322–3; Männchen, *Dalmans Leben*, 54 with n. 212.

[35] Franz Rosenthal, *Die Aramaistische Forschung seit Th. Nöldekes Veröffentlichungen* (Leiden: Brill, 1939).

[36] Gustaf H. Dalman, *Grammatik des jüdisch-palästinischen Aramäisch* (Leipzig: Hinrichs, [1]1894, [2]amplified 1905 = 1960, 1978, 1981, 1989). From hereon: *GJPA*.

[37] Gustaf H. Dalman, *Aramäischen Dialektproben* (Leipzig: Hinrichs, [1]1896, [2]amplified 1927 = 1960, 1978, 1981, 1989).

[38] Gustaf H. Dalman, *Aramäisch-neuhebräisches [Hand-] Wörterbuch zu Targum, Talmud und Midrasch, mit Vokalisation der targumischen Wörter nach südarabischen Handschriften*

and others which were cautious about etymologies and supplied material provided by Onkelos and Jemenite vocalisation—are still in use and are published to this day. Clearly modern studies diverge at many points from Dalman's more summarizing publications like "Die Worte Jesu"[39] and the work of his Greifswald period "Jesus-Jeschua".[40] They show, by the way, that for Dalman the starting point of even Aramaic studies was the initial questions, "wie die Worte Jesu in der Ursprache haben lauten müssen, und welchen Sinn sie in dieser Gestalt für den Hörer hatten."[41]

Dalman will retain his place in the history of Aramaic studies alone for the following two reasons: First, he takes seriously the elementary difference between Biblical Aramaic and the Aramaic of the rabbinical literature—a differentiation already underlined by Samuel David Luzzatto in the title of his treatise of 1832/33 (published only in 1865): "Elementi grammaticali del caldeo biblico e del dialetto talmudico babilonese."[42] Secondly, Dalman reminds scholarship urgently of the need for critical text editions. At this point one has to refer to the fact that Dalman frequently and meticulously consulted the fine collection of early Hebrew printings from the Gustaf-Dalman-Institut.[43] Of course, Dalman as well as his contemporaries, had no precise idea of the importance and the dimensions of Old Aramaic as the breeding ground for Official Aramaic. Therefore Dalman was wise to confine himself to Middle Aramaic in *Grammatik des jüdisch-palästinischen Aramäisch* (*GJPA*) and to describe it "nach den Idiomen des palästinischen Talmud und Midrasch, des Onkelostargums (Cod. Soc. 84) und der jerusalemischen Targume zum Pentateuch."[44] He

---

*und besonderer Bezeichnung des Wortschatzes des Onkelostargums, Teil I–II* (Frankfurt: Kauffmann, ¹1897–1901, ²corr. and amp. 1922, ³1938 = 1967, 1987, 1997 . . . 2007).

[39] Gustaf H. Dalman, *Die Worte Jesu I* (Leipzig: Hinrichs, 1898).

[40] Gustaf H. Dalman, *Jesus-Jeschua* (Leipzig: Hinrichs, 1922).

[41] Dalman, *Die Worte Jesu*, 57, emphasized in the original.

[42] David Luzzatto, *Elementi grammaticali del Caldeo Biblico e del Dialetto Talmudico Babilonese* (Padova: Bianchi, 1865); to the long years between conception and publication cf. ibid., 3.

[43] In addition to the volumes noted above at n. 10 I would like to note here the books that *GJPA*, VII, gathers as "Druckausgaben": Pentateuch with Targum Onkelos (ed. pr. Lisbon 1491), Sabbioneta 1557: J I 14; Pentateuch with three Targumim (Ed. princ. for Targum Jerushalmi I), Venise 1591: J I 15; First Biblia rabbinica (Ed. princ. for the Targum of the Ketubim as well as for Targum Jerushalmi II) [Felix Pratensis with Daniel Bomberg], Venise 1517: J I 25; Midrash chamesh Megilloth, Pesaro 1519, Venise 1545, Saloniki 1593: J VI 1; Midrash [Ber.] rabba, Constantinople 1512: J VII 1; Midrash Tehillim, Constantinople 1512, Venise 1547: J VI 1; Talmud jerushalmi [Ed. princ.], Venise 1523/24: J V 1; En Jaakob, Venise 1546: J XIII 5; Sefer Aruk, Pesaro 1517: J XXI 50.

[44] This is the sub-title of the first edition of Dalman's *GJPA*.

reaches positions that later on would be qualified and corrected in certain aspects, but remain valid in terms of his formulation of the problems and the methods he used to solve them. Among others it is Dalman's quite correct impression that the Western-Aramaic linguistic material emerged from a thoroughly common earlier stage.[45]

His voice is likely to be heard in other aspects of Aramaic research. First, in the question about the language spoken by Jesus, Dalman was the one who "es wohl als erster mit der philologischen Seite des Problems wirklich genau nahm."[46] And in the dispute with Julius Wellhausen and his follower Friedrich Schulthess, Dalman held firmly to the "als solide Arbeitsgrundlage in philologischer Hinsicht doch nur zu berechtigten Grundsatz . . .: quod non est apud Rabbinos, non est judaicum."[47] Second, enquiring into the supposed "original" Aramaic language underlying the Gospels, Dalman proved to be much more critical than, for example, Eberhard Nestle or Julius Wellhausen who both assumed an Aramaic source for Matthew. Third, it was Dalman who, as a pioneer, in the introductory part of *GJPA*[48] divided the Jewish-Palestinian Aramaic literature into three major branches, namely a) the *Jewish, sc. Judaean writings*, e.g., the Aramaic portions of the OT; the "Book of the Hasmoneans";[49] the Aramaic words in the NT and in Josephus; Meg. Ta'an. as well as Targum Onkelos and the Targum of the Prophets;[50] b) the *Galilaean*, into which he places mainly the Aramaic portions in the Palestinian Talmud, in the Palestinian Midrashim;[51] and c) the "Sprachdenkmäler mit gemeinsamem Sprachtypus," which was not homogenous and therefore rightly critized by Paul Kahle as non-useful, and which contained the Palestinian Targum to the Pentateuch, the Targums to the Hagiographa[52] (though Dalman himself held of them, "dass sie nur Kunstprodukte sind"),[53] and apocryphal Aramaic writings such as the Aramaic version of Tobit. Quite recently,

45 Rosenthal, *Aramaistische Forschung*, 104 n. 2.
46 Rosenthal, *Aramaistische Forschung*, 106.
47 Rosenthal, *Aramaistische Forschung*, 107, by referring to the opposite position of Julius Wellhausen, *Einleitung in die drei ersten Evangelien* (Berlin: Reimer, 1905), 41, and the explicit reasoning in the second edition (1911).
48 *GJPA*, 6–39.
49 "Das er [pp. 7–8] als eine Nachahmung in der aramäischen Sprachform des Alten Testaments erkannte, also ganz hätte aus dem Spiel lassen müssen," Rosenthal, *Aramaistische Forschung*, 124.
50 *GJPA*, 6–16.
51 Ibid., 16–27.
52 Ibid., 27–39.
53 Ibid., 35.

Abraham Tal insisted on this last point, that "apparently, Dalman was closer to the real nature of Neubauer's Aramaic version of Tobit... The document in question justifies Dalman's assertion regarding its age as *Sprachtypus*."[54] Indeed, Dalman with his dating "nicht vor dem siebten Jahrhundert,"[55] was right over against Theodor Nöldeke who saw in it "eine wirkliche lebendige Sprache" and dated it back as far as 300 CE.[56] Fourth, concerning Christian-Palestinian Aramaic, Dalman held that there were no proofs for a relation to the Galilaean dialect as often contended. In this he categorically disproved Julius Wellhausen's "Forderung, das Evangelium Hierosolymitanum bei der Erörterung der Muttersprache Jesu zu Grunde zu legen."[57]

Last but not least, Dalmans' studies on Jewish-Palestinian Aramaic were embedded in a broader semitic frame of reference. He spoke and wrote fluently, even composed poems in Arabic and was especially interested in the "Volkssprache"[58] with which he tried to familiarize himself as early as his first journey to the Near East in 1899/1900 and that he used daily in his Jerusalem years from 1902 to 1914. One may not forget his expeditions to Petra—ten times between 1904 and 1910! The Aramaic studies constitute in many respects a sort of *continuum* from Leipzig to Jerusalem. Jerusalem gave him new opportunities. Starting with the second edition of *GJPA* he chose with keen insight the Yemenite vocalization he had in his hands in a Genesis/Exodus manuscript belonging to the Edler-von-Lämel-library, and he verified the texts by "praktische Kenntnisnahme der jemenischen Aussprache des Hebräischen und Aramäischen, zu welcher Jerusalem Gelegenheit bietet" (*GJPA*, VIII).

## III. Conclusions

From a modern point of view one may ask why mission among the Jews played such an important role for Dalman. In sum, it was no less than the

[54] Abraham Tal, "The Role of Targum Onqelos in Literary Activity During the Middle Ages," in *Aramaic in its Historical and Linguistic Setting* (ed. Holger Gzella and Margaretha L. Folmer; Wiesbaden: Harassowitz, 2008), 164–67.

[55] *GJPA*, 37.

[56] Theodor Nöldeke, *Berichte über die Verhandlungen der königl. Akademie der Wissenschaften zu Berlin* (Berlin: Verlag der königlichen Akademie der Wissenschaften, 1879), 65–69, cf. Rosenthal, *Aramaistische Forschung*, 125.

[57] *GJPA*, 41 with n. 1.

[58] "Die arabische Volkssprache, für welche mich Prof. Socin vor meiner Abreise in grosser Freundlichkeit noch privatim geschult hatte...," Dalman, *Religionswissenschaft der Gegenwart*, 13.

starting point for his Judaic studies as well as for his Aramaic and Holy Land studies. The influence of his revered mother's engagement with the Jewish people was only one motive. Dalman realized very soon how massive was the ignorance about Jews and Judaism in the second half of the 19th century, so that antisemitism found easily a nourishing soil. And the roots of such a development reached even deeper. Following his *mentor* Delitzsch, Dalman felt compelled to resist the ongoing alienation of biblical exegesis and theology as a whole from its Jewish origins. He was quite aware how helpless the Protestant church was in the face of these trends. *Zionism* was for him one of the foremost factors promoting indifference and secularization. He charged it with an a-religious modernism and pure nationalism. Against such a lack of religion he unceasingly proclaimed, not without a certain apologetic undertone; the personality of Jesus was for him the only real difference between Judaism and Christianity.

This appears somewhat paradoxical. For just to understand Jesus better and deeper, Dalman—the Christian, the philologist, the lover of the Holy Land—turned to Jesus' *Jewish* world, to the language of the *Jewish* tradition and to the land of the Bible. Lastly he was convinced that even the developments in Palestine would disclose themselves only to someone who acknowledged God's word upon which Jews as well as Christians, yet in different ways, relied—the word with its Jewish, that means, human aspect *and* with its divine origin.

# PART II

# HEBREW LANGUAGE AND TEXTUAL TRADITIONS

# TRACES OF ERGATIVITY IN BIBLICAL HEBREW

John Barton

One of the first things one learns in studying biblical Hebrew is that the definite direct object takes the particle את.[1] Apart from the construct state, a kind of inverted genitive,[2] Biblical Hebrew does not have inflections for case, but it does have this strange *nota accusativi*, as it is technically called, which at least in prose appears to be obligatory when the object of a verb is definite. There is no agreement about the origin of the particle or its usage as a marker of the accusative. An early study, an unpublished Yale doctoral thesis by Alfred M. Wilson,[3] argued that it was in origin a marker of emphasis, but this has not been generally accepted and in any case does not account for the usage in the Hebrew Bible, where it is undoubtedly a case-marker. Segal notes that the use as a mark of the accusative continues in Mishnaic Hebrew, though with some exceptions,[4] and it is still in use in Modern Hebrew to mark the definite direct object.

But it is well known that there is a small but significant number of instances in the Bible where the particle is prefixed not to the object but to the subject of the sentence. Gesenius-Kautzsch lists some twelve instances, and a few more were added in an article by P. P. Saydon in 1964, though some of his examples seem to me unlikely or simply mistaken.[5] More recently Waltke and O'Connor have listed some others.[6] I present below a consolidated list:

> Gen 4:18, 17:5, 21:5, 27:42; Num 3:46 (?), 5:10, 35:6, 35:7; Deut 11:2, 15:3; Josh 22:17; Judg 20:44, 20:46; 1 Sam 17:34, 26:16 (?); 2 Sam 11:25; 2 Kgs 6:5, 10:15; 2 Chr 31:17; Neh 9:19, 9:34; Jer 36:22; Ezek 10:22, 17:21, 35:10, 44:3; Dan 9:13.

---

[1] It is a great pleasure to offer this essay to Hugh Williamson, a valued colleague for so many years and such an expert on Biblical Hebrew.

[2] At least synchronically one could analyse the construct as an 'antigenitive,' but from a historical point of view it is not really a case, simply a reduction of the governing noun in front of a noun in the genitive—thus it occurs in Semitic languages that do have a case-system, such as Akkadian.

[3] Summarized in Alfred M. Wilson, "The Particle את in Hebrew," *Hebraica* 6/2–3 (1899–90): 139–50, 212–24.

[4] Moses H. Segal, *A Grammar of Mishnaic Hebrew* (Oxford: Clarendon Press, 1927), 168.

[5] Paul P. Saydon, "Meanings and uses of the particle את," *VT* 14 (1964): 192–210.

[6] Bruce K. Waltke and Michael O'Connor, *An Introduction to Biblical Hebrew Syntax* (Winona Lake, Indiana: Eisenbrauns, 1990), 182–3 (§10.3.2).

GKC adds Ezek 20:16; Saydon, Gen 29:27, 1 Sam 19:10, Jer 45:4, and Ezek 24:4; and Waltke and O'Connor, Deut 14:12 and 14:14, and Hag 2:17. But none of these seems to me to contain the particle prefixed to the subject of the sentence.[7] Waltke and O'Connor also mention Gen 13:15, 1 Kgs 15:13, and Ezek 20:16, but these are simply cases where the object is fronted in the sentence.

There seems so far to be no satisfactory explanation for the use of the same particle to mark both the subject and the object of a sentence. Waltke and O'Connor suggest that there may be a clue in the three passages just mentioned, where the object is fronted, and one might translate 'as to X' (*quoad* in Latin): "as for all the land you see, I will give it to you" (Gen 13:15). Perhaps when the particle is prefixed to the subject a similar effect is intended: the particle simply draws attention to the noun rather than indicating its case. But so far as I can see this does not work in most of the cases listed, though Joüon also mentions this as a possible use of the particle את.[8] GKC claim that the particle with the nominative always has an implied *ecce* in front of it, which amounts to the same thing, and is related to the explanation of the particle as a kind of demonstrative or intensifier: thus also J. MacDonald in *Vetus Testamentum* in 1964.[9]

One possible reaction is to regard the use of the same particle for both nominative and accusative as so counter-intuitive that there is no choice but to emend the passages in question, and this is the approach of Muraoka. He writes that את "is never used with a genuine subject noun," and "after having exhausted all the possibilities imaginable, there remain a considerable number of passages for which we have no alternative but to suggest emendation, ranging from mere change in the pointing to alteration of the consonantal text itself."[10] Naturally there may be cases where emendation is reasonable, but in general I believe there are too many examples of the particle with the subject to make this a satisfactory solution in every case.

---

[7] Jer 45:4 ends with ואת־כל־הארץ היא, which is strictly speaking an example of a verbless clause in which the subject (or rather the complement) is preceded by את, but in context the היא looks like an afterthought.

[8] Paul Joüon, *Grammaire de l'hébreu biblique* (2nd ed.; Rome: Pontifical Biblical Institute, 1947), 170 (§125j).

[9] John MacDonald, "The Particle את in Classical Hebrew: Some New Data on its Use with the Nominative," *VT* 14 (1964): 264–75, referring to the use of the particle at Josh 7:9 in the Samaritan Chronicle.

[10] Takamitsu Muraoka, *Emphatic Words and Structures in Biblical Hebrew* (Jerusalem/Leiden: Magnes Press/Brill, 1985), 146–58; the quotation is from p. 157.

An observation that seems to me to lead in the direction of a possible way of analysing this puzzling phenomenon, though not necessarily of explaining it, is made by Waltke and O'Connor. This is that (with one exception, Neh 9:34) את with the subject occurs only with intransitive or passive verbs or in verbless clauses, never when the noun is the subject of a transitive verb. And this suggests to me that the phenomenon should probably be analysed as showing a degree of ergativity in Biblical Hebrew—at least in its late phase, from which most of the examples appear to come. Waltke and O'Connor mention this possibility, although they are not very hospitable to it; but I think it may have some mileage. However, I have the impression that the concept of ergativity is not very familiar in biblical studies, so I must spend a little time in explaining what is meant.

## I. The Concept of Ergativity

In nearly all of the languages of Europe two main functions are recognized in a sentence, which we call subject and object. In inflected languages the subject stands in the nominative case and the (direct) object in the accusative; in minimally inflected languages such as English the two functions may be marked by word order rather than morphology, so that we distinguish 'the dog bit the man' from 'the man bit the dog.' Biblical Hebrew for the most part is like most European languages in similarly distinguishing nominative from accusative, with accusative sometimes marked with the particle את and with word order often disambiguating where there is no marking.

If we move out to other languages—the main examples being, in Europe, Basque, which is unrelated to any other known language; outside Europe, the native languages of Australia and some of the languages of the North American Arctic and Sub-Arctic; and, historically, Sumerian and (the Indo-European) Hittite—we find that the simple subject-object distinction is no longer adequate. In these languages a crucial distinction exists between transitive and intransitive verbs, and the cases of nouns and pronouns differ according to that distinction. We may say that there are in principle three possible functions in a sentence or clause. One is the direct object. But the others are the subject of an intransitive verb, and the agent of a transitive one. These three functions are conventionally dubbed S (subject of an intransitive verb), A (subject or agent of a transitive verb), and O (direct object of a transitive verb). In theory one could have a language that had separate inflections for all three functions, but in practice in nearly all languages two of the functions work morphologically or syntactically in the same way. Most of the languages with which most of us are familiar merge S and A, and where there are inflections these nouns or pronouns are in the nominative case, while O is in the accusative. (In a largely uninflected language such as English S and A both precede the verb, and O follows it.) But it is possible to have languages that merge S and O, and in these languages S and O are said to be in the absolutive case, while A, the agent of the transitive verb, is in the ergative case. The first type of language is called, somewhat confusingly, an accusative language, while the second type is known as an ergative language. The following chart represents the two systems:

| | | |
|---|---|---|
| | Transitive subject | A---------------Ergative |
| Nominative--------------- | | |
| | Intransitive subject S | |
| | | ---------------Absolutive |
| Accusative---------------- | Direct object O | |

A formal definition of ergativity is provided by R. M. W. Dixon, the leading authority on the subject and expert in Australian languages, in his standard work *Ergativity*: "The term 'ergativity' is, in its most generally accepted sense, used to describe a grammatical pattern in which the subject of an intransitive clause is treated in the same way as the object of a transitive clause, and differently from transitive subject."[11]

To imagine how this works, we can play with an imaginary ergative version of English. Since English nouns do not inflect for case except in the possessive, we shall have to use pronouns throughout. In normal English, 'she' is the nominative, used for the subject of both transitive and intransitive verbs, and 'her' is the accusative, used for the direct object of transitive verbs. But in our imaginary ergative English, 'she' is the ergative case, used for the subject of transitive verbs, and 'her' the absolutive, used for the subject of intransitive verbs and for the direct object of transitive verbs. As in the English we are familiar with, in 'ergative English' we

[11] Robert M. W. Dixon, *Ergativity* (Cambridge Studies in Linguistics; Cambridge and Melbourne: Cambridge University Press, 1994), 1. See also the helpful discussion in Barry J. Blake, *Case*, (Cambridge Textbooks in Linguistics; Cambridge: Cambridge University Press, 1994).

would say 'She delivered a lecture'—transitive verb. But with an intransitive verb we would have to say 'Her came in' and 'Her is a lecturer.' This 'her' would be identical with the object pronoun, as in 'He saw her.' (In fact, the word order would need to change too, since the accusative—and hence, in our imagined language, the absolutive—follows the verb, but for simplicity's sake I have left the normal English word order alone.)

In normal English, one does not have to repeat the subject of a sentence in a co-ordinate clause: thus 'She came in and delivered a lecture' (not, at least not obligatorily, 'She came in and she delivered a lecture')—because S, the subject of the intransitive 'came' and A, the agent of the transitive 'gave,' are treated the same way, and so the subject is nominative in both clauses and hence does not need to be repeated. In our ergative version of English, it would be the subject of an intransitive verb (S) and the object of a transitive one (O) that would be the same. So we should say, 'Her came in and the students saw'—no need to repeat 'her' because it is already there. But of course we should have to say 'Her came in and she delivered a lecture,' because S and A are in different cases.

My impression is that to speakers of most European languages ergativity seems counter-intuitive. How can one treat the subjects of transitive and intransitive verbs as different, and treat the subjects of intransitive verbs as the same as the direct objects of transitive ones? Surely the distinction between acting and suffering, which is the nominative/accusative distinction, is somehow natural, whereas the distinction between the subject (or agent) of a transitive verb and the subject of an intransitive verb, is of a second order? The fact that accusative languages are more widespread than ergative ones might tend to underpin this sense of what is 'natural': about 80% of languages are accusative, and 20% significantly ergative (I say 'significantly' because many languages are only partly ergative, as I shall go on to explain). Nevertheless even the languages with which we are familiar, though they have no traces of ergativity, do have features that can hint at why, psychologically, a culture might develop an ergative language. Here are a few thoughts.

In saying that to most speakers of European languages the equivalence of S and A is much more obvious than the equivalence of S and O, we are in effect saying that for us the distinction between transitive and intransitive verbs seems less significant than that between subject and object. But even in Indo-European languages the two sorts of verb do have striking differences. An everyday definition of a verb is that it is a word of doing, an action-word. But this is only very moderately true of many intransitives. 'To die' is a verb (an intransitive one), but dying is not in any usual sense an action. 'To be' is an even more obvious case. Furthermore, verbs that are intransitive in English often have equivalents in other languages that are reflexive or middle: 'I get up' in French is 'je me lève,' 'I wash' is 'je me lave,' compare English 'I get washed.' In Greek 'die' can be an active verb ἀποθνησκω but it can also be middle, ἀποθανομαι. The sense of self-involvement that we tend to learn as essential to the middle voice means that the subject of a middle verb is also to a degree its object, as is clear in languages that use reflexives to convey a middle sense, such as French. (In Hebrew the middle is most often expressed through the Niphal or in some cases the Hithpael, and it may be that the Niphal is in origin a middle, which has now usurped the place of the obsolete passive Qal and is used also to express the passive.) It would be quite easy to imagine a language in which there was a special form of the subject for middle verbs, or in which in fact the 'middleness' of the verb was expressed wholly through such a special form rather than being marked on the verb itself. That might produce a system in which S, A, and O all had separate forms, a logical possibility that, as I remarked before, seems hardly ever to occur in practice.

Another factor relevant to the issue is that while formally transitivity is an absolute (verbs either have an object or they do not), semantically there is a sliding scale between transitive and intransitive. 'To die' is definitely intransitive, 'to kill' is definitely transitive; but 'to suffer,' 'to resist,' and 'to attack' represent stages in between. 'To see' is a transitive verb in English but it has an intransitive side, in that it suggests that something impinges on our vision, as opposed to 'to look' where we are stressing an active seeking after perception. It would not be surprising if various languages differed in how far they treat these various verbs as transitive or intransitive, and that is in fact what we find. Once the S/A distinction is recognized, it is easy to see that different languages might then encode this distinction in different ways depending on the degree of transitivity that is perceived in the verb.

Especially in the case of verbs in the middle voice, it is not difficult to see that the subject might perfectly well be expressed in the same form as the object of a transitive verb rather than in the same form as the agent of a transitive verb—and that is the position in ergative languages. Such languages highlight the person who is *affected* by the verb. In the case of transitive verbs, this is the object; in the case of intransitives, and especially middles, it is what we call the subject. In 'I hit you,' you are the person affected; but in 'I go,' or 'I die,' or 'I get up,' I am the person affected. These two functions are expressed through the same morphological or syntactic means: S=O, both in the absolutive case. The agent of plainly *transitive* verbs (A) is another matter, expressed in the ergative case. Accusative languages, on the other hand, concentrate on who is doing the 'action' expressed in the verb, and express that function in the nominative irrespective of whether it is that person or the object that undergoes the action expressed by the verb. These are simply two different ways of slicing the cake, neither really more intuitive than the other. Apparently in learning English children sometimes show an awareness of the difference between the intransitive subject and the transitive agent, which is the classic ergative distinction, in that "verbs expressing actions which are overtly agentive and require some degree of control on the part of the (first person) subject are used with a subject pronoun *my*, while those that were not expressive of agentivity were (*sic*) marked with a subject pronoun *I* (e.g. *I like cookies*)."[12]

A second point is this. In Indo-European languages that have a neuter gender, the nominative and accusative of the neuter are always identical. Of languages known by most biblical scholars, this is true of Greek, Latin, and German. Even in the barely inflected English language it holds true in the pronouns, the one place where nominative and accusative are morphologically distinguished: we have he/him and she/her, but it/it. It is possible that this is related to the fact that neuter nouns are typically the names of inanimates: and inanimates initiate action much less frequently than animates, so that they are seldom in the agent function A. There may thus be a kind of underlying feeling that a neuter noun is typically accusative, typically the patient rather than the agent. Certainly, to speak for myself, when I began learning inflected languages I used to try to grasp this phenomenon about the neuter by telling myself that neuter nouns are somehow already accusative even when they're nominative. This is not a formulation that would appeal to a linguist, but there is some intuitive value in it. A neuter noun, on the rare occasions that it does name the subject of a sentence or clause, is morphologically identical to a neuter noun when, more typically, it names the object. (Even when neuter nouns are agents, they exhibit one particular property in Greek at least, in that the plural of neuter nouns takes a singular verb, which marks the neuter

---

[12] Sonja Eisenbeiss, Bhuvana Harasimhan, and Maria Voeikova, "The Acquisition of Case," in *The Oxford Handbook of Case* (ed. Andrej Malchukov and Andrew Spencer; Oxford: Oxford University Press, 2009), 369–83; the quotation is from p. 376, citing Nancy Budwig, "The Linguistic Marking of Agentivity and Control in Child Language," *Journal of Child Language* 16 (1989): 263–84.

out as different from the other genders.) The peculiarities of the Indo-European neuter may not be a million miles away from the equivalence of S and O in ergative languages. I do not mean to suggest that it is an actual example of ergativity, which it certainly is not, but simply that it may help us to get into the mindset that produces ergative ways of organizing a language, and make this seem less alien and counter-intuitive.

A third aspect of familiar languages that may help us to understand ergativity is the prevalence in many languages of impersonal clauses, such as 'it seems to me' (archaically with an oblique case, 'me thinks,' compare archaic German 'mich dünkt'). Here the person concerned is in the oblique case, either accusative or dative, rather than in the nominative, and there is an 'empty' nominative 'it.' This again is not a case of ergativity, but it can help to loosen up our ideas of how verbs work and so make ergativity comprehensible. The feature it has in common is that the person actually concerned is not in the nominative, since (s)he is not 'doing' anything but rather is in the position of the recipient of the action: we conceptualize 'thinking that something is the case' as an event that happens to us, rather than as something we do. We are in a sense the subject, but we are not the agent, which is exactly the distinction that ergative languages make between S and A, between absolutive and ergative. This is also apparent in some ideas that are expressed in English with a transitive verb but in other languages with an impersonal or some other construction. For example, 'to like' is regarded as transitive in English—'I like this colour'—but in German, despite the fact that 'ich mag diese Farbe' is possible, it is probably more usual to say 'diese Farbe gefällt mir,' 'this colour pleases me.' 'Liking,' so one may interpret this construction, is not something I do, but something that happens to me: it is the colour that does the appealing rather than I that do the liking—compare the comment above about children's use of the verb 'to like.'

## II. Ergativity in the Hebrew Bible

Now we are in a position to turn to the evidence from the Hebrew Bible about את with the 'nominative,' and to see whether an analysis in terms of ergativity can contribute anything to understanding this strange phenomenon. On the face of it I think it can. The phenomenon we have here is that an intransitive subject is marked in the same way as a direct object, and that is the classic feature of ergativity. An analysis in terms of ergativity solves the puzzle about 'את with the nominative' in these passages in a way that nothing else seems to do. There are instances among those listed where there may be a more traditional explanation. In the examples from Gen 4:18 and 21:5, we have את followed by the name of someone who was born, and a plausible explanation is that the accusative marker has been retained even though the word in the accusative has now become the subject of the passive verb, either wrongly or as part of some kind of fixed idiom, when a typical active construction—'PN1 bore את PN2'—was passivized to produce 'את PN2 was born to PN1.' This is the kind of thing that happens in languages without its necessarily having any wider significance. It is noteworthy that GK do not list these examples at all in their enumeration of cases of את with the nominative.[13] (In parenthesis, however, it might be noted that verbs for 'being born' sit uneasily in the active/middle/passive system of voice in a number of languages. In French *naître* is active, but in English and German the corresponding verb is passive, and in Latin *nascor* is morphologically passive, but might be analysed as middle—traditionally called 'deponent.')

But other examples do seem to me to suggest an ergative interpretation. As I commented before, all but one of the verses listed involve intransitive verbs, including the verb to be, or are verbless and imply a copula which is not expressed. These are exactly the sorts of instance that occur in ergative languages. The subject is expressed using the same morphological or syntactic devices as with the object of transitive verbs, which in Hebrew means the particle את. One of the clearest cases is Neh 9:19:

> You in your great mercies did not forsake them in the wilderness; את-the pillar of cloud that led them in the way did not turn from them by day, nor את-the pillar of fire by night that gave them light on the way by which they should go.

Here we clearly have 'את with the nominative,' as it is traditionally expressed, but an analysis of the nouns with את as in effect absolutives, indicating the subject of an intransitive verb, is preferable. The same is true in 2 Sam 11:25:

> David said to the messenger, "Thus you shall say to Joab, 'Do not let את-this matter trouble you, for the sword devours now one and now another; press your attack on the city, and overthrow it.' And encourage him."

[13] See also Karl Albrecht, "את vor dem Nominativ und beim Passiv," *ZAW* 47 (1929): 274–83.

"Do not let the matter trouble you," literally "may the matter not seem bad to you," just the kind of clause where, as we saw, ergative languages use the absolutive. A number of the other examples are verbless, since in Hebrew as in many languages the verb 'to be' remains unexpressed in clauses with an implied copula, and here again ergative languages use the absolutive case for what we call the subject.

I can envisage three major objections to my analysis. The first is that it surely seems odd to have just a few examples of ergativity in a language which, as all would agree, is essentially accusative, as are all the Semitic languages. Could there be this handful of examples? But this misunderstands the distribution of ergativity among the world's languages. Whereas there are wholly accusative languages—English, French, and German, indeed all the Romance and Germanic languages as well as most other Indo-European languages—there are very few wholly ergative languages. Basque is apparently an almost pure example. But most ergative languages are so-called 'split-ergative,' meaning that in some areas they are ergative and in some accusative: this is true of Sumerian. Typically nouns will work ergatively, but pronouns accusatively. Even in the Indo-European family, which is overwhelmingly accusative, there are a few languages that exhibit occasional ergative features: this is true of Hindi-Urdu in perfective aspect, and in Iranian languages in past tenses. The Indo-European Hittite had an ergative case, but—oddly—only with neuter nouns (but compare my comments above about the Indo-European neuter). The suggestion that biblical Hebrew might have had a *measure* of ergativity, while remaining predominantly accusative, is thus not all that outlandish. And ergativity does not correlate necessarily with language families: there is no reason why one Semitic language should not exhibit occasional ergative features even if the rest do not—though H.-P. Müller in fact has argued that Akkadian, as well as archaic Hebrew, had ergative features.[14] It is possible, indeed relatively normal, for languages to move from ergativity to accusativity and vice versa. Thus it is entirely possible that at some stage there were traces of ergativity in Hebrew, even though it was overwhelmingly accusative in character throughout its history. From the examples I have listed I think we should probably think of it as predominantly a late rather than archaic feature, though the sample is so small that it is hard to be definite about this, and one or two of the examples would be

[14] Hans-Peter Müller, "Ergativelemente im akkadischen und althebräischen Verbalsystem," *Bib* 66 (1985): 385–417.

reckoned pre-exilic on many current datings of biblical books (e.g. 1 Sam 17:34, 2 Sam 11:25).

A second, and I think more serious objection, is that the absolutive form in ergative systems is normally the unmarked form of the noun or pronoun, whereas forms with את are clearly marked in Hebrew, having an extra element that the noun in its unmarked form does not possess. In ergative languages it is regularly the ergative case that is marked. I suspect that some linguists might regard this as a fatal flaw in my proposed analysis: I do not know whether there are ergative languages or phases of languages in which the absolutive is the marked form. This is an area where further thought is needed. One could imagine, however, a Hebrew writer sensing an affinity between direct object and intransitive subject and so using the same form occasionally: it would be correct to analyse the usage in terms of ergativity, even though it would not represent a major trend.

A third problem is that there is one single example among those listed where the 'nominative with את' governs a transitive verb, which ought not to be possible in an ergative structure. This is Neh 9:34: "את-Our kings, our officials, our priests, and our ancestors have not kept your law or heeded the commandments and the warnings that you gave them." It is noticeable here that the את is prefixed only to the first of the people listed, which is irregular in itself, and BHS proposes that it be emended to אף.[15] But emending to get rid of a problem is poor practice, and we might want to register this example as anomalous. It is, to make the best of a bad job, the only case in the entire Hebrew Bible where את is prefixed to the agent/subject of a transitive verb: all the other examples involve intransitives or verbless clauses, as one would expect from the usual functioning of ergativity.

## III. Concluding Remarks

Have I succeeded in showing that Biblical Hebrew shows traces of ergativity? I think I have, and in a sense a language is as ergative as it looks: if the subject of intransitive verbs takes the same morphology or syntax as the object of finite verbs, then to that extent there is ergativity. It doesn't make sense to ask 'Is this *really* ergativity?': ergativity is a descriptive category that sums up in one word a particular phenomenon, and if I have

[15] Following Wilhelm Rudolph, *Esra und Nehemia samt 3 Esra* (HAT 1/20; Tübingen: J. C. B. Mohr [Paul Siebeck], 1949), 168, who draws on Albrecht (see note 13 above).

shown that the phenomenon exists in certain passages, then in those passages there *is* ergativity. The only thing that would call this in question would be a textual argument for emending each of the passages to get rid of the particle את. But more important is the question what if anything follows from the demonstration that Hebrew has traces of ergativity. My tentative answer is that nothing much does follow from it. It does not call in question the general point that Semitic languages are accusative, any more than the evidence, from Hittite, Persian, and Hindi-Urdu calls in question the general accusativity of the Indo-European family. But it is interesting in itself that Hebrew has this additional complexity. And it provides a satisfying analysis, even though not an explanation, of a phenomenon that has puzzled grammarians for a long time: how the same form can be both a *nota accusativi* and a *nota nominativi*. The phenomenon remains unexplained: we don't know why at some time or other a few writers (for we know nothing about *speakers* of Hebrew) started occasionally to use את to mark function S. But at least we have some categories with which to describe what the phenomenon is. In a wider linguistic context it is less puzzling than it seems at first sight.

For me, the exploration of ergativity has been a fascinating one, giving insight into the different ways in which human languages are configured, and reminding us that matters that seem obvious within one system are far from obvious in another. In learning languages even as far removed from each other as the Indo-European and Semitic families, we never need to call in question our basic assumption that verbs have subjects and objects and that one can expect these to be different either morphologically or syntactically. The study of ergativity shows us that such an assumption is false: there are two different sorts of subject, and some languages correlate them with each other, while some languages correlate one of them with objects. Studying phenomena like these opens up new horizons on how human beings encode their world in language.

# ISAIAH 30:15 בשובה ונחת AND AKKADIAN *ŠUBAT NĒḪTI/ŠUBTU NĒḪTU*, 'QUIET ABODE'

Kevin J. Cathcart

On 5th April 1860, Edwin Norris, one of the pioneers of Assyriology and the editor of the first Akkadian dictionary,[1] wrote to Edward Hincks, the decipherer of Akkadian cuneiform, in these words:

> I quite agree with you as to the progress that will be made in Assyrian when we have unity of effort. I think too that more must be made of Hebrew above Arabic or anything else. What I am myself doing, to forward the work, is classifying alphabetically all the words I find; and fancy I often light upon a correction of former readings in that way. I saw the other day a couple of words together in Tiglath Pileser who says he left his kingdom in *subta va nukhta*. I forget how it is rendered by Rawlinson, but I saw at once peace and rest, from שׁבת and נוח.[2]

Norris was referring to a passage in an inscription of Tiglath-pileser I, *šīri nišēya uṭīb šubta nēḫta ušēšibšunūti*,[3] which he translates in his *Assyrian Dictionary* as follows: "The conditions of my people I ameliorated, (in) a seat of repose I made them sit."[4] Today the passage is more accurately rendered: "I improved the well-being of my people (and) settled them in a quiet abode." Norris seems to have been in two minds about the meaning of *šubtu* because in another place in his dictionary he gives this version of the text of Tiglath-pileser I: "The condition of my people (in) abundance and rest I established them."[5] He may have been influenced by his mentor, Rawlinson, whose version in the celebrated "Comparative Translations" of 1857 reads: "I improved the condition of the people, and I obtained for

---

[1] Edwin Norris, *Assyrian Dictionary* (3 vols.; London: Williams and Norgate, 1868–72). See the entry for Edwin Norris in *ODNB*.

[2] See Kevin J. Cathcart, ed., *The Correspondence of Edward Hincks* (3 vols.; Dublin: University College Dublin Press, 2007–2009), 3:72.

[3] A. Kirk Grayson, *Assyrian Rulers of the Early First Millennium* BC: *I (1114–859* BC) (RIMA 2; Toronto: University of Toronto Press, 1991), 27, vii 33–35 (hereafter RIMA 2).

[4] Norris, *Assyrian Dictionary*, 3:1015.

[5] Norris, *Assyrian Dictionary*, 3:1008. The translation "abundance" suggests that he derived *šubtu* from the Semitic root *šbʿ* instead of *yšb*. Compare Akk. *šēbû* and *wašābu*. In the letter to Hincks he seems to regard Hebrew שׁבת, "to rest" as a cognate of the root of *šubtu*.

them abundance and security."[6] Norris's version is all the more puzzling because in another place on the same page he translates *šubat nēḫti* by "a place of rest." Although Norris writes *subta va nukhta* in his letter to Hincks, he does not refer to Isa 30:15, בשובה ונחת.

As far as I know, Avishur is the only scholar who has clearly recognised the importance of Akkadian *šubat nēḫti/šubtu nēḫtu*, 'abode (or seat) of rest, quiet abode,' for the possible clarification of the etymology and meaning of the expression in Isaiah.[7] De Jong, who shares the view that שובה in Isa 30:15 must be derived from ישב, 'to sit, dwell,' mentions the combination of *nāḫu* and *wašābu* in an Akkadian text, but not the expression *šubtu nēḫtu*.[8] In this paper I shall discuss the arguments for and against the derivation of שובה from ישב (or a Nebenform שוב), 'to dwell, sit,' and examine the possible association of Isa 30:15 בשובה ונחת with Akkadian *šubat nēḫti/šubtu nēḫtu*, 'quiet abode, peaceful dwelling.'

Hugh Williamson has made outstanding contributions to the study of the Old Testament, especially to the Book of Isaiah, so it is a pleasure to dedicate this paper to him, a friend over many decades, to whom I owe much gratitude.

## I. Isaiah 30:15 בשובה ונחת in Ancient and Modern Translations

The etymology and meaning of the word שובה, which is a *hapax legomenon*, are much disputed. Many modern exegetes still derive the noun from שוב, 'to return' and translate it by 'returning,' 'conversion' or 'repentance.' Some scholars, however, hold opinions similar to those of the early medieval Jewish commentators Rashi, Kimḥi and Ibn Ezra, who were of the view that שובה is to be understood with the sense of 'rest' and to be derived from ישב. In his commentary on Isaiah, Rashi comments that בשובה is an

[6] Edward Hincks, Jules Oppert, Henry C. Rawlinson and W. H. F. Talbot, "Comparative Translations of the Inscription of Tiglath Pileser I," *JRAS* 18 (1861): 150–219 (206). Although the translation "abundance" for *šubtu* is wrong, it should be noted that other words for "abundance" occur together with "rest" and "tranquillity" in the inscriptions to be examined below.

[7] Yitshak Avishur, *Stylistic Studies of Word-Pairs in Biblical and Ancient Semitic Literatures* (AOAT 210; Kevelaer: Butzon & Bercker; Neukirchen-Vluyn: Neukirchener, 1984), 709–11.

[8] Matthjis J. de Jong, *Isaiah Among the Ancient Near Eastern Prophets: A Comparative Study of the Earliest Stages of the Isaiah Tradition and the Neo-Assyrian Prophecies* (VTSup 117; Leiden: Brill, 2007), 114 n. 300. See *CAD* N$^{I}$, 145: "Quiet down (*nūḫ*), sit down (*tišab*), compose yourself, provide well-being for the house you have entered."

expression of restfulness and tranquillity. He compares Num 10:36, "Rest (שׁובה), O Lord, with the ten thousands of the thousands of Israel." In this case, however, Moran would emend שׁובה to שׁבה (see *BHS*).[9] In the modern period Ehrlich, who does not believe that שׁובה has anything to do with 'repentance,' proposes the emendation of שׁובה to שׁבת with the sense of 'sitting' and 'resting.'[10] Lexicographers in general derive the word from שׁוב: 'retirement, withdrawal (from war),'[11] 'Umkehr,'[12] 'turning back, returning,'[13] 'reversio ad Deum, conversio.'[14] Gesenius and Fürst prefer a derivation from שׁוב, but they recognize the possibility that שׁובה might be from ישׁב, 'to sit, dwell.'[15] Ewald is more decisive and translates שׁובה as 'Ruhe,' deriving it from ישׁב.[16]

The majority of translators, ancient and modern, also connect שׁובה with שׁוב, 'return.' For Isa 30:15 בשׁובה ונחת, the LXX has ὁταν ἀποστραφεις στεναξῃς, "When you come back and groan,"[17] and the Vulgate has *si revertamini et quiescatis*, "If you return and be quiet." Symmachus has ἐν μετανοια και ἀναπαυσει, "in conversion and rest." The Targum, with some expansion, has אמרית דתתובון לאוריתא תנוחון, "I thought, you will return to my law, you will rest"[18] or "I thought that you would return to my law, that you would rest." All these versions, with the exception of the LXX, derive נחת from נוח, 'to rest.' The LXX interpreted נחת as if from אנח, 'to groan, sigh.' Among modern translations of the Bible, NRSV ("in returning and rest"), NJB ("in conversion and tranquility") and NIV

---

[9] See William L. Moran, Review of Richard Hentschke, *Die Stellung der vorexilischen Schriftpropheten zum Kultus*, *Biblica* 41 (1960): 420–21, where he says: "Num. 10,36 cannot be cited to show that Yahweh's presence is not bound to the Ark; the antithesis with *qûmâ yhwh* and the virtual parallelism with 'when it comes to rest' (*b*ᵉ*nūḥô*), especially in view of the parallelism of *nāḥ* and *yāšab* in Ugaritic, Phoenician and elsewhere in the OT, shows that we must vocalise *š*ᵉ*bâ*."

[10] Arnold B. Ehrlich, *Randglossen zur hebräischen Bibel* (7 vols.; Leipzig: J. C. Hinrich, 1908–14), 4:108.

[11] *BDB*, 1000.

[12] Gesenius-Buhl, 812.

[13] *HALOT*, 1435.

[14] Franz Zorell, *Lexicon hebraicum et aramaicum Veteris Testamenti* (Rome: Pontificium Institutum Biblicum, 1957), 827.

[15] Wilhelm Gesenius, *Thesaurus philologicus criticus linguae hebraeae et chaldaeae Veteris Testamenti* (3 vols.; Leipzig: F. C. W. Vogel, 1835–53), 3:1375; Julius Fürst, *Hebräisches und chaldäisches Handwörterbuch über das Alte Testament* (3rd ed.; Leipzig: B. Tauchnitz, 1876), 418.

[16] Heinrich Ewald, *Ausführliches Lehrbuch der hebräischen Sprache des Alten Bundes* (8th ed.; Göttingen: Dieterich, 1870), 396.

[17] See Vetus Latina: *Cum conversus fueris gemueris* (var. *et ingemueris*).

[18] Bruce Chilton, *The Isaiah Targum* (ArBib 11; Wilmington, Del.: Michael Glazier, 1987), 60.

("in repentance and rest") clearly follow the traditional interpretation of שׁובה. NAB ("by waiting and by calm") and JPS ("in sitting still and rest" [1917], "by stillness and quiet" [1978]) understand the nominal form as if it is derived from שׁוב/ישׁב, 'to rest, sit, dwell.'

The elucidation of Isa 30:15 בשׁובה ונחת was taken a step further in 1958 when Dahood presented what he described as "pertinent material from Ugaritic which tilts the balance in favour of those who derive the noun in question from *yāšab*."[19] He cites the words of Dani'el in the Ugaritic Aqhat story, which he spoke when he heard the news that he would be blessed with a son: *aṯbn ank wanḫn wtnḫ birty npš*, "I shall sit and take my rest, and my soul shall be at ease within my breast" (CTA 17 [2 Aqht] II:12–14). In the Ba'al myth El says the same words when he learns in a dream the news that Ba'al is alive and that "the heavens rain down oil and the wadis run with honey" (CTA 6 [49] III:18–19).[20] In Dahood's view, the collocation of the verbs *yṯb* and *nḫ* in these Ugaritic texts supports the view that שׁובה, with which נחת from נוח is collocated in Isa 30:15, is derived from ישׁב. Dahood believes that there is further support for his position in the Phoenician inscription of Azitawadda, KAI 26 A II:7–8, 13, ושׁבת נעמת ונחת לב, "and pleasant dwelling and tranquility of heart."[21] Mention must also be made of other lines in the same inscription, KAI 26 A I:17–18, לשׁבתנם דננם בנחת לבנם, "that the Danunites might dwell in peace of mind." Phoenician נחת לב, 'tranquillity of heart, peace of mind,' recalls Akkadian *libbaka nēḫtum linīḫ*, "May she (Aya) calm your heart," and *libbaka linūḫ*, "let you heart rest."[22] In the Ahiram inscription, KAI 1:2, "and may peace (נחת) flee from Byblos," נחת is associated with the power and duty of a king, an association which will be mentioned below in the examination of Assyrian texts.

---

[19] Mitchell J. Dahood, "Some Ambiguous Texts in Isaias," *CBQ* 20 (1958): 41–49 (42).

[20] Dennis Pardee translates *aṯbn* in these two Ugaritic passages differently. In CTA 6 [49] III:18, "(Now) I can again get some rest," he seems to understand *aṯbn* as an auxiliary verb expressing repetition. See the usage of Hebrew שׁוב in Joüon, §177b. In CTA 17 [2 Aqht] II:12–13, "I can sit and be at rest," *aṯbn* is taken as a main verb. See *COS* 1:271, 345.

[21] Dahood, "Ambiguous Texts," 43.

[22] See *CAD* N$^{II}$, 150, where the paranomastic construction of *nēḫtu*, "peace, tranquility," with the verb *nāḫu* is noted; and *CAD* N$^{I}$, 243, 245–46. Note also *CAD* R, 134: *nūḫi mārat Sin rimî šubtukki*, "calm down (Ishtar), daughter of Sin, take your seat." See also the examples given in Hayim Tawil, *An Akkadian Lexical Companion for Biblical Hebrew* (Jersey City, N.J.: Ktav, 2009), 235.

Dahood's views are clearly at variance with those of Loewenstamm, who argues that שׁוב, 'to return,' is the root of Hebrew שׁובה and Phoenician שׁבת.[23] Loewenstamm renders Phoenician שׁבת נעמת by Modern Hebrew שובה נעימה ('pleasant returning'), an unlikely translation. Just as unconvincing is his derivation of Ugaritic *aṯbn* from *ṯb*, 'to return'; and his translation אשוב אנוכי ואנוח ("let me return and rest") for *aṯbn ank wanḫm* can scarcely be correct. Ahuvya has proposed the existence of two synonymous roots, ישׁב and שׁוב, 'to dwell, sit,' comparing יטב and טוב, 'to be good.'[24] Joüon places יטב among seven verbs with primitive *yod* as the first radical, and points out that they are all stative.[25] Although Dahood had originally derived שׁובה from ישׁב, he subsequently stated that he preferred a derivation from a by-form שׁוב, 'to sit.'[26] However, it is completely unnecessary to insist on the occurrence of a by-form שׁוב. Just as *šubtu* is derived from *wašābu* in Akkadian, so is שׁובה derived from ישׁב in Hebrew. With regard to the long vowel in שׁובה, we must mention an observation by Albright. When he wrote a footnote on Aramaic בירתא, Late Hebrew בירה, 'fortified town, citadel,' pointing out that it was ultimately a loanword from Akkadian *birtu*, he explained the long vowel of the Aramaic borrowing as secondary.[27] He compared the form of Akkadian *birtu* with *šubtu* (**šibtu*), 'abode,' from *wašābu*, but he did not mention any possible Hebrew cognate for *šubtu*. Is it conceivable that Hebrew שׁובה is a loanword from Akkadian *šubtu* with the long vowel to be explained as secondary? The sibilant indicates that the borrowing would have been from Babylonian and not Assyrian.

## II. *Šubat nēḫti/šubtu nēḫtu* in Akkadian Texts

The lack of agreement surrounding the meaning of Hebrew שׁובה is not matched by any disagreement about the meaning of Akkadian *šubtu*, which

---

[23] Samuel E. Loewenstamm, "ספר חדש של גורדון בחקר האוגריתית": Review article of Cyrus H. Gordon, *Ugaritic Manual, Tarbiz* 25 (1956): 468–72 (470).

[24] Avraham Ahuvya, "והנה 'ישב' ו'שוב' כמו 'יטב' ו'טוב'," *Leš* 39 (1975): 21–36.

[25] Joüon, §76a–e.

[26] Mitchell J. Dahood, *Proverbs and Northwest Semitic Philology* (Rome: Pontificium Institutum Biblicum, 1963), 7; idem., *Psalms I: 1–50* (AB 16; Garden City, N.Y.: Doubleday, 1966), 44 (Ps 7:8), 148 (Ps 23:6).

[27] William F. Albright, "The Nebuchadnezzar and Neriglissar Chronicles," *BASOR* 143 (Oct. 1956): 28–33 (33 n. 22). See also Paul V. Mankowski, *Akkadian Loanwords in Biblical Hebrew* (HSS 47; Winona Lake, Ind.: Eisenbrauns, 2000), 46–47.

is derived from *ašābu/wašābu*, 'to sit, to dwell,' and means 'seat, chair, throne; residence, abode, dwelling, home.'[28] The meaning 'seat, place' is found, for example, in Gilgamesh III: 97, "Let a restful seat (*šubtu nēḫtu*), a bed [for the night] be *laid out* for you."[29] The paranomastic expression *šubta nēḫta šūšubu*, "to settle (people) in a peaceful abode" occurs frequently,[30] especially in royal inscriptions. We have already given an example from Tiglath-pileser I at the beginning of this article. To it may be added the following examples: "The remainder of their troops [who] had fled from my weapons (but then) returned [I settled] in peaceful dwellings" (*šubtu nē[ḫtu ušēšibšunu]*) (Adad-narari II);[31] "I established (them) in abandoned cities (and) settled them in peaceful dwellings" (*šubtu nēḫtu ušēšibšunu*) (Tukulti-Ninurta II);[32] "I built ten strong fortresses around it and settled its inhabitants in a peaceful abode" (*nišēšu šubat nēḫti ušēšib*) (Sargon II);[33] "Who gathered the people (of Babylon) and settled (them) in a peaceful abode" (*ušēšibu šubat nēḫti*) (Esarhaddon).[34] In some texts the reference is to the settling of deities: "who returned the captured gods of all the lands from Assur to their place and settled them in a peaceful abode" (*ušēšibu šubtu nēḫtu*) (Esarhaddon);[35] "I brought her in there and I settled her

---

28 *CAD* Š$^{\text{III}}$, 172–85.

29 Andrew George, *The Babylonian Gilgamesh Epic: Introduction, Critical Edition and Cuneiform Texts* (2 vols.; Oxford: Oxford University Press, 2003), 1:578–79. In his commentary (2:814) George tentatively restores *mayal* [*mūši*], "a bed [for the night]." The expression *šubtu nēḫtu* also occurs in VII: 139–43 (640–41), "Now Gilgamesh, your friend and brother, [will] lay you out on a great bed. [On] a bed of honour he will lay you out, [he will] set you on a restful seat, the seat to his left (*ušeššebka šubta nēḫta šubat šumēli*); [the princes] of the earth will all kiss your feet." See also the nearly parallel text in VIII: 84–87 (656–57).

30 *CAD* A$^{\text{II}}$, 408. It must be mentioned here that *nēḫtu* in the phrase *šubat nēḫti* is a noun. In *šubtu nēḫtu* it is the feminine form of the adjective *nēḫu*. See *CAD* N$^{\text{II}}$, 150–52: *nēḫtu*, "peace, tranquility, quiet, security"; *nēḫu* (fem. *nēḫtu*), "quiet, peaceful, calm, undisturbed, safe, secure." *Pace* Avishur, *Stylistic Studies of Word-Pairs*, 710–11, Akkadian *šubtu nēḫtu* is not an example of asyndetic parataxis. The nouns *tanīḫu* and *tanīḫtu* are less common, but note *šubat tanīḫti*, "quiet abode, relaxing dwelling place" (*CAD* T, 171); *tanēḫtum u šupšuḫum kûmma Ištar*, "rest and giving rest are in your power, Ishtar" (*CAD* P, 228).

31 Grayson, RIMA 2, 144, obv. 19.

32 Grayson, RIMA 2, 172, 23–24.

33 Andreas Fuchs, *Die Annalen des Jahres 711 v. Chr. nach Prismenfragmenten aus Ninive und Assur* (SAAS 8; Helsinki: The Neo-Assyrian Text Corpus Project, University of Helsinki, 1998), 127, 324. See also "I settled the oppressed Mannaeans in a peaceful abode" (*šubat nēḫtu ušēšib*), 76, 308; "I settled the inhabitants of Ellipi in its totality in a peaceful abode" ([*šub*]*tu nēḫtu ušēšib*), 181, 339.

34 Riekele Borger, *Die Inschriften Asarhaddons, Königs von Assyrien* (AfO 9; Graz: Im Selbstverlage des Herausgebers, 1956), Assur §53, 43.

35 Borger, *Die Inschriften Asarhaddons*, §27 Nin. A Episode 3 ii 24. On this text, see Mordechai Cogan, *Imperialism and Religion: Assyria, Judah, and Israel in the Eighth and Seventh Centuries BCE* (Missoula, Mont.: Scholars Press, 1974), 29–30, 39.

(Ishtar) in a quiet dwelling" (*šubtu nēḫtu ušēšibši*) (Esarhaddon).[36] Gelb published a clay nail of Hammurabi on which the following words occur: "(When) he (Shamash), with his pure word, which cannot be altered, had given orders to let the people of Sippar and Babylon dwell in a peaceful habitation (*šubat nēḫtim šūšubam*)."[37]

It was the duty of the Assyrian king to establish and maintain justice, to bring peace and prosperity. The expansion of the land, the protection of the borders, and the maintenance of order and peace and care of the inhabitants were important obligations of the king. A successful monarch was one who attracted peace and tranquillity. Oded has treated this role of the Assyrian king at length, and he pays particular attention to the Assyrian texts which we have given above.[38] In these texts, he points out, the Assyrian kings are depicted as redeemers of the inhabitants of Assyria and other lands, and they boast of their favourable treatment of foreign people.[39] The opposite of *šubtu nēḫtu* is a state of chaos with disorder, desolation and hunger. In ancient Mesopotamia nothing could be done without the consent of the gods. Oded deals at length with the Assyrian gods' authority to declare war and a requirement on the part of the kings to request permission from the gods to wage war. The gods also determined the borders of the nations. The making of peace, the maintenance of peace and living in peace were all subject to the authority of the gods.

During the eighth and seventh centuries BC, specialists in divination reported to the Assyrian kings celestial observations, which were interpreted as omens. The events, which were predicted by certain 'signs,'

[36] Borger, *Die Inschriften Asarhaddons*, §64 r. 39. Other examples from royal inscriptions include "[I settled] them in cities (and) houses [which were suitable] (and) they dwelt in peaceful abodes" (*šubtu nēḫtu ušbu*) (Assur-dan II) (RIMA 2, 134–35, 61–63); "I settled them in a peaceful abode" (*šubtu nēḫtu ušēšibšunu*) (Ashurnasirpal II) (RIMA 2, 261, 95). Two interesting examples are found in Hanspeter Schaudig, *Die Inschriften Nabonids von Babylon und Kyros' des Großen* (AOAT 256; Münster: Ugarit-Verlag, 2001), 379–81, 2.8a Tiara cylinder, II: 25, "Gesetzt, die Blase hat sich verdoppelt: Sichere Fundamente, ruhige Wohnung" (*šubat nēḫti*); and 549, K1.2a, Cyrus cylinder: "Die großen Götter haben alle Länder in meiner Hand gefüllt und daraufhin ließ ich daß Land in ruhiger Wohnung wohnen" (*šubti nēḫti ušēšib*). In a bilingual building inscription of Ammi-Ditana we find, "I let the widespread people live a peaceful life" (*šubat nēḫtim ušēšibšunūti*). See Raphael Kutscher, *The Brockmon Tablets: Royal Inscriptions* (Haifa: Haifa University Press, 1989), 105.

[37] Ignace J. Gelb, "A New Clay-Nail of Hammurabi," *JNES* 7 (1948): 267–71 (268, line 19; 270).

[38] Bustenay Oded, *War, Peace and Empire: Justifications for War in Assyrian Royal Inscriptions* (Wiesbaden: Ludwig Reichert Verlag, 1992), especially the chapter, "To Enforce Order and Peace," 102–20. See also Oded, "'ונתתי שלום בארץ' (ויקרא כ"ו 6): נוסח אשורי פרק באידיאולוגיה המלכותית האשורית," *Eretz Israel* 24 (1993): 148–57 (Eng. summary 236*). On p. 151 he uses the biblical expression בשובה ונחת.

[39] Oded, *War, Peace and Empire*, 104–105.

messages sent by the gods, were important for the king and the country. The expression *šubat nēḫti/šubtu nēḫtu*, 'peaceful dwelling, quiet abode,' occurs in a number of these reports of celestial omens which merit attention. In these texts, as in most of the others we have seen, *šubtu nēḫtu* has a real sense of security and stability. There are many examples of its occurrence in favourable omens and two are given here. One is a report from a lunar observation, the other from a planetary observation.

> If the moon becomes visible on the 1st day: reliable speech; the land will become happy. If the moon at its appearance wears a crown: the harvest of the land will prosper; [the king] will reach the highest rank. If the moon's horns both equal each other: quiet dwelling (*šubtum nēḫtum*) for the land. If the horns of the moon at its appearance are very pointed: the king will rule the land wherever he goes, variant: he will knock down wherever he wants to subdue.[40]

> [If] Neberu (Jupiter) rises and the gods get peace: confused (things) will be made bright, blurred (things) will clear; rains and floods will come; the harvest-time grass will last until winter, the winter grass until harvest time; all lands will dwell in quiet (*matāti šubta nēḫta uššabu*); enemy kings will be reconci[led; the gods] will accept sacrifices, listen to [pray]ers; they will keep answering the di[viner]'s queries.[41]

There are numerous omen and extispicy texts in which the expression *mātu šubta nēḫta uššab*, 'the land will dwell in peace' is found. Extispicy was a necessary prerequisite before any important undertaking. Examples include "If a woman gives birth, and (the child) has two eyes on the right—an abandoned canal will be redug, and there will be grain (growing) on its banks; the land will live undisturbed" (*mātum šubtam nēḫtam uššab*);[42] and "In battle the army of the prince will have no equal, in future days: The land of the prince will abide by his word forever or they will have prosperity, the land of the prince will live undisturbed" (*māt rubê šubat nēḫti uššab*).[43]

---

[40] Hermann Hunger, *Astrological Reports to Assyrian Kings* (SAA 8; Helsinki: Helsinki University Press, 1992), No. 389. See also Nos. 505 and 108: 9–10.

[41] Hunger, *Astrological Reports to Assyrian Kings*, No. 254: r. 2–10. See No. 323: 7–r. 4 for a similar text. Also noteworthy are No. 323:1–2, "[If J]upiter passes to the west: quiet [dwelling] and complete well-being will come down on the land" ([*šubat*] *nēḫti sulum damiqti ana māti urada*); No. 329: r. 2–3, "Jupiter is passing to the west: quiet dwelling (*šubat nēḫti*), peace and good for the land;" No. 456: 6–7, "(If) Jupiter passes to the west: the land will dwell in quiet" ([*šubat*] *nēḫti*).

[42] Erle Leichty, *The Omen Series Šumma Izbu* (TCS 4; Locust Valley, N.Y.: J. J. Augustin, 1970), Tablet II:53'. See also Tablets II:55; III:18, 20, 60; X:71'; XII:15.

[43] Ulla S. Koch, *Babylonian Liver Omens* (Copenhagen: Carsten Niebuhr Institute of Near Eastern Studies, Museum Tusculanum Press, 2000), 56:18. See also 7:1–8:13; 16:20;

## III. Isaiah 30:15 בשׁובה ונחת in Modern Biblical Scholarship

It is probably accurate to say that most modern commentators on Isaiah regard שׁובה as a nominal form from שׁוב, 'to return,' and interpret it as 'conversion, returning (to God).' Duhm thought it meant 'turning away from war,' and pointed to Mic 2:8 שׁובי מלחמה, which may mean something like "men returning from the battle" (REB),[44] but the interpretation and translation of this text are unclear. Fohrer adopts a translation similar to Duhm's but suggests that שׁובה has the notion of turning away from a military alliance.[45] He interprets נחת as 'treaty faithfulness' which he derives from נוח, allegedly having the meaning 'to enter into a treaty,' following a suggestion made by Eissfeldt.[46] Clements regards Isa 30:15–17 as belonging to the time of Hezekiah's rebellion against Sennacherib and, preferring the translation 'in returning' for בשׁובה, suggests that Isaiah was in favour of "returning to accept allegiance to Assyria and staying quiet," that is, remaining submissive to Assyria.[47]

Among more recent commentators, Wildberger is quite animated in his defence of the traditional understanding of בשׁובה, which he renders 'in return': "If scholars cannot be satisfied with translating שׁובה as 'come back,' [sic] that has to do with the fact that they cannot believe that Isaiah would speak of coming back."[48] He discusses Dahood's proposal but decides that the Ugaritic and Phoenician evidence does not support the

---

20:61; 20:88; 25:43; 26:1; 27:26; 59:28; Koch, *Secrets of Extispicy: The Chapter Multābiltu of the Babylonian Extispicy Series and Niṣirti bārûti Texts mainly from Aššurbanipal's Library* (AOAT 326; Münster: Ugarit-Verlag, 2005), *Multābiltu* 8:37 (Tablet 10, text 2); 12:6 and 12:8 (Tablets 12–13, text 2).

[44] Bernhard Duhm, *Das Buch Jesaia* (HKAT 3/1; 4th ed.; Göttingen: Vandenhoeck & Ruprecht, 1922), 221.

[45] Georg Fohrer, *Das Buch Jesaja* (2 vols.; ZBK 19; 2nd ed.; Zurich: Zwingli, 1966–67), 2:101–103.

[46] Otto Eissfeldt, "*nûaḥ* 'sich vertragen,'" in *Kleine Schriften* (6 vols.; ed. Rudolph Sellheim and Fritz Maass; Tübingen: J. C. B. Mohr, 1962–79), 3:124–28 (= *Festschrift für Ludwig Köhler zu dessen 70. Geburtstag 14. April 1950* (Bern: Büchler, 1950), 23–26.

[47] Ronald E. Clements, *Isaiah 1–39* (NCB; Grand Rapids: Wm. B. Eerdmans; London: Marshall, Morgan & Scott, 1980), 248–49.

[48] Hans Wildberger, *Isaiah 28–39* (trans. Thomas H. Trapp; Minneapolis: Fortress Press, 2002), 156. See also 157: "Why deny to Isaiah this traditional meaning that seems obvious at every turn?" He is opposing in particular the view of Georg Sauer, "Die Umkehrforderung in der Verkündigung Jesajas," in *Wort, Gebot, Glaube: Beiträge zur Theologie des Alten Testaments. Walther Eichrodt zum 80. Geburtstag* (ed. Hans J. Stoebe, Johann J. Stamm and Ernest Jenni; Zürich: Zwingli Verlag, 1970), 277–95, esp. 286–89. A search in a concordance of the Hebrew Bible does not reveal as many examples of שׁוב, 'to return (to God)' in First Isaiah as Wildberger suggests.

case for שׁוב as a byform of ישׁב.[49] We have seen, however, that Dahood originally derived שׁובה from ישׁב[50] and only later did he argue the case for a byform שׁוב.[51] Furthermore, his proposal for a byform שׁוב is not based on Ugaritic. In any case this is a separate issue and the derivation of שׁובה from ישׁב is not in any way weakened. Wildberger believes that Isa 9:12 is "an unassailable and undisputed passage to show that the prophet kept hoping for a return."[52] Wong has also mounted a strong defence of the traditional interpretation of שׁובה, 'returning to YAHWEH,' and בטחה, 'trusting in YAHWEH.'[53] He sees no reason to attribute to בטחה "the Stoical idea of calmness and composure."[54] The interpretation of בשׁובה, 'in returning,' as a call to repentance has been cogently expressed recently by Kratz in his examination of Isa 28–31 in which he sees a "successive rewriting" of earlier forms of Isa 1–12.[55] He is sure that 1–12 and 28–31 did not come into being independently of each other and he finds that "the process of reformulation of older material within chs. 1–12 begins with the units in 28:11–22; 29:9–16 and 30:8–17 which are modelled on chs. 5–10."[56] In taking account of the inner-Isaianic literary connections, he finds it significant that 30:15 picks up the warning to be still from 7:4 and begins with the call to repentance.[57]

---

49 Wildberger, *Isaiah 28–39*, 156–57.

50 Dahood, "Some Ambiguous Texts in Isaias," *CBQ* 20 (1958): 41–43.

51 Dahood, *Psalms I*, 148.

52 Wildberger, *Isaiah 28–39*, 157.

53 Gordon C. I. Wong, "Faith and Works in Isaiah XXX 15," *VT* 47 (1997): 236–46. This is a clearly presented and fair critique of views opposing the traditional interpretation. The author believes that "the arguments advanced have shown the plausibility of the alternatives, but have not demonstrated the implausibility of the traditional views" (238).

54 Wong, "Faith and Works," 243. Wong (240) has misunderstood Dahood's remarks on בטחה in *Proverbs and Northwest Semitic Philology* 7 n. 1. Dahood does not give "Ugaritic *baṭiḥtî*, 'at ease'." He refers to El-Amarna 147:56 in which *nu-uḫ-ti* (*nuḫti*), "I am at rest" is glossed by *ba-ṭì-i-ti*, "I am at ease," and he regards both verbs as Canaanite, following William F. Albright, "The Egyptian Correspondence of Abimilki, Prince of Tyre," *JEA* 23 (1937): 190–203 (199 n. 12, *ba-ṭì-i-ti* = **baṭiḥtî*). Both verbs are regarded as West Semitic by Tawil, *An Akkadian Lexical Companion for Biblical Hebrew*, 48, 235. See also *CAD* B, 177. Until there is further evidence, it seems to be no more than a possibility that the Amarna form is related to Hebrew בטח. See Anson F. Rainey, *Canaanite in the Amarna Tablets: A Linguistic Analysis of the Mixed Dialect Used by the Scribes from Canaan* (4 vols.; HO; Leiden: Brill, 1996), 2:286, 301.

55 Reinhard Kratz, "Rewriting Isaiah: The Case of Isaiah 28–31," in *Prophecy and Prophets in Ancient Israel* (ed. John Day; LHBOTS 531; New York & London: T&T Clark International, 2010), 245–66.

56 Kratz, "Rewriting Isaiah," 263.

57 Kratz, "Rewriting Isaiah," 261.

De Jong takes the view that Isa 30:15–17 "continues the theme of the people having rejected YAHWEH's blessings, represented by earlier prophecies of salvation."[58] He mentions Isa 28:12, "This is the resting place (המנוחה), give rest (הניחו) to the weary; here is repose—but they would not listen," noting that both passages contain prophecies from earlier times, which depict how YAHWEH long ago had promised to save the people. The present disaster has come as a result of their past refusal of YAHWEH's help and promise of salvation. In de Jong's layout of Isa 30, v. 15 is an original saying, which is now part of a literary reworking (vv. 15–17) from the exilic period, highlighting disobedience and judgement.[59] Verses 27–33, obviously anti-Assyrian, are from the seventh century and vv. 18–26 are a post-exilic extension. In the case of Isa 28, vv. 7b–10, 12 are original sayings and vv. 14–22 represent a literary reworking. This analysis of the redactional complex is entirely convincing.

De Jong translates בשׁובה by 'in staying' and points out that שׁוב and נוח are never found together but ישׁב and נוח are juxtaposed in Deut 12:10; 2 Sam 7:1; Jer 27:11.[60] He rightly mentions the picture of the quiet and peaceful life, without military oppression, enjoyed by the people of Laish found in Judg 18:7, where we have a vocabulary similar to that in Isa 30:15, "They saw the people living securely (יושׁבת לבטח) after the manner of the Sidonians, quiet and safe" (שׁקט ובטח).[61] He interprets נחת in Isa 30:15 as 'rest' in the sense of quietly accepting Assyrian rule and prospering. As we have mentioned already, although de Jong points out the combination of *nāḫu* and *wašābu* in Akkadian, he does not mention the relevant *šubtu nēḫtu* with its sense of peaceful living and prosperity.

In this short study we have seen that there are sound philological reasons for relating בשׁובה ונחת in Isa 30:15 to the Akkadian expression *šubat*

58 De Jong, *Isaiah Among the Ancient Near Eastern Prophets*, 113.

59 De Jong, *Isaiah Among the Ancient Near Eastern Prophets*, 83–89, esp. 84.

60 De Jong, *Isaiah Among the Ancient Near Eastern Prophets*, 114. Among other commentators who accept the derivation of שׁובה from ישׁב, see Walter Dietrich, *Jesaia und die Politik* (BEvT 74; Munich: Chr. Kaiser Verlag, 1976), 149–50, esp. n. 83; Francolino J. Gonçalves, *L'Expédition de Sennachérib en Palestine dans la littérature hébraïque ancienne* (Études Bibliques 7; Paris: J. Gabalda, 1986), 172–74; Jesper Høgenhaven, *Gott und Volk bei Jesaja: eine Untersuchung zur biblischen Theologie* (Leiden: Brill, 1988), 206: "*šûbâ* ist mit den Rabbinern und Gesenius von *jšb*, nicht, wie es die alten Versionen wollen, von *šwb* abzuleinten."

61 In later biblical texts there are various combinations of vocabulary from the roots ישׁב, נוח, שׁקט and בטח. See Isa 14:7; 32:17–18; Ezek 38:11; Zech 1:11; 1 Chr 22:9; 2 Chr 14:5 [ET 6], 20:30. Space does not allow for a wider investigation of the concepts of "rest," "tranquillity" and "spaciousness" of the land, which time and again surface in reading not just the relevant Old Testament texts but also an informative range of Akkadian texts.

*nēḫti, šubtu nēḫtu*, 'quiet abode, dwelling (or seat) of rest.' In a broad selection of Akkadian texts, we have seen that 'peaceful abode, quiet dwelling' and other aspects of security and stability were brought about by the king, subject to the authority of the gods. Isa 30:15 represents an early prophecy in which YAHWEH promised salvation through 'quiet dwelling, rest and security.' In the 'literary reworking' and 'successive rewriting' of early material, to use the terms employed by de Jong and Kratz, שׁובה may have acquired an ambiguous significance. There was no ambiguity by the time the LXX and other ancient versions appeared.

# WHO "BEGAN TO CALL ON THE NAME OF THE LORD" IN GENESIS 4:26B?: THE MT AND THE VERSIONS

Robert P. Gordon

"Then it was begun to call upon the name of the LORD" is a literal rendering of the last few words of Gen 4:26, and they are usually read as a statement about the beginnings of YHWH-worship in early human history. That they come at this point and not earlier, in the narrative about Adam and Eve in the garden of Eden, is itself cause for reflection; nevertheless it is their relationship to the texts in early Exodus about the revelation of the divine name to Moses (see Exod 3:13–15; 6:2–3) that usually brings them to attention. Whereas Exodus is commonly read to mean that the divine name has been previously unknown to Moses, who must now announce it to the Hebrew slaves in Egypt, Gen 4:26 claims that worship of God, apparently by the name YHWH, began already in the time of Seth and Enosh. This apparent equivocation would be sufficient grounds for expecting divergence within the textual and translational traditions, but probably no less significant in antiquity was the unique form הוחל, the only occurrence in the Hebrew Bible of the verb חלל ("begin") in the Hophal conjugation. Since this use of the passive denies the sentence a clear and unambiguous subject—Hendel describes the clause as "ungrammatical and semantically obscure in its context"[1]—the opportunity is there for differing identifications of those involved in the worship. The exegetical possibilities of the half-verse ramify through centuries of Jewish, Samaritan and Christian interpretation.[2]

## I. THE SEPTUAGINT

The earliest translation-cum-interpretation of Gen 4:26 is provided by the Septuagint: "This one (=he) hoped to call upon the name of the LORD God." "LORD God" corresponds to the simple use of the Tetragrammaton in the

---

[1] Ronald S. Hendel, *The Text of Genesis I–II: Textual Studies and Critical Edition* (New York: Oxford University Press, 1998), 49.

[2] See the excellent study by Steven D. Fraade, *Enosh and His Generation: Pre-Israelite Hero and History in Postbiblical Interpretation* (SBLMS 30; Chico: Scholars Press, 1984).

MT and is of uncertain textual status. This fuller designation may derive from the Septuagintal *Vorlage*, or may be a translator's flourish, in either case connecting with the occurrences of the composite form used throughout most of the Eden narrative in Gen 2–3. Wevers claims that the LXX's use of the composite designation "the Lord God" actually "negates the Hebrew notion that invoking the name YAHWEH began with Enos."[3] The claim is difficult to justify, and we shall return to it briefly. There are more palpable differences between the Hebrew and the Greek at the beginning of this half-verse, where "This one (= he) hoped" in the Greek corresponds to MT "Then it was begun." In theory, the Greek could represent an independent, and even the "original," reading. On the other hand, it seems likely that the two divergences "then"/"this one" and "was begun"/"hoped" are interdependent. If this is granted, two main lines of approach are possible. If אז was misread as זה, or if אז was taken as a rare equivalent of זה, the passive verb would have had to be converted to the active, since "this one was begun" would have conveyed no sense. Conversely, the rendering of הוחל by an active verb could have triggered the inclusion of a more explicit subject than would have been indicated within the simple (active) verb-form. Wevers represents the first of these options, concluding that LXX οὗτος is the result of a misreading of אז, with dittography a possible factor; with this divergence it became necessary, on Wevers' view, to render the passive verb of the MT by an active.[4] Others, as we shall see, have simply assumed that the LXX more faithfully reflects the original reading.[5] At the same time, normal Hebrew usage would favour הוא in the kind of situation that the LXX creates, with οὗτος frequently enough translating MT הוא.[6] This seems to raise a question about the status of any presumed *Vorlage* that had זה corresponding to אז in the MT.

---

[3] John W. Wevers, *Notes on the Greek Text of Genesis* (SBLSCS 35; Atlanta: Scholars Press, 1993), 66–67.

[4] Wevers, *Notes on the Greek Text of Genesis*, 66. Susan Brayford, *Genesis* (SCS; Leiden: Brill, 2007), 257, is in broad agreement with Wevers. Kenneth A. Mathews, *Genesis 1–11:26* (NAC IA; Nashville: Broadman and Holman, 1996), assumes a variant *Vorlage*, with both dittography and haplography involved (291 n. 332).

[5] Cf. John Skinner, *A Critical and Exegetical Commentary on Genesis* (ICC; 2nd ed.; Edinburgh: T&T Clark, 1930), 126, and Sandmel's reservations: Samuel Sandmel, "Genesis 4:26b," *HUCA* 32 (1961): 19–29 (27–28).

[6] זה (LXX οὗτος) in direct speech in Gen 5:29 is in a different category; cf. also Gen 12:12; 38:28. For הוא//οὗτος in Genesis see 4:20, 21; 10:8, 9. See also Ilmari Soisalon-Soininen, "Die Wiedergabe des Hebräischen, als Subjekt Stehenden Personalpronomens im Griechischen Pentateuch," in *De Septuaginta: Studies in Honour of John William Wevers on his Sixty-Fifth Birthday* (ed. Albert Pietersma and Claude Cox; Mississauga, Ont.: Benben Publications, 1984), 115–28 (122), referring to Gen 2:11, 13, 14, among other texts.

## II. The Implication of "Hoped"

More probably, it is the unique form הוחל rather than the familiar אז that drives the rendering in the LXX. As has long been recognized, LXX's "hoped" easily retroverts into the 3 m. sg. perfect of BH יחל (Hi.) ("wait, hope"), which, with the second vowel represented *defective*, would produce the same consonantal form as the MT. Nevertheless, the Septuagint's "he hoped" still raises an interesting question about the Greek translator's choice of term, for, whatever precisely greeted him in his *Vorlage*, it would have required minimal manipulation to produce "begin," the obvious verb in the context, for which there is evidence in the Samaritan Pentateuch,[7] in *Jub.* 4:12, and also in Philo (*Det.* 138; *Abr.* 7).[8] Moreover, Gen 4:26 is the only place where חלל and יחל are confused in the LXX.[9] We are entitled to inquire, therefore, whether there is any special reason why "hoped" was preferred to "began."

Most obviously, "hoped to call" is not the same as "called," and even leaves open the possibility that the subject of the verb never did "call." This becomes relevant when we recall the apparent conflict between Gen 4:26 and Exod 3 and 6 on the revelation of the divine name. In particular, Exod 6:3, as usually interpreted, says that, whereas God appeared to Abraham, Isaac and Jacob as El Shaddai, "by my name 'the Lord' I did not make myself known to them." It is an obvious possibility that the Greek translator chose his form of words in order to ease this tension, and it is mentioned by, for example, Marguerite Harl in her commentary on LXX Genesis.[10] Wevers thinks that LXX "hoped" may mean that Enosh "did not actually succeed in doing so"; he describes as "interesting" Harl's suggestion that perceived tension between the Genesis and Exodus texts may have motivated the Greek translator, though, strictly, he has ruled out the need of any such expedient on the Greek translator's part by suggesting that the LXX use of the double appellation "Lord God" negates the

[7] See August F. von Gall, *Der Hebräische Pentateuch der Samaritaner* (Giessen: Töpelmann, 1918), 7. The Samaritan Targum to Gen 4:26 likewise has "Then he began to call upon the name of the Lord." See Abraham Tal, *The Samaritan Targum of the Pentateuch: A Critical Edition*, I (Tel-Aviv: Tel-Aviv University, 1980), 14.

[8] In *Abr.* 7 Enosh is called "the *first* lover of hope"; according to *Det.* 138 Enosh "*first* hoped" to call on the name of the Lord God. It appears that Philo was aware of both readings ("began" as in the MT, and "hoped" as in the LXX).

[9] Fraade, *Enosh and His Generation*, 6. The OL *hic speravit* follows the LXX; for the OL text see Bonifatius Fischer, ed., *Genesis* (VL 2; Freiburg: Herder, 1951–4), 92.

[10] Marguerite Harl, *La Genèse* (La Bible d'Alexandrie; Paris: Cerf, 1986), 119.

idea that it was Enosh who first invoked the divine name.[11] In his monograph on Gen 4:26, Fraade does not address the possibility that tension between Genesis and Exodus explains the LXX's use of "hoped" in the verse. He allows that the translator may have had difficulty with the idea that Enosh "instituted divine worship,"[12] but thinks it more likely that it was the translational problem posed by the unique form הוחל, as in the MT, that led him to favour "hoped."[13]

Fraade's disinclination to explain LXX Gen 4:26 on the basis of perceived tension with Exod 6:3 probably arises from his awareness that this was not an issue for later Jewish interpreters who, if they were at all concerned about the matter, at any rate interpreted Exod 3:13–15; 6:3 as referring to the revelation of the *content or meaning* of the divine name.[14] We need not, however, make such an assumption about the Septuagintal translator of Gen 4:26, who may even have been unaware of the line of interpretation that later commended itself to the rabbis (see below on Aquila). To say of Enosh that he *hoped* to call on the name of the LORD would certainly take care of any problem as between Genesis and Exodus. The idea that Enosh's hoping implied failure of execution is indeed expressed by later writers. At one point Philo interprets Enosh's hoping as an indication that, despite his aspirations, he fell short of the attainment of true excellence.[15] Origen, also on the basis of the Septuagintal "hoped," finds Enosh deficient: *Cur speravit, et cur non statim invocat, sed dissimulat et moratur* ("Why did he hope, and why does he not immediately call, but dissembles and delays?").[16] Such readings of "hoped" have, of course, nothing to do with the specific issue of the cultic propriety of Enosh, in pre-Mosaic times, calling upon the name of the LORD, but they are useful as illustrating how the substitution of "hoped" could be seen as relativizing an assertion about Enosh and worship, and they show that "hoped" does not necessarily imply that Enosh "hoped" in the sense of "enthused" about the prospect of engaging in divine worship (which he may later have carried out).[17]

---

[11] Wevers, *Notes on the Greek Text of Genesis*, 67. In his footnote 50 Wevers refers infelicitously to the "inherent contradiction between Exod 3:14 and 6:3," whereas it is the relationship of Gen 4:26b to Exod 6:3 that requires attention.

[12] *Enosh and His Generation*, 7–8.

[13] *Enosh and His Generation*, 8.

[14] Fraade, *Enosh and His Generation*, 200.

[15] Philo, *Abr.* 47.

[16] *In Epistolam B. Pauli ad Romanos*, Book 5 (PG 14:1011–12).

[17] *Pace* Fraade, *Enosh and His Generation*, 8.

## III. A Targumic Analogy

If "hoped" substitutes desire or intention for actual cultic performance in LXX Gen 4:26, we have analogous situations in the Targum to the Prophets. First, MT Jonah 1:16 says that the sailors on board Jonah's troubled ship "offered a sacrifice to the Lord and made vows." This, however, raised issues about the cultic appropriateness of the worshippers and their ersatz altar, so that the Targum offers the mitigating "and they *promised* (lit. 'said') to offer a sacrifice before the Lord and they made vows."[18] Secondly, a similar question arises at 2 Sam 23:16, where David's men bring him water from the well at Bethlehem, and he, feeling unworthy of their devotion, *pours it out* before the Lord. Since the verb used is נסך, which mainly denotes the pouring of libations, a question of cultic appropriateness could be said to be involved. The Targum deals with this by having David *promise* to pour the water out as a libation before the Lord. This use of "said"/"promised" is paralleled elsewhere in the Targums, where its introduction enables the Targumists to refine biblical statements about the divine presence in the Jerusalem temple so that they do not conflict with the historical realities of their and their readers' world (see *Tg.* Isa 12:6 ["has promised to make his presence dwell in your midst"]; cf. *Tg.* Zeph 3:5, 15; similarly *Tg.* Hab 2:20 ["the Lord was pleased to make his presence dwell in his holy temple"], for MT "the Lord is in his holy temple").[19] If the Septuagintal use of "hoped" in Gen 4:26 has a comparable function, then it belongs with a number of other "transversional" translation features that are of sufficient substance to be distinguished from the minor standardizations and suchlike that are a feature of biblical translations in all periods.[20]

---

[18] There is discussion in the author's "*Terra Sancta* and the Territorial Doctrine of the Targum to the Prophets," in *Interpreting the Hebrew Bible: Essays in Honour of E. I. J. Rosenthal* (ed. John A. Emerton and Stefan C. Reif; Cambridge: Cambridge University Press, 1982), 119–31 (120–24); repr. in Robert P. Gordon, *Hebrew Bible and Ancient Versions* (Aldershot: Ashgate, 2006), 317–26 (318–20).

[19] There is a formal equivalent to this Targumic circumlocution in MT 1 Kgs 8:12 ("promised [lit. said] to dwell").

[20] See my essay, "Dialogue and Disputation in the Targum to the Prophets," *JSS* 39 (1994): 7–17 (17); repr. in *Hebrew Bible and Ancient Versions*, 338–346 (346).

## IV. The Significance of ΟΥΤΟΣ

If the pedigree of the Septuagint's "hoped" in Gen 4:26b is questionable, this casts further doubt on the first word of the sentence, οὗτος. Fraade was able to find two instances of אז "translated with a form of the demonstrative pronoun *houtos* in the LXX (Jer 11:15; Mal 3:16),"[21] but even if the equation אז=זה is conceded as a slight possibility, manipulation on the part of the Greek translator still remains highly probable. As we have noted, זה would not necessarily be in accordance with the best Hebrew style.[22] Most probably, the translator wished to make a statement about Enosh (or even Seth[23]), and he may have been influenced by adjacent references to individuals—descendants of Cain—whom the text associates with other new "beginnings" ("he [LXX οὗτος] was the father of..." [4:20, 21]).[24] This is the explanation favoured by Mathews who, while allowing that a Hebrew text may underlie the LXX (and Vulgate) version of Gen 4:26b, thinks that, on the analogy of Cain's pioneering descendants in vv. 20–22, the ancient translator(s) associated the beginnings of "public worship" with Seth's firstborn: "Cain's firstborn and successors pioneer cities and the civilized arts, but Seth's firstborn and successors pioneer worship."[25] This may, however, be putting it too strongly. Since the Septuagint says that Enosh *hoped* to call upon the name of the Lord, he is not quite an innovator in worship.

The presence of οὗτος in Gen 4:26b may be compared with other Septuagintal occurrences of the word where an element of deliberateness is involved.[26] Perhaps the best-known instances come in the account of the tabernacle in LXX Exod 38:18–26, where a sequence of activities in connection with the making of the tabernacle and its furnishings is attributed to Bezalel by repeated use of οὗτος, which occurs ten times in the section.[27] Wevers notes that in these verses Bezalel's skill in metalwork is highlighted over against the preceding account of Eliab (=Oholiab) and

---

[21] Fraade, *Enosh and His Generation*, 9, n. 14.

[22] Skinner (*Genesis*, 126) favours הוא rather than זה as subject in his retroverted text of 4:26b.

[23] Cf. Fraade, *Enosh and His Generation*, 89.

[24] Cf. also Gen 10:8, 9.

[25] Mathews, *Genesis 1–11:26*, 291–92.

[26] I leave out of consideration the question of underlying Hebrew *Vorlagen*, which is a frequent imponderable in this kind of study.

[27] Cf. David W. Gooding, *The Account of the Tabernacle: Translation and Textual Problems of the Greek Exodus* (TS 6; Cambridge: Cambridge University Press, 1959), 47. On the unusual character of this section in the Greek see the comments by Anneli Aejmelaeus,

his skilled assistants who were responsible for working with textiles: "The translator thus contrasts Beseleel's (sic) efforts as climactic over against his (lesser) fellow architect's work."[28] Again, the alternative account of the rise of Jeroboam in 3 Kgdms 12:24a–z notes, with some apparent emphasis, that "οὗτος (=Jeroboam) built the citadel with the levies of the house of Ephraim," and that "οὗτος closed up the city of David, and was aspiring to the kingdom" (12:24b). The equivalent statements in MT 1 Kgs 11:27 have Solomon as subject, whereas 3 Kgdms 12:24b attributes the activity to Jeroboam in illustration of his thrusting ambition.[29] In citing these texts from Exodus and 3 Kingdoms one is not overlooking the use of οὗτος where there appears to be no special emphasis involved, as in 3 Kgdms 12:24h, "and this man was sixty years old," though the presence of the connective may in any case put this example and its like in a different class from the others already cited.[30]

## V. An Exegetical Bonus

There is an exegetical bonus arising from the Greek translator's use of "hoped" that should not be overlooked. If the LXX or its *Vorlage* intentionally deflects the text from saying that Enosh, or anyone else in his time, actually "called upon the name of the Lord," this has the effect of making Abraham the first to "call upon the name of the Lord": the only other occurrences of the expression in Genesis associate worship of this order with Abraham (12:8; 13:4; 21:33) and Isaac (26:25).[31] Moreover, Isaac is said to have done so upon being reassured by Yhwh that he was

*On the Trail of the Septuagint Translators: Collected Essays* (rev. ed.; Leuven: Peeters, 2007), 118.

[28] John W. Wevers, *Notes on the Greek Text of Exodus* (SBLSCS 30; Atlanta: Scholars Press, 1990), 620.

[29] See Zipora Talshir, *The Alternative Story of the Division of the Kingdom: 3 Kingdoms 12:24a–z* (Jerusalem Biblical Studies 6; Jerusalem: Simor, 1993), 204. For comment on both the Exodus and the Kings passages see David W. Gooding, "Two Possible Examples of Midrashic Interpretation in the Septuagint Exodus," in *Wort, Lied und Gottesspruch: Festschrift für Joseph Ziegler*, 1 (ed. J. Schreiner: Würzburg: Echter Verlag, 1972), 45–48.

[30] Martha L. Wade, *Consistency of Translation Techniques in the Tabernacle Accounts of Exodus in the Old Greek* (SBLSCS 49; Leiden: Brill, 2003), 154 n. 11 (continued from p. 153), comments not only on the use of οὗτος but also on the absence of conjunctions, which she interprets as indicating a shift from sequential narrative to descriptive list. She compares several texts in both MT and LXX Genesis in this respect (2:11, 13, 14; 4:20–21; 10:8–9). Note also her comment on referentiality and the use of οὗτος (167 n. 35).

[31] This point has been made independently by Fraade, *Enosh and His Generation*, 7 n. 6.

heir to the promises given to Abraham ("I am the God of Abraham your father; do not fear for I am with you, and I shall bless you and multiply your descendants for the sake of Abraham my servant" [v. 24]). In three of these instances of calling upon the name of YHWH there is mention of an altar (12:8; 13:4; 26:25).

## VI. Rabbinic Interpretation

As Fraade has well shown, rabbinic interpretation of Gen 4:26b contrasts sharply with pre-rabbinic Jewish and Christian exegesis of this half-verse. Rabbinic interpretation refers it to the generation of Enosh, rather than to Enosh himself or his descendants, and it finds here the beginnings of idolatry. This importation of idolatry into the interpretation of Gen 4:26b is often explained on the basis that MT הוחל has been associated with חלל in the sense of "profane."[32] However, as Fraade points out, although there is plenty of play on the root חלל and similar-sounding forms in rabbinic literature, the connection of חלל in the sense of "profane" with Gen 4:26b is not clearly attested until the Jewish mediaeval commentators Ibn Ezra and Kimchi.[33] Moreover, it seems much more likely that, rather than the meaning "profane" for חלל, it is the occurrence of BH קרא in the verse that has generated the rabbinic view, succinctly represented in the Palestinian Targums, that in the days of Enosh people began to misuse the divine name in their pursuit of idolatry. It is not consciousness of tension with the statements in Exod 3 and 6 that has impelled the rabbis to this explanation of the biblical text. Since they interpreted the Exodus passages to mean that it was God's character as implicit in the divine name YHWH, and not the actual Tetragrammaton itself, that was revealed to Moses, they did not have cause to shape their explanation of Gen 4:26b to fit Exodus. Indeed, the very wording of the Targums (to go no further) assumes the knowledge of the divine name in the time of Enosh. Thus Neofiti translates, "Then people began to make idols for themselves and to call them by the name of the Memra of the LORD," while the Fragment-Targum has, "In his days, then, people began to worship foreign [deities] and to call them by the name of the Memra of the

[32] E.g., Mathews, *Genesis 1–11:26*, 292; Harl, *La Genèse*, 119.
[33] See Fraade, *Enosh and His Generation*, 184.

LORD."[34] These Targums assume the knowledge of the divine name in the earliest generations, which is why people were able to misappropriate it. There is a translational crux in the Onkelos rendering of the verse, but a likely English translation would run: "Then in his days people ceased from praying in the name of the LORD." This too implies the knowledge of the divine name in antediluvian times.

The near unanimity of the rabbinical tradition on the interpretation of Gen 4:26b is impressive. This reading of the half-verse is probably not influenced, as we have noted, by the statements on the divine name in Exod 3 and 6. Rather, as Fraade observes, it seeks to account for the placement of the statement about Enosh's generation immediately after the Cainite genealogy and the achievements of Cain's descendants, negatively viewed, in Gen 4:17–24. For the rabbis, not the beginning of true worship, but its perversion, is represented in 4:26b.

## VII. The Reason for the Hophal

In the remainder of this discussion of Gen 4:26b we shall maintain that the biblical text itself is concerned with Enosh's generation, *pace* the LXX and other ancient witnesses, and those modern interpreters who follow their lead in referring the text to Enosh and his personal initiative.

The clause beginning אז הוחל plainly intends to say something about the worship of YHWH. As already noted, the first thing to be observed about the expression is its uniqueness. Whereas the verb חלל ("begin") occurs approximately fifty times in the Hebrew Bible in the Hiphil conjugation, this is the only instance of the Hophal. This is sufficient reason to inquire whether there is a special explanation for this unique occurrence. Earlier in the verse there is an occurrence of ילד in the Qal passive[35] ("was born"), which already exemplifies the *u-a* vowel pattern, but assonance is an unlikely explanation for the precise form הוחל. Occurrences of ילד in the Qal passive, albeit sometimes classified as Pual, are relatively common in Biblical Hebrew. The occurrence in Gen 4:26a is unlikely to have occasioned such an unusual construction as is found in the second half of the verse.

[34] Text in Michael L. Klein, *The Fragment-Targums of the Pentateuch According to their Extant Sources*, I (AnBib 76; Rome: Biblical Institute Press, 1980), 48.

[35] See Bruce K. Waltke and Michael O'Connor, *An Introduction to Biblical Hebrew Syntax* (Winona Lake: Eisenbrauns, 1990), 374–76 (§22.6b–d).

Clearly, it is not the intention of the MT to associate the beginnings of YHWH-worship specifically with Enosh. If this had been the case, a simpler statement to that effect could have been made, such as is represented in those ancient texts that appear to reflect a *Vorlage* with the reading, "This one/he began." If, on the other hand, it was the intention of the author to say that in Enosh's time people in general set about the worship of God by the name YHWH, we may perhaps help our cause by asking what alternative ways of saying the same thing were available to the author. And most obviously "Then people began to call" would be expressed in the form אז החל האדם, which construction is paralleled in a statement about early human activity in 6:1:

ויהי כי־החל האדם לרב על־פני האדמה

If we reconstruct 4:26b on this basis the following text-form results:

אז החל האדם לקרא בשם יהוה

Other statements in the Genesis protohistory about what humans "began" to do are likewise rendered by חלל (Hi.). Noah "began to be a husbandman" (9:20); Nimrod "began to be a mighty hunter on the earth" (10:8). If, then, the author of 4:26 had used the verb "begin" in the normal way, in a statement about humans beginning to call upon the name of the LORD, the natural way to express this would have been as set out above. The citing of 6:1 in this regard is particularly relevant, given that, within the material customarily attributed to the J source, 6:1 follows immediately on 4:26.[36] If the Genesis author had so phrased himself at 4:26b, however, he would have introduced an ambiguity into his text, since such a form of words could also be made to say that "the man" (i.e. Adam) began to call upon the name of the LORD. Throughout Gen 2:7–4:1 the first man is regularly indicated by האדם;[37] in 4:25 אדם, without the definite article, is the first unambiguous occurrence of the word as a proper name. It may be, therefore, that in the unique use of the Hophal of חלל the writer has sought to avoid the possibility of his statement being referred to "the man"/Adam who, after some narrative absence, has just been reintroduced in the preceding verse. As to any underlying reason for such avoidance,

[36] This is to say nothing about the possibility of intervening material in the hypothetical original source.

[37] The pointing in MT 2:20; 3:17, 21 should probably be emended to represent the definite article, in keeping with the occurrences of the article elsewhere when referring to "the man" in Gen 2–3.

we can only surmise, but a misconstrued statement about Adam and the beginnings of worship would, at the least, have raised questions about the religious life of Adam and Eve in their Eden phase. For if Adam began to call on the name of the LORD only in the days of Enosh, what had he been doing hitherto?[38]

If this explains why Gen 4:26b has אז הוחל, and not אז החל האדם, then emendation is unnecessary. Hendel cites J usage at Gen 6:1; 10:8 in support of reading the Hiphil form, and he follows the LXX (etc.) in reading "This one" for "Then," so making Enosh the one who began to call on the name of the LORD.[39] Earlier, August Dillmann was also inclined to think that the original text had "This one began," and he made the suggestion, largely neglected since, that the passive form in the MT was somehow connected with the rabbinic interpretation, as represented in the Targums, that the divine name was profaned through the introduction of idolatry.[40] This, however, depends too much on the assumption that it is הוחל that generates the reference to idolatry, which explanation, as we have seen, appears only with the mediaeval commentators. As Dillmann himself observes, Aquila (τοτε ἤρχθη) and, probably, Symmachus (τοτε ἀρχη ἐγενετο) were already acquainted with the MT reading: Aquila represents the pre-rabbinic interpretation suggested by the MT itself: "Then calling on the name (of the LORD) was begun."[41] N. H. Tur-Sinai adopted a more radical approach, suggesting that יהוה at the end of the verse replaced an original הזה. He translated the supposed original, "Then men began to be called by this name," by which he meant Enosh's name, which word is more familiar in Biblical Hebrew as a common noun meaning "man, mankind."[42]

---

38 The religious status of Adam and Eve in Eden is the subject of a further study ("Evensong in Eden: As It Probably Was *Not* in the Beginning") in the forthcoming Festschrift in honour of A. A. Macintosh (*Leshon Limmudim*; ed. David A. Baer and Robert P. Gordon).

39 Hendel, *The Text of Genesis I–II*, 49.

40 August Dillmann, *Genesis Critically and Exegetically Expounded* (translated from the 4th German edition by William B. Stevenson; Edinburgh: T&T Clark, 1897), I, 210. See G. J. Spurrell, *Notes on the Text of the Book of Genesis* (2nd ed.; Oxford: Clarendon, 1896), 64.

41 See Frederick Field, *Origenis Hexaplorum Quae Supersunt*, I (Oxford: Clarendon, 1875), 20.

42 Naftali H. Tur-Sinai (H. Torczyner), *Pešuṭo šel miqra'*, I (Jerusalem: Kiryath Sepher, 1962), 21–22. Tur-Sinai compares Josh 8:8 in the MT ("word of YHWH") and LXX ("this word").

As I have noted elsewhere,[43] there are various signs of authorial ingenuity in Gen 4, and the same observation could be invoked in connection with הוחל. In particular, it will be appropriate to recall here the suggestion of our honorand, Hugh Williamson, that the writer uses two forms of the infinitive construct of the verb נשא, in vv. 7 and 13, so that the meaning of the verb in v. 7 should not be carried over to v. 13.[44] This suggests a sensitivity on the part of the biblical writer such as we are claiming for the statement about the origins of YHWH-worship in v. 26b. In other words, what may have exercised the Septuagint translator in one direction—namely, the desire for clarity and consistency in the Hebrew text—may already have influenced the biblical author in another.

I have greatly valued the friendship and support of Hugh Williamson over many years, and I welcome this opportunity to pay tribute to his outstanding achievements in the field of Hebrew and Old Testament study.

[43] In "'Couch' or 'Crouch'?: Genesis 4:7 and the Temptation of Cain," in *On Stone and Scroll: Essays in Honour of Graham Ivor Davies* (BZAW 420; ed. James K. Aitken, Katharine J. Dell, and Brian A. Mastin; Berlin: De Gruyter, 2011), 195–209.

[44] Hugh G. M. Williamson, "On Getting Carried Away with the Infinitive Construct of נשא," in *Shai le-Sara Japhet: Studies in the Bible, its Exegesis and its Language* [Heb.] (ed. Moshe Bar-Asher, Dalit Rom-Shiloni, Emanuel Tov and Nili Wazana; Jerusalem: Bialik Institute, 2007), 357*–367*.

# THE SEPTUAGINT OF ISAIAH AND PRIESTHOOD

Arie van der Kooij

The book of Isaiah is well known for its focus on the holy city, Jerusalem/Zion, and its temple, but it does not display a great interest, at least not explicitly so, in priests and priesthood. The passages referring to priests are small in number; see 8:2; 24:2; 28:6; 37:2; 61:6, and 66:21, the latter instance being the only place where also the term 'Levites' occurs.[1] The Septuagint of Isaiah (LXX Isaiah), however, displays a different picture as there are several instances where, different from MT, its vocabulary reflects an interest in priests and priesthood.[2] The first place to be mentioned is 40:2, since here the LXX offers the term 'priest' where MT (cf. 1QIsa[a], 1QIsa[b], 4QIsa[b]) does not: 'O priests, speak to the heart of Jerusalem, comfort her.' The Greek version makes explicit who, to the mind of its translator, are the ones that are being addressed.[3] In his view, 'priests' are the appropriate authorities to comfort the people of Jerusalem.

Another passage which is of great interest is to be found in ch. 22: it contains a prophecy (vv. 15–25) about Sebna and Eljakim who in MT are presented as high officials of the court, fully in line with Isa 36–37, but who in LXX turn out to be priestly leaders.[4] Furthermore, there is reason to believe that LXX Isa 9:5–7 (MT, vv. 4–6) allude to priestly leaders as well—to illegitimate high-priests in v. 5, and to a legitimate high-priestly leader to be expected, in vv. 6–7.[5]

---

[1] But see also 43:28 ('the princes of the sanctuary').

[2] In Isa 8:2 ('Uriah, the priest'), on the other hand, LXX has no equivalent of 'priest.'

[3] Compare the explicitation in *Tg.* Isa 40:2 ('prophets').

[4] See Arie van der Kooij, *Die alten Textzeugen des Jesajabuches. Ein Beitrag zur Textgeschichte des Alten Testaments* (OBO 35; Freiburg: Universitätsverlag; Göttingen: Vandenhoeck und Ruprecht, 1981), 56–60.

[5] See Arie van der Kooij, "Wie heisst der Messias. Zu Jes 9,5 in den alten griechischen Versionen," in *Vergegenwärtigung des Alten Testaments. Beiträge zur biblischen Hermeneutik. Festschrift für Rudolf Smend zom 70. Geburtstag* (ed. Christoph Bultmann, Walter Dietrich, and Christoph Levin; Göttingen: Vandenhoeck and Ruprecht, 2002), 156–69; idem, "The Septuagint of Isaiah and the Mode of Reading Prophecies in Early Judaism. Some Comments on LXX Isaiah 8–9," in *Die Septuaginta—Texte, Kontexte, Lebenswelten. Internationale Fachtagung veranstaltet von Septuaginta Deutsch (LXX.D), Wuppertal 20.–23. Juli 2006* (ed. Martin Karrer und Wolfgang Kraus; WUNT 219; Tübingen: Mohr Siebeck 2008), 597–611. For different suggestions as to LXX Isa 9:6–7, see John J. Collins, "Isaiah 8:23–9:6

In this contribution I will deal with two other instances in LXX Isaiah, which, in my view, also testify to a strong interest in priesthood: 6:13 and 29:22.[6]

## I. Isaiah 6:13 (LXX)

> And the tenth is still/again on it, and it will again be for plunder, like a terebinth, and like an acorn when it falls from its husk.
>
> (MT: And though a tenth remain in it, it will be burned again, like a terebinth or an oak, whose stump remains standing when it is felled. The holy seed is its stump [RSV])

LXX offers a text which is shorter than MT (and 1QIsa[a]). There is no rendering of several words found in MT. On the basis of the version of Theodotion (σπέρμα ἅγιον τὸ στήλωμα αὐτῆς) it was thought that the final clause of v. 13 was the part missing in the Greek.[7] However, scholars have pointed out that, since the word αὐτῆς ('its [husk]') plausibly shows that the last word in Hebrew (מצבתה) was read, the words not translated are קדש מצבת בם זרע.[8] The minus can be explained as due to homoioarkton.[9]

The clause 'And the tenth is on it,' interestingly, uses a present tense, ἐστι—MT has a non-verbal clause—whereas the context of v. 12 and the remainder of v. 13 is in the future. How should one interpret the present tense in the first part of the verse? Troxel is the only one who has dealt with this issue, and according to him, this feature is best explained in the

in its Greek Translation," in *Scripture in Transition. Essays on Septuagint, Hebrew Bible, and Dead Sea Scrolls in Honour of Raija Sollamo* (ed. Anssi Voitila and Jutta Jokiranta; Supplements for the Journal for the Study of Judaism 126; Leiden: Brill, 2008), 205–21; Rodrigo de Sousa, "Problems and Perspectives on the Study of Messianism in LXX Isaiah," in *The Old Greek of Isaiah: Issues and Perspectives* (ed. Arie van der Kooij and Michaël N. van der Meer; CBET 55; Leuven: Peeters, 2010), 135–52.

[6] It is a great pleasure to contribute to this volume in honour of Hugh Williamson who has contributed significantly among other things to the study of the book of Isaiah.

[7] See e.g. Joseph Ziegler, *Untersuchungen zur Septuaginta des Buches Isaias* (ATA 12/3; Münster: Aschendorff, 1934), 48.

[8] Hans Wildberger, *Jesaja* (BKAT 10; Neukirchen-Vluyn: Neukirchener Verlag, 1971), 234; John A. Emerton, "The Translation and Interpretation of Isaiash vi.13," in *Interpreting the Hebrew Bible. Essays in Honour of E. I. J. Rosenthal* (ed. John A. Emerton and Stefan C. Reif; University of Cambridge Oriental Publications 32; Cambridge: Cambridge University Press, 1982), 85–118 (89); Dominique Barthélemy, *Critique textuelle de l'Ancien Testament.* Tome 2. *Isaïe, Jérémie, Lamentations* (OBO 50/2; Fribourg: Éditions universitaires, and Göttingen: Vandenhoeck & Ruprecht, 1986), 42.

[9] Emerton, "Translation and Interpretation," 89; Barthélemy, *Critique textuelle*, 42. Ronald L. Troxel ("Economic Plunder as a Leitmotif in LXX-Isaiah," *Bib* 83 [2002]: 375–91 [387 n.]) suggests that "G's *Vorlage* had suffered parablepsis."

light of the context, i.e., vv. 11–13. In order to understand his explanation it is necessary first to have a look at the preceding verses, 11–12. In the Greek version, both verses read as follows (in English translation):

> v. 11: Then I said, How long, O LORD? And he said:
> Until cities become desolate because they are not inhabited,
> and houses, because there are no people,
> and the land will be left desolate.
> v. 12: And after these things, God will put the men far away,
> and those who have been left will be multiplied on the land.

This version differs from MT (and 1QIsa[a]) in v. 12 in particular. 'After these things' (μετὰ ταῦτα) in v. 12 is a plus indicating a situation after the events, the desolation of the land, announced in v. 11. Unlike MT, where v. 12 provides a description in line with the desolation of the land as announced in v. 11, LXX v. 12 refers to a new situation, to a period *after* the desolation of v. 11.

In the phrase 'God will put the men far away' MT refers to the deportation of people from the land, in line with v. 11. However, since LXX refers to a later situation, v. 12a in Greek is likely to be understood in a different way. This is even more plausible in light of the rendering of v. 12b. MT has it that 'the forsaken places are many in the midst of the land,' again alluding to a situation in line with v. 11. LXX, however, reads, 'and those who have been left will be multiplied on the land.' The Hebrew עזובה has not been taken here in the sense of a desolation of the land, but it has been interpreted as referring to a group of people that had been left.[10] Seeligmann speaks of a "community left behind and spared."[11] In line with this interpretation, Hebrew רבה has been read in the sense of being numerous; hence the rendering: '(those who will be left) will be multiplied.' So, instead of desolation, LXX v. 12b is about a growing population, thus conveying the notion of salvation.

From this perspective, the removal of 'the men' in v. 12a is likely to be understood as a reference to the occupiers of the land, as has been proposed by Baer,[12] and not in the sense of a depopulation, as in MT. For 'the

[10] Cf. Wildberger, *Jesaja*, 233; Troxel, "Economic Plunder," 385; David A. Baer, "It's All about Us": Nationalistic Exegesis in the Greek Isaiah (Chapters 1–12)," in *"As Those who are Taught." The Interpretation of Isaiah from the LXX to the SBL* (ed. Claire Mathews McGinnis and Patricia K. Tull; SBLSymS 27; Atlanta: Society of Biblical Literature, 2006), 29–48 (37).

[11] Isaac Leo Seeligmann, *The Septuagint Version of Isaiah. A Discussion of its Problems* (Mededelingen en verhandelingen Ex Oriente Lux 9; Leiden: Brill, 1948), 116.

[12] Baer, "Nationalistic Exegesis," 37. Troxel ("Economic Plunder," 386) sees 'the men' as equivalent to the (bad) rulers in 3:12.

men' in the sense of oppressors, LXX Isa 25:4a, 5 may be compared. The verb μακρύνω is also found in 49:19, where it is also used in connection with enemies ('those who swallow you up').

Let us return to the issue of the present tense in the first part of v. 13. Troxel offers the following explanation: "While all the actions of vv. 11–13 are yet future in the MT, the LXX, after describing desolation (v. 11) and portraying a day beyond that desolation (v. 12), turns to what it regards as *current* troubles, as indicated by its choice of ἐστι in translating the non-verbal clause." Thus, the tenth part "must envision conditions before the desolation augured in v. 11."[13] In this view, the troubles indicated in the first part of v. 13 are to be seen as referring to the time before the desaster announced in v. 11, that is to say, to the time of the prophet (cf. vv. 1–10). However, the difficulty with this reading of the first clause of v. 13 is that it does not do justice to the fact that this clause is embedded in the whole of vv. 12–13, i.e., the passage introduced by 'after these things.' It therefore is more plausible to read this clause as part of this context, and not as referring to a state of affairs preceding that of v. 11. Moreover, ἐπ' αὐτῆς in v. 13 is clearly related to ἐπὶ τῆς γῆς 'on the land' in v. 12. The use of the present tense expresses a durative sense: in the time after the desolation (v. 11), when the oppressors will be put away, and the ones who had been left will multiply—in this period there will be a tenth part, continually.[14]

Turning to the word 'the tenth', according to MT, a tenth, a small part, will be left in a situation as described in v. 12. "Even though a fraction of the population, a tenth, is left behind in Judah when YAHWEH exiles the rest (v. 12a), it will not escape, but it too must be exterminated."[15] Things are different, however, in the Greek version. As v. 12b in LXX depicts a positive situation—the remaining ones will grow in number in the land (of Judah)—it follows that 'the tenth' should not be understood in the light of MT. Moreover, since the tenth is considered, in the Greek, to be present continually (cf. the present tense), one gets the impression that this part is to be distinguished from the growing number of people in v. 12b. The latter will grow, while the former is there constantly.

An important question in this regard concerns the meaning of the Greek equivalent of the Hebrew for '(the) tenth': ἐπιδέκατον. This term

---

13 Troxel, "Economic Plunder," 386.

14 For other cases of a present tense embedded in a context alluding to the future, see LXX Isa 9:6; 13:19 (καλειται in both cases).

15 George B. Gray, *A Critical and Exegetical Commentary on the Book of Isaiah 1–27* (ICC; Edinburgh: T&T Clark, 1912), 111.

is commonly understood as the tenth part of the population, in line with MT.[16] However, the difficulty is that a reading based on MT does not fit the meaning of v. 12 in Greek (see above). Moreover, elsewhere in the LXX τὸ ἐπιδέκατον always refers to *the tithe*.[17] If 'the/a tenth part' would have been the intended meaning, then one would expect τὸ δέκατον in Greek.[18] It therefore is more correct to render the first clause of v. 13 as follows: "and the tithe is again on the land."[19]

This raises the question of what this text might mean. The tithe was something which was to be offered in the temple. According to Num 18 this was important for the sons of Levi, since they were the ones who should receive the tithes offered by the Israelites, because, as is stated in v. 21: "I have given to the sons of Levi every tithe in Israel for an inheritance for their services" in the temple. The tribe of Levi did not receive a portion of the promised land—God is their portion and inheritance (v. 20)— and that is why the tithes should be given to them. Instead of having a landed inheritance, the priests and Levites receive the tithes offered by the Israelites to the LORD.

If read from this perspective one could say that the beginning of v. 13 is about the offering of tithes to the priests in the temple in the period after the desolation. However, I would propose another interpretation, which is more plausible in the light of the simile at the end of the verse (on this, see below). According to Num 18, there is a close link between the tithes and the tribe of Levi, the priests; but interestingly, writings at the time of LXX Isaiah—Jubilees and Aramaic Levi—contain a story about Levi which provides a clue for another understanding of the term 'tithe.' In *Jub.* 32 we are told that Levi had a dream at Bethel that he had been made a priest (v. 1). "V. 2 then has it that Jacob tithed all of his belongings and his children to complete the vow he had made at Bethel (Gen 28:22). Verse 3 offers an explanation of how Levi could be the tithe-son among Jacob's twelve male offspring."[20] As to this explanation, "the composer of Jubilees

---

16 Cf. Richard R. Ottley, *The Book of Isaiah according to the Septuagint* (*Codex Alexandrinus*) (vol. 1; London: Cambridge University Press, 1904), 85; Seeligmann, *Septuagint Version*, 45; Troxel, "Economic Plunder," 385; *The New English Translation of the Septuagint*; Takamitsu Muraoka, *A Greek-English Lexicon of the Septuagint* (Leuven: Peeters, 2009), 271.

17 See Num 18:21, 26; Deut 12:11, 17; 14:23, 28; 26:12; Amos 4:4; Mal 3:8; 2 Chr 31:5, 6, 12.

18 Cf. the variant reading attested in Eusebius's Commentary on Isaiah (GCS 9): τὸ δέκατον.

19 Cf. *Septuaginta Deutsch* ("der Zehnt"). 'Again' is to be preferred to 'still' because the clause refers to the period after a desolation (v. 12).

20 Robert A. Kugler, *From Patriarch to Priest. The Levi-Priestly Tradition from Aramaic Levi to Testament of Levi* (SBLEJL 9; Atlanta: Scholars Press, 1996), 164–5.

has Jacob count his sons from the youngest up, beginning with Benjamin, still in the womb. Counting upwards in this way the 10th son is Levi [...], who becomes Jacob's tithe to the LORD."[21] In the light of this evidence—Levi as the tithe-son of Jacob—'the tithe' in v. 13 can be interpreted metonymically as a reference to Levi/the priesthood.[22] This also sheds light on the difference between v. 12b and v. 13a, noted above: the former then is about the lay-people of Judah, whereas the latter passage refers to another part of the nation, namely, the priesthood.

In the clause, 'And it will again be for plunder like a terebinth, and like an acorn when it falls from its husk, contextually, 'it' is best understood as referring to 'the tithe.'[23] As for the phrase 'for plunder' (εἰς προνομήν), in LXX Isaiah the Hebrew root בער is usually rendered in the sense of burning (see e.g., εἰς καῦσιν in 44:15 for לבער), but in this case, as well as in 5:5 (εἰς διαρπαγήν), it has been interpreted differently.[24] According to our verse, it will be for plunder 'like a terebinth.' It is not clear what is implied here, but in the light of LXX Isa 1:30, the only place in the book where the same comparison occurs, it may well be that it should be understood as 'like a terebinth that had shed its leaves.'[25] The second simile of our verse is more explicit: 'like an acorn when it falls from its husk.' Greek βάλανος can refer to an oak-tree, but, as has been pointed out by Troxel, here it is the 'acorn' because in 2:13 the tree is designated as 'the tree of the acorn' (for the same Hebrew word as in 6:13 [אלון]!).[26] The verb ἐκπίπτω with ἀπό, is used here as the equivalent of Hebrew שלך, just as in Job 15:33

[21] Sidnie White Crawford, *Rewriting Scripture in Second Temple Times* (Studies in the Dead Sea Scrolls and Related Literature; Grand Rapids: Eerdmans, 2008), 77.

[22] One may wonder whether the expression זרע קדש, if present in the underlying Hebrew text, has triggered this interpretation.

[23] Ronald L. Troxel (*LXX-Isaiah as Translation and Interpretation. The Strategies of the Translator of the Septuagint of Isaiah* [Journal for the Study of Judaism in the Persian, Hellenistic, and Roman Period Supplements Series 124; Leiden: Brill, 2008], 271) holds that 'it' refers to 'the land', but it seems more plausible to regard the subject of 'it will be' the same as that of the preceding clause of the verse ('the tithe').

[24] It may well be that the rendering of 'plunder' is based on the meaning 'to graze' (for which, see LXX Exod 22:4).

[25] As to the relationship between 6:13 and 1:30 in the Hebrew text, see H. G. M. Williamson, "Isaiah 6,13 and 1,29–31," in *Studies in the Book of Isaiah. Festschrift Willem A. M. Beuken* (ed. Jacques van Ruiten and Marc Vervenne; BETL 132; Leuven: Peeters, 1997), 119–28. Furthermore, it is interesting to note that in antiquity there was a tradition of rendering the Hebrew שלכת in v. 13 as referring to the shedding of leaves (Targum and Symmachus).

[26] Troxel, "Economic Plunder," 387 n. See also Emerton, "Translation and Interpretation," 89.

('But may he [i.e. the impious] [...] fall off like an olive blossom'). This expression is to be taken in the literal sense ('to fall from'), just as in LXX Deut 19:5 ('and the iron slips from the wood').

What does this simile mean? An acorn falling from its husk evokes the idea of an object that falls from the place where it belongs. The same is true of other passages where the verb ἐκπίπτω is found. For instance, Isa 14:12: 'How is *fallen from* heaven the morning-star.' The falling from its place in this passage has to do with the loss of a position of power. The same is true of LXX Dan 7:20: 'And concerning its ten horns, that were upon its head, and the one, which was growing, and three *fell out* because of it.' Because of the one horn three horns fell out, i.e., lost their position of power (upon the head). This meaning is also attested in LXX Isa 28:1 (and see v. 4) where the loss of glory and power of particular leaders, referred to as 'the crown of pride, the hired workers of Ephraim,' is expressed by the image of 'the flower that has fallen from its glory.' Compare also Diodorus Siculus, 31, 18.2: 'Ptolemy the king of Egypt having been fallen from the kingship (ἐκπεσὼν τῆς βασιλείας),' i.e., having lost and deprived of the kingship (by his own brother).

Thus, the simile 'like an acorn when it falls from its husk' is likely to be understood in the sense of the loss of a position of glory and power. This fits the idea of 'the tithe' as a reference to the priesthood. The final part of v. 13 in Greek then means to say that the priesthood will lose their place and postion of power.

Finally, a note on the choice of θήκη for Hebrew מצבת is in order. The Greek term fits the imagery (referring to the husk or cup of an acorn), but how does one explain this term as a rendering of מצבת? It seems to me that this Hebrew word has been taken in the sense of מצב as attested in 22:19, 'position, office' (LXX: οἰκονομία 'office'), which then was applied to the image of an acorn. This would mean that the notion of position or office was indeed the underlying idea of the simile.

All in all, the imagery in LXX Isa 6:13 is quite different from that in MT. Whereas the latter is about a terebinth or oak whose stump remains when it is felled, as the verse is usually understood, the Greek speaks of a terebinth (shedding its leaves) and of an acorn when it falls from its husk. It strikes one that LXX is not speaking of two trees as in MT, but reflects a particular choice as far as the second part of the comparison is concerned—'acorn' instead of 'oak.' This choice was made, likely so, to evoke the idea of losing a position or office. Another choice made concerns the rendering 'for plunder' as noted above. It may be observed that, unlike the alternative ('for burning'), this equivalent fits the similes of the verse. The notion of plunder conveys the idea of losing glory[27] and the position is due to an act of violence.[28]

## II. Isaiah 29:22 (LXX)

> Therefore thus said the Lord concerning the house of Jacob, which he separated from (the descendants of) Abraham

According to MT ('Therefore thus says the Lord concerning the house of Jacob, [the Lord] who redeemed Abraham') it is the Lord who redeemed Abraham,[29] but in the LXX the relative clause is related to 'the house of Jacob,' which fits the word order in Hebrew more easily. As a result, the Greek version does not speak of God as the one who 'redeemed' (פדה) Abraham, but as the one who 'separated' (ἀφώρισεν) the house of Jacob from Abraham, i.e., from the descendants of Abraham. The Greek verb employed here is nowhere else in the LXX used as an equivalent of פדה. How does one explain this unusual rendering?

Ziegler has suggested that the verb 'to separate' was introduced in order to express the idea of God's election of Israel from among the nations, in line with a passage such as Lev 20:26: 'You shall be holy to me; for I the Lord am holy, and have separated (בדל Hi.) you from the peoples, that you should be mine' (RSV).[30] The difficulty of this proposal, however, is that the text in LXX Isaiah does not refer to a separation 'from the peoples,' but 'from Abraham.'

Eusebius of Caesarea read the Greek of Isa 29:22 in the light of a passage in the New Testament, John 8:39 ([Jesus to the Jews:] 'If you were Abraham's children, you would do what Abraham did'). In his view, God separated, in the negative sense of the word, those who are called 'the house of Jacob,' because they did not do what Abraham did, and hence could not be considered Abraham's children.[31] Jerome interpreted the Greek version in a similar way: sic intellegi potest, quod scribas et pharisaeos, qui

---

27 Cf. the image of a terebinth shedding its leaves.

28 An interesting passage in this regard is to be found in LXX Isa 22: "you will be removed from your office and from your position" (v. 19).

29 This reading is also attested by 'the three,' Theodotion, Aquila, and Symmachus.

30 Ziegler, *Untersuchungen*, 120. For a similar view, see Léo Laberge, *La Septante d'Isaïe 28–33. Étude de tradition textuelle* (Ottawa: chez auteur, 1978), 38.

31 GCS 7.

Dominum blasphemabant, separaverit ab Abraham, qui vidit diem Domini, et laetatus est. Si enim fuissent filii Abraham, fecissent opera Abraham.[32]

However, in the light of what follows in LXX Isa 29:22 ('Jacob shall not be ashamed now'), the verb 'to separate' is not to be taken in a negative sense. Read from the perspective of the laws of Moses, the idea of being separated from (the offspring of) Abraham is best understood as referring to the marking out of Levi and his tribe for the priesthood. They were set apart for the service of the temple. This interpretation also explains the relationship between 'to redeem' in Hebrew and 'to separate' in Greek, because the Levites were taken from among the people of Israel instead of every first-born of this people (Num 3:11; 8:18), that is to say, the Levites were the ones who 'redeemed' the first-borns of Israel (for the notion of 'redeeming' first-borns, see Exod 13:13, 15). So the underlying Hebrew text of Isa 29:22, which was read thus: 'the house of Jacob that redeemed Abraham,' was interpreted in the light of the idea that the tribe of Levi was set apart in order to redeem the first-borns of the offspring of Abraham.

One may object, however, that it is difficult to take the expression 'the house of Jacob' as a reference to Levi/the priesthood. This is unusual indeed, but it is not impossible as soon as the term 'house' is taken in the sense of 'ruling, reigning house,' and not as referring to the people of Jacob as a whole. In this connection it is interesting to note that in Isa 22:21 and 37:31 where the expression 'the house of Judah' occurs, and clearly refers to the people of Judah as a whole, the LXX does not provide a literal rendering: in 22:21 it reads,'those who dwell in Judah' and in 37:31, 'those who are left in Judah' (MT, 'the surviving remnant of the house of Judah'). Moreover, as we know from sources of the time, the priests were seen as the leaders of the Jewish nation. For instance, Hecataeus of Abdera (ca. 300 BC) tells his readers:

> He [Moses] picked out the men of most refinement and with the greatest ability to head the entire nation, and appointed them priests; [...] These same men he appointed to be judges in all major disputes, and entrusted to them the guardianship of the laws and customs.[33]

---

32 CCSL 73.

33 Menahem Stern, ed., *Greek and Latin Authors on Jews and Judeans, Vol. I: From Herodotus to Plutarch* (Jerusalem: Israel Academy of Sciences and Humanities, 1974), 28. See also *Jub.* 31:15.

## III. Conclusion

As I have argued elsewhere,[34] LXX Isaiah contains passages which reflect a strong interest in a particular group of Jews in Egypt, in the Hellenistic era. These passages are 10:24, 11:16, and 19:18–19. The first one is about their going to Egypt, the second one about their return from Egypt (to Jerusalem), whereas the third passage alludes to their stay in Egypt and the existence of a temple there. In the light of what we know through Josephus, it makes perfect sense to assume that in these places LXX Isaiah is referring to a particular group that fled from Jerusalem at the time of the crisis in the sixties of the second century BC: Onias, member of the high-priestly family, and his followers, among them priests and Levites. He got permission from the Ptolemaic king, Ptolemy VI, to build a temple in the nome of Heliopolis. The building of a Jewish temple in Egypt was legitimized on the basis of the prophecy to be found in Isa 19:19 ('There shall be an altar in Egypt to the Lord'; see *Ant.* 13.67–68). All this strongly suggests that LXX Isaiah was produced by the group of Onias, which, in my view, explains the interest in priesthood as reflected in several passages in LXX Isaiah.

[34] Van der Kooij, *Die alten Textzeugen*, 52–55; idem, "'The Servant of the Lord': A Particular Group of Jews in Egypt according to the Old Greek of Isaiah. Some Comments on LXX Isa 49,1–6 and Related Passages, in *Studies in the Book of Isaiah: Festschrift Willem A. M. Beuken* (ed. Jacques van Ruiten and Marc Vervenne; BETL 132; Leuven: Peeters, 1997), 383–96.

# PROVERBS 30:32 AND THE ROOT נבל

A. A. Macintosh

"The words of Agur the son of Jakeh of Massa," if wise words, present a number of severe problems for the translator and interpreter. The penultimate verse of his collection of aphorisms (30:32) constitutes one such[1] and it runs as follows:

אם נבלת בהתנשׂא ואם זמות יד לפה

The sentence appears to consist of a conditional clause, with a second protasis in apposition to the first, and a single apodosis. The whole is extremely laconic and its three parts ambiguous, each for somewhat different reasons. These will first be reviewed.

## I. The Root נבל

The verb נבל (II) is rare in the *Qal*, though it is well attested in the *Piel* where it has a declarative sense, e.g., 'to treat with contumely' (BDB, cf. Gesenius, 16 and 18);[2] *'als nichtig erklären,' 'für nichtig halten'* (HALOT, נבל II). The difference in emphasis between these renderings depends to some extent on the view taken as to the meaning of the cognate noun נבל which is also common and plays a special part in the Wisdom Literature of the Hebrew Bible. Here, under the influence of the ancient Versions,[3]

[1] Wilhelm Frankenburg (*Die Sprüche* [HKAT 2/3; Göttingen: Vandenhoeck, 1898], 165) e.g., regards the words as *'unverständlich'* and, apart from the last phrase, leaves the verse untranslated.

[2] Gesenius 16 refers to Frants Buhl and Heinrich Zimmern, eds, *Wilhelm Gesenius' Hebräisches und Aramäisches Handwörterbuch über das Alte Testament* (16th ed.; Leipzig: Vogel, 1915). Gesenius 18 refers to Rudolph Meyer and Herbert Donner, eds, *Wilhelm Gesenius' Hebräisches und Aramäisches Handwörterbuch über das Alte Testament* (18th ed.; Berlin: Springer, 2007).

[3] See Gillis Gerleman, "Der Nicht-Mensch. Erwägungen zur hebräischen Wurzel *NBL*," *VT* 24 (1974): 147–58 (145); the LXX generally uses the following terms: ἀφρων 'foolish,' μωρος 'stupid' and, less frequently, ἀπαιδευτος 'ignorant,' ἀσυνετος 'stupid'; cf. the Peshiṭta with the equivalent terms ܣܟܠܐ and ܫܛܝܐ, the Vulgate with *stultus* and *insipiens* and the Targum with טפשא. It should be noted that in both the Peshiṭta and the Targum the renderings ܚܒܠܐ, ܡܣܪܝܐ, רשיעא 'wicked,' 'vile' are also attested, on which see below.

the traditional rendering of the term is 'fool,' '*Tor,*' '*törich*' specifically in an intellectual and ethical sense. An important article by G. Gerleman, however, has demonstrated that these traditional renderings are not adequate because they do not fit a number of instances where the noun נבל occurs. Examples include 2 Sam 3:33, where David's protest following the assassination of Abner is founded upon his view that Abner should not have died the death of a נבל, i.e., a criminal "bound hand and foot." Abner, then, did not die as a 'fool.' Another is Isa 32:5–8, where the virtues of the נדיב 'the generous' are contrasted with the vices of the נבל. Here the antithesis is not between the generous, noble נדיב and the נבל understood as a foolish man; rather it is between the generous, warm, liberal נדיב and the nihilistic, amoral, mean, and heartless נבל. To Gerleman such an estimate of the true sense of the noun נבל suggests an etymological explanation offered by reference to the bi-radical root בל 'negation,' prefixed by an augmental *nun*.[4] It is difficult to suggest a single English word which captures the 'taste' of נבל with its notions of self-centred cynicism and heartless selfishness and so, for the moment and for convenience, the simple expression 'mean' will suffice. If the נבל is mean and heartless, then he is very much more discreditable than the fool, and the traditional translations which use these terms must be discounted. In that early they became established, rests, perhaps, on the tendency for the Wisdom tradition to put words denoting various aspects of wicked and undesirable behaviour into the straight-jacket of that tradition, whereby the abiding and ultimate antithesis is between the wise and the foolish.[5] If the *qal* perfect form נבלת is unlikely to mean "If thou hast done foolishly…" (so, e.g., RV, RSV), it would seem rather to denote "If thou hast behaved meanly…" or, if stative, "If you are mean…"; cf. the NEB's "If you are churlish…".

The second word בהתנשא, a *hithpa'el* infinitive of the very familiar root נשׂא 'to lift up, carry, etc.,' prefixed by the preposition ב, follows closely the finite verb. The meaning of the expression is 'rising,' '(self-) exaltation.' In Num 23:24 it describes the aggressive stance taken by a lion which will

---

[4] Cf. the similar (and earlier) suggestion of Theodor Nöldeke, *Neue Beiträge zur semitischen Sprachwissenschaft* (Strassburg: K. J. Trübner, 1910), 94–95; for further comments see below.

[5] See my assessment of the word ליץ ("Light on ליץ," in *On Stone and Scroll: G. I. Davies Festschrift* [ed. Brian Mastin and James K. Aitken; BZAW; Berlin: de Gruyter, 2011], 479–492), for another example of a word which has suffered this fate.

not be relinquished until it has devoured its prey. Elsewhere the term is used in a good sense as well as pejoratively. For the former, 1 Chr 29:11 praises YAHWEH as "exalted over all as head," and in Num 24:7 Israel's "kingdom will be exalted" just as his king will be "higher than Agag." Yet kingdoms, societies, and constituent elements of them are recorded as 'exalting themselves' in rebellion—usually marked with a distinct element of arrogance (cf. Num 16:3, 1 Kgs 1:5, Ezek 17:14, 29:15, Dan 11:14). The decision as to whether the word has a good or a bad sense, then, depends greatly upon the particular context. In the verse under discussion the matter is difficult to judge by reason of its extremely terse nature.

The second, alternative, clause of the protasis אם זמות presents another problem in that the verb זמם 'to purpose, devise' is attested in a good sense as well as a pejorative one. The good sense is predicated only of YAHWEH (often with just punishment as its object); the pejorative is otherwise predominant. Similarly, the cognate noun זמה is found only once in a good sense (Job 17:11) and some 30 times in the pejorative. A similar weighting as between a good and a bad sense attaches to the other cognate noun מזמה, though a number of verses in Proverbs[6] use the words 'discretion,' 'understanding,' and 'knowledge' as products of devising and purpose in the context of Wisdom. Again the context is crucial in determining which sense obtains in any particular verse.

Finally, the apodosis consists of the noun clause יד לפה, literally, 'hand to mouth.' The words seem to imply a command to keep silence, cf. the very similar (but not identical) phrases in Judg 18:19, Mic 7:16, Job 21:5, 29:9, 40:4 and Wis 8:12.

In the light of these observations the verse as a whole would seem to mean "If thou hast behaved meanly in promoting thyself, if thou hast schemed, keep silent!" The rendering, however, is based upon a number of assumptions which may be, but are not certainly, correct. Further, the terse form of the saying reveals little of the exact nature of the exhortation it contains and the reader, in attempting to understand it, cannot help seeking further explanation of its words. The renderings of the ancient versions and the comments of medieval rabbinic commentators reflect just such uncertainty and consequent need for amplification.

---

[6] See 1:4, 2:11, 3:21, 5:2, 8:12.

## II. The Versions and the Rabbinic Commentators

Considerations of space preclude the inclusion here of a detailed account of this evidence and a short indication must suffice.

The LXX renders:

> ἐαν προῃ σεαυτον εἰς εὐφροσυνην
> και ἐκτεινῃς την χειρα σου μετα μαχης, ἀτιμασθησῃ
>
> If thou abandonest thyself in merriment and extendest thy hand (i.e. in friendship) during battle, thou wilt be condemned.

It is very difficult to relate this rendering to the MT, with which it seems to bear little resemblance. It seems likely, however, that "if thou abandonest thyself in merriment" corresponds to the words of the first MT protasis and that the reference to the 'hand' has some tenuous relation to the apodosis. The phrase "... thou wilt be condemned," i.e., the apodosis of the LXX version, is either supplied *ad sensum* or represents a second translation of נבלת; cf. the Peshiṭta (below) and Rashi's rendering, "If you have suffered disgrace..." (אם נתנבלת).[7]

The Vulgate:

> *et qui stultus apparuit postquam elatus est in sublime si enim intellexisset ori inposuisset manum.*
>
> ... and he who has been shown to be a fool after he has been exalted to a high position, since, if he had had the wit, he would have put his hand on his mouth.

The limitations of *stultus* 'fool' as a rendering of נבל have been noted above. The phrase "... exalted on high" clearly corresponds to בהתנשא and "... if he had had the wit, he would have put his hand on his mouth," to the second protasis and the apodosis. In the interests of a coherent, unified translation the subject of the sentence as a whole has been modified from the second to the third person singular and the imperative of MT's apodosis, now conjoined to its second protasis, is made a single conditional clause in its own right. Jerome's solution is cleverly crafted and creates a coherent whole.[8]

---

[7] Rashi, מקראות גדולות, vol. 11 (ed. Akivah Frenkel [פרענקעל]; Warsaw: J. Lebensohn, 1864), 134a.

[8] The relationship ('*et qui*') to what precedes this verse and to what follows it is obscure.

The Targum:

לא תתרורם דלא תטפש ולא תושיט אידך לפומך

> Do not exalt thyself so as not to be foolish and do not stretch forth thy hand to thy mouth.

'Foolish' presumably answers to נבלת and consequently, with inversion of the order of MT's words, בהתנשא (the ב ignored) is taken as a prohibition.

The Peshiṭta:

ܠܐ ܬܪܓ ܕܠܐ ܬܬܒܣܪ ܘܠܐ ܬܘܫܛ ܐܝܕܟ ܠܦܘܡܟ ܒܢܟܠܐ

> Do not covet lest thou be brought into contempt and do not stretch forth thy hand to thy mouth in deceit.

"Do not covet" is likely to correspond to בהתנשא; and "brought into contempt" to נבלת, cf. the LXX and Rashi above. The shape of the rendering is similar to that of the Targum and has points of contact with the LXX.

The rabbinic commentators, like the ancient versions, are under some constraint to expand considerably the sense in their elucidation of the text. Thus, for example, Rashi offers two variant renderings of the verse[9] and Ibn Ezra suggests no fewer than four alternative interpretations of אם נבלת,[10] investing the verb with meanings from foolishness to wickedness, transgression and, apparently, arrogance.

Ibn Janaḥ, in his *Book of the Hebrew Roots*,[11] believes that אם נבלת in Prov 30:32 is to be explained by reference to the fundamental meaning of the root נבל.[12] Its occurrences in Isa 24:4, 28:1, 34:4, Ps 1:3, Exod 18:18 suggest that the fundamental meaning, predicated of flowers, leafage, vegetation etc., is 'to wilt,' 'sink down,' 'fade,' 'depreciate,' 'degrade' (Arabic ألسقوط والأنحطاط). The word is not restricted to vegetation, however, and Moses is warned (Exod 18:18) that he is in danger of 'degenerating' i.e., 'wearing himself out' by overworking (Hebrew, 2nd pers. sing., נבל תבל). Again

---

9 Rashi, מקראות גדולות, 134a.

10 Ibn Ezra, in מקראות גדולות, vol. 11 (ed. Akivah Frenkel [פרענקעל]; Warsaw: J. Lebensohn, 1864), 134a–b.

11 Abu 'l-Walîd Marwân Ibn Janaḥ, *Book of the Hebrew Roots* (ed. Adolf Neubauer; Oxford: Clarendon, 1875), cols. 401–2.

12 It should be noted that he does not consider or indicate the existence of separate homonymous roots as do, e.g., BDB, HALOT, and Gesenius 16 and 18; one root denotes wilting and decay, the other folly or nihilism in an ethical sense. The treatment of ibn Janaḥ may render this distinction otiose.

this same meaning is detected when it is used of persons who are described as belonging to the class of deviant, degenerate persons (נבלים/־ות) who speak and practice נבלה (2 Sam 13:13; Isa 32:6; Job 2:10). This is the meaning, then, that Ibn Janaḥ detects for אם נבלת in the proverb under review. The verse means (my translation of Ibn Janaḥ's Arabic):

> If circumstances overwhelm you and you sink down and decline then (it should be) in raising yourself and ascent from the despicable; i.e. if you decline from your true status, and from your wealth, rise up from the despicable and do not decline to what takes away your dignity and honour; it is the situation reflected in the (Arabic) proverb, You will see the (true) sage exalted whenever he suffers disgrace.[13]

Ibn Janaḥ continues by stating that another aspect of good manners and noble character is set out in the second protasis: ואם זמות יד לפה: "If you think of something and there arises in your mind a concern, then do not articulate it, seal your secret and do not reveal it to anybody and no one will come upon it and keep your mouth from disclosing it."

Ibn Janaḥ appears to make a clear distinction between the first protasis of the text on the one hand and the second protasis with the (single) apodosis on the other. If his treatment of the second protasis and the apodosis, with its insistent repetition, is clear in meaning and emphatic in tone, his understanding of the first apodosis appears to include the perception of a subtle play upon the notions of descent and elevation, of deprivation and wealth, of disgrace and honour. The two words which constitute the clause could themselves, of course, constitute this antithesis, נבלת conveying the former notions and בהתנשא the latter. But, the adverbial, defining use of בהתנשא prompts the suspicion that the antithesis is conveyed by נבלת. Confirmation that this is Ibn Janaḥ's view may be found in his treatment of the word נבלה 'corpse.'[14] Naturally he explains the word in terms of the fundamental meaning of the root outlined above ('to wilt,' 'decline,' 'degrade' etc.) and he illustrates his point by reference to Judg 14:8. Here Samson is said to have made a detour in order to see the carcass of the lion which he had previously killed. The word translated 'carcass' is מפלת and, from the root נפל 'to fall,' it parallels very closely Ibn Janaḥ's definition of נבלה. Indeed he states explicitly that נבלה and מפלת are one and the same in meaning. Following these observations, Ibn Janaḥ notes that Arabic uses نَبِيلة (*nabīlah*) as a synonym for the more usual جِيفَة (*jīfah*) 'corpse.' The

13 تري الحكيم يعز حيث يهون. Ibn Janaḥ, *Book of the Hebrew Roots*, col. 402, line 12.

14 Ibn Janaḥ, *Book of the Hebrew Roots*, col. 402, lines 19–27.

reason behind this usage differs from that of Hebrew with its etymological link to the notion of 'wilting,' 'declining' etc. Rather, because Arabic uses the word نبيلة (*nabīlah*) to denote 'elevation,' 'rising,' it is appropriate to use it of a corpse by reason of its elevation, its rising up as it swells in distension and inflation (ارتفاعها بالانتفاخ). This analysis is summarily dismissed by Ibn Barūn on the grounds that such a metaphorical use in relation to a corpse is 'far-fetched.'[15] The objection does not, however, affect the argument set out here to the effect that Ibn Janaḥ believes that the root נבל was capable of meaning 'elevation, rising up' as well as 'wilting,' 'sinking down,' 'depreciating,' 'degrading,' 'declining.'

## III. Aḍdad

The phenomenon characteristic of some Semitic languages whereby particular words have opposite meanings is well-attested and given the name in Arabic grammars *Aḍdad* (اضداد). While there are some occurrences of *Aḍdad* within Arabic and Hebrew severally, the greater number are found when Hebrew has one meaning for a particular word and Arabic its opposite (and *vice-versa*). Nöldeke has provided a full treatment of a considerable number of examples (largely from Arabic) but amongst those which relate wholly to Hebrew the following may serve as examples:[16] פחד with the sense 'tremble,' 'be alarmed,' but contrast Jer 33:9 where the context demands 'be excited through joy.' רנן frequently denotes 'cries of rejoicing,' but in Lam 2:9 the context demands 'cries of distress,' cf. Arabic رن (*rnn*) with the meaning 'lament.'[17]

The question now arises whether נבל belongs to the *Aḍdad* class and whether it was capable of opposite meanings within Hebrew or in Hebrew and Arabic. Arabic was, of course, Ibn Janaḥ's mother tongue, and it was in Arabic that he wrote his works on the Hebrew language. It is understandable, then, that his ear would be attuned to the possibility of a word in the Hebrew Bible having a meaning better attested for its cognate in Arabic. Lest any suggestion in this sense, and in respect of a particular

---

[15] Pinchas Wechter, *Ibn Barūn's Arabic Works on Hebrew Grammar and Lexicography* (Philadelphia: Dropsie College, 1964), 13. Eli'ezer Ben Yehudah (*Thesaurus totius Hebraitatis* [Jerusalem/Berlin: Talpioth/Langenscheidt, 1908–59], 3490n) thinks that Arabic نبيلة (*nabīlah*) is likely to be a loan word from Hebrew on the grounds that there is no root *nbl* in Arabic which corresponds to this meaning.

[16] Nöldeke, *Neue Beiträge*, 67–101.

[17] For further examples, see James Barr, *Comparative Philology and the Text of the Old Testament* (Oxford: Clarendon, 1968), 173 –77.

word, be attributed to an arbitrary judgment, it is important, if possible, to seek other indications that confirm its likelihood. Proverbs 30:32 is the only verse for which Ibn Janaḥ appears to detect a meaning for נבל akin to its Arabic cognate.[18] The question arises whether other examples may be found. In answer, it is here suggested that there is one such: it is the proper name Nabal of 1 Sam 25.[19] Before considering this suggestion it is expedient to set out the evidence of the dictionaries for the meaning of Arabic *n-b-l*.

1. Lane, I 8 (Supplements), 3026,[20] records (*nubl*$^{un}$) نُبْلٌ as meaning *'Sharpness, acuteness*, or *sagacity*' as well as '*generosity*, or *nobility*' and again '*Excellence*,' for which he cites the synonym نجابة (*najābah*)'nobility, eminence, exalted rank.' He continues by quoting the proverb which is currently still in use:[21]

   كَفَى المَرْءَ نُبْلًا أَنْ تُعَدَّ مَعَايِبُهُ

   "It is sufficient eminence (i.e. merit) for a man that his faults may be numbered" (i.e., are finite in number).

2. Significant entries in Dozy's account of the root include his note that the verb *n-b-l* (I) may be defined by reference to the phrase حذق الشيء "he had mastered the matter, he was competent in it" (my translation).[22] He lists the adjective نبيل (*nabīl*) with the meanings '*noble*,' '*honorable* (*accueil, réception*)' as in the phrase تلقّاه لقاءً نبيلا "he greeted him with a sincere (*nabīl*$^{an}$) welcome" (my translation).

3. Wehr gives for the verb نَبُلَ (*nabula*) 'to be noble, noble-minded, generous, magnanimous.'[23] For the noun نُبل *nubl*$^{un}$, he reports very much as the authorities already mentioned above. The adjective نبيل *nabīl* means, e.g., 'noble, exalted, distinguished, generous, magnanimous. Finally he

[18] Ibn Janaḥ, *Hebrew Roots*, col. 402.

[19] So Guillaume in a short note; see Alfred Guillaume, *Hebrew and Arabic Lexicography: A Comparative Study* (Leiden: Brill, 1965), 2,24.

[20] Edward W. Lane, *An Arabic-English Lexicon*, vol. 8 (London: Williams and Norgate, 1893), 3027.

[21] I am grateful to my colleague, T. J. Winter, for this information.

[22] Reinhart Dozy, *Supplément aux dictionnaires Arabes*, vol. 2 (Leiden: E.J. Brill, 1881; reprinted Beirut: Liban, 1968) 645, col. 2.

[23] So Hans Wehr, *A Dictionary of Modern Written Arabic* (ed. J. Milton Cowan; Ithaca, N.Y.: Spoken Language Services, 1994), 1103–41107.

notes that *en-nabīl* was formerly the title of members of the Egyptian royal family.

The evidence for a favourable meaning for the Arabic root *n-b-l* is, then, as firm as is that for a pejorative meaning for its Hebrew cognate נבל, and the conclusion that the word belongs to the *Aḍdad* class, as between the two languages, seems reasonably secure. Here, however, the further question should be considered whether the Arabic word *n-b-l* is *Aḍdad*, i.e., within the confines of Arabic itself. It does not appear that this is the case from a perusal of the dictionaries cited above which show no trace of evidence pointing in that direction. Two authorities, however, do mention a pejorative meaning for the Arabic root. First, Ibn Barūn, referring to the 'fool' (נבל) who has said in his heart "There is no God" (Pss 14:1, 53:2), states that the noun is akin to نَبَل (*nabal*) with the meaning خسيس (*ḫasis*) 'vile' and تِنْبَال (*tinbāl*) 'lazy, slothful.'[24] Secondly, Nöldeke explicitly lists Arabic نبل (*nbl*) under his heading of *Aḍdad* words.[25] He cites as meanings 'miserable things' (*elendes Zeug*)' and 'fool (*Tor*),' on the one hand, and, on the other (for *nabīl*, pl. *nabal*, cf. *nubl*$^{un}$), 'noble, highborn (*edel, hervorragend*).' He is inclined to conclude, however, that this evidence points to two separate bilateral roots, the first בל akin to בלה, בלל, and the second נב, akin to נבע and נבט.[26] This conclusion is strictly inconsistent with the identification of a true *Aḍdad* word which requires opposite meanings in a single root; rather it is consistent with the mere appearance of *Aḍdad*. We may conclude that the first of these notices may point to *Aḍdad* within Arabic, but, without further evidence, it seems prudent to stick to the firm conclusion indicated above that *n-b-l* belongs to the *Aḍdad* class in relation to the two languages.

## IV. The Story of Nabal in 1 Samuel 25

It is now convenient to return to the story of Nabal in 1 Sam 25 and the question whether his name reflects the *Aḍdad* phenomenon. Nabal is

---

24 Wechter, *Ibn Barun's Arabic works*, 103.

25 Nöldeke, *Neue Beiträge*, 94–5.

26 The meanings of these verbs do not seem to me to support Nöldeke's theory; thus, בלה 'wear out'; בלל 'confound,' 'confuse'; נבע 'pour forth' and נבט 'look to.' Ibn Janaḥ's understanding that most, if not all, uses of the root נבל derive from the notions of 'wilting, falling declining' etc., seems to me to be preferable, not least for its simplicity; Ibn Janaḥ, *Book of the Hebrew Roots*, cols. 401–2.

reported as being a rich and successful sheep farmer of Maon who was active (in sheep shearing) in nearby Carmel. If his wife Abigail was as intelligent as she was beautiful, Nabal is said to have been "hard and mean in deed" (קשה ורע מעללים). His home town Maon is generally understood to have been some thirteen kilometres south of Hebron. Carmel (not of course the mountain overlooking modern Haifa and the scene of Elijah's contest with the prophets of Baal) was nearby, some twelve kilometres south of Hebron. We are also informed that Nabal was a Calebite,[27] a member of the tribe which inhabited the region to the south of Hebron, stretching down further south and east to the Arabah. They were thus neighbours of the Edomites to the south-east with whom also they shared certain constitutive tribal elements, notably the Kenizzites (cf. Gen 36:11, 42). Indeed a number of references indicate that the eponymous Caleb was called a Kenizzite (Num 32:12; Josh 14:6; cf. Judg 1:13, 3:9).[28] Here it is important to recognise that the area of Caleb was to the south of Judah, the latter tribe originally inhabiting the mountainous area south of Jerusalem which did not extend to Hebron. At some stage this city seems to have been appropriated by the Calebites from their Canaanite predecessors. David, a Judaean from Bethlehem, following his time at Ziklag, where he had continued assiduously to develop contacts with the southern tribes, on receipt of the news of Saul's demise, moved into Hebron and settled there with his followers (2 Sam 2:1–3). Thereafter he consolidated his position and the 'house of Judah' began to control all the southern tribal area including that of Caleb.[29]

The story of David's dealing with Nabal belongs to the period just before he entered an alliance with the Philistines at Ziklag. A fugitive from Saul, he was supporting himself and his men as a brigand and cultivating contacts with the southern tribes. The outline of the story itself is clear. David's polite overtures to Nabal for cooperation and immediate help were rudely rebuffed, provoking the former to call his men to arms in retaliation. Abigail, demonstrating her shrewd resourcefulness, intervened, persuading David not to resort to violence. In the course of her intervention she made the all-important definitive statement: Nabal was a 'son of Belial' with whom David should not concern himself. Her husband's name was

[27] Following some MSS, the *qere*, cf. LXX κυνικος.

[28] See further, Martin Noth, *The History of Israel* (trans. Stanley Godman; London: A. & C. Black, 1958), 56, 76–7.

[29] See further Roland de Vaux, *Ancient Israel: Its Life and Institutions* (transl. John McHugh; London; Darton, Longham, and Todd, 1973), 6; and Noth, *History*, 179–81.

Nabal, she said, and he lived up to his name (כי כשמו כן־הוא); if Nabal was his name, then he was characterized by נבלה 'cynical meanness' (נבל שמו ונבלה עמו). For the rest, it is recorded that Nabal died following a drunken sheep-shearing festival and David, impressed by her, married his widow.

It is, of course, difficult to assume that Nabal's parents gave him so pejorative a name, a name which would eventually readily suit Abigail's purpose in her timely and shrewd depreciation of her husband's worth. The argument that his name was not a birth name but rather a name by which he had become known in recognition of his mean character is hardly convincing.[30] A number of suggestions[31] have been made to resolve the problem, amongst them that the true nature of the name may be illustrated by its Arabic cognate.[32] None, however, can be said to have been entirely convincing simply because they may be characterized as mere guesses and are not supported by any evidence, even that of a circumstantial kind. But there is one factor which has not, so far as I am aware, been adequately noticed. It is that Nabal was not a Judaean, but a Calebite who lived and worked in the territory of his tribe before it was incorporated into the 'house of Judah' and David's burgeoning empire. This tribe, as has been noted above, contained ethnic elements which were common to the neighbouring kingdom of Edom. That Edom existed as a kingdom (as did its northern neighbour, Moab) before Israel is stated in Gen 36:31. From the few inscriptions that have survived from Edom, it is concluded that the Edomite script and language represented a variant of north-west Semitic, sometimes further classified as south Palestinian. It should be noted that, since the earliest evidence for the use of the script belongs to the eighth century BC, there can be no certainty concerning

---

[30] Kimchi records that his father took this view of the matter; but fundamentally it is likely to constitute a recognition of the problem rather than a reliable historical notice; Kimchi, מקראות גדולות, vol. 7 (Warsaw: J. Lebensohn, 1862), 125b.

[31] See the discussion of possibilities in James Barr, "The Symbolism of Names in the OT," *BJRL* 52 (1969): 11–29 (25–6).

[32] So, particularly, Johann Jacob Stamm, "Der name Nabal," in *Beiträge zur Hebräischen und altorientalischen Namenkunde* (ed. Johann Jacob Stamm, Ernst Jenni, and Martin A. Klopfenstein; OBO 30; Freiburg: Universitätsverlag, 1980), 205–13 (205–12), whose conclusions, similar to mine, are not identical. Most importantly he is inclined to posit *Aḍdad* within Hebrew itself for which I find no clear evidence; rather the matter depends, as I think, upon tribal and dialectal considerations. The editor of ben Yehudah's *Thesaurus* (p. 3488n) records in a marginal note ben Yehudah's suggestion that the root here may have its Arabic sense and denote a person of esteemed virtues (בעל מעלות חשובות).

what obtained in Edom at an earlier stage.[33] It is possible, however, that its early status as a kingdom facilitated the rise of administrative lists and records, cf. the king-list of Gen 36: 31–39.[34]

Geographically Edom's south-eastern boundary is marked by the descent to the deserts of North Arabia. This is the area where Job's native 'land of Uz' was likely to have been situated (cf. the reference to the "daughter of Edom that dwellest in the land of Uz" in Lam 4:21).[35] In Gen 36:20–28 Uz is connected with "Seir in the land of Edom" (v. 28) and Seir frequently occurs as a synonym for Edom. Job 1:15 speaks of a plundering raid on Job's residence by Sabaeans. This people are named by reference to their city of Sheba (שבא) which was close to Teima; both cities, mentioned in the annals of Tiglath-Pileser III, were situated in the north-west of Arabia.[36] The widespread threat to the area by the Assyrians at the end of the eighth century BCE is likely to be reflected in the oracle(s) of Isa 21:11–17.[37] Originally a single[38] oracle constituting a sympathetic warning to Edom under the cipher of Dumah, the prophet envisages Edomite fugitives from the Assyrians being met with water and provisions by the inhabitants of Teima and Dedan. Again the 'caravans of the Dedanites' refers to a well-known merchant tribe who, according to Ezek 25:13, lived in the same area of Arabia, to the south of Edom. Such passages indicate both the proximity of Arabia to Edom and the natural contacts in terms of culture and language that such proximity will have generated. The language of the passage from Isa 21 is marked by a number of dialectal peculiarities and it seems likely that the prophet has adapted the register of the language he deploys (? Edomite) to reflect the people referred to.[39]

The collection entitled "The words of Agur of Massa" in Prov 30 is widely thought to have a foreign origin. If, as many suppose, Massa is a

---

33 John R. Bartlett, *Edom and the Edomites* (JSOTSup 77; Sheffield: JSOT, 1989), 209–10.

34 For the general correlation between royal courts and the rise of administrative writing, see, e.g., Alexander Rofé, *Introduction to the Literature of the Hebrew Bible* (Jerusalem Biblical Studies 9; Jerusalem: Simor, 2009), 18–30. For recent archaeological evidence that 'state formation began several centuries earlier that the eighth and seventh centuries BC,' see Thomas E. Levy et al., "Reassessing the Chronology of Biblical Edom: New Excavations and $^{14}$C Dates from Khirbet en-Nahas (Jordan)," *Antiquity* 78 (2004): 865–79.

35 For a full review of the evidence for the location of Uz, see Edouard Dhorme, *A Commentary on the Book of Job* (trans. Harold Knight; London: Nelson, 1967), xxi–xxv.

36 See Dhorme *Job*, 9–10, for the evidence and the relevant literature.

37 See A. A. Macintosh, *Isaiah xxi: A Palimpsest* (Cambridge: Cambridge University Press, 1980), 96–102.

38 Macintosh, *Isaiah xxi*, 131–43.

39 Macintosh, *Isaiah xxi*, 79 and 137.

place name, attention is drawn to Gen 25:14 where Massa is listed with other places, such as Teima, Dumah, sons of Ishmael "by their villages and by their encampments." The area matches precisely that described above. Again there are a number of apparent dialectal features[40] and McKane's commentary, for example, records a number of appeals to Aramaic[41] and Arabic[42] by scholars in their quest to elucidate the difficult words and expressions.[43] These considerations of provenance and of dialectal character suggest that the problems of v. 32, cited at the beginning of this paper, may be illuminated by the *Aḍdad* nature of the word נבל in relation to Hebrew and Arabic. On this view and on the basis of the evidence for the meanings of the root in Arabic, we may suggest the following translation of the verse:

If you have become eminent in your career, and if you have planned diligently, keep your counsel.

אם־נבלת—literally, "if you have become elevated, exalted, distinguished."

בהתנשא—the reflexive can have a pejorative sense and denote arrogance (e.g., 1 Kgs 1:5; Num 16:3; Ezek 29:15). It is also capable of a positive sense (e.g., 1 Chr 29:11; Num 24:7). The basic sense of 'elevation,' 'exaltation' appears to mirror in word-play the meaning attributed here to נבלת.

ואם־זמות—Again the verb may have a pejorative sense but does not necessarily do so. For an example of a beneficial use, see, e.g., Zech 8:15; note the contrast with the previous verse, where the verb is predicated of malevolent action. The verb in the verse here under consideration implies purposeful thinking and planning and, consequently, 'diligently' is added *ad sensum*.

יד לפה—literally 'hand to mouth'; the words imply a command to keep discrete silence. See further above.

If this is the original sense of the saying with its Edomite/Arabian flavour, the question arises whether, as it settled into the Hebrew tradition, the prevailing (Hebrew) sense of the root נבל asserted itself. The evidence of the ancient versions and of the rabbinic commentators cited above suggests that this is inevitably what happened. Indeed the occurrence of the noun נבל with a pejorative sense within the Words of Agur (Prov 32:22)

---

[40] An indication, perhaps, is furnished by the NEB which notes no fewer than eight cases in which either their renderings are "probable" on the basis of "meaning uncertain" or because "the Hebrew is unintelligible."

[41] See vv. 1, 15, 21.

[42] See vv. 9, 15, 16, 28, 31.

[43] William McKane, *Proverbs: A New Approach* (OTL; London: SCM, 1970), 643–64.

may indicate the early beginnings of this process within what is generally understood to be a somewhat diverse collection of aphorisms.[44] Ibn Janaḥ seems to have detected in the proverb the *Aḍdad* nature of the root and to have sought to represent both meanings in his translation which, in his attempt to explain the verse, is necessarily expansive.

> *If you decline* from your true status and from your wealth, *rise up* from the despicable and do not decline to what takes away your dignity and honour.

The words in italics indicate the two senses of נבל while 'dignity' and 'honour' are related to the infinitive construct בהתנשא. The result is that he posits for the saying an elegant play on the notions of downwards and upwards, of decline and elevation. While, as usual, Ibn Janaḥ's comments belong to the "sum of unusual thoughts and noteworthy opinions which no one else has expressed or noticed,"[45] it seems unlikely that so complicated an aphorism was originally formulated by a mere two words.

## V. Conclusion

We return finally to the story of Nabal and to the question of the meaning of his name. Noth in his *Personennamen* lists נבל under the heading "Names indicating personal intellectual characteristics."[46] At the end of this category, and prefaced with a laconic '*sogar,*' he gives to the name the traditional meaning 'fool,' 'foolish' (*Tor, töricht*). Following the work of Gerleman (see above), this view of the matter cannot be sustained. Elsewhere Noth offers an assessment of biblical names which have Arabic origins.[47] Apart from names mentioned in (Arabic) literature, and in the inscriptions of north-western and southern Arabia, an important source for such names (and from a very early stage) are the Edomite

---

[44] McKane (Proverbs, 660) notes that the נבל in this number saying is 'the odd man out', since there appears to be no contrast between 'a former and present condition'. The servant who becomes a king, the שנואה who achieves marriage and the maid-servant who displaces a wife, all reflect a radical change of status. While it is clear that well-fed נבל is a seriously unpleasant phenomenon, there is no indication of his status before, with full stomach, he became such. It is possible, then, that the term נבל is deployed here because it retained something of its Aḍdad nature and thus conveyed the notion of degeneration as a transition comparable to the manifest transitions of the other persons indicated.

[45] *Roots*, col. 93, under בלל.

[46] Martin Noth, *Die Israelitischen Personennamen in Rahmen der gemeinsemitischen Namengebung* (BWANT 3/10; Hildesheim; G. Olms, 1966), 229.

[47] Noth, *Die Israelitischen Personennamen*, 51.

names preserved in Gen 36:31–39.[48] It is readily apparent from their non-composite nature that these names differ markedly from contemporary, as also from earlier and later, Israelite names. The connection between these names and Arabic names is so close that they may be designated as 'simply Arabic.' It seems likely from what has been argued above that this Calebite, from the far south of what was later to become part of Judah, was given a name which, so far from being deprecatory, had a benign sense. That sense may be determined by reference to Arabic *n-b-l* and accords with the likelihood that Nabal's dialect was closely related to the speech of nearby Edom and Arabia. When his wife Abigail, in an urgent and dangerous situation, addressed the powerful brigand David, she was addressing a Judaean. It is explicitly said of her that she was intelligent (טובת־שכל—1 Sam 25:3) and consequently we may assume that she was familiar with David's Judaean dialect (as well as that of her husband) and that she determined to exploit her knowledge in the course of arguing her case. Thus, urging David not to resort to bloodshed in assuaging his anger, she indicates that her husband is not worth such radical action and the ensuing risk of blood-guiltiness. Nabal's provocation of David naturally resulted from his defective character in accordance with which, as a "son of Belial" (v. 25), he took mean, ungenerous and short-sighted decisions. By the expediency of using an aspect of dialect familiar to David, the point that she makes is the more directly and effectively addressed *ad hominem*. Thus, he whose parents expressed the wish that their child be 'noble,' 'magnanimous,' was, at his end, more accurately characterized by Abigail's

> 'Mean' is his name, and mean is his behaviour.

[48] Noth (*Die Israelitischen Personennamen*, 51 n.) argues that there is no reason to doubt the statement of Gen 36:31 that the list belongs to the period "before there were kings in Israel."

# THE ROLE OF AQUILA, SYMMACHUS AND THEODOTION IN MODERN COMMENTARIES ON THE HEBREW BIBLE

Alison Salvesen

## I. The Identity of the Three

In the textual notes of modern philological commentaries on the Hebrew Bible there are sometimes references to Aquila, Symmachus, and Theodotion (henceforth Aq., Sym., Theod., or 'the Three'), or to their sigla in Greek, α′, σ′, θ′. Often the introduction to a commentary explains that the major versions of the LXX, Peshiṭta, Targumim, and Vulgate will be cited, and less frequently the significance of these versions for the textual history of the Hebrew book commented upon. Yet it is rare for any commentary to explain the importance of the later Jewish Greek versions.[1] In this essay it will be argued that for modern study of the biblical text, the 'Three' are valuable witnesses both to the emerging MT between the turn of the Era and 200 CE, and to the meaning as it was understood at a time much closer to that of the biblical writers than our own.

Almost all that we have of the Jewish Greek versions of Aq., Sym., and Theod. depends ultimately on the work of the early third century scholar Origen. Perturbed by the differences between the Church's LXX and the contemporary Hebrew text used by Jews, Origen had assembled a number of later Greek translations known to him. He set them out synoptically along with the Hebrew text and a transliterated version of the Hebrew, in the multi-columned work known subsequently as the Hexapla.[2]

Apart from the entire version of the book of Daniel bearing Theod.'s name,[3] almost all of the versions of the Three are preserved only in a

[1] The fullest and most accurate account to date remains that of N. Fernández Marcos, *The Septuagint in Context. Introduction to the Greek Versions of the Bible* (Leiden: Brill, 2000), 109–61.

[2] As well as the 'Three,' he sometimes included anonymous versions he had found, 'Quinta,' 'Sexta,' and 'Septima,' the 'fifth,' 'sixth,' and 'seventh' versions. The Latin names are derived from Jerome's use of the Hexaplaric versions: naturally, Origen and Eusebius employed the Greek terms. (The 'first' version is the LXX, and the second to fourth the Three.)

[3] Theod.'s version of Daniel survived in its entirety because for unknown reasons it replaced the Church's LXX version of the book.

fragmentary state. The Hexapla perished, probably sometime after its LXX column was translated into Syriac in 616 to become the Syrohexapla version. Most of the remaining material from the Three has been preserved by Christians, often recorded precisely because it differs from LXX at that point. Preservation has been sporadic: more readings of the Three survive for certain books such as Genesis, Isaiah, and Psalms because Christians were especially interested in those.[4] Some LXX manuscripts even have marginal notes recording readings from the Hexapla. Such notes and citations are not confined to Greek sources, but were translated into Latin, Syriac, Armenian, and Georgian. These can be retroverted back into Greek with care, but obviously there is an element of uncertainty involved.[5]

## II. Modern Collections and Editions

Collections of Hexaplaric readings were made by scholars from the sixteenth century onwards, up until Frederick Field's *Origenis Hexaplorum quod supersunt*.[6] Field's 1875 edition can still be useful. However, it is no longer an adequate tool for biblical textual criticism without updating and considerable supplementation. Field had drawn on the work of his predecessors and made few fresh collations of the material, though he did add material from the Syrohexapla.[7] Furthermore, there have been several important discoveries of new readings since his day, especially from the Cairo Geniza.[8] There is also the Tur ʿAbdin manuscript of the Syro-

[4] Eusebius of Caesarea often cites the Three to demonstrate that the renderings of these supposedly anti-Christian Jewish translators could support a Christian interpretation of Isaiah. Later, Jerome's commentaries on the prophetic books had a similar aim, though he also used the Three to show that the Hebrew text was superior to the LXX. Thus a large number of surviving readings are associated with passages presenting theological difficulties in antiquity, rather than with places where modern scholars identify a textual crux.

[5] In Field's edition of Hexaplaric fragments, the retroversions appear in smaller Greek type. However, the Göttingen LXX edition translates Syriac readings into Latin, which can be misleading.

[6] Frederick Field, *Origenis Hexaplorum quae supersunt sive Veterum interpretum Graecorum in totum Vetus Testamentum fragmenta* (2 vols; Oxford: Clarendon, 1875). See T. Michael Law, "A History of Research on Origen's Hexapla," *BIOSCS* 40 (2007): 30–48.

[7] Gerard J. Norton, "Collecting Data for a New Edition of the Fragments of the Hexapla," in *IX Congress of the International Organization for Septuagint and Cognate Studies, Cambridge 1995* (ed. Bernard A. Taylor; SBLSCS 45; Atlanta: Scholars Press, 1997), 251–62.

[8] Francis Crawford Burkitt, *Fragments of the Books of Kings according to the Translation of Aquila* (Cambridge: Cambridge University Press, 1897) (1 Kgs 20:7–17; 2 Kgs 23:11–27); Charles Taylor, *Hebrew-Greek Cairo Genizah Palimpsests from the Taylor-Schechter Collection including a fragment of the twenty-second Psalm according to Origen's Hexapla* (Cam-

hexapla for the Pentateuch, which covers parts of the Pentateuch that are not extant in earlier copies of the Syrohexapla.[9] New editions of patristic commentaries and catenae have been published, such as a new and more reliable edition of Eusebius' commentary on Isaiah[10] and Françoise Petit's editions of catena material.[11]

Since the inception of the Göttingen Septuaginta Unternehmen in 1908, the editions of LXX books have incorporated most of this new material in the second, 'Hexaplaric,' apparatus at the bottom of each page. However, the function of this apparatus is primarily to indicate where the later revisions influenced the mainstream LXX tradition, rather than to provide a guide to the renderings of the Three. Moreover, the second Göttingen edition of Psalms published in 1967 did not include a Hexaplaric apparatus, and the new edition of the Psalter is still a long way off completion, owing to the complexity of the manuscript tradition.

Although patristic tradition suggests that 'Theodotion' was a translator living in the late second or early third century CE, the evidence of the version points to circles working in the early first century CE, if not before.[12] It seems very likely that 'Theodotion's' work is associated with a pre-Christian movement of revision that sought to 'improve' the older

bridge: Cambridge University Press, 1900) (Pss 22:15–18 and 90:17–103:17); a Cairo Geniza fragment containing Pss 68.13–14,30–33 and 80:11–14 published by Charles Wessely ("Un nouveau fragment de la version grecque du Vieux Testament par Aquila," in *Mélanges offerts à M. Émile Chatelain* [Paris: A. Champion, 1910], 224–29) was immediately re-identified as Sym. Giovanni Mercati (*Psalterii Hexapli Reliquiae. Pars prima. Codex rescriptus Bybliothecae Ambrosianae O 39 sup. Phototypice Expressus et Transcriptus* [Bibliotheca Apostolica Vaticana; Città del Vaticano: In Bybliotheca Vaticana, 1958]) published a ninth century text of Hexaplaric Psalms.

9 Arthur Vööbus, *The Pentateuch in the Version of the Syro-Hexapla: A Facsimile Edition of a Midyat Manuscript discovered 1964* (CSCO 369; Subsidia 45; Leuven: Peeters, 1976).

10 Joseph Ziegler, *Eusebius Werke*, Vol. 9. *Der Jesajakommentar* (GCS; Berlin: Akademie, 1975).

11 A catena is an ancient bible commentary consisting of excerpts culled from noted patristic authorities. The tradition is often very complex. For an example, see Françoise Petit, *La chaîne sur la Genèse* (TEG 3; Leuven: Peeters, 1995). The Psalter also has a rich catena tradition.

12 Frederick Field (*Origenis Hexaplorum quae supersunt sive Veterum interpretum Graecorum in totum Vetus Testamentum fragmenta* [2 vols; Oxford: Clarendon Press, 1875], xxx–viii) suggested that Theod. was prior to Sym., but no earlier than 180–192 CE. A date in the early first century CE was put forward in the revolutionary work of Dominique Barthélemy, *Les devanciers d'Aquila: première publication intégrale du texte des fragments du Dodécaprophéton* (VTSup 10; Leiden: Brill, 1963). See the summary of the current consensus on the 'kaige' Revision and 'Theodotion,' in Jennifer M. Dines, *The Septuagint* (London: T&T Clark, 2004), 81–87. However, Fernández Marcos (*Septuagint in Context*, 150) wishes to retain the 'historical' figure Theodotion as the last stage of an earlier revisional process.

LXX by conforming it more closely to the Hebrew text of that time. The principles of this movement culminated in Aq.'s revision. Aquila's version has an etymologizing style that is very consistent, and reflects the increasing importance of the details of the Hebrew text for exegesis. Symmachus' translation may have been a reaction in the other direction, because he is interested in fidelity to the Hebrew without the compromises of Greek style that Aq.'s approach entailed.[13] An analysis of Sym.'s renderings in the Pentateuch shows clear affinities with Palestinian Judaism of the second to fourth centuries CE. Sometimes the sigla denoting attribution to a particular reviser has become confused or omitted in the course of transmission. However, someone thoroughly familiar with the style, common equivalences, and translation technique of each of the Three is often able to assign readings to the appropriate reviser.

This overview demonstrates why the versions of the Three are important for the biblical scholar. Theodotion's version may have its roots in the period at the turn of the Era, Aq. dates from 130 CE, and Sym. from 200 CE. These two centuries represent a significant period when MT was being consolidated in terms of its text form and reading tradition. So the readings of the Three witness to the development of MT and to possible variants of their period.[14] They also offer a window onto how the Hebrew text was understood both linguistically and theologically by Palestinian Jews during this key period between the formation of the 'Old Greek' LXX translations and Qumran bible texts on the one hand, and of the Peshiṭta, Old Latin, Vulgate, and Targum versions on the other.

A note of caution should be sounded, however. As James Barr noted, the conjectural element involved in using any biblical text in a language other than Hebrew means that none of the versions can provide direct evidence for Hebrew variants.[15] In addition, the very partial state of preservation of the Three is a further limitation on their usefulness. However, where readings of the Three do survive, they sometimes attest to possible

---

[13] It is difficult to determine how far the Three are revisions of the LXX and how far they are new translations. Theodotion is likely to depend on OG, and Aquila on Theod., but whether Sym. knew an unrevised LXX, Theod. and/or Aq., is hard to demonstrate. The situation may vary from book to book.

[14] See especially T. Michael Law, "Do 'the Three' reveal anything about the textual history of the Books of Kings? The Hebrew Text behind the later Greek Jewish versions in 1 Kings," in *After Qumran: Old and New Editions of Biblical Texts. The Historical Books* (ed. Hans Ausloos, Bénédicte Lemmelijn and Julio Trebolle Barrera; BETL; Leuven: Peeters, forthcoming).

[15] James Barr, *Comparative Philology and the Text of the Old Testament* (Oxford: Oxford University Press, 1968), 239–40.

variants in a pre- or early rabbinic Hebrew text, with regard to the consonantal text or the vocalization. More frequently they indicate how Jewish scholars of the first and second centuries CE analysed and understood the Hebrew text before them. Below there are some examples of recent commentaries and how they use evidence from the Three.

## III. Use of the Three by Modern Commentators

### 1. *Hanhart on Zechariah*

Robert Hanhart has been involved for a long time with the Göttingen LXX Unternehmen, and displays familiarity with the Hexaplaric material in his commentary on Zechariah.[16] Hanhart renders the phrase at Zech 4:7 תְּשֻׁאוֹת חֵן חֵן לָהּ as "unter dem Jubelruf Gnade, Gnade über ihn."[17] The difficulty is with the word תְּשֻׁאוֹת: Hanhart notes the versions' false etymology of תְּשֻׁאוֹת as from שׁוה 'to be like, equal.' This sense is reflected in the renderings of LXX, Peshiṭta, Aquila, and Jerome's *Iuxta Hebraeos* version (often known as the Vulgate),[18] but is rejected by Hanhart. He also comments that Theod. alone of the versions understands the phrase as a cry of jubilation (καταπαυσις καταπαυσις αὐτῃ), though evidently with metathesis of חן to נח: "rest, rest for it!"[19] The textual implications of this reading are not discussed, however.

At Zech 5:1-2 where MT has the 'flying scroll' מְגִלָּה עָפָה, Hanhart notes the sole variant among the versions, the LXX reading, δρεπανον πετομενον, 'sickle.' He believes this presupposes an ancient Hebrew variant *מַגָּל, influenced by the text of MT in v. 2 and in Joel 4 (*LXX* 3:13) and Jer 50:16 (*LXX* 27:16) where a sickle appears in the context of harvesting. He argues that in Zech 5:1–2 what was originally a tradition from Palestine was adopted and perpetuated by Hellenistic Judaism in the form of the LXX reading. This image of the flying sickle increases the eschatological-apocalyptic emphasis of the vision. However, Hanhart notes that the

---

16 Robert Hanhart, *Sacharja 1,1–8,23* (BKAT XIV/7.1; Neukirchen-Vluyn: Neukirchener, 1998).

17 Hanhart, *Sacharja*, 249–50.

18 However, Hanhart (*Sacharja*, 249–50) says that the renderings of Aq. and Jerome suggest they took the Hebrew word as a verbal form (ἐξισωσει and *exaequabit*). Jerome seems to have relied on Aq., but as Ziegler's edition of the Minor Prophets suggests, in all probability Aq. originally rendered with the very similar plural noun ἐξισωσεις to reflect the Hebrew plural.

19 Hanhart, *Sacharja*, 250.

Three restore the MT reading within the Greek tradition since Aquila and Theod. have διφθερα 'prepared hide, leather,' and Sym. either κεφαλις (as reported by Jerome) or *εἵλημα (suggested by Syh ܟܘܪܟܐ) 'volume, roll.'[20] (The likelihood that all three versions originated in Palestine would also fit this reconstruction). Thus Hanhart uses the Three to plot the trajectory of the Greek tradition in its relationship to MT.[21]

In the introduction to his commentary on 2 Samuel, Hans Joachim Stoebe does not mention the Three explicitly,[22] though he is certainly aware of the issues of 4QSam[a] and 4QSam[b] and of the *kaige* recension of the Old Greek. The difficulty is that there is as yet no Göttingen edition of the historical books,[23] so commentators have to depend on Field and the larger Cambridge edition for readings from the Hexapla. It is possible that more material from the Three has emerged since publication of the latter in 1927.[24]

## 2. *Stoebe on 2 Samuel*

In 2 Sam 6:7 the LORD is described as striking Uzzah עַל־הַשַּׁל. The word שַׁל in MT is otherwise unknown. Stoebe states that Codex Vaticanus of the LXX omits it.[25] Furthermore, when Stoebe adds that Codex Alexandrinus has ἐπι τῃ προπετειᾳ 'because of (his) recklessness,' he could have added that in 2 Samuel and some other books, Alexandrinus frequently represents Origen's revised text, and that this very reading is under asterisk. Usually such asterisked readings have been drawn from one of the Three, and often from Theodotion.[26] However, Stoebe notes that the versions all interpret the Hebrew word as indicating ignorance or reckless

20 Hanhart, *Sacharja*, 324–25.

21 See also Hanhart (*Sacharja*, 544–45) on 2 Sam 8:19[a–a] and the pre-hexaplaric Greek witnesses, where he also criticises Ziegler's note in the hexaplaric apparatus as misleading.

22 Hans Joachim Stoebe, *Das zweite Buch Samuelis* (KAT 8/2; Gütersloh: Gütersloher, 1994), 53.

23 2 Samuel for the Göttingen edition was recently assigned to Philippe Hugo and T. Michael Law.

24 Alan E. Brooke, Norman McLean, and Henry St. J. Thackeray, *The Old Testament in Greek: according to the text of Codex Vaticanus. Vol. 2: The later historical books. Part 1: I and II Samuel* (Cambridge: Cambridge University Press, 1927).

25 Stoebe, *Das zweite Buch Samuelis*, 190. Stoebe does not mention here that Vaticanus is regarded as largely representative of the Old Greek translation of Samuel before Origen's revisional activity influenced much of the subsequent LXX tradition.

26 Jerome, *Epist.* 112 to Augustine §19, cf. also *Comm. Dan. Prol.* However, Jerome may be extrapolating from books such as Job where the many 'minuses' of LXX were indeed all supplied from Theod.

behaviour, perhaps through a supposed etymology from Aramaic שלי, 'to be careless' (Aq. ἐκνοιᾳ, *Vg temeritate*).

At 2 Sam 1:21, where MT has נִגְעַל 'defiled' to describe the shield of heroes on Mount Gilboa, Stoebe sees the renderings of LXX (προσωχθισθη 'reviled'), the Vulgate (*abjectus*), and Aq. (ἀπεβληθη 'rejected') as referring to the throwing away or rejection of the heroes' shields.[27] Since this seems an inappropriate idea in a song commemorating heroes, he thinks it preferable to render the word נִגְעַל as 'defiled,' without emending it to the later form *נִגְאַל. Stoebe could also have included Theod.'s reading ἐξηρθη, 'lifted up, removed,' as it indicates an association of נִגְעַל with a Niph'al form (perf. or ptc.) of עלה, i.e. *נעלה, and thus bears witness to MT form with *'ayin* rather than *'alef*.

### 3. *Baltzer on Deutero-Isaiah*

The focus of Klaus Baltzer's commentary on Deutero-Isaiah is his thesis that the book represents 'liturgical drama.' However, he also pays close attention to text-critical matters and makes intelligent use of the Three for their philological and text-critical value.[28]

On Isa 41:14, where MT reads מְתֵי יִשְׂרָאֵל ('men of Israel,' construct of מְתִים, 'men'), he notes that 1QIsa[a] has מיתי, and that the translations of Aq., Theod., and Vg suggest that they also interpreted this as 'dead ones of Israel.'[29] Baltzer observes that similar phrases to that of MT here often occur in contexts suggesting a small number (e.g., Gen 34:30 מְתֵי מִסְפָּר '[small number of] people,' Deut 28:62 בִּמְתֵי מְעָט 'remnant'). However, he could have included in his comments Sym.'s rendering ἀριθμος Ἰσραηλ (or for that matter, LXX ὀλιγοστος Ἰσραηλ and Peshiṭta ܡܢܝܢܐ ܕܐܝܣܪܝܠ), which also supports both MT's vocalization and Baltzer's own preferred meaning for this phrase, 'the few people of Israel.'

In Isa 53:2, there is a long-standing difficulty over whether to understand וַיַּעַל כַּיּוֹנֵק לְפָנָיו as 'he went up like a *shoot* before him' (which would provide synonymous parallelism with וְכַשֹּׁרֶשׁ מֵאֶרֶץ צִיָּה, 'and like a *root* from thirsty ground'), or 'he went up like an *infant* before him'

[27] Stoebe, *Das zweite Buch Samuelis*, 91.

[28] Klaus Baltzer, *Deutero-Isaiah: a commentary on Isaiah 40–55* (Hermeneia; Minneapolis: Fortress, 2001), 2–3 (original German version, idem, *Deutero-Jesaja* [KAT 10/2; Gütersloh: Gütersloher, 1999]).

[29] These are in fact Aq. τεθνεωτες Ἰσραηλ, Theod. οἱ νεκροι Ἰσραηλ, Jerome (no doubt following Aq. and Theod.) 'qui mortui estis in Israel' (Baltzer, *Deutero-Isaiah*, 104).

(cf. LXX ἀνηγγειλαμεν[30] ἐναντιον αὐτου ὡς παιδιον)? Though Baltzer notes that the words יונק and שׁרשׁ associate this passage with the messianic prophecy in Isa 11:1–10 (v. 1: וְיָצָא חֹטֶר מִגֵּזַע יִשָׁי וְנֵצֶר מִשָּׁרָשָׁיו יִפְרֶה), he opts for the understanding 'infant,' since it fits his interpretation of the Servant as identified with Moses:[31] יונק is a reference to the infancy stories of Moses.[32] Baltzer does not mention any of the Three here. Yet Aq. and Theod. favor a similar interpretation to his, though they both take it as a prophecy rather than a reference to a past event: 'he shall go up like a suckling' (Theod. ἀναβησεται ὡς θηλαζον, Aq. ἀναβησεται ὡς τιθιζομενον), in contrast to Sym. 'he went up like a branch' (ἀνεβη ὡς κλαδος). Symmachus clearly reflects the converted imperfect verb and takes it as referring to a past event.

In Isa 53:5 Baltzer observes that the vocalized form in MT, מְחֹלָל, is a Polal ptc. of חלל II, indicating the interpretation 'pierced through.' However, he comments that the Pu'al ptc. of חלל I, מְחֻלָּל 'desecrated,' should be read instead.[33] This alternative is also noted by BHS, though only Baltzer mentions that Aq.'s rendering βεβηλωμενος, 'profaned' supports this conjectured vocalisation. Yet neither BHS nor Baltzer mentions that the earlier, LXX, rendering ἐτραυματισθη 'wounded' supports MT's vocalisation מְחֹלָל 'pierced.' Aquila's rendering may suggest that in Palestine of the second century CE either there was not yet uniformity of the reading tradition, or Hebrew philology was not sufficiently refined to distinguish between the two very similar forms at an oral level and reflect such differences consistently in translation.[34]

Baltzer renders the rather difficult Hebrew of MT Isa 53:10 וַיהוָה חָפֵץ דַּכְּאוֹ הֶחֱלִי as 'But it has pleased YAHWEH to smite him. He let him become sick.'[35] However, he prefers to see a deliberate textual change having taken

[30] Sic, with Rahlfs and the entire Greek tradition. Joseph Ziegler (*The Hebrew University Bible: The Book of Isaiah* [Jerusalem: Magnes, Hebrew University of Jerusalem, 1995]) assumes a very early corruption and therefore reconstructs *ἀνετειλε μεν (=וַיַּעַל) in his edition. However, Moshe H. Goshen-Gottstein (*The Hebrew University Bible: Book of Isaiah* [Jerusalem: Magnes Press/Hebrew University, 1995], 244) notes that ἀνατελλειν is appropriate for plants but less so for child-rearing.

[31] As did the rabbis in bSota 14a.

[32] Baltzer, *Deutero-Isaiah*, 392, 405.

[33] Baltzer, *Deutero-Isaiah*, 392, 410.

[34] See David Weissert, "Alexandrian analogical word-analysis and Septuagint translation techniques. A case study of חלל–חיל–חול," *Textus* 8 (1973): 31–44. Since this approach can also be found in Aq. and Sym., it is clear that the technique continued in second century CE Palestine.

[35] Baltzer, *Deutero-Isaiah*, 393, 419.

place, over the original form which he argues is preserved in 1QIsa[a] as ויחללהו, pointed by C. R. North as וַיְחַלְלֵהוּ, 'He (God) had profaned him.'[36] Thus his preferred understanding of the whole phrase is: 'But it had pleased Yahweh to let him become dust. He had desecrated him.' As for LXX και κυριος βουλεται καθαρισαι αὐτον της πληγης 'the Lord wished to purify him of the plague,' Baltzer argues that πληγης assumes the consonants of MT, החלי read as a noun plus article, 'the sickness.' He does not consider that πληγη could also mean 'wound' and that therefore (regardless of the exact form of the consonants before him) the LXX translator could have made an association with the root חלל. Baltzer does not mention Sym.'s rendering Κύριος ἠθελησεν ἀλοησαι[37] αὐτον ἐν τῳ τραυματισμῳ 'the Lord desired to thresh him through wounding,' which implies a similar association. Analysis of Hebrew by interpreters in antiquity often reflects a biconsonantal understanding of the root system, with the association of forms sharing two letters. Thus we cannot be certain from his rendering what Hebrew form Sym. had in front of him in 200 CE: either MT's החלי (perhaps understood as a noun) or something like 1QIsa[a] ויחללהו could have been rendered in much the same way on this basis.[38] The interpretative tradition he inherited is more likely to have guided his translation than a scientific analysis of the grammar.

## 4. *Wenham on Genesis*

The Word Biblical Commentary series often includes textual remarks, though these can vary in scope. In his commentary on Gen 1–15, Gordon Wenham uses the versions in cases of textual difficulty. In Gen 4:26 Wenham identifies MT אָז הוּחַל as 3rd masc. sg perf. Hoph'al of חלל, 'begin,' in the impersonal sense 'people began.'[39] Wenham states that LXX (οὑτος) ἠλπισεν 'mistranslates' this as '(he) hoped.' This is a little unfair, since even if the LXX translator had the same consonantal text before him as MT, it would be more obvious to take it as Hiph'il of הוֹחִל*, יחל, rather than the unique Hoph'al of חלל of MT. (However, it is clear that LXX was able to

36 Christopher R. North, *Isaiah 40–55: The Suffering Servant of God* (2nd ed.; London: SCM Press, 1956), 231.

37 MS 86 and Eusebius read ἐλεησαι, evidently a corruption of ἀλοησαι 'thresh,' which represents דַּכְּאוֹ much more closely. Hence Ziegler's correction.

38 The Hebrew University Bible edition of Isaiah records several medieval variants of this word, including הֶחֱלִי, החלו, and החליא, reflecting long-standing difficulties with this word (Goshen-Gottstein, *Book of Isaiah*, 244).

39 Gordon Wenham, *Genesis 1–15* (WBC 1; Waco: Word Books, 1987), 96.

recognise the verb in the active forms, hence Gen 9:20 וַיָּחֶל LXX ἤρξατο, and Gen 10:8 הוּא הֵחֵל LXX οὗτος ἤρξατο).

Wenham could have added the testimony of Aq. and Sym. in support of MT. Aquila renders, 'then it was begun,' τοτε ἠρχθη, and Sym. τοτε ἀρχη ἐγενετο, 'then there was a beginning.' However, LXX, the Vulgate, and a reading misattributed to Aquila (Theod.'s?), οὗτος,[40] all support what could be a genuine early variant reading זֶה for אָז, if a possible association with Gen 10:8 is ruled out (see above).

### 5. *Childs on Exodus*

The Old Testament Library series does not emphasise text-criticism and philology, but there are some textual notes in Childs's volume on Exodus.[41] In Exod 5:16 the MT text does not make much sense: וְחָטָאת עַמֶּךָ. Gesenius-Kautzsch §74g suggests reading *לְעַמְּךָ וְחָטָאתָ on the basis of LXX ἀδικησεις οὖν τον λαον σου, and Childs takes the same line. He also cites Sym.'s rendering, 'the fault lies with you,' και ἁμαρτιαν ἐχεις, which would suggest *עִמְּךָ וְחַטָּאת.[42] Childs could have cited the readings of Aq. and Theod., which reflect a similar text to that represented by LXX, and midway between that of LXX and Sym. (Theod. και η ἁμαρτια εἰς τον λαον σου and Aq. και ἁμαρτια λαῳ σου = *לְעַמֶּךָ וְחַטָּאת). Since Aq. is generally very faithful to his Hebrew text, it may be that this was a genuine variant, also reflected in the presumed לְ of LXX. Symmachus' rendering apparently reflects a different reading tradition that makes sense of MT consonants.

### 6. *Zimmerli on Ezekiel*

Zimmerli's commentary on Ezekiel is also included in the Hermeneia series.[43] He explains the major versions, but though he refers to the Three, he nowhere explains what they are and their significance in the textual picture.[44]

---

[40] Also a Greek reading attributed to 'the Hebrew,' ὁ Ἑβραιος, which shares affinities with Aq. and Theod. here.

[41] Brevard S. Childs, *The Book of Exodus* (OTL; Philadelphia: Westminster, 1974), 93.

[42] Childs, *Exodus*, 93.

[43] Walther Zimmerli, *Ezekiel* (2 vols.; Hermeneia; Philadelphia: Fortress 1979, 1983): original German version *Ezechiel* (BKAT 13; Neukirchen-Vluyn: Neukirchener, 1969).

[44] Zimmerli, *Ezekiel*, 1.74–77.

The problem in Ezek 12:18a MT בֶּן־אָדָם לַחְמְךָ בְּרַעַשׁ תֹּאכֵל is that the word רַעַשׁ is used of earthquakes and not of people quaking. Zimmerli cites LXX μετ' ὀδυνης, Aq. ἐν σεισμῳ, Sym. ἐν ἀκαταστασια, Theod. ἐν σαλῳ.[45] His purpose in so doing is not clear, unless as further evidence against Koehler-Baumgartner's proposed emendation to כעשׂ, since the renderings of Theod. and Aq. show that at least by the first century CE the Hebrew text had רַעַשׁ. In contrast LXX and Sym. reflect difficulty with the word in its context rather than a different Hebrew Vorlage.

On Ezek 19:7 MT has וַיֵּדַע אַלְמְנוֹתָיו וְעָרֵיהֶם הֶחֱרִיב 'and he knew his widows (and destroyed their cities'). Zimmerli regards this as 'unintelligible' and tentatively emends to 'he did evil to their palaces,' since the MT form is unattested before the Peshiṭta and Vulgate. His suggestion makes better sense and gives a better parallel to the following half. He also notes LXX 'he pastured in his boldness' (και ἐνεμετο τῳ θρασει αὐτου), reflecting either a different Vorlage or a misreading of the verbal form with *resh*, *רעה.[46] Zimmerli cites Aq. και ἐκακωσε χηρας (αὐτου) 'and he maltreated (his) widows,' to demonstrate that Aq. also must have had a consonantal text with *resh*, not the *dalet* of MT, though interpreted from the root *רעע.[47]

However, Zimmerli passes over the fact that Aq.'s 'widows' reflects MT, while that of Theod. reflects a verb with *dalet* but does not involve widows: και ἐγνω βαρεις αὐτου 'he knew his palaces,' cf. Targum Jonathan's בירנייתיה. Sym., not cited by Zimmerli, knows a text closer to MT than either the earlier revisers Aq. or Theod. did: 'he knew *how to make* widows' (και ἐγνωσεν χηραποιειν), which is presumably an interpretation of the difficult MT.

## 7. *Macintosh on Hosea*

Andrew Macintosh's commentary on Hosea makes frequent use of all the versions including the Three, and supplies a good introduction to them.[48]

---

45 Zimmerli, *Ezekiel*, 1.276. LXX translators often use σεισμος for רַעַשׁ, whereas ὀδυνη occurs only in this case.

46 Zimmerli, *Ezekiel*, 1.389.

47 Once again we encounter the phenomenon of ancient biconsonantal understandings of the root system, especially in the case of 'weak' verbs: geminates, hollow verbs and those with a final *hê*.

48 Andrew A. Macintosh, *Hosea* (ICC; Edinburgh: T&T Clark, 1997), and Introduction, lxxix–lxxx. Joseph Ziegler, *Beiträge zum griechischen Dodekapropheton* (Göttingen: Vandenhoeck & Ruprecht, 1943).

Yet having consulted Ziegler's *Beiträge*, Macintosh apparently did not use Ziegler's edition of LXX Hosea and states that he uses Field's edition for the Three.[49] However, in the case of Hosea there is not much in Ziegler's edition beyond what one can find in Field, apart from some new readings preserved in the commentary of Basilius of Neopatrae.[50]

Macintosh notes that the entire phrase וְגָדַרְתִּי אֶת־גְּדֵרָהּ in Hos 2:8b (= LXX 2:6b) 'I will build up her wall' i.e., 'I will block her path with a wall' is absent from 4QpeshHos[a].[51] He speculates that in MT it may therefore reflect an attempt to explain the unusual word שָׂךְ in the previous phrase. He quotes LXX (και ἀνοικοδομησω τας ὁδους αὐτης) 'I will wall up [sic] her roads,' and Vulgate (*sepiam eam maceria*), 'I will fence her with a wall.' Macintosh posits three stages of development from the Ur-Text, where וְגָדַרְתִּי was added, and then *את דרכה (as suggested by LXX) and finally *את דרכה was replaced by אֶת־גְּדֵרָהּ. However, this hypothesis has minimal support from the versions (LXX seems to have been guessing or influenced by the following וּנְתִיבוֹתֶיהָ in rendering as τας ὁδους αὐτης), and Macintosh fails to cite the Three, all of which support MT even though we are reliant on retroversions from the Syrohexapla and Sym. is evidently rendering freely: Theod. *…το τειχος αὐτης, Aq. *και φραξω τον φραγμον αὐτης, Sym. *και ἐμφραγμον κατ'αὐτης περιοικοδομησω.

## 8. *Williamson on First Isaiah*

Finally, in this brief survey of modern philological commentaries we may turn to another International Critical Commentary volume, that on Isaiah chs. 1–5, published by the honorand of this volume, Hugh Williamson.[52] Readings from the Three are cited on at least fifteen occasions, and the evidence is carefully employed.

[49] Joseph Ziegler, *Duodecim Prophetae* (vol. 13 of *Septuaginta: Vetus Testamentum Graecum*; ed. Auctoritate Societatis Litterarum Gottingensis editum; Göttingen: Vandenhoeck & Ruprecht, 1943). For readings preserved in Syriac, see Michael P. Weitzman, "The Reliability of Retroversions of the Three from the Syrohexapla: A Pilot Study in Hosea," in *Origen's Hexapla and Fragments: Papers presented at the Rich Seminar on the Hexapla, Oxford Centre for Hebrew and Jewish Studies, 25th July–3rd August 1994* (ed. Alison G. Salvesen; TSAJ 58; Tübingen: Mohr Siebeck, 1998), 317–59.

[50] Ziegler, *Duodecim prophetae*, 102.

[51] Macintosh, *Hosea*, 50, 52.

[52] H. G. M. Williamson, *Isaiah 1–5* (Vol. 1 of *A Critical and Exegetical Commentary on Isaiah 1–27*; ICC; Edinburgh: T&T Clark, 2006).

In Isa 1:4 Williamson renders נָזֹרוּ אָחוֹר as 'they have become estranged (and gone) backwards.'[53] He notes that the phrase is a minus in LXX, but possibly present in Qumran manuscripts. It is also rendered by Theod., and 'some later Greek texts' which 'clearly follow MT,' with ἀπηλλοτριωθησαν εἰς το ὀπισω. This reading is under asterisk (meaning that in his Hexapla Origen supplied the addition from one of the later Greek versions). Though the attribution differs in each source it is evident that by Origen's time a Greek equivalent for the 'missing' phrase in LXX was known. As Williamson says, this Greek rendering (using a passive form) supports MT vocalization as a Niph'al perf. of זור I.

In this sampling of commentaries, perhaps the best example of a scholar's effective assessment of the Three in terms of their semantic information is Williamson's incisive discussion of the problematic phrase in Isa 2:6, וּבְיַלְדֵי נָכְרִים יַשְׂפִּיקוּ.[54] He notes the loose rendering of LXX, και τεκνα πολλα ἀλλοφυλα ἐγενηθη αὐτοις, and takes Barr's treatment of Jerome's comments a stage further by connecting *adhaeserunt* with ש/ספח and observing that Aq. χορηγησουσιν and Theod. ἠρκεσαντο evidently derived the verb from שפק II.[55] He also demonstrates that Sym.'s interpretation ἐκροτησαν relates to שפק I, thus correcting Jerome's view that Sym.'s reading implied pederasty. In this way he places the Three in the context of the history of interpretation of this verse along with the Vulgate, Peshiṭta, and Targum.

## IV. Summary of Modern Use of the Three

The foregoing examples are broadly illustrative of the two main ways in which those modern commentaries that use the Three employ their readings: to demonstrate the possible existence of a non-Masoretic consonantal text or a pre-Masoretic vocalisation; or to provide semantic information in the case of a hapax legomenon or difficult phrase.

Sometimes commentators do not take the implications of the Hexaplaric renderings far enough, or they overlook readings that would prove helpful in reconstructing the history of the text. Few commentaries explain why Aq., Sym., and Theod. are cited, in contrast to other more familiar

---

[53] Williamson, *Isaiah 1–5*, 36.
[54] Williamson, *Isaiah 1–5*, 193–95.
[55] Barr, *Comparative Philology*, 233.

versions. Thus users may turn to outdated information in encyclopedias and the Web.

## V. Non-use of the Three in Commentaries and Editions of the Hebrew Bible

A few philological commentaries appear not to cite the Three at all, or do so very rarely,[56] yet regularly include readings from later versions. Certainly the Targums as we have them are a good deal younger than the Three and frequently reflect MT, while Jerome at the end of the fourth century was reliant on a combination of the Three, the contemporary Hebrew consonantal text, and live Jewish informants.[57] It is particularly odd that the editorial guidelines of the Oxford Hebrew Bible Project appear to ignore the Three totally, given the project's stress on textual criticism for restoring the oldest possible Hebrew text and its professed use of the Gottingen edition where available.[58] However, the editorial policy of Biblia Hebraica Quinta does advocate use of the Three, even if some fascicles are forced to rely on Field in the absence of a recent Gottingen LXX edition of the book in question.[59]

---

[56] There is little or no apparent use of the Three in the following philological commentaries: Hans Strauss, *Hiob 19.1–42.17* (BKAT 16/2; Neukirchen-Vluyn: Neukirchener, 2000) (contrast Friedrich Horst, *Hiob 1–19*, BKAT 16/1; Neukirchen-Vluyn: Neukirchener, 1968); Werner Schmidt, *Exodus 1.1–6.30* (BKAT 2/1; Neukirchen-Vluyn: Neukirchener, 1988); William McKane, *Jeremiah* (ICC; Edinburgh: T&T Clark, 1986); Leslie C. Allen, *Ezekiel 1–19, 20–48* (WBC 28, 29; Waco: Word Books, 1990); Hans Wildberger, *Jesaja 1–12* (BKAT 10/1; Neukirchen-Vluyn: Neukirchener, 1972); Hans W. Wolff, *Hosea* (Hermeneia; Philadelphia: Augsburg Fortress, 1974). Marvin A. Sweeney (*I & II Kings: A Commentary* [OTL; Louisville: Westminster John Knox, 2007]) frequently refers to the LXX, but the Three do not appear in the commentary, nor is there mention of the Cairo Geniza texts of Aquila for 1 Kgs 20:7–17 and 2 Kgs 23:11–27. See now T. Michael Law, "Aquila, *Kaige*, and Jewish Revision," in *The Greek Bible and the Rabbis* (ed. T. Michael Law and Alison G. Salvesen; CBET; Leuven: Peeters, forthcoming).

[57] James Adair ("A Methodology for using the Versions in the Textual Criticism of the Old Testament," *JNSL* 20/2 [1994]: 111–42) overlooks the Three.

[58] See Ronald Hendel, "The Oxford Hebrew Bible: Prologue to a New Critical Edition," *VT* 58 (2008): 324–51 (348).

[59] Carmel McCarthy (*Deuteronomy* [ed. Adrian Schenker et al.; BHQ 5; Stuttgart: Deutsche Bibelgesellschaft, 2007], 7*–8*) used Wevers's edition, Jan de Waard ("Ruth," in Megilloth [BHQ 18; Stuttgart: Deutsche Bibelgesellschaft, 2004], *5–*7, *25–26, *37–38*, *51–56*, 3–10 [5*–7*]) consulted Udo Quast, editor of LXX Ruth, before the recent Göttingen edition appeared, and Rolf Schäfer ("Lamentations," in *Megilloth* [BHQ 18; Stuttgart: Deutsche Bibelgesellschaft, 2004], 17*–20*, 30*–34, 43*–46*, 113*–136*, 54–72 [18*–19*]) used Ziegler's 1957 Göttingen edition.

## VI. Conclusions

What we have left of Aquila, Symmachus, and Theodotion is unfortunately fragmentary. However, for the Hebrew biblical text these versions represent a vital textual link between the Qumran fragments and the Old Greek on the one hand, and the Masoretic tradition, Peshiṭta,[60] Targum, Samaritan Pentateuch, and Vulgate on the other. This is because:

1) The Three date from the period when the Hebrew consonantal text was becoming standardized. Sometimes their renderings suggest the persistence of small variations in the consonantal form. More often the Three also represent variant vocalization traditions from that recorded in MT.
2) The Three also preserve Jewish traditions about the meaning of obscure words, whether correct or not. Sometimes their interpretations are adopted by Jerome in his Vulgate version or commentaries, and so antedate the Vulgate.

At present there is no up-to-date edition of the surviving readings of the Three and other later versions, since Field now requires much supplementation and the Göttingen edition's second apparatus is more complete but harder to use due to the lack of annotation. The Hexapla Project is working to produce fascicles of edited and annotated Hexaplaric readings.[61] It is hoped that this work will encourage commentators to make further use of this valuable material in their text-critical work.[62]

---

[60] Michael P. Weitzman (*The Syriac Version of the Old Testament: An Introduction* [University of Cambridge Oriental Publications 56; Cambridge: Cambridge University Press, 1999]) argued for a date in the second half of the second century CE for most of the Old Testament Peshiṭta books. Their northern Mesopotamian and probable non-rabbinic provenance should also be borne in mind when the Peshiṭta is used as a textual witness.

[61] The first fascicle is likely to be Canticles by Reinhart Ceulemans, based on his PhD dissertation, "A Critical Edition of the Hexaplaric Fragments of the Book of Canticles, with Emphasis on their Reception in Greek Christian Exegesis" (PhD. diss., Katholieke Universiteit Leuven, 2009), to be published by Peeters Press.

[62] See R. Bas ter Haar Romeny and Peter J. Gentry, "Towards a New Collection of Hexaplaric Material for the Book of Genesis," in *X Congress of the International Organization for Septuagint and Cognate Studies, Oslo 1998* (ed. Bernard A. Taylor; SBLSCS 51; Atlanta: Scholars Press, 2001), 285–99.

# PART III

# ISAIAH AND THE PROPHETS

# THE MANY VOICES OF ISAIAH 40

David J. A. Clines

In Isa 40 there is a veritable medley of voices, not all of them ascribed to their speakers. In reading the poem, we have the impression of overhearing a conversation among people we do not know and cannot identify. That is the way the poet wanted it to be, no doubt, and I am not so sure I should be thwarting his desire by attempting to make clear what he has chosen to leave obscure, to identify where he has concealed. But commentators are intrigued by mysteries and authorial ruses, as the esteemed recipient of this volume, a long-time friend and colleague, well knows.

## I. Analysis of the Voices

First, let me determine what is said to be spoken in this poem. I have numbered, within square brackets, the various voices in the order in which they appear in the poem. The translation is that of the NRSV, but I have adjusted its quotation marks and its divisions between strophes.

1 [1] "Comfort, O comfort my people,"
    [2] says your God.
2 "Speak tenderly to Jerusalem,
    and cry to her
[3] that she has served her term,
    that her penalty is paid,
that she has received from the LORD's hand
    double for all her sins."

1. Already in this first strophe there are three speakers. First, God speaks, to persons unknown, the words of the "comfort" speech (vv. 1a, 2).

2. It is of course a different voice, the reporting voice of the narrator, that tells us that, saying, "says your God" (v. 1b), and that then reports the words that the comforters are to use (v. 2b–c).

3. The third voice is that of the comforters. Their words are embedded in the words of God, which are themselves embedded in the words of the narrator. In vv. 2b–c the narrator reports the words that God says that the unnamed comforters are to use. They are to be spoken to God's "people," or, to "Jerusalem" (vv. 1a, 2aα).

3 [4] A voice cries out:
[5] "In the wilderness prepare the way of the Lord,
make straight in the desert a highway for our God.
4 Every valley shall be lifted up,
and every mountain and hill be made low;
the uneven ground shall become level,
and the rough places a plain.
5 Then the glory of the Lord shall be revealed,
and all people shall see it together,
[6] for the mouth of the Lord has spoken."

4. In this strophe, a reporting voice (v. 3a) says everything else that is in the strophe (vv. 3b–5).

5. What is reported is an unnamed voice that is calling out to road workers, commanding them to prepare a way for Yahweh (vv. 3–5).

6. At some point, the "mouth of Yahweh" has spoken (v. 5c); it is not clear whether the words it has spoken are all the words of vv. 3–5 or just those of v. 5a–b. Perhaps it is implied that these words Yahweh has spoken have been reported by the voice that cries out (v. 3a).

6 [7] A voice says, [8] "Cry out!"
[9] And I said, [10] "What shall I cry?
All people are grass,
their constancy is like the flower of the field.
7 The grass withers, the flower fades,
when the breath of the Lord blows upon it;
surely the people are grass."
8 [11] "The grass withers, the flower fades;
but [12] the word of our God will stand forever."

7. A reporting voice (v. 6aα) now tells us of a dialogue between "a voice" and another person.

8. First, an unnamed voice says, "Cry out!," to a person unnamed. What that person should "cry out" is not stated.

9. Then, another voice, noticing that there has been a command to cry out but there is no message to cry out, reports a question in reply. According to the MT, this is a further unnamed voice (וְאָמַר "and one, i.e. another, said"); but if we follow the LXX, it may be the voice of the narrator, who would be referring to himself for the first and only time as "I" (LXX καὶ εἶπα implies a Hebrew וָאֹמַר: "and I said"). Either way, the voice is the reporting voice of the person who replies to the command, "Cry!"

10. Now that voice tells us the content of his reply, which is a question: "What shall I cry?" (v. 6b). It is not certain how much this speaker says.

My belief—against the NRSV—is that to this voice belongs the rest of v. 6 and also v. 7; that is, the speaker says that it is not worth saying anything, since the situation is hopeless. The people are grass that has wilted under the hot breath of YAHWEH.

11. Unless voice #10 repeats itself ("the grass withers, the flower fades"), which I think unlikely, I take it that a different voice answers in v. 8. I prefer to assume that the voice that earlier commanded, "Cry!," now responds. This voice begins by repeating the downbeat words of the prophet, "The grass withers, the flower fades," and acknowledging their truth; but then it moves into a different key with the contrasting statement, "But the word of our God will stand for ever" (v. 8b).

12. The voice that responds (voice #11) says that the word of "our God" will stand for ever. This word of God is yet another voice, for it does not speak in v. 8b, but is only referred to. It is for the readers to decide whether this "word" of God has already been spoken, or is still in the future.

9 [13] Get you up to a high mountain,
O Zion, herald of good tidings;
lift up your voice with strength,
O Jerusalem, herald of good tidings,
lift it up, do not fear;
say to the cities of Judah,
[14] "Here is your God!
10 See, the LORD GOD comes with might,
and his arm rules for him;
his reward is with him,
and his recompense before him.
11 He will feed his flock like a shepherd;
he will gather the lambs in his arms,
and carry them in his bosom,
and gently lead the mother sheep."

13. Now there is heard another voice, an important and authoritative one, which speaks in vv. 9–11; unlike the downbeat voice of vv. 7–8, it delivers a command to Jerusalem. Now the narrator's voice is no longer heard, and the voice that speaks directs itself immediately to Jerusalem.

14. It will be a different voice when Jerusalem obeys the authoritative voice by announcing a message to the villages of Judah, "Behold your God!" (v. 9cβ). There is no clear marker of where Jerusalem's voice concludes, but I believe that it continues to the end of the strophe, i.e. to the end of v. 11, promising that YAHWEH is coming (v. 10aα) on his way to Jerusalem with his flock.

12 [15] Who has measured the waters in the hollow of his hand
and marked off the heavens with a span,
enclosed the dust of the earth in a measure,
and weighed the mountains in scales
and the hills in a balance?
13 [16] Who has directed the spirit of the LORD,
or as his counselor has instructed him?
14 Whom did he consult for his enlightenment,
and who taught him the path of justice?
Who taught him knowledge,
and showed him the way of understanding?
15 Even the nations are like a drop from a bucket,
and are accounted as dust on the scales;
see, he takes up the isles like fine dust.
16 Lebanon would not provide fuel enough,
nor are its animals enough for a burnt offering.
17 All the nations are as nothing before him;
they are accounted by him as less than nothing and emptiness.

15. It is a different voice again that speaks in vv. 12–17. It is not an authoritative voice, as in vv. 9–11; it does not makes demands but rather it asks rhetorical questions; it does not address any particular person, but throws out its question to anyone who may care to listen and answer.

16. There occurs within the words of that voice, in vv. 13–14, not a quotation of another voice, but a reference to another voice, a prior one, that of the Heavenly Counsellor, who instructed the spirit of YAHWEH, which seems to mean YAHWEH himself ("the spirit of YAHWEH" in v. 13a is parallel to "him" in v. 13b). Now this is a very strange voice among the voices of this poem, for it is a voice that is not a voice, a voice of a non-existent speaker. In fact, there never was anyone who told YAHWEH how to build the universe, and there was in reality no Heavenly Counsellor, and he never said a word. But if such a Heavenly Counsellor had existed, we know what his words would have been.

18 [17] To whom then will you liken God,
or what likeness compare with him?
19 An idol?—A workman casts it,
and a goldsmith overlays it with gold,
and casts for it silver chains.
20 As a gift one chooses mulberry wood
—wood that will not rot—
then seeks out a skilled artisan
to set up an image that will not topple.

21 Have you not known? [18] Have you not heard?
Has it not been told you from the beginning?
Have you not understood from the foundations of the earth?
22 It is he who sits above the circle of the earth,
and its inhabitants are like grasshoppers;
who stretches out the heavens like a curtain,
and spreads them like a tent to live in;
23 who brings princes to naught,
and makes the rulers of the earth as nothing.
24 Scarcely are they planted, scarcely sown,
scarcely has their stem taken root in the earth,
when he blows upon them, and they wither,
and the tempest carries them off like stubble.

17. The voice that speaks in vv. 18–24 seems to be different from the previous voice, since it is not asking rhetorical questions in general, but is directly addressing "you"; and it not only asks the rhetorical questions of vv. 18–19aα and 21 but it answers its own rhetorical questions also (vv. 19aβ–20, 22–24).

18. Within the speech of voice #17 is reference to a prior voice that has told the audience "from the beginning" about YAHWEH's power (v. 21).

25 [19] "To whom then will you compare me,
or who is my equal?," [20] says the Holy One.
26 Lift up your eyes on high and see:
Who created these?
He who brings out their host and numbers them,
[21] calling them all by name;
because he is great in strength,
mighty in power,
not one is missing.

19. The new voice that speaks in v. 25 is that of the Holy One, asking a question of the "you" ("to whom will you compare me?").

20. The voice of the Holy One is quoted by a reporting voice. Perhaps this reporting voice also becomes in v. 26 a challenging voice, uttering a command and a question (not rhetorical), and answering it itself (v. 26). Or perhaps v. 26 is a continuation of the voice of the Holy One in v. 25, though that would involve God referring to himself in the third person (not without parallels in the poem; see vv. 2c, 5, 8 for other possible examples).

21. Within that speech, there is an allusion to a further voice, a daily divine speech by YAHWEH to the stars of heaven, "calling them all by name" so that they will present themselves in the morning sky (v. 26bβ).

27 [22] Why do you say, O Jacob,
  and speak, O Israel,
[23] "My way is hidden from the LORD,
  and my right is disregarded by my God"?
28 Have you not known? Have you not [24] heard?
The LORD is the everlasting God,
  the Creator of the ends of the earth.
He does not faint or grow weary;
  his understanding is unsearchable.
29 He gives power to the faint,
  and strengthens the powerless.
30 Even youths will faint and be weary,
  and the young will fall exhausted;
31 but those who wait for the LORD shall renew their strength,
  they shall mount up with wings like eagles,
they shall run and not be weary,
  they shall walk and not faint.

22. Now a voice speaks throughout the whole of vv. 27–31, which addresses Jacob/Israel by name. It is a reproachful voice to begin with (v. 27), but it is increasingly encouraging as it continues.

23. Another voice is heard within it, when it quotes an earlier speech by Jacob/Israel, complaining that its rights have been disregarded by YAHWEH (v. 27b).

24. And the voice of vv. 27–31 also alludes to a prior voice, no doubt the same one as in v. 21, that has told Jacob/Israel that YAHWEH is the eternal God (v. 28).

All in all, I count twenty-four voices, each with its own speech event, in this chapter. Quite a few of the voices may merge into one another when we come to consider the *identity* of the voices, but all I have done so far is to identify all the voices that speak within the poem.

## II. Identity of the Speakers

This is not the place for a line-by-line argumentation about the identity of the voices that I have analysed; sad to say, here I can do little more than present my conclusions.

In v. 1, I take it that it is God who says נחמו נחמו to his heavenly council. They are commissioned to 'encourage' Jerusalem—the verb נחם being much more positive than our word "comfort"—with the news that its time of hard service (צבא) in exile has come to an end. Jerusalem, or rather the nation for which it stands by synecdoche, has now received full and adequate punishment (I understand כפלים to mean 'equivalent' and not 'double'). God says נחמו to the heavenly council, and the heavenly council will speak encouragingly to Jerusalem. Those identities are clear enough, but who is it that says, "Says your God"? This reportorial voice is perhaps best understood as the voice of the prophet who speaks throughout this prophetic book. It is he, we may suppose, who overhears the exchanges in the divine council and reports what he has heard to his audience, which is the people. The "you" of "your God" must then be the same "you" as in v. 27, "Why do you say, O Jacob, and speak, O Israel?"

In v. 3 the voice that cries (קול קורא) could be the voice of God, or of a heavenly subordinate; but the latter would be strange if in v. 1 we have met with a plurality of heavenly counsellors. So I prefer to think it is the voice of God himself. The persons addressed must be superhuman beings, for they are required to perform the superhuman earth-moving tasks of lifting up every valley and making low every hill. It is only the valleys and the hill that stand on the line of the road they are building that they must remove, of course; it is not every valley and hill in the world. Nevertheless, the task they are called upon to fulfil is a task beyond the capacity of humans with their picks and shovels.

In v. 6 the voice that commissions the prophet is presumably the same voice as in v. 3. But the person addressed appears to be different. In vv. 3–5 the addressees are plural, and they are to do road construction, whereas here it is a singular addressee and he is to do "crying." Most think he is a prophet, since prophets do a lot of crying (e.g. Jer 2:2). I will agree with that. After the prophet demurs (as prophets do), the voice begins by echoing his negative words but ends with a positive affirmation: "the word of our God will stand for ever." No doubt it is God himself who commissions the prophet. It is, admittedly, a little strange that YAHWEH should refer to himself as "our God"; but it is probably a case of YAHWEH putting into the prophet's mouth the very words *he* should use: "the word of our God" (it would be the same third-person usage as when, in v. 2, the words of God include a reference to "the LORD's hand").

In v. 9, who is speaking, telling Jerusalem to bring a message to its villages? It could be God, it could be the heavenly council. But since there is no preface of "A voice says," I am more inclined to think it is the prophet, whose voice I think is that of the narrator.

From v. 12 to the end of the poem it has to be the prophet who is speaking, but as well as speaking in his own voice the prophet is also both referring to and quoting the prior speeches of others. He refers to the non-existent speech of the Heavenly Counsellor to YAHWEH at creation (vv. 13–14); to the speech of religious traditionists about the universal God (v. 21); and to the speech of the deity to the heavenly bodies, calling them each by name (v. 26). And he quotes a challenge by the Holy One, presumably to the people (v. 25), and a complaint of Jacob/Israel, presumably to God (v. 27), but certainly about God.

So, after identifying the twenty-four voices of Isa 40 we can narrow the speakers themselves down to seven: there are five who actually speak: God, the heavenly council, the prophet who is the narrator, Jerusalem as herald, and Jacob/Israel as complainant, and there are two whose speech is only referred to: the Heavenly Counsellor and the traditionists. Seven speakers are not as many as twenty-four voices; but it is still a lot of talking.

## III. Non-Speaking Voices

We have nevertheless not yet identified all the characters whose voices are to be heard in this poem. There is as well a whole crew of non-speaking voices, if the oxymoron will be allowed.

The first is the *narrator*. When we are speaking of poetry, and not of narrative, we will often refer to the narrator as the 'speaking voice.' I cannot do that here, since I am using the term 'voice' for the speech acts of each of my characters. So I will stick with 'narrator.' It is the person who says in v. 1, "Says your God." I have been referring to him so far as 'the prophet,' but I do not mean a prophet who actually lived or who wrote this book of Isaiah. For in the book of Isaiah there are no actual people, because you cannot fit people into books. Calling the narrator 'the prophet' is systematically misleading, I admit, and it might be better to keep the term for a real person. But since the voice is a prophetic voice, perhaps we can accept the usage that calls it 'the prophet.'

Then there are the *narratees*, i.e. the addressees of the narrator. It is often the case that the addressees of a work are hard to identify, but in Isa 40 they are obviously Jacob/Israel and Jerusalem, which is a synecdoche for Jacob/Israel—not the real or physical Jerusalem, of course, but the character Jerusalem in the book. They are those who are directly addressed by name in vv. 9–11 and in v. 27, and perhaps also directly addressed, though not by name, in vv. 12–31 as a whole. The whole of the poem is addressed to them, directly or indirectly.

We must not overlook the *implied author* of Isa 40, who is neither a character in the poem nor a real person outside it. While the implied author is not a voice within the poem, it is he who gives voice to the whole poem. The implied author is a construct on the part of us real readers. Among many features we imply about the implied author of Isa 40 is that he writes at the time when the exiles have not yet returned from Babylon but are expected to arrive in the near future. The real author of Isa 40 may have lived much later (or, for that matter, much earlier), and have written imaginatively about what it must have been like to find oneself in that historical situation.

The *implied readers* are analogously our construct of those who would be reading this poem as a work of this implied author. They too have no voice within the poem, but their presence is a necessary part of the voicing of the poem. The implied author's audience will have had a basic competence in understanding his poetry (as well as knowing Hebrew), and will not, for example, mistake poetic hyperbole about lifting up every valley (v. 4) for an actual production of seismic change. We can probably distinguish from an average or typical implied audience the *ideal* audience of the implied author, who will probably also know about the heavenly council as a site of decision-making for earth (v. 1)—even though there is no direct reference to it in the text. They will understand that a solemn poem can contain humorous sarcasm (about idol-making, vv. 19–20) without lowering its tone. They will probably be in accord with the implied author's ideology, e.g. that the other nations of the earth are like grasshoppers to God, whereas the nation of Israel is going to be made ever more powerful by God.

And then of course there is the *real author*, without whom there is no Isa 40 and no voicing of Isa 40, and the *real readers*, many and various, both ancient and modern, without whom there is a risk that there will be no Isa 40 (for if there are no readers, there will be no copies), and certainly there will be no voicing of Isa 40. All in all, we have identified a collection of six or more 'non-speaking voices' who contribute to the performance of the poem.

Here now again is the whole poem, with my markers of the identities of the voices, i.e. of the speakers, as I understand them:

1 [GOD] "Comfort, O comfort my people,"
[NARRATOR] says your God.
2 [GOD] "Speak tenderly to Jerusalem,
and cry to her

[COMFORTERS] that she has served her term,
that her penalty is paid,
that she has received from the LORD's hand
double for all her sins."

3 [NARRATOR] A voice cries out:
[GOD] "In the wilderness prepare the way of the LORD,
make straight in the desert a highway for our God.
4 Every valley shall be lifted up,
and every mountain and hill be made low;
the uneven ground shall become level,
and the rough places a plain.
5 Then the glory of the LORD shall be revealed,
and all people shall see it together,
for the mouth of the LORD has spoken."

6 [NARRATOR] A voice says, [GOD] "Cry out!"
[NARRATOR] And I said, "What shall I cry?
All people are grass,
their constancy is like the flower of the field.
7 The grass withers, the flower fades,
when the breath of the LORD blows upon it;
surely the people are grass."
8 [GOD] "The grass withers, the flower fades;
but the word of our God will stand forever."

9 [NARRATOR] Get you up to a high mountain,
O Zion, herald of good tidings;
lift up your voice with strength,
O Jerusalem, herald of good tidings,
lift it up, do not fear;
say to the cities of Judah,
[JERUSALEM] "Here is your God!"
10 [NARRATOR] See, the Lord GOD comes with might,
and his arm rules for him;
his reward is with him,
and his recompense before him.
11 He will feed his flock like a shepherd;
he will gather the lambs in his arms,
and carry them in his bosom,
and gently lead the mother sheep.

12 [NARRATOR] Who has measured the waters in the hollow of his hand
and marked off the heavens with a span,
enclosed the dust of the earth in a measure,
and weighed the mountains in scales
and the hills in a balance?

13 Who has directed the spirit of the LORD,
or as his counselor [HEAVENLY COUNSELLOR] has instructed him?
14 Whom did he consult for his enlightenment,
and who taught him the path of justice?
Who taught him knowledge,
and showed him the way of understanding?
15 Even the nations are like a drop from a bucket,
and are accounted as dust on the scales;
see, he takes up the isles like fine dust.
16 Lebanon would not provide fuel enough,
nor are its animals enough for a burnt offering.
17 All the nations are as nothing before him;
they are accounted by him as less than nothing and emptiness.

18 [NARRATOR] To whom then will you liken God,
or what likeness compare with him?
19 An idol? — A workman casts it,
and a goldsmith overlays it with gold,
and casts for it silver chains.
20 As a gift one chooses mulberry wood—
wood that will not rot—
then seeks out a skilled artisan
to set up an image that will not topple.

21 Have you not known? [TRADITIONISTS] Have you not heard?
Has it not been told you from the beginning?
Have you not understood from the foundations of the earth?
22 [NARRATOR] It is he who sits above the circle of the earth,
and its inhabitants are like grasshoppers;
who stretches out the heavens like a curtain,
and spreads them like a tent to live in;
23 who brings princes to naught,
and makes the rulers of the earth as nothing.
24 Scarcely are they planted, scarcely sown,
scarcely has their stem taken root in the earth,
when he blows upon them, and they wither,
and the tempest carries them off like stubble.

25 [GOD] "To whom then will you compare me,
or who is my equal?," [NARRATOR] says the Holy One.
26 Lift up your eyes on high and see:
Who created these?
He who brings out their host and numbers them,
[GOD] calling them all by name;
because he is great in strength,
mighty in power,
not one is missing.

27 [NARRATOR] Why do you say, O Jacob,
and speak, O Israel,
[ISRAEL] "My way is hidden from the LORD,
and my right is disregarded by my God"?
28 Have you not known? Have you not [TRADITIONISTS] heard?
[NARRATOR] The LORD is the everlasting God,
the Creator of the ends of the earth.
He does not faint or grow weary;
his understanding is unsearchable.
29 He gives power to the faint,
and strengthens the powerless.
30 Even youths will faint and be weary,
and the young will fall exhausted;
31 but those who wait for the LORD shall renew their strength,
they shall mount up with wings like eagles,
they shall run and not be weary,
they shall walk and not faint.

## IV. Signification

"There are," says Paul, "so many kinds of voices in the world, and none of them is without signification" (1 Cor 14:10 KJV). He meant of course "languages," but the line will serve well enough as my slogan for this final section. Let me spend a moment wondering about the signification of the many voices of Isa 40.

### a. *Conflicted voices*

The more voices, the less likelihood of unanimity. It is especially interesting to see traces of conflict among the voices in this poem.

The first I will mention is the protest by Jacob/Israel in v. 27: "My lot is hidden from the LORD, my cause goes unheeded by my God" (REB). This signifies a judgment on the part of some within Israel that the exile is simply a political disaster, without any theological significance, and that it is God's fault that it is without theological significance. In particular, it implicitly denies that Israel has deserved its fate or that the exile has been a punishment for sin, as v. 2 insists. The poet of Isa 40 wants to resist this judgment, but he can only do so by acknowledging that it exists among his countrymen and women.

The second is the resistance of the prophet to his vocation. Such a resistance by a prophet is not unheard of, but elsewhere prophets make their *incapacity* their excuse: one is too young and does not know how to speak (Jeremiah, Jer 1:6), another will not be believed and is not eloquent (Moses, Exod 4:1, 10). Here it is not the prophet's incapacity, but his sense of the improbability of any word of prophecy (v. 6, "What shall I cry? All flesh is grass"). His reason is a theological one: he doubts God. In a way, his resistance is the same as the resistance of the people in v. 27. Although he ultimately accedes to the divine message, his initial reaction authenticates the resistance of his people, and shows that even a prophet agrees with them. When he eventually overcomes his resistance, and delivers the encouragement of his poem, he is submitting to the divine voice; he is not manufacturing it or merely assenting to it.

### b. *Voice begets voice*

We notice how often a voice that speaks in this poem urges another voice to speech. "Encourage my people," says God (v. 1)—which means that first God speaks and only then the comforters will speak. A voice says, "Cry!" (v. 6)—which means that first a voice commands, and then another voice gives utterance. "Up to a high mountain, Zion the herald; say to the cities of Judah, "Behold your God!" (v. 9)—which means that one voice summons Zion, who will then become the second voice that speaks. There is a sense of the transmission of orders, from the mouth of God to the divine courtiers to the people of Jerusalem, from YAHWEH to the prophet, from the prophet to the city. The urgency and the authority of the messages derive from this transmission and forwarding. That is where their authenticity is grounded.

### c. *Speech demanding reason*

All this speaking is in the interest of creating rationales for what is happening to the Jewish people at this time of the return from exile. To the outside observer, it would no doubt seem that all that is happening is that a migration of exiles is taking place under Persian auspices, a pretty normal event in the political realm. Our poem knows nothing of politics or human agency or historical causes; it insists on theorizing the events it depicts as acts of God, fraught with meaning, explanatory of the past century of its history, definitive for the coming centuries of its existence. Jacob/Israel must recognize what is happening to it as the deeds of the creator God (v. 28), who is self-determining (vv. 12–14) and never tiring (v. 28), enthroned as the supreme ruler of the universe (v. 22). These meanings implicit in current history, the poet recognizes, are not self-evident, and will gain assent only by dint of persuasive speech, multi-voiced. It is in this way that he is God's spokesman.

### d. *Speech as inter-personal*

Everything in religion, according to this poem, is personal—especially as between the people and its God. They are to regard themselves as personally addressed, whether with encouragement (v. 1) or with reproach (vv. 27–28), by their deity. He may be incomparable (v. 25), wise beyond conception (v. 28), and universally powerful (vv. 10, 25–26, 28), but he also shares his power with the faint (v. 29), and his coming to the land of Israel is not as a warrior but as a Jacob-like figure returning from a land where he too has been serving as a shepherd in exile, but is now bringing his wages with him in the form of the sheep he gathers and carries and leads (vv. 10–11). At a different time and from the pen of a different author, the return from exile will be portrayed as being for the sake of the rebuilding of the temple and the restitution of its cult (Ezra 1:3). Our poet, however, cares nothing for the cult; his only allusion to cult is to say that Lebanon itself would not suffice for fuel for a sacrificial cult worthy of this God, nor its beasts for a single burnt offering (v. 16). That must mean that the poet thinks that the Jerusalem cult, even in Solomonic splendour, can only be pitifully inadequate to YAHWEH's grandeur. Religion, for our poet, lives in the world of speech, not of ritual; it is constituted by the interchange of voices—dialogue, debate, command, reproach, rhetoric, question. The many voices it takes to create Isa 40 signify the poem's conception of religion—not as a matter of deeds, but—as a verbal negotiation between a people and their God about meaning, the meaning of what is happening before their eyes.

## TYRE AND THE MEDITERRANEAN IN THE BOOK OF ISAIAH

Anselm C. Hagedorn

The existence of the Mediterranean Sea serves as subject of a variety of discourses,[1] which are determined by the different national, scholarly, and popular positions of the partakers in such a discourse.[2] Defining the Mediterranean is almost impossible since the term alone evokes multiple responses that elude clear distinctions and concepts.[3] However, most of these responses to the existence of the Mediterranean and the various concepts connected to it serve as an exchange between the past and the present.[4]

The Hebrew Bible's relationship to the Mediterranean can at best be described as being ambiguous.[5] Despite the undeniable fact that ancient Israel borders the Mediterranean, it never became one of the great seafaring nations.[6] "By and large, the Israelites were not a nautical people,

---

[1] Peregrine Horden, "Mediterranean Excuses: Historical Writing on the Mediterranean since Braudel," *History and Anthropology* 16 (2005): 25–30.

[2] This pluriform nature is, for example, expressed in the collection of booklets under the title *Les représentations de la Méditerranée* that speak of la méditerranée grecque, allemande, tunisienne etc.

[3] Iain Chambers, *Mediterranean Crossing: The Politics of an Interrupted Modernity* (Durham and London: Duke University Press, 2008), 12, rightly observes: "The 'Mediterranean' as an object of study is fundamentally the product of modern geographical, political, cultural, and historical classifications." See also Fernand Braudel, *Les Mémoires de la Méditerranée: Préhistoire et Antiquité* (Paris: Éditions de Fallois, 1998), 23, who opens his study with a statement about the interconnectedness of the Mediterranean Sea with history and the self of the spectator, thus forming a bridge to the present.

[4] See Fernand Braudel, "Mediterrane Welt," in *Die Welt des Mittelmeeres: Zur Geschichte und Geographie kultureller Lebensformen* (ed. Fernand Braudel, Georges Duby, and Maurice Aymard; Frankfurt am Main: Fischer, 1987), 7–10.

[5] This ambiguity is mirrored in contemporary Israeli anthropological thought; see Lisa Anteby-Yemini, "Israël et la Méditerranée; des relations ambiguës," in *La Méditerranée des anthropologues. Fractures, filiations, contiguïtés, L'atelier méditerranéen* (ed. Diogini Albera and Mohamed Tozy; Paris: Maisonneuve & Larose, 2005), 247–268.

[6] Cf. Chantal Reynier, *La Bible et la mer* (Lire la Bible 133; Paris: Cerf, 2003), 7; Bernard Renaud, "La 'Grande mer' dans l'Ancien Testament: de la géographie au symbole," in *La Biblia i el Mediterrani: Actes del Congrés de Barcelona 18–22 de setembre de 1995* (ed. Agustí Borrell, Alfonso de la Fuente, and Armand Puig; Barcelona: Abadia de Monserrat, Associació Bíblica de Catalunya, 1997), 75–101; and Raphael Patai, *The Children of Noah: Jewish Seafaring in Ancient Times* (Princeton: Princeton University Press, 1998), on later Jewish seafaring.

and indeed they seem to have been deeply suspicious of most things to do with the sea."[7] In Num 34:6 the Mediterranean Sea is envisaged as the (Western) border of the Promised Land. The verse makes it quite explicit that the Sea is seen as a border, since the 'Western' border is equivalent with the shores of the Mediterranean. This view departs from other concepts in antiquity where the Mediterranean Sea is regarded as a bridge that connects people and countries rather than as a barrier that separates them. In societies where ships are an essential form of communication it is hardly surprising that not having ships is seen as an indication of being uncivilized.[8] The Mediterranean is described in the Hebrew Bible as "Great Sea," a term used elsewhere in the Bible to distinguish the Mediterranean from other seas (Num 34:7; Josh 1:4; 9:1; 23:4; Ezek 47:10, 15, 19, 20). It is by no means the only term used, since we also find "Western Sea" (Deut 11:24; 34:2; Joel 2:20; Zech 14:8). This use is hardly surprising because biblical authors look at the sea from an Eastern perspective.[9] In contrast to Greek authors who employ special terminology for the Mediterranean Sea such as "sea inside the pillars" (ἡ θάλαττα ἡ ἐντὸς Στηλῶν, Strabo, *Geogr.* 11.1.4) the Hebrew language does not possess such a term. Rather, there are some indications that the Mediterranean is regarded as something outside the mental framework of the biblical writers. In Exod 23:31—again a description of the extent of the Israelite territory—the Western border is labelled Sea of the Philistines (ים פלשתים), pointing to the fact that the coastlands were never part of biblical Israel (cf. Zeph 2:5) as well as indicating by the name who rules the sea. Despite texts like 1 Kgs 10:22 that seem to allude to Israelite seafaring, for the biblical sages sailing the seas is simply listed among the things one cannot understand (Prov 30:18–19).

However, we have to note that the biblical authors are aware of the other nations that populate the Mediterranean basin. Already in the Table of Nations in Gen 10:1–32 the Greek world is mentioned (Gen 10:4) and the references to Crete and Cyprus indicate that those territories that could only be reached by ship were known and were part of the picture of the biblical world.[10] Moreover, despite the above mentioned suspicion towards the sea there are some passages that deal explicitly with the sea and with what lies beyond. Isaiah 23 is such a text to which we will now turn.

---

[7] H. G. M. Williamson, *Isaiah 1–5* (ICC; London/New York: T&T Clark, 2006), 226.

[8] Cf. Homer, *Odyssey*, 9.125–129.

[9] Anselm C. Hagedorn, *Between Moses and Plato: Individual and Society in Deuteronomy and Ancient Greek Law* (FRLANT 204; Göttingen: Vandenhoeck & Ruprecht, 2004), 54.

[10] Ibid., 53–60.

## I. Isaiah 23 in Context

Isaiah 23:1–18 concludes a series of oracles against foreign nations in the book of Isaiah.[11] Isaiah 13–23 represents a collection of various literary material, collected over a long period and brought into its current form by complex redactional processes.[12] The beginning of the collection in Isa 13:1 wants to make clear that Isaiah son of Amoz is the author of the word against Babel and probably of the cycle as a whole. The superscriptions of the various oracles, however, indicate—at least as far as the final form of the biblical text is concerned—that the chapters are to be understood as a unity.[13] At the same time, these superscriptions help to structure the collection. Here the oracles against Babel, Moab, Damascus, Egypt, the Wilderness of the Sea, Duma, which possibly refers to Edom, Arabia, the Valley of Vision, and Tyre all carry the simple 'title' משא. The oracle against Philistia (14:28–32) deviates slightly from this pattern as the superscription also contains a dating. The oracles against Cush in Isa 18:1–7 and against Shebna, an officer of the palace (Isa 22:15–25), do not fit this pattern. Isaiah 18:1–7 is introduced like a woe oracle and Isa 22:15–25 contains a YHWH speech formula followed by a commission proper. In this context, "the oracle concerning Tyre is shaped in such a way that it serves as the culmination of God's word to the nations, a fitting conclusion for all that precedes."[14] Within the larger context of the Book of Isaiah as a whole Isa 23 seems to put into practice what 2:12–17 announces.[15] "Judgment is pronounced on human pretensions with special reference to the Syro-Palestinian and Levantine regions."[16]

---

[11] Ulrich Berges, *Das Buch Jesaja: Komposition und Endgestalt* (Herders Biblische Studien 16; Freiburg: Herder, 1998), 139, has drawn attention to the fact that the form-critical label 'Oracles against Foreign Nations' insufficiently explains the nature of Isa 13–22 as Isa 22 is directed against Jerusalem and Isa 20:1–6 contains a symbolic action report, which is unique in the collection of such oracles.

[12] Uwe Becker, *Jesaja—Von der Botschaft zum Buch* (FRLANT 178; Göttingen: Vandenhoeck & Ruprecht, 1997), 271.

[13] H. G. M. Williamson, *The Book Called Isaiah: Deutero-Isaiah's Role in Composition and Redaction* (Oxford: Clarendon Press, 1994), 162–167, has shown that an older order of the texts can be detected in Isa 13–23. Here Isa 14:28 is especially relevant as it connects the word against the Philistines (Isa 14:29–32) with Isa 6:1.

[14] Christopher Seitz, *Isaiah 1–39* (Interpretation; Louisville: John Knox Press, 1993), 169.

[15] See especially the catchword connection with אניות תרשיש. This connection is destroyed by the Septuagint that renders תרשיש here as θαλάσσης.

[16] Joseph Blenkinsopp, *Isaiah 1–39* (AB 19; New York: Doubleday, 2000), 196.

The collection is followed in Isa 24–27 by the so-called 'Isaiah-apocalypse,'[17] "whose connection with the preceding collection by way of a generalizing or universalizing tendency is widely recognized."[18]

Isaiah 23 moves into a different geographic realm than the other oracles against foreign nations in the book of Isaiah and as such into the unknown.[19] The sea and the people who traverse it are the focus.[20] Thus the text stretches the boundaries of the known world and the imaginative realm. The mentioning of the inhabitants of the islands (ישבי אי),[21] who remain anonymous, are a case in point, reminding the reader that the events in Syro-Palestine also affect the unknown parts of the world, or more precisely spread around the Mediterranean.[22]

## II. An Oracle Against Tyre—or Phoenicia?

The superscription in Isa 23:1 (משא צר) suggests that we are dealing with an oracle against the Phoenician city of Tyre here.

[17] Thus first Bernhard Duhm, *Das Buch Jesaia* (HAT 3/1; Göttingen: Vandenhoeck & Ruprecht, 1922), 143.

[18] Williamson, *The Book Called Isaiah*, 156.

[19] In the following we will only consider Isa 23:1–18 MT and not address the various problems of the Septuagint version of the chapter. On this see Arie van der Kooij, *The Oracle of Tyre: The Septuagint of Isaiah XXIII as Version and Vision* (VTSup 71; Leiden: Brill, 1998), and Peter W. Flint, "The Septuagint Version of Isaiah 23:1–14 and the Massoretic Text," *BIOSCS* 21 (1988): 35–54. On the Septuagint of Isaiah in general see Joseph Ziegler, *Untersuchungen zur Septuaginta des Buches Isaias* (ATA 12/3; Münster: Aschendorff, 1934), and Isaac L. Seeligmann, *The Septuagint Version of Isaiah and Cognate Studies* (FAT 40; ed. R. Hanhart and H. Spieckermann; Tübingen: Mohr Siebeck, 2004), 124–294.

[20] See Francis Landy, "The Oracle against Tyre (Isa 23)," in *Berührungspunkte: Studien zur Sozial- und Religionsgeschichte Israels und seiner Umwelt. Festschrift für Rainer Albertz zu seinem 65.Geburtstag* (AOAT 350; ed. Ingo Kottsieper, Rüdiger Schmitt, and Jakob Wöhrle; Münster: Ugarit-Verlag, 2008), 239–251.

[21] Heb. אי can denote the islands in the West (איי הים as in Isa 11:11; 24:15; Esth 10:1); or the island of the people (איי הגוים, as in Gen 10:5; Zeph 2:11); or simply far-flung places (e.g. Isa 40:15; 41:1.5; 42:4, 10, 12; 49:1; 51:5; 59:18; 66:19).

[22] Campegius Vitringa, *Commentarius in librum prophetiarum Jesaiae. Pars Prior et Pars Posterior* (Basel: Editio Nova, 1732), 675, equates the islands with the Aegean, Italy and Northern Africa, i.e. all the places with which the Phoenicians are said to have trade relationships.

(1) Oracle[23] concerning Tyre[24]
Wail, ships of Tarshish,[25]
for it[26] is laid to waste, without[27] house [or] harbour;
from the land of Kittim (i.e. Cyprus)
it is announced to them.

In the course of the text, however, Sidon and Canaan are also addressed, so that it is probably more accurate to speak of an oracle against Phoenicia when describing Isa 23.[28]

---

23 משא in Isa 13:1; 14:28; 15:1; 17:1; 19:1; 21:1, 11, 13; 22:1; 23:1; 30:6 (משא בהמות נגב). LXX renders משא as ὅραμα here (see also Isa 15:1; 21:1.11; 22:1); in Isa 13:1; 19:1; 30:6 משא is translated as ὅρασις, and ῥῆμα is found in Isa 14:28; 15:1; 17:1. The rendering λῆμμα, common in the Book of the Twelve and Jeremiah, is not found in Isaiah. On the relationship between Isaiah and the Twelve in the Septuagint see Cécile Dogniez, "L'indépendance du traducteur grec d'Isaïe par rapport au Dodekapropheton," in *Isaiah in Context. Studies in Honour of Arie van der Kooij on the Occasion of His Sixty-Fifth Birthday* (VTSup 138; ed. Michaël N. van der Meer, Percy van Keulen, Willem Th. van Peursen, and Bas Ter Haar Romney; Leiden: Brill, 2010), 229–246.

24 צר in Isa 23:1, 8, 15, 17. The name Tyre is first attested in Herodotus 2.44 (ἔπλευσα καὶ ἐς Τύρον τῆς Φοινίκης); in cuneiform sources Tyre is called *ṣurri* (see e.g. the treaty between Esarhaddon and Ba'al, king of Tyre [SAA II 5.iii.23']). Strabo, *Geogr.* 16.2.22, adds to the fame of Tyre, when he states that Tyre is the oldest Phoenician city, with colonies even beyond the Pillars: ... αἱ δ' εἰς τὴν Λιρύην καὶ τὴν Ἰβηρίαν ἀποικίαι, μέχρι καὶ ἔξω Στηλῶν τὴν Τύρον πλέον ἐξυμνοῦσιν. On Strabo's view of Phoenicia in general see Johannes Engels, "Syrien, Phönikien und Judäa in den Geographika Strabos von Amaseia (Strab. Geog. 16,2,1–46)," in *Die Septuaginta—Texte, Theologien, Einflüsse: 2. Internationale Fachtagung veranstaltet von Septuaginta Deutsch (LXX.D), Wuppertal 23.–27.7.2008* (WUNT 252; ed. W. Kraus and M. Karrer; Tübingen: Mohr Siebeck, 2010), 85–98. Nonnos, *Dionysiaca* 40.521–534, reports that Tyre was founded by gods themselves (and maybe this is echoed in the statement מימי קדם קדמתה in Isa 23:7); a little earlier he relates that Tyre was founded upon two rocks joined together by an olive tree (*Dionysiaca* 40.468–492 [αἷς ἔνι θάλλει | ἥλικος αὐτόρριζον ὁμόζυγον ἔρνος ἐλαίης, | πέτρης ὑγροπόροςο μεσόμφαλον (469–471)]); on Nonnos see Robert Shorrock, *The Challenge of Epic: Allusive Engagement in the Dionysiaca of Nonnus* (MnS 210; Leiden: Brill, 2001). The history of Tyre is treated in detail in H. Jacob Katzenstein, *The History of Tyre. From the Beginning of the Second Millenium* BCE *until the Fall of the Neo-Babylonian Empire in 538* BCE (Jerusalem: Schocken Institute for Jewish Research, 1973). The status of the Phoenician cities in the Hellenistic period has been assessed in F. Verkinderen, "Les cités phéniciennes dans l'Empire d'Alexandre le Grand," in *Studia Phoenicia V. Phoenicia and the East Mediterranean in the First Millennium* BC (OLA 22; ed. Edward Lipiński; Leuven: Peeters, 1987), 287–308 and John D. Grainger, *Hellenistic Phoenicia* (Oxford: Oxford University Press 1991).

25 אניות תרשיש in 1 Kgs 22:49 (אני תרשיש [2x]); 10:22; Isa 2:16; 23:1, 14: 60:9; Ezek 27:25; Ps 48:8; 2 Chr 9:21; תרשיש alone Gen 10:4; Isa 23:6, 10; 66:19; Jer 10:9; Ezek 27:12; 38:13; Jonah 4:2; Ps 72:10; 1 Chr 1:7.

26 This is a masculine form referring to a female entity, i.e. Tyre; see GKC §110k.

27 On the use of מן here see GKC §119y.

28 See also Jer 25:22 and Zech 9:2–4, where Tyre and Sidon are mentioned together.

(2) Lament,[29] inhabitants of the islands,
merchants of Sidon,
crossing the sea,[30] they replenish you.[31]

It is difficult to determine why an oracle against Phoenicia concludes the prophecies against foreign nations, but it is unlikely that the latest of the oracles was simply placed at the end.[32] Since Tyre and Sidon only occur in Isa 23 we cannot use the view of the Phoenicians from other passages from the book of Isaiah to illuminate the passage. Maybe it was intended that Jerusalem in Isa 22 was flanked by political powers in the East and West.[33]

The oracle is structured by the *Kehrvers* in Isa 23:1bα and 23:14a. Here the ships of Tarshish are asked to bemoan the destruction of Tyre, followed by an individual explanation. This *Kehrvers* indicates that Isa 23:1bα–14 have to be treated as a larger unit. The two bases for the command to wail (שדד Perf. Pu'al) indicate that Isa 23 is not to be treated as a prophetic pronouncement of an event to occur in the future but rather a retrospective over an incident that has already happened.[34] This retrospective character makes it difficult to relate Isa 23 to the events of Sennacherib's third campaign of 701 BCE or to the third campaign of Ashurbanipal in 664 BCE.[35] Sennacherib succeeds in replacing Lūlī, king of

---

29 If the imperative of דמם I 'to keep quiet' (see e.g. Pss 30:13; 35:15; 37:7) or 'to be rigid' (Exod 15:6) is kept here, it can only be explained by referring to the shock triggered by the news of the fall of Tyre (thus Ges[18], 255). The word is, however, generally thought of as being derived from דמם II (Isa 23:3; Ps 4:5; 31:18; Lam 2:10), which is related to Akk. *damāmu* (see CAD 3 "D," 59–61), which can refer to human beings or things, or to Ug. *dmm*.

30 The participles סחר and עבר are to be read as plural.

31 The translation is supported by Ezek 27:25 (תמלאי); 1QIs[a] thinks of messengers here that cross the sea (עברו ים מלאכיך).

32 See Erich Bosshard-Nepustil, *Rezeptionen von Jesaia 1–39 im Zwölfprophetenbuch: Untersuchungen zur literarischen Verbindung von Prophetenbüchern in babylonischer und persischer Zeit* (OBO 154; Göttingen: Vandenhoeck & Ruprecht, 1997), 265.

33 See Willem A. M. Beuken, *Jesaja 13–27* (HTKAT; Freiburg: Herder, 2007), 289.

34 Accordingly, Hans Wildberger, *Jesaja 13–27* (BKAT 10/2; Neukirchen-Vluyn: Neukirchener Verlag, 1978), 861, understands Isa 23:1–14 as a lament rather than an oracle. See also Reed Lessing, "Satire in Isaiah's Tyre Oracle," *JSOT* 28 (2003): 81–112.

35 Thus the proposal by María E. Aubet, *The Phoenicians and the West* (2nd ed.; translated by Mary Turton; Cambridge: Cambridge University Press, 2001), 120, followed by Reed Lessing, *Interpreting Discontinuity: Isaiah's Tyre Oracle* (Winona Lake: Eisenbrauns, 2004), who once again argues for literary unity as well as an Assyrian setting of the passage; see also Thomas Renz, "Proclaiming the Future: History and Theology in Prophecies against Tyre," *TynB* 51 (2000): 17–58. Marvin A. Sweeney, *Isaiah 1–39 with an Introduction to Prophetic Literature* (FOTL 16; Grand Rapids: Eerdmans, 1996), 306–307, argues that Isa 23 is placed in the 5th century edition of the Book of Isaiah, but "that it is based on an earlier

Sidon ([I]*Lu-li-i-LUGAL*(*šar*) [uru]*Ṣi-du-un-ni*), who probably also ruled Tyre,[36] but does not destroy any of the Phoenician cities, since they continue to provide food and water for the Assyrian garrisons.[37] Both Esarhaddon and Ashurbanipal bound the Phoenician cities as vassals that are important for the campaigns against Egypt.[38] The geographical location of Tyre saves the city from being ransacked by the Assyrians.

והיה ביום ההוא and והיה מקץ שבעים שנה in v. 15 and v. 17 indicate additions to the oracle, a view further supported by the change from poetry to prose. 23:15–18 are a prophetic announcement of future events. They refer exclusively to Tyre, showing that a later author clearly understood 23:1–14 as an oracle against Tyre. Here we find two *Fortschreibungsschübe* that use metaphors common to classic prophetic announcements of doom but at the same time seem to problematize the attitude towards the Phoenicians.[39] The restoration of Tyre has a distant parallel in Strabo, who reports that the Phoenicians have the cunning ability to recover from disaster; here both the maritime trade and the purple industry are the main reasons for the regaining of economic strength.[40]

Within Isa 23:1–14, vv. 5 and 13 also interrupt the flow of the text. The context does not help to illuminate v. 5. If one retains MT—supported by 1QIsa[a]—the events are relayed to Egypt that will 'sway in anguish.'[41] Via the root חיל the verse is connected to the preceding verse, equating the pain at birth with the pain about the news of the destruction. By introducing Egypt here, the author emphasizes the spreading of the destruction of Phoenicia around the Mediterranean basin. Egypt denotes the Southern part of the Levant, while Cyprus in v. 1 represents the Northern part. Thus, the news is carried to the places with which Sidon and Tyre normally traded.[42] In the larger context of Isa 13–23, v. 5 reverses the view of 20:6

---

Isaianic call to lament in vv. 1b–14 that dates to the capitulation of Phoenicia to Sennacherib in 701."

36 See Daniel D. Luckenbill, *The Annals of Sennacherib* (Chicago: University of Chicago Press, 1924), 68–69.

37 Chicago-Taylor-Prism (*COS* II, 302).

38 See e.g. Esarhaddon's treaty with Baal of Tyre (text and translation in Simo Parpola and Kazuko Watanabe, *Neo-Assyrian Treaties and Loyalty Oaths* [SAA II; Helsinki: Helsinki University Press, 1988], 24–27).

39 See Markus Saur, *Der Tyroszyklus des Ezechielbuches* (BZAW 386; Berlin/New York: W. de Gruyter, 2008), 272–275.

40 Strabo, *Geogr.*, 16.2.23: ... ἀλλὰ τῶν τοιούτων συμφορῶν κατέστη κρείττων καὶ ἀνέλαβεν αὑτὴν τῇ τε ναυτιλίᾳ ... καὶ τοῖς πορφυρείοις.

41 Thus the translation of Blenkinsopp, *Isaiah*, 340.

42 Beuken, *Jesaja*, 296.

where the events in Egypt have an impact on the inhabitants of the coast (ישב האי).

Especially 23:13 has puzzled exegetes. Maintaining the Masoretic punctuation, it reads:

(13) Behold the land of the Chaldeans,
this is the people which is not.
Assur determined it for wild animals.[43]
They erected his siege-towers,
they destroyed her citadels
he made her into a heap.

Isaiah 23:13 reads like an explanatory gloss to v. 12. Such an explanation is made difficult, however, by the mentioning of the Chaldeans in v. 13aα (ארץ כשדים).[44] Maybe the verse as it stands now is intended to form a link to the beginning of the cycle against the foreign nations, since כשדים only occurs in Isa 13:19 and 23:13. In 13:19 Babylon, the proud splendour of the Chaldeans will be like Sodom and Gomorrah when YHWH overthrows it; the gloss in 23:13 would then report the result. Furthermore, there is an additional connection to the destruction of Babylon in 13:19–21 via the word ציים. In 13:21aα it is stated that wild animals will lay down in devastated Babylon (ורבצו שם ציים) after it has been destroyed.

Naturally the mentioning of Assur as destroyer of Babylon remains problematic. If one wants to find an accurate historical allusion here, one is forced to refer to the Assyrian destruction of Babylon under Sennacherib (689 BCE).[45] Such a reading does not explain why an author during the Hellenistic period would remember the event; especially so as Babylon/Chaldea is not seen as the victim of Assur elsewhere in the Hebrew Bible but almost exclusively as the oppressor of the people of YHWH. Since Assur can be used as a cipher for other empires such as Persia (e.g. Isa

[43] Several commentators (Wildberger; Blenkinsopp) prefer to read ציים I (a loanword related to Egyptian *ḏ3j*; see Ges[18], 1114) denoting a ship; they point to Num 24:24 and Dan 11:30.

[44] 1QIsa[a] col. xviii.19 (כשדיים) supports MT; 4QIsa[c] does not preserve the verse. Duhm, *Jesaia*, 141 (following a proposal first made by Maier), corrects to כתיים; Otto Kaiser, *Der Prophet Jesaja: Kapitel 13–39* (ATD 18; Göttingen: Vandenhoeck & Ruprecht, 1983), 131, and Wildberger, *Jesaja*, 858, follow this proposal.

[45] John N. Oswalt, *The Book of Isaiah. Chapters 1–39* (NICOT; Grand Rapids: Eerdmans, 1986), 434–435.

19:23–25; Ezra 6:22), the same might be happening here,[46] i.e. Assur is used to denote the Persians who in fact conquered Babylon in 539 BCE.[47]

## III. Tarshish and the Islands

Isaiah 23 begins in the far West, where the ships of Tarshish are commanded to wail.[48] The mention of Cyprus (ארץ כתים) in the same verse makes it clear that Tarshish or at least the point of origin of the Tarshish-ships is beyond the island of Cyprus.[49] As such the text—right at its very beginning—approaches the Mediterranean coast of Syro-Palestine from the outside, i.e. travelling across the sea. This travelling is explicitly mentioned in 23:2 (עבר ים). The wailing of the ships from Tarshish is set in parallel to the lament of the island population.

This movement is reversed again in 23:6 when the inhabitants of Sidon are told to cross the Mediterranean and to travel (עבר) to Tarshish. Again as the islands are passed, they wail (ילל) because of the news received from the motherland. In a way the text mimics the crossing of the Mediterranean by the Phoenician vessels. Despite all the crossing and returning

---

46 On such a use of Assur see Odil H. Steck, *Der Abschluß der Prophetie im Alten Testament: Ein Versuch zur Frage der Vorgeschichte des Kanons* (BThSt 17; Neukirchen-Vluyn: Neukirchener Verlag 1991), 76–83.

47 It remains a problem that none of the ancient sources mention that the Persians destroyed Babylon. The Cyrus Cylinder states explicitly: "He [Marduk] made him enter his city Babylon without fighting or battle; he saved Babylon from hardship" (*COS* II, 315); the Babylonian Chronicle for the year 539 BCE reports a battle between Cyrus and the army of Babylon at Opis, but then confirms the statement of the Cyrus Cylinder (*COS* I, 468). Herodotus, *Hist.* I.190–191, reports a siege of Babylon (ἐνθαῦτα οὗτοι μὲν λόγον εἶχον τῆς πολιορκίης οὐδένα); here Cyrus conquers Babylon by diverting the Euphrates so that his soldiers could march into the city by the riverbed.

48 The root ילל in the book of Isaiah is clustered in the passages against the foreign nations, see Isa 13:6; 14:31; 15:2, 3; 16:7; 23:1, 6, 14, with the only two occurrences outside such a context in Isa 52:5; 65:14.

49 The location of Tarshish has been debated in recent years; see Lemaire, "Tarshish-Tarsisi," 44–62 (editors' note: see the article in this volume by John Day). On the basis of the book of Jonah I would equate biblical Tarshish with Tartessos in Spain; Josephus, *Ant.* 1.6.1, locates the place in Cylikia, while the inscriptions of Esarhaddon mention Tarsisi together with Cyprus and Greece: *šárrâni*$^{meš}$ *šá qabal tam-tim kalî-šú-nu ultu mât Ia-da-na-na mât Ia-man a-di mât Tar-si-si a-na šêpê*$^{II}$*-ia ik-nu-šu bilta-*[*šunu*] (Riekele Borger, *Die Inschriften Asarhaddons, Königs von Assyrien* [Afo. B9; Graz: Im Eigenverlage des Herausgebers, 1956], 86). Rather than looking for a place here, the inscription wants to describe the Mediterranean as a whole. In 2 Chron 9:21 it is said that Tarshish-ships actually travel to Tarshish. Manfred Görg, "Ophir, Tarschisch und Atlantis: Einige Gedanken zur symbolischen Topographie," *BN* 15 (1981): 76–86, has proposed to see in Tarshish a mythical name that does not denote an actual geographical place.

evident in the text, the Mediterranean remains a mysterious entity in Isa 23. Islands remain anonymous and one wonders whether the author's knowledge of the Phoenician colony of Tartessos extends beyond the stereotypical picture of the name Tarshish as a rhetorical cipher for the last place on the western fringe of the known world.[50]

The mystery of the sea is paired with the striking absence of it, or (better) reluctance to acknowledge its importance, in Isa 23. The term for sea (ים) only occurs three times in the chapter (vv. 2, 4, 11). Twice it is simply the object: and only in 23:4 does take the sea an active role when it appears to speak:

(4) Be ashamed, O Sidon, for the Sea has spoken,
  [the fortress of the sea, saying:][51]
I have not laboured, I have not given birth
I have not reared young men,
  nor raised girls of marriageable age.

Here the Sea makes a prominent statement, implying "a transference of gender."[52] Suddenly the source of Phoenicia's riches speaks and adopts a feminine experience. The prosperity of Sidon is linked to childbirth and a multitude of children. It becomes clear that the barrenness envisaged has to be understood in economic terms.[53] If the Sea that guaranteed prosperity and was seen almost as an ally now turns against oneself, times are indeed dire.

---

[50] Herodotus, 4.152, locates Tartessos to the west of the Pillars of Heracles, i.e. the border of the Mediterranean; in Herodotus Tartessos has become a fantastical city/country whose king lived 120 years (Herodotus 1.162). The longevity of the kings of Tartessos seems to have been proverbial, since we read in a fragment of the lyric poet Anacreon (*fr.* 361 *apud* Strabo 3.2.14): ἐγὼ δ' οὔτ' ἂν Ἀμαλθιης | βουλοίμην κέρας οὔτ' ἔτεα |πεντήκοντά τε κἀκατὸν | Ταρτησσοῦ βασιλεῦσαι.

[51] Isa 23:4aβ is probably a gloss explaining that Sidon is meant by the sea that speaks. Thus it takes up a word used elsewhere in the passage describing the Phoenician cities (מעוז in vv. 11.14); Kaiser, *Jesaja*, 130 n. 8, notes that כי אמר ים is also problematic, since 23:4a can only be spoken by a woman and ים is masculine. As a result he emends to השמרת. Edward Lipiński, "The Elegy on the Fall of Sidon in Isaiah 23," *Eretz Israel* 14 (1978): 79*–88* (82*), draws attention to *KAI* 15, arguing that Sidon was originally called צידון ים, denoting the harbour town as opposed to the inland territory "Sidon-in-the-Fields." A later glossator then adds כי אמר...לאמר. 1QIsa[a] also understands ים as being the subject and corrects the text to כי אמרה ים.

[52] Landy, "Oracle," 243.

[53] See Wilhelm Rudolph, "Jesaja 23,1–14," in *Festschrift Friedrich Baumgärtel zum 70. Geburtstag 14. Januar 1958 gewidmet von den Mitarbeitern am Kommentar zum Alten Testament* (*KAT*) (Erlanger Forschungen 10; ed. J. Herrmann; Erlangen: Universitätsbund Erlangen, 1959), 166–74 (172); differently Landy, "Oracle," 243, who thinks that such an interpretation "is to transpose the mythic dimension onto the human plane and to reduce the pathos of the image."

The economic impact of the destruction of Phoenicia is furthermore mentioned in 23:10, where a change of the economic basis is envisaged:

> (10) Cross over your land, like the Nile—daughter of Tarshish—
> there is no more harbour.

Here Tarshish is *addressed* for the first and only time in the chapter. Before that, Tarshish was only mentioned as a place of refuge for Phoenicians in verse 6 (עברו תרשישה) or as an attribute defining the ships that cross the Mediterranean. This has puzzled commentators, leading either to the expulsion of בת תרשיש or to alternative explanations. Campegius Vitringa, for example, argued that Tarshish was regarded as the second or other Tyre and therefore it was possible to use both names.[54] It is, however, unlikely that the mother-city was addressed by the name of the colony; rather I would propose that in the current context the disaster of the motherland also affects the colony. In the current context we seem to have a certain movement here, where one moves from the far West via the kingdoms to Canaan, i.e. Phoenicia.

The verse is notoriously difficult and already the Septuagint offers a vastly different text, when it reads: ἐργάζου τὴν γῆν σου, καὶ γὰρ πλοῖα οὐκέτι ἔρχεται ἐκ Καρχηδόνος. Much depends on the interpretation of מזח. The word only occurs twice in the Hebrew Bible, in Isa 23:10 and Ps 109:19. In Ps 109 it seems to denote a girdle, since it is parallel to בגד. As such it would be related to Akkadian *mēze/aḫu* or *māzaḫu*.[55] If such a translation is preferred one is forced to interpret the girdle as describing the Tyrian/Phoenician shackles on their colonies. Maybe this interpretation is already found in the Targum when מזח is rendered as 'strength' (תקוף).

Bernhard Duhm, in his commentary on the basis of Ps 107:30, has proposed that we read מזח as מחז, denoting 'harbour' or 'harbour-town.'[56] Such an interpretation now finds support in KTU 4.81.1, a list of ships and their owners which is headed with *anyt .miḫd*, i.e. "the ships of *Ma'ḫâdu*." *Ma'ḫâdu* seems to be the name of the harbour of Ugarit.[57] As the ' can be elided or assimilated to the *ḫ*, / *māḫādu*/ or /*maḫḫādu* / is cognate to

54 Vitringa, *Commentarius*, 681: "*Suppono autem, orationem hanc verti ad* Tyrios: *quod tamen dubium videri posset. Quomodo enim Tyrus appellatur* filia Tarsis *sive* Tartessi, *cum Tartessii sive Gaditani potius* filia Tyri, *quam Tyrii* filia Tartessi *dicendi videantur? Equidem dubium facile expeditur. Propheta sic elegantiae caussa scripsit, quod cum alias Tyrii tantum deberent Gadibus, quantum Gaditani Tyro.*"

55 See CAD 10 "M/II," 46.

56 Duhm, *Jesaia*, 169, followed by Rudolph, "Jesaja 23,1–14," 169.

57 See Michael C. Astour, "Ma'ḫâdu, the Harbor of Ugarit," *JESHO* 13 (1970): 113–127.

Hebrew מחוז.[58] Possibly the LXX also understood the מזח as a reference to the harbour, when it introduces Carthage as the most famous harbour-city in the Hellenistic period.[59]

A further problem is represented by the first part of the verse. MT reads עברי ארצך, which has been understood as referring to Tarshish's possibility to expand, after the yoke of Tyre is broken.[60] But such an interpretation depends too much on מזח describing an object or form of oppression.[61] 1QIsa[a] changes עבר to עבד,[62] which allows us to understand the imperative as referring to agriculture.[63] Of course ר and ד can be easily confused but in the light of the mention of the Nile in the same verse, עבר should probably be maintained. If בת תרשיש is eliminated for metrical or other reasons, the feminine imperative at the beginning of the verse is lacking a reference. The reference to the Nile may offer the key to the passage here. It refers back to v. 3, where the grain of Shihor (זרע שחר) is mentioned. שחור, which appears in Jer 2:18 as a synonym for Egypt, is glossed in Isa 23:3 with קציר יאור, thus making a clear reference to the rich harvest of grain in Egypt.[64] The Nile and its annual flood that irrigates the fields is then a synonym for farming here. If that is the case then v. 10 would indicate a change in the economic basis—the seafaring nation is transformed into a population of immobile farmers. Crossing over the land (עבר) would then be the opposite to crossing the sea (עבר) in 23:2 and 6,[65] and the verse would be a command addressed to the citizens of Tarshish to forget their maritime trade which was dependent on their Phoenician mother-city, now destroyed.[66]

---

[58] See Michael L. Barré, "A Rhetorical-Critical Study of Isaiah 2:12–17," *CBQ* 65 (2003): 522–534 (529).

[59] Ges[18], 653, thinks of 'shipyard' or 'harbour' for מזח[I] and relates it to Egyptian *mḏḥ* 'to timber.' This translation is already favoured by Wildberger, *Jesaja*, 854, and by Thomas Fischer and Udo Rüterswörden, "Aufruf zur Volksklage in Kanaan (Jesaja 23)," *WO* 12 (1981): 41.

[60] E.g. Oswalt, *Isaiah*, 433.

[61] Vitringa, *Commentarius*, 681, however argues that מזח stands for a *cingulum* that holds society and the state together.

[62] 4QIsa[c] (עבורי) supports MT and in 4QIsa[a] only עב are legible; there are ink traces of the third letter but it cannot be identified.

[63] For such a use of עבד see e.g. Gen 2:5; 3:23; 4:2, 12; Deut 15:19; 28:39 (of a vineyard); 2 Sam 9:10; Zech 13:5; Prov 12:11.

[64] שחור only occurs in Josh 13:3; 1 Chron 13:5, denoting creeks or canals of the Nile; and Isa 23:3 and Jer 2:18, where it is used for the Nile proper.

[65] Whether this is meant ironically, as argued by Beuken, *Jesaja*, 299, remains doubtful.

[66] See Ronald E. Clements, *Isaiah 1–39* (NCB; Grand Rapids and London: Eerdmans and Marshall, Morgan & Scott, 1980), 194.

The islands of the Mediterranean remain anonymous, despite the fact that they are passed regularly. Cyprus is the only island of the Mediterranean mentioned in the text of Isa 23. This reflects the importance of this place, which is mirrored in the view of other ancient authors.[67]

Isaiah 23:6 and 23:12 urge the inhabitants to flee. Verse 6 reverses the movement from v. 2 where the ships from Tarshish return home. Verse 12 mentions a movement to Cyprus.[68] Cyprus seems to be a place of refuge for Phoenicians—this is hardly surprising if one takes the close relationship between Phoenicia and Cyprus into account. The first contacts between Phoenicia and Cyprus are attested during the 11th century BCE and Kition on Cyprus was the first Phoenician colony overseas.[69] So it is only natural that Lūlī, King of Sidon, flees to Cyprus, where he died.

A further feature of the text is the limitation of religious overtones in the chapter. Only 23:8–9 and 11 mention YHWH, depicting him as the Lord over sea and land, and maybe the verses were later added to the oracle.[70] Be that as it may, a religious overtone and moral condemnation is only found in Isa 23:8–9 and 11.[71] Here the verses appear to be a compilation of motifs taken from Isa 14:24, 26–27 and Isa 19:12–17.[72] Isaiah 23:8–9 and 11 have a universalistic outlook that differs from the rest of 23:1–14. The passage emphasizes that the fall of Phoenicia is not the result of general historical developments but the plan of YHWH. Again the verses seem to link back to Isa 2:12–17, where YHWH wants "to defile the pride of all beauty" (v. 9). The announcement of judgement on pride (גאון) is a stereotypical theme of oracles against foreign nations (e.g. Isa 13:11; Jer 13:9; etc.).[73] The titles of honour for Tyre/Phoenicia described in 23:9 are regarded as *hubris*

---

[67] Strabo, *Geogr.*, 14.6.5, calls Cyprus one of the best islands that does not have to fear comparison.

[68] כתי(י)ם only in Gen 10:4; Num 24:24; Isa 23:1, 12; Jer 2:10; Ezek 27:6; Dan 11:30; and 1 Chr 1:7.

[69] See Aubet, *Phoenicians*, 51–54.

[70] See Lipiński, "Elegy," 82*–83*, who attributes the verses to a later redactor because they seem to concern Tyre and are not written in the קינה-rhythm that characterizes his base-layer. See also Jacques Vermeylen, *Du prophète Isaïe à l'apocalyptique: Isaïe, I–XXXV, miroir d'un demi-millénaire d'expérience religieuse en Israël. Tome I* (Etudes Bibliques; Paris: Gabalda, 1977), 343–344.

[71] ויאמר in 23:12aα transforms the verse into a divine speech, but the context makes it quite clear that it is not YHWH but the prophetic voice that speaks here.

[72] Blenkinsopp, *Isaiah*, 343.

[73] גאון with a negative connotation in Isa 13:11, 19; 14:11; 16:6; 23:9.

by the prophetic voice.[74] The main thrust of these verses is against pride and arrogance, as is the case in the much more elaborate oracle against Tyre in the book of Ezekiel.[75]

Only in Isa 23:11 does God stretch his hand over the sea (in Ezek 25:16 YHWH stretches his hand over the coastline [חוף הים]); in all the other instances it is Moses who does that (Exod 14:16, 21, 26, 27). Whether 23:11 is an allusion to the tradition of the Exodus remains doubtful.[76] Rather the verse seems to stress that God's command over the sea far exceeds Phoenician rule over it.[77] God's outstretched hand will first shake kingdoms and then destroy the fortresses of Phoenicia. Again the text moves from the outside in—"kingdoms" may refer here to the Phoenician colonies around the Mediterranean.[78] Such an interpretation of ממלכות would fit very well to the description of Tyre as "the bestower of crowns" in v. 8. That Phoenicia is called Canaan here fits well with the use of the term in late biblical texts (Zeph 1:11; Prov 31:24), as well as with the self-designation of the Phoenicians in later periods.[79]

[74] המעטירה may echo the fact that Tyre set up independent monarchies in its colonies. This is mentioned again in Strabo, when he states that every Phoenician city had its own king (Strabo, *Geogr.*, 16.2.14).

[75] Blenkinsopp, *Isaiah*, 344.

[76] Thus Wildberger, *Jesaja*, 877.

[77] In the book of Isaiah צוה is only used with YHWH as subject; see Isa 5:6; 10:6; 13:3; 34:16; 38:1; 45:11–12: 48:5; 55:4.

[78] Wildberger, *Jesaja*, 854, transposes vv. 11b and 11a, creating a *lectio facilior* as well as giving the impression that the text moves from a concrete destruction to a more universal judgement.

[79] See Karen Engelken, "Kanaan als nicht-territorialer Terminus," *BN* 52 (1990): 47–63. Philo of Byblos reports that the hero Χνᾶ was the first one to be called a Phoenician: … ὧν ἦν καὶ Εἰσίριος <ὁ> τῶν τριῶν γραμμάτων εὑρετής, ἀδελφὸς Χνᾶ τοῦ πρώτου μετονομασθέντος Φοίνικος (FGH 790 *fr.* 2,39). In Stephanus of Byzantium, *Ethnika*s.v. Χνᾶ (Meineke), this is further developed—Phoenicia was originally called Χνᾶ: οὕτως ἡ Φοινίκη ἐκαλεῖτο, ὥσπερ Λᾶ ἡ Λακωνιὴ πόλις. Τὸ εθνικὸν ταύτης Χνᾶος, ὡς τῆς Λᾶ Λᾶος. The ethnicon "Canaanite" must have spread from the Phoenician mother-land to the colonies, since Augustine, *Epistolae ad Romanos Inchoata Exposito* 13.5, reports in the 5th century CE that Punic peasants are still called "Canaanite": *unde interrogati rustici nostri quid sint, Punice respondentes: Chanani, corrupta scilicet, sicut in talibus solet, una littera, quid aliud respondent quam: Chananaei* (text according to Paula Fredriksen Landes, *Augustine on Romans: Propositions from the Epistle to the Romans: Unfinished Commentary on the Epistle to the Romans* [SBL.TT 23; Chico: Scholars Press, 1982], 68).

## IV. Concluding Remarks

The deep suspicion of the biblical writers in regard to the Mediterranean Sea, seafaring, and maritime trade noted at the beginning of the article is quite obvious throughout Isa 23.[80] Actual knowledge of the Mediterranean, however, does not go beyond some basic information.

Isaiah 23 and the Bible as a whole do not propagate the idea of a shared Mediterranean identity, driven by the desire "to represent themselves as exercising cultural choice in parallel with other, neighbouring populations doing exactly the same thing."[81] This attitude, however, does not prevent the biblical world-view from comparison and interaction, i.e. being "as comparative as anti-Mediterraneanism recommends."[82] The significance of the Mediterranean Sea, however, is being silenced by reducing much of the geographical area to anonymity. The same can be said about actual knowledge about Phoenicia. Most of the verses use allusion or difficult-to-understand phrases when dealing with Tyre and Sidon. This absence of historical clues is especially remarkable as the historical books of the Hebrew Bible are at pains to show a relationship between the court in Jerusalem and the Phoenician cities.[83] The positive assessment of Tyre (and Sidon) in those books is possible because the city's prosperous maritime existence remains secondary to Solomon and his economic and political influence.[84] When reality hits the biblical authors the portrayal becomes negative. Now the socio-economic competitiveness becomes an issue—in Isa 23 this is not very prevalent especially in comparison with texts like Amos 1:9 and especially Ezek 26–28 where a whole chapter (Ezek 27) is devoted to the consequences of a fall of Tyre for trade in the Mediterranean.

The departure from the common description of Phoenicia's doom in other prophetic collections has given rise to a description of Isa 23 as a satirical oracle full of *Schadenfreude*.[85] The delight at the destruction is

---

[80] Blenkinsopp, *Isaiah*, 343, even speaks of "the typical Israelite allergy to the sea."

[81] Michael Herzfeld, "Practical Mediterraneanism: Excuses for Everything, from Epistemology to Eating," in *Rethinking the Mediterranean* (ed. William V. Harris; Oxford: Oxford University Press, 2005), 57.

[82] Peregrine Horden and Nicolas Purcell, *The Corrupting Sea. A Study of Mediterranean History* (Oxford: Blackwell, 2000), 523.

[83] On this relationship see Françoise Briquel-Chatonnet, *Les relations entre les cites de la côte phénicienne et les royaumes d'Israël et de Juda* (Studia Phoenicia 12; OLA 46; Leuven: Peeters 1992).

[84] Here we have to note that any assessment of the cult of Tyre is missing in the historical books; this is in contrast to the role ascribed to Sidon; see e.g. Judg 1:31; 1 Kgs 11:5.

[85] See Lessing, "Satire," 109–110, and Blenkinsopp, *Isaiah*, 343.

apparent, though the reluctant attribution of the event to YHWH is slightly surprising. Maybe the sack of Tyre at the hands of Alexander the Great was still too much an event of the present for the authors.

Though Isa 23 transcends geographical boundaries as the chapter looks at areas normally beyond the reach of an Israelite, this process is limited by suspicion. The Mediterranean is seen as a border here. It is a border that can be crossed, but this crossing is only done by the Phoenicians, and Isa 23 is a powerful reminder as to what will happen if the mastery of the sea leads to pride.

# THE ONE WHO BRINGS JUSTICE: CONCEPTUALIZING THE ROLE OF 'THE SERVANT' IN ISAIAH 42:1–4 AND MATTHEW 12:15–21

Elizabeth R. Hayes

Who is the servant in Isa 42:1–4 and what is his brief from God?[1] This question is relevant both to Isaiah studies and to New Testament exegetes as well, since the author of Matthew quotes the passage in full (and nearly word for word) with regard to Jesus in Matt 12:15–21. A range of possible candidates have been proposed by various interpreters: Cyrus, the prophet himself, the Messiah, the Israelite nation, Jesus.[2] H. G. M. Williamson devotes a number of pages to this passage in his volume *Variation on a Theme*, before concluding that Israel is the referent of the passage.[3] If this is the case, how is a New Testament exegete to make sense of the claim that Jesus' actions in Matt 12:9–14 (his healing actions on the Sabbath and his subsequent withdrawing from the Pharisees) are meant to fulfill Isa 42:1–4? This essay will review the evidence using a conceptual blending approach to the interrelated questions surrounding the identity of the servant, the role of the servant and the claim that Jesus is the fulfillment of the passage.

## I. Vital Relations: Roles and Values

Conceptual blending provides a fresh approach to understanding quotations and allusions in biblical text, as both quotations and allusions represent complex conceptual blends involving the shifting of vital relations

---

[1] Westermann observes that this section is clearly written but is difficult to interpret precisely because of the ambiguity surrounding the identity of the servant and the nature of his task. Claus Westermann, *Isaiah 40–66*, (trans. D. M. G. Stalker; Philadelphia: Westminster Press, 1969), 99.

[2] Benjamin Sommer acknowledges that the identity of the servant in Isa 42:1 is "hotly debated." Rabbinic sources are not in agreement: Saadia Gaon claims that Cyrus is the servant. For ibn Ezra the prophet himself is the servant. The Targums and Radak agree that the servant is the Messiah, while the Septuagint and Rashi identify the servant as the Israelite nation. See the note to Isa 42:1–4 in Adele Berlin and Marc Zvi Brettler, eds., *The Jewish Study Bible* (New York: Oxford University Press, 2004), 867.

[3] H. G. M. Williamson, *Variations on a Theme: King, Messiah and Servant in the Book of Isaiah*, Didsbury Lectures, 1997 (Carlisle: Paternoster Press, 1998), 130–146.

between contexts that are often widely separated in time, space and culture. In their landmark volume *The Way We Think*, Fauconnier and Turner explain a number of ways that blended mental spaces are created as we think and talk.[4] Elsewhere, it has been argued that similar mental-space construction also occurs during the writing and reading processes.[5]

According to Fauconnier and Turner, one way that blended spaces are structured and linked is by 'vital relations,' such as identity, role, analogy, disanalogy, property, similarity, category, intentionality and uniqueness.[6] Thus, questions regarding the identity and role of the Servant in Isa 42:1–4 and Matthew's use of this quotation in conjunction with Jesus centre upon vital relations that are fundamental to human conceptualization.

Leaving the vital relation *identity* aside for the moment, it is notable that Fauconnier and Turner state, "Role is a ubiquitous vital relation."[7] They cite examples of role such as *president* and *queen*. Additionally, they claim that roles have *values*. At present, Elizabeth is a value for *queen*, while president is a value for *head of state*. Finally, elements or entities are roles and values in relation to other elements. They state, "*President* is both a role for the value *Lincoln* and a value for the role *head of state*."[8] Hence, differentiating between *role* and *value* is one way to differentiate between the identity of the servant and the role that the servant is to play in establishing God's intentions for the people. Williamson makes just this point in *Variations on a Theme*, where he notes that the role of the servant in Isa 42:1–4 is that of one who "... will bring forth justice to the nations."[9]

---

[4] Gilles Fauconnier and Mark Turner, *The Way We Think: Conceptual Blending and the Mind's Hidden Complexities* (New York: Basic Books, 2002). For a full exposition of Mental Spaces Theory, see Gilles Fauconnier, *Mental Spaces: Aspects of Meaning Construction in Natural Language* (Cambridge: Cambridge University Press, 1994); idem, *Mappings in Thought and Language* (Cambridge: Cambridge University Press, 1997).

[5] Many thanks are due to Professor Williamson, who patiently and ably supervised my D.Phil thesis on this topic. I am very grateful for his guidance. See Elizabeth R. Hayes, *The Pragmatics of Perception and Cognition in MT Jeremiah 1.1–6.30: A Cognitive Linguistics Approach* (BZAW 380; Berlin and New York: Walter de Gruyter, 2008).

[6] Fauconnier and Turner, *The Way We Think*, 93–101. See also Gilles Fauconnier and Mark Turner, "Blending as a Central Process of Grammar," in *Conceptual Structure, Discourse and Language* (ed. Adele E. Goldberg; Stanford: CSLI, 1996), 113-29; Gilles Fauconnier and Eve Sweetser, *Spaces, Worlds, and Grammar* (Chicago: University of Chicago Press, 1996).

[7] Fauconnier and Turner, *The Way We Think*, 98.

[8] Ibid., 99.

[9] The term משפט proves only slightly less problematical for translators than the identity of the Servant. Temba Mafico notes that uses of the term exhibit a tendency to be "multifarious in meaning." Mafico mentions terms such as justice, judgment, rights, vindication, deliverance, custom and norm before explaining that originally the substantive

Furthermore, it is the role of 'justice-bringer' rather than the identity of the servant that provides the key to understanding this passage.[10] Might this also be true of the Matthew passage, which overtly identifies Jesus as the servant?

Utilizing a conceptual blending approach, it can be demonstrated that, on one level the role of the servant in Isa 42:1 and the 'fulfillment' role of Jesus in Matthew 18 are similar. Isa 42:1 states:

הן עבדי אתמך־בו רצתה נפשי
נתתי רוחי עליו משפט לגוים יוציא

Here God announces that he has placed his spirit upon his beloved servant who will 'bring משפט (justice) to the nations.' In this case, the servant is a *value* for the *role* 'justice-bringer.'

Turning to the fulfillment passage in the Gospel, Matt 12:18 states:

> ἰδου ὁ παις μου ὁν ἡρετισα,
> ὁ ἀγαπητος μου εἰς ὁν εὐδοκησεν ἡ ψυχη μου
> θησω το πνευμα μου ἐπ αὐτον,
> και κρισιν τοις ἐθνεσιν ἀπαγγελει.

In this text, God announces that he has placed his spirit upon ὁ παις μου, 'my child,' and that this chosen child will 'proclaim κρισιν to the nations.' In this instance the term κρισιν proves to be difficult. Luz states that "the meaning of κρισις is an old *crux interpretum*." He suggests that the term might be translated 'right, justice' or 'judgment.'[11] Clearly, though, the role of 'justice-bringer' is assigned the value 'my child.'[12]

Thus, it is possible to associate both the value of God's servant in Isaiah and that of God's child in Matthew with the role of 'justice-bringer': For

"referred to the restoration of a situation or environment which promoted equity and harmony in a community." T. M. Mafico, "Just, Justice," *ABD* 2:1128. This resonates with Williamson's assessment that the term in this context points toward "... the total ordering of the well-being of a society." Williamson, *Variations*, 135.

[10] Williamson shares this view with C. R. North. Williamson, *Variations*, 135.

[11] Ulrich Luz, *Matthew 8–20* (ed. Helmut Koester; trans. James E. Crouch; Hermeneia; Minneapolis: Fortress Press, 2001), 193–94.

[12] For the purposes of this paper, the term 'my child' will be retained when discussing the Matthew passage. However, it is worth noting that commentators are not in agreement regarding the translation of the term ὁ παις μου. Luz translates the term 'my child,' while Hagner argues convincingly that ὁ παις μον reflects the LXX translation of the Hebrew term עבד. He uses the term 'servant' and sees this play upon the terms 'child' and 'servant' as a deliberate ambiguity that points to the father-son relationship at both Jesus baptism (Matt 3:17) and at the Transfiguration (Matt 17:5). Donald A. Hagner, *Matthew 1–13* (WBC 33a; Dallas, Tex.: Word Books, 1993), 337; Luz, *Matthew 8–20*, 190.

Isaiah, the term 'my servant' is a value for the role; while for Matthew the term 'my child' is a value for the role.

## II. Role-Value Compression and Analogy

With regard to analogy, Fauconnier and Turner state, "Analogy depends upon role-value compression."[13] A pair of conceptual blending diagrams will help to illustrate what is meant by "role-value compression." In the case of the Isaiah text, a network diagram may be created with 'justice-bringer' in one input space and 'my servant' in the other input space. These two input spaces contribute to a blended space that could be labeled 'Isaiah 42:1 Justice-Bringer,' as follows:

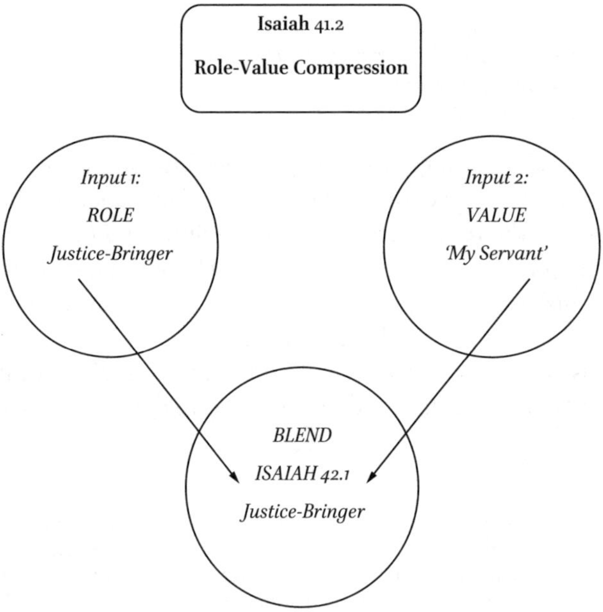


A similar network can be developed for the Matt 12:18, with 'my child' in one input and 'justice-bringer' in the other. These input spaces then contribute to a blended space that could be labeled 'Matt 12:18 Justice-bringer':

---

[13] Fauconnier and Turner, *The Way We Think*, 98–99.

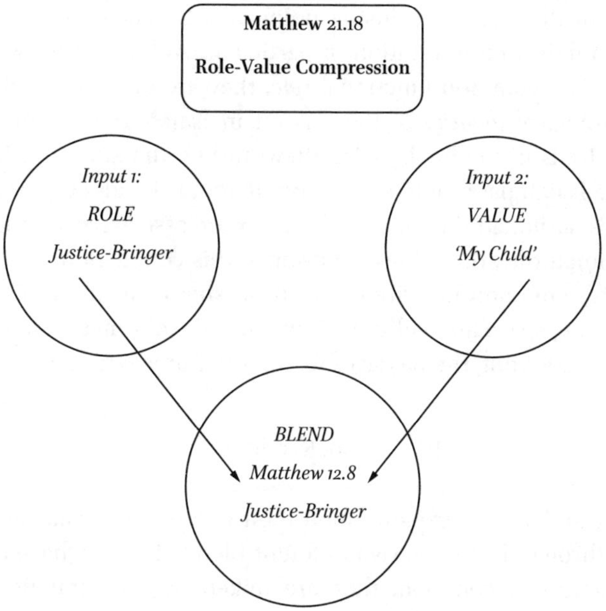


According to Fauconnier and Turner, these two blended spaces can be considered analogous because '... we have two Role-Value compression networks that have the same Role input.'[14]

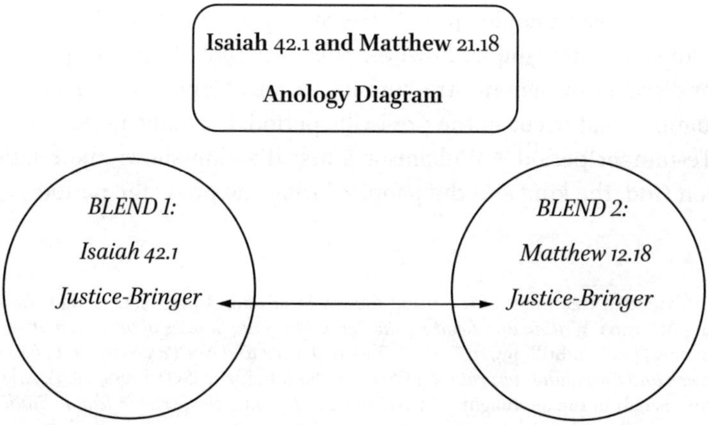


14 Ibid., 99.

This diagram illustrates a valuable point about analogy in general and analogy in biblical interpretation in particular. Although the two spaces are linked via a common functional *role*, they are not necessarily linked by the ontological *identity* of the servant in Isaiah and the ontological identity of Jesus in the book of Matthew: rather, the author of Matthew is using the Isaiah passage to make a point about the identity of Jesus. In other words, although the servant and Jesus are associated via their common functional role, that of justice-bringer, this connection in itself does not establish common identity or fill in missing contextual information regarding time, space and culture.[15] Some of this information may be discovered by examining the passages for shared frame structure.

## III. Frame Structure

Fauconnier and Turner expand upon their definition of analogy, stating "... when, through blending, two different blended spaces have acquired frame structure in common, they are linked by the Vital Relation of Analogy."[16] The first set of diagrams, above, illustrate role-value compression in the Isaiah and Matthew passages. It now becomes possible to look at the passages and examine them for common frame structure: how tightly are these spaces associated by the vital relation of analogy?

Williamson moves in this direction when he adds diagrams to explain the role of a human being/group of human beings as a conduit of God's wishes for a given people-group.[17] He readily admits that the diagrams might appear to be simple: however this apparent simplicity paves the way for discovering generic structure for various blends as he tracks similar situations that occur in the pre-exilic period, the exilic period and the New Testament period.[18] Williamson's first diagram shows the relations between God, the king and the people during the pre-exilic period:

[15] For extended treatment of reception history issues and Isaiah, see: Craig C. Broyles and Craig A. Evans, *Writing and Reading the Scroll of Isaiah: Studies of an Interpretive Tradition* (2 vols.; Leiden: Brill, 1997); Craig A. Evans, *To See and Not Perceive: Isaiah 6.9–10 in Early Jewish and Christian Interpretation* (JSNTSup 64 (Sheffield: JSOT Press, 1989); Arie van der Kooij, "Isaiah in the Septuagint," in *Writing and Reading the Scroll of Isaiah: Studies of an Interpretive Tradition* (ed. Craig C. Broyles and Craig A. Evans; Leiden: Brill, 1997).

[16] Fauconnier and Turner, *The Way We Think*, 99.

[17] Williamson, *Variations*, 123–50.

[18] A full conceptual blending diagram includes a generic space, positioned above the two input spaces. Elements that are common to both input spaces are documented in this generic space.

Williamson notes that the diagram would be actualized effectively when there was motion both from bottom to top: faithful obedience by the people (including the king); and from top to bottom: God's blessing upon the people.

However, by the time of Isa 40–55, the people have moved up into the position formerly filled by the king and the nations then moved to the position formerly filled by the people:

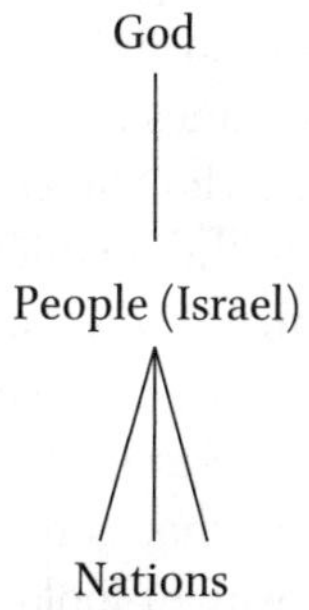


Israel has taken the place of the royal figure and the nations have taken the place of the people of Israel.[19] When discussing Matthew's quotation of Isaiah, Williamson is able to create a similar diagram that includes God, Jesus, and the Church to illustrate the fulfillment of the Isaiah passage.

In terms of Conceptual Blending theory the diagrams do indeed demonstrate shared frame structure. In each there is a divine designator (God), a designate (the king, idealized Israel, Jesus), a functional role (justice-bringer) and a people-group (Israel, the nations, the church). However,

---

19 See Williamson's discussion regarding the ideal nature of Israel as represented in this passage. Williamson, *Variations*, 142–43.

not all features exhibit a one to one correspondence. This may be illustrated as follows:

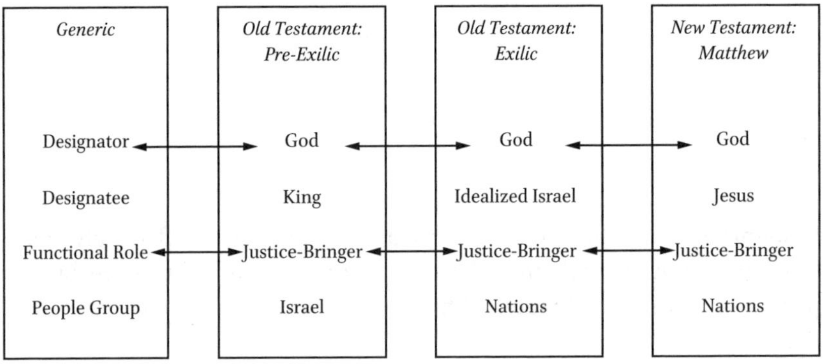


The frame on the left includes generic information, or frame knowledge. The next three frames illustrate the situations in two Old Testament settings and the New Testament setting in Matt 12.[20] When placed side by side, the identity connections (and disjunctions) become apparent. The constants in the three biblical frames are God and his designation of one who is to be the justice-bringer. The values for the role of justice-bringer are different in each case, as are the recipients of the promised justice.

The conjunctions/disjunctions in these diagrams support Williamson's claim that finding a strict one-to-one correspondence between the servant in Isa 42:1 and Jesus' fulfillment of the role (as predictive prophecy only) results in a view of the situation that is too narrow. Rather, as he points out "... there is an alternative way of looking at the situation, namely to say that Jesus fulfils, but does not thereby exhaust the prophecy."[21]

Thus, these diagrams are useful for displaying the connections and disjunctions between given instances of frame structure. On one level, the separate instances can be considered analogous because they demonstrate both a shared *role*-input (the God of Israel is the same in each) and a shared functional role input (justice-bringer). On another level, the differences in time, space and culture place a demand for more extra-textual study upon

20 Understanding the quotation within the book of Matthew is complicated by the text, which has some affinities with both the MT and the LXX, but also has features that belong to neither. For a full discussion, see Hagner, *Matthew*, 336; Luz, *Matthew 8–20*, 191–92.

21 Ibid.

the exegete. This is particularly important when analyzing role of the Isa 42:1–4 quotation in the book of Matthew.[22]

## IV. Conclusion

This short essay has explored a few ways in which a conceptual blending approach can contribute to the exegesis of biblical text. Differentiating between roles and values helps to clarify the connection between the servant in Isa 42:1–4 and Jesus in Matt 12:18: both are values for the role of justice-bringer. Role-value compression creates specific blends that include both a role and a value. These blends are analogous because they share a role, yet they are not necessarily ontologically identical because they do not share a value. Hence, there is a need for careful exegesis that does not demand more from the text than it can offer. Finally, the entities created by role-value compression can be included as part of a formalized structure, or frame. These frames can be interconnected by identity and analogy. In the case of Isa 42:1–4 and Matt 12:18–21, there are direct identity connections between God and the role of justice-bringer, while there are disjunctions between the identities of the justice-bringer: the servant/Jesus.

A cognitive approach is also open to geographical, historical and cultural features that form the greater context for a given text. In this way, a cognitive approach provides a principled way of addressing both the text itself and extra-textual knowledge from a variety of sources. Thus, the Matthean claim that 'this' servant is Jesus finds coherence within the larger schema of the Matthean corpus, with its emphasis upon fulfillment as a means of persuading his audience that Jesus is indeed the awaited Messiah.

---

[22] R. T. France notes that of the eleven formula quotations, two are taken from the servant passages in Isaiah, yet neither "refers to the distinctive role of redemptive suffering…" Rather, in both cases, justice comes in the form of healing. All in all, Matthew's use of fulfillment passages points to his purpose: building a case for the identity of Jesus as Messiah for an audience that may have been largely Jewish. See R. T. France, "Servant of Yahweh," in *Dictionary of Jesus and the Gospels* (eds Joel B. Green, Scot McKnight, and I. Howard Marshall; Downers Grove: InterVarsity Press, 1992), 744-47.

# WHO OR WHAT IS ISRAEL IN TRITO-ISAIAH?

Gary N. Knoppers

In an important essay published over two decades ago, H. G. M. Williamson charted evolving notions of corporate identity in the biblical literature of the Neo-Babylonian and Persian periods, querying: "What now *is* Israel?"[1] The question is most apt. In late writings, Israel can refer to the ancestor (Jacob), the descendants of Jacob/Israel, a tribal alliance, a territory, the northern tribes, the united kingdom, the northern kingdom, Judah, the Babylonian exiles, the people of God, laypeople (as opposed to priests and Levites), and the future community of YHWH's people.[2] The transformations in meaning are fascinating, because they provide insights into disputes among ancient writers in Neo-Babylonian, Persian, and Hellenistic times about foundational issues of ethnicity, religious practices, (dis)ability, social memory, and diaspora-homeland relations.

If there is a trend to be discerned in the tremendous diversity of meanings ascribed to Israel during these times, it is usually understood as one of constriction. Over time, Israel is construed more and more narrowly. The long development of the book of Isaiah may serve as a case study.[3] In First Isaiah, Israel often refers to the northern kingdom or to the people as a whole, but in Second Isaiah the title Israel is sometimes applied to

[1] H. G. M. Williamson, "The Concept of Israel in Transition," in *The World of Ancient Israel* (ed. Ronald E. Clements; Cambridge: Cambridge University Press, 1989), 142. See also his earlier work, *Israel in the Books of Chronicles* (Cambridge: Cambridge University Press, 1977). Hugh Williamson is a wonderful friend and scholar whose research has transformed the way in which scholars approach the biblical literature of the Neo-Babylonian and Persian periods. It is a pleasure to dedicate this essay to his honour.

[2] Hans-Jürgen Zobel, "יִשְׂרָאֵל; *yiśrāʾēl*," *TDOT* 6: 397–420; Ehud Ben Zvi, "Inclusion and Exclusion from Israel as Conveyed by the Use of the Term Israel in Post-Monarchic Biblical Texts," in *The Pitcher is Broken: Memorial Essays for Gösta W. Ahlström* (ed. Steven W. Holloway and Lowell K. Handy; JSOTSup 190; Sheffield: Sheffield Academic Press, 1995), 95–149; Silvio Sergio Scatolini Apóstolo, "On the Elusiveness and Malleability of 'Israel,'" *JHS* 6 (2006): 1–27.

[3] Leonhard Rost, *Israel bei den Propheten* (BWANT 19; Stuttgart: Kohlhammer, 1937), 91–94; Gustaf A. Danell, *Studies in the Name Israel in the Old Testament* (Uppsala: Appelbergs Boktryckeriaktiebolag, 1946), 186–89, 261–64; Jesper Høgenhaven, *Gott und Volk bei Jesaja: Eine Untersuchung zur biblischen Theologie* (ATDan 24; Leiden: Brill, 1988), 17; Williamson, "Concept," 144–59; Reinhard G. Kratz, "Israel in the Book of Isaiah," *JSOT* 31 (2006): 105.

the Babylonian exiles. In Third Isaiah the title can be further restricted "to a faithful individual or group within the community" (in the land or in the diaspora).[4] For some, the most narrow meanings are also the most revealing. According to Danell, the vision of Israel found in Trito-Isaiah is limited to the "little Jewish community."[5]

Whether the survival of older concepts can be subordinated, however, to the development of newer highly restrictive notions is an open question. Williamson and Kratz separately point out that the latest editorial layers of Isaiah provide evidence for broader concepts of Israelite identity, including a more theologically-oriented reconfiguration of Israel as the people of YHWH.[6] In what follows, I would like to broaden yet further such carefully-nuanced ways of reading pertinent texts in Trito-Isaiah. My essay will revisit the issue of Israelite identity in two different oracles in order to contest a uniformly narrow and highly restrictive interpretation of Israelite identity.[7] Traditional scholarly treatments have been too limited in dealing with the demographic complexities of the Persian and

---

[4] Williamson, "Concept," 147–50; cf. Gösta W. Ahlström, *Who were the Israelites?* (Winona Lake, Ind.: Eisenbrauns, 1986), 110–18.

[5] Danell, *Studies*, 264. Similarly, Rost, *Propheten*, 93–94.

[6] H. G. M. Williamson, *The Book Called Isaiah: Deutero-Isaiah's Role in Composition and Redaction* (Oxford: Clarendon, 1994); Reinhard G. Kratz, *Kyros im Deuterojesaja-Buch: redaktionsgeschichtliche Untersuchungen zu Entstehung und Theologie von Jes 40–55* (FAT 1; Tübingen: Mohr, 1991); idem, "Israel," 103–28.

[7] For the sake of this study, Third Isaiah comprises chs. 56–66. Space constraints do not permit a larger discussion of the compositional history of Isa 56–66 and how these chapters relate to earlier chapters. See Bernhard Duhm, *Das Buch Jesaia übersetzt und erklärt* (4th ed.; HKAT III/1; Göttingen: Vandenhoeck & Ruprecht, 1922), 13–15; Willem A. M. Beuken, "Isa. 56:9–57:13—An Example of the Isaianic Legacy of Trito-Isaiah," in *Tradition and Reinterpretation in Jewish and Early Christian Literature* (ed. Jan Willem van Henten et al.; StPB 36; Leiden: Brill, 1986), 48–64; Odil Hannes Steck, "Tritojesaja im Jesajabuch," in *The Book of Isaiah/Le livre d'Isaïe: les oracles et leurs relectures unité et complexité de l'ouvrage* (ed. Jacques Vermeylen; BETL 81; Leuven: Peeters, 1989), 403–6; idem, *Studien zu Tritojesaja* (BZAW 203; Berlin: de Gruyter, 1991), 217–28; Paul A. Smith, *Rhetoric and Redaction in Trito-Isaiah: The Structure, Growth and Authorship of Isaiah 56–66* (VTSup 62; Leiden: Brill, 1995); Benjamin D. Sommer, "Allusions and Illusions: The Unity of the Book of Isaiah in Light of Deutero-Isaiah's Use of Prophetic Tradition," in *New Visions of Isaiah* (ed. Roy F. Melugin and Marvin A. Sweeney; JSOTSup 214; Sheffield: Sheffield Academic Press, 1996), 156–86; idem, *A Prophet Reads Scripture: Allusion in Isaiah 40–66* (Contraversions; Stanford: Stanford University Press, 1998), 187–98; Jan L. Koole, *Isaiah III, Volume 1: Isaiah 40–48* (trans. Anthony P. Runia; Historical Commentary on the Old Testament; Kampen: Kok Pharos, 1997), 5–38; Konrad Schmid and Odil Hannes Steck, "Restoration Expectations in the Prophetic Tradition of the Old Testament," in *Restoration: Old Testament, Jewish, and Christian Perspectives* (ed. James M. Scott; JSJSup 72; Leiden: Brill, 2001), 41–81; Joseph Blenkinsopp, *Isaiah 40–55: A New Translation with Introduction and Commentary* (AB 19A; New York: Doubleday, 2002); idem, *Isaiah 56–66: A New Translation with Introduction and Commentary* (AB 19B; New York: Doubleday, 2003).

Hellenistic periods and too limiting in their engagement with the range of designations Israel could have during these times.[8] My argument is not that certain understandings of Jacob/Israel—the eponymous ancestor, the Judean community (or some subset thereof), the future community of God—are somehow all invalid. They are clearly not. My argument is that one can discern within Trito-Isaiah a multiplicity of different, sometimes overlapping, constructions of Israelite identity. Alongside new restrictive designations, one may detect the survival of traditional meanings and the creative redefinition of old concepts.

## I. Israel, Jacob, and Judah in Third Isaiah

In discussing the appearances of the name Israel in the prophetic wrings, Rost described the use of Israel in Trito-Isaiah as obscure.[9] Similar things may be said of Jacob. Israel (six appearances) and Jacob (five appearances) are fairly rare in Isaiah 56–66 and the latter never parallels the former. Interestingly, the term Judah is also rare in Trito-Isaiah, occurring only once.[10] The statistics pertaining to Israel, Jacob, and Judah are significant, suggesting that Israelite identity is not as much a concern in Trito-Isaiah as it is in Deutero-Isaiah. The low numbers involved should also caution us against automatically assuming that Trito-Isaiah is completely obsessed with Judah.[11] Other concerns predominate—the divine promises to Jerusalem (Isa 59:20; 61:10–62:12), the gathering of the nations to Zion (Isa 60:4–8; 66:18–21), the state of the temple (Isa 56:5, 7; 60:7, 13; 66:1–2, 6), the role of foreigners and eunuchs in temple worship (Isa 56:3–6), the text and texture of corporate lament (Isa 59:9–15; 63:7–64:11), the plight of the poor (e.g., Isa 58:6–10; 59:1–15), the contested significance of religious practices, such as fasting, mourning, sacrifice, mortuary rituals, and Sabbath observance (Isa 56:2; 57:18; 58:13; 59:9–15; 61:2–3; 62:6–7; 65:24; 66:10), cultic misbehavior (Isa 57:3–13; 65:1–7), and the roles of community leaders, including priests (Isa 56:9–12; 66:1–4, 17–18, 21).[12]

---

[8] See Konrad Schmid, *Buchgestalten des Jeremiabuches: Untersuchungen zur Redaktions- und Rezeptionsgeschichte von Jer 30–33 im Kontext des Buches* (WMANT 72; Neukirchen-Vluyn: Neukirchener Verlag, 1996), 110–81 (and the references listed there).

[9] Rost, *Propheten*, 114.

[10] Benjamin never appears. Cf. Ezra 1:5; 4:1; 10:9; Neh 11:1, 4, 7, 20, 25, 31, 36; Obad 19; Zech 14:10; Esth 2:5.

[11] By comparison, Judah appears three times in Second Isaiah (40:9; 44:26; 45:1).

[12] Space constraints do not permit a full discussion.

Given the range of pronouncements appearing in Third Isaiah, the corpus defies easy categorization. It might be reductive to say that the concerns of Trito-Isaiah are entirely parochial because certain passages are quite sweeping in their imaginative engagement with a range of social, cultic, ethnic, and international themes.[13] Some propose to reorder relationships between God's people and those foreigners, who worship YHWH and adhere to his covenant, while others creatively call for the reformation, if not delimitation, of the people from within. There are also some lines of continuity among all three major sections of Isaiah.[14] It may be helpful to take a closer look at Israel and Jacob in Trito-Isaiah to consider whether its usage is exclusively focused on Judah (or on some group within Judah).[15]

Of the six times Israel appears, the term appears twice as part of the divine epithet, "the Holy One of Israel" (Isa 60:9, 14).[16] The soubriquet "the Holy One of Israel" is quite common in Isaiah and Deutero-Isaiah (25 of its 31 appearances in the HB appear in Isaiah), but uncommon in Trito-Isaiah. The two appearances in Trito-Isaiah are significant insofar as they occur in a section (Isa 60–62) that is generally agreed to be the most like Deutero-Isaiah in style and content. Israel in "the Holy One of Israel" (קדוש ישראל) seems to refer to the people as a whole (however one would define that entity).[17] Given Isaiah's close attachment to the Jerusalem cult, the epithet also connotes a special connection to temple worship.[18] Of the other occurrences of the term Israel, three refer to the population or body politic (Isa 56:8; 63:7; 66:20) and one refers to the eponymous ancestor (parallel with Abraham in Isa 63:16).

Of the five times Jacob appears, one reference involves the patriarch (Isa 58:14), while another recalls the divine epithet, "the Mighty One of

[13] Høgenhaven, *Gott*, 15–26; Schmid and Steck, "Restoration Expectations," 46–81; Saul M. Olyan, *Disability in the Hebrew Bible: Interpreting Mental and Physical Differences* (Cambridge: Cambridge University Press, 2008).

[14] Blenkinsopp, *Isaiah 56–66*, 27–37. But connections with Jeremiah are also prominent, Bernhard Duhm, *Jesaia*, 8–9; Odil Hannes Steck, *Gottesknecht und Zion: Gesammelte Aufsätze zu Deuterojesaja* (FAT 4; Tübingen: Mohr [Siebeck], 1992), 197–204; Reinhard G. Kratz, "Der Anfang des Zweiten Jesaja in Jes 40,1f. und das Jeremiabuch," *ZAW* 106 (1994): 243–61; Schmid, *Buchgestalten*, 315–19; Sommer, "Allusions and Illusions," 178–83; idem, *Prophet*, 32–72.

[15] For some (e.g., Danell, *Studies*, 263–64), the paucity of references to Israel/Jacob comports with a redefinition of Israel as the Jerusalemite community. But see below.

[16] Williamson, "Concept," 141–60.

[17] Danell, *Studies*, 156, 162.

[18] Høgenhaven, *Gott*, 15–26.

Jacob" (אביר יעקב; Isa 60:16) in a variety of earlier writings. There are two references to Jacob involving the people or body politic (Isa 58:1; 65:9) and one reference is territorial (Isa 59:20). The last case confirms, theoretically at least, the possibility of a restrictive understanding of Jacob: "He [YHWH] will come as redeemer to Zion, to those turning back from sin in Jacob." If one grants, as is usually the case in most readings of this poem, that this is an instance of synonymous parallelism, Jacob seems to stand parallel with Zion. Rather than being associated with the northern tribes, Jacob is associated with Jerusalem. Admittedly, there are issues, when interpreting the verse in this manner. Two elements in a parallelism may not be identical or synonymous with one another. There are different kinds of parallelism (synonymous, antithetic, synthetic, etc.) and some cases of parallelism are not rigidly framed.[19] Indeed, the two elements standing parallel in some fashion to one another may be considerably different in meaning.[20] Such considerations are quite important to bear in mind, when attempting to construe unusual pairings in Hebrew verse.[21]

In any event, assuming, for the sake of argument, the traditional restrictive understanding of Isa 59:20, is the constriction of Jacob to Jerusalem typical of the entire corpus? A couple of pericopes within Trito-Isaiah intimate broader understandings of the Israelite people and the territories they inhabit. In both texts, I would argue that the references to Jacob and Israel encompass more than Judeans. Yet, it must be kept in mind that the two passages present distinctive portraits of YHWH's involvement in his people's future. Given the dense clusters of images found within the poetry, it will be useful to examine each passage separately.

## II. Gathering the Dispersed of Israel

The material in Isa 56:1–8 plays a critical function inasmuch as it introduces the final section of the book—Isa 56–66. This passage, along with the conclusion in Isa 66, provides the intervening material with a "universalist

---

19 On these complications, see the thoughtful discussion of J. Barr, *Comparative Philology and the Text of the Old Testament* (Oxford: Clarendon, 1968 [repr. Winona Lake, Ind.: Eisenbrauns, 1987]), 277–82.

20 There are also important questions as to what "synonymous" parallelism actually comes to. See further below (n. 43).

21 So, e.g., if one were to argue that Isa 59:20 is a case of synthetic parallelism, the poem may promote a Zion-centered vision of Jacob (which is, however, left undefined in this context).

accent."[22] The final chapter depicts YHWH as intending to gather (לקבץ) all nations (כל־הגוים) and tongues to come and see his glory (Isa 66:18). The nations, in turn, will escort "all your kin" (כל־אחיכם) back to Jerusalem (Isa 66:20), "just as the children of Israel bring an offering in a pure vessel to the House of YHWH."[23]

In keeping with this universal theme, the stress on practicing justice and Sabbath observance encompasses not only Israelites (56:1–2), but also foreigners (בני הנכר; 56:6–7).[24] Indeed, in a new dispensation, the offerings of foreigners, those holding fast to YHWH's covenant, will be welcome on YHWH's "holy hill" (56:7).[25] The divine speech thus announces a major new initiative that effectively reforms the community and its worship. But lest the reader think that the oracle only has to do with the integration and participation of eunuchs and aliens, as important as these initiatives might be, the conclusion to the oracle returns to Israel itself.[26] YHWH is identified as the one who gathers (קבץ) the scattered of Israel (נדחי ישראל). The author of repatriation announces that he will gather

---

[22] Koole, *Isaiah III*, 1, 30. Raymond de Hoop ("The Interpretation of Isaiah 56:1–9: Comfort or Criticism?," *JBL* 127 [2008]: 671–95) provides a useful discussion of the larger literary context.

[23] Claus Westermann, *Isaiah 40–66: A Commentary* (OTL; Philadelphia: Westminster, 1969), 305–6; Ulrich Berges, *Das Buch Jesaja: Komposition und Endgestalt* (Herder's biblische Studien 16; Freiburg: Herder, 1998), 414–534; Philipp A. Enger, *Die Adoptivkinder Abrahams: Eine exegetische Spurensuche zur Vorgeschichte des Proselytentums* (BEATAJ 53; Frankfurt am Main: Lang, 2006), 373–90; C. Nihan, "Ethnicity and Identity in Isaiah 56–66," in *Judah and the Judeans: Negotiating Identity in an International Context* (ed. Oded Lipschits, Gary N. Knoppers, and Manfred Oeming; Winona Lake, Ind.: Eisenbrauns, 2011), 67–104.

[24] On the contrast with (and refutation of) Ezek 44:9–16, see Michael A. Fishbane, *Biblical Interpretation in Ancient Israel* (Oxford: Clarendon, 1985), 138–43; Joachim Schaper, "Rereading the Law: Inner-Biblical Exegesis of Divine Oracles in Ezekiel 44 and Isaiah 56," in *Recht und Ethik im Alten Testament: Beiträge des Symposiums 'Das Alte Testament und die Kultur der Moderne' anlässlich des 100. Geburtstags Gerhard von Rads (1901–1971) Heidelberg, 18.–21. Oktober 2001* (ed. Bernard M. Levinson and Eckart Otto; Altes Testament und Moderne 13; Münster: Lit Verlag, 2004), 125–44; Steven S. Tuell, "The Priesthood of the "Foreigner": Evidence of Competing Polities in Ezekiel 44:1–14 and Isaiah 56:1–8," in *Constituting the Community: Studies on the Polity of Ancient Israel in Honor of S. Dean McBride, Jr.* (ed. John T. Strong and Steven S. Tuell; Winona Lake, Ind.: Eisenbrauns, 2005), 183–204.

[25] The situation may be compared to that pertaining in Lev 22:18–25 and Num 15:14–15 in which the sacrifices of resident aliens (גרים) are welcome at the Tabernacle. On the prayers of foreigners at the temple, see 1 Kgs 8:41–43. But the Trito-Isaianic text goes further than the passages in the Pentateuch do by allowing foreigners to minister (שרת) to YHWH (Isa 56:6).

[26] Referencing the antique accentuation of Isa 56:8–9, de Hoop ("Comfort," 671–75, 686–90) defends the delimitation of the pericope as Isa 56:1–9. He argues that Isa 56:8–9 function as a bridge to the material in Isa 56:10–59:21.

yet more to Israel to those already gathered.[27] In this manner, the divine initiative announced at the beginning (Isa 56:1) becomes more fully developed. A new day is dawning not only for foreigners and eunuchs, but also for Israelite expatriates. Israel remains central to YHWH's larger purpose, even as that purpose is remarkably extended and redefined.[28]

But to whom does the expression "the dispersed of Israel" apply? The text does not identify whether the "dispersed of Israel" refers only to Judeans or is more encompassing. Nevertheless, a comprehensive, rather than a narrow, meaning is likely to hold true. To begin with, "Israel" is by definition an inclusive term for the descendants of Jacob/Israel.[29] There are examples of Israel designating the Babylonian exiles or the southern kingdom, but the number of such cases pales by comparison to the usage of Israel as a larger entity.[30] One can hold, of course, that Israel has a very particular meaning in this literary context, but the point has to be demonstrated and not simply assumed.

Second, if the writer wished to speak of the scattered of Judah, he could have done so (cf. Isa 40:9; 44:26; 48:1). Trito-Isaiah does speak of the return of Jerusalem's children (60:1–4; cf. 62:11–12; 65:23) and Zion is mentioned regularly in the work (59:20; 60:14; 61:3; 62:1, 11; 64:9; 66:8), but a more general term (Israel) appears here. To be sure, the promises here are also very much Jerusalem-directed, but the point is that the poem takes a broad view of the people who are to be called back to Zion. Third, the phraseology recalls that used in the concluding chapters of Deuteronomy to depict YHWH's future restoration of the people back to the land (30:1–10).[31] In both instances, orthopraxis is stressed. YHWH pledges that he will gather (קבץ) again the Israelite deportees from all the peoples (מכל־העמים) among whom he had banished them (Deut 30:3). The assurance extends even "to those scattered (נדח) to the ends of heaven; from there YHWH

[27] Cf. Isa 27:13; 66:18; Jer 31:10–11; Ps 147:2; Sir 51:12. See also Jer 23:2–4; 29:14; 32:37; Zeph 3:19.

[28] Jan L. Koole, *Isaiah III, Volume 3: Isaiah 56–66* (trans. Anthony P. Runia; Historical Commentary on the Old Testament; Leuven: Peeters, 2001), 5–6, 26–27.

[29] Zobel, "יִשְׂרָאֵל," 398–99.

[30] In this case, Zobel ("יִשְׂרָאֵל," 398–403) thinks that Israel refers to the Israel of the prophet's day, but it is not entirely clear what this means. Most, albeit not all, of the cases in which Israel designates the southern kingdom (or some subsection of Judah) occur in Chronicles, Ezra, and Nehemiah. But even in Chronicles the use of Israel for Judah sometimes has larger (pan-Israelite) implications, Williamson, *Israel*, 97–131.

[31] Roy D. Wells, "'Isaiah' as an Exponent of Torah: Isaiah 56.1–8," in *New Visions of Isaiah* (ed. Roy F. Melugin and Marvin A. Sweeney; JSOTSup 214; Sheffield: Sheffield Academic Press, 1996), 151–52.

your God will gather you" (קבץ; Deut 30:4).[32] Clearly, the divine assurance does not distinguish among individual tribes or among phratries within such sodalities. The promise extends to all. Some have suggested also (or alternatively) a link between Isa 56:8 and another Isaianic text, which foretells YHWH's regathering of those banished from the land (Isa 11:12).[33] If so, such a link would only strengthen the pan-Israelite interpretation of our text because the promise in Isa 11 extends both to YHWH assembling (אסף) the outcasts of Israel (נדחי ישראל) and to his gathering (קבץ) the dispersed of Judah (נפצות יהודה).[34]

Fourth, it would be odd, albeit not impossible, to include foreigners among those allowed to offer sacrifices and prayers at the Jerusalem temple, but to disallow descendants of Israelite tribes other than Judah (or other than Judah, Benjamin, and Levi), from doing so. It has been argued that the opening lines of the oracle contain a series of allusions to Pentateuchal texts.[35] Certainly, it was incumbent upon all Israelites, and not simply Judahites, to practice justice and to honor the Sabbath. Finally, it is quite possible, as many commentators have maintained, that the whole point of the oracle is to challenge, if not transcend, traditional ethnic and physical boundaries.[36] If so, the question of whether Israel carries narrow, as opposed to broad, connotations in Isa 56:8 may be moot.

## III. New Wine Found in the Cluster (Isa 65:8–10)

A somewhat different perspective on corporate renewal is found within the oracle of Isa 65:1–16, responding to the long communal lament of Isa 63:7–64:11.[37] The piece cannot be categorized simply as a salvation oracle,

---

32 The allusions to and transformation of Deut 30:1–10 in Nehemiah's prayer (Neh 1:9) are also striking, H. G. M. Williamson, *Ezra-Nehemiah* (WBC 16; Waco: Word, 1985), 166–75.

33 Steck, *Studien*, 41, 248.

34 That the parallel between Israel and Judah (as representative of north and south) is deliberate is confirmed by the parallelism between Ephraim and Judah in Isa 11:13.

35 Recently, Wells ("Exponent," 140–45) in reference to the Sabbath stipulations of Exod 31:12–17.

36 See Jill Middlemas, "Trito-Isaiah's Intra- and Inter-nationalization: Identity Markers in the Second Temple Period," in *Judah and the Judeans: Negotiating Identity in an International Context* (ed. Oded Lipschits, Gary N. Knoppers, and Manfred Oeming; Winona Lake, Ind.: Eisenbrauns, 2011), 105–23; Nihan, "Ethnicity," and the references listed in these works.

37 In Smith's view (*Rhetoric*, 132) the entire section of Isa 65:1–66:17 responds to the lament. On this matter, see also the earlier comments of Steck, *Studien*, 217–28. For a somewhat different perspective, see Blenkinsopp, *Isaiah 56–66*, 27–66, 266–83. See

because it alternates punishment with promise.[38] Our focus will be on one section, depicting the future repopulation of the land (Isa 65:8–10). Unlike the previous oracle (Isa 56:1–8), this oracle speaks of renewal from within, rather than an ingathering from without. At first glance, the divine promises within vv. 8–10 would appear to contain evidence to counter my argument for a more inclusive understanding of Israel/Jacob in certain literary contexts within Trito-Isaiah. When YHWH declares: "As when new wine is found in the cluster and one says, 'Do not destroy it, for there is a blessing in it'" (Isa 65:8), the text alludes to a surviving remnant of some kind and not to the renewal of the whole.[39] The repeated references to "my servants" (vv. 8–9), generally understood as the successors to "the servant of YHWH" in Deutero-Isaiah, point toward the same conclusion.[40] As with some other texts, this poem calls attention to a particular group as playing a critical role in the divine economy.[41]

To complicate matters further, one finds Judah and Jacob listed in parallel fashion: "I shall bring forth seed (זרע) from Jacob//from Judah one

now also, Judith Gärtner, "'...Why Do You Let Us Stray from Your Paths...' (Isa 63:17): The Concept of Guilt in the Communal Lament in Isa 63:7–64:11," in *Seeking the Favor of God: Volume 1—The Origin of Penitential Prayer in Second Temple Judaism* (ed. Mark J. Boda, Daniel K. Falk, and Rodney A. Werline; Atlanta: Society of Biblical Literature, 2006), 145–63.

[38] So, for instance, Paul D. Hanson, *The Dawn of Apocalyptic: the Historical and Sociological Roots of Jewish Apocalyptic Eschatology* (rev. ed.; Philadelphia: Fortress, 1979), 144.

[39] In the judgment of Smith (*Rhetoric*, 141–42) "Jacob and Judah are designations of the whole." The faithful among people are to inherit the land (cf. Isa 65:1–2). In some older interpretations, the distinction between the faithful (i.e., "my servants") and "the whole" was thought to differentiate returned Judeans from the mixed population of the land, especially the Samaritans. See, e.g., Duhm, *Jesaia*, 7–22; Johann Wilhelm Rothstein, *Juden und Samaritaner: die grundlegende Scheidung von Judentum und Heidentum: eine kritische Studie zum Buche Haggai und zur jüdischen Geschichte im ersten nachexilischen Jahrhundert* (BWANT 3; Leipzig: Hinrichs, 1908) 1–82.

[40] Willem A. M. Beuken, "The Main Theme of Trito-Isaiah 'The Servants of Yhwh,'" *JSOT* 47 (1990): 67–87; idem, "Isaiah Chapters LXV–LXVI: Trito-Isaiah and the Closure of the Book of Isaiah," in *Congress Volume: Leuven, 1989* (ed. John A. Emerton; VTSup 43; Leiden: Brill, 1991), 204–21; Blenkinsopp, *Isaiah 56–66*, 132–43, 274–78.

[41] Alexander Rofé, "Isaiah 66:1–4: Judean Sects in the Persian Period as Viewed by Trito-Isaiah," in *Biblical and Related Studies Presented to Samuel Iwry* (ed. Ann Kort and Scott Morschauer; Winona Lake, Ind.: Eisenbrauns, 1985), 205–17; idem, "The Onset of Sects in Postexilic Judaism: Neglected Evidence from the Septuagint, Trito-Isaiah, Ben Sira, and Malachi," in *The Social World of Formative Christianity and Judaism: Essays in Tribute to Howard Clark Kee* (ed. Jacob Neusner et al.; Philadelphia: Fortress, 1988), 39–49; Beuken, "Main Theme," 67–87; Joseph Blenkinsopp, "A Jewish Sect of the Persian Period," *CBQ* 52 (1990): 5–20; Berges, *Jesaja*, 512–15; Christophe Nihan, "Trois cultes en Ésaïe 57,3–13 et leur signification dans le contexte religieux de la Judée à l'époque perse," *Transeu* 22 (2001): 143–67.

possessing my hills" (Isa 65:9). If in parallel poetic lines, the second element defines the first more precisely, Judah defines Jacob.[42] But is this a case of synonymous parallelism or of synthetic parallelism?[43] If one looks at the geographical areas in which God's chosen ones (בחירי) are to take possession, a large, rather than a highly restricted, area is in view. The general reference to "my hills" (הרי) suggests a broad perspective. The text does not speak specifically about the hills of Judah, the hills of Manasseh, the hills of Benjamin, or the hills of Ephraim. Rather, YHWH speaks of repopulating the (central) hill country by those whom he has freely elected to possess this territory.

That an expansive perspective is in view is confirmed by the geographic reference points in the following lines of the oracle: "Sharon will become a fold for flocks//the valley of Achor a place for cattle to lie down" (Isa 65:10). The Sharon coastal plain extends from the Carmel range in the north to Joppa in the south and the Achor valley is located near Jericho.[44] The Sharon designates, therefore, the northwestern extreme of the land, while the Achor valley marks the southeastern extreme of the land. Given this wide geographical perspective, it is likely that the author is employing Jacob as a northern reference point and Judah as a southern one.[45] The poet is envisaging the reemergence of a repopulated Israel and Judah,

[42] In one Lamentations text (2:2), the phrase the "settlements of Jacob" parallels the "fortresses of the daughter of Judah." The specification may be compared with that of the earlier usage in Ps 79:6–7 and the reuse of that imagery in Jer 10:25.

[43] Indeed, James L. Kugel (*The Idea of Biblical Poetry: Parallelism and Its History* [New Haven: Yale University Press, 1981]) and Adele Berlin (*The Dynamics of Biblical Parallelism* [Bloomington: Indiana University Press, 1985]) have maintained that (synonymous) parallelism in biblical poetry has been construed too mechanically as "A restated by B." Kugel argues that *parallelismus membrorum* often has an inherently synthetic function ("A; what is more, B").

[44] The precise location of עמק עכור is disputed (Josh 7:24, 26; 15:7; Isa 65:10; Hos 2:17). Some locate it between Qumran and Kh. el Mird. Wâdī Nuwēʿime northwest of Jericho has also been suggested (HALOT 823b–824a). See, further, Zecharia Kallai, *Historical Geography of the Bible: The Tribal Territories of Israel* (Jerusalem: Magnes, 1986), 118–20. For a somewhat different view, situating the Valley of Achor south of Jericho between Benjamin and Judah (cf. Josh 15:7, 9), see Yohanan Aharoni, *The Land of the Bible: A Historical Geography* (rev. and enl. ed.; Philadelphia: Westminster, 1979), 208; Anson F. Rainey and R. Steven Notley, *The Sacred Bridge: Carta's Atlas of the Biblical World* (Jerusalem: Carta, 2006), 180–81.

[45] Perhaps the translators of the NJPS grasped the force of the geographical merism and therefore took the highly unusual step of suggesting a textual emendation from "the Sharon" (השרון) to "the Yeshimon" (הישימון) in the southeastern corner of the Jordan Valley (Num 21:20; 23:18). By emending the text, the editors achieve an inner-Judahite (or an inner Judahite-Benjaminite) geographic merism. But so far as I am aware, the versions do not support the proposed emendation.

recalling the familiar distinction made between North and South in older writings.[46] To be sure, such a broad geographic vantage point does not correspond to an equally broad demographic referent for Jacob/Judah. The prophecy promises only the chosen seed the heritage of progeny and land originally afforded to all of Jacob and Judah. The piece encourages YHWH's servants to trust that not all has been lost. The God of Israel will create new offspring from his people to dwell (שכן) within the land. The reference by the deity "to my people" (לעמי) underscores the sense of continuity between the servants of YHWH and the Jacob/Judah of ages past.

Responding to the pleas of the people, the oracle underscores the deity's sovereign choice in decision-making. He will punish some (65:1–7) and deliver others (65:8–10). The stress on choices and their consequences establishes a larger point. The determining factor is not where precisely the people stem from within Jacob and Judah, but whether and how they respond to YHWH. The seed of Jacob and Judah, those who seek (דרש) YHWH (v. 10), will yet possess the land and enjoy its benefits.[47] By contrast, those who have abandoned YHWH and forgotten his holy mountain are destined for the sword (vv. 11–12).

To this, it could be objected that in reality the oracle only has a small genealogically and geographically circumscribed group in view. Hence, "salvation [is] limited to Judah."[48] It may be readily admitted that Trito-Isaiah espouses a very Jerusalem-centric vision of God's people. The temple cultus in Zion is never very far from the attention of the writers.[49] But this is hardly a fatal objection to a geographically expansive understanding of the oracle. Samuel-Kings and Chronicles also promote a vision of Israel centered on Jerusalem and Judah, but that vision encompasses more than Jerusalem and Judah. In any event, if Judah (or a small party therein) is the sole focus, such an entity would control a tremendous amount of land in northwestern Israel that lay far beyond the traditional boundaries

---

46 He is, however, employing an unusual set of geographic expressions to do so (compare "from Dan to Beersheba"). In some late texts, the progression is from south to north (e.g., "from Beersheba to the hill country of Ephraim" in 2 Chr 19:4). For other late possibilities, see 1 Chr 13:5; 21:2; 2 Chr 30:5. Interestingly, beginning with a focus on the central hill country, the poem retains the traditional north/south orientation.

47 On the cultic overtones of דרש, see also Isa 8:19; 19:3; 55:3 (HALOT 233b). Such a meaning is common in Late Biblical Hebrew, Gary N. Knoppers, *I Chronicles 10–29* (AB 12A; New York: Doubleday, 2004), 523–24.

48 Hans-Jürgen Zobel, "יְהוּדָה; *yᵉhûdâ*," *TDOT* 5:498.

49 Ronald E. Clements, "Zion as Symbol and Political Reality: A Central Isaianic Quest," in *Studies in the Book of Isaiah: Festschrift Willem A. M. Beuken* (ed. Jacques T. A. G. M. Van Ruiten and Marc Vervenne; BETL 132; Leuven: Peeters, 1997), 3–17.

attributed to the tribe or province. This consideration undermines the viability of the Judah-alone interpretation of Jacob in Isa 65:8–10.

## IV. Conclusions

To return to the issues raised at the beginning of this essay, there are good reasons to doubt a unilinear progression over the centuries that would entail broad definitions of Israelite identity in the Neo-Babylonian period becoming ever-so-narrow definitions of Israelite identity in the Achaemenid period. Such a simplistic typology fails to do justice to the complexity of the evidence, even though it recognizes one important development. Rather than attempting to force the imagery of Trito-Isaiah into a single mold, it may be more helpful to recognize that the work presents a variety of hopes for the future of Israel/Jacob. Like Deutero-Isaiah, Trito-Isaiah gives imaginative and, at times, forceful expression to diverse aspirations within the community.[50]

Before one jumps to the conclusion that such hopes were altogether unrealistic, given the underpopulated and impoverished status of Yehud during the postmonarchic age, one should recall that Judaism had become an international phenomenon already in the seventh-sixth centuries BCE. During the Neo-Babylonian, Persian, and early Hellenistic eras, Judeans (or, at least, Yahwists) could be found in Judah, other parts of Syria-Palestine, Cyprus, Babylon, and Egypt (e.g., 2 Kgs 25:22–26; Jer 37:1–43:13).[51] To the north of Yehud, there were many Yahwists residing in the province

[50] Gary N. Knoppers, "Did Jacob become Judah?: Assessing Israel's Reconstitution in Deutero-Isaiah," in *Samaria, Samarians, Samaritans: Studies on Bible, History and Linguistics—Proceedings of the Sixth International meeting of the Société d'Études Samaritaines, Pápa, Hungary, 20–25 July 2008* (ed. József Zsengellér; Studia Samaritana 6. Berlin: de Gruyter, 2011), 39–67.

[51] On the Egyptian question, reference is often made to the colony at Elephantine (Bezalel Porten, *Archives from Elephantine: The Life of an Ancient Jewish Military Colony* [Berkeley: University of California Press, 1968]), but reference may also be made to Judeans residing in the Delta, John S. Holladay, "Judeans (and Phoenicians) in Egypt in the Late Seventh to Sixth Centuries," in *Egypt, Israel, and the Ancient Mediterranean World: Studies in Honour of Donald B. Redford* (ed. Gary N. Knoppers and Antoine Hirsch; Probleme der Ägyptologie 20; Leiden: Brill, 2004), 405–37. The analysis of Sophocles Hadjisavvas, André Dupont-Sommer, and Hélène Lozachmeur documents the appearance of some Yahwistic personal names on fourth-century BCE funerary stelae in Cyprus, "Cinq steles funéraires découvertes sur le site d'Ayios Georghias à Larnaca-Kition, en 1979," in *Report of the Department of Antiquities, Cyprus 1984* (Cyprus: Department of Antiquities, 1984), 101–15 (pls. xix–xxi).

of Samaria, who likely laid claim to the name Israel/Jacob.[52] That one finds various projections of Israelite identity in Deutero-Isaiah and Trito-Isaiah is not surprising, considering the demographic and social complexities attending Yahwistic communities during the times in which these texts were composed.

Moreover, one should note that both oracles acknowledge that the land was underpopulated. In one case, the people are to be strengthened by a divinely initiated ingathering of Israelites from without (Isa 56:1–8), while in the second case, renewal results from an initiative undertaken by YHWH on behalf of his servants to repopulate and resettle the land with the offspring of Jacob and Judah (Isa 65:8–10). In negotiating the perennial issue of corporate identity, the novel contribution of Trito-Isaiah consists, therefore, not simply in its application of the name Israel/Jacob to Judah (or to a group within Judah), but also in its creative deployment of Israel/Jacob to prophesy the reconstitution of a larger community.

[52] Gary N. Knoppers, "In Search of Postexilic Israel: Samaria after the Fall of the Northern Kingdom," in *In Search of Preexilic Israel* (ed. John Day; JSOTSup 406; Edinburgh: T&T Clark, 2004), 150–80; idem, "What has Mt. Zion to do with Mt. Gerizim? A Study in the Early Relations between the Jews and the Samaritans in the Persian Period," *SR* 34 (2005): 307–36; idem, "Revisiting the Samarian Question in the Persian Period," in *Judah and the Judeans in the Persian Period* (ed. Oded Lipschits and Manfred Oeming; Winona Lake, Ind.: Eisenbrauns, 2006), 265–89.

# THE TWO HOUSES OF ISRAEL

Reinhard G. Kratz

In this contribution I shall deal with the question, who or what are the 'two houses of Israel' which are mentioned in Isa 8:14:

> He shall be for a sanctuary, a stone men strike against, a rock men stumble over for the two Houses of Israel, and a trap and a snare for those who dwell in Jerusalem.
>
> והיה למקדש ולאבן נגף ולצור מכשול לשני בתי ישראל לפח ולמוקש ליושב ירושלם

Although I know that Hugh Williamson already has his own view and has commented on this verse, I would like to take this opportunity since when I was writing this contribution, only the first volume of his excellent commentary on the book of Isaiah had been published.[1] Because of this I am free to express my humble remarks on that verse on which he himself has certainly already reflected. Nonetheless, I hope that he will enjoy my remarks, whether we coincidentally agree with each other or whether he has already disproved my view on this verse.

## I. The Exegetical Problem

Already the textual tradition in the Septuagint and in the Targum prove that behind the expression 'the two houses of Israel,' which is unique in the Old Testament, there is an exegetical problem.[2] The Septuagint divides the text in vv. 13–14 differently and changes its meaning. The translator either omitted the end of v. 13 (והוא מערצכם) or did not find it in the Hebrew *Vorlage*; instead, v. 14—in line with Isa 28:16 and the Targum—begins with a conditional clause, opening with this the way for the pious to escape all terrors as announced in v. 14. This, however, does not apply to the 'two houses of Israel,' which the Septuagint connects with the following and reads in accordance with v. 17 with the singular 'house of Jacob':

[1] H. G. M. Williamson, *Commentary on Isaiah 1–5* (vol. 1 of *A Critical and Exegetical Commentary on Isaiah 1–27*; ICC; London: T&T Clark, 2006).

[2] See Joseph Ziegler, *Untersuchungen zur Septuaginta des Buches Isaias* (ATA 12/3; Münster: Aschendorff, 1934), 95–96.

> If you trust in him, he will become your holy precinct, and you will not encounter him as a stumbling caused by a stone nor as a fall caused by a rock, but the house of Jacob is in a trap, and those who sit in Jerusalem are in a pit.
>
> καὶ ἐὰν ἐπ' αὐτῷ πεποιθὼς ᾖς, ἔσται σοι εἰς ἁγίασμα, καὶ οὐχ ὡς λίθου προσκόμματι συναντήσεσθε αὐτῷ οὐδὲ ὡς πέτρας πτώματι· ὁ δὲ οἶκος Ιακωβ ἐν παγίδι, καὶ ἐν κοιλάσματι ἐγκαθήμενοι ἐν Ιερουσαλημ

The 'house of Jacob' in the Greek text seems to be not as problematic as the 'two houses of Israel,' probably because the expression is more common in biblical language. It stands for the twelve sons of Jacob and, therefore, for God's people, the social group of the twelve tribes of Israel, defined by family relation with religious connotations. Here the 'house' does not have a political but a social meaning; it refers to a family group. But the expression 'the two houses of Israel' in the Hebrew text is different. 'The house' in the singular, just like the name 'Israel,' could mean both the 'house of Israel' in the sense of the 'house of Jacob,' i.e., the people of the twelve sons of Jacob-Israel, or the 'house of Israel' as opposed to the 'house of Judah', i.e., the northern kingdom. In the plural, however, 'house' has clearly a political meaning and refers to the dynasty. This does not comply with the genitive in the construct state in which 'Israel' can only refer to God's people as a whole.

Since the Septuagint is the easier version, which also brings the text into line with 8:17, this variant must be considered as secondary according to the rules of textual criticism. Following the more difficult and original reading of the Hebrew text, the two ways of using the word 'house' and the word 'Israel' seem to be intermingled: the political meaning of 'house' with the social meaning of the name 'Israel.' Thus, the question arises, what is the reason for the semantic combination and what is actually the meaning of this unique formulation in the book of Isaiah?

Unfortunately, I cannot look it up in Williamson's commentary yet. Therefore, I started to leaf through some older or newer commentaries and some monographs on the book of Isaiah in order to find out what exegetes had to say or noticed about this phrase. The result was not really surprising. Some do not seem to see a problem here at all and do not waste a word on the phrase in question.[3] Quite naturally, either the political

---

[3] Wilhelm Gesenius, *Commentar über den Jesaja: Ersten Theiles erste Abteilung enthaltend die Einleitung und Auslegung von Kapitel 1–12* (Leipzig: FCW Vogel, 1821), 540; Bernhard Duhm, *Das Buch Jesaja übersetzt und erklärt* (HKAT 3/1; Göttingen: Vandenhoeck & Ruprecht, 1892), 62; Antoon Schoors, *Jesaja* (BOT 9; Roermond: J. J. Romen & Zonen, 1972),

(two kingdoms) or the social meaning (the people of God) is assumed, or even both.[4] Others, at least, mention that the phrase is unique but still do not investigate it any further.[5] The same applies to the textual variant or, rather, different text of the Septuagint.[6] More attention is given to the difficult למקדש at the beginning of the verse, which is easily changed and put in line with vv. 12–13,[7] and to the singular participle יושב in the phrase 'to the inhabitants of Jerusalem,' which in some Hebrew manuscripts and versions appears in the plural.[8]

However, there are commentators who have recognized the problem and suggested a solution. Thus, for instance, Campegius Vitringa in the 18th century deals expressively with the question "why is there a mention of the two houses of Israel?" ("Cur hic binarum Domuum Israelis mentio fiat").[9] Vitringa identifies "the two houses of Israel" with Judah and Ephraim (or Joseph or Judah and Israel) which in the time of the prophet were divided into two parts ("illo tempore, quo Propheta hanc prophetiam edidit, in duas partes, duos Populos, duo Regna divisi") and only after

78–79; Joseph Blenkinsopp, *Isaiah 1–39: A New Translation with Introduction and Commentary* (AB 19; New York: Doubleday, 2000), 241–42; Brevard S. Childs, *Isaiah* (OTL; Louisville: Westminster John Knox, 2001), 74–75; John Goldingay, *Isaiah* (New International Biblical Commentary on the Old Testament 13; Peabody, MA: Hendrickson, 2001), 69, 72.

[4] See e.g., Ludwig Knobel, (*Der Prophet Jesaja* [4th ed.; Kurzgefasstes exegetisches Handbuch zum Alten Testament 5; Leipzig: Hirzel, 1872], 80) and Bernhard Duhm (*Das Buch Jesaja übersetzt und erklärt* [4th ed.; HKAT 3/1; Göttingen: Vandenhoeck & Ruprecht, 1922], 84) for the first meaning, or Willem M. A. Beuken (*Jesaja 1–12: Unter Mitwirkung und in Übersetzung aus dem Niederländischen von Ulrich Berges* [HTKAT; Freiburg: Herder, 2003], 214, 216, 218, 229–30) for the second. Both meanings without any further explanation can be found in Franz Delitzsch, *Commentar über das Buch Jesaja* (4th ed.; Biblischer Commentar über das Alte Testament 3/1; Leipzig: Dörffling & Franke, 1889), 158; ET: Carl F. Keil and Franz Delitzsch, *Isaiah* (vol. 7 of *Commentary on the Old Testament*; trans. James Martin; Edinburgh: Clark, 1866–1891; repr., Peabody, MA: Hendrickson, 2001), 154. More carefully based on the text is August Dillmann, *Der Prophet Jesaja* (5th ed.; Kurzgefasstes exegetisches Handbuch zum Alten Testament 5; Leipzig: Hirzel, 1890), 85; Geoffrey W. Grogan, "Isaiah," in *Proverbs–Isaiah* (rev. ed.; vol. 6 of *The Expositor's Bible Commentary*; ed. Tremper Longman III and David E. Garland; Grand Rapids: Zondervan, 2008), 523.

[5] Otto Kaiser, *Isaiah 1–12: A Commentary* (trans. John Bowden; OTL; Philadelphia: Westminster, 1983), 193; translation of *Das Buch des Propheten Jesaja: Kapitel 1–12* (5th ed.; ATD 17; Göttingen: Vandenhoeck & Ruprecht, 1981), 186.

[6] See John D. W. Watts, *Isaiah 1–33* (rev. ed.; WBC 24; Nashville: Thomas Nelson 2005), 156: "But there is no compelling reason to change it."

[7] See the commentaries and furthermore Godfrey R. Driver, "Two Misunderstood Passages of the Old Testament," *JTS* 6 (1955): 82–87 (82–84); Norbert Lohfink, "Isaias 8,12–14," *BZ* 7 (1963): 98–104.

[8] See Arnold B. Ehrlich, *Jesaia, Jeremia* (vol. 5 of *Randglossen zur Hebräischen Bibel: Textkritisches, Sprachliches und Sachliches*; Leipzig: J. C. Hinrichs'sche Buchandlung, 1912), 35.

[9] Campegius Vitringa, *Commentarius in Librum Prophetarium Jesaiae* (Pars Prior; Herborn: Johan. Nicolai Andreae, 1715), 270 (= Editio Nova; Basel, 1932, 221).

the return from Exile were united (again) into one nation ("inter se jam conjunctis et coadunatis in *unum Populum*, post reditum ex Exilio, juxta clarissimam Ezechielis [note: Cap. XXXVII. 19.20.seqq.] prophetiam"). The prophet Isaiah, says Vitringa, wanted to address not only Judah but both parts of the people of Israel. Interestingly Vitringa uses an exilic or post-exilic prophecy in order to demonstrate the unity of the two monarchies.

Karl Marti and Otto Procksch see it as a case for textual criticism and give a different explanation. Marti does not like the all-Israel perspective, which does not fit the context:

> Actually, Jerusalem is not really the opposite of the two houses of Israel, and Ephraim does not fit at all into the picture; as often in Hosea, Judah is used..., the relation with Ephraim has been inserted, and originally לאיש יהודה, or ליהודה has been used, whereby it is still possible that earlier ליושב ירושלם stood on the first position.[10]

Conversely, Procksch sees the point of the text as it stands, which he would like to restore with few changes. Referring to the Septuagint, he suggests the reading 'for the house of Israel' as

> Israel does not seem to be either Judah or Ephraim but the entire people because Isaiah, at the time, calls the northern kingdom Ephraim (7,2.9a) and the southern kingdom Judah (8:8). As opposed to Judah and Ephraim as political powers, Israel is the significant religious entity of God's people, the religious capital of which is Jerusalem.[11]

Both proposals are still mentioned in the literature occasionally, but generally they are rejected. However, scholars have, at least, been made aware of the problem. Hans Wildberger for example can just dismiss the text critical discussion with a short remark on the parallelism,[12] but has to make a great effort in order to explain the problem on the semantic level,

---

[10] Karl Marti, *Das Buch Jesaja* (KHC 10; Tübingen: J. C. B. Mohr [Paul Siebeck], 1900), 87: "Übrigens ist Jerusalem kein richtiger Gegensatz zu den beiden Häusern Israels, und Ephraim kommt hier gar nicht in Frage; wie in Hosea oftmals Juda eingesetzt ist [...], so ist hier die Beziehung auf Ephraim eingetragen und ursprünglich stand dafür לאיש יהודה, oder ליהודה, wobei noch möglich ist, dass ליושב ירושלם früher an erster Stelle stand." See George B. Gray, *Introduction, and Commentary in I–XXVII* (vol. 1 of *A Critical and Exegetical Commentary of the Book of Isaiah I–XXXIX*; Edinburgh: T&T Clark, 1912), 153.

[11] Otto Procksch, *Jesaja* (KAT 9/1; Leipzig: Deichert, 1930), 136, 137–38: "Israel [...] scheint weder Juda noch Ephraim als das Gesamtvolk zu sein, da Jesaja damals das Nordreich Ephraim (7,2.9[a]) und das Südreich Juda (8:8) nennt. Gegenüber Juda und Ephraim als politische Größen ist Israel die religiöse Größe des Gottesvolkes, dessen religiöse Hauptstadt Jerusalem ist."

[12] Hans Wildberger, *Isaiah 1–12: A Continental Commentary* (trans. Thomas H. Trapp; Minneapolis: Fortress, 1991), 356; translation of idem, *Jesaja* (2nd ed.; BK X/1; Neukrichen-Vluyn: Neukirchener 1980), 335.

historicising the phrase in a rather naïve way. His solution: "The judgment applies to all of Israel. No one in Jerusalem should think it possible to stand by as merely an observer of the tragedy of the Northern Kingdom and stay untouched." In his explanation he hopelessly confuses the political and the social meaning of the word 'house': "Isaiah wants to stress the fact that both of these individual countries belong together, like two houses, in which sons of just one father live in close proximity."[13]

More concise is the short remark by Peter Höffken: "The formulation of 'the two houses of Israel' is unusual and possibly already a sign of a post-Isaianic period."[14] The consequence drawn by him may also be the background for the proposal to treat the problem neither as a case for textual criticism nor for semantics or (pseudo-) historical explanations, but as a case for literary-criticism, dismissing the phrase in question and any related parts of the text in Isa 8:11, 14–15.[15] Even Jörg Barthel, who is rather inclined to favour a historicising explanation, thinks of this suggestion as "worth considering," although he rejects it in the end.[16] In fact, there is not much in favour of dismissing the phrase in question only for the reason that it does not fit into the (Isaianic or one's own) concept. The solution must, therefore, be found through a different approach.

## II. CD VII:13

Let us begin with a look at the reception within the Damascus Document (CD) which quotes the phrase in question from Isa 8:14 in CD VII:12 and combines it with Isa 7:17.

09 וכל המואסים בפקד אל את הארץ להשיב גמול רשעים
10 עליהם בבוא הדבר אשר כתוב בדברי ישעיה בן אמוץ הנביא
11 אשר אמר יבוא עליך ועל עמך ועל בית אביך ימים אשר <לא>
12 באו מיום סור אפרים מעל יהודה בהפרד שני בתי ישראל
13 שר אפרים מעל יהודה וכל הנסוגים הוסגרו לחרב והמחזיקים
14 נמלטו לארץ צפון

[13] Quotations from Wildberger, *Isaiah 1–12*, 360; idem, *Jesaja*, 339–40.

[14] Peter Höffken, *Das Buch Jesaja: Kapitel 1–39* (Neuer Stuttgarter Kommentar Altes Testament 18/1; Stuttgart: Katholisches Bibelwerk GmbH, 1993), 102: "Die Rede von den 'zwei Häusern Israels' ist ungewöhnlich und vielleicht Anzeichen schon erheblich nachjesajanischer Zeit."

[15] Wolfgang Werner, "Vom Prophetenwort zur Prophetentheologie. Ein redaktionsgeschichtlicher Versuch zu Jes 6,1–8,16," *BZ* (NS) 29 (1985): 1–30 (7–11).

[16] Jörg Barthel, *Prophetenwort und Geschichte: Die Jesajaüberlieferung in Jes 6–8 und 28–31* (FAT 19; Tübingen: Mohr Siebeck, 1997), 217, 219–20.

> 9 But all those who despise shall be rewarded with the retribution of the wicked when God visits the land, 10 when the word shall come which is written in the words of Isaiah, son of Amoz, the prophet, 11 who says: 'There shall come days upon you and upon your people and upon your father's house, such as did [not] 12 come since the day Ephraim departed from Judah.' When the two houses of Israel were divided, 13 Ephraim deviated from Judah, and all the apostates were given up to the sword, but those who held fast, 14 escaped to the land of the north.

The combination of quotations from Isa 7:17 and 8:14 opens a kind of midrash or pesher which also quotes and interprets Amos 5:25–26; 9:11, and Num 24:17. This midrash is part of the last three or, if one also takes 4QD[a] (4Q266) 1 into account, four exhortations which open CD (4QD[a] 1–4 par; CD I–VIII/XIX–XX), before the laws for the community of the 'new covenant' begin (4QD[a] 5–11 par; CD XV–XVI; IX–XIV). Just at that place where we find the quotations from Isaiah, the textual tradition differs enormously. The quotations from Isaiah and the following Amos-Numbers Midrash are only attested in one of the medieval manuscripts of CD, A VII, but not in the manuscript B XIX, where, instead, we find quotations from Zechariah (13:7; 11:11) and Ezekiel (9:4).[17] There has been much speculation about the relationship of the two versions.[18] Many reasons, however, support the hypothesis that we have the earlier version, at least in respect to the Isaiah quotations, in manuscript A, which has been secondarily augmented by the Amos-Numbers Midrash and which has also been literarily edited in manuscript B.[19]

The combination of Isa 8:14 with Isa 7:17 in CD VII is most informative for the understanding of the expression 'the two houses of Israel.' The quotations are to be found within the third or fourth exhortation respectively (A II:14–VIII:21, with a continuation in B XIX:34b–XX:34 and 4Q266 4:9–13). For the author of CD and his contemporaries the fulfilment of the

[17] The parallel manuscripts 4Q266 and 4Q269, which only begin with VII,16 at the place in question, support the version of A but do not contribute anything to the clarification of the relationship between the two versions A and B.

[18] See Stephen Hultgren, *From the Damascus Covenant to the Covenant of the Community: Literary, Historical, and Theological Studies in the Dead Sea Scrolls* (STDJ 66; Leiden: Brill, 2007), 5–41; Menahem Kister, "The Development of the Early Recensions of the Damascus Document," *DSD* 14 (2007): 61–76; Christian Metzenthin, *Jesaja-Auslegung in Qumran* (ATANT 98; Zürich: Theologischer Verlag Zürich, 2010), 139–52. A comprehensive comparison is offered by Jean Carmignac, "Comparaison entre les manuscrits 'A' et 'B' du Document de Damas," *RevQ* 5 (1959): 53–67; Sidnie A. White, "A Comparison of the 'A' and 'B' Manuscripts of the Damascus Document," *RevQ* 48 (1987): 537–53.

[19] See Reinhard G. Kratz, "Jesaja in den Texten vom Toten Meer," in *Prophetenstudien: Kleine Schriften II* (FAT 74; Tübingen: Mohr Siebeck, 2011), 243–271.

prophetic sayings lies in the future, and they are introduced as proof of the future fate of 'those who despise.'[20] For them the days are announced which the prophet Isaiah once announced to the king of Judah (Ahaz), his people, and the house of his fathers, comparing them with the day when Ephraim split with Judah.[21] The split of Ephraim with Judah—i.e., the so-called division of the two kingdoms which in the prophetic announcement is the point of comparison with the judgment of the dynasty of Judah and in the biblical (deuteronomistic) historiography is designated as 'the sin of Jeroboam' which caused the downfall of Israel and Judah as well as the exile as a consequence—serves here as an example of the 'retribution of the wicked' yet to come. 'Those who despise' and the 'wicked' take over, so to say, the role of the dynasty of Judah in Isa 7:17, to whom the future judgement is being announced with reference to the past biblical history. The *tertium comparationis* is not only the split of Ephraim from Judah and the damage to the Judaean dynasty but, in particular, the fate of the 'apostates' (CD VII:14) of earlier times which will hit 'those who despise' today, just like the prophecy of Isaiah according to Isa 7:17 should hit the dynasty of Judah.

The following reference to Isa 8:14 has the purpose of underlining the analogy. Just as at the time of the division of the two kingdoms when the 'two houses of Israel' split, Ephraim splitting from Judah, and the apostates were delivered to the sword, so also will this happen to the king of Judah, his people, and the house of his fathers according to the word of the prophet and, during the future 'visitation of the land,' also to 'those who despise' and to the 'apostates' of present-day Judah which leave the covenant and the law. They, too, will be, as one should assume, delivered to the sword.[22] From the combination with Isa 7:17 it becomes clear that in CD VII the 'two houses of Israel' are thought of as the two monarchies, Ephraim and Judah, the separation of which, however, is seen as a shame

[20] On the absolute use of מאס see Ps 89:39; Job 42:6. There has been much discussion about whether this was an outsider or an apostate of the community of Qumran. See Philip. R. Davies, *The Damascus Covenant: An Interpretation of the "Damascus Document"* (JSOT 25; Sheffield: JSOT Press, 1983), 143–72; Jerome Murphy-O'Connor, "The Damascus Document Revisited," *RB* 92 (1985): 223–46; Hultgren, *Covenant*, 5–41. Looking at the context, it seems to me absolutely clear that only in VIII:1b the apostates of the community come into view.

[21] In CD VII:11–12 the לא of the biblical text is missing; see, however CD XIV:1.

[22] The version B differs in that the quotations from Zechariah aim directly at the future judgement of "those who despise" and only then draw a parallel to the "earlier visitation" to Israel (Judah), referring to Ezekiel. In both versions no differentiation within the community can be observed.

and, indeed, as a sin against God. The split between the two 'houses' is seen as an offence against the biblical idea of the unity of the kingdom under David and Solomon and, therefore, as an offence against the biblical idea of the divinely chosen one and whole people of 'Israel.' In CD the offence and the fate of the king of Judah in Isa 7:17 as well as of the opponent against the community in his own people, i.e., 'those who despise' and the 'apostates,' are seen as analogy to the division of the two kingdoms and the divine punishment which would follow this offence.

Qumran scholarship wants to see even more in this analogy. It tends to find in the kingdoms of Judah and Ephraim and the 'two houses of Israel' in CD VII:10–13 ciphers or sobriquets which would be identified historically with certain political or religious parties at the time of CD. Thus, one identifies 'Judah' as the 'Community of the New Covenant,' the group responsible for CD, and 'Ephraim' as their opponent in the 1st century BC, the Pharisees. Based on this identification, Menahem Kister suggested that we should apply the 'two houses of Israel' in CD VII:13 not to Judah and Ephraim but to Ephraim and Manasseh; in the Pesharim of Qumran these are codes for Pharisees and Sadducees, from which 'Judah,' i.e., the members of the community of Qumran and 'the new covenant,'[23] separated.[24] To me, however, this hypothesis seems to read more into the text of CD than is actually in it. The hypothesis is based on the presupposition that the sobriquets of the Pesharim may be applied to CD and overlooks the contextual embedding of the quotation of Isa 7:17 which relates the judgement, i.e., the fate of the king of Judah, to the opponents of the community. There is no talk about Manasseh either in Isa 7:17, 8:14 or in CD VII, and there is no relation to Isa 9:19–20 where we find the constellation of Ephraim against Manasseh, and both against Judah.

Thus, we must take it that Judah and Ephraim are first of all geographical and political entities in biblical history.[25] As such they are also mentioned in CD, where the conflict in 'Israel' between Ephraim and Judah, i.e., the 'two houses of Israel,' serves as an historical example for the conflict between the community of the (new) covenant and its opponents

---

[23] They are identical with the 'I' in Isa 8:11 or the 'us' of Isa 8:11 in 1QIsa[a]; see also CD A VIII:16 = B XIX:26; 4QMidrEschat[a] (4Q174) III:14; 11Q13 (Melch) II:23–24.

[24] Menahem Kister, "Biblical Phrases and Hidden Biblical Interpretations and Pesharim," in *The Dead Sea Scrolls. Forty Years of Research* (ed. Devorah Dimant and Uriel Rappaport; STDJ 10; Jerusalem/Leiden: Magnes/Brill, 1992), 27–39 (35–37).

[25] See Reinhard G. Kratz, "Der Pescher Nahum und seine biblische Vorlage," in *Prophetenstudien: Kleine Schriften II* (FAT 74; Tübingen: Mohr Siebeck, 2011), 99–145.

within Judah. CD, therefore, differs substantially from the (older) way of speaking in QS, QH, and QM where the name of 'Israel' is used exclusively, and it initiates a differentiation within 'Israel,' historically speaking in Judah, by means of the biblical entities Ephraim and Judah. These entities are, however, not (yet) identified with certain groups in 'Israel' or Judah respectively.

The use of the geographical, political, and sociological names of Judah, Ephraim and Manasseh as a code for the different parties of Judaism in the 1st century BC, we do not find in CD but first in the Pesharim of Qumran, which are later.[26] If we are not mistaken, the way from the historical example in CD VII to the contemporary code can be comprehended even within the Pesharim. Thus, 1QpMi (1Q14) and 4QpHos[b] (4Q167), where the conflict of Judah and Ephraim is given in the biblical text, may indicate the beginning of a trend to relate this conflict to that of the Qumran community with its opponents within Judah ('Israel'), the Pharisees. This is probably presupposed in 4QpPs[a] (4Q171) and 4QpNah (4Q169), where the conflict is introduced without any reference to the biblical text, and in 4QpNah where it is evaluated in different directions with Ephraim and Manasseh (Pharisees and Sadducees) and other groups within 'Ephraim' itself in view (מתעי אפרים and פתאי אפרים). Judah and Ephraim, the 'two houses of Israel,' have thus become ciphers, which, however, have not lost their identity as representatives of the biblical 'Israel' by any means, not even in the Pesharim.

## III. Isaiah 8:14

The combination of Isa 7:17 with 8:14 in CD VII is an important hint for where to look for the solution of the problem of the expression 'the two houses of Israel' in the text of Isa 8:14 itself. The text-critical, historical, or literary-critical speculations in respect to this verse are, therefore, superfluous. Also, the isolated look at 8:11–15 as a 'small unit' (*kleine Einheit*) of the oral preaching of the historical prophet[27] or the literary-critical fragmentation and bold rephrasing of the text, as suggested by Walter Dietrich,[28] have but rather little probability. The answer to our question

26 See Metzenthin, *Jesaja-Auslegung*, 195–266.

27 Barthel, *Prophetenwort*, 216–27.

28 Walter Dietrich, *Jesaja und die Politik* (BEvT 74; München: Kaiser, 1976), 69–74, 96–97.

of who or what are 'the two houses of Israel' in Isa 8:14, may be found in the context and, therefore, in the composition of the book of Isaiah itself. It is here where the differentiation between the names of Israel, Ephraim, Judah etc. play an important role, as I have tried to show elsewhere.[29]

The pericope Isa 8:11–15 is placed at the end of the so-called memorandum of Isaiah (*Denkschrift*) in chs. 6–8, which have a rather complicated history.[30] Isaiah 6 and 8:1–8 can, disregarding some supplements, be taken as the core of the memorandum, and 8:16–18 as its original conclusion. The word of salvation in Isa 8:(8b), 9–10[31] and the complete chapter of Isa 7 (with its literary core in 7:1–9), which in terms of style and content is differentiated from its context in Isa 6 and 8 and which is also followed by several supplements (e.g., 8:18),[32] are generally considered to be later insertions.

The beginning of the literary development could have been a word of salvation by the prophet Isaiah for Judah from the time of the so-called Syro-Ephraimite war at the end of the 8th century BC (8:1–4), to which one may factually add also 7:4 and 7:7–9a (and 17:1–6; 28:1–4). In the context of the memorandum, the word of salvation in Isa 8:1–4 was put into a literary context by the supplement (*Fortschreibung*) in 8:5–8 and the framing by Isa 6 and 8:16–18. In this frame the original oracle of salvation was interpreted as an oracle of doom. Not only Samaria, the enemy in the north of Judah, but (also) Judah itself was going to be destroyed according to the will of YHWH. The original oracle of salvation of the prophet is meant to close the eyes and ears of 'this people' so that it would not escape by any means the catastrophe, which God had decided for them (6:9–10).[33]

---

[29] See Reinhard G. Kratz, "Israel in the Book of Isaiah," *JSOT* 31 (2006): 103–28.

[30] On the analysis see Hermann Barth, *Die Jesaja-Worte in der Josiazeit: Israel und Assur als Thema einer produktiven Neuinterpretation der Jesajaüberlieferung* (WMANT 48; Neukirchen-Vluyn: Neukirchener Verlag, 1977); Uwe Becker, *Jesaja—von der Botschaft zum Buch* (FRLANT 178; Göttingen: Vandenhoeck & Ruprecht, 1997); Barthel, *Prophetenwort*; Thomas Wagner, *Gottes Herrschaft: Eine Analyse der Denkschrift (Jes 6,1–9,6)* (*VTSup* 108; Leiden: Brill, 2006); Matthijs. J. de Jong, *Isaiah among the Ancient Near Eastern Prophets: A Comparative Study of the Earliest Stages of the Isaiah Tradition and the Neo-Assyrian Prophecies* (VTSup 117; Leiden: Brill, 2007).

[31] Becker, *Jesaja*, 109–110; for 8:9–10, see also Barthel, *Prophetenwort*, 208–15; de Jong, *Isaiah*, 72–73.

[32] Becker, *Jesaja*, 21–60; see also Barthel, *Prophetenwort*, 62–63, 192–93.

[33] See Kratz, "Israel"; idem, "Das Neue in der Prophetie des Alten Testaments," in *Prophetie in Israel: Beiträge des Symposiums "Das Alte Testament und die Kultur der Moderne" anlässlich des 100. Geburtstags Gerhard von Rads (1901–1971) Heidelberg, 18–21 Oktober 2001* (ed. Irmtraud Fischer, Konrad Schmid, H. G. M. Williamson; Altes Testament und Moderne 11; Münster: LIT, 2003), 1–22.

As far as the literary addenda are concerned, it is Isa 7, and especially 7:17, which is of particular interest for our question. Only with Isa 7, which borrows from the relevant chapter in 2 Kgs 16, do we see an integration of the conflict between Ephraim and Judah into the framework of the biblical history. Also the historical memory of the division of the two kingdoms in Isa 7:17 serves this purpose and is the example used to warn that the conflict between Ephraim and Judah will be a disaster for both of them. According to the literary fiction of the book of Isaiah, which probably refers to 701 BC (Isa 36-39), this disaster fits the situation of the Syro-Ephraimite war as well as the downfall of Judah and Jerusalem (2 Kgs 20–25), which follows the division of the two kingdoms (1 Kgs 12–14) and the downfall of Israel (2 Kgs 17) due to the 'sin of Jeroboam.'

Among scholars it is disputed where within the literary-historical development of Isa 6–8 the piece 8:11–15 had to be placed. Some would attribute it to the prophet himself and his original memorandum.[34] Others hold that it is a later supplement, which also in itself is not a literary unity.[35] The second possibility is supported by the fact that the text gives up the usual opposition between God and his prophet on the one side and Ephraim or 'this people' (Judah) on the other side, and that there is for the first time a differentiation within the people between the person addressed by the prophet and 'this people,' meaning here all of Israel and not just Judah as in Isa 6 and 8:1–9. This differentiation has been taken up and expanded by the tradition of Qumran (1QIsa[a] et al.) as well as the rendering of the Septuagint. In both traditions the prophet and his followers have become a group of pious people obeying the Torah and separating themselves from 'this people.'[36]

The pericope shows some literary connections with its context in Isa 6–8. Referring to his call in Isa 6, the role of the prophet gets a new definition. According to this, the prophet is responsible not only in the sense of the mission of Isa 6:9–10 (see also 8:11) in order to lay out the snares for Ephraim and Judah (8:14–15), but also to open up the possibility to escape from the judgement for a chosen group of people (vv. 12–13). This group

[34] Barthel, *Prophetenwort*, 216–27.

[35] Becker, *Jesaja*, 110–14; see also de Jong, *Isaiah*, 70–71.

[36] More on this and the relevant literature in Kratz, "Jesaja in den Texten vom Toten Meer." On the separation of different groups within Isa 8:11–14 and whether they are to be identified with "the two houses of Israel" or not see already Vitringa, *Commentarius*, 267 (editio nova, 219) discussing Kimchi's explanation of the problem to whom God 'shall be for a sanctuary' and to whom 'a stone men strike against.'

seems to be supposed to be the 'disciples' and 'children' of the prophet from 8:16–18. In 8:11–15 they do not only appear as the ones who represent the prophetic tradition or as signs and portents of the judgement, but they themselves are being addressed and exhorted to obey the law and to fear God. Insofar, this text is rather in line with the word of salvation Isa 8:8b–10, with the difference that here the whole land is protected by God and Immanuel from the peoples, and there it is only a chosen group to be saved within 'this people' which has become the enemy of YHWH in vv. 11–15.[37]

Furthermore, it seems that Isa 8:11–15 and the expression 'the two houses of Israel' also presuppose Isa 7 and the biblical (deuteronomistic) construction of history. As is the case in Isa 8:11 also here the versions (see section I. above) and the early reception (see section II. above) are evidence for the particularity of the text which, as we can see, in CD VII has expressively been associated with Isa 7:17. This association must, however, already have been in view in the text of Isa 8:14 itself. Also here, the unique expression after Isa 7 can mean only the two kingdoms of Ephraim and Judah to which YHWH will become the 'rock men stumble over', and of which the inhabitants of Jerusalem are not to be distinguished but mentioned as a part of them. With 7:17 the verses 8:11–15 look at the conflict between Ephraim and Judah in the sense of the prophet who announces the judgement to both of them as an all-Israel problem. Insofar, one may say with Jörg Barthel: "The announcement of the judgement summarizes the words against the northern (8,1–4; see also 7,1–9a.16) and the southern kingdom (8,5–8 [one may add: and 7:17])."[38] However, in view of the differences this does not speak for the authenticity of the unity at all but, rather to the contrary, that it is a literary supplement, which does not only give the role of the prophet a new definition and introduces a special group of disciples of the prophet, but also, following Isa 7, pinpoints the implications of the memorandum for all Israel: "This prophecy is in truth a retrospective judgment on the causes of the decline of the 'two houses of Israel' . . ."[39]

The all-Israel perspective was, at least in a certain phase, a particular concern of the tradition. This is shown also by the literary extensions in Isa 5 and 9–10, which have been composed in a double ring fashion (5:25–

---

[37] Barthel, *Prophetenwort*, 227.

[38] Barthel, *Prophetenwort*, 220: "Die Gerichtsankündigung faßt die vorangehenden Worte gegen das Nord- (8:1–4; vgl. 7:1–9a.16) und das Südreich (8:5–8) zusammen."

[39] Kaiser, *Book*, 192; idem, *Buch*, 186.

30/9:7–20 and 5:1–24/10:1–4) around the memorandum.[40] There are in particular two texts which expressively articulate this concern: the famous Song of the Vineyard in Isa 5:1–7 and the poetic account in Isa 9:7–20, to which also 10:27b–32 may be added.[41] We can see in both texts how within the book of Isaiah a concept of all-Israel is being drawn up and becomes formulated in even greater detail, which transfers the prophet's sayings about the two kingdoms, Ephraim and Judah, to a new, also terminologically comprehensive concept of (all-)'Israel.' In my opinion, this development also explains the expression 'the two houses of Israel,' which combines and highlights both the two kingdoms and the ideal of a unified 'Israel.' The concept of all-Israel developed in different directions in the course of the literary history of the book of Isaiah.[42] It remained, however, preserved up to the later prophecies of salvation and the areas of Deutero- and Trito-Isaiah, and offered a possibility, together with the increasing distinction between the wicked and the righteous one within the people of Israel, for the reception and interpretation of Isa 7:17 and 8:14 in the textual history as well as in CD VII and the further development in the Pesharim.

[40] See Becker, *Jesaja*, 124–60; for a different interpretation see Barthel (*Prophetenwort*, 46–51) who basically follows Barth, *Jesaja-Worte*.

[41] See Erhard Blum, "Jesajas prophetisches Testament: Beobachtungen zu Jes 1–11 (Teil II)," *ZAW* 109 (1997): 12–29 (17–19).

[42] See Kratz, "Israel"; idem, "Rewriting Isaiah: The Case of Isaiah 28–31," in *Prophecy and the Prophets in Ancient Israel* (ed. John Day; Proceedings of the Oxford Old Testament Seminar; London: T&T Clark International, 2010), 245–66.

# 'I AM LIKE A LUXURIANT JUNIPER': LANGUAGE ABOUT GOD IN HOSEA

J. G. McConville

## I. Yahweh and the Image of a Tree

Hosea 14:9b [Eng. 8b] contains the only case in the Hebrew Bible in which YAHWEH is likened to a tree: "I am like a luxuriant juniper" (אני כברוש רענן).[1] As most commentators note, this is remarkable in view of the Hebrew Bible's usual caution about trees in the context of worship. Some interpreters of the present passage find it so disturbing that they attempt to mitigate the force of it in certain ways. Macintosh, for example, finds it "most unlikely that Hosea would be inclined to make such use of the simile." He therefore takes Hos 14:9 [Eng. 8] as a dialogue between YAHWEH and Ephraim, so that the second half of the verse reads: "[Ephraim] 'I am like a luxuriant juniper.' [YAHWEH] 'It is from me that your fruit will be assured.' "[2] Already the Targum had transferred the image to Ephraim, with its rendering of verse 9b [Eng. 8b] as "I, by my Memra, will make them like a beautiful cypress tree," and its introduction of a messianic figure.[3] B. Seifert, in her work on metaphors for God in Hosea, thinks that the tree-image serves the purpose of attributing to YAHWEH powers that in the Canaanite world were attributed to other gods. However, she finds that the book's typical use of simile for YAHWEH, with the preposition כ as here in כברוש, has a mitigating effect, guarding against the possibility of attributing mythological concepts to YAHWEH. For good measure, she also makes Hos 14:6–9 [Eng. 5–8] 'post-Hosean,' and its divine metaphors distinct from Hosea's own, which are informed, in her view, by historical thinking.[4]

---

[1] I am delighted to dedicate this essay to Hugh Williamson, in deep appreciation both of an old friendship and of his enormous contribution to the understanding of Hebrew, the prophets, and the theology of the Old Testament.

[2] Andrew A. Macintosh, *Hosea* (ICC; Edinburgh: T&T Clark, 1997), 576–77.

[3] Ehud Ben Zvi, *Hosea* (FOTL XXIA/1; Grand Rapids: Eerdmans, 2005), 308; Kevin J. Cathcart and Robert P. Gordon, *Targum of the Minor Prophets* (ArBib 14; Collegeville, MN: Liturgical Press, 1989), 61–62.

[4] Brigitte Seifert, *Metaphorisches Reden von Gott im Hoseabuch* (FRLANT 166; Göttingen: Vandenhoeck & Ruprecht, 1996), 251, 259, 262. A number of scholars see Hos 14:5–9 [Eng. 4–8] *in toto* as secondary; see Ben Zvi (*Hosea*, 301) for a range of scholarly views.

Are commentators right to be nervous about this particular image? Part of the context of the question is the book's range of metaphorical language for God, who is variously husband and parent of Israel (Hos 1–3; 11:1–4), several ferocious animals that tear and devour (5:14; 13:7–8), a moth or maggot, and rottenness (5:12), rain and dew (6:3; 14:6 [Eng. 5]). The persona of YAHWEH in the book is conveyed extensively by metaphorical language, much of it provocative.

The use of the tree-image for YAHWEH has a further dimension in the modern scholarly recognition of the complex relationship between metaphorical language and the reality that it seeks to express. Macintosh calls Hosea 'a master of language,' and speaks of the 'mystery' of his speech.[5] And indeed, mystery and mastery are inseparable here, for there is no easy passage in Hosea from language to meaning. The language draws attention to itself, so as to suggest that it is inescapably part of the meaning. It has an adventurous quality, exemplified in the range of daring metaphors used for YAHWEH, as already noted, and also in other kinds of verbal dexterity. Macintosh documents rhetorical repetition (e.g., ענה in 2:23–24 [Eng. 21–22]), alliteration and assonance (e.g. סררה סרר ישראל, 4:16), and word-play. The name Ephraim (אפרים), for example, attracts several word-plays, including פרא, 'wild ass' (8:9), פרה, 'heifer' (4:16–17), פרי 'fruit'/'fruitful' (9:16), רפא, 'heal' (11:3),[6] and also פרח, 'flourish' (14:8 [Eng. 7]). These word-plays on Ephraim, mostly also based on metaphors or similes, are part of the powerful prophetic depiction of Ephraim's situation, evoking variously the people's aimlessness, stubbornness, inability to embrace the full, rich life that YAHWEH intended for his people, or to recognize where their chief good lay. Yet in the end they would indeed 'flourish' (14:8 [Eng. 7]).

## II. THE TREE-IMAGE AND HOSEA'S LINGUISTIC WEB

Figurative speech in the book does not consist simply in individual tropes, however, but in an interweaving of expression which defies complete description. Chapter 14 echoes motifs that run through the preceding discourse. Ben Zvi finds in 14:2–9 [Eng. 1–8] "a system of textual signposts,"

[5] Macintosh, *Hosea*, lxi.
[6] Macintosh, *Hosea*, lxiv.

which "conveys much of the meaning of the book of Hosea as a whole."[7] The first clue to a reading of the chapter comes at vv. 2–3 [Eng. 1–2], with the double exhortation to 'return' (שובה ישראל...ושובו אל־יהוה). This is echoed in v. 5 [Eng. 4] with another double use of שוב, in which YAHWEH first declares that he will 'heal' Israel's 'faithlessness' (משובתם, a form which connotes Israel's frequent or habitual 'turning' away from him), and then that his anger has 'turned back' (שב) from them. This word-play corresponds to a complex development of the theme of 'return' in the book, including Israel's failure to do so (5:4; 11:5, 7), their 'turning' to Baal (7:16), their 'returning' to Egypt (8:13; 11:5), YAHWEH's 'turning' away from them in anger (5:15), and indications of a successful future 'return' of Israel to YAHWEH (3:5; cf. 2:16–25 [Eng. 14–23]). Israel's ultimate 'returning' to YAHWEH has never been certain of accomplishment. In 6:11–7:1, for example, the notion of YAHWEH's taking an initiative to 'return' Israel to himself meets resistance. The re-emergence of the theme in ch. 14 now looks, at last, like closure. The correlation of שוב, 'return,' and רפא, 'heal,' in both 14:5 [Eng. 4] and 6:11b–7:1a, and the word-play אפרים/רפא in the latter place, strengthens the sense that the discourse of ch. 14 is shaped in relation to the development of the theme up to that point.

The sense of a definitive change in Israel's fortunes comes at v. 5 [Eng. 4]), in which Yahweh himself becomes the speaker and remains so to the end of the poem. The new action and attitude which he announces are signalled plainly, not only in the convergence of 'healing' and 'turning,' but also in his declaration that he will 'love them freely,' with its echoes of his former frustrated love and their misdirection of theirs. This declaration is given strength and texture by the web of verbal echoes in the discourse.

The tree-image in 14:9 [Eng. 8] is part of this linguistic web, and the culmination of a range of tree-imagery in the book. In ch. 2, fruit-bearing trees, along with other food crops, are part of what is at stake in the controversy between YAHWEH and Baal, and a word of judgment threatens to return the cultivated trees of the land back to untamed forest, capable only of sustaining wild creatures (2:14 [Eng. 12]). Oaks, poplars, and terebinths symbolize the misguided worship that Hosea castigates, and offer a

[7] Ben Zvi, *Hosea*, 291. He identifies an array of verbal resonances between ch. 14 and the rest of the book, including: כשלת בעונך (14:2 [Eng. 1]), cf. 4:5; כל תשא עון, (14:3 [Eng. 2], cf. 4:8; 'healing' 14:5 [Eng. 4], cf. 5:13; 6:1; 7:1; 11:3; 14:9) ענה [Eng. 8], cf. 2:23–24 [Eng. 21–22]; טל (v. 6 [Eng. 5], cf. 6:4; 13:3); שרש, v. 6 [Eng. 5], cf. 9:16; דגן, v. 8 [Eng. 7], cf. 2:10, 11, 24 [Eng. 8, 9, 22], cf. 7:14, 8:7; 9:1; Ben Zvi, *Hosea*, 291, 297.

'shade' which seems good to the people (4:13). Related imagery speaks of failed fertility (9:2) and return to wildness (9:6; 10:8). In the latter chapters, tree-images become more directly predicated of Israel. It is like the fruit of vine and fig tree (9:10); then a tree whose root has dried up, so that it yields no fruit (9:16); then a vine, whose fruitfulness ironically matches its religious perversity (10:1). YAHWEH's speech in the final poem (14:6–8 [Eng. 5–7]) concentrates tree-images so as both to lead up to v. 9 [Eng. 8] and also to echo language that has occurred previously. The striking three-fold appearance of Lebanon attributes the grandeur of its proverbially majestic trees to Israel, and the people is depicted besides as flourishing like lily, olive, and vine. Here is an Edenic scene, having affinities with the Song of Songs, in which barrenness and devastation have turned again to life in its richness and beauty. Israel is now in the presence of YAHWEH, who is not only life-giving 'dew' (v. 6 [Eng. 5]), in a re-application of a previously negative image (6:4; 13:3), but also towers over all, for Israel shall dwell beneath his 'shadow' (not the false shade given by pretenders, 4:13), a first hint of YAHWEH's attribution of a tree-image to himself.

The first half of v. 9 [Eng. 8] switches to direct address to Ephraim. This line poses its own difficulties for the interpreter, but it is clear, I think, that it makes a final pointed antithesis between YAHWEH and other gods or putative sources of life.[8] The line serves rhetorically to allow a pause before YAHWEH's closing words and thus heighten their impact. In the second line then, the predication of YAHWEH as being like an evergreen tree is part of a declaration of his own capacity to sustain Israel rather than anyone else's, as is also evident in the prominent placement of ממני ('from me'), at the beginning of the second half-line.

The tree itself is not just any tree, but a ברוש רענן. The tree has been variously taken as cypress, cedar and (perhaps likeliest) juniper,[9] and is in any case one of the tall trees of Lebanon (cf. 1 Kgs 5:22 [Eng. 8]). The image of YAHWEH as ברוש therefore makes a connection with the luxuriance of

[8] In the difficult verse 9 [Eng. 8], MT's dissociation of YAHWEH from idols (MT) is sometimes transposed to Ephraim; Macintosh, *Hosea*, 576; LXX. Ben Zvi (*Hosea*, 299) finds the possible meanings converging: Ephraim "will not be joined to idols any more," nor "confuse its deity/provider with them."

[9] The last is preferred by, among others, Macintosh (*Hosea*, 576, 581) and Oestreich, who specifies *juniperus excelsa*, because it fits his criteria of a majestic tree, suitable for large building projects, such as the construction of the temple, where the ברוש had to be imported from Lebanon along with the cedar (1 Kgs 5:22, 24 [Eng. 8, 10]), and thus was not native to Palestine; Bernhard Oestreich, *Metaphors and Similes for YAHWEH in Hosea 14:2–9(1–8): A Study of Hoseanic Pictorial Language* (Friedensauer Schriftenreihe. Reihe A, Theologie 1; Peter Lang, Frankfurt, 1998), 192–95.

Lebanon predicated of Israel in vv. 6–8 [Eng. 5–7], and so belongs to the picture of mutual intimacy between YAHWEH and Israel that is being built up in the poem. As a majestic tree, the 'juniper' is probably a metaphor for a king, who is powerful to care and protect, and who can secure peace and order.[10] The adjective רענן, 'luxuriant,' may connote particularly the shade given by the great tree, a function of royal protection.[11] The words of YAHWEH continue somewhat unexpectedly, however, with "from me comes your fruit" (ממני פריך נמצא), since the ברוש is not a fruit-tree. There is no prosaic inconsistency here; rather, the shift in the image illustrates the capacity of metaphor for rapid change and development. The essentially royal metaphor is joined, as Oestreich has argued, with traditions about creation and Paradise, by means of the motif of Lebanon.[12] Not only is YAHWEH Israel's true ruler and protector, but also the people draws its very life from its intimate relationship with him.

YAHWEH's comparison of himself to a 'luxuriant juniper,' therefore, pulls together certain strands in the book. It is he, not another, who is Israel's true protector and provider. His relationship with them is set in the land, indeed in the creation, which is his to give, together with its capacity for fruitfulness, and over which he holds sway. That relationship, moreover, is close and intimate, as portrayed by the notion of Israel's fruitful life deriving from the life of YAHWEH himself. Fruitfulness here may be taken in a broad sense, to embrace all manner of human flourishing; yet the fruitfulness of land is at the core of this. These words of Yahweh, and the poem as a whole, help articulate the book's theology of 'reversal,' or 'turning' (14:5 [Eng. 4], cf. 14:8 [Eng. 7]).[13]

## III. The Tree-Image and Human Metaphors for God

A further question arises, however, from the book's closure with this particular metaphor, namely, how does it relate to the dominant human metaphors for God in the prophecy? Since human metaphors have attended some of the most powerful moments in the depiction of YAHWEH, why

---

[10] Oestreich, *Metaphors*, 212–13.

[11] Oestreich, *Metaphors*, 216.

[12] Oestreich, *Metaphors*, 218–22. He argues that Lebanon can symbolize a fruitful garden and the abode of God (Ps 80:11 [Eng. 10]; 104:16; Ezek 31:9, 16, 18); Oestreich, *Metaphors*, 219; cf. v. 3 in the same chapter.

[13] See Ben Zvi, *Hosea*, 291, 305; Göran Eidevall, *Grapes in the Desert: Metaphors, Models and Themes in Hosea 4–14* (ConBOT 43; Stockholm, Almqvist & Wiksell, 1996), 240–42.

does the book close on a completely different note, especially one that is so dramatic?

The answer to this lies, I believe, in the nature of metaphor itself. Metaphors can suggest new ways of seeing, by bringing entities imaginatively into new relationships with each other. But by the same token they convey that there is more to understanding any reality than the particular metaphor can achieve. This is true supremely of speech about God, and Hosea's language illustrates the point forcefully. Paradoxically, 'knowledge of God' is one of Hosea's key demands (4:1–3), yet such knowledge is elusive. On one hand, Israel is held to account because of its failure to tell the difference between the worship of YAHWEH and the worship of Baal (2:10 [Eng. 8]—"she did not know…"). A great deal is said about what YAHWEH is like, much of it by YAHWEH himself. Twice he declares: "I am YAHWEH your God, from the land of Egypt" (12:10 [Eng. 9]; 13:4), echoing language of self-disclosure in Exodus, especially Exod 3:14; 20:2, and (in 13:4b) what looks like an allusion to the First Commandment, with its demand of exclusive allegiance (Exod 20:3). This passage leads into one of Hosea's well known reflections on Israel's history with YAHWEH (13:4–8). Twice statements of YAHWEH are made with the personal pronoun in emphatic initial position (vv. 4, 5); and in v. 7, the opening ואהי recalls the אהיה of Exod 3:12, 14.[14] The allusions to what may be taken to be known from history contribute to the portrayal of YAHWEH. The meaning of Hosea, therefore, is predicated on a knowledge of who YAHWEH is.

Yet in spite of the language of disclosure, there remains that which is undisclosed. This is true in a number of ways. It has been observed, for example, that the delineation of YAHWEH from Baal is not as obvious as the rhetoric of exclusive allegiance suggests.[15] It is true of the historical postulates, as well as of the metaphorical language. The history is not simply a given, for it poses some conundrums,[16] and is apparently being created afresh here, while drawing on shared knowledge between author and readership.[17] In the same way, the identity of YAHWEH is constructed in the language of the book. In 13:7, the 'I am' saying, far from introducing

[14] Note BHS, which suggests reading ואהיה, following LXX, and cf. ואקרע in v. 8.

[15] See Yvonne Sherwood, *The Prostitute and The Prophet: Hosea's Marriage in Literary-Theoretical Perspective* (JSOTSup 212; Sheffield: Sheffield Academic, 1996), 251–53.

[16] For example, did YAHWEH first know Israel in Egypt (11:1; 12:10 [Eng. 9]; 13:4), or in the wilderness (9:10)? How does the judgment saying about Jehu (12:4) relate to the story of his zeal for YAHWEH in 2 Kgs 10?

[17] On the use of place names in 5:1–2, 8; 6:7–9, see Ben Zvi, *Hosea*, 139.

a promise of divine protective presence, continues with metaphors of lion, leopard, and bear waiting to pounce on prey. Historical reflection and metaphorical language combine to ask a hard question about the nature of YAHWEH. As for the metaphors and similes used for YAHWEH, we have noticed above their range and provocative nature. They both make sharp points and draw attention to the limitations of such language to disclose him fully. If YAHWEH is like a lion, there is also some sense in which he is not like a lion. Furthermore, YAHWEH who is like a lion is also like a husband, or dew, or a maggot. None of these, obviously, is absolute. There is even mobility within metaphors, as when YAHWEH the lion who tears his prey (5:14; 13:7–8) can elsewhere be the lion who roars as he accompanies his people protectively home from exile (11:10). Similarly, the great tree of 14:9 [Eng. 8] connotes both royal protector and giver of life, the force of the image being composed, not entirely by meanings attributable to it from usage of the image in general, but in part by its place in the discourse of Hosea as a whole.

Hosea demonstrates an awareness of both the power and the limitations of language in the portrayal of the deity. This is equally true of the human metaphors for God, which play a leading part in the book and are in an important sense different in kind from other metaphors. For a human being to hear that God is like a human being is in the nature of the case different from their hearing that God is like a lion or a tree. The close affinity between God and human beings is present otherwise in Israel's theological traditions in the notion of humans as the 'image of God' (Gen 1:26–28), as well as in visions of the deity (Exod 24; Isa 6:1–8), and in anthropomorphic theophanies (e.g., Gen 18; Josh 5:13–14; Judg 13). The human metaphor for YAHWEH, therefore, is at first glance as unsurprising as certain others are surprising. However, it too partakes of some of the features of language about God that we have already observed.

In an extended analogy in chs. 1–3, YAHWEH's love for Israel is likened to that of a husband for his unfaithful wife (explicitly in 3:1). In the same place, the image shades over to his love (after anger) for the children of the unfaithful wife, who in their turn stand in the place of Israel (1:8–9; 2:1–2 [Eng. 1:10–11]). The parental image re-emerges in ch. 11, in the prophecy's most compelling expression of the divine love. Already we see something of the mobility or instability of Hosea's metaphorical language for God even in this central trope. Indeed, its precise nature in chs. 1–3 is more elusive than appears at first. Is the woman a wife or a harlot? Who are the 'children,' and do they stand with YAHWEH or against him (2:4–6

[Eng. 2–4])?[18] Interpretation of the sexual imagery applied to YAHWEH's love for Israel has seen a significant shift in recent scholarship. Whereas it used to be common to find an occasion for the depiction of Israel as unfaithful wife and prostitute in supposed sexual practices in the cult of Baal,[19] the connection between sexual image and religious practice has now been widely challenged. The grounds for this include the paucity of evidence for the alleged cultic practices, the fact that they have been largely spun out of the language of Hosea in the first place, and the specifically linguistic difficulty of pressing the recalcitrant images logically into the mould that the theory requires.[20]

## IV. "I AM GOD AND NOT A MAN"

There is a further striking clue to the status of the human metaphor for YAHWEH, in two contrary statements involving the term איש, 'man.' In 2:16–25 [Eng. 14–23], where YAHWEH speaks of his intention to draw Israel back into relationship with himself, he says: "... in that day... you will call me 'my husband' [אישי] and no longer 'my baal' [בעלי] (2:18 [Eng. 16])." This makes sense within the controversy with Baal-worship because both words are capable of meaning 'husband.' Even so, the attribution of the term איש to YAHWEH is the strongest anthropomorphism in the elaboration of human metaphors in chs. 1–3.

In stark antithesis to this stands Hos 11:9. Chapter 11 to this point is strongly anthropomorphic. YAHWEH has loved his child, his son Ephraim, whom he called out of Egypt (11:1). The exodus tradition thus alluded to also calls Israel YAHWEH's 'son' (Exod 4:22–23), but the concept is developed here in touching images of parental care for the small child (v. 3). The parent-child metaphor may continue in v. 4 (so NRSV), though

---

18 This aspect of the imagery in chs. 1–3 has been elaborated by Sherwood, *Prostitute*, 245–47.

19 Mays puts it thus: "Here metaphor and reality are almost synonymous"; James L. Mays, *Hosea* (OTL; London: SCM, 1969), 25. See also Hans Walter Wolff, *Hosea: A Commentary on the Book of the Prophet Hosea* (Hermeneia; Philadelphia; Fortress, 1974; German 1965), 14–16; Francis I. Andersen and David Noel Freedman, *Hosea* (AB 24; New York: Doubleday, 1980), 157–58.

20 The argument has been well made by, among others, Alice A. Keefe, *Woman's Body and Social Body in Hosea* (JSOTSup 338; London: Sheffield Academic, 2001), e.g., 73–75. Keefe finds Hosea's concern to lie in the kind of confidence Israel put in alliances and commercial relations with foreign powers, such as Tyre.

MT changes the image to the lifting of a yoke from a beast of burden.[21] Ben Zvi helpfully suggests that the connotation of tenderness to the child can co-exist with MT's strict meaning, because of "the precise, and somewhat unusual, textual choices represented in the expression."[22] This is consonant with what we have seen concerning shifting and mutually supporting metaphors. The notions of 'yoke' and 'child' can even come together in the frame supplied by exodus from, and possible return to, Egypt (vv. 1, 5). In any case, v. 4 contains the strong anthropomorphism: בחבלי אדם אמשכם, "I led them with human ropes/bonds." 'Human bonds' might denote some restraining or guiding lead, but the usage is no doubt metaphorical.[23] In the occurrence of אדם in a speech of YAHWEH about himself we have another remarkable anthropomorphism.

The passage continues with an expression of YAHWEH's resolve to punish his people in anger at their persistent apostasy (vv. 5–7), but then takes a dramatic turn in vv. 8–9. These verses resume the theme of YAHWEH's love for Ephraim. The 'child'-image is not explicit, but fits well with the emotive quality of YAHWEH's speech, in which he apparently wrestles with conflicting impulses to punish and to show compassion. When his desire to show compassion prevails, the explanation of this decision comes in what is perhaps YAHWEH's most telling self-predication in the book: כי אל אנכי ולא־איש, "For I am God/a god and not a man" (11:9b). The significance of this declaration for Hosea's portrayal of YAHWEH can hardly be overstated. It occurs in one of those parts of the book that contributes to its theology of 'turning,' a thorough transformation from judgment on sin to hope of restoration. In that sense it corresponds to the image of YAHWEH as 'luxuriant juniper' in 14:9 [Eng. 8], also in a context of climactic 'turning.' But here, the anthropomorphic current that has run through the chapter collides with the postulate of YAHWEH as God.[24] For our present

---

21 The difficult phrase is כמרימי על לחיהם, literally, 'like those who lift a yoke upon their cheeks/jaws,' perhaps meaning the lifting of the yoke from the animal's head for feeding; Macintosh, *Hosea*, 446. Many emend to עול, 'child,' and find an image of a parent lifting the child to their cheeks in affection; Mays, *Hosea*, 150, 154–55; Wolff, *Hosea*, 191, 199–200; NRSV.

22 Ben Zvi, *Hosea*, 234. This is consonant with what we have seen concerning shifting and mutually supporting metaphors. The notions of 'yoke' and 'child' can even come together in the frame supplied by exodus from and possible return to Egypt (v. 5).

23 Ben Zvi, *Hosea*, 234; Macintosh, *Hosea*, 446.

24 The point of this is, I think, to affirm YAHWEH's deity in contrast to humanity, rather than to attribute the divine name El, *pace* R. Scott Chalmers, *The Struggle of YAHWEH and El for Hosea's Israel* (Hebrew Bible Monographs 11; Sheffield: Sheffield Phoenix, 2008); cf. Andersen and Freedman, *Hosea*, 589–90.

purposes, what is striking about it is the tension in which it stands not only with 2:18 [Eng. 16],[25] but also with its immediate context in ch. 11. The paradox of this is as tense as the expression of emotive conflict of which it is part. Besides the anthropomorphic language in the verses preceding, YAHWEH's emotional self-address in the very moment of declaring 'I am not a man' is thoroughly anthropomorphic: in its powerfully constraining love informed by the underlying human metaphors in the chapter, and in its language of 'heart,' 'compassion,' and anger, all based on human physiology, and expressing a powerful inner struggle.[26]

These conflicts in the deployment of human metaphors are immensely revealing about Hosea's language for God. The human analogy reaches far in Hosea, embracing even speech itself, and creating a commonality of experience between God and humans, that lies close to incarnational.[27] However, at this moment of YAHWEH's profoundest self-utterance (11:9b), a crucial reservation is entered, which shows that even this apparently indispensable metaphor is inadequate to express the nature of YAHWEH. In this regard the human metaphors are of a piece with the language for God generally in the book, with its range of metaphors and mobility within them. If the book of Hosea has a meaning, it is inseparable from the interplay of its metaphorical language, which constitutes the book's unique way of asserting that in all such language there is both like and unlike.

## V. The Tree-Image and the Limits of Language About God

So we return to the prophecy's finale in the likeness of YAHWEH to a luxuriant juniper. In the discourse of the book, this may function precisely to conclude with a non-human metaphor. Indeed, the unique adoption

[25] Cf. Gerald Morris, *Prophecy, Poetry and Hosea* (JSOTSup 219; Sheffield: Sheffield Academic, 1996), 128–29.

[26] For accounts of the meaning of 11:8 see Joy Philip Kakkanattu, *God's Enduring Love in the Book of Hosea: A Synchronic and Diachronic Analysis of Hosea 11:1–11* (FAT 2/14; Tübingen: Mohr Siebeck, 2006), 77–85; J. Gerald Janzen, "Metaphor and Reality in Hosea 11," *Semeia* 24 (1982): 7–44.

[27] The classic statement of this is Ulrich W. Mauser, *Gottesbild und Menschwerdung: Eine Untersuchung zur Einheit des Alten und Neuen Testaments* (BHT 43; Tübingen: Mohr, 1971); cf. Paul Fiddes, "The Cross of Hosea Revisited," *RevExp* 90 (1993): 175–90; Terence E. Fretheim, *The Suffering of God: an Old Testament Perspective* (OBT 14; Philadelphia: Fortress, 1984), e.g., 54; 119–23. Fretheim provides some important caveats about the use of language that attributes perplexity or indecision to God.

of a tree-metaphor for YAHWEH is one last twist in the tale, not just one more metaphor, but a daring one. If the likeness of YAHWEH to a juniper functions to relativize the human metaphors, what does it add in particular to the whole picture? We have seen above that the poem in 14:5–9 [Eng. 4–8] deploys paradisal, and thus creational, language and concepts. It thus complements the strong theme of Israel's experience of YAHWEH through his actions in history.[28] In addition, I have now suggested that it belongs to the book's strategy of showing the limitations of all language to convey the reality of YAHWEH.[29]

Can such a theological project succeed, however? Or does Hosea's heavy use of wordplay and figurative language suggest that meaning itself is undermined? Gerald Morris claims that ambiguous wordplay, as in Hosea, "permits meaning to play against meaning in such a way as to put all meanings into question."[30] If this is true of Hosea's language, it clearly affects the book's capacity to speak clearly about God. For Francis Landy, while the 'knowledge of God' is what ultimately matters in Hosea, "[the] diversity of metaphor expresses an uncertainty of identity."[31] Furthermore, "God's unity is as fissile and contingent as that of the human self."[32] Sharon Moughtin-Mumby doubts whether Hosea succeeds in 'turning' the language of sin and punishment into 'love-language' in 14:6–9: "We are left with the question of whether such a reversal is possible."[33]

However, it seems to me that the theological challenge taken up by Hosea, of speaking truly about YAHWEH, does not consist simply in the problem of linguistic indeterminacy. Rather, the deployment of metaphors for God in Hosea functions theologically in the context of the controversy between YAHWEH and Baal. The use of language is an integral part of the

---

28 In contrast, Hosea's historical tendency was one reason why Seifert thought the tree-metaphor is 'post-Hosean.' See above, n. 4.

29 Kirsten Nielsen has also argued that the human metaphors for YAHWEH in Hosea are relativized by others, specifically animal metaphors. She sees this, however, as an echo in the Old Testament of ancient Near Eastern (mainly Egyptian) patterns in which human and animal imagery combines in portrayals of God; Nielsen, "I am like a lion to Ephraim: Observations on animal imagery and Old Testament theology," *ST* 61 (2007): 184–97, especially 191–95.

30 Morris, *Prophecy*, 97. Here he says that "Israel's fate remains unresolved at the end," citing 14:9 and 11:9. Yet a little later he adds: "By ch. 14, the puns have been redeemed; every negative connotation has been wiped away," Morris, *Prophecy*, 126.

31 Francis Landy, *Hosea* (Readings; Sheffield: Sheffield Academic, 1995), 18.

32 Landy, *Hosea*, 19. Cf. Sherwood (*Prostitute*, 250) citing Proust: "Yhwh is impossible to 'conceive of as a single person.'"

33 Sharon Moughtin-Mumby, *Sexual and Marital Metaphors in Hosea, Jeremiah, Isaiah, Ezekiel* (Oxford Theological Monographs; Oxford: Oxford University Press, 2008), 76–77.

prophecy's concern to affirm what can be said of YAHWEH while maintaining a necessary distinction between YAHWEH and Baal. That distinction has been too readily expressed in such unsustainable polarities as transcendence versus immanence, or history versus nature. YAHWEH's claim upon Israel, for Hosea, rests on his love for them as demonstrated in his care for them since the distant past, and in his provision for all their needs in the good things of the land. Hosea's achievement is to have discovered language that is fitting for his highly nuanced theological purpose. In the natural world, it shows how YAHWEH does everything that might be claimed by Baal, yet is independent of natural process, since he is known through word and act in history. It expresses profound intimacy, with imagery for divine love drawn from the closest human relations; at the same time it guards YAHWEH's 'otherness,' in the sense that likeness is always attended by unlikeness ('I am not a man'). It does this, not by treading timorously among dangers, but with a kind of liberty and *élan*. The book's final metaphor perfectly illustrates the brilliance of this. The image of YAHWEH like a tree that gives both shade and fruitfulness at once reinforces the anthropomorphic disclaimer from ch. 11, and thus YAHWEH's freedom from being fully captured in any kind of earthly likeness, and also imaginatively affirms YAHWEH's presence in the natural world, and expresses his life-giving power in an image of natural growth.

# FROM WOE TO WEAL: COMPLETING A PATTERN IN THE BIBLE AND THE ANCIENT NEAR EAST

Alan Millard

## I. Oracles of Woe in Israel and the Ancient Near East

Isaiah 5 has six verses beginning with the word 'Woe.' For many readers that typifies the message of the Hebrew prophets, heralding destruction and doom, in line with Jeremiah's response to Hananiah, "From early times, the prophets... have prophesied war, disaster and plague..." (Jer 28:8). Those forecasts, Jeremiah implies, were fulfilled and so prophets who spoke like him were to be believed, but anyone who prophesied peace implausibly could only gain credibility when his prediction came true (v. 9). There were two classes of prophets, therefore, those foreseeing 'woe' and those predicting 'weal.' Consequently, where oracles of 'weal' follow oracles of 'woe' commentators commonly detach the prophetic promises of prosperity from the warnings of doom, ascribing them to later redactors or editors. Julius Wellhausen most memorably characterized the golden future Amos describes in vv. 11–15 of ch. 9, following the expectation of judgement and destruction in the previous verses, as "roses and lavender in place of blood and iron."[1] While Ernst Würthwein perceived a radical shift in Amos' career from being initially a prophet of 'weal' to becoming a prophet of 'woe,' almost all introductions to Old Testament prophecy assume oracles of 'weal' stem from post-exilic editors.[2] However, the pattern of deterioration or destruction followed by restoration or renewal can be traced in ancient Near Eastern texts where there is no question of later insertion and so it has been argued that Hebrew prophets may have used the same scheme.

In 1926 Hugo Gressmann drew attention to several texts in which the scheme appears:

> A... peculiarity of the Egyptian oracle is the typical combination of threat and promise. The order of events is understood and therefore left unstated:

---

[1] Julius Wellhausen, *Die kleinen Propheten übersetzt und erklärt* (3rd ed.; Berlin: Reiner, 1898), 96.

[2] Ernst Würthwein, "Amos-Studien," *ZAW* 62 (1950): 10–52.

> first must come calamity, then prosperity; the threat always precedes the promise. Except in details the two parts are antithetic, and they are as truly complementary as the two shells of the mussel.[3]

The two clearest examples from Egypt are *The Admonitions of Ipuwer* and *The Prophecy of Neferti*. Written about 2000 BC, *Ipuwer* gives a string of cases where the normal structure of society is reversed, and then appears to reproach the pharaoh for letting the land fall into this state; were a king to rule correctly, the land would prosper again.[4] *The Prophecy of Neferti* (earlier read as Nefer-rohu), composed a few decades later than *Ipuwer*, also laments the sorry state of the country, which would be reversed with the rise of a new king.[5] From Babylonia Gressmann cited the *Epic of Erra* which depicts the land suffering under the oppression of an angry god who eventually repents and blesses the country.[6] (The historical contexts of these compositions are irrelevant to the present study.)

## II. The Pattern of Woe and Weal in Babylonian History

In their exploitations of the theme, Gressmann and others had connected it with creation narratives, the New Year Festival, and other rituals. When reviewing the material in 1971, Bertil Albrektson brought into the discussion some Akkadian texts which H. G. Güterbock had investigated in an important study of Babylonian history writing.[7] Babylonian records show an almost regular rise and fall of dynasties under successful or ill-fated rulers, whom Güterbock categorized as *Heils-* or *Unheilsherrscher* ('sound' or 'unsound'). Besides rulers in the *Sumerian King List*, the principal examples are in stories about the great kings of Akkad in the latter half of the third millennium BC, Sargon and Naram-Sin. The former, the founder of the dynasty, is victorious; the latter, in at least one line of tradition, suffers for ignoring divinely written omens, yet in another ultimately conquers

---

[3] Hugo Gressmann, "Foreign Influences in Hebrew Prophecy," *JTS* 27 (1926): 241–54 (244).

[4] See "The Admonitions of an Egyptian Sage: The Admonitions of Ipuwer," translated by Nili Shupak (*COS* 1.42:93–98).

[5] See "The Prophecies of Neferti," translated by Nili Shupak (*COS* 1.45:106–110).

[6] See Benjamin R. Foster, *Before the Muses: An Anthology of Akkadian Literature* (3rd ed.; Bethesda, MD: CDL, 2005), 880–911.

[7] Hans G. Güterbock, "Die historische Tradition und ihre literarische Gestaltung bei Babyloniern und Hethitern bis 1200," *ZA* 42 (1934): 1–91; 44 (1938): 45–145.

his enemies.[8] In the *Weidner Chronicle*, a document apparently composed late in the second millennium BC, there is a deliberate narration of the incidence of 'woe' and 'weal.' It presents itself as advice from a king of Isin to another ruler, perhaps a king of Babylon. The text takes the form of a letter advising the recipient of the need to perform all the cultic duties carefully in order to win Marduk's favour, using the fates of earlier kings to illustrate the success which met the observant and the calamities which befell the careless.[9] All those cuneiform documents are primarily interpretations of past events. A group of texts from the seventh century BC and later, published as *Akkadian Prophecies*, is different, for they present as happening in the future events which seem to mirror episodes of earlier Babylonian history, each ending badly or well.[10] In neither of these types of text is there a regular alternation or an assumption of final bliss.

## III. Woe and Weal in Enuma Elish and Genesis 1

The idea of a bad period giving way to a good one claimed support from ancient mythology. Hermann Gunkel, reading the texts of the Babylonian 'creation epic' *Enuma elish* which had been recovered by the last decades of the nineteenth century, deduced that the Babylonians believed the gods had to conquer the threatening forces of chaos before they could create the world, chaos being personified as the ocean, Tiamat and her spouse Apsu. Gunkel published his study in 1895, drawing on the fragments of *Enuma elish* that George Smith had identified a few years earlier, with additions made afterwards, and in the light of ensuing discussions.[11] The

---

[8] See Joan Goodnick Westenholz, *Legends of the Kings of Akkade: The Texts* (Mesopotamian Civilizations 7; Winona Lake, IN: Eisenbrauns, 1997). A tablet from the Old Assyrian merchant colony at Kanesh (Kültepe) is now to be added, studied by Bendt Alster and Takayoshi Oshima, "Sargonic Dinner at Kaneš: The Old Assyrian Sargon Legend," *Iraq* 69 (2007): 1–20.

[9] For the most recent edition, see Jean-Jacques Glassner, *Mesopotamian Chronicles* (ed. Benjamin R. Foster; SBLWAW 19; Atlanta: Society of Biblical Literature, 2004) 263–68, cf. 268–71. See Glassner's discussion on pp. 20–27.

[10] Albert K. Grayson and Wilfred G. Lambert, "Akkadian Prophecies," *JCS* 18 (1964): 7–30; "The Dynastic Prophecy," translated by Tremper Longman III (COS 1.150:481–82); see Albert K. Grayson, *Babylonian Historical-Literary Texts* (Toronto Semitic Texts and Studies 3; Toronto: University of Toronto Press, 1975), 6–9; and Wilfred G. Lambert, *The Background of Jewish Apocalyptic* (London: University of London, Athlone Press, 1978).

[11] Hermann Gunkel, *Schöpfung und Chaos in Urzeit und Endzeit* (Göttingen: Vandenhoeck & Ruprecht, 1895). The translation of Enuma elish by Heinrich Zimmern is given in a Beilage on pp. 401–17. Cf. Hermann Gunkel, *Creation and Chaos in the Primeval Era*

poem describes how the gods learn that Tiamat and Apsu plan to destroy them, so one god, Ea, kills Apsu and then, after others have failed, Marduk kills Tiamat. Thereafter Marduk creates the world. Gunkel argued that "At some point these monsters of chaos [i.e., Tiamat and Apsu] rebelled against the power of the deities of the upper realm," referring to Tiamat as "a frightful being of a primeval era," "the chaos monster" and "the pernicious monster." Gunkel saw relics of this *Chaoskampf* motif in the 'without form and void' (תהו ובהו), the 'darkness' and the 'deep' (תהום) of Gen 1:2, equating 'the deep' (תהום) with Tiamat. Before the presently visible world was created there existed a situation of chaos. Only after God had overcome those elements of chaos could he establish an ordered universe. Thus there was in ancient Israel a belief that God subjugated a chaos monster before he could create the world. Various verses scattered through the Psalms, Prophets, and Job, which mention God as subduing the sea or creatures including those named as Rahab and Leviathan, could accordingly be interpreted as references to the same conflict. Gunkel's proposal gained acceptance with most Old Testament scholars during the first half of the twentieth century and remains influential. Gressmann proceeded to correlate the pattern noticed in the prophetic texts with the scheme of chaos and order Gunkel had perceived in creation accounts, with a god triumphing over disorder, setting the world aright.

## IV. In the Beginning there was no Chaos according to *Enuma Elish*

Since Gunkel worked with *Enuma elish* further fragmentary manuscripts of the poem have been recovered so that more complete and better translations can be made, with significant consequences for Gunkel's interpretation of it. Already in 1902, L. W. King could state, "From the new fragments of the poem we now know that the rebellion of the forces of disorder, which was incited by Apsu and not Tiamat, was due, not to the creation of light, but to his hatred of the way of the gods which produced order in place of chaos."[12] It has been clear for several decades that the opening

*and the Eschaton: A Religio-Historical Study of Genesis 1 and Revelation 12* (trans. K. William Whitney, Jr.; The Biblical Resource Series; Grand Rapids: Eerdmans, 2006).

[12] Leonard William King, *The Seven Tablets of Creation* (Luzac's Semitic Text and Translation Series 12–13; London: Luzac, 1909), lxxxii. For W. G. Lambert's authoritative translation, used here, see pp. 37–59 of his "Mesopotamian Creation Stories" in *Imagining Creation* (ed. Markham J. Geller and Mineke Schipper; Institute of Jewish Studies

lines of *Enuma elish* do not depict a chaotic world.[13] Firstly, they tell of two primary beings, the male Apsu and the female Tiamat, whose waters mingled, but no gods existed. Secondly, "The gods were created within them" (Tablet I.9), two pairs followed by two single gods, Anu and his son Ea, who then, as children do, disturbed their mother who wanted to quieten them: "The divine brothers came together, their clamour got loud, throwing Tiamat into a turmoil. They jarred the nerves of Tiamat... Their conduct was displeasing to her, yet though their behaviour was not good, she wished to spare them" (I. 21–23, 26, 27). Apsu was less lenient: "Their behaviour has become displeasing to me and I cannot rest in the day-time or sleep at night. I will destroy and break up their way of life that silence may reign and we may sleep" (I. 37–40). (Note that it was their rumbustious conduct which angered him; their activity did not "produce order in place of chaos," as L. W. King thought.) Although Tiamat was grieved, she wanted punishment, not destruction, "How can we destroy what we have given birth to? Though their behaviour causes distress, let us tighten discipline graciously" (I. 45, 46). Despite her opposition to Apsu's plan, he did not relent, but the gods heard of it and the youngest of the six, Ea, forestalled him, overcame and killed him, setting up his home on Apsu and there begetting Marduk, his glorious son (I. 61–99). Encouraged by other gods, Tiamat, whom Marduk had already provoked, prepared monstrous forces to combat her troublesome offspring. Her children were unable to confront her until Marduk, armed with dread magic powers, slew her and split her into two halves, forming the heavens from one and the earth from the other (Tablet IV. 93–105, 128–40, V. 47–62). Clearly, the chaos was not primordial; the gods frolicking within Tiamat and Apsu caused it! Prior to their creation all had been peaceful and calm; Tiamat was their mother, reluctant to harm them. Only when Ea had killed Apsu was her anger turned into active hostility. After Marduk had killed her, the gods needed a new home, so that is why *Enuma elish* is a creation myth, for Marduk provided that new home by creating heaven and earth from her corpse, founding his seat at Babylon. There was, therefore, no chaos in the way Gunkel assumed. The gods did not have to conquer chaos to produce order, they made war to preserve themselves; they had to subdue their previously peaceful parents since their own behaviour, the turmoil they

in Judaica; Leiden: Brill, 2008), 15–59. It is also accessible on the web-site ETANA. Cited 17 March 2011. http://www.etana.org.

[13] For example, Alexander Heidel, *The Babylonian Genesis: The Story of Creation* (2nd ed.; Chicago: Chicago University Press, 1951), 3, 89.

themselves had created, had pushed them to the limit. In this light, the widely assumed idea of a Babylonian source for a battle between God and a monster of chaos before the creation of the world in Gen 1 should be abandoned. In the Babylonian myth there were battles before the world came into being, but the watery beings the gods defeated were not in the first place chaotic; only after they were provoked did they harness their horrid powers, and then the gods did the same! No other Mesopotamian creation stories involve such elements, except the report of Berossus, which may echo *Enuma elish*.

## V. In the Beginning there was no Chaos according to *Genesis 1*

In addition, the direct linking of Tiamat with תהום that Gunkel made has long been discarded; the two words are cognate, the Hebrew is not a loan word from the Babylonian. Furthermore, scrutiny of the term "formlessness" (תהו ובהו) of the earth denotes its unsuitability for human habitation, but not a state of chaos. This is the case in Gen 1:2, in the two other occurrences of the phrase (Jer 4:23; Isa 34:11) and those involving תהו alone (e.g., Deut 32:10; Isa 24:10; 45:18; Job 6:18; 12:24; 26:7; Ps 107:40). *Enuma elish* gives no grounds for supposing the Israelites believed God defeated a monstrous chaos before he created the world.[14] Removing the concept of a primeval *Chaoskampf* also removes the basis for the supposed commemoration or re-enactment of God's defeat of the forces of chaos in an Israelite New Year Festival.

## VI. No Primeval Chaos so no Primeval *Chaoskampf*

The discovery of Ugaritic tablets which relate a battle between the god Baal and the sea (ים) has led many to prefer a Levantine, or 'Canaanite' source for Gen 1:2, rather than the Babylonian. Arguments in support of this view have been marshalled by John Day who, following previous writers,

[14] Wilfred G. Lambert, "A New Look at the Babylonian Background of Genesis," *JTS* 16 (1965): 287–300; repr. with additions in *I Studied Inscriptions from Before the Flood: Ancient Near Eastern, Literary, and Linguistic Approaches to Genesis 1–11* (ed. Richard S. Hess and David Toshio Tsumura; Sources for Biblical and Theological Study 4; Winona Lake, IN: Eisenbrauns, 1994), 96–113. David Toshio Tsumura, *Creation and Destruction. A Reappraisal of the* Chaoskampf *Theory in the Old Testament* (Winona Lake: Eisenbrauns, 2005).

took the scattered passages Gunkel had identified in other biblical books as evidence of the *Chaoskampf* and explained them all in the light of Ugaritic and other Levantine myths.[15] On the other hand, a strong case has been made for all those verses being references to the Exodus events or to God's control of creation without chaos having any role, and, as has often been noted, no Canaanite creation narrative has been discovered. Indeed, it is probably true that the concept of chaos followed by creation only entered Old Testament scholarship as a result of the way Gunkel interpreted the fragments of *Enuma elish* available in his time. The reference to the storm god Addu defeating the sea (*têmtum*) in a tablet of the eighteenth century B.C. from Mari is not necessarily a reference to a primordial battle any more than is Baal's battle with the sea, for the ocean always held a threat to human life (e.g., Ps 107:23–30).[16]

## VII. The Pattern: Weal—Woe—Weal

In each of the ancient Near Eastern texts mentioned there is an assumption of well-being which has been or will shortly be overturned, although that is not explicit. *The Prophecy of Neferti* is given in a stable society, but foresees a time when "everything good has disappeared,"[17] and *Ipuwer* depicts a kingdom in which people are bewildered because the normal conduct of life has been turned upside down. In other words, 'weal' exists, or has existed, prior to the 'woe' and its succeeding 'weal.' The Babylonian narratives and prophecies tell of some kings whose reigns began well and who were successful, then met difficulties or disasters. The revised interpretation of *Enuma elish* reveals that it begins with a peaceful situation, then descends into warfare before the world is created; chaos was not primary. Likewise, the Hebrew oracles of woe were precipitated by bad circumstances which the prophets expected to worsen, or by their forecasts of bad circumstances which they expected would arise. They presume, therefore, that a better situation had existed, or was existing, from which

[15] John Day, *God's Conflict with the Dragon and the Sea: Echoes of a Canaanite Myth in the Old Testament* (University of Cambridge Oriental Publications 35; Cambridge: Cambridge University Press, 1985).

[16] Jean-Marie Durand, "Le mythologème du combat entre le dieu de l'orage et la mer en Mésopotamie," *MARI* 7 (1993): 41–61; Pierre Bordreuil and Dennis Pardee, "Le combat de Ba'lu avec Yammu d'après les textes ougaritiques," *MARI* 7 (1993): 63–70.

[17] "The Prophecies of Neferti," translated by Nili Shupak (*COS* 1.45.46:109).

there would be a severe decline, a factor some have recently recognized.[18] The references to the Exodus and wilderness experience and to the days of David are evidence they recognized such times of 'weal' in the past (e.g., Hos 3:5; Ezek 37:15–28).

Gressmann's observation, extended by Albrektson, should give cause to pause before divorcing oracles of weal from oracles of woe. The contradiction between them which leads commentators to treat 'weal' oracles as additions to 'woe' oracles, often seeing them as post-exilic additions, may be more apparent than real. Although the Egyptian *Prophecy of Neferti* and *The Admonitions of Ipuwer* and the Babylonian *Erra Epic* are understood as *post eventum* compositions, the Neo-Assyrian prophecies, which are prophecies of weal, overall, are obviously not. Jeremiah's condemnation of false prophets who were forecasting imminent peace when he knew disaster loomed (e.g., chs. 23, 28) does not preclude the possibility of true prophets foretelling catastrophe and subsequent restoration; after all, he did that in Jer 30–33! Where prophecies of weal follow oracles of woe, therefore, there may be cause to pause before detaching them as secondary—as additions from later hands—although, of course, it does not preclude that.[19]

While the progress from 'woe' to 'weal' is evident in many prophetic texts (e.g., Isa 27–29), it is not confined to prophecy. In psalms of lament the speaker passes from present distress to assurance that God will rescue him, e.g., Pss 6, 12, 31, 79. Several of those psalms look back to the ways God had acted for the good of the Psalmist or of Israel in the past as grounds for their assurance of his future care, e.g., Pss 80, 143. In those Psalms, too, the complete pattern appears; it is not simply from 'woe' to 'weal' but from 'weal' to 'woe' to 'weal.' The acts of God in the past, in Israel's history, most notably in the redemption from Egypt, and in the individual's experience, contrast with the present sad circumstances the

[18] Erhard Blum, "Israels Prophetie im altorientalischen Kontext. Anmerkungen zu neueren religionsgeschichtlichen Thesen," in *"From Ebla to Stellenbosch": Syro-Palestinian Religions and the Hebrew Bible* (ed. Izak Cornelius and Louis C. Jonker; Abhandlungen des deutschen Palästina-Vereins 37; Wiesbaden: Harrassowitz, 2008), 81–115; Matthijs J. de Jong, *Isaiah among the Ancient Near Eastern Prophets: A Comparative Study of the Earliest Stages of the Isaiah Tradition and the Neo-Assyrian Prophecies* (VTSup 117. Leiden: Brill, 2007), 448–49. Robert Gordon drew my attention to these two studies and Graham Davies kindly provided a copy of the first.

[19] For examples, see Gösta W. Ahlström, "Isaiah VI.13," *JSS* 19 (1974): 169–72; and H. G. M. Williamson, *Isaiah 1–5* (ICC; London: T&T Clark, 2006), 254–60 on Isa 3:10.

Psalmists describe and give the basis for assurance of God's future acts of rescue and restoration.

Therefore, the pattern 'weal > woe > weal' appears to be basic in this literature, in the thought of its authors and thus familiar to their audiences. In fact, the scheme is discernible throughout the Hebrew Bible in short and in lengthy sequences. Genesis begins with 'weal' in Eden, rapidly moves to 'woe,' then passes to the promise to Abraham of 'weal' for his descendants. The Sinai covenant begins with Israel's rescue, promises prosperity for obedience, warns of woe for failure, yet even then envisions return to 'weal' (see Deut 29, 30). In Isa 4, vv. 2–6 function "effectively as a climactic conclusion to the whole section comprising Isaiah 2–4,"[20] as 11:1–12:6 conclude chs. 7–10. Israel's history runs from the 'weal' of the Promised Land to the fulfilment of the prophesied woes, then to a degree of restoration as recorded in the final verses of 2 Chronicles. The Old Testament span from Genesis to Malachi covers similar ground, with Malachi looking forward to the rise of "the sun of righteousness" (4:2). May Hugh Williamson delight in this evangelic pattern, and encounter much 'weal' in the coming years.

---

20 Williamson, *Isaiah 1–5*, 305 n. 16.

# ON TRIPLETS IN A TRIO OF PROPHETS

David J. Reimer

Of the many well-known texts from the book of Isaiah, perhaps the best known is the Trisagion, the proclamation of the seraphim before the throne of God in Isa 6:3, familiar as it is to both Jews and Christians in liturgical settings, and in the Christian context in both Western and Orthodox traditions. In his detailed investigation into the saying, Hugh Williamson argues persuasively for the surmise of many commentators: that it is liturgical in origin, too. As Williamson further demonstrates, this celebration of God's "holiness and glory" in the handling of Isaiah of Jerusalem is "no longer an expression of a simplistic form of nationalism but rather give[s] expression to divine freedom and sovereignty in the choice of agent of the divine will, even if that comes at the expense of his own people."[1] For the prophet's audience, the celebratory resonances of this saying take on deeply ominous overtones.

Williamson devotes the lion's share of attention to the complexities of the latter part of the saying, rendered in the RSV by "the whole earth is full of his glory." By contrast, the opening "holy, holy, holy" is thought to be relatively straightforward—even if the triplet form is "certainly unusual in Hebrew."[2] Williamson notes that Isa 6:3 is not the only text of the Hebrew Bible to contain a triple repetition: the others typically set alongside it are Jer 7:4 (citing the RSV for the moment: "This is the temple of the LORD, the temple of the LORD, the temple of the LORD"); 22:29 ("O land, land, land, hear the word of the LORD!"); and Ezek 21:32 (Eng. 27; "A ruin, ruin, ruin I will make it"). This list exhausts the examples in the whole of the Bible.[3] Such three-fold statements may be found in many times, in many places, and in literature of many kinds. For example, the narration of Joseph

---

[1] H. G. M. Williamson, *Holy, Holy, Holy: The Story of a Liturgical Formula* (Julius-Wellhausen-Vorlesung 1; Berlin: Walter de Gruyter, 2008), 32.

[2] Williamson, *Holy, Holy, Holy*, 21.

[3] This set of texts is already noted in the comments of Rashi and Kimchi, who sometimes explain them together. Bernhard Stade ("Die Dreizahl im Alten Testament," *ZAW* 26 [1906]: 124–41 [124]) extends the list to include Isa 8:9; 33:10; Hos 2:21–22; and Nah 1:2. While these texts are of interest in further illustrating the rhetorical rhythms of a three-fold pattern, none of them contains an unbroken triplet of the kind found in our four verses.

Conrad's maritime masterpiece *Lord Jim* contains manifold repetitions—two-fold, three-fold, four-fold, and more—but only rarely a "triplet" (statement, repeated twice further). A telling example occurs during Marlow's account of Jim's account of his experience on the stricken *Patna*. In the deep darkness, Jim takes stock and draws the only conclusion he can: that the ship and its passengers are doomed, there is nothing he can do to avert disaster.

> Nothing could save them! There were boats enough for half of them perhaps, but there was no time. No time! No time! It did not seem worthwhile to open his lips, to stir hand or foot. Before he could shout three words, or make three steps, he would be floundering in a sea whitened awfully by the desperate struggles of human beings, clamorous with the distress of cries for help.[4]

This is the moment of climax which provokes Jim's actions and subsequent anguish which in turn form the substance of the novel. The triply-stated "no time" which cuts Jim off from one possible course of action reinforces (and is reinforced by) the "three words" he cannot speak and "three steps" he cannot take. The triplet makes for a powerful literary device.

It is the purpose of this essay to ask whether the standard explanations of the biblical "triplet" texts are satisfactory; to investigate the force of the triplets in those texts where one occurs; and finally to reflect on the possibility of some theological resonance between them.

## I. Language

The triplet texts as a set tend not to receive sustained attention by handbooks of classical Hebrew grammar and syntax. This might in part be due to some uncertainty about what kind of phenomenon they present. Should they be classed among the syntactic elements of the language? Or are they, rather, a distinctive and expressive style of speaking?

When treated as an aspect of syntax, these triplets are as a rule simply seen as a flavour of the more common doublet repetition, and these in turn were generally included in older grammars as a species of "apposition."[5]

---

[4] Joseph Conrad, *Lord Jim: A Tale* (Edinburgh and London: William Blackwood and Sons, 1900), 91.

[5] E.g., *inter alia*, Andrew B. Davidson, *Hebrew Syntax* (3rd ed.; Edinburgh: T & T Clark, 1902), 43 (§29, rem. 8), substantially retained by John C. L. Gibson, *Davidson's Introductory Hebrew Grammar: Syntax* (Edinburgh: T & T Clark, 1994), 43 (§39 rem. 4), citing Isa 6:3.

They may also be treated under the rubric of the comparative,[6] the construct,[7] or even the number of the noun.[8] Repetitions are typically classified as having the nuance of a "distributive" or "emphatic" construction.[9] While the former clearly does not bear on our small corpus, the latter definitely does. The notion of a sort of superlative being expressed attracts many. Although attempts are often made to render doublets in this manner, e.g., Eccl 7:24 for ועמק עמק as "exceeding deep" (GKC §133k), such is seldom ventured for the triplet texts.[10] Even with doublets, however, it is difficult to discern what the value of this "syntax" might be. One of the parade examples, 2 Kgs 25:15 (//Jer 52:19), provides a useful litmus test. Linguistic treatments, and some English versions, often translate its זהב זהב as "pure gold," adhering to the "superlative" notion.[11] Commentators justifiably reject this interpretation. The context is the removal of the bronze pillars and temple vessels by the pillaging Babylonians, with the items of the precious metals, gold and silver, sandwiched between an account of the bronze vessels and columns, in particular how the latter were smashed for transport (2 Kgs 25:13–17//Jer 52:17–23). As such, Holladay's explicit rejection of GKC's suggestion has merit: what is at issue is the handling of the metals, not the purity of the gold and silver.[12]

---

[6] E.g., GKC, §133k–l (but cf. §123e), often cited to with reference to the triplets: Isa 6:3 cited at §133k, the others in §133l, cf. Williamson, *Holy*, 21 n. 17: "*qāḏōš* is repeated three times to express particular emphasis, similar to the superlative; cf. Jer 7:4; 22:29; Ezek 21:32; GK §133*k*."

[7] So Joüon-Muraoka, §129r in conjunction with apposition, although not citing any triplet text.

[8] As in Christo H. J. Van der Merwe, Jackie A. Naudé, and Jan H. Kroeze, *A Biblical Hebrew Reference Grammar* (Sheffield: Sheffield Academic, 1999), 184 (§24.3[2] iv–vi); cf. Joüon-Muraoka, §135e.

[9] This was essentially Kimchi's understanding as well (cf. commentary at Jer 22:29). Further refinements are sometimes offered: cf. Bruce K. Waltke and Michael O'Connor, *An Introduction to Biblical Hebrew Syntax* (Winona Lake: Eisenbrauns, 1990), main treatment at pp. 115–16 (§7.4.1[a]), but cf. pp. 233–34 (§12.5); Ronald J. Williams, *Williams' Hebrew Syntax* (3rd ed. rev. and expanded by John C. Beckman; Toronto: University of Toronto Press, 2007), 4 (§15–16).

[10] Davidson is among the exceptions here, glossing Isa 6:3 as "most holy" (retained by Gibson; see n. 5, above).

[11] E.g., GKC §123e; *Williams' Hebrew Syntax*, §16a; Waltke-O'Connor, §7.2.3(c) #12; cf. NIV, NASB. At its conclusion, the verse includes a second doublet, כסף כסף, "pure silver" according to this understanding.

[12] William L. Holladay, *Jeremiah 2: A Commentary on the Book of the Prophet Jeremiah Chapters 26–52* (ed. Paul D. Hanson; Hermeneia; Philadelphia: Fortress, 1989), 442. So too, e.g., Charles F. Burney, *Notes on the Hebrew Text of the Books of Kings* (Oxford: Clarendon, 1903), 369.

On the other hand, GKC (§133k) makes the further observation that these repetitions—doublets and triplets alike—are a feature of rhetoric rather than syntax. Wilfred Watson classes it among the typical techniques of Hebrew poetry and provides a catalogue of its various guises and effects.[13] Although set in a different linguistic context, E. J. Revell remarks: "the purpose of repetition is, in general, . . . to mark [some item] as significant. The reader or hearer is left to determine the reason why it is so marked."[14] So in the most basic sense, repetition calls attention to itself, giving the repeated item some "significance" (so Revell) or emphasis that requires discernment. However, identifying "emphasis" as the key feature of repetition is not the end of the matter, rather its beginning. As Barry Bandstra writes:

> Emphasis has tended to become "the great explanation" of syntactic irregularities in many commentaries and grammatical studies. . . . [But] the attempted explanation of syntactic phenomena by means of emphasis is really a non-explanation, at least until the notion is given empirical linguistic definition. After all, who can say a claim for the presence of emphasis is wrong?

Bandstra proceeds to look at emphasis in relation to word order and to build a more refined account of its workings in his particular text.[15]

It does not seem likely that there is anything intrinsically significant to the trebling itself. Of the commentators on our texts, the one to explore this aspect most thoroughly is Jack Lundbom in his remarks on Jer 7:4.[16] His short catalogue of three-fold repetitions shows the persistence of the pattern across the years, with a common property between them being a heightened emotional intensity. He is also among those who draw attention to J. Herrmann's observation of triplets found in the *Maqlû* incantation texts.[17] Herrmann thought Isa 6:3 unlike the other triplets, owing to

---

[13] Wilfred G. E. Watson, *Classical Hebrew Poetry: A Guide to Its Techniques* (JSOTSup 26; Sheffield: JSOT Press, 1984), 52–53, 264–82.

[14] E. J. Revell, "The Repetition of Introductions to Speech as a Feature of Biblical Hebrew," *VT* 47 (1997): 91–110 (92).

[15] Barry Bandstra, "Word Order and Emphasis in Biblical Hebrew Narrative: Syntactic observations on Genesis 22 from a Discourse Perspective," in *Linguistics and Biblical Hebrew* (ed. Walter R. Bodine; Winona Lake: Eisenbrauns, 1992), 109–23 (quote from pp. 112–13).

[16] Jack R. Lundbom, *Jeremiah 1–20* (AB 21A; New York: Doubleday: 1999), 462; cf. Karl-Martin Beyse, "שָׁלֹשׁ [*sic*] *šālōš*," *TDOT* 15: 119–28.

[17] Johannes Herrmann, "Zu Gen $41_{43}$, Jer $22_{29}$, $7_{4}$," *ZAW* 62 (1950): 321–22; further on the *Maqlû* texts, see the studies collected as chs. 6–14 in I. Tzvi Abusch, *Mesopotamian Witchcraft: Toward a History and Understanding of Babylonian Witchcraft Beliefs and Literature* (Ancient Magic and Divination 5; Leiden: Brill/Styx, 2002).

its formulaic, liturgical character. Herrmann believed that while the other three examples had attractive explanations in the commentaries (or, like Ezek 21:32, needed none), the possibility of an original connection with the Babylonian incantations ought at least to be held open. It should be noted, however, that Herrmann put forward the suggestion in an expressly tentative manner. There are good reasons for doing so: the *Maqlû* texts have distinctive features that make the parallel less than compelling. They have a distinctive context and shape, marked by formal directions for the delivery of the incantations intended to ward off evil. None of the biblical triplet texts resonates with these features, and it is a small irony that the text nearest in a purely formal sense to the Babylonian parallels—the Trisagion of Isa 6:3, the liturgical setting of which has at least some contact with the quasi-liturgical incantations—is excluded by Herrmann himself. The *Maqlû* texts are also marked by a high degree of repetitiveness: the triplets are not distinctive, but occur alongside frequent two-, four-, five- and even six-fold repetition. This substantially reduces the value of the parallel. Thus Herrmann's superficially attractive suggestion fails to offer any explanatory power for the biblical triplet texts.[18]

For our texts, then, the question remains concerning the nature of the emphasis provided by repetition. It is time to turn to the texts themselves.

## II. Triplets in Focus: Commentary

The force of the three-fold repetition must be judged case-by-case, attending to context. As such, I begin with Jer 22:29 which appears to offer the clearest line of interpretation. It is followed by Ezek 21:32; then Jer 7:4; finally returning to Isa 6:3.[19]

### 1. *Jeremiah 22:29*

An oracle against Jehoiachin (= Coniah) concludes a collection of sayings against the Davidic line which begins at Jer 21:11.[20] As one finds elsewhere

[18] Still more distant, yet still noteworthy, are the three-fold cultic utterances in classical Greek texts, described by Gerhard Delling, "τρεῖς, τρίς, τρίτος," *TDNT* 8: 216–17.

[19] Space precludes handling the text critical problem of evidence for a doublet for each of these texts: 1QIsa[a] for Isa 6:3, and the LXX for the Jeremiah and Ezekiel texts. I am satisfied, however, that there is a triplet to contend with in each case.

[20] Unless 23:1–8 should be seen as the concluding pericope; the boundaries of this section remain somewhat fluid, with the oracle against Zedekiah's prospects in 21:1–10 seen as a trigger for the royal collection which follows.

in Jeremiah, a prose saying (22:24–27) stands in close relation to an accompanying poetic oracle (22:28–30). It spells the end of the line for David through Jehoiachin in which "land" has prominence. Aside from the triplet of interest in v. 29, the pivotal thought of both prose and poetry has to do with Jehoiachin's expulsion from the land, with the key term, הארץ, found in vv. 26, 27, and 28.

It is not unusual for ארץ to be addressed with a vocative, especially as a witness in the set pair "heavens and earth" (e.g., Deut 32:1; Isa 1:2; Mic 1:2; 6:2; cf. Isa 49:13). ארץ also forms a natural partner when the earth's inhabitants are addressed (e.g., Isa 34:1; Jer 6:18–19; cf. 1 Kgs 10:24). That the "land" should be addressed in the second person, then, comes as no surprise. What does come as a surprise is that it should be invoked with a three-fold repetition, and the usage does not quite tally with either of the patterns just noted. Obviously, too, there can be no quasi-superlative meaning here, as the term is not adjectival, but rather a vocative.

The oracle holds within it some ambiguities. As Rudolph points out, v. 28 can be taken as the expression of a people who cannot believe this is the fate of their young king.[21] Beyond this, the ה...אם...מדוע formulation of v. 28—a particular favourite in Jeremiah—could lead one to expect that a future is being held open for Jehoiachin. Typically the rhetorical questions of the ה...אם elements create the frame of reference for seeing the situation described by the final מדוע as wrong in some way.[22] Thus here, the first two questions expect a "no": "(ה) Is this man Coniah a despised, broken pot?", no, "(אם) a vessel no one cares for?," no again. So it follows, according to the rhetorical pattern, that it must be wrong or at least unreasonable for him and his offspring to be ejected from the land.

This is the point at which the cry goes out, "O Land, land, land!" (v. 29). Again, as Rudolph comments, the connection is entirely appropriate in showing "wie wichtig dem Propheten das folgende Orakel 30 ist."[23] The three-fold vocative alerts all who might be listening that the faint hopes that any ambiguity might have aroused are about to be dashed. It is perhaps only coincidence that there are three previous mentions of ארץ in

---

[21] Wilhelm Rudolph, *Jeremia* (3rd ed.; HAT 1/12; Tübingen: Mohr Siebeck, 1968), 143.

[22] Cf. Jer 2:14, 31; 8:4–5, 19, 22; 14:19; 22:28; 49:1. There are other examples of ה...אם without the concluding מדוע in Jeremiah and beyond, but this third element is the crucial one which gives rhetorical force to the whole construction. For secondary literature and discussion see David A. Diewert, "Job 7:12: *Yam, Tannin* and the Surveillance of Job," *JBL* 106 (1987): 203–15 (211–12).

[23] Rudolph, *Jeremia*, 143.

the preceding material.[24] Be that as it may, the triple invocation of ארץ to attend to the following prophetic word provides a marked insistence on the land itself as witness to the judgment on Jehoiachin. Here "land" is not a partner in cosmic witness, nor a metonym for the people of Judah.[25] The triplet signals by its insistent personification on the part of the prophet that place from which Jehoiachin's presence and future is excluded.

### 2. *Ezekiel 21:32 [Eng. 27]*[26]

GKC lists this text among those whose repetition exhibits "a periphrasis for the superlative," but in a note (§133l n. 2) declares this instance to be "different in kind from the triple utterances of the same words in 2 S $18^{33}$, Jer $7^{4}$ and $22^{29}$, and the double exclamation in Jer $4^{19}$ and La $1^{16}$ (?)"—texts in which a "superlative" meaning is inappropriate. Is it, however, also appropriate here?

The passage as a whole contains other repetitive language, as well as some ambiguities and obscure language. Twice a double invocation of the "sword" itself is heard (חרב חרב, vv. 14b, 33b). The sword's very action is described in repetitive terms (v. 19b, RSV: "let the sword come down twice, yea thrice [שלישתה]"—too far from our "triplet" to have any influence there). In the immediate context, the "prince of Israel" is identified in a four-fold vocative, while the initial statement of degradation is announced, unusually, with four infinitives having the force of imperatives, three of which (השפיל, הסיר, הרים, more unusual still) are infinitive constructs.[27] There is ambiguity in the final clause in v. 32bβ (עד־בא אשר־לו המשפט ונתתיו ) as to whether the one who is to come brings "judgment" or has "right" depending on how one understands משפט at this point. Context inclines the better understanding to the former; further, nowhere else in

---

[24] Aside from other considerations, this would have some implications for the composition of this text which can be no more than speculative. Meanwhile, it is noteworthy that there is other repetition in the immediate context, *viz.* the four-fold reiteration of ביד in v. 25, itself reinforcing the metaphor of the torn-off signet ring of v. 24.

[25] *Pace* Kimchi; Rashi offered possibilities in which each of the three individual invocations takes on a distinct meaning: Jehoiachin's native land, new land, and the land of Israel; or the three lands contained within the land of Israel (Judah, trans-Jordan, Galilee); further, it could express a kind of superlative: "a land that is a land among lands."

[26] Further citations from this passage will refer to verse numbering of the Hebrew text only.

[27] Following Daniel Block (*inter alia*) on both points: *The Book of Ezekiel: Chapters 1–24* (NICOT; Grand Rapids: Eerdmans, 1997), 683, 690. There may be another example of the infinitive construct with imperatival force in Ezek 24:17 (האנק) although the text is obscure and often emended.

Ezekiel does משפט have this meaning of "right."[28] A slightly more resistant ambiguity is found in the antecedent for the 3fs pronominal suffix on אשׂימנה ("I will make it"). The most natural antecedent in context is the "crown" of v. 31: I take the two parallel terms (מצנפת, "turban"; עטרה, "crown") to be poetic variation, both referring to the same, royal object. Both are feminine nouns and, as Block points out, although "turban" is commonly used of priestly headdress, occurrences are limited and a related term occurs in connection with royalty at Isa 62:3.[29]

This leaves the difficulty inherent in the tripled term itself, for עַוָּה is a *hapax legomenon*. Although the translation of "ruin" is offered by many English versions,[30] the supposed root, עי, does not easily explain the form found here with a medial ו.[31] The more attractive explanation relates it to the root עוה, with the occurrence in Isa 24:1 (*piel* verb, עִוָּה, "twist") providing an apt analogy for our text. In contrast to the English versions, commentators rightly prefer this explanation, and offer some variation of "twisting" in their translations. I am not aware of any commentators who combine this explanation with that of the antecedent of אשׂימנה, although Kimchi may be one.[32] The royal headdress referred to in v. 31, whether "turban" or "crown," are both "wound": מצנפת obviously so, but עטרה, "crown," can refer to a garland or wreath—indeed, other words for "crown" might have been used which would not lend themselves to this meaning.[33] It makes very good sense for this symbol of high estate to be twisted beyond use, which the tripled עוה states emphatically.

---

[28] For the possessive construction cf. also Hos 5:1 where a similar ambiguity holds, again best resolved as judgment rather than "right" (*contra* NJPS, NJB in both cases).

[29] Block, *Ezekiel 1–24*, 690 n. 189. Cf. Alison Salvesen, "עֲטָרָה," *Semantics of Ancient Hebrew* (ed. Takamitsu Muraoka; Abr-Nahrain Sup 6; Louvain: Peeters, 1998), 106–13: "Ezk 21.31, where the word is coupled with מִצְנֶפֶת, does seem to point to עֲטָרָה being a sign of kingship, but even that passage seems to have more to do with utter humiliation than with loss of kingship *per se*" (p. 111).

[30] It appears to be the consensus choice, found in each of NASB, NIV, NJB, NJPS, RSV, and REB. Rashi appealed to עִי in Mic 1:6 to explain the meaning as "ruin" (חרבה).

[31] So (*inter alia*) William L. Moran, "Gen 49,10 and Its Use in Ez 21,32," *Bib* 39 (1958): 405–25 (420).

[32] At least, Kimchi asserts that it is the "crown" which is made עוה. Both Kimchi and Rashi understood the tripling in terms of succession of leadership, Rashi taking a cue explicitly from the Targum's reference to Seraiah, Gedaliah, and Zechariah. Kimchi, on the other hand, explained the threefold reference in terms of generations which the עטרה would be void.

[33] See Salvesen, "עֲטָרָה," for further discussion.

### 3. *Jeremiah 7:4*

This is certainly the better known of Jeremiah's two triplets, but it has complexities of its own. The two central, interrelated, issues are these: it is unclear who is (or are) the speaker (or speakers) of the "deceptive words"; and the verse concludes with the syntactic problem of the referent of המה. To begin with the latter, the problem is the unexpected plural. If one is to understand the saying as "*this* is the temple of the LORD ...," then a singular would be expected. By far the most widely accepted explanation for the plural is that it refers to the plurality of buildings which comprised the temple complex (Ps 84:2 and 2 Chr 8:11 often cited in support) which goes back at least as far as Kimchi.[34] Another often mooted suggestion is that it is an abbreviation of המקום הזה.[35] However, whatever the merits of this suggestion, as Lundbom points out the phrase itself occurs elsewhere in the immediate context with reference to the land rather than the temple. This suggestion, then, makes for confusion, not clarity.[36] Carolyn Sharp attempts to link "them" to the priests and false prophets who have duped the people into trusting the "wrong advisors," so the reference is not directly to the mantra-like recitation of the "deceptive words" themselves. However, such a reading seems unnecessarily allusive, although her stricture stands, *viz.* that a "persuasive exegetical reading should account for the semantic correspondence between the multiple occurrences of the phrase היכל יהוה and the plural status of המה in some way."[37]

Such comments lead back to the first problem: who speaks the "deceptive words"? The wider context addresses all Judaeans entering the Temple precincts (7:2, cf. v. 8), but this is little help in deciding the identity of the speakers themselves. Commonly the "words" are understood as

---

[34] Kimchi related the threefold saying to "the hall, the temple, and the devir."

[35] Suggested by Harry Torczyner ("Dunkle Bibelstellen," in *Vom Alten Testament: Karl Marti zum siebzigsten Geburtstage gewidmet von Freunden, Fachgenossen und Schülern* [ed. Karl Budde; BZAW 41; Giessen: Töpelmann, 1925], 276) recorded as a possibility in the notes to *BHS* by Rudolph, preferred by Robert P. Carroll (*Jeremiah: A Commentary* [OTL; London: SCM, 1986], 207) alone among modern commentators. Peter C. Craigie, Page H. Kelley and Joel F. Drinkard, Jr., (*Jeremiah 1–25* [WBC 21; Dallas: Word, 1991], 116) prefer (and slightly misunderstand) Alan Corré's suggestion that here המה stands for המה הדברים, "indicating that the unusual wording that precedes it is correct despite its peculiarity." Corré is not suggesting an "abbreviation," however ("*'ēlle, hēmma = sic*," *Bib* 54 [1973] 263–64); rather המה signals "that the thrice-repeated היכל ה׳ is *not* a dittography," much as the modern convention of using [*sic*].

[36] Lundbom, *Jeremiah 1–20*, 1.462.

[37] Carolyn J. Sharp, *Prophecy and Ideology in Jeremiah: Struggles for Authority in the Deutero-Jeremianic Corpus* (OTS; London: T&T Clark, 2003), 45–47.

the fervent, mantra-like expression of the safety afforded by the presence of the LORD's temple, or perhaps the LORD's presence in it. Reventlow proposed a very different setting for the recital of these words, however, which puts them in the mouths of the people. Noting the connection to the *Maqlû* incantations, he thought that a cultic recitation made good sense, especially as sung by pilgrims as they made their way towards Jerusalem.[38] In any case, as Sharp notes, this remains a speculative proposal which further fails to help with the problem of the plural המה.[39]

A more plausible reading takes its cue from some of the observations seen in this brief survey. The three-fold saying *is* unusual, but the use of המה is not. One way of explaining the syntax of the verse works this way: v. 4a warns against trusting deceptive speech, ending in לאמר which merely serves to introduce the direct speech following;[40] what follows in v. 4b has the character of a nominal clause with the three-fold recitation of direct speech the predicate for which the final המה is the subject. In translation: "Do not trust in deceptive words: they are 'The temple of the LORD, the temple of the LORD, the temple of the LORD.'" המה, then, functions somewhat like a resumptive pronoun with its antecedent דברי השקר from v. 4a (cf. Est 9:1 *fin*; also הוא in Jer 32:8 *fin*), but in a separate clause (cf. Ps 55:22; Prov 18:8).[41]

While this discussion helps to clarify the text, it does not offer a clear explanation for the presence of the tripled saying itself. Here there is a reasonable consensus, however, that the mantra-like repetition of the דברי השקר rhetorically portrays both the ubiquity and the banality of the slogan, often associated with an overly simplistic "Zion theology."[42]

---

[38] Henning Graf Reventlow, "Gattung und Überlieferung in der 'Tempelrede Jeremias', Jer 7 und 26," *ZAW* 81 (1969): 315–52 (328–29). Rashi's relating the triplet to the three pilgrimage festivals might resonate with Reventlow's suggestion, but it is not a connection that he makes himself.

[39] Sharp, *Prophecy and Ideology*, 46.

[40] Thus *HALOT*: "often it has no other sense than our colon, a breathing space before direct speech" (*q.v.* אמר, qal[2]).

[41] This is not too far from Corré's sense of how the verse works, but the explanation is rooted in the typical syntax of the independent pronoun rather than in a hypothetical meaning for the particles he examines. Cf. also Edmund F. Sutcliffe ("A Gloss in Jeremiah VII 4," *VT* 5 [1955]: 313–14) who argued that the final repetition plus pronoun was a marginal gloss confirming the "deceitful words"—the work of a pedantic, or zealous, copyist. Again, there is no need to resort to an imagined scribal scenario for which there is no evidence, although the relationships between the terms is as Sutcliffe had it.

[42] For an analysis of the verse in terms of formal rhetoric—which, however, pays no particular attention to the triplet itself—see Michael Avioz, "A Rhetorical Analysis of Jeremiah 7:1–15," *TynBul* 57 (2006): 173–89 (182–84). In addition to the commentaries, cf. also

The "sermon" which follows acerbically denounces the iniquity of trusting a name and a place (cf. v. 14) when the behaviour demanded by them is flagrantly offended. The point is sharpened by Holladay's observation that היכל is not the common way of referring to the Temple in Jeremiah: why should it be used here?[43] He notes that it is the phrase used in the narrative which features the Shiloh sanctuary in 1 Samuel (1:9; 3:3). But beyond that, the phrase appears in Samuel-Kings at particular moments of crisis: Hezekiah's capitulation to the threatening Assyrians (2 Kgs 18:16), the fall of Jerusalem to the Babylonians in 597 BCE (2 Kgs 24:13), and positively, in Josiah's reforms (2 Kgs 23:4).[44] Each of these moments could be seen as illustrative of the point Jeremiah's "sermon" is making here. Holladay also notes, however, another connection: "The choice of the word 'temple' may be governed... by the fact that that word appears in Isa 6:1 (if there is an echo here of the trisagion of Isa 6:3)." To this text we now turn.

## 4. *Isaiah 6:3*

So we return to the text that launched this study. Isaiah 6:3 differs from the previous texts: while the other three texts could not easily (or simply could not) bear a "superlative" nuance, so that some other understanding of the effect of the triplet in context was required, here the adjectival קדוש has often been understood in "superlative" terms (often under the influence of GKC §133k). Given the discussion above, it is not clear that doubled (let alone tripled) terms should be understood in comparative (or superlative) terms. Beyond that, there are reasons for explaining the triplet along different lines. Although, as was seen above (n. 6), Williamson subscribes to the view that the superlative is an adequate explanation for the three-fold repetition of קדוש, there are within his own observations seeds of a slightly more nuanced understanding.[45]

If Jeremiah was at the gate of the earthly בית יהוה and speaks of the היכל יהוה (Jer 7:2–3), Isaiah is given a glimpse into the היכל which is

R. W. L. Moberly, "'In God We Trust'? The Challenge of the Prophets," *ExAud* 24 (2008): 18–33 (25–28).

[43] Holladay, *Jeremiah 1*, 242.

[44] It is also frequent in post-exilic texts looking towards the rebuilding of the Temple: Ezra 3:6, 10; Hag 2:15, 18; Zech 6:12–15.

[45] In addition to *Holy, Holy, Holy* (see n. 1, above), see also his "Isaiah and the Holy One of Israel," in *Biblical Hebrews, Biblical Texts: Essays in Memory of Michael P. Weitzman* (ed. Ada Rapoport-Albert and Gillian Greenberg; JSOTSup 333; Sheffield: Sheffield Academic, 2001), 22–38; "Temple and Worship in Isaiah 6," in *Temple and Worship in Biblical Israel* (ed. John Day; LHBOTS 422; London: T & T Clark, 2005), 123–44.

the abode of the LORD (Isa 6:1). As he sees, he also hears the cries of the worshipping seraphim. Their worship asserts that the LORD of Hosts is "holy, holy, holy"—that is, the triplet is what is predicated of the LORD, the grammatical subject. However, although it may surprise modern readers, this was not the most obvious ascription to make of Israel's deity.[46] Still, there are good reasons why it is entirely appropriate here. As one of the "absolute" uses of the term in Isaiah, Williamson notes it is differentiated from the nationally specified "Holy One *of Israel*" which is the more common title in the tradition.[47] In context, this declaration suits well the heavenly court which transcends national interests. This perception is reinforced by the second part of their praise which invokes "the fullness of the whole earth."[48] "Holiness" is further that quality which sets the Creator apart from the creature and which transcends also moral categories, even if the association of holiness and morality is readily made (cf. Isa 5:16).[49] It is that quality which by virtue of its simple presence brings judgment (cf. Lev 10:1–3), experienced acutely by the prophet as the scenario of Isa 6 unfolds.

The intersection of this language especially with certain of the Psalms is often noted. That with Ps 99 is especially noteworthy, given its three-fold declaration that the LORD is "holy" (99:3, 5, 9).[50] Mays suggests that "the entire psalm is meant to be an exposition of the holiness of the LORD."[51] This psalm forges a conjunction between the cosmic rule of the LORD and the worship life of Israel *via* its mediators *par excellence*, Moses, Aaron, and Samuel. Just as the psalm registers the need for forgiveness before

---

[46] Williamson, "Isaiah and the Holy One of Israel," 33–35; "Temple and Worship," 132–33; *Holy, Holy, Holy*, 18–21.

[47] "Isaiah and the Holy One of Israel," 24. Baruch Levine notes this usage and, taking a cue from Samuel D. Luzzatto, suggests that the first part of the declaration by the seraphim is not subject-predicate, but two acclamations: "The Holy One, the Holy One, the Holy One! The LORD of [the heavenly] Hosts!" That is, they do not provide a description, but rather, as "heralds" they announce the One seated on the throne. "The Language of Holiness: Perceptions of the Sacred in the Hebrew Bible," in *Backgrounds for the Bible* (ed. Michael P. O'Connor and David Noel Freedman; Winona Lake: Eisenbrauns, 1997), 241–55 (citation from p. 253).

[48] For my point, it is immaterial whether this phrase is the grammatical subject or predicate (Williamson prefers the former: *Holy Holy, Holy*, 25).

[49] Cf. the older but still valuable discussion of James Muilenburg, "Holiness," *IDB* 2: 616–25.

[50] Otto Kaiser, *Isaiah 1–12* (2nd ed.; OTL; London: SCM, 1983), 126; Hans Wildberger, *Isaiah 1–12: A Commentary* (Minneapolis: Fortress, 1991), 265–66. Cf. also Williamson's observations on the work of Ruth Scoralick, *Holy, Holy, Holy*, 21 n. 17.

[51] James L. Mays, *Psalms* (IBC; Louisville: John Knox Press, 1994), 316.

such a God, so too does the prophet in Isa 6. In both Ps 99 and Isa 6, the Lord is the king on the throne, whose universal rule extends from Zion. To suggest that the Trisagion registers a "superlative" of holiness seems to me to be impossible in this context. One might refer to some created thing in these terms (e.g., the frequent קֹדֶשׁ קָדָשִׁים for "most holy," e.g., Exod 29:37). But here, as applied to the Lord, it is an absolute quality, not one which can be graded.

This, then, is the point of the tripling: the three-fold declaration emphatically forces this "otherness" of the Lord into the foreground. It may not be precisely as G. B. Gray has it, that here Isaiah fills "holiness" with ethical content.[52] Gray's impulse, though, to see that the moral demand follows inevitably on the vision of holiness, captures well what the "thrice repeated" acclamation accomplishes.

## III. Conclusion

Studying these triplet texts as a small but distinct corpus—as they were by the medieval Jewish exegetes—permits a different perspective on the meaning and effect of the tripled terms. If the notion of a quasi-superlative was deemed unhelpful, the aspects of emphasis and intensification come to the fore. In each case, the tripled term provided a focal point for the judgment stated or implied in the wider context. It is natural enough that this should be the case. Consider another text, not this time a "triplet," but a "multiple" all the same. In the pathos-laden, tragic *dénouement* to Absalom's attempted coup, the news of Absalom's death finally reaches the almost naively hopeful David. The statement of his grief in 2 Sam 19:1 [Eng. 18:33] gives vent to his breaking heart (cf. 19:5 [Eng. 4]):

> And the king was deeply moved, and went up to the chamber over the gate, and wept; and as he went, he said, "O my son Absalom, my son, my son Absalom! Would I had died instead of you, O Absalom, my son, my son!"

His son's name is uttered three times, "my son!" a total of five. The reader is left in no doubt as to the all-consuming grief into which David has plunged. The repeated elements form the foreground and focus for characters and readers alike. So too, in only slightly less dramatic fashion, for

[52] George B. Gray, *A Critical and Exegetical Commentary on the Book of Isaiah I–XXXIX*, vol. 1 *Introduction, and Commentary on I–XXVII* (ICC 18; Edinburgh: T & T Clark, 1912), 106.

our prophetic triplet texts. As the judgment is pronounced, the triplet provides a fulcrum for the prophetic rhetoric.

There are some striking surface similarities between our four texts, even while their differences are readily apparent. Each of them appears as direct speech, although the speakers vary from the seraphim of Isa 6:3, once the voice of the prophet introducing an oracle (Jer 22:29), once the voice of the prophet speaking on behalf of the LORD (Ezek 21:32), and once the voice(s) of indeterminate speakers (Jer 7:4). Each is bound up with the court and/or the king: the heavenly king in Isa 6:3, twice the human king in (Jer 22:29; Ezek 21:32), and once with the temple itself (Jer 7:4). Each states (Jer 22:29; Ezek 21:32) or implies (Isa 6:3; Jer 7:4) a moral judgment.

It is worth noting, too, the broad historical relationships between these texts. Without entering the debate about the precise placement of Isa 6 within the career of Isaiah of Jerusalem, we can at least locate the text broadly in the latter part of the eighth century. This makes it significantly older than the examples from Jeremiah and Ezekiel in the Babylonian period. Taking the most straightforward cues for the dating of these texts: Jer 26:1 provides a date of 609 BCE for Jeremiah's "temple sermon" (thus 7:4); the oracle against Jehoiachin (Jer 22:29) must fit the small window of his three-month reign in 597 BCE; Ezek 21:32 is more difficult to fix, but probably follows the chronological notice of Ezek 20:1 (591 BCE), and could be placed tentatively in the campaign of Nebuchadnezzar in 588/587 BCE.[53] Evidence is lacking for a bold claim that the Isaianic Trisagion inspired the triplets of the Babylonian crisis, but there is an attraction to Holladay's suggestion that this may be the case for Jer 7:4 (n. 64, above), which sets a trajectory to the two remaining triplets.

The Trisagion of Isa 6:3 reinforces the supreme exaltation of the God of Israel which in consequence implies a judgment on a sinful people, but effects repentance in a particular individual—the prophet who received the vision. Using some of the same language, and countering false assumptions about the nature of the LORD's temple, Jeremiah (7:4) calls his contemporaries to just the sort of repentance confessed by Isaiah. The triplet of Jer 22:29 signals the finality of the judgment against Jehoiachin that brings an apparent end to his royal line as he is ejected from his native land. Ezekiel's oracle (21:32) condemns his contemporary as monarch of

---

[53] So Block, *Ezekiel 1–24*, 685 n. 167.

Judah, Zedekiah, who is utterly demoted and degraded in the threefold "knotting" of the "crown" which stood as the insignia of his office.

One cannot go beyond noting these intertextual resonances, but at the same time, these resonances are there to be noted in this small yet distinctive corpus of texts. Their echoes may well have continued, although another prophet of the Babylonian period voiced one appropriate response to the broad theme of the prophetic triplet texts: "But the LORD is in his holy temple; let all the earth keep silence before him" (Hab 2:20).

It is a privilege to contribute this essay in honour of Hugh Williamson who has been to me an examiner, mentor, colleague, and friend, and whose scholarship exemplifies faith seeking understanding.

# ZECHARIAH AND THE AMBIGUITY OF KINGSHIP IN POSTEXILIC ISRAEL

Wolter H. Rose

In the first part of this article a brief survey will be given of how the prophet Zechariah envisaged kingship and its future after the exile.[1] The main purpose of this survey is to provide a background for the second part of the article which will look at the significance of Zech 9:9 for answering the question as to the identity of the king in the book of Zechariah.

## I. Kingship and Its Future

### 1. *A Dating Formula With a Foreign Ruler*

The first time we find the word מלך in the book of Zechariah is in 7:1. Once we have arrived at this verse, we realise that we have to start all over again: the king mentioned there was already mentioned earlier in the book, in 1:1 and 1:7. We have learned an important lesson: looking for the theme of kingship is not the same as looking for the word מלך.

In his first appearance (1:1), the reference to Darius only gives his name. His title is not mentioned, and the name of the empire is also missing. The second occurrence of Darius (1:7) is exactly identical to the first. Such

---

[1] This article is written in appreciation and gratitude to Hugh Williamson for what I have learned in the years as his (first) D.Phil. student in Oxford and afterwards. With respect to Zech 1–6 the survey builds on the thesis written under his supervision (published as Wolter H. Rose, *Zemah and Zerubbabel: Messianic Expectations in the Early Postexilic period* [JSOTSup 304; Sheffield: Sheffield Academic, 2000]). My interpretation of kingship in Zech 7–14 is explored in more depth in a commentary published in Dutch in 2010: Wolter H. Rose, "Zacharia," in *Daniël – Ezra – Haggai – Zacharia – Esther – Nehemia – Maleachi: Zeven bijbelboeken uit de Perzische periode* (Geert W. Lorein and Wolter H. Rose; Commentaarreeks op het Oude Testament De Brug 11. Heerenveen: Groen, 2010), 247–329. The title of the article is borrowed from the title of an article written by Peter Machinist, "Hosea and the Ambiguity of Kingship in Ancient Israel," in *Constituting the Community: Studies on the Polity of Ancient Israel in Honor of S. Dean McBride, Jr.* (ed. John T. Strong and Steven S. Tuell; Winona Lake, Ind.: Eisenbrauns, 2005), 153–81. I will employ a canonical approach to the text of the book of Zechariah, basing my interpretation on the final form of the text as the author or editor(s) left it to us. Quotations are from the NRSV, unless otherwise noted.

a sober description of a king in a dating formula is somewhat unusual (though not unique), particularly when it is the first time the king is mentioned.[2] Darius is not a local king, but a foreign emperor in a remote capital. This is a painful moment in the book: every dating formula in Zechariah is a reminder of the fact that there is no king in Jerusalem.

## 2. *Responsibilities of a King*

Having learned our lesson, we move on to consider the absence of a king in Zech 3–4. In 3:7 the high priest is given some new responsibilities, probably government and administration of the temple precincts, as ביתי as direct object of the verb דין seems to indicate. Before the exile this was part of the responsibilities of the king. Now these responsibilities are transferred to the high priest. The reasons for this transferral are not stated.

Another case of someone taking over responsibilities of the king is found in ch. 4. The vision of the lampstand and the two olive trees is explained with reference to the temple rebuilding project which was in progress at that moment. In 4:9 Zerubbabel, the governor appointed by the Persian king, is presented as the temple builder, the one who was there at the beginning and the one who will see the project to its completion. Temple building was the responsibility of the king, and once again we have a case where in the absence of the king someone else has to do the job. This time it is not the high priest, but the governor.

The prophetic oracles referring to Zerubbabel's role as chief temple builder would have been an excellent opportunity for Zechariah to highlight the Davidic ancestry of Zerubbabel. In my view it is noteworthy that the prophet does not mention it, here or anywhere else in the book (the same reticence is found in Haggai and Ezra).[3]

---

[2] Zechariah's contemporary Haggai uses the title the first two times he refers to Darius in a dating formula (דריוש המלך, Hag 1:1, 15) and only the name the third and final time (2:10).

[3] In Zech 4:14 the "two sons of oil" are not anointed ones, a priestly one and a royal one, and there is no model here for a diarchy of priest and prince. They are members of the heavenly court, most likely angels (not prophets, as I had argued earlier); see now Wolter H. Rose. "Messianic Expectations in the Early Postexilic Period," in *Yahwism After the Exile: Perspectives on Israelite Religion in the Persian Era* (ed. Rainer Albertz and Bob Becking; Studies in Theology and Religion 5; Assen: van Gorcum, 2003), 168–85 (184).

### 3. *Temple Building and Ruling, No Title*

There seems to be a second king without a title in the book of Zechariah: the royal figure in ch. 6. He does have a name, צמח, but no title. The main features in the portrait of Zemah are his involvement in building the temple and his rule. He does what a king is supposed to do, but the noun מלך is not used, and neither is the cognate verb. The name Zemah should be interpreted against the background of Jer 22–23 (not Isa 11:1, where the noun צמח does not occur, but other nouns do, which refer to parts of plants). The end of Jer 22 seems to spell the end of the Davidic dynasty, but then in the following chapter (23:5) YHWH provides a future for (ל, not מן) 'David' in an unexpected way, of which 'David' is the recipient, not a contributor. This is expressed using plant imagery in which the noun צמח, 'vegetation, greenery,' figures.[4] As the details in the description in the second half of v. 5 indicate, the prophecy is about a royal figure.

In Zech 6 Zemah is presented as someone who, as the verbal forms indicate, will be present in the future. A crown is given to the high priest (compare 3:8) as a sign of YHWH's faithfulness and to guarantee the fulfilment of his promise of the coming of Zemah. Taken together, the name, the future reference, and the function of the crown make an identification of Zemah as a contemporary figure, whether Zerubbabel or someone else, implausible. Zemah is a messianic figure.[5]

---

[4] My interpretation of the meaning of צמח has drawn criticism from Anthony R. Petterson (*Behold Your King: The Hope For the House Of David in the Book of Zechariah* [LHBOTS 513; New York: T&T Clark, 2009], 125) who writes: "Rose has relied too much on the semantics of the word צמח and has not paid close enough attention to the context of both Zechariah and the earlier prophets at this point." In my view the contexts are more different than Petterson suggests, and his conclusion "differing terminology, but a common metaphor" (p. 92) can only be reached when one ignores the semantics of צמח (my view that צמח grows directly out of the ground, not from some other plant or tree, is not a new view, but was "correctly noted by several scholars before him [= Rose]," so H. G. M. Williamson, *Isaiah 1–5* [Vol. 1 of *A Critical and Exegetical Commentary on Isaiah 1–27*; ICC; London: T&T Clark, 2006], 301).

[5] Zemah is not a priest, in spite of what Marko Jauhiainen ("Turban and Crown Lost and Regained: Ezekiel 21:29–32 and Zechariah's Zemah," *JBL* 127 [2008]: 501–11 [509]) and Petterson (*Behold*, 111) have argued recently. YHWH is indeed mentioned twice in the context (so Jauhiainen), however not as a subject but merely as a complement in the phrase היכל יהוה. Petterson's syntactical argument in support of "he will be a priest" seems unfounded: as Num 24:17–18 shows, there are cases that contradict Block's statement: "The initial *waw* consecutive precludes a change in subject from the previous clause": Daniel I. Block, "My Servant David: Ancient Israel's Vision of the Messiah," in *Israel's Messiah in the Bible and the Dead Sea Scrolls* (ed. Richard S. Hess and M. Daniel Carroll R.; Grand Rapids: Baker, 2003), 17–56 (36 and n. 69). Finally, it seems arbitrary to find YHWH already present in the

### 4. *A New Beginning, Where Is the King?*

Zechariah 7–8 link back to 1:1–6 and explore in more detail the main elements of the introduction of the book. A new generation is not doomed to repeat the wrong behaviour of a previous generation: they can make a new beginning. In that way they will experience that YHWH's anger is something of the past: now he will richly bless Jerusalem, the city for which YHWH is burning with passion. The prophet presents a picture of a peaceful and prosperous society, which has so much appeal that people of other nations will notice and make an effort to join God's people.

What is striking in this picture is that there seems to be no connection between this new society and the royal figure portrayed just before these two chapters, at the end of Zech 6. However, it would be too quick a conclusion to say that there is no king in Zech 7–8, because he has been there all the time, almost unnoticed, yet painfully real: Darius the king (7:1), now, in contrast to 1:1 and 1:7, with the title מלך. The section of the book where the absence of the king is almost tangible[6] is introduced by a dating formula which mentions a foreign ruler complete with the title מלך.

### 5. *The King of Jerusalem*

We have to wait until Zech 9 to find the first unmistakable reference to the king (מלך) of Jerusalem. Finally he arrives, and the inhabitants of the city are called to welcome him with passion. The manner of his coming is spelled out in great detail. He is righteous, he is one to whom victory is given, he is humble and rides on a donkey. His coming will result in the destruction of the tools of military conflict, the announcement of peace, and his rule will have global proportions. Many of the features of the rule of the king echo parts of Ps 72, including the words expressing the notion of global rule (Ps 72:8).

### 6. *Shepherd Metaphors*

Shepherd metaphors are used in Zech 9–14 both of God and of human leaders. The shepherd metaphor is not necessarily used to refer to king-

suffix of כסאו; even in the verse which Petterson mentions as the only other place which has the combination "sit [...] rule [...] throne," the throne is not the throne of YHWH: ישב על־כסא דוד ומשל עוד ביהודה (Jer 22:30).

[6] Compare Machinist's comment in the opening paragraph of his article: "How does the Hebrew Bible conceive of the good society? There is no easy or uniform answer to this question. But whatever answer is given must reckon with the institution of kingship" ("Hosea," 153).

ship. At the same time there is no need to exclude kingship from the world of shepherd metaphors in Zech 9–14. The noun מלך is used once explicitly in a context where the shepherd metaphor is used (11:6), not to refer to a specific king, but in a general description of turmoil in society. Used of God, one finds the shepherd metaphor only a few times and in an implicit way. YHWH's intervention for his people is compared to what a shepherd is supposed to do for his flock. He will save (ישׁע Hiphil) his people, because they are his sheep (צאן; 9:16); he looks after (פקד) his flock (עדר; 10:3). The noun רעה is here not used of God.

Used of human leaders the shepherd metaphor occurs a number of times, employing the noun רעה in singular and plural. The acting shepherds provoke the anger of YHWH and he announces that their punishment is coming (10:3; 11:17). The prophet is called by YHWH to act as a virtuous shepherd but the flock does not like him and give him little credit for his efforts (11:4–14). The good shepherd is deemed a failure. Then, for a second time the prophet is called to impersonate a shepherd, this time a dysfunctional one: this prefigures the careless shepherd whom YHWH will raise up (11:15–17). The last time we hear about a shepherd is when the sword of YHWH is called to execute the punishment against the shepherd. This also affects the sheep, including the little ones: only a third will survive and this remnant will now be God's covenant people (13:7–9).[7]

## 7. *The House of David*

In Zech 12 we find the name of David for the first time in the book. In ch. 12 and then also in ch. 13 the name of David usually occurs in the phrase בית דויד, "house of David." The one exception concerns a comparison (12:8) in which the feeblest among the inhabitants of Jerusalem are said to be "like David," most likely a reference to the historical David. So apart from this comparison we are not dealing with an individual, but with a collective: the "house of David." Five actions are mentioned in which the

---

[7] With Rex Mason ("The Use of Earlier Biblical Material in Zechariah 9–14: A Study in Inner Biblical Exegesis," in *Bringing Out the Treasure: Inner Biblical Allusion and Zechariah 9–14* [ed. Mark J. Boda and Michael H. Floyd; JSOTSup 304; Sheffield: Sheffield Academic Press, 2003], 1–208 [129-30]) I consider the shepherd in 13:7 to be the same as the one in 11:17, and therefore not a good shepherd, as, e.g., Iain Duguid, "Messianic Themes in Zechariah 9–14," in *The Lord's Anointed: Interpretation of Old Testament Messianic Texts* (ed. Philip E. Satterthwaite, Richard S. Hess, and Gordon J. Wenham; Tyndale House Studies; Carlisle/Grand Rapids: Paternoster/Baker, 1995), 265–80 (274). If of the flock entrusted to the shepherd "two-thirds shall be cut off and perish" (13:8), it is highly problematic to see the shepherd of 13:7 as suffering vicariously for the flock (so, e.g., Petterson, *Behold*, 241, 250).

house of David are involved: receiving victory from YHWH (12:7); exercising leadership (12:8); receiving a spirit of compassion and supplication (12:10); mourning for the pierced one (12:10, 12–14);[8] and receiving cleansing from a freshly opened fountain (13:1).

None of these actions is explicitly or uniquely royal, and in all cases but one the distance between the house of David and other entities (inhabitants of Jerusalem, [tents of] Judah, other families) seems to be decreasing. The one exception is 12:8 where the inhabitants of Jerusalem are clearly set apart from the house of David and only the house of David is given a position in which they will lead and as such "be like God."

## 8. *God to Be the King of the Whole Earth*

In the vision reports in Zech 1–6 one finds several references to the authority of YHWH over the whole earth. The horsemen figuring in the first vision are said to be "those whom the LORD has sent to patrol the earth" (1:10). In the vision of the lampstand and the two olive trees YHWH is called "the Lord [אדון] of the whole earth" (4:14). This title also occurs in the final vision where the four chariots are explained in this manner (6:5): "These are the four winds of heaven going out, after presenting themselves before the Lord of all the earth."

In the final section of the book a similar idea is expressed but with a different title: after the final battle of Jerusalem is over, YHWH will become (14:9) "king over all the earth" (מלך, rather than אדון). The interpretation of הארץ as "the earth" is confirmed by the references to the nations (גוים) and the families of the earth (משפחות הארץ) in vv. 16–17 who "will worship the King, the LORD of hosts."

## 9. *Conclusion*

Machinist writes about the "centrality of [the] institution" of kingship in Israelite history on the one hand and "ambiguity and ambivalence over its place and achievements" on the other.[9] Space constraints allow

[8] It seems extremely difficult to establish the identity of this pierced one. The fact that the "house of David" side with the inhabitants of Jerusalem both in mourning and in receiving cleansing (which possibly suggests involvement in the piercing), makes it problematic to see the pierced one as a royal figure (so, e.g., Duguid, "Messianic Themes," 275-76). The comparison with the mourning of Josiah seems to reflect more on the unusual intensity of the mourning, than on the identity of the one mourned for. The presence of the comparison is therefore insufficient reason for speaking of "royal overtones" in 12:10.

[9] Machinist, "Hosea," 154–55.

him to illustrate this only "through one biblical text and personality, the prophet Hosea, who reflects the tensions and possibilities in a particular pronounced way."[10] Looking at the material presented so far, one could point to something similar in the book of Zechariah. A number of features indicate a certain level of restraint with respect to kingship.

Aspects of the message of the prophet which lead me to notice this restraint include the provisions for the high priest taking over responsibilities which once belonged to the king in ch. 3; the governor under Persian authority being responsible for the rebuilding of the temple (without any hint of his Davidic lineage) in ch. 4; and the absence of the word מלך in the portrait of the messianic figure in ch. 6,[11] followed by a blueprint of a new society without a king (introduced by a dating formula which now for the first time mentions Darius' title מלך). This restraint can also be detected in the mainly negative use of shepherd imagery in Zech 10–13 (with one notable exception); and finally in the late introduction (Zech 12–13) of the house of David and the portrayal of the unique, yet in a number of ways, shared role this institution will play standing side by side with other sections of the people of God (in several actions including repentance and receiving cleansing).

## II. The Identity of the King

In the second part of the article I will look at the identity of the king in the book of Zechariah, zooming in on Zech 9:9. There is a broad consensus that the king in Zech 9:9 is human.[12] I would like to argue that a plausible case can be made for the view that the prophet wants his audience

---

[10] Machinist, "Hosea," 154–55.

[11] Compare Meyers' remark on the vagueness of ch. 6 and its intention "to deflate the final burning embers of monarchist feelings that might have existed at the time" (Eric M. Meyers. "Messianism in First and Second Zechariah and the 'End' of Biblical Prophecy," in *"Go to the Land I Will Show You": Studies in Honor of Dwight W. Young* [ed. Joseph E. Coleson and Victor H. Matthews; Winona Lake, Ind.: Eisenbrauns, 1996], 127–42 [130]) and his phrase "the muted messianism of First Zechariah" (p. 135).

[12] To be more precise: a human individual. Adrian M. Leske ("Context and meaning of Zechariah 9:9," *CBQ* 62 [2000]: 663–78 [665, compare 671-73]) is able to string together an impressive array of allusions to other prophetic texts in his argument for the identity of the king as the community of God's people: "the 'king' is God's faithful people who are to present God's gracious rule through their faithfulness to covenant and their consequent witness to God's blessings before the nations." In the end, though, his proposal concerning the identity of the king of Zech 9:9 fails to carry conviction, because king and people are clearly distinguished entities in Zech 9:9-17.

to identify the king as YHWH.[13] The case is cumulative and is based on three clues located in different parts of the book of Zechariah which when taken together point to this identification.

### 1. *The First Clue: Zechariah 9:9 and 9:1–8*

First we will look somewhat more closely at what comes before Zech 9:9. It may be that the connection of 9:1–8 and the following section is closer than is usually thought. One of the most striking features of 9:1–8 is the high number of topographical names. There seems to be some order in the names: the movement is going from north (Hadrach, known as Hatarikka in Assyrian sources) to south (Judah). Many different interpretations have been put on this passage.

One of the more fruitful approaches takes its cue from the genre of military campaign reports of Assyrian or Babylonian kings. This would explain the high number of topographical names, the movement from north to south and the language of encamping (חנה) towards the end of the passage. It is possible that a very specific historical period has been the model for Zech 9:1–8: most of the topographical names fit into the period of the military exploits of Sargon II (721–705), but it is more difficult to fit them all in one campaign.[14]

---

[13] One of the few scholars who defend this identification is Joachim Becker (*Messiaserwartung im Alten Testament* [SBS 83; Stuttgart: Katholisches Bibelwerk, 1977], 67–68): "Meines Erachtens tritt in Sach 9,9f Jahwe im Gewand des irdischen Königs auf. Das Königtum wird also nicht auf das Volk, sondern auf Jahwe übertragen." The identification of the king as YHWH has recently been challenged by Mark Boda ("Figuring the Future: The Prophets and Messiah," in *The Messiah in the Old and New Testaments* [ed. Stanley E. Porter; McMaster New Testament Studies; Grand Rapids: Eerdmans, 2007], 35–74 [60]) who takes the identification of the king as YHWH together with the identification as the remnant of Judah and mentions three reasons why these two proposals cannot be accepted: "(1) this is a speech of YHWH to the personified city of Zion about a 'king'; (2) YHWH calls him 'your king' (your = Zion); and (3) the speech contains significant allusions to Psalm 72." I will respond briefly to these objections. At first sight the fact that someone is #1 speaking *about* a king and #2 calling him "your king" may seem to suggest that YHWH and the king are two separate persons. As I will argue shortly, reading 9:9 in the context of the chapter as a whole makes clear that speaking about the king in the third person is not necessarily supposed to distinguish him from YHWH. The point of objection #3 is that the allusions to Ps 72 suggest the Davidic nature of kingship. I agree that the words about the global scope of the rule of the king have their origin in Ps 72. But in my view it remains an open question whether all aspects of this original setting (including a context of specifically Davidic kingship) of these words have to be brought along when one reads the words in their new context in Zech 9.

[14] Abraham Malamat, "The Historical Setting of Two Biblical Prophecies on the Nations," *IEJ* 1 (1950–1951): 149–59 (149–54), now in idem, *History of Biblical Israel* (Culture and History of the Ancient Near East 7; Leiden: Brill, 2001), 370–74. Compare William W. Hallo and

The passage imitates the genre of the military campaign report and reserves the twist for the very last moment. YHWH is portrayed in this passage as a king marching down towards the south of Palestine. The audience expects another attack on Jerusalem, and the language of encamping is foreboding. The king is indeed setting up his camp, but in this case not to attack Jerusalem, but to protect his house in the city.

Immediately after this twist follows the call to Zion/Jerusalem to cheer their new king at his arrival. If 9:1–8 had been a campaign report of an ordinary king, it would have been natural to see a close connection between the king leading the military campaign heading for the south and the king arriving in Jerusalem. Moving on from 9:1–8 to what follows, it is as if the perspective changes and we now look at the approach of the king from within the walls of Jerusalem. The approach of the king is no reason to be afraid, but to rejoice, because this king is not going to attack, but to protect and defend the city.

In this case the king leading the military campaign is not an ordinary king, but God. In my view that is not a reason suddenly to cut the strong connection between 9:1–8 and what follows. It is quite possible that we still have to consider what would have been natural in a different scenario: the leader of the military campaign aiming for the south and the king arriving in Jerusalem are one and the same person.

The fact that the king is spoken of in the third person, while YHWH is spoken of in the first person in what immediately precedes (v. 8) and then again in the first half of v. 10, is certainly noteworthy, but does not create an insurmountable hindrance for the interpretation I propose. However strange such a shift from one grammatical person to another may seem for the modern reader, a careful reading of Zech 9 shows that this is a characteristic of this chapter as a whole (see figure 1), a possible indication of the close connection between 9:1–8 and 9–17.

More than once in this chapter we find a switch from third to first person or vice versa, sometimes even for just one or two clauses. The passage begins with a third person section, then a first person section starts in v. 6b, is briefly interrupted by a third person section in v. 7b, and then in v. 8 we are back again in first person. In all these eight verses with their switches between third and first person there is only one protagonist:

William Kelly Simpson, *The Ancient Near East: A History* (Forth Worth: Harcourt Brace, 1998), 135, based on William W. Hallo, "From Qarqar to Carchemish: Assyria and Israel in the Light of New Discoveries," *BA* 23 (1960): 33–61 (53–55).

| Zechariah 9 | 3rd | 2nd | 1st |
|---|---|---|---|
| 1–6a | YHWH | | |
| 6b–7a | | | YHWH |
| 7b | "our God" | | |
| 8 | | | YHWH |
| 9 | the king | Zion/Jerusalem | |
| 10a | | | YHWH |
| 10b | the king | | |
| 11–12 | | city/residents | YHWH |
| 13 | | | YHWH |
| 14–17 | YHWH | | |

Figure 1: Third to First Person Switch in Zechariah 9

YHWH. So, in Zech 9 a switch from 3rd to 1st person does not necessarily imply the introduction of another character.[15]

Similarly, the third person section starting in v. 9 is briefly interrupted by a first person section in v. 10a (if we follow MT; LXX and Peshiṭta have a third person at the beginning of v. 10, in which case there is no interruption). Then in v. 10b we are back again to third person, and return once more to first person in vv. 11–13, while the chapter closes with a third person section in vv. 14–17. Significantly, the king is never in these verses presented as the object of an action performed by God.

### 2. *The Second Clue: Zechariah 9:9 and 14:9*

The second pointer is found when one reads Zech 9:9 in connection with the end of the book. Zechariah 14 describes what one could call "the last battle," in which the nations are gathered (by YHWH) to fight against Jerusalem. The casualties are many and the details are horrifying. Then YHWH comes to the aid of Jerusalem. The battle assumes cosmic proportions, the countryside is remodelled, and an unprecedented climate-change occurs: it marks the end of the world as we know it. It is in the context of this battle that we read: "And the LORD will become king over all the earth." This creates an *inclusio* enveloping chs. 9–14. The passages at the beginning and at the end share the elements of battle, Jerusalem, YHWH defending the city, and the presence of a king. It is important to notice that the

[15] In my opinion there is therefore no need to take the third to first person switch in Zech 9:9–10 as a reason to find two kings in this passage, so Paul D. Hanson, *The Dawn of Apocalyptic* (Philadelphia: Fortress, 1975), 320: "the anointed ruler here is celebrated alongside the divine king."

notion of global rule is part of this literary structure. The king of Jerusalem of 9:9–10 already was said to exercise a worldwide rule in 9:10: "his dominion shall be from sea to sea, and from the River to the ends of the earth." The *inclusio* is interpreted by some[16] as an indication of contrast or development, from the king of Jerusalem at the beginning to YHWH as the king of the whole earth at the end of the section, with no more mention being made of a human king. There is contrast or development when the king in 9:9 is human. However, when we consider the suggestion of YHWH as king, then the absence of the human king is seen not in a perspective of contrast or development but continuity.

### 3. *The Third Clue: Zechariah 9:9 and 2:14*

The third pointer is found when one reads Zech 9:9 in connection with a passage from the first part of the book. The first half of Zech. 9:9 can be divided into three constituents:

1. call to rejoice
2. city addressed in second person singular
3. announcement of arrival

There is a remarkable parallel to this in an earlier passage in the book: Zech 2:14. Even though the wording is in many ways different, all three constituents are there. In both verses the city is addressed in second person singular, there is a call to rejoice, and there is someone arriving. Nowhere else in the book of Zechariah does one find this combination of constituents.

גילי מאד בת־ציון הריעי בת ירושלם
הנה מלכך יבוא לך

9:9

רני ושמחי בת־ציון
כי הנני־בא ושכנתי בתוכך נאם־יהוה

2:10 [Heb. 14]

Looking at the details, one sees that the identity of the one who is arriving is different: God in ch. 2, and the king in ch. 9. What we observe here is that a sequence of constituents which was used in Zech 2:14 to describe the coming of God to live with his people is used in Zech 9:9 to describe the coming of the king of Jerusalem. The two passages are so unique

[16] E.g., Boda, "Figuring," 60.

within Zechariah that we are compelled to conclude that this similarity is deliberate. This state of affairs is another challenge for the reader to consider the possibility of God and the king being identical.

In a recent study, Collins has broadened the picture by looking at a number of other passages in the prophets which share elements found in Zech. 9:9 and 2:14. His list is somewhat different from mine and contains seven elements in total:[17]

1. imperative, indicating the response expected
2. vocative proper noun, revealing the identity of the recipients
3. interjection particle הנה
4. identity of the one who is coming (namely God by various titles)
5. the verb בוא
6. mode of coming
7. effects of coming

Collins uses the presence of these seven elements to identify a literary form, which he calls "prophetic proclamation of the coming of the Lord."[18] He finds all seven elements in Zech 9:9–10. My discussion of the three constituents which are similar in Zech 9:9 and 2:14 covers elements 1–5. Collins writes:

> Up to this point, therefore, Zech 9:9 has the typical form of a prophetic proclamation of the coming of the Lord. Consequently, the form points the reader familiar with the convention towards the conclusion that the one who is coming is none other than God himself. This expectation is reinforced by the immediate context of the oracle which contains a reference to the Divine Warrior in 9:8.[19]

Collins shows how the two remaining elements are also present in the two passages under discussion in v. 9b (#6, the mode of coming) and v. 10

[17] The list is found in Terry Collins, "The Literary Contexts of Zechariah 9:9," in *The Book of Zechariah and Its Influence* (ed. Christopher Tuckett: Aldershot: Ashgate, 2003), 29–40 (35). The items in the list show interesting overlap with elements used by Crüsemann more than forty years ago to identify the literary form of the *Aufruf zur Freude* (Frank Crüsemann, *Studien zur Formgeschichte von Hymnus und Danklied in Israel* [WMANT 32; Neukirchen-Vluyn: Neukirchener, 1969], 55–60).

[18] Collins, "Literary Contexts," 37; he finds main examples in Isa 35:4; 30:27; 49:9–11; 62:11; Zeph 3:14–17; Zech 2:10 (p. 35), and related examples in Isa 30:2; 52:7–10; 60:1–3 (p. 40 n. 16); compare Leske ("Context and meaning of Zechariah 9: 9," 671), who lists Zeph 3:14; Isa 40:9–11; 52:1–2, 7–9; 62:11 and comments: "In all cases, Yahweh is king [...]," but then continues, "Whoever this king is, his function will be to act on behalf of Yahweh's kingship."

[19] Collins, "Literary Contexts," 37.

(#7, effects of the coming). However, Collins refrains from concluding that Zech 9:9–10 are about the coming of the Lord. The expectation raised by the form is "foiled in the contents":

> The second half of Zech 9:9, however, steers us in a completely different direction by telling that the king will be meek and humble and will come riding on an ass. The introduction of a human king does not fulfill the expectation set up in the opening line.[20]

For Collins, the content of element #6 (the mode of the coming) subverts the form of the proclamation of the coming of the Lord. Apparently, the possibility that God can be presented as coming "humble and riding on a donkey, on a colt, the foal of a donkey" is excluded from the outset. Admittedly, this is a bold picture of the coming of YHWH. However, if all seven elements are present, and one of the elements is unusual, maybe even highly unusual, then one should surely consider the possibility that what is subverted here is not the literary form, but the limits of the imagination of how YHWH can come and be present in the world. This is all the more so, when, as I have argued, there are other pointers to the divine identity of the king in Zech 9:9.

## III. Conclusion

In the first part of this article I have pointed to a number of details in the book of Zechariah which indicate a considerable level of restraint in the book of Zechariah with respect to kingship. There seems to be one exception to this ambiguity of kingship.

This exception is found in the portrayal of the arrival of the king of Jerusalem in Zech 9. He is an unusual king in a number of ways. I have argued that Zechariah intends his audience to identify the king as YHWH. This way of reading Zech 9:9 is based on observations of the connection of this verse with three other passages in the book. Zechariah 9:1–8 presents YHWH like a king on a military campaign marching down towards the south, heading for Jerusalem, the city whose new king arrives in 9:9. The *inclusio* of Zech 9:9 and 14:9 includes the aspect of global rule by a king who is clearly identified as YHWH in 14:9. The form of the first part of 9:9 invites a comparison with a verse from the first part of the book (2:14) with the same constituents, which proclaims the return of YHWH to live in Jerusalem.

[20] Collins, "Literary Contexts," 37.

# THE COMING OF THE LORD—AN INTER-TEXTUAL READING OF ISA 40:1–11; 52:7–10; 59:15B–20; 62:10–11 AND 63:1–6

Lena-Sofia Tiemeyer

This paper will explore the ways in which the later material in Isa 56–66 reused and developed the earlier material in Isa 40–55. It will focus on the specific example of the motif of God's return to Jerusalem after a period of absence. I shall suggest that Isa 59:15b–20, 62:10–11, and 63:1–6 transformed the extant motif in Isa 40:3–5, 9–11, and 52:7–10. It is an honour to dedicate this paper to Prof. H. G. M. Williamson.[1]

## I. Dating

We need to establish first the relative dating of these passages. Although any exact dating is impossible, the primacy of the material in Isa 40–55 is commonly accepted.

Beginning with the material in Isa 40–55, it is debatable whether Isa 40:1–11* is exilic or post-exilic. Some exegetes differentiate between Isa 40:(1–2)3–5, part of a core-text composed prior to 539 BC, and 40:9–11, part of a later edition from the early post-exilic period.[2] Others include all of Isa 40:1–5, 9–11 in this post-exilic edition.[3] In my view, the affinity in terms of content and theological outlook between vv. 1–5 and 9–11 invites reading these verses as a textual unity. Furthermore, as they highlight some of the key themes of Isa 40–55 and, in this manner, function as a prelude to the subsequent material, they probably contain among the latest material in Isa 40–55.[4] The text of Isa 52:7–10 mentions many of the same themes

---

[1] Prof. H. G. M. Williamson was my doctoral supervisor from 1998–2002. I am forever indebted to his knowledge of the book of Isaiah.

[2] See, e.g., Klaus Kiesow, *Exodustexte im Jesajabuch: Literarkritische und motivgeschichtliche Analysen* (OBO 24; Fribourg: Editions Universitaires, 1979), 201–2; and Reinhard G. Kratz, "Der Anfang des Zweiten Jesaja in Jes 40,1f. und seine literarischen Horizonte," *ZAW* 105 (1993): 400–19 (404–5).

[3] See, e.g., Jürgen van Oorschot, *Von Babel zum Zion: Eine literarkritische und redaktionsgeschichtliche Untersuchung* (BZAW 206; Berlin: de Gruyter, 1993), 105–27, 273–75.

[4] See further Lena-Sofia Tiemeyer, *For the Comfort of Zion: The Geographical and Theological Location of Isaiah 40–55* (VTSup 139; Leiden: Brill, 2011), 333–45.

as Isa 40:1–11.* This affinity has caused many scholars to view these two passages as together forming a framework around an early edition of Isa 40–55.[5] I prefer seeing Isa 52:7–10 as the earlier text to which Isa 40:1–11 alludes.[6] As to the date of these two passages, the predominant Jerusalem perspective in them suggests that they were composed in Judah, either by the returned exiles sometime after 539 BC or, in my view more likely, by the people of Judah shortly before 539 BC.[7]

Turning to the material in Isa 56–66, Isa 62:10–11 is clearly dependent on Isa 40:1–11. Isa 62:11b is identical with Isa 40:10b, and Isa 62:10 and Isa 40:3 share key vocabulary. Some scholars interpret these similarities to mean that Isa 62:10–12 is the ending of an early version of the whole book of Isaiah (1–39* + 40–55 + 60–62).[8] Others maintain that the author(s) responsible for Isa 60–62 composed Isa 62:10–12 in order to emphasize the connection to the earlier material in Isa 40–55.[9] These two views are compatible with each other, and both highlight that Isa 62:10–12 is later than Isa 40–55 yet earlier than the rest of Isa 56–66.

Finally, scholars disagree about the relative dating of Isa 59:15b–20 and 63:1–6. Much depends on the textual relationship between Isa 60–62 and 63:1–6: if the person(s) responsible for Isa 60–62 also composed Isa 63:1–6, then Isa 63:1–6 is among the oldest material in Isa 56–66 and thus predates Isa 59:15b–20. The perceived difference in outlook regarding foreigners speaks against shared authorship,[10] as does the disparate literary character of the two texts.[11] Yet, the difference in attitude towards foreigners between Isa 60–62 and Isa 63:1–6 is smaller than it is often claimed to be.[12] Likewise, the apocalyptic character of Isa 63:1–6 agrees with that of

---

[5] See, e.g., Christina Ehring, *Die Rückkehr JHWHs: Traditions- und religionsgeschichtliche Untersuchungen zu Jesaja 40,1–11, Jesaja 52,7–10 und verwandten Texten* (WMANT 116; Neukirchen-Vluyn: Neukirchener, 2007), 90–95.

[6] See Tiemeyer, *Comfort of Zion*, 341–43.

[7] See Tiemeyer, *Comfort of Zion*, 50–51.

[8] E.g. Odil Hannes Steck, *Studien zu Tritojesaja* (BZAW 203; Berlin: de Gruyter, 1991), 143–66.

[9] E.g. Joseph Blenkinsopp, *Isaiah 56–66: A New Translation with Introduction and Commentary* (AB 19B; New York: Doubleday, 2003), 241–45.

[10] See, e.g., Claus Westermann, *Das Buch Jesaja: Kapitel 40–66* (ATD 19; Göttingen: Vandenhoeck & Ruprecht, 1966), 243; Pierre E. Bonnard, *Le second Isaïe, son disciple et leurs éditeurs Isaïe 40–66* (EBib; Paris: J. Gabalda, 1972), 434.

[11] Westermann, *Jesaja*, 243, 305.

[12] Paul A. Smith, *Rhetoric and Redaction in Trito-Isaiah: The Structure, Growth and Authorship of Isaiah 56–66* (VTSup 62; Leiden: Brill, 1995), 38–39.

Isa 60:19–20.[13] In addition, the lexical similarities between Isa 60–62 and 63:1–3 speak in favour of shared authorship.[14]

A comparative study of Isa 59:15b–20 and 63:1–6, two texts that are clearly related as evidenced by the large amount of shared significant vocabulary,[15] confirms the primacy of Isa 63:1–6. As pointed out by Whybray, the depiction of God as a warrior fits better the context of Isa 63:5 which deals with foreign nations than that of Isa 59:15b–20 which reflects the struggle within the community in Judah.[16] There is, however, no consensus regarding this matter. Several scholars detect a development from Isa 59:15b–20 to Isa 63:1–6,[17] and yet others maintain that Isa 59:15b–20 and 63:1–6 were written by the same hand.[18] Although we cannot reach a conclusive decision, the evidence in favour of the primacy of Isa 63:1–6 is convincing.

To sum up, the five texts in question date relatively in the following order: Isa 52:7–10; 40:1–5, 9–11; 62:10–12; 63:1–6 and Isa 59:15b–20.

## II. Dependency of Isa 59:15b–20 and 63:1–6 upon other texts

It has often been noted that the motif of God's return (to Zion) and his vengeance over his enemies (for the sake of Zion) in Isa 63:1–6 and 59:15b–20 depends on earlier Isaianic and non-Isaianic traditions:

---

13 Fredrich Holmgren, "Yahweh the Avenger: Isaiah 63:1–6," in *Rhetorical Criticism: Essays in Honor of James Muilenburg* (ed. Jared J. Jackson and Martin Kessler; PTMS 1; Eugene, OR.: Pickwick, 1974), 133–48 (144).

14 Smith, *Rhetoric*, 43.

15 See further Hugo Odeberg, *Trito-Isaiah* (UUA 1; Uppsala: A.-B. Lundequistska Bokhandeln, 1931), 210–15, 274–76; and Claire R. Mathews, *Defending Zion: Edom's Desolation and Jacob's Restoration (Isaiah 34–35) in Context* (BZAW 236; Berlin: de Gruyter, 1995), 80. See also Lena-Sofia Tiemeyer ("The Watchman Metaphor in Isaiah lvi–lxvi," *VT* 55 [2005]: 378–400 [395–97]) in which I argue for the primacy of Isa 63:1–6.

16 R. Norman Whybray, *Isaiah 40–66* (New Century Bible Commentary; London: Marshall, Morgan & Scott, 1975), 226. See also Bernhard Duhm, *Das Buch Jesaia: Übersetzt und Erklärt* (HAT 3/1; Göttingen: Vandenhoeck & Ruprecht, 1892), 445; Karl Elliger, *Die Einheit des Tritojesaia (Jesaia 56–66)* (Stuttgart: W. Kohhammer, 1928), 18; and Westermann, *Jesaja*, 279.

17 Paul Volz, *Jesaja*, II (KAT; Leipzig: Deichertsche, 1932), 263; Jacques Vermeylen, *Du prophète Isaïe á l'apocalyptique* (EBib; Paris: J. Gabalda, 1978), 489; John J. Scullion, *Isaiah 40–66* (OTM 12; Wilmington: Michael Glazier, 1982), 189; Bernard Gosse, "Detournement de la vengeance du Seigneur contre Edom et les nations en Isa 63,1–6," *ZAW* 102 (1990): 105–10 (109–10), Henrik Pfeiffer, *Jahwes Kommen von Süden: Jdc 5; Hab 3; Dtn 33 und Ps 68 in ihrem literatur- und theologiegeschichtlichen Umfeld* (FRLANT 211; Göttingen: Vandenhoeck & Ruprecht, 2005), 84–85.

18 Holmgren, "Yahweh the Avenger," 145–48. Cf. Klaus Koenen, *Ethik und Eschatologie im Tritojesajabuch* (WMANT 62; Neukirchen-Vluyn: Neukirchener, 1990), 83–87.

1. The notion that God returns from Edom is probably part of the larger tradition that God comes from the south. This notion is associated with the traditions around Jethro/Reuel, Moses' father-in-law, and the origin of YHWH-ism in the southern parts of the Negeb/Sinai.[19] The same notion occurs in Deut 33:2–3; Judg 5:4 and Hag 3:3.[20]

2. It is also possible that the imagery of Lam 1:15 where God treads the winepress is a source of influence for the imagery in Isa 59:15b–20 and 63:1–6.

3. Isa 63:1–3 shares significant vocabulary and imagery with Isa 61:1–2; Isa 34:1–8 (vengeance) and 35:4 (return).[21] In this case, however, the imagery in Isa 34:1–8 and 35:4 probably depends on that in Isa 60:1–63:1. It is likely that the material in Isa 34–35 was added later to serve as a bridge between Isa 1–39* and the subsequent Isa 40–55 which, at this point, was already supplemented with Isa 60:1–63:6.

4. There is probably also a link between the notion of a "Day of Vengeance" (יום נקם) in Isa 34:8; 61:2; 63:4 and the idea of a "Day of Salvation" (יום ישועה) in the earlier Isa 49:8. Following Steck and Beuken, it is likely that the author of Isa 61:2 transformed the expression יום ישועה in the earlier Isa 49:8 into the opposite expression יום נקם.[22]

The present paper suggests yet another set of passages upon which Isa 59:15b–20 and 63:1–6 depend, namely Isa 40:1–11; 52:7–10 and 62:11.

## III. Exegesis of Isaiah 40:1–5, 9–11; 52:7–10; 62:11; 63:1–6 and 59:15b–20

Let us therefore take a closer look at these passages. Beginning with Isa 40:1–11,* verses 1–2 contain a command to comfort Jerusalem and to announce to the city that its guilt has been exonerated, and the following vv. 3–5 depict God's journey through the wilderness. Nature will be transformed and God's glory will be visible for all humanity. Verse 9 commands a (female) messenger[23] to announce God's arrival in Jerusalem and

---

[19] See further John R. Bartlett, *Edom and the Edomites* (JSOTSup 77; Sheffield: JSOT Press, 1989), 89.

[20] See further Pfeiffer, *Jahwes Kommen von Süden*, 82–86.

[21] See, e.g., Holmgren, "Yahweh the Avenger," 137–43; Koenen, *Ethik*, 81–82; Steck, *Studien*, 116–18, 210.

[22] Steck, *Studien*, 116–18; and Willem A. M. Beuken, "Servant and Herald of Good Tidings: Isaiah 61 as an Interpretation of Isaiah 40–55," in *The Book of Isaiah—Le Livre d'Isaie: Les oracles et leurs relecteurs: unité et complexité de l'ouvrage* (ed. Jacques Vermeylen; BETL 81; Leuven: Leuven University Press, 1989), 411–42 (420–24).

[23] See Tiemeyer, *Comfort of Zion*, 279–85.

the other cities in Judah. Finally, verses 10–11 portray God's arrival like a victorious warrior (v. 10) and like a shepherd who cares for his flock (v. 11). In this manner, Isa 40:1–5, 9–11 is a message to Zion in the form of a theophany[24] that accentuates God's kingship yet also his just and merciful character.[25] Moreover, given the focus on Zion in vv. 1–2, 9, this passage describes God as returning to his home in Zion from his abode in the south.[26] In a similar manner, the material in Isa 52:7–10 speaks of God's visible return to Jerusalem. The (male) messenger announces God's kingship (v. 7), the watchmen of Zion shout for joy because God will return to the city (v. 8) in order to comfort his people there (vv. 8–9), his power visible for all the nations (v. 10).[27] Isaiah 62:11 conveys the same imagery of God arriving to Zion with salvation.

Isaiah 63:1–6 depicts how God comes from Edom and Bozrah in strength, declaring that he speaks in righteousness and is mighty to save (v. 1). There is a verbal exchange between a watchman (v. 2) and God (vv. 3–6).[28] The watchman asks why God's clothes are red as if stained by grapes, and God responds that as he treaded the nations like grapes in his anger, his clothes became stained by their blood (v. 3, cf. v. 6).[29] It is unclear whether the people of Edom are included among those nations,[30] or whether Edom is merely the battleground, situated alongside the route upon which God travels on his way to Jerusalem from his abode in the south.[31] The destruction of the nations is part of God's planned Day of Vengeance and Year of Salvation (v. 4).[32] God laments the absence of a

---

24 Jan L. Koole, *Isaiah. Part 3, Volume 1: Isaiah 40–48* (Historical Commentary on the Old Testament; Kampen, the Netherlands: Kok Pharos, 1997), 59.

25 Ehring, *Rückkehr JHWHs*, 47, 60–63.

26 Michael D. Goulder, *Isaiah as Liturgy* (SOTSMS; Aldershot, England: Ashgate, 2004), 113.

27 For a discussion of the similarities and the differences between Isa 40:3–5, 9–11 and 52:7–10, see Ehring, *Rückkehr JHWHs*, 90–95.

28 See further James Muilenburg, "The Book of Isaiah Chapters 40–66," *IB* 5 (Nashville: Abingdon, 1956), 381–773 (726); Westermann, *Jesaja*, 302–3; and Whybray, *Isaiah*, 252. Cf. Isa 21:11–12.

29 It can be inferred from v. 6 that the object suffixes on the verbs ואדרכם and וארמסם refer to the "nations." See further the discussion in Mathews, *Defending Zion*, 78–79.

30 See, e.g., Koenen, *Ethik*, 79; Pfeiffer, *Jahwes Kommen von Süden*, 83.

31 See, e.g., Bert Dicou (*Edom, Israel's Brother and Antagonist: The Role of Edom in Biblical Prophecy and Story* [JSOTSup 169; Sheffield: Sheffield Academic, 1994], 192) who emphasizes that Edom is described as the geographical battleground rather than as the enemy. Cf. Steck, *Studien*, 210.

32 The word גאולי can be read in two ways: it may be derived from the root גאל II = "defile" (BDB, 146, cf. Isa 63:3, אגאלתי = "I have defiled" [probably a rare *Aphel* form or Aramaizing form of *Hiphil*, cf. Blenkinsopp, *Isaiah 56–66*, 246, note j]), or from the root גאל I, with the specific meaning suggested by BDB (145b, 1.e.) for Num 35 (גאל הדם)

person willing to fight on behalf of his people (v. 5), an absence that has motivated God to act himself for his people against the nations (v. 6).

The parallel passage in Isa 59:15b–20 likewise describes God as acting alone on behalf of his people because nobody else is present. God laments the absence of justice (v. 15b), and the absence of anybody (v. 16aa) who can intervene (v. 16ab). Given this unsatisfactory situation, God then decides to intervene himself (v. 16bb), dressed in armour and fuelled by his anger (v. 17). He will fight his adversaries (v. 18), thus causing his name and glory to be known from west to east (v. 19a). God will come in rage (v. 19b), yet also as a redeemer for those penitent in Zion (v. 20).

## IV. Similarities and Differences

We shall now look more closely at the similarities and differences between these five texts and explore how the later set of texts in Isa 59:15b–20 and Isa 63:1–6 transforms and reinterprets the earlier set of texts in Isa 40–55 (and Isa 62:11).

### 1. *God's Strength/God's Arm*

Both sets of texts describe God as coming in *strength*. This idea is expressed in several different ways. Isaiah 40:10 describes God as coming in strength (בחזק יבוא).[33] Isaiah 63:1 picks up this notion, although using different terminology, as it depicts God as coming in great might (ברב כחו). In yet another manner, Isa 59:17 conveys God's strength through its imagery in which God is dressed in a coat of mail (כשרין) and wearing a helmet (כובע). Likewise, the metaphors in Isa 59:19, which denote God's arrival as a pent-up flood (כנהר צר), emphasize God's might. In addition, both sets of texts use the phrase "God's arm" (זרע) to signify God's strength. Isa 40:10 (וזרעו משלה לו) and 40:11 (בזרעו יקבץ טלאים) employ this term as a metaphor for God's executive power and strength, and Isa 52:10 states that God will reveal "his holy arm" (חשף ה' את זרוע קדשו). Likewise,

"the avenger of blood." Cf. Westermann, *Jesaja*, 304–5 ("Jahr meiner Vergeltung"); and Odil Hannes Steck, *Bereitete Heimkehr: Jesaja 35 als redaktionelle Brücke zwischen dem Ersten und dem Zweiten Jesaja* (SBS 121; Stuttgart: Katholisches Bibelwerk, 1985), 52. Alternatively, the term גאולי in Isa 63:4 may be a conscious wordplay on both roots as well as on the similar expression in Isa 61:2a. The semantic range remains positive.

[33] It is possible that the descriptions of the "mighty one" and the "awe-inspiring one" in Isa 49:24 refer to God. If so, this may be yet another source of influence in Isa 40–55. For the translation of this verse, see Tiemeyer, *Comfort of Zion*, 199.

Isa 63:5 (ותושע לי זרעי) and Isa 59:15b–16 (ותושע לו זרעו) both refer to "God's arm." Finally, both sets of texts portray God as coming in strength to *Zion-Jerusalem* (Isa 40:9; 52:8; 59:20).

In view of these similarities, it is likely that the image of "God's arm" as a metaphor for God's strength, as used in Isa 40:1–5, 9–11 and 52:7–10, constituted a source of influence for the later material in Isa 63:1–6 and 59:15b–20. In this case, there is hardly any change in the ways in which the two sets of texts use the imagery.

### 2. *Justice and Righteousness*

Both sets of texts state that the main reason for God's coming to Jerusalem is the lack of *justice* there. Beginning with the earlier material in Isa 40–55, although Isa 40:1–2 contains no specific word denoting "justice," there is a sense that the "comfort" that Jerusalem is supposed to receive relates to justice. Verse 2 states that the Lord has punished Jerusalem "double for all her sins" (כפלים בכל חטאתיה). Although scholars differ in their exact interpretation of this expression, the general impression is that the punishment of Judah was not "just."[34] In this sense, Isa 40:1–2 addresses a situation in which God needs to intervene and establish justice. Isaiah 52:7–10 contains the same notion that God needs to restore the current situation to what it used to be. In particular, the contrast between the reference to "ruins" and the reference to God's redemption in v. 9 suggests a scenario in which God will redress the situation in Zion to its former status quo. As to the material in Isa 56–66, Isa 59:15 states that there is *no judgment* (כי אין משפט); with the result that *God's own righteousness* will come to his help (v. 16b, וצדקתו), whereupon he will put on armour of *righteousness* (וילבש צדקה כשרין, v. 17). Likewise, Isa 63:1 depicts how God will speak in *righteousness* (מדבר בצדקה).

In this case, there are no clear verbal ties between the two sets of texts, yet both sets get across the general sense that God is coming in order to bring justice to Jerusalem, something which the city has not experienced in recent times. At the same time, there is a marked contrast between the two sets of texts. While the earlier material conveys the hope that justice will be re-established in the near future, the material in Isa 56–66 communicates the disappointment that this has not yet happened.

---

[34] See discussion in John Goldingay and David Payne, *Isaiah 40–55* (vol. 1; ICC; London: T&T, Clark, 2007), 71–72.

### 3. *Salvation/Redemption (roots* ישע *and* גאל*) of Zion-Jerusalem*

The notion that God will *redeem* Jerusalem, communicated by the use of the two roots ישע and גאל, is a key feature in both sets of texts. In Isa 52:7–9, a messenger proclaims peace and *salvation* (מבשר ישועה) as he informs Zion that its God reigns (v. 7). He further encourages Jerusalem to rejoice because God, now as he is returning to Zion (v. 8), has *redeemed* Jerusalem (גאל ירושלם). Likewise, Isa 62:11 (modelled after Isa 40:10, the counterpart of Isa 52:7–10) states that God is coming and with him, or even embodied in him, comes Zion's *salvation* (הנה ישעך בא). The same two roots also appear in the later Isa 59:15b–20 and 63:1–6. Isaiah 59:17 speaks of a "helmet of *salvation*" that God will wear (כובע ישועה). Later in the same passage, Isa 59:20 picks up the theme that God will come as a *redeemer* to Zion (ובא לציון גואל) from Isa 52:9 and 62:11. In addition, both Isa 59:16 and Isa 63:5 use a *Hiphil* form of the root ישע in the phrase תושע לי/ו זרעי/ו (cf. above). In addition, Isa 63:1 employs the root ישע when describing God as "mighty to *save*" (רב להושיע), and Isa 63:4 speaks of the year of God's *redemption* (ושנת גאולי). Both sets of texts thus maintain that God is coming to Jerusalem in order to bring salvation to the city, and both attribute salvation to God as a defining characteristic.

### 4. *God as a Coming Victor*

Both sets of texts ascribe to God military victory over his enemies, but they employ distinct terminology and imagery. The material in Isa 40–55 has the salvation of Jerusalem in focus when describing God's victory over his enemies. Isaiah 40:10b depicts God as coming with "his *reward*" (שכרו) and "his *deeds*" (ופעלתו) before him. The idea of God's "deeds," a phrase often translated as "recompense," is that of God bringing some form of restitution. Likewise, the notion of God's "reward" carries the connotation of compensation. The 3rd masculine singular suffix on both words implies that the reward and the recompense alike belong to God, as befitting the powerful deity (cf. v. 10a).[35] At the same time, the focus on Jerusalem (v. 9) suggests that the city is the beneficiary of God's reward and recompense which, in turn, form some kind of compensation for its past suffering. From a different angle, the messenger in Isa 52:7 speaks of "*peace*" (שלום) alongside "*salvation*" (ישועה, cf. above). In a sense, the notion of tidings of

[35] Cf. Koole, *Isaiah*, III/3, 324–25, speaking about Isa 62:11.

peace suggests that the past of Jerusalem was less than peaceful. As such, the text of Isa 52:7 implies that God has won a victory over those who brought havoc upon Jerusalem.

The idea of victory is present also in the material of Isa 56–66. Isaiah 62:11b reuses the image in Isa 40:10b *verbatim* (הנה שכרו אתו ופעלתו לפניו) with similar connotations. Isaiah 62:12a suggests that God has acted on behalf of Jerusalem, as its population will be called "God's redeemed ones" (גאולי ה'). As in Isa 40:10, the reward and the deeds belong to God but are carried out for the benefit of the people of Jerusalem. In contrast, Isa 59:15b–20 and 63:1–6 place less stress on Jerusalem and its salvation and instead emphasize God's vengeance over its enemies. Notably, Isa 59:17 speaks of "clothes of vengeance" (בגדי נקם) and a "robe of zeal" (מעיל קנאה). As do Isa 40:10 and 62:11, Isa 59:18 refers to "recompense" but uses different words (גמול/גמלות) and a different syntactical construction: God will pay in accordance with (the enemies') deeds (כעל גמלות כעל ישלם) (cf. JPS, KJV). In other words, rather than bringing reward to Jerusalem as in the earlier material, God will bring punishment to his enemies. Finally, from a broader perspective and again using distinct vocabulary, Isa 63:1–6 tells of God's victory over the peoples. Thus, while the notion of God as the victor over his enemies, the nations, is a prominent feature in both sets of texts, they focus on the opposite sides of the same coin. While the material in Isa 40–55, as well as the clearly related text of Isa 62:11–12, accentuates God's victory over the nations *for the sake of Jerusalem*, Isa 59:15b–20 and 63:1–6 highlight God's victory *against the nations*. This change reflects the change of expectations within the group of people responsible for the growing body of literature of Isa 40–66. It can be assumed that when the situation in Jerusalem did not change drastically with the Persian take-over in 539 B.C., the concerns of this group of prophets turned from trust to distrust in the nations.

### 5. *Seeing*

Both sets of texts contain the notion of "seeing," yet use it in diverse ways. Isaiah 40:5 declares that all flesh will see God's glory (וראו כל בשר). In fact, Isa 40:3–5 as a whole proclaims the way in which nature itself will enable all of humankind to see God's return (to Jerusalem). Isaiah 40:9 contains the same notion although without using any terminology related to "seeing." It encourages the messenger to Zion-Jerusalem to climb a high mountain, presumably to permit everyone to see her, as she announces God's arrival. Her message, found in vv. 10–11, begins with the interjection

הנה ("behold") which often serves to call attention to something visible. This idea of "seeing" is picked up in Isa 59:15b. Here, however, it is *God* who sees the lack of justice and, as a result, is displeased (וירא ה' וירע בעיניו). Likewise, v. 16a depicts God as seeing, or rather not seeing (וירא), anyone who is able or willing to intervene (on behalf of God's people). Finally, Isa 63:5 speaks of God seeing, although using a different verb (ואביט).

As above, the transformation of the concept of "seeing" reflects the changes in the Judahite community in the early post-exilic period. The community responsible for Isa 40–55 expressed their confidence in God though the hope that the surrounding *nations* would see God's mighty deeds. In the subsequent years when Judah remained an insignificant cultural and political backwater, this hope was transmuted into the hope that *God* would see the people of Judah and their current situation of need.

### 6. *Glory and Honour*

Both sets of texts speak of God's *glory/honour* (כבוד ה'). Isaiah 40:5 predicts that God's glory/honour will be revealed so that all flesh can see it (ונגלה כבוד ה' וראו כל בשר יחדו). Isaiah 59:19 reflects the same idea, although instead of using the verb "to see" (root ראה) it employs the orthographically similar verb "to fear" (root ירא): "they shall fear God's name from the west (וייראו ממערב את שם ה'), and from the (place of the) rising of the sun his glory/honour (וממזרח שמש את כבודו)". It is possible that this change from "to see" to "to fear" is a conscious play on the similarity between the two roots, yet it also reflects the changed attitude towards the nations (cf. above).

### 7. *Watchmen and Messengers*

The motifs of messengers and watchmen bind the two sets of texts together. In this case, the link between the two motifs is conceptual rather than verbal. A messenger and a watchman are interconnected to that extent that both deal with news. The watchman's task is to spot a person approaching the city and to discover his origin and his business (cf. Isa 63:1). He thus *obtains* news from the outside. The messenger is his equivalence insofar as his task is to *deliver* news from the outside. Both professions furthermore have as their task to alert people of danger. A messenger often brings military information of attacking armies and, as such, serves as a herald of danger. In a similar manner, a watchman is often the first person to notice oncoming enemies and is therefore in a position to alert the leaders of the city of the imminent danger.

Isa 40–55 features both types of people. Isa 40:9a speaks of a *messenger* to Zion (מבשרת ציון) and Isa 52:7a refers to a *messenger* who will proclaim peace and salvation (מבשר משמיע שלום מבשר טוב משמיע ישועה),[36] while Isa 52:8aa mentions *watchmen* (צפיך) who will raise their voices in joy. It is furthermore possible that the people[37] who are commanded to comfort God's people (in Jerusalem) in Isa 40:1–2 should be understood as some kind of messengers. After all, their task was to bring a message of "comfort". As to Isa 56–66, although Isa 63:1–6 contains neither the term "watchman" nor "messenger," verse 1 depicts the exchange between a messenger and a watchman (cf. above). In contrast, Isa 59:15b–20 does not contain any references to messengers or watchmen.

### 8. *Missing people*

While the material in Isa 40:1–11 and 52:7–10 describes a situation in which God sends watchmen and messengers to proclaim good news to Jerusalem, the material in Isa 63:1–6 and 59:15b–20 depicts a scenario in which God bemoans the absence of a person who can help and, as a result of this absence, decides to act himself. In my view, these two scenarios are interconnected and show a theological development.

Isaiah 63:5 bewails the absence of a "helper" (m.sg. part. עזר) and a "supporter" (m.sg. part. סומך). This missing person is probably meant to signify an actual warrior who should have fought on behalf of Judah against the nations. When he fails to appear, God decides to step in and fight himself. In a similar manner, although using different vocabulary, Isa 59:16 bemoans that there is no מפגיע, a word which probably denotes an intercessor, i.e., a person who could intervene between the people and God. I suggest that Isa 59:16 transformed the original warrior motif in Isa 63:5 into a motif related to intercession in order to make it fit its new context of domestic conflict in Isa 59:15b–20.[38]

I further propose, although somewhat speculatively, that the scenario depicted in Isa 59:15b–20 has fused not only the concept of the missing warrior in Isa 63:1–6 but also the commands in Isa 40:1–2, 9 to comfort and bring good news to Zion. Thus, what we see here is a sequence of development. First, Isa 40:1–11 seeks a person who can comfort Zion and proclaim

[36] See Tiemeyer, *Comfort of Zion*, 276–85.

[37] Scholars identify the recipients of the command in Isa 40:1–2 with either prophets or members of the heavenly court. The former identification fits the present context better, cf. Tiemeyer, *Comfort of Zion*, 16–18.

[38] Tiemeyer, "The Watchman Metaphor," 392–94, 396–97.

to her the good news about God's imminent arrival (cf. Isa 52:7–10), for the entire world to see (Isa 40:3–5). The awaited comforters and messengers apparently fail to appear and the nations fail to note God's arrival in Jerusalem. In view of this disappointing situation, God decides to act on his own. God will tell the ends of the earth about his arrival in Jerusalem (Isa 62:11) and he will fight against the nations (Isa 63:1–6). Even later, the disappointment has reached into the community of Judah itself. Yet again, God decides to act on his own, but now for the sake of a select group of faithful ones among his people (Isa 59:15b–20).

## V. Summary

As we have seen, the many thematic and semantic similarities between Isa 40:1–5, 9–11; 52:7–10 and 62:11 on the one hand and Isa 59:15b–20 and 63:1–6 on the other make a strong case for literary dependency. Both sets of texts describe God as coming in strength and glory to Jerusalem, and both give the lack of justice for the people in Jerusalem as the reason for God's arrival. Moreover, both sets of texts maintain that God will come to Jerusalem as its redeemer, both see God's military victory over their shared enemies as an important aspect of Jerusalem's salvation, and both regard God's acts of salvation as one of his defining features. Finally, both sets of texts employ the same types of literary personae (e.g., warrior, watchmen, and messengers) to put their message across. At the same time, there are significant differences between the two sets of texts which can be explained by changes in the sociological and theological circumstances in Judah. Primarily, while the earlier texts speak solely of comfort, in this manner reflecting their authors' hope for a brighter future, the latter material contains elements of vengeance and violence that mirror its authors' own disappointments. In these later texts, God is indeed coming but he is coming alone because he did not receive the help that he pleaded for in Isa 40:1–2.

# PART IV

# CHRONICLES-EZRA-NEHEMIAH

# FLASHFORWARD: FUTURE GLIMPSES IN THE PAST OF EZRA 1–6

Mark J. Boda

The historiographic character of the first six chapters of Ezra-Nehemiah has long been debated and it is well known that our honoured professor has been one of the key contributors to this debate.[1] In light of this it is my intention to reflect once again on the historiography of this section of the Hebrew Bible in conversation with the past work of Hugh Williamson which lays the foundation for new insights in the present essay. In investigating this historiography I will address first the question "how?": how have the ones responsible for Ezra 1–6 shaped this presentation of the history of the early Persian period, that is, what are some key techniques employed by the ones responsible for Ezra 1–6 to present the history of the early Persian period? Seeing as a full investigation is not possible in the present context, I will focus attention on a particular set of literary techniques. Having accomplished this, I will consider the question "why?": why did the ones responsible for Ezra 1–6 shape their presentation in this particular way, that is, what purpose is there in the employment of these techniques?

## I. Literary Structure and Temporal Notations

The literary structure of these chapters appears to be set at the outset of the section with the twofold invitation of Cyrus to the exilic community: "let them go up (עלה) . . . and rebuild (בנה)" (1:3).[2] These invitations drive the remainder of the narrative. Two chapters are devoted to the first invitation (עלה) and the remaining four to the second (בנה). It is clear that the first chapter (Ezra 1) is presented as taking place in the historical

[1] My first paper at Cambridge as I began my doctoral studies under Hugh Williamson was on the thorny issue of the relationship between the Chronicler and Ezra-Nehemiah and Ezra 1–6 played a key role in that work. His insightful response to that initial offering oriented me to the world of graduate studies and pushed me to new levels in my research. For his supervision during that first phase of my doctoral studies I am deeply grateful.

[2] See Bezalel Porten, "Theme and Structure of Ezra 1–6: From Literature to History," *Transeuphratene* 23 (2002): 27–44, esp. 29–30.

context of the earliest phase of the reign of Cyrus (539 BCE and following; see Ezra 1:1), and it is equally clear that the last two chapters (Ezra 5–6) are presented as taking place in the historical context of the earliest phase of the reign of Darius (522 BCE and following; see Ezra 4:24; 6:15).[3] What is not clear and has been the point of greatest debate, however, is the historical context and flow of the events described, and the sources utilized, in the intervening chapters (Ezra 2–4).

Temporal notations are offered by the narrator at several junctures in Ezra 2–4. Ezra 3:1 links the restoration of the altar and reinstitution of the cult to the "seventh month," with 3:6 identifying a particular day, "the first day," of this seventh month, although in neither case is a particular year given. Ezra 3:8 identifies "the second year of their arrival at the house of God at Jerusalem in the second month" as the time when work on the house of God began. The date of this arrival is not made clear, although an initial reading suggests that the arrival in view is that described at the end of the list in Ezra 2:68, where similar vocabulary appears. In Ezra 4:4–5 a period stretching from the entire reign of Cyrus to that of Darius is linked to a campaign by the people of the land to discourage the people of Yehud and frighten them from rebuilding the temple. Then two historical references are made to the reigns of the later kings Ahaseurus (Xerxes) and Artaxerxes in 4:6 and 4:7, each linked to correspondence written to frustrate rebuilding efforts in Jerusalem. The final historical reference is found in 4:24, which speaks of the cessation of the rebuilding effort on the temple until the second year of Darius. There are two other references to Persian royal reigns in Ezra 2–4 (3:7; 4:3), both emphasizing Cyrus' authorization of the reconstruction effort.

---

[3] See Sara Japhet, "Composition and Chronology in the Book of Ezra-Nehemiah," in *Second Temple Studies: 2. Temple and Community in the Persian Period* (ed. Tamara C. Eskenazi and Kent H. Richards; JSOTSup 175; Sheffield: JSOT, 1994), 189–216, who notes how the inner structure of the two major sections of Ezra-Nehemiah (Ezra 1–6; Ezra 7–Neh 13) entails "a concentration of events at two points in time, in the beginning of the period and at the end." In the case of Ezra 1–6 it is the beginning of Cyrus' reign and the beginning of Darius' reign and "between these two extremes is an interim period which, chronologically speaking, is the lion's share of the period, though there is nothing to tell about it." Such an agenda of fusing the efforts of Cyrus and Darius to complete the prophetic agenda related to the Persians can be seen in the night visions of Zech 1:7–6:15 and possibly also Isa 40–55 and Dan 6:28; cf. Rainer Albertz, "Darius in Place of Cyrus: The First Edition of Deutero-Isaiah (Isaiah 40.1–52.12) in 521 BCE," *JSOT* 27 (2003): 371–88; Mark J. Boda, "Terrifying the Horns: Persia and Babylon in Zechariah 1:7–6:15," *CBQ* 67 (2005): 22–41.

As this evidence highlights, dealing with the flow of history in Ezra 1–6 and Ezra 2–4 in particular is clearly a challenge.[4] For some the answer is to be found in denying historical validity to most of what is found in these chapters. At best, these chapters belie an unsophisticated amalgamation of competing traditions concerning the temple restoration.[5] Others, however, have investigated the literary techniques employed by those responsible for Ezra 1–6 in order better to understand their historical perspective.[6] It is in this latter camp that one finds H. G. M. Williamson.

## II. Literary Historiographic Techniques in Ezra 1–6

It appears that it was Shemaryahu Talmon's 1976 dictionary article which proved most helpful to Hugh Williamson for understanding the historiographic role of some of the material found in Ezra 1–6.[7] Talmon identified three literary techniques used by the various historiographers responsible for Ezra-Nehemiah. First were the "closing invocations" employed in

[4] See the superb chart in Japhet, "Composition," 202, and attendant discussion (pp. 201–6). She shows how the flow of kings in Ezra 1–6 would fit a much longer period in Persian history, but how this is untenable historically. For one who argued for a similar flow of history in Ezra 1–6, placing the building of the temple in the period of Darius II, see Luc Dequeker, "Darius the Persian and the Reconstruction of the Jewish Temple in Jerusalem (Ezra 4, 23)," in *Ritual and Sacrifice in the Ancient Near East* (ed. Jan Quaegebeur; OLA 55; Leuven: Peeters, 1993), 67–92; Luc Dequeker, "Nehemiah and the Restoration of the Temple After Exile," in *Deuteronomy and Deuteronomic Literature: Festschrift C. H. W. Brekelmans* (ed. Marc Vervenne and Johan Lust; BETL 133; Leuven: Peeters/Leuven University, 1997), 547–67.

[5] For the former see Diana V. Edelman, "Ezra 1–6 as Idealized Past," in *A Palimpsest: Rhetoric, Ideology, Stylistics, and Language Relating to Persian Israel* (ed. Ehud Ben Zvi, Diana V. Edelman, and Frank Polak; Piscataway, N.J.: Gorgias, 2009), 47–59; for the latter see Lester Grabbe, *Judaism from Cyrus to Hadrian: Volume 1—The Persian and Greek Periods* (Philadelphia: Fortress, 1992), 279; James Maxwell Miller and John H. Hayes, *A History of Ancient Israel and Judah* (2nd ed.; Louisville, Ky.: Westminster John Knox Press, 2006), 512. Edelman speaks of this as "fictionalized reality" (p. 47), while Grabbe writes of the author that he "clearly has not the faintest idea of the relationship of the Persian kings to one another, and has placed his documents to produce what in his opinion is the best argument without being aware that it makes nonsense of Persian history," Lester L. Grabbe, *Ezra-Nehemiah* (Old Testament Readings; London/New York: Routledge, 1998), 134.

[6] See Joseph Blenkinsopp, *Ezra-Nehemiah: A Commentary* (OTL; Philadelphia: Westminster, 1988), 41–43; Japhet, "Composition," 189–216, although the former speaks of events in ch. 3 as being "telescoped" into the early Persian period (p. 100).

[7] Shemaryahu Talmon, "Ezra and Nehemiah (Books and Men)," in *IDB Supplementary Volume* (ed. Keith Crim; Nashville: Abingdon, 1976), 322; cf. H. G. M. Williamson, "The Composition of Ezra i-vi," *JTS* 34 (1983): 1–30, esp. 23. On repetitive resumption in Ezra-Nehemiah see the earlier work of Jean de Fraine, *Esdras en Nehemias* (Roermond: J. J. Romen & Zonen, 1961), 43.

Neh 5:19; 6:14; 13:14, 22, 29, 31, short prayers which bring closure to literary sections. Second were "summary notations" which comprised "condensed summaries at the end of a given unit," which "recapitulate the contents, and thus also delineate the extent of a preceding textual unit. The catch phrases catalogue major issues touched upon in the unit and thus help in identifying it." According to Talmon these occur in Ezra 4:4–5bα (summarizing 3:1–5:3); 6:13–14 (summarizing 5:1–6:12); Neh 12:26 (summarizing 12:10–25); 12:47 (summarizing 12:44–46); and 13:29b–31 (summarizing chs. 10–13). The third historiographic technique is seen in the "repetitive resumptions" which "mark the insertion of a self-contained unit into a given context" and which are "characterized by the partial repetition after the insert of the verse which closed the preceding part of the comprehensive unit, generally with some textual variation."[8] These can be discerned in Ezra 2:1b/2:70–3:1 (marking off 2:2–67 or 69); 4:5bβ/24b (marking off 4:6–23); 6:16b/22b (marking off 6:19–22a); and Neh 7:4–5a/11:1 (marking off 7:5b–10:40 [E39]).

In his study of Ezra 1–6 Williamson capitalized especially on Talmon's work in his analysis of Ezra 4:4–5.[9] Talmon identified two of his literary techniques within these verses: first, a "summary notation" in Ezra 4:4–5bα and, second, a "repetitive resumption" in 4:5bβ which links to 4:24b. This had major implications for Williamson's understanding of the historical presentation found in Ezra 1–6. By using catchwords and themes in the summary notation of 4:4–5bα which echo words and themes found in 3:3 (בלה//אימה; עמי הארצות//עם־הארץ) the ones responsible for Ezra 1–6 were signaling by the summary notation in 4:4–5bα that the events of 3:1–6 were linked to the period of Cyrus (4:5a).[10] In addition to this, 4:5b then "implies that no work at all was done on the temple until the second year of Darius," and so the events in 3:7–4:3 should be linked to the

[8] Many scholars today refer to this technique using the term "resumptive repetition." However, in keeping with Talmon's original article and Williamson's practice (see Williamson, *Ezra, Nehemiah*, 57; *Ezra and Nehemiah*, 45), I will use Talmon's terminology.

[9] See Williamson, "The Composition of Ezra i–vi," 17, 23–24; H. G. M. Williamson, *Ezra, Nehemiah* (WBC; Waco: Word Books, 1985), 43–44, 57; H. G. M. Williamson, *Ezra and Nehemiah* (OTG; Sheffield, UK: JSOT, 1987), 45, 53; cf. H. G. M. Williamson, "The Origins of the Twenty-Four Priestly Courses: A Study of 1 Chronicles 23–27," in *Studies in the Historical Books of the Old Testament* (ed. John A. Emerton; VTSup 30; Leiden: Brill, 1979), 251–68, esp. 265.

[10] The traditional critical view has been that the Hebrew narrative of 3:1–4:5 and the Aramaic narrative of 5:1–6:12 are "virtually parallel or at least cover two different aspects of the same period," Peter R. Ackroyd, *Exile and Restoration: A Study of Hebrew Thought of the Sixth Century BC* (OTL; Philadelphia: Westminster, 1968), 146.

recommencement of work during the reign of Darius.[11] The catchwords in the repetitive resumption of 4:5bβ/24b reveal that the writer is most likely marking off the material in 4:6–23, which is linked to the reigns of Xerxes I (Ahaseurus) and Artaxerxes I, as later material which does not fit in the temporal flow of his narrative, but does relate to it thematically.[12] Williamson's work confirmed, bolstered and refined that of Talmon and has had a major impact on the field of Ezra–Nehemiah studies.

One of Talmon's observations that has great potential for the study of Ezra 1–6 is his identification of another repetitive resumption in 2:1/70.[13] Much has been written about the list which is incorporated into Ezra 2 and appears also in Neh 7. For some, those responsible for Ezra 1–6 drew upon Neh 7, while others have challenged this by arguing that those responsible for Neh 7 have drawn upon Ezra 2 or both have drawn on an independent document.[14] If one accepts Talmon's argument that a repetitive resumption can be discerned in 2:1/70, thus identifying the list in ch. 2 as included as evidence backing up the narrative presentation, then ch. 2 would appear to be the original list. Many have noted that the list in ch. 2 does not reflect an early list of those who returned in a single caravan, and it is possible that it was a later record of those who had settled in the land at the end of the first phase of return (possibly as part of the official inspection in Ezra 5:3–4).[15] The list is clearly not a mere continuation of the account

---

[11] Williamson, "The Composition of Ezra i–vi," 23. The claim that no work was done on the temple may be a bit strong since 3:1–6 actually demonstrates perseverance in the face of opposition (taking the כי as concessive in 3:3), while 4:4–5 only speaks of discouraging, frightening and political maneuvering. Clearly the work is presented as stopped at some point (as per 4:24b), but this is only mentioned closer to Darius' reign.

[12] See now Porten, "Theme and Structure," 36. Although entertaining the other option that the writer of Ezra 1–6 was confused in his chronology of Persian kings, "on balance" Williamson concludes that the repetitive resumption theory "faces fewer difficulties" than that of a chronologically-challenged editor; Williamson, "The Composition of Ezra i–vi," 18.

[13] Talmon, "Ezra," 322. Porten ("Theme and Structure," 34) also highlights an inclusion formed by 2:1, 70.

[14] See Williamson, "The Composition of Ezra i–vi," 2–8, for dependence of Ezra 2 on Neh 7; for dependence of Neh 7 on Ezra 2 see Blenkinsopp, *Ezra-Nehemiah*, 43–44; Jacob L. Wright, *Rebuilding Identity: The Nehemiah-Memoir and its Earliest Readers* (BZAW 348; Berlin: de Gruyter, 2004), 301–3. See my "Redaction in the Book of Nehemiah: A Fresh Proposal," in *Unity and Disunity of Ezra-Nehemiah: Redaction, Rhetoric, Reader* (ed. Mark J. Boda and Paul Redditt; Hebrew Bible Monographs; Sheffield: Sheffield Phoenix Press, 2008), 25–54, esp. 44, 46, where I suggest that one can discern evidence of a document from the early Persian period being drawn on for both uses of the list.

[15] See Kurt Galling, "The 'Gōlā-List' According to Ezra 2//Nehemiah 7," *JBL* 70 (1951): 149–58, esp. 153–54; cf. Kurt Galling, "Die Liste der aus dem Exil Heimgekehrten," in *Studien zur Geschichte Israels im persischen Zeitalter* (Tübingen: Mohr Siebeck, 1964), 89–108,

in ch. 1.[16] If this is the case, then once again repetitive resumption marks material from a later period that has been inserted into a narrative and is related not temporally, but rather thematically.[17]

There is, however, a third candidate for this technique in Ezra 1–6 that was not highlighted by either Talmon or Williamson. Williamson concluded that the summary notation of Ezra 4:4–5bα identified 3:1–6 is material from the reign of Cyrus. He also claimed that this summary notation in 4:4–5bα implicitly identified 3:7–4:3 as material from the reign of Darius, since it claims that the people were frightened from building during the reign of Cyrus up until the reign of Darius. According to Talmon, however, summary notations do not signal the insertion of self-contained material into a narrative. That role is played by repetitive resumption. Nevertheless, this does not mean that the material in 3:7–4:3 is entirely comprised of material from the reign of Cyrus, since there is a third example of repetitive resumption that can be discerned in this section.

The closing words of Ezra 3:6 clarify for the reader that although the sacrificial cult had been restored through the perseverance of the people in Ezra 3:1–6, "the foundation of the temple of YHWH had not been laid"

whose view is entertained by Williamson, *Ezra, Nehemiah*, 31. Blenkinsopp looks to Nehemiah's era; cf. Blenkinsopp, *Ezra-Nehemiah*, 83.

[16] First, ch. 2 begins with a list of returnees which does not include the only returnee mentioned in ch. 1 (Sheshbazzar); and second, both ch. 1 and ch. 2 end with unique accounts of the return to Jerusalem and contributions to the rebuilding project. Kratz and Wright argue that Ezra 3:8 was the original continuation of Ezra 1; however, reliance on the evidence of "first year" in 1:1 and "second year" in Ezra 3:8 is unconvincing, since the former refers to Cyrus' reign and the latter to an arrival of Jews in Jerusalem Reinhard G. Kratz, *Die Komposition der erzählenden Bücher des Alten Testaments: Grundwissen der Bibelkritik* (UTB 2157; Göttingen: Vandenhoeck & Ruprecht, 2000), 63–64; Wright, *Rebuilding Identity*, 301.

[17] This does not mean that repetitive resumption only marks the insertion of material reflecting a period different from (here later than) that of the main narrative. For example, it is commonly used to identify narrative events occurring at the same time as the main narrative, but in a different location (e.g., Gen 37:36/39:1), or to share information about a character which is relevant to the story (e.g., 2 Sam 14:24/28). On the role of repetitive resumption, see Curt Kuhl, "Die 'Wiederaufnahme'—ein literarkritische Prinzip?" *ZAW* 64 (1952): 1–11; Isaac L. Seeligmann, "Hebräische Erzählung und biblische Geschichtsschreibung," *TZ* 18 (1962): 314–24; Shemaryahu Talmon, "The Presentation of Synchroneity and Simultaneity in Biblical Narrative," *ScrHier* 27 (1978): 9–26; Henry Van Dyke Parunak, "Oral Typesetting: Some Uses of Biblical Structure," *Bib* 62 (1981): 153–69; E. J. Revell, "The Battle with Benjamin (Judges XX 29–48) and Hebrew Narrative Techniques," *VT* 35 (1985): 417–33; Burke O. Long, "Framing Repetitions in Biblical Historiography," *JBL* 106 (1987): 390–392; Moshe Anbar, "La 'Reprise'," *VT* 38 (1988): 384–98; Shimeon Bar-Efrat, *Narrative Art in the Bible* (JSOTSup 70; Sheffield: Almond Press, 1989), 215–16; Isaac Kalimi, *The Reshaping of Ancient Israelite History in Chronicles* (Winona Lake: Eisenbrauns, 2005), 275–94.

(והיכל יהוה לא יסד). What follows in 3:7 is an account of the purchase of cedar wood from the Phoenicians to be used presumably for the construction of the temple, the foundation of which was noted in 3:6 as not yet laid. Ezra 3:8 then provides a date notation ("in the second year of their arrival at the house of God at Jerusalem in the second month"), which introduces an account stretching from 3:8–13 concerning the foundation-laying of the temple (cf. 3:10) and its attendant ceremonies (3:11–13).

Since 3:7 describes the purchase of a key material for the reconstruction of the temple, one might assume that this verse is more closely associated with the material which follows in 3:8–13 rather than that which precedes it in 3:1–6. However, two features in 3:7–8 speak against this conclusion. First, 3:7 relies on the verbal subjects which were introduced in 3:2 and function as the subjects of the main verbs through 3:2–6. Explicit reference to verbal subjects of the main clauses occurs after 3:2 only in 3:8. Second, 3:8 begins with a dating formula ("in the second year of their coming to the house of God at Jerusalem in the second month"), further evidence that it represents the aperture of a new literary unit. The unit that begins in 3:8 then stretches all the way to 4:3, first describing the foundation laying of the temple (3:8–13) and then, in response, the approach of "the enemies of Judah and Benjamin" seeking to join in the building project (4:1–3). What follows in 4:4–5bα is what Talmon identified as a summary notation, followed by a clause in 4:5bβ which is echoed in the repetitive resumption of 4:24b. However, Talmon's characterization of 4:4–5 needs to be revisited.

First, 4:4–5bα stands out among the summary notations identified by Talmon for Ezra-Nehemiah in that it is the only one in the book which does not occur at the conclusion to the section it summarizes (for Talmon that section is 3:1–5:3). Williamson modified Talmon's observation, by arguing that 4:4–5bα functioned as a summary notation for 3:1–4:3. In reality, however, it does not summarize the events in 3:1–4:3, since according to Williamson the events of 3:7–4:3 do not take place during the period outlined in 4:5b (from Cyrus' reign to the beginning of Darius' reign). Second, it may be suggested that 4:4–5 represents not only the beginning of a repetitive resumption pair (4:5bβ/24b), but the close of another repetitive resumption pair represented by 3:7b and 4:4–5bα. The same phrase "Cyrus king of Persia" (כורש מלך־פרס) which closes 3:7 also appears in 4:5 (כורש מלך פרס)[18] just prior to the phrase "until the reign of Darius

[18] There is a reference to Cyrus king of Persia at the end of the speech in 4:3; however, there the phrase is different from those found in 3:7 and 4:5, since it uses an initial המלך.

king of Persia" (ועד־מלכות דריוש מלך־פרס) whose counterpart in 4:24b (until ... the reign of Darius king of Persia; עד...למלכות דריוש מלך־פרס) represents a repetitive resumption. If the phrase "Cyrus king of Persia" in 4:5 functions as a repetitive resumption which returns to the narrative flow ending in 3:7, then what is the function of 4:4–5bα? This can be understood by examining 4:24a. While the second half of this verse (4:24b) represents a repetitive resumption, the first half of the verse resumes the narrative which was left off in 4:4–5bα. Whereas 4:4–5bα speaks of the people of the land discouraging, frightening, hiring and frustrating, 4:24a represents the next step: the ceasing of work on the house of God. In the same way, 4:4–5bα represents the actions which followed 3:7. After the people had paid for the supplies for the building of the temple, their efforts were thwarted by the people of the land, already introduced in 3:1–6. Furthermore, the actions described in the material just prior to the repetitive resumption in 4:24 (4:24a: "then work on the house of God in Jerusalem ceased and it was stopped ...") connects directly to the material from a later period identified by the repetitive resumption; in the case of 4:24, the material in 4:6–23 has been included to provide an instance where cessation of building activity was caused by forces outside the Yehudite community. Similarly, the actions described in the material just prior to the repetitive resumption in 4:4–5 (that is, in 4:4–5bα) connects this to the material found in 3:8–4:3, which represents an instance in which there was intimidation from the enemies of Judah which frustrated the building program.

For those responsible for Ezra 1–6 the material in 3:8–4:3 provides evidence from a later period that the foundation laying stage was completed (a key phase in the construction of any temple project),[19] but more importantly further evidence of the kind of opposition which frustrated the project which had been authorized by Cyrus.

This means that, according to the historiographers of Ezra 1–6, Zerubbabel and Jeshua returned to the land sometime in the reign of Cyrus and were involved in a restoration of the altar and the sacrificial cult at the

19 As per Mark J. Boda, "From Dystopia to Myopia: Utopian (re)visions in Haggai and Zechariah 1–8," in *Utopia and Dystopia in Prophetic Literature* (ed. Ehud Ben Zvi; Publications of the Finnish Exegetical Society 92; Helsinki/Göttingen: Finnish Exegetical Society/ Vandenhoeck & Ruprecht, 2006), 211–49; cf. the contributions of John Kessler and Antti Laato in Mark J. Boda and Jamie R. Novotny, *From the Foundations to the Crenellations: Essays on Temple Building in the Ancient Near East and Hebrew Bible.* (AOAT 366; Münster: Ugarit-Verlag, 2010).

temple site in Jerusalem (3:1–6). Opposition was evident from the outset, but they persevered in this initial stage of reconstruction (3:3), reinstituted the sacrificial cult and festal calendar (3:3–6), and began preparations for the reconstruction of the temple by obtaining building materials authorized by Cyrus (3:7). It was at this point that the people of the land frustrated the people's efforts (4:4–5bα), a continuation of their actions already noted in 3:1–6, bringing the work to a standstill (4:24).

The identification of 3:8–4:3 as material depicting a later period which has been employed by the ones responsible for Ezra 1–6, explains the striking similarity between the date notation in 3:8 and material found in the list in 2:2–69 (compare Ezra 2:68 with 3:8). Both of these sections (2:2–69 and 3:8–4:3) may reflect material from the same later period and possibly even the same source.

Thus, using repetitive resumption the historiographers of Ezra 1–6 have introduced material from a later period at three junctures in their account in order to strengthen or clarify their presentation. In this light, there is no reason to doubt the historiographers' understanding of the flow of Persian emperors and events in Judah in the early Persian period.

## III. Rhetorical Sophistication in Embedded Material

Nevertheless, a closer look at the cases of repetitive resumption reveals that the ones responsible for Ezra 1–6 embed inserted material into their respective contexts with such rhetorical sophistication that the material becomes part of the narrative flow. Such rhetoric explains why traditionally readers of Ezra have been tempted towards a "flat reading,"[20] which, of course, creates problems when reference is made to broader ancient Near Eastern history.

Evidence of this sophisticated embedding can be discerned in the repetitive resumption found in Ezra 4:24. While 4:24b takes up catchwords from 4:5bβ—evidence of the presence of a repetitive resumption—many have noted how twice 4:24a echoes the word "stop" (בטל), which is a key term at the end of the inserted later material. It appears in the letter of Artaxerxes in 4:21, and also in the concluding narrative link in 4:23.[21] Furthermore, the Aramaic term באדין in 4:24a normally designates

[20] For this term see Williamson, *Ezra and Nehemiah*, 51.

[21] E.g., Porten, "Theme and Structure," 38, 40, who also notes catchword connectivity between the embedded material in 4:6–23 and Darius' decree in ch. 6; see further Baruch

the next temporal phase in a narrative, subtly drawing the reader to the previous event described in 4:23.[22] While the inserted material is marked off by repetitive resumption, it is embedded creatively into its context to make the embedded material serve a rhetorical purpose that subtly increases its punch and makes the inserted piece implicitly part of the story of an earlier era.

A similar trend can be seen in the repetitive resumption that brackets the list in Ezra 2. While Ezra 2:70b twice employs the phrase בעריהם ("in their cities") to echo the earlier phrase איש לעירו ("each to his city") in Ezra 2:1, Ezra 2:70a echoes categories from the list that precedes it. Further evidence of integration into the context may be seen in 2:68, where a description of the arrival at the temple site includes willing offering to restore the temple on "its place" (מכונו)—a term repeated immediately in 3:3 in reference to the restoration of the altar. One can also discern rhetorical integration in the first part of the repetitive resumption in 2:1. Many have noted how in this verse the writer omits any historical notation, leaving vague the temporal relationship between chs. 1 and 2. The use of catchwords like Nebuchadnezzar, Babylon, Jerusalem and exiles (גולה) only bolsters the continuity between chs. 1 and 2. Not only does this repetitive resumption embed the list in the earlier context of the later part of Cyrus' reign, when Zerubbabel and Jeshua returned to the land, but it also subtly embeds the initial phase of the work of Zerubbabel and Jeshua in Sheshbazzar's era.

This trend can also be discerned in the repetitive resumption bracketing the material in Ezra 3:8–4:3. Reference to the lack of foundation laying (לא יסד) in 3:6 finds an echo in its reversal in the phrases in 3:11, "the foundation of the house of Yahweh was laid" (הוסד בית־יהוה) and 3:12 "when the foundation of this house was laid" (ביסדו זה הבית). Furthermore, references to building a house to our God and the allusion back to the authorization by Cyrus in 4:3 embeds this event from a later

---

Halpern, "A Historiographic Commentary on Ezra 1–6: Achronological Narrative and Dual Chronology in Israelite Historiography," in *The Hebrew Bible and Its Interpreters* (ed. William H. Propp, Baruch Halpern, and David Noel Freedman; Winona Lake: Eisenbrauns, 1990), 81–142, esp. 114, 124.

[22] So also the reference to the Assyrian deportation (and a king responsible for such) in both the letter (4:10) and the narrative preceding it (4:1–3), creates connectivity between the two. However, there are clear differences between them (different king and vocabulary), evidence that the letter has not been created *ex nihilo* by the editor; contra Wright, *Rebuilding Identity*, 35–43.

period (that of Darius) into this narrative depiction from an earlier period (that of Cyrus).

## IV. Summary and Conclusions

What we see in these three instances of repetitive resumption is creative tension between inclusion and exclusion of the material embedded into the context. On the one side, the use of this historiographic technique signals to the reader that the material is not to be related chronologically to the era being presented, but is only related thematically (exclusion). On the other side, the employment of catchwords creates connectivity between the inserted material and the main narrative line (inclusion). What appear to be competing strategies serve to explain the tension throughout interpretive history between a "flat" and "critical" reading of Ezra 1–6.

Can one find any source for the historiographical approach used by those responsible for Ezra 1–6? A very similar strategy is evident in the historiography of the Jews reported in Tattenai's letter in 5:11–16. There the Jews link their work in the period of Darius with that of Sheshbazzar in the period of Cyrus.[23] The work begun under Sheshbazzar is continuous with that of their work in the present ("from then until now it has been under construction and it is not completed"). Reference is even made to the foundation of the house of God being laid in Sheshbazzar's time, and while it may be that there was some initial foundation-laying activity by Sheshbazzar, we have no confirmation of it. Instead we have an account of Zerubbabel and Jeshua beginning work on the base of the temple (2:68), seen in their reconstruction of the altar on its base (3:3), and followed by the embedded piece in 3:8–13 concerning the future refounding of the temple. While the historiographers responsible for Ezra 1–6 correctly identify Zerubbabel and Jeshua with the foundation-laying in their account (based on his access to Haggai and Zechariah 1–8),[24] their historiographic techniques in chs. 1–4 have linked the work of Zerubbabel and Jeshua subtly with the era of Sheshbazzar, envisioning him (as the report of the Jews in 5:11–16 reveals) as the ultimate overseer of this activity.

---

[23] See Jacob Wright ("Ezra," in *The New Interpreter's Bible: One Volume Commentary* [ed. Beverly Roberts Gaventa and David Petersen; Nashville: Abingdon, 2010], 263–70, esp. 264, 266–67), for the seeking-finding motif. This motif forges a link between these two eras in Ezra 1–6.

[24] For the reliance on Haggai and Zech 1–8 by those responsible for Ezra 1–6, see Williamson, *Ezra, Nehemiah*, xxiv.

One can understand why the Jews would mention Sheshbazzar and foundation-laying in their appeal. First, Ezra 1 reveals that Sheshbazzar was the one commissioned by Cyrus and thus probably the only name that would be connected with Cyrus' permission in the Persian records. Secondly, foundation-laying was the most important stage in the construction of temples in the ancient Near East, and thus work on this would have been essential evidence for a royal sponsored project.[25] For the Jewish contingent appealing to Tattenai, foundation-laying was linked to Sheshbazzar and not Zerubbabel and Jeshua, with the understanding that the activity of the latter two was done under the authority of the former.

It is possible that those responsible for Ezra 1–6 have taken their lead from the testimony of the Jews in their key source.[26] They know from the books of Haggai and Zechariah that Zerubbabel and Jeshua were responsible for the foundation-laying, but link them with the era of Sheshbazzar (and possibly Sheshbazzar was still in authority when their initial foundation work on the altar was done) and subordinate them to Sheshbazzar by not providing Zerubbabel's status as governor (again, possibly Zerubbabel was not governor at this point yet).[27]

---

[25] See Boda and Novotny, *From the Foundations*.

[26] Some might respond to this that the letter with its reply did not prompt this historiographic agenda, but rather itself is a byproduct of this historiographic agenda, even though this view would not undermine the dominance of this agenda within Ezra 1–6. However, besides past defense of the authenticity of this letter within the Persian context, there is an indication that although close to the agenda found in Ezra 1–6 it is not a complete match. While the writer of Ezra 1–6 admits to a stoppage at least just immediately prior to the appeal of the Jews to Tattenai, the letter focuses entirely on continuous progress. Although the phrase "from then until now it has been under construction and it is not completed" does not necessarily preclude stoppages in construction (that is, it was in a state of construction), if those responsible had set out to create a letter from scratch that would fit his historical account one might think that they would have included something in the speech about the frustrating actions of the Jews' enemies which is also found in their historiography as well. Possibly, they thought that this would be inappropriate in a letter to the king, since these stoppages could be linked to the crown (as is the case in the "future" evidence of 4:6–23), but if creating it from scratch those responsible could have allowed for this as well, so as to have the letter match their agenda exactly.

[27] See Wilhelm Rudolph (*Esra und Nehemia* [HAT 20; Tübingen: J. C. B. Mohr (Paul Siebeck), 1949], xxvi) who argued that Zerubbabel was younger contemporary of Sheshbazzar who took over the governorship from him; cf. Jacob M. Myers, *Ezra, Nehemiah* (AB 14; Garden City, N.Y.: Doubleday, 1965), xlvii. Some have sought to equate Sheshbazzar and Zerubbabel either historically or in terms of the writer's perspective, e.g., Johan Lust, "The Identification of Zerubbabel with Sheshbassar," *ETL* 63 (1987): 90–95; Myers, *Ezra, Nehemiah*, 15; but this has largely been rejected in scholarship. Derek Kidner, *Ezra and Nehemiah: An Introduction and Commentary* (Downers Grove, Ill.: Inter-Varsity, 1979), 139–42, considers Sheshbazzar as a Persian official and Zerubbabel as the people's choice, serving

What purpose lies behind this infusion of later events into an earlier era? Many have rightly noted how the account of Ezra 1–6 is driven by a historiography which seeks to legitimize the activities of the early Persian Jewish community by creating links to the past: whether to the first temple, the exodus, or prophecy.[28] However, one can see in the regular use of the technique of repetitive resumption that the historiography also seeks to legitimize the activities of the early Persian Jewish community by infusing future events and materials into this early period. The historiographers are not ignorant of the flow of Persian history, but rather creatively embed material into the account using a literary convention of the day (repetitive resumption). And yet they do this in such creative ways that the result makes this embedded material come alive in this earlier period. Not only do the writers use flashbacks to earlier scenes and visions in Israel's history in their historiography, but also employ "flashforwards" to future scenes.[29] This fusion of the activities of multiple generations reveals

under Sheshbazzar's authority. Ackroyd (*Exile*, 147) notes in passing an important point that brings into question the appointment of Zerubbabel as late as the reign of Darius: no mention is made by Darius of his recently appointed governor in his reply to the Tattenai. This point forces Ackroyd to push the appointment "back somewhat further." He suggests the time of Cambyses or even the later years of Cyrus.

[28] For the First Temple see Williamson, "The Composition of Ezra i–vi," 27–28; Williamson, *Ezra, Nehemiah*, 47–48; Williamson, *Ezra and Nehemiah*, 53; for the Exodus see e.g., Mark A. Throntveit, *Ezra-Nehemiah* (Int; Louisville, Ky.: John Knox, 1992), 15–18, 23, 35–36; cf. Williamson, *Ezra, Nehemiah*, 15–20; Johanna W. H. Van Wijk-Bos, *Ezra, Nehemiah, and Esther* (Westminster Bible Companion; Louisville, Ky.: Westminster John Knox, 1998), 20–21; for prophecy see Edelman, "Ezra 1–6," 47–59; Wright, "Ezra," 264. Others have looked to ancient Near Eastern building rituals and pilgrimage as key to the historiography of Ezra 1–6; for the former see Lisbeth S. Fried, "The Land Lay Desolate: Conquest and Restoration in the Ancient Near East," in *Judah and Judeans in the Neo-Babylonian Period* (ed. Oded Lipschits and Joseph Blenkinsopp; Winona Lake: Eisenbrauns, 2003), 21–54; Lisbeth S. Fried, "Temple Building in Ezra 1–6," in *From the Foundations to the Crenellations: Essays on Temple Building in the Ancient Near East and Hebrew Bible* (ed. Mark J. Boda and Jamie R. Novotny; AOAT 366; Münster: Ugarit-Verlag, 2010), 319–38; Lisbeth S. Fried, "*Deux ex Machina* and Plot Construction in Ezra 1–6," in *Prophets and Prophecy in Ancient Israelite Historiography* (ed. Mark J. Boda and Lissa Wray Beal; Winona Lake: Eisenbrauns, forthcoming); for the latter see Melody D. Knowles, "Pilgrimage imagery in the returns in Ezra," *JBL* 123 (2004): 57–74 (at least for Ezra 1–2, and Ezra 7–8).

[29] This also may explain the reference to Artaxerxes in Ezra 6:15, which foreshadows already his key role in the rest of Ezra-Nehemiah; cf. Tamara C. Eskenazi, *In an Age of Prose: A Literary Approach to Ezra-Nehemiah* (SBLMS 36; Atlanta: Scholars, 1988), 55; Porten, "Theme and Structure," 36, and Wright, *Rebuilding Identity*, 38, 40, note how the Artaxerxes' note in 4:21 prepares the way for the rest of the narrative in Ezra-Nehemiah. See my "Redaction," 25–54, for the way Neh 7–13 (at the end of the Ezra-Nehemiah complex) reverses this rhetorical strategy and embeds earlier documents into the account of Nehemiah in order to create multi-generational links. There I suggest that "the one(s)

their response to the divinely prompted imperial permission, justifying the enduring validity of the imperial edict, and highlighting the response of the community even against difficult opposition after the exile.[30]

responsible for Ezra 1–6 was (were) responsible for much of the transformation of the Nehemiah materials into their present form" (p. 53). This would explain the close connections Jacob Wright has noted between the material in Ezra 1–6 and the book of Nehemiah; cf. Wright, *Rebuilding Identity*, esp. 323.

30 With thanks to Jacob Wright and Iain Provan for honest and helpful comments on an earlier draft of this essay. All views and errors which remain are mine.

# NEHEMIAH—THE BEST KING JUDAH NEVER HAD

Iain Duguid

It is a particular pleasure for me to contribute this essay for the *Festschrift* for Hugh Williamson, since it had its genesis in work I did for him during my first year of Ph.D. studies. I am deeply grateful to have had the opportunity to study with someone who was not only vastly acquainted with the academic subject, but who also showed such personal interest and pastoral care for all of his students. His approach has profoundly impacted my life.

Without exploring here the much-discussed question of the common authorship of Chronicles and Ezra-Nehemiah, there are at least similarities of style and common themes between the books. Rex Mason speaks of "echoes" of the speeches of Chronicles in Ezra-Nehemiah.[1] We find in Ezra-Nehemiah the same devices of periodisation and the modeling of events after the pattern of earlier biblical events that were used by the Chronicler. Thus the return under Cyrus is presented as a second Exodus,[2] and Ezra and Nehemiah's activities are related in the same way as those of David and Solomon.[3] I suggest that one aspect of this relationship is the fact that the figure of Nehemiah is depicted as embodying the ideal king, as described in the book of Chronicles. For the person responsible for the present form of the book of Nehemiah, he represents all that a king should be, in a way that was quite unparalleled even at the height of the monarchy.[4]

[1] Rex Mason "Some Chronistic Themes in the Speeches of Ezra-Nehemiah," *ExpTim* 101 (1989): 72–76 (72); for a discussion of the issues concerning common authorship, see Kyung-Jin Min, *The Levitical Authorship of Ezra-Nehemiah* (JSOTSup 409; London & New York: T&T Clark, 2004), 6–30.

[2] H. G. M. Williamson, *Ezra-Nehemiah* (WBC; Waco: Word, 1985), li, 16.

[3] Otto Plöger, "Reden und Gebete im deuteronomistischen und chronistischen Geschichtswerk," *Festschrift für Günther Dehn* (ed. W. Schneemelcher; Neukirchen-Vluyn: Neukirchener Verlag, 1957), 35–49.

[4] J. David Pleins calls the description of Nehemiah a "royally charged figure," in *The Social Visions of the Hebrew Bible: A Theological Introduction* (Louisville, KY: Westminster John Knox, 2001), 183.

## I. Nehemiah, the Man of Prayer

The book opens with a portrayal of *Nehemiah the prayerful leader*. On hearing of the deplorable state of affairs in Jerusalem, his response is to weep, mourn, fast and offer a prayer (1:5b–11) which is based very closely on Solomon's prayer at the dedication of the temple (1 Kgs 8:23–53).[5] To be sure, there are also other influences at work in the prayer, notably from the book of Deuteronomy, and some of the similarities may simply be due to common "liturgical language," but the number and detail of the similarities to Solomon's prayer suggest that a deliberate parallel is being invoked. These are as follows:

- Nehemiah 1:5b is a free paraphrase of 1 Kgs 8:23. Both assert God's heavenliness, his incomparability and his "covenant of love" (הברית וחסד) with those who are wholeheartedly obedient. This incidentally provides an explanation for the use in this passage of the divine name Yahweh, uncharacteristic of Nehemiah. The source text employs the divine name.[6]
- Nehemiah 1:6 appeals for the Lord's ears to be attentive and his eyes open to Nehemiah's prayer, a combination found also in 1 Kgs 8:28–9. In particular, the phraseology: "hear... the prayer that your servant is praying in your presence this day" (לשמע אל־תפלת עבדך אשר אנכי מתפלל לפניך היום) is almost exactly copied from 1 Kgs 8:28. The notion of praying "day and night" is found both here and in 1 Kgs 8:29.
- The focus of Nehemiah's prayer is the possibility envisaged in 1 Kgs 8:46–53: the sin of the people has resulted in exile, followed by repentance and the confession of sin, which is met by the promise of restoration on return to God. Both prayers appeal to the example of "your servant Moses" (Neh 1:8; 1 Kgs 8:53) and the role of "the place chosen as a dwelling for my name" (Neh 1:9; 1 Kgs 8:29, 48). In both the object of the appeal is "your people" redeemed out of Egypt (Neh 1:10; 1 Kgs 8:51).

---

[5] As Eep Talstra says, "it redesigns and updates parts of the text known from 1 Kings 8, adjusting it to the actual situation of early Judaism as described in the book of Nehemiah"; see his "The Discourse of Praying: Reading Nehemiah 1," in *Psalms and Prayers* (eds. Bob Becking and Eric Peels; Leiden: Brill, 2007), 219–236 (230). See also the discussion in Jacob L. Wright, *Rebuilding Identity: The Nehemiah Memoir and its Earliest Readers* (BZAW 348; Berlin: De Gruyter, 2004), 15–17.

[6] Williamson, *Ezra-Nehemiah*, 167.

- The purpose of both prayers is also the same: Solomon asks that the people's conquerors would show them "mercy" (רחמום; 1 Kgs 8:50) and Nehemiah seeks "favour" (רחמים; Neh 1:11) from King Artaxerxes.

Thus the opening chapter of the book of Nehemiah presents him as re-enacting Solomon's prayer at the dedication of the temple. Nehemiah is not just shown as a man of prayer but as a veritable Solomon of prayer. The expectation is perhaps that this humble, repentant approach will receive the merciful answer promised to Solomon in 2 Chr 7:14: God will hear from heaven, forgive their sin and heal their land.

## II. Nehemiah, the Holy Warrior

Having established the picture of Nehemiah in prayer, the writer goes on to show him in action as the *rebuilder of the walls of Jerusalem*. This in itself is a Davidic theme in the Books of Chronicles: not only did David build the walls of Jerusalem (1 Chr 11:8) but so did several faithful Davidic kings (Uzziah, 2 Chr 26:15; Jotham, 2 Chr 27:3; Hezekiah, 2 Chr 32:5; Manasseh—afterhis conversion—2 Chr 33:14).[7] Even the words used to describe the people's response to Nehemiah's challenge to rebuild (Neh 2:18) have Davidic overtones: "let us arise" (נקום) and "strengthen the hands" (חזק ידים) echo the charge of David to Solomon and the people to build the temple (1 Chr 22:13,16,19), as does his assurance that God will give success to the work (צלח; Neh 2:20; 1 Chr 22:11,13).[8]

Rebuilding the wall was much more than a civil engineering project, however: it was nothing less than holy war, as Nehemiah's response to the plotting of their enemies shows: the people were gathered together and instructed not to fear (Neh 4:14); the fighting—if it should come to that—would be begun by the sounding of the trumpet (Neh 4:18,20) and the Lord himself would fight on their behalf (Neh 4:14).[9] In fact, Judah was not required to strike a blow; God intervened to throw their enemies into confusion (Neh 4:15). In his leadership, Nehemiah epitomized the behavior expected of the Davidic king, stirring up the people to trust in God and recognizing the victory as the Lord's (Neh 4:15; 6:15). Perhaps

[7] Mason, "Chronistic Themes," 73.
[8] Mason, "Chronistic Themes," 73.
[9] Ulrich Kellermann, *Nehemia: Quellen, Überlieferung und Geschichte* (BZAW 102; Berlin: Töpelmann, 1967), 18.

the closest parallels lie in Jehoshaphat's victory over the Moabites and Ammonites (2 Chr 20), and Hezekiah's triumph over Sennacherib (2 Chr 32). Both of these were victories won in dependence upon God without actual fighting on Judah's part, but other Davidic kings also conducted holy war against God's enemies (Abijah, 2 Chr 13:12–16; Asa, 2 Chr 14:11–12). As well as showing trust in the LORD, Nehemiah also repudiated any foreign alliances of the kind for which Asa and Jehoshaphat were rebuked (2 Chr 16:8; 19:2).[10] The rebuilding of Jerusalem was a task for Judah alone: foreigners have no share or claim in Jerusalem (Neh 2:20). This motivation lies behind Nehemiah's continued attempts to keep foreign influence out of Jerusalem (Neh 9:2,30; 13:18).

## III. Nehemiah, the Just Ruler

Nehemiah's responsibilities were not limited simply to building the walls of Jerusalem: he had the much more difficult task of establishing an equitable community. Thus in Neh 5 particularly we see him depicted as *the just ruler*.[11] It was the king's primary duty to guarantee the true administration of justice throughout the land,[12] especially in protecting the poor and needy from their exploiters (Ps 72:4). In Nehemiah's time, the poorest members of the community were in danger of losing their children to debt-slavery and also whatever land they possessed. This problem may have been caused by Nehemiah's special measures to protect Jerusalem from her enemies (Neh 4:22), which, combined with the efforts to rebuild the wall, may have led to a shortage of labor to gather in the harvest. Alternatively, there may simply have been a poor harvest to begin with. Whatever the cause, Nehemiah acted to stop this exploitation immediately (Neh 5:9–13), in the process forgoing the opportunity of personal gain.

Even beyond that, Nehemiah laid no heavy tax burden on the people, though he was entitled to their financial support as governor (Neh 5:14–15). He neither lorded it over the people nor acquired great wealth, but rather himself supported others out of his private resources (Neh 5:16–18). This was quite a contrast to the behavior of many of the Davidic kings: Solomon

---

[10] Rex Mason, *Preaching the Tradition: Homily and Hermeneutics After the Exile* (Cambridge: Cambridge University Press, 1990), 56.

[11] Pleins, *Social Visions*, 183.

[12] Keith Whitelam, *The Just King* (JSOTSup 12; Sheffield: Sheffield Academic Press, 1979), 29.

placed a heavy yoke upon the people and Rehoboam would gladly have made it heavier (1 Kgs 12:3–11); Ahab used his position to procure for himself Naboth's vineyard (1 Kgs 21). This kind of behavior was the "custom" of the kings of those days, as Samuel explained: it was considered normal for a king to exploit the people's children and take for himself much of their produce (1 Sam 8:11–16). The ideal for the king in Israel was quite different, however: he was not to multiply horses or wives or silver and gold, nor to consider himself better than his brothers (Deut 17:16–20). It is this ideal pattern into which Nehemiah fitted: he apparently possessed only one mount (Neh 2:12), freed the people from the governor's tax of forty shekels of silver (Neh 5:15), and both he and his men were fully engaged alongside everyone else in the work on the wall (Neh 4:23; 5:15–16). In all of this, he compares favorably with any of the kings of Israel or Judah.

## IV. Nehemiah, the Reformer of the Cult

The leadership of those kings also extended into the cultic arena. Similarly, we also find Nehemiah depicted as *the cultic administrator*.[13] It is particularly remarkable to note how small a part the High Priest plays in Nehemiah's activities. Eliashib has the honor of being listed first in the catalogue of wall builders (Neh 3:1), but then largely disappears from view. He played no part in either the reading of the law (Neh 8) or in the dedication ceremony for the wall (Neh 12). The omission of his name from the list of those signing the pledge to keep the law of God (Neh 10:1–27) may perhaps be explained by the fact that many of the names are family names, and his family name—Seraiah—is not only listed but prominent.[14] However, if the Eliashib of Neh 13:4–9 is the same as that of Neh 3:1 and 13:28—and the simple title *kohen* is the most common designation of the High Priest[15]—then it may be that the High Priest of the day had very little sympathy with Nehemiah's reforms.[16] The fact that his grandson was involved in a mixed marriage (Neh 13:28) reflects at the very least

---

[13] Frank C. Fensham, *The Books of Ezra and Nehemiah* (NICOT; Grand Rapids: Eerdmans, 1983), 262.

[14] Williamson, *Ezra-Nehemiah*, 328. Deborah Rooke still finds its absence here surprising, though: *Zadok's Heirs: The Role and Development of the High Priesthood in Ancient Israel* (Oxford: Oxford University Press, 2000), 172.

[15] John Bailey: "Usage of Post Restoration Period Terms Descriptive of Priest and High Priest," *JBL* 70 (1951): 217–225 (217).

[16] Lisbeth S. Fried, *The Priest and the Great King: Temple-Palace Relations in the Persian Empire* (Winona Lake, IN: Eisenbrauns, 2004), 207–8.

an inability to keep his own family under control. Yet his power to resist Nehemiah's authority as the civil leader seems to have been limited, even when it came to the control of the temple building itself (Neh 13:7–8). In terms of his reform of the cult, Nehemiah appears again after the pattern of a godly Davidic monarch.

At the dedication of the wall (Neh 12:27–47), it was Nehemiah who gave the procession its marching orders and appointed a large praise choir (Neh 12:31), just as David had done before him (1 Chr 16:4). The description of the dedication service seems to cast a backward glance toward the dedication of the temple under Solomon (compare Neh 12:40,43 with 2 Chr 7:6–7). Nevertheless, Nehemiah was careful not to intrude into cultic areas which were not rightly his: he followed the levitical choir among the lay people, and when it came to the offering of the sacrifices, the subject is the indeterminate "they," which presumably indicates the priests (Neh 12:43). In another context, it was suggested to him that to escape a threat to his life he should hide in the sanctuary, an area reserved for priests (Neh 6:10–11).[17] Here too he resisted the temptation to arrogate to himself priestly prerogatives, unlike at least one of his Davidic predecessors (2 Chr 26:16–18).

Under his direction, after the dedication of the wall, storerooms were prepared in the temple for the contributions and tithes for the priests and Levites (Neh 12:44), just as Hezekiah had done (2 Chr 31:11–16). The result was that the priests and Levites were able to be wholly devoted to the temple service (Neh 12:45; compare 2 Chr 31:4). This action under Nehemiah's direction is seen as the capstone of the whole restoration process: now the central cult was once again fully functional. In appointing and purifying the priests and the Levites (Neh 7:1; 13:30), Nehemiah followed in the footsteps of David (1 Chr 23–26), Solomon (2 Chr 8:14) and Hezekiah (2 Chr 31:2). The renewal of the order of the days of David and Solomon, begun with the rebuilding of the temple under Zerubbabel, was now completed under Nehemiah (Neh 12:47).

It is Nehemiah too who is viewed as the prime mover behind the agreement to keep the law of God (Neh 10:1 [9:38]). His was the first name on the list of signatories and he took the initiative to enforce the measures (Neh 13). In this, he was following David's charge to Solomon to "follow the teachings of YAHWEH your God" and "observe the statutes and the

---

[17] Williamson, *Ezra-Nehemiah*, 259.

decrees which YAHWEH imposed on Moses for Israel (1 Chr 22:12–13).[18] The focus of the agreement rested on the practical issues of avoidance of intermarriage, keeping the Sabbath and provision for the needs of the temple and its personnel. That these were not merely theoretical concerns may be seen from the steps Nehemiah took in ch. 13 to counter abuses. Neither were they new concerns, though: intermarriage with foreigners was the cause of Solomon's apostasy (Neh 13:26; 1 Kgs 11:1–6); the continuing desecration of the Sabbath was part of an earlier pattern of unrighteousness which had led to the exile (Neh 13:18; 2 Chr 36:21; Ezek 22:26) and the neglect of the house of God had been a common complaint (Neh 13:4–13; 2 Chr 24:18; 28:24; Hag 1:3,9). Often, the kings had been more part of the problem in these areas than of the solution (Jer 17:20).

In the past, the answer to such failures by king and people was a reform by the incoming king, sometimes in the form of a covenant renewal. Most of the good Davidic kings had initiated such reforms (Asa, 2 Chr 15:8–15; Jehoshaphat, 2 Chr 19:4–11; Joash, 2 Chr 24; Hezekiah, 2 Chr 29–31; Manasseh, 2 Chr 33:15–17; Josiah, 2 Chr 34:1–35:19).[19] Indeed, so close was the control of the cult by the king that as the king went, so went the temple. A godly king would reform and purify temple worship, a godless king would neglect it, or lead it into apostasy and idolatry. Thus the covenant renewal in Neh 8–10 serves to show Nehemiah acting as a godly king would, reforming the community. Even if Nehemiah 8:9a is a gloss, artificially introducing the name of Nehemiah into the context of Ezra's reforms, it merely serves to make explicit what is implicit in the ordering of the material: Ezra's reforms were to be understood as an integral part of Nehemiah's program. Concern for the law of God was an essential virtue of the godly king (Deut 17:18–19). Like Josiah before him, therefore, Nehemiah led the people in reading the law and renewing covenant (Neh 8; 2 Chr 34:30–32).

## V. Why this Portrait?

The data gathered above, taken together, suggests that the author of the final form of Ezra-Nehemiah was seeking to portray Nehemiah as the very

[18] Mason, "Chronistic Themes," 73.

[19] Dennis J. McCarthy, "Covenant and Law in Chronicles-Nehemiah," *CBQ* 44 (1982): 25–44 (29).

picture of a pious king. The questions then arise: "Why was Nehemiah presented in this way? What was the writer seeking to demonstrate?"

Certainly the writer was not attempting to assert that Nehemiah ever was, or should have been, the Davidic king. There is no clear evidence that Nehemiah was actually of Davidic descent,[20] and he personally rejected allegations that he sought the crown for himself (Neh 6:7). In any event, the author of Ezra-Nehemiah shows little interest in Davidic lineage even where it is unquestionable, as in the case of Zerubbabel.[21] At the simplest level, this depiction of Nehemiah in terms strongly reminiscent of the best of the pre-exilic kings meets the need of the people for a feeling of continuity, the "reassurance that they and their institutions indeed stood in direct line with those of pre-exilic history."[22] The godly kings of the golden age had not all died out with the end of their era: their spiritual descendants remained in place. This presentation also fits the strain of quietism in Ezra-Nehemiah: Nehemiah was after all the appointee of the Persian government, and the appointment of such a man as this was further evidence of God's ability to work through the Persian authorities to achieve his purposes.

But this depiction also points to deeper longings: according to the theology of immediate retribution of the book of Chronicles, a king of the godly stature of Nehemiah ought to have been able to expect numerous progeny, successful building operations, military armaments, victory in warfare, cultic reforms, religious instruction, tribute from the nations, honor and fear in the sight of the nations and the direct conferring of prosperity and rest.[23] A brief glance at the book of Nehemiah will show that only some of these benefits have thus far accrued to Judah:

---

[20] Williamson, *Ezra-Nehemiah*, 179, 257.

[21] Sara Japhet: "Sheshbazzar and Zerubabbel against the Background of the Historical and Religious Tendencies of Ezra Nehemiah," *ZAW* 94 (1982): 66–98 (72).

[22] Williamson, *Ezra-Nehemiah*, li.

[23] Roddy L. Braun: "Chronicles Ezra Nehemiah: Theology and Literary History," in *Studies in the Historical Books of the Old Testament* (ed. John A. Emerton; VTSup 30; Leiden: Brill, 1979), 52–64 (54). "Retribution" is not perhaps the best term for this idea since it focuses our attention on the negative connection between action and consequences, while as this list shows, the linkage can just as easily be positive. Brian Kelly has also pointed out the role of covenant and grace in tempering the negative aspects of retribution theology: "Retribution Revisited: Covenant, Grace and Restoration," in *The Chronicler as Theologian: Essays in Honor of Ralph W. Klein* (eds. M. Patrick Graham, Steven McKenzie and Gary N. Knoppers; JSOTSup 371; Sheffield: Sheffield Academic Press, 2003), 206–27.

- numerous progeny: of Nehemiah himself, we are not even given any information concerning his marriage status, let alone any children. Because of his position as Artaxerxes' cupbearer, some have speculated that he would have been a eunuch, but this is far from certain.[24] The people at large had experienced population growth—but under the present circumstances it was proving a mixed blessing (Neh 5:2).
- building operations: Nehemiah's construction of the wall was an unqualified success. The celebration at its completion (Neh 12:43) was even greater than at the rededication of the temple (Ezra 6:16) or the presentation of the law (Neh 8:12,17), for on those occasions the rejoicing was mixed with weeping.[25]
- military armaments: the people were not well armed, possessing only light hunting weapons (Neh 4:7[13]).[26] They lacked the chariots and horsemen of the days of Solomon (2 Chr 9:25) and the large armies of his successors (e.g. 2 Chr 11:1; 14:8).
- victory in warfare: since the building of the wall in the face of opposition constituted holy war, its completion counts as a military victory.
- cultic reforms: Nehemiah 8–10 represent a major cultic reform in the best traditions of the Davidic kings. But the contents of Neh 13 leave a question mark against the final success of these reforms. Nehemiah found a society corrupt in all its major institutions: nobles (Neh 5:6), prophets (Neh 6:14) and priests (Neh 13:29). Under his leadership society was reformed, but that reform was not an automatic, "once for all" event. The gains made could easily be lost unless constant vigilance were to be exercised.
- religious instruction: Ezra's reading of the law constituted a major blessing in this regard, in contrast to the former days when Israel was without a teaching priest and without the law (2 Chr 15:3).
- tribute from the nations: this aspect of God's blessing is largely absent. True, the king of Persia provided the timber for the wall, the gates of the citadel and Nehemiah's house, but this would have been small consolation to a people who were bowed down to the point of breaking under the tribute burden of the Persians (Neh 5:4; 9:37).
- honor and fear in the sight of the nations: the nations were powerless to prevent the building of the wall (Neh 4:15; 6:16), which once rebuilt

---

24 Joseph Blenkinsopp, *Ezra-Nehemiah: A Commentary* (OTL; Philadelphia: Westminster, 1988), 213.

25 Williamson, *Ezra-Nehemiah*, 376.

26 Williamson, *Ezra-Nehemiah*, 227.

would remove the "disgrace" of Judah (Neh 2:17). On a more positive note, the supplying of food from Nehemiah's table to "those who came to us from the surrounding nations" is a faint echo of the theme of the pilgrimage of the nations to Zion (1 Kgs 10), though the provisions of Nehemiah's court (Neh 5:18) were certainly scant by comparison with those of Solomon (1 Kgs 4:22).

- prosperity and rest: these are the elements of divine blessing which were most obviously lacking. Even though Nehemiah acted to resettle Jerusalem (Neh 7:4–5; 11), the people were trapped in the most desperate poverty (Neh 5:1–5,18b), and from beginning to end they faced difficulties and opposition (Neh 2:10,19; 4:1–3,7–12; 6:1–13,17–18; 13:4–7). Their condition could be summed up in the conclusion to the prayer of Nehemiah 9:

> But see, we are slaves today, slaves in the land you gave our forefathers so that they could eat its fruit and the other good things it produces. Because of our sins, its abundant harvest goes to the kings you have placed over us. They rule over our bodies and our cattle as they please. We are in great distress. (Neh 9:36–37)

This state of "partial blessing" suggests that the quietism of Ezra-Nehemiah should not be caricatured as complete contentment with Persian rule. Certainly there were no overheated messianic hopes, nor incitements to rise up and throw off the Persian yoke, but included in the underlying tone are both gratitude for what God has already done through the Persian authorities in the "now," and a patient expectation that there is still more to come in the "not yet." As Gordon McConville puts it, "The books express deep dissatisfaction with the exiles' situation under Persian rule; the situation is perceived as leaving room for a future fulfilment of the most glorious prophecies of Israel's salvation and the cause of the delayed fulfilment is Israel's sin."[27]

This fits with the emphasis elsewhere in Ezra-Nehemiah (and indeed in the book of Esther).[28] The repeated cycle of sin, repentance and deliverance in Neh 9 is deliberately broken off in the last cycle at the end of the repentance stage, which points to a recognition of the possibility of, and the people's need for, a future deliverance by the LORD.[29] So too the "semi-

---

[27] J. Gordon McConville, "Ezra-Nehemiah and the Fulfilment of Prophecy," *VT* 36 (1986): 205–24 (223).

[28] See Iain M. Duguid, "But Did They Live Happily Ever After? The Eschatology of the book of Esther," *WTJ* 68 (2006): 85–98.

[29] Williamson, *Ezra-Nehemiah*, 315.

realized eschatology" seen above necessarily looks to God for the consummation of his covenant of love (Neh 1:5; 9:32). The glorious future that the LORD has promised his people cannot be brought in by human effort, for even a leader as godly as Nehemiah was unable to give the people rest. Instead, it would have to come from God's sovereign intervention on their behalf, as it did in the past for Abraham (Neh 9:7), in the Exodus (Neh 9:9–12), and in the conquest of the land (Neh 9:22–25). In the meantime, the people found themselves in a situation analogous to that of Israel in the wilderness, experiencing God's blessing (Neh 9:19–21) but not yet having entered God's rest. The necessary response on the part of the people in that situation was patient waiting for God to act and present obedience to God's law while they waited—a response that had begun in Neh 10, but was not free from the threat of relapse (Neh 13). The challenge—and the promise—that the book of Nehemiah presented to Judah is the same as that of Ps 95:6–11: those who enter God's rest are those who trust in the LORD and wait faithfully for his deliverance.

# 2 CHRONICLES 32:30 AND THE WATER SYSTEMS OF PRE-EXILIC JERUSALEM

Judith M. Hadley

Most Hebrew Bible scholars contend that the construction of the Siloam Tunnel in Jerusalem, which was hewn out of the bedrock under the City of David, and which carries water from the Gihon Spring on the eastern side of the Ophel ridge along a winding course to the Pool of Siloam (located in the Tyropean Valley on the western side of the Ophel ridge), was carried out during the reign of King Hezekiah of Judah, in anticipation of King Sennacherib of Assyria's siege of the city in 701 BCE. Indeed, the identification of this tunnel with Hezekiah is so widespread that the tunnel is popularly known simply as 'Hezekiah's Tunnel,'[1] although that identification is not without its critics.[2] The attribution to Hezekiah is commonly based on discussions in 2 Kgs 20:20; 2 Chr 32:3, 30; Isa 22:9–11 and Ben Sira 48:17. Crucial to this argument is 2 Chr 32:30, which asserts that "Hezekiah closed the upper outlet of the waters of Gihon and directed them down to the west side of the city of David" [NRSV]. This verse is generally considered to correspond to the earlier 2 Kgs 20:20, which reads: "The rest of the deeds of Hezekiah, all his power, how he made the pool and the conduit and brought water into the city, are they not written in the Book of the Annals of the Kings of Judah?" [NRSV]. Not everyone interprets 2 Chr 32:30 (or its assumed Vorlage) in just this way, however. Among the dissenters is Hugh Williamson, who notes that Hezekiah's water system is mentioned only in the course of the summary of Hezekiah's reign

---

[1] Cf. e.g., John A. Thompson, *1, 2 Chronicles* (NAC 9; Nashville: Broadman & Holman Publishers, 1994), 361; Raymond B. Dillard, *2 Chronicles* (WBC 15; Waco, Tex.: Word Books, 1987), 257; Steven S. Tuell, *First and Second Chronicles* (IBC; Louisville, Ky.: John Knox Press, 2001), 226; Yigal Shiloh, "City of David: Excavation 1978," *BA* 42 (1979): 165–71, esp. 168.

[2] Cf. e.g., Robert North, "Does Archeology Prove Chronicles Sources?" in *A Light Unto My Path: Old Testament Studies in Honor of Jacob M. Myers* (ed. Howard M. Bream, Ralph D. Heim and Carey A. Moore; Philadelphia: Temple University Press, 1974), 375–401; and more recently John Rogerson and Philip R. Davies, "Was the Siloam Tunnel Built By Hezekiah?" *BA* 59/3 (1996): 138–49; but for counter arguments see Ronald S. Hendel, "The Date of the Siloam Inscription: A Rejoinder to Rogerson and Davies," *BA* 59/4 (1996): 233–37; Jane Cahill, "A Rejoinder to 'Was the Siloam Tunnel Built by Hezekiah?'" *BA* 60/3 (1997): 184–85; Stig Norin, "The Age of the Siloam Inscription and Hezekiah's Tunnel," *VT* 48 (1998): 37–48, among others.

that is given in Kings and Chronicles, and not in the context specifically of Hezekiah's preparations for the siege earlier (as outlined for example in 2 Chr 30:3–4). Therefore, Williamson believes that "from a historical point of view... it had probably been built earlier. It is in any case unlikely that so large an undertaking could have been completed in time after the immediate Assyrian threat had become known."[3]

This essay offers a fresh assessment of the textual and archaeological evidence bearing on this matter, attempting to determine the connection, if any, between Hezekiah and some of the water systems of Jerusalem, and whether or not any of the water systems was built in preparation for the siege of Sennacherib. I am honoured and extremely delighted to have been asked to contribute the essay to this Festschrift for Professor Williamson, and I offer it with great respect—and with some fear and trembling, as I tread on his 'turf' in the book of Chronicles.

## I. Textual Discussion

It has long been the consensus that the Chronicler's history is to be dated to a much later time than the Deuteronomistic History, of which the book of Kings is a part, and that the author of Chronicles used the book of Kings as a source[4] (albeit there have been a few dissenters).[5] Assuming that this is so, it is interesting to note that 2 Chr 32:30 and 2 Kgs 20:20, although they are certainly similar to each other, also differ from each other signifi-

---

[3] H. G. M. Williamson, *1 and 2 Chronicles* (NCB; Grand Rapids: Eerdmans, 1982), 380.

[4] An examination of the dating of the book of Chronicles is beyond the scope of this article. See among others Martin Noth, *The Chronicler's History* (trans. H. G. M. Williamson; JSOTSup 50; Sheffield: JSOT Press, 1987); Isaac Kalimi, *An Ancient Israelite Historian: Studies in the Chronicler, His Time, Place and Writing* (Assen: van Gorcum, 2005); Williamson, *Chronicles*; Sara Japhet, *I & II Chronicles: A Commentary* (OTL; Louisville, Ky.: Westminster/John Knox Press, 1993). For comparisons between DtrH and Chronicles see Ehud Ben Zvi, "Are There any Bridges out There? How Wide was the Conceptual Gap between the Deuteronomistic History and Chronicles?" in *Community Identity in Judean Historiography: Biblical and Comparative Perspectives* (ed. Gary N. Knoppers and Kenneth A. Ristau; Winona Lake, Ind.: Eisenbrauns, 2009), 59–86; and Mark J. Boda, "Identity and Empire, Reality and Hope in the Chronicler's Perspective," in *Community Identity in Judean Historiography: Biblical and Comparative Perspectives* (ed. Gary N. Knoppers and Kenneth A. Ristau; Winona Lake, Ind.: Eisenbrauns, 2009), 249–72.

[5] Some believe that Kings and Chronicles had common sources but that Chronicles was not directly dependent on Kings, or else that Chronicles had a different Vorlage of Samuel-Kings; we may note Graeme Auld, *Kings Without Privileges: David and Moses in the Story of the Bible's Kings* (Edinburgh: T&T Clark, 1984), 22–29; and Steven L. McKenzie, *The Chronicler's Use of the Deuteronomistic History* (HSM 33; Atlanta: Scholars Press, 1985), 187.

cantly. Chronicles omits mention of the pool (ברכה) and conduit (תעלה), and therefore does not specify how the waters were moved to the west side of the city. The Kings account, on the other hand, does not mention the closing of the outlet (מוצא) of the Gihon. Williamson's assessment of the data appears sound: that although the Kings account does seem to refer to the same water system as Chronicles, "the greater detail of this verse [2 Chr 32:30], together with considerations of the Hebrew style at this point, strongly suggest that he drew this notice from an alternative source."[6] Japhet notes that 2 Chr 32:30 "is an addendum with a different topic, its own opening and an additional conclusion."[7] The alternative source is arguably less specific than Kings, with its reference to the pool and the conduit. The Chronicler does nevertheless at least identify both the source of the water ("the upper outlet of the waters of Gihon") as well as its destination ("the west side of the city of David"), and in this Chronicles is more specific than Kings, with its more general "brought water into the city."

Vaughn acknowledges that independent verification of the Chronicler's chronology is impossible: "in the end... ascription of the Siloam Tunnel to Hezekiah's reign is a result of biblical references and is not based solely on archaeological data."[8] Therefore, although the Chronicler's claim in v. 30 seems reliable, it is more difficult to substantiate than the activities related to vv. 27–29.[9] However, Vaughn believes that the fact that the data in vv. 27–29 can be substantiated helps to support the view that the author of Chronicles is relating known events. "Even though the modern interpreter cannot corroborate 32:30 in the same way that is possible for 32:27–29, it is reasonable to posit that the reference to the establishing of the Siloam Tunnel by Hezekiah is an additional datum that the Chronicler's community would have recognized as authentic."[10]

Even if this were so, of course, it is clear that our biblical texts do not help us to understand the circumstances surrounding Hezekiah's work on Jerusalem's water system. In both Kings and Chronicles, reference to Hezekiah's work in this area is found in the midst of a summary evaluation of

---

6 Williamson, *Chronicles*, 387; cf. Japhet, *Chronicles*, 995; and see Noth, *Chronicler's History*, 57, who believes this verse "must be a word-for-word citation from some source otherwise unknown to us."

7 Japhet, *Chronicles*, 994.

8 Andrew G. Vaughn, *Theology, History, and Archaeology in the Chronicler's Account of Hezekiah* (Atlanta: Scholars Press, 1999), 174.

9 Japhet, *Chronicles*, 995.

10 Vaughn, *Theology*, 174.

his reign. This is not a reliable guide as to exactly when the work was carried out, as Japhet notes with respect to the Chronicler in particular: "for the Chronicler, the placing of Hezekiah's prosperity and economic activity where they are [at the end of the account] was more likely determined by literary and theological considerations, but they may nevertheless reflect Hezekiah's economic and building activity in various periods of his reign."[11] It is not the date, but the significance of his work on the water system that is indicated in 2 Chr 32:27–30, which prefaces the information about the waters with information about Hezekiah's great wealth. This passage indicates, as Knoppers notes, that Hezekiah used "his resources to enhance the living conditions of his people."[12] Immediately following the diversion of the waters in v. 30 is a description of how Hezekiah prospered in all his works, whenever they were accomplished during his reign.

## II. Archaeological Discussion

We now turn to a discussion of the water systems associated with the Gihon Spring. In August 2010, I explored the 'Warren's Shaft System' with Dr. Gabriel Barkay of Bar Ilan University.[13] Numerous water systems of various periods have been identified, associated with the Gihon Spring.[14] Today one must descend from the present valley floor to reach the spring; however since the valley has silted up over the millennia, in antiquity the valley floor was quite a bit lower (exactly how much is not known, as the valley floor has never been excavated), and so the spring would have emerged from the side of the slope. The earliest water system discovered to date was a simple shaft system consisting of a hole in the ceiling of the natural cave where the Gihon Spring is located. Then, in the Middle Bronze period several systems were built. One of these was the channel[15] referred to in 2 Chr 32:3–4 which Hezekiah and his people blocked up, and which

[11] Japhet, *Chronicles*, 979.

[12] Gary N. Knoppers, "History and Historiography: The Royal Reforms," in *The Chronicler as Historian* (ed. M. Patrick Graham, Kenneth G. Hoglund and Steven L. McKenzie; JSOTSup 238; Sheffield: Sheffield Academic Press, 1997), 178–203 (192), and cf. 2 Chr 32:27–29.

[13] I am grateful to Dr. Barkay for explaining the intricacies of this system to me.

[14] For earlier descriptions and plans, see Yigal Shiloh, *Excavations at the City of David I: 1978–1982* (Qedem 19; Jerusalem: Institute of Archaeology of the Hebrew University of Jerusalem, 1984), 21–24, figs 30–32, plates 37:1–40:2.

[15] Channel II of Louis-Hugues Vincent, *Underground Jerusalem: Discoveries on the Hill of Ophel (1909–11)* (trans. from the French; London: Horace Cox, 1911), 6–8; Jan Simons, *Jerusalem in the Old Testament: Researches and Theories* (Leiden: E. J. Brill, 1952), 176–78.

many scholars identify as the Shiloah channel of Isa 8:6.[16] (There is a second channel of uncertain date, taking water from the Gihon Spring down into the Kidron Valley along the eastern side of the City of David.[17] Reich and Shukron date it to Iron Age II.[18]) Also in the Middle Bronze Age a tunnel system was excavated in the softer limestone rock from above, using stone tools. The tunnel descended down rock-hewn steps to a horizontal tunnel, used to bring people to a place right above a rock-cut pool, which was fed by another tunnel which brought water from the spring to the bottom of the pool.[19] The water would probably have been drawn while people stood on a wooden platform suspended above the pool.[20] A second tunnel system was dug in the Middle Bronze Age, perpendicular to the first and reinforced by stone walls. This was probably never completed. On the basis of deposits of Iron I pottery and fill material in the pool, the Middle Bronze tunnel and pool system may be judged to have been abandoned by the Iron IIa period (ninth century BCE). Then, later in Iron II, builders first attempted to reuse the Middle Bronze tunnel in order to access water from the Gihon Spring. The horizontal tunnel was deepened into a harder limestone layer, as is clear by the chisel marks in this lower rock stratum. As the workers were digging through this lower, harder rock layer, they encountered a natural karstic shaft which is popularly known as 'Warren's Shaft.'[21] Gill notes that the top of 'Warren's Shaft' is 4.25 metres below the top of the harder limestone layer, or Mizzi Ahmar. He continues, "[i]t should be pointed out that, from an engineering standpoint, there was no reason whatsoever to deepen the tunnel into the hard Mizzi Ahmar rather than remain within the softer Meleke; the latter would have made the hewing much easier and would have resulted in an almost horizontal

[16] Cf. (among others) Ronny Reich and Eli Shukron, "Jerusalem: 2. The Gihon Spring and Eastern Slope of the City of David," in *NEAEHL* 5 (ed. Ephraim Stern; Jerusalem: Israel Exploration Society, 2008), 1801–07, esp. 1803; Williamson, *Chronicles*, 381; Thompson, *1, 2 Chronicles*, 361; David Tarler and Jane M. Cahill, "David, City of," in *ABD* 2: 52–67, esp. 62; and most recently H. G. M. Williamson, "The Waters of Shiloah (Isaiah 8:5–8)," in *The Fire Signals of Lachish: Studies in the Archaeology and History of Israel in the Late Bronze Age, Iron Age, and Persian Period in Honor of David Ussishkin* (ed. Israel Finkelstein and Nadav Na'aman; Winona Lake, Ind.: Eisenbrauns, 2011), 331–43.

[17] Channel I of Vincent, *Underground Jerusalem*, 6; also known as Masterman's channel; Simons, *Jerusalem*, 176.

[18] Reich and Shukron, "Jerusalem," 1806.

[19] Channel III of Vincent, *Underground Jerusalem*, 8; offshoot of channel II; see fig 23 in Simons, *Jerusalem*, 174.

[20] Reich and Shukron, "Jerusalem," 1803.

[21] Reich and Shukron, "Jerusalem," 1805.

tunnel, an important convenience in itself."[22] This natural shaft is only part of the 'Warren's Shaft System,' which includes the artificially hewn tunnels. Another tunnel[23] was dug at the base of this shaft to connect with the spring, so that the water from the spring could be accessed by means of the 12.3 metre shaft.[24] It had been thought that 'Warren's Shaft' formed a part of the earlier, pre-Israelite water system,[25] perhaps even the צנור through which Joab gained access to the city in order to secure it for King David (so interpreting 2 Sam 5:6–8).[26] It is now clear that this natural karstic shaft was not revealed until Iron Age II, with this later deepening of the Middle Bronze tunnel.

It is not likely that this system was used as the primary means to access the spring by most of the city dwellers, since there is only room for a few people at the top of the shaft, and the process of lowering wooden or leather water buckets on ropes through the rough and uneven natural shaft down to a depth of 12 metres and bringing them back up full would have been a difficult and inefficient, time-consuming method. Therefore, another system had to be built, which is the Iron Age II system known as the Siloam Tunnel or, more popularly, 'Hezekiah's Tunnel.'[27]

The winding nature of the tunnel has long been a source of speculation, especially since the tunnels of other Iron Age water systems at other sites are straight (cf. especially Megiddo). The tunnel is roughly S-shaped,[28] as it makes its way west and south from the Gihon Spring and east and north from the Pool of Siloam. The fact that the tunnel was created simultaneously by two crews, one working from the Gihon Spring and the other from the Pool of Siloam is clear, not only from the inscription (to be discussed below), but also by the orientation of the chisel marks and the several false 'dead ends' as the two teams drew closer.[29]

---

[22] Dan Gill, "The Geology of the City of David and its Ancient Subterranean Waterworks," in *Excavations at the City of David 1978–1985: Directed by Yigal Shiloh IV* (ed. Donald T. Ariel and Alon de Groot; Qedem 35; Jerusalem: Institute of Archaeology of the Hebrew University of Jerusalem, 1996), 1–28, esp. 5–6. This is exactly what the earlier Middle Bronze excavators did when they stayed in the softer limestone layer to dig their tunnel to access the pool.

[23] Channel VI of Vincent, *Underground Jerusalem*, 10–11.

[24] Shiloh, *Excavations*, 21.

[25] P. Kyle McCarter, Jr., *Ancient Inscriptions: Voices from the Biblical World* (Washington, D.C.: Biblical Archaeology Society, 1996), 113.

[26] Cf. Vincent, *Underground Jerusalem*, 34; Tarler and Cahill, "David, City of," 61–62, among others.

[27] Channel VIII of Vincent, *Underground Jerusalem*, 16–24.

[28] Vincent, *Underground Jerusalem*, Plate IV.

[29] Tarler and Cahill, "David, City of," 62.

The base fall of the tunnel is very consistent, falling at a rate of approximately 0.06%[30] over the 533 metre-long distance of the tunnel.[31] The height of the ceiling, on the other hand, varies considerably. In some places the ceiling is little over one metre, whereas in other places the ceiling is far overhead. In some places where the ceiling is high overhead it is due to fissures in the rock which extend far upwards. In the southern part, there are places where the tunnel is quarried to a height of five metres,[32] no doubt in order to lower the floor after the two teams met so as to allow the water to flow consistently.

There have been many suggestions in an effort to explain the circuitous route the tunnel takes. Some of these include:

1) The ancient engineers were unable to accurately plot the line of the tunnel.[33]
2) The northern curve was an attempt to intersect some springs along the route, and the southern curve was to avoid the royal necropolis of the kings of Judah.[34]
3) The line of the tunnel followed a softer stratum of the rock.[35]
4) The line of the tunnel followed a fissure in the rock that had dissolved a passageway that created a karstic solution channel all the way from the Gihon to the Pool of Siloam.[36]
5) Workers above sent sound signals down to guide the workers below.[37]
6) The tunnel started at both ends with natural dissolution channels, and then the ancient engineers worked out how to join them above ground to close the gap in between, and then transferred that information to the workers below.[38]

---

30 Shiloh, *Excavations*, 23, erroneously printed as 0.6%.

31 Naseeb Shaheen, "Siloam End of Hezekiah's Tunnel," *PEQ* 109 (1977): 107–12, esp. 107.

32 Ronny Reich and Eli Shukron, "Reconsidering the Karstic Theory as an Explanation to the Cutting of Hezekiah's Tunnel in Jerusalem," *BASOR* 325 (2002): 75–80.

33 Stephen G. Rosenberg, "The Parker Mission and Hezekiah's Tunnel," *Strata* 27 (2009): 79–87, esp. 81, citing Warren and Conder.

34 Vincent, *Underground Jerusalem*, 21, citing Clermont-Ganneau; cf. Rosenberg, "Parker Mission," 81.

35 Vincent, *Underground Jerusalem*, 23.

36 Ruth Amiran, "The Water Supply of Israelite Jerusalem," in *Jerusalem Revealed: Archaeology in the Holy City 1968–1974* (ed. Yigael Yadin; New Haven: Yale University Press, 1976), 75–78, esp. 77–78; and cf. Gill, "Geology," 1–28.

37 Naseeb Shaheen, "The Sinuous Shape of Hezekiah's Tunnel," *PEQ* 146 (1979): 103–08.

38 Rosenberg, "Parker Mission," 82–83.

Most scholars now follow some variation of the theory that the workers were following natural fissures or karstic solution channels in the rock, although most believe that Gill's suggestion of a karstic channel for the whole distance is overstated.[39]

## III. The Siloam Tunnel Inscription

Although the tunnel was rediscovered by the early 1800's, it was not until 1880 that some boys (in some earlier reports, students of Conrad Schick[40]) discovered the Siloam Tunnel inscription while they were swimming about six metres up the tunnel from the Pool of Siloam end. Originally the inscription was engraved directly into the side of the tunnel, but some time after its discovery it was illicitly gouged out of the rock, and later recovered by the Turkish authorities who were in control of Jerusalem at that time. Unfortunately, the inscription broke in several places due to its rough handling, but it has subsequently been restored and is now in the Istanbul Archaeological Museum. It is important to be clear that there is no mention of Hezekiah, or any other king, official, or any other person—or even a deity's name, for that matter—on the inscription.

A full discussion of the Siloam Tunnel inscription is beyond the scope of this article.[41] However, a few comments are in order. The inscription reads:[42]

---

[39] Steven P. Lancaster and G. A. Long, "Where They Met: Separations in the Rock Mass Near the Siloam Tunnel's Meeting Point," *BASOR* 315 (1999): 15–26; cf. Reich and Shukron, "Karstic Theory," 75–78.

[40] Cf. Simons, *Jerusalem*, 183.

[41] For this, see Shmuel Aḥituv, *Handbook of Ancient Hebrew Inscriptions: from the Period of the First Commonwealth and the Beginning of the Second Commonwealth* (Jerusalem: Musad Bialek, 1992; Hebrew), 13–16; F. W. Dobbs-Allsopp *et al., Hebrew Inscriptions: Texts from the Biblical Period of the Monarchy with Concordance* (New Haven: Yale University Press, 2005), 499–506; John C. L. Gibson, *Textbook of Syrian Semitic Inscriptions. Volume 1: Hebrew and Moabite Inscriptions* (Oxford: Clarendon Press, 1971), 21–23; Simon B. Parker, *Stories in Scripture and Inscriptions: Comparative Studies on Narratives in Northwest Semitic Inscriptions and the Hebrew Bible* (New York and Oxford: Oxford University Press, 1997), 36–42; Victor Sasson, "The Siloam Tunnel Inscription," *PEQ* 114 (1982): 111–17; K. Lawson Younger, "The Siloam Tunnel Inscription: An Integrated Reading," *UF* 26 (1994): 543–56; Ian Young, Robert Rezetko and Martin Ehrensvärd, *Linguistic Dating of Biblical Texts. Volume 1: An Introduction to Approaches and Problems* (London & Oakville: Equinox Publishing, 2008), 149–56, among others.

[42] Sasson, "Siloam Tunnel Inscription," 111.

1. [ym] hnqbh. wzh. hyh. dbr. hnqbh. b‘wd [. mnpm. hḥṣbm.]
2. hgrzn. ’š̌. ’l. r‘w. wb‘wd. šlš. ’mt. lhn[qb. wyš̌]m̊‘. ql. ’š̌. q
3. r’. ’l. r‘w. ky. hyt. zdh. bṣr. mymn. [wmhśm]’l̊̊. wbym. h
4. nqbh. hkw. hḥṣbm. ’š̌. lqrt. r‘w. grzn. ‘l. [g]rzn. wylkw[.]
5. hmym. mn. hmwṣ’. ’l. hbrkh. bm’tym. ẘ’lp. ’mh. wm[’]
6. t. ’mh. hyh. gbh. hṣr. ‘l. r’š̌. hḥṣb[m.]

The text may be translated:[43]

> /1/ [The day of] the tunnel. This is the record of how the tunnel was breached: while [the excavators were wielding] /2/ their axes, one crew progressing towards the other, and while there were yet three cubits for the brea[ching to take place,] the voices of the men [were hea]rd ca/3/lling to each other; for there was a fissure (?) in the rock extending from south [to north]. So on the day the /4/ tunnel was breached the excavators struck, crew progressing towards crew, axe against [a]xe. Finally, the water flowed /5/ from the spring to the pool, a distance of one thousand and two hundred cubits. One hun[d]/6/red cubits was the height of the rock above the heads of the excavat[ors.]

As can be seen, the inscription seems to begin in the middle of the account. It also begins about half way down the smoothed panel, which might suggest that the upper part was also smoothed to prepare for some type of carving, which was never completed. (There are three other smoothed panels without any inscription in the tunnel.)[44] The inscription has been dated to the end of the eighth century BCE, partly based on the shape of the letters but also on the similarity of the events detailed in the inscription to the events related in 2 Chr 32:30, which pertain to Hezekiah's reign. Williamson notes a particular connection beyond the general ones: that the word in 2 Chr 32:30 used for 'outlet' (מוצא) is exactly the same word used here in line 5 in the Siloam Tunnel inscription, "which is a contemporary record of the undertaking."[45] Nevertheless, it will be noted that this dating of the tunnel and the inscription is based more on the biblical references than it is on archaeological data.[46]

Scholars have proposed that the blank space at the top of the inscription was left for the name and the titles of the king to be supplied, but that time ran out before the Assyrian siege was upon the city and the

---

43 Sasson, "Siloam Tunnel Inscription," 111.

44 See Younger, "Siloam Tunnel Inscription," 545 n. 4; cf. Simons, *Jerusalem*, 183 n. 2.

45 Williamson, *Chronicles*, 387, among others.

46 Vaughn, *Theology*, 174.

inscription was never completed. As one would expect the king to be mentioned if this inscription was intended as a royal inscription, this interpretation is not likely. Hezekiah reigned for about 15 years after the 701 BCE invasion, so if this inscription were meant to celebrate this achievement, he presumably would have had time to have it completed. Additionally, if the inscription was intended to publicize the creation of the tunnel, why place it so far into the tunnel, where anyone who wished to view it had to wade six metres further in the city's water supply? Furthermore, if the account in 2 Kgs 20:20 refers to the same enterprise, it is vastly different in tone. There only Hezekiah is responsible for bringing water into the city—he is front and centre of the account. The inscription, on the other hand, does not even refer to the king in order to date the event.[47] It thus cannot be considered a building inscription. If the biblical account were to be written in the first person, that could be a building inscription; but the Siloam Tunnel inscription cannot. Parker thinks it may have been put up by the overseer, or 'civil engineer,' out of sight in the tunnel so the king would not know about it;[48] and Sasson believes that the space above the inscription was to be used for a relief of the workmen, which was never carved.[49] But there are three other smoothed panels in the tunnel which are not engraved. At least two of these panels "are joined to a black line on the wall sometimes interpreted as a levelling-device."[50] Therefore, it may be that all of the smoothed panels were somehow used in the levelling of the tunnel, and the panel that bears the inscription was larger because more levelling was needed once the two crews met each other, in order to allow the water to flow. Then, once the tunnel was completed, someone (one of the original excavators?) decided to use the bottom of the smoothed panel to commemorate the wondrous achievement.

This may go too far; but it is clear that we do not have a royal inscription here. There is no evidence that it was officially sponsored, and it almost certainly has nothing to do with any "Book of the Annals of the Kings of Judah."[51] It is rather both the sense of achievement and the efforts of the tunnelers that are celebrated here. Only the climactic breakthrough is

47 Ben Sira 48:17 attributes even more: "he [Hezekiah] tunneled the rock with iron tools, and built cisterns for the water" [NRSV]; and cf. Parker, *Stories*, 39, 42.

48 Parker, *Stories*, 39.

49 Sasson, "Siloam Tunnel Inscription," 111; and cf. Gibson, *Textbook*, 21.

50 Simons, *Jerusalem*, 183 n. 2.

51 2 Kgs 20:20 and cf. 2 Chr 32:32; cf. Sasson, "Siloam Tunnel Inscription," 116; and Parker, *Stories*, 39.

described. Not only the king is ignored, but so is God. This is unlike any other ancient Near Eastern monumental inscription. It is a purely secular document.[52]

## IV. Conclusion

In summary, although most scholars contend that the construction of the tunnel was done in anticipation of Sennacherib's siege, there may be other options. In an attempt to determine how long it may have taken to construct the Siloam Tunnel, Rosenberg has estimated that the workers moved on average 1.8 metres (length) of rock per day.[53] With two teams working, one from each end, it would have taken approximately five months to dig the total 533 metres of the tunnel, although since the two ends of the tunnel where the two crews started were natural formations, which needed no digging, the work might have gone more quickly. Depending on how much advance notice Hezekiah had (and one might suspect it well may have been several months), it remains possible that this task could have been achieved in time to prepare for an impending invasion. However, neither Kings nor Chronicles specifically mentions the tunnel's construction (Kings mentions the pool and the conduit, and Chronicles merely refers to diverting the waters). Furthermore these statements are related only in their summary accounts of Hezekiah's reign; and neither text attributes this activity to the invasion. Most scholars are not concerned about this odd placement of the notice, and cite other achronistic reports.[54] And yet it is also interesting that the Siloam Tunnel inscription does not mention any king, invasion or deity. There is nothing in the tunnel itself to connect it with Sennacherib's invasion.

It is also possible, then, that the tunnel's construction took place some time before the Assyrian siege, as Williamson has proposed. It is equally possible, however, that it took place after the Assyrian siege. It is not difficult to reconstruct a plausible sequence of events. Even though the Chronicler's account in 2 Chr 32:3–4 has the springs and channels blocked, so that the Assyrians would not have access to the city's water

[52] Cf. Judith M. Hadley, "Hebrew Inscriptions," in *Dictionary of the Old Testament Historical Books* (ed. Bill T. Arnold and H. G. M. Williamson; Downers Grove, Ill.: InterVarsity Press, 2005), 366–80, esp. 367–68.

[53] Stephen G. Rosenberg, "The Siloam Tunnel Revisited," *Tel Aviv* 25 (1998): 116–30, esp. 128.

[54] Knoppers, "History," 178–203, esp. 190 n. 29.

supply, Jerusalem's residents could still have accessed the spring by way of the shaft system, which preceded the tunnel, and which may have been excavated to help divert the Gihon Spring water away from the Shiloah channel and the hillside. Furthermore, the construction of a reservoir between the two walls in Isa 22:11 may have been an attempt to try to control the overflow of the now backed-up and blocked-off spring. Then, after the Assyrian siege was lifted and the water flow restored to normal, Hezekiah would have had a problem with providing water to the residents of the western hill, whose former extra-mural settlements were now enclosed within the second wall of the city, and who would have had easy access only to water collected in cisterns from rain-water run-off. In this scenario, the tunnel was created to bring water into this new addition to the city. If most of the expansion to the western hill had in fact occurred early in Hezekiah's reign, as a result of people moving to Jerusalem in the aftermath of the fall of the Northern Kingdom, this itself would provide a motive for creating the tunnel, earlier, to bring fresh water closer to the new settlements on the western hill. In either case, whether the construction was before or after the siege, it is unlikely that the creation of the so-called 'Hezekiah's Tunnel' was an immediate result of the invasion by Sennacherib.

# PAIN IN CHILDBIRTH? FURTHER THOUGHTS ON "AN ATTRACTIVE FRAGMENT" (1 CHRONICLES 4:9–10)

Iain Provan

Buried in the midst of the nine chapters of genealogies that form the introduction to the books of 1–2 Chronicles lies the brief account of a man named Jabez who prayed (1 Chr 4:9–10). It is a pericope to which until very recently hardly anyone, scholar or lay person, had paid much attention, and to which relatively little significance had been attached.[1] For example, writing in his 1982 commentary on 1–2 Chronicles, my own mentor H. G. M. Williamson, to whom I gratefully dedicate this essay (and whose commentary was indeed published in the very year in which I began my doctoral studies under him in Cambridge), deals with this "attractive fragment" in short order. He restricts his comments to the word-play involved in the naming of Jabez and to his prayer that "the ill omen of his own name" might not hurt him. As to *why* the passage might have found its way into 1 Chronicles, Williamson comments that it "accords well with the Chronicler's belief in the efficacy of prayer."[2] These same elements are well represented in the other commentaries—usually just as brief in their treatment of the passage—published during the last thirty years. A brief and highly selective review down to the present will suffice to illustrate the point. Sara Japhet (1993), for example, thinks of Jabez as "irrevocably burdened with a name which was determined by his mother's experience and is now to determine his own fate." God's power alone can save him; and so he prays.[3] Gary Knoppers (2004) thinks that "the story treats the circumstances of Jabez's birth as an omen…Jabez asks the God of

[1] All this changed at least in the world of popular religion with the publication of Bruce Wilkinson's little book, *The Prayer of Jabez: Breaking Through To The Blessed Life* (Sisters, OR: Multnomah, 2000)—allegedly the fastest-selling book in history, with worldwide sales exceeding 20 million. No such dramatic change in perspective has marked academic writing on this hitherto little-regarded text, although it should be noted that it has a strikingly important role to play within 1 Chr 2:3–4:43 in James T. Sparks' interesting monograph, *The Chronicler's Genealogies: Towards An Understanding of 1 Chronicles 1–9* (Academia Biblica 28; Atlanta: Society of Biblical Literature, 2008), 236–43.

[2] H. G. M. Williamson, *1 and 2 Chronicles* (NCB; Grand Rapids and London: Eerdmans and Marshall, Morgan and Scott, 1982), 59–60.

[3] Sara Japhet, *I and II Chronicles*, (OTL; Louisville: Westminster John Knox, 1993), 109–10.

Israel to free him from an association between his name and his fate."[4] The pericope "anticipates an important theme in the Chronicler's narration of the monarchy: the importance of prayer."[5] For Ralph Klein (2006), "[Jabez's] prayer was meant to counteract the threatening character of his name... he desired that his name would not be his fate."[6] Finally by way of example, Mark Boda (2010) writes that

> the story shows how someone whose name means 'he causes pain,' and thus has a destiny of pain, experienced the very opposite in his life by being 'more honorable than any of his brothers' (4:9). It was due to his prayer to the God of Israel... This foreshadows a strong emphasis in the Chronicler on prayer as a sign of human covenant fidelity and blessing.[7]

For all these commentators, the problem that Jabez must overcome is his name; and efficacious prayer is the means by which this is achieved. This is indeed a settled line of interpretation in the commentaries in general.[8] Commentators may not have *much* to say about Jabez; but *this much* they do know.

It is my intention in this brief essay to unsettle this settled line of interpretation. It is not that I doubt that there was an ancient belief that "a person's name revealed the character and personality as well as the reputation, authority, vocation, and even the destiny of the bearer,"[9] and that Jabez's 'name' might well have suggested to him and to others that he was fated to experience pain, in an ancient Mediterranean context in which some, at least, believed that genealogies themselves had a predictive aspect.[10] What I doubt is that his name is the only problem that Jabez had to overcome. I believe, to the contrary, that there is in 1 Chr 4:9–10 a far closer connection between the pain of the mother and the pain of the son than has usually been recognized, and that indeed the context in

---

[4] Gary N. Knoppers, *1 Chronicles 1–9* (AB; New York: Doubleday, 2004), 346.

[5] Knoppers, *1 Chronicles 1–9*, 346.

[6] Ralph W. Klein, *1 Chronicles* (Hermeneia; Minneapolis: Fortress, 2006), 132–33.

[7] Mark J. Boda, *1–2 Chronicles* (Cornerstone Biblical Commentary; Carol Stream, IL: Tyndale House, 2010), 57.

[8] So also, e.g., J. A. Thompson, *1, 2 Chronicles* (NAC; Nashville: Broadman and Holman, 1994), 73; Andrew E. Hill, *1 & 2 Chronicles* (NIVAC; Grand Rapids: Zondervan, 2003), 95–96; and Thomas Willi, *Chronik: 1 Chr 1–10* (BKAT; Neukirchen-Vluyn: Neukirchener Verlag, 2009), 125–28.

[9] Hill, *1 & 2 Chronicles*, 62.

[10] "The regard of ancient Mediterranean peoples for matters genealogical must be connected to the significance they attributed to origins and the original ancestor in determining the character of future generations. In ancient Greece... one's identity was intimately tied to one's roots and social context" (Knoppers, *1 Chronicles 1–9*, 250–51).

which the prayer is uttered is defined by this ongoing pain. The name is not merely an omen; it does not speak only to a future threat or destiny. It is expressive of Jabez's life from the moment of his birth until he prays.

## I. Does 1 Chr 4:9 Refer to Pain Endured in Childbirth?

This reality has been obscured from most scholars reading 1 Chr 4:9–10, I propose, because they have been working with a shared, unexamined assumption with respect to the meaning of 4:9 (ויהי יעבץ נכבד מאחיו ואמו קראה שמו יעבץ לאמר כי ילדתי בעצב). It is the assumption that the pain suffered by Jabez's mother (עצב), which results in the naming of her child (יעבץ), is pain that is endured in the course of childbirth. This assumption certainly comes to explicit expression in Hill, for example, and in Knoppers.[11] It is also reflected in Klein, who notes a possible allusion to the first part of Gen 3:16, which he renders: "I will greatly increase your pangs in childbearing; in pain (בעצב) you shall bring forth children."[12] Klein refers by way of analogy to Gen 35:18, where Rachel, as she dies in childbirth, names her son Ben-Oni "son of sorrow."[13] We may deduce that it is also the view of Jarick, since in the preface to his commentary he entertainingly shares with us his temptation to name his commentary "Jabez," on account of the pain of the process by which it was birthed.[14] Some other recent commentaries do not provide us with any explicit guidance as to their author's opinion on such matters, although they certainly do not clearly proceed from a different starting-point either. We are dealing with a firmly established reading, it seems.[15] But does the reading have merit?

My first question about it is this: leaving aside for the moment Gen 3:16a, and passing over the obvious point (relevant to both that verse and also to 1 Chr 4:9) that the Hebrew verb ילד does not itself necessarily refer

[11] Hill, *1 & 2 Chronicles*, 95; Knoppers, *1 Chronicles 1–9*, 339, 346.

[12] Klein, *1 Chronicles*, 132. The allusion is also explicitly noted in Isaac Kalimi, *Zur Geschichtsschreibung des Chronisten* (BZAW 226; Berlin/New York: De Gruyter, 1995), 218.

[13] Klein, *1 Chronicles*, 132.

[14] John Jarick, *1 Chronicles* (Readings: A New Biblical Commentary; Sheffield: Sheffield Academic, 2002), vii.

[15] The reading is so firmly established that even Sparks (*The Chronicler's Genealogies*, 240) who is otherwise quite prepared to strike out and explore new ground, does not even hint at doing so in this case, simply assuming that "for Jabez' mother [the pain] was the pain of childbirth."

in the Old Testament to the birth process as such,[16] are there any other occasions in the Old Testament upon which this root עצב is used to refer to labour-pains?[17] A survey of the literature quickly reveals that there are not. It is used of emotional pain[18] and of the pain involved in work.[19] It can also be used of a more generalized kind of pain.[20] It is never used elsewhere in the Old Testament, however (with the possible exception of Gen 3:16a), to refer to labour-pains or 'birthpangs.' Conversely, there is a well-established vocabulary which is routinely used to refer to such realities: צרר, חבל and חול.[21]

Secondly: does anything in 1 Chr 4:9 itself suggest that we should, nevertheless (and unusually), interpret עצב in this verse as referring to birthpangs, rather than to some other kind of pain? We must again reply in the negative. All that we are actually told in 1 Chr 4:9 is that Jabez's mother gave birth to him or "begat" him in pain. The reference *may* be (unusually) to her physical pain in giving birth. However, taking our lead from our review of texts just completed, we might more plausibly understand it as a reference either to the mother's emotional state at the time of Jabez's birth or to her challenging (painful) economic circumstances. The first of these options was in fact long ago adopted by the KJV, which rendered the line: "I bare him with sorrow." The second, however, fits better with what we read in v. 10, where Jabez prays that he himself will be "free from pain."[22] On that occasion, of course, עצב certainly does not refer to birth-

---

[16] See Carol Meyers, *Discovering Eve: Ancient Israelite Women in Context* (New York/Oxford: OUP, 1988), 105–6.

[17] I refer to עצב-I, which the vast majority of scholars have taken to be the verbal root with which we are dealing both in Gen 3:16–17 and in 1 Chr 4:9–10. I find unconvincing the recent attempt by Tzvi Novick ("Pain and production in Eden: Some philological reflections on Genesis iii 16," *VT* 58 [2008]: 235–44) to find עצב-II in Gen 3:16a and 3:17 (as well as in 5:29), but not in 3:16b—not least because it requires "the attribution of gestation to the mother... even though, in most other biblical passages, it is naturally God to whom formation of the child is attributed" (pp. 241–42 n. 20).

[18] Gen 6:6; 2 Sam 19:3; Ps 139:24; Prov 15:1.

[19] Gen 3:17; 5:29; Ps 127:2; Prov 5:10; 10:22, 14:23.

[20] Isa 14:3.

[21] In this overall conclusion I find myself in agreement with Meyers, *Discovering Eve*, 103–9. However, I do not find convincing the sharp contrast she draws in her discussion of עצב between the use of the verbal root עצב generally and the use of the noun עצבון in particular, relating the former to psychological or emotional discomfort and latter to physical labour. I can see no good reason to limit either the verbal root or the noun in such a manner. I do in fact think that "the meanings of physical toil or labor, and of emotional turmoil or grief, are inherently related and indeed are derived from the same verbal root" (p. 107).

[22] So, rightly, R. Christopher Heard, "Echoes of Genesis in 1 Chronicles 4:9–10: An Intertextual and Contextual Reading of Jabez's Prayer," *JHS* 4 (2002): 1–28, on p. 7—an

pangs. The context, in which Jabez also asks God to enlarge his territory, strongly suggests that it does not refer primarily to emotional or more generalized pain either, but specifically to economic pain. He is looking for economic prosperity—for what Prov 10:22 refers to as "the blessing of the LORD [that] makes rich... [to which] he adds no pain (עצב, i.e., painful toil)." He is asking to escape the difficult economic circumstances in which his mother found herself on the day of his birth (and to which his own birth no doubt added), and to avoid such a fate in the future. We need not exclude entirely, of course, the reality of emotional or more generalized pain, since these things are often also associated with economic hardship. We probably *should* exclude, I propose, any allusion to birthpangs. Jabez had known a hard life; his name promised little in the way of change; but now he asks God for a different kind of existence.

## II. Does Gen 3:16a Refer to Pain Endured in Childbirth?

It is not anything in the passage itself, I suspect, that has led commentators to think it self-evident that 1 Chr 4:9 refers to birthpangs. Nor has consideration of the normal range of meanings of the root עצב within the Old Testament played much of a role. I suspect that at the heart of the 'problem,' if that is what we have here, lies a settled, received opinion about the meaning of Gen 3:16a, inherited ultimately from ancient authorities like John Chrysostom,[23] such that any commentator who (rightly) adduces a connection between Gen 3:16a and 1 Chr 4:9 is likely to assume that the latter refers to childbirth—because the former "clearly" does. Certainly it is this settled, received interpretation of Gen 3:16a that we find reflected in major English-language Bible translations. It is also the interpretation commonly and explicitly offered of the whole line in many of the commentaries on Genesis.[24] Even where it is not entirely clear what commentators think of the first part of the line, or where they explicitly take a different view of that part of the line (i.e., they do not believe that

interesting essay which I came across after my own convictions about 1 Chr 4:9–10 had already taken shape.

[23] See Andrew Louth, ed., *Genesis 1–11* (Ancient Christian Commentary on Scripture; Downers Grove, IL: InterVarsity, 2001), 92–93.

[24] For example, Ephraim A. Speiser, *Genesis* (AB; Garden City, NY: Doubleday, 1964), 22; Gordon J. Wenham, *Genesis 1–15* (WBC; Nashville: Thomas Nelson, 1987), 81; Victor P. Hamilton, *Genesis 1–17* (NICOT; Grand Rapids: Eerdmans, 1990), 200; Robert Alter, *Genesis*, (New York/London: W. W. Norton, 1996), 13; and Bruce K. Waltke, *Genesis* (Grand Rapids: Zondervan, 2001), 94.

*it* refers to birthpangs), they typically refer the second part, at least, to birthpangs.[25]

Yet is this assumption that Gen 3:16a refers to birthpangs *itself* well-founded? Again, we must reply in the negative. Wenham, who adopts this view, nevertheless concedes in writing about the second part of the verse (and in line with my comments above), that "neither the word used here for 'pain,' עצב, nor the earlier one, עצבון, is the usual one for the pangs of childbirth."[26] If we were to take our lead from what is "usual" elsewhere in the Old Testament, we would certainly understand the "pain" (עצב) with which "you will give birth to children" in the second part of Gen 3:16a as referring to the "agony, hardship, worry, nuisance, and anxiety"[27] of the circumstances into which children are born and then raised, and in which they die (note the use of עצב in 2 Sam 19:3). Indeed, nothing forbids us from understanding it as referring, in part, to the same kind of challenging (painful) economic circumstances that are in view, I have proposed, in 1 Chr 4:9–10, and which might be considered to contribute greatly to trouble within a home. The noun עצבון in the first part of Gen 3:16a, for its part, is the *very* noun that appears in the adjacent v. 17, where the man is told: "cursed is the ground... in pain (עצבון) shall you eat of it." This is the man's fate, to match the woman's—he knows עצבון, as she does; and in this case the noun *certainly* refers to challenging (painful) economic circumstances, as the man is locked in a struggle with the land, hoping through "painful toil" to grow sufficient "green plants" (עשב השדה) in the midst of "thorns and thistles" to survive. There was work to be done in the field before the events of Gen 3 transpired, just as there was work to be done in the home (the woman's עצבון is said greatly to *increase*, not to *begin*). Human beings were created to rule and subdue the earth (1:28) and to "serve the garden and keep it" (2:15), in an environment in which we are probably meant to imagine there were already thorns and thistles (included under the heading of שיח) as well as עשב השדה (Gen 2:5 for both; cf. 1:11–12, 29). But much harder work is now required

[25] So John Skinner, *Genesis* (ICC; 2nd ed.; Edinburgh: T&T Clark, 1930), 82; Gerhard von Rad, *Genesis* (OTL; rev. ed.; Philadelphia: Westminster, 1972), 93; and John Walton, *Genesis* (NIVAC; Grand Rapids: Zondervan, 2001), 227. The same general line of interpretation is found even in the most recent of commentaries on Genesis, down to and including Bill T. Arnold, *Genesis* (New Cambridge Bible Commentary; Cambridge: CUP, 2009), 69–70: "... the woman will experience pain in childbirth and pain in relating to the man."

[26] Wenham, *Genesis 1–15*, 81.

[27] The language is Walton's (*Genesis*, 227) as he describes that to which nouns from this root refer elsewhere in the Old Testament.

in both spheres, as the human relationship with God and with the rest of creation is fractured.

If Gen 3:17 thus helps to explain *why* the "agony, hardship, worry, nuisance, and anxiety" bound up with the woman's experience in the home might relate partially to economic circumstances, Gen 3:16b helps to explain further dimensions of it. For Gen 3:16b tells us that it is not just the human relationship with God and with the rest of creation that is fractured; it is the human relationship with other humans, specifically the husband with the wife. The man is not only locked in a struggle with the land; he is also locked in a struggle with his spouse: "your desire will be for your husband, and he will rule over you." Men and women were created to work in partnership, according to Gen 1:27–28 and 2:20–23, ruling jointly over the earth (and in that context building their families). Psalm 8 describes this reality in the language of "rule" (משל) over the works of God's hands. Genesis 3 insists, on the other hand, that the future of the woman from this point onwards in the story is to be "ruled" (משל) by her husband. This verb has occurred before in Genesis, in Gen 1:16 and 18, where the sun and the moon "rule" the day and the night. It will occur later again in Gen 4:7, where Cain is told: "[Sin] desires to have you, but you must master it." משל refers to mastery. It seems likely then that the man is envisaged in Gen 3:16 as relating to the woman as if she were a *part* of the creation over which humans were given dominion, rather than co-ruler *over* creation along with the man.

She, for her part, is not envisaged by the text as blameless in this increased dysfunctionality in male-female relations, for "your desire [תשוקה] will be for your husband." In the same way that our understanding of the occurrence of עצבון in Gen 3:16 should be informed by its occurrence in the adjacent Gen 3:17, so too should our understanding of the equally rare noun תשוקה in the close-by Gen 4:7—especially when משל itself appears there. Here the noun is used of sin's desire to gobble up Cain, like a wild animal lying in wait for its victim. This implies that in Gen 3:16 we are to think of a female desire to control, even to consume, her husband.[28] Intended for partnership, the human pair will in fact find themselves embroiled in a struggle for dominance, as they

[28] So, rightly, Susan Foh, "What is the Woman's Desire?" *WTJ* 37 (1974): 376–83. Walton's objection (*Genesis*, 227–9) on the basis of Song 7:10 is not compelling; see Iain W. Provan, *Ecclesiastes/Song of Songs* (NIVAC; Grand Rapids: Zondervan, 2001), 356–59.

themselves struggle for dominance over the earth.[29] This is, in part, why family life will be more painful for the woman than it would have been if the human pair had not turned away from God. Dysfunction marks not only the human relationship with the environment outside the home; it also marks the human relationships within the home. The remainder of the book of Genesis powerfully illustrates this dysfunction and the sorrow that it brings.

Such an interpretation of עצב and עצבון as referring to pain of body and of mind in general, as children are brought into the world, rather than to birthpangs in particular, has the merit (among other things) of allowing us to translate והרנך in Gen 3:16a in a much more plausible way than has often been managed. For if "neither the word… עצב, nor the earlier one, עצבון, is the usual one for the pangs of childbirth," it is equally the case that the word הרן is of very questionable connection to the birthing of children. הרן is a by-form of הריון,[30] which in its two occurrences within the Old Testament clearly refers to conception, and not to birth. In Hos 9:11 "Ephraim's glory will fly away like a bird—no birth (לדה), no pregnancy (בטן), no conception (הריון)"; and Ruth 4:13 tells us that Boaz "went to her [Ruth], and the Lord enabled her to conceive (lit. gave to her conception, הריון), and she gave birth (ילד) to a son." What is it that God increases, then, in Gen 3:16? It is "pain and conception." Perhaps we have a reference to the multiplication (separately) of pain and conception—there will be more of both. Perhaps, though, we have here an example of 'hendiadys,' in which case the reference is to the multiplication of painful conception.

What we do not get, in either case, is any reference to painful birthing. The invocation of hendiadys does not magically allow the transformation of הרן (conception) into בטן (pregnancy) or לדה (birth)—although it is such alchemy that commentators and translators have nonetheless attempted to deploy, when they have read עצבונך והרנך as referring to pains in pregnancy or birth. Skinner, for example, in the space of a few lines moves without blinking (and without explanation) from a literal reading involving "suffering and pregnancy" to a rendering arising out of the acceptance of hendiadys, which involves "the pain of thy conception,"

[29] Contra Meyers (*Discovering Eve*, 109–17) who argues implausibly that Gen 3:16b speaks only about females acceding to male sexual advances, in spite of the fear of pregnancy, because of the passion they feel towards their men.

[30] For a discussion, see Novick, "Pain," 237–40.

appearing to equate both these with the pangs of childbirth.[31] Speiser tells us that this "parade example of hendiadys" signifies "your pangs that result from your pregnancy," but his translation of the *text* offers "your pangs in childbearing" and he confusingly tells us that a literal rendering (not assuming hendiadys) would be "your pangs and your childbearing."[32] Westermann refers to "a typical hendiadys," translating the phrase "the pains that childbearing will bring you," even while explicitly acknowledging that this is a unique rendering of הריון/הרן.[33] Cassuto proposes that the second term specifies the first: "your suffering in general, and more particularly that of your childbearing."[34] Into this alchemist's guild comes, refreshingly, Walton. "Despite the NIV's 'childbearing,'" he writes (and we could multiply the translations and spread the blame), "the Hebrew word is specifically concerned with conception."[35] He does accept that the phrase is a hendiadys; but he renders it "conception anxiety," arguing that the first half of v. 16 "is an extended merism . . . referring to the anxiety that a woman will experience through the whole process from conception to birth."[36] If we accept the hendiadys, I propose simply adjusting this idea (in line with my overall comments above about Gen 3:16–17) so as not to limit the "pain" to the woman's experience of anxiety between the period in which conception takes place and the period of the birth of her child. She conceives in painful circumstances just as she gives birth in painful circumstances, including economic circumstances, and no doubt raises children and watches some of them die in those same circumstances (e.g., Abel in Gen 4).[37] If there is no hendiadys, then the intimation of suffering and death may well be even more strongly expressed here; for then it is the greater number of conceptions as such, rather than the increase of

[31] Skinner, *Genesis*, 82.
[32] Speiser, *Genesis*, 22–24.
[33] Claus Westermann, *Genesis 1–11* (trans. J. J. Scullion; Minneapolis: Augsburg, 1984), 262. See further Wenham (*Genesis*, 81) who begins with "your pains and your pregnancies, which is "probably hendiadys for 'your pains of pregnancy,' " yet only two lines later refers to "the pain of childbirth."
[34] Umberto Cassuto, *A Commentary on the Book of Genesis, Part I: From Adam to Noah* (trans. Israel Abrahams; 2nd ed.; Magnes: Jerusalem, 1973), 165.
[35] Walton, *Genesis*, 227.
[36] Walton, *Genesis*, 227. So, similarly, John Calvin, *Genesis* (Wheaton/Nottingham: Crossway, 2001), 48: "all the trouble women sustain during pregnancy" (including giving birth in pain).
[37] This way of interpreting the line, if hendiadys is present, goes some way towards meeting Meyers' objection to the link that is thus forged between pain and pregnancy (*Discovering Eve*, 103), when she states that pain is "neither an accurate nor a suitable part of the description of pregnancy."

their pain specifically, that is emphasized with the mention of הרן, and this implies significant infant mortality such that more numerous conceptions (in the absence of the continuous breast-feeding that would prevent the female body from ovulating) are the natural result of sexual intercourse. On either understanding of the line, it would perhaps be best to avoid the word 'pain' in translation, because of its strong associations now in the Bible-reader's mind with labour-pains. The old KJV provides a helpful foundation for a fresh translation: "I will greatly multiply thy sorrow and thy conception; in sorrow thou shalt bring forth children."[38] We need to add something, though, in order to capture the idea in עצב of struggle or toil. We might translate in this way: "I will greatly multiply your sorrow and your conception; in sorrow and hardship you shall bring forth children."

In translating in such a manner we depart from the received opinion about the meaning of Gen 3:16a that is inherited ultimately from ancient authorities like John Chrysostom. Inevitably, however, we do not depart from tradition as such; for in the line of interpreters behind the KJV we may cite an ancient interpreter like Jerome, whose Vulgate translation speaks of the multiplication of "your toils and your conceptions" and predicts that "in grief you will bear children" (*multiplicabo aerumnas tuas et conceptus tuos in dolore paries filios*). Such a broad interpretation of עצב and עצבון in Gen 3:16 is in fact the one reflected in many ancient sources which, even when they refer to or may mean to include the difficulties of childbirth in connection with the verse, only do so as one aspect of a woman's 'pain.' LXX, for example, translates עצב and עצבון in Gen 3:16 with λυπη, a broad term covering both pain of the body and pain of the mind; and according to Hanneke Reuling, in the Old Latin versions that are based upon LXX, "the psychological connotation is [in fact] prevalent over the physical."[39] The Alexandrian scholar Didymus the Blind (310/313–398) understands the woman's ordeal in Gen 3:16 in terms of "the generation of children in the widest sense of the word, i.e. pregnancy, childbirth and raising of progeny." Genesis Rabbah 20:6–7 (fifth century) similarly speaks of the suffering of the woman in conception, through pregnancy and birth, and in the upbringing of children, quoting R. Eleazar b. R. Simeon as follows: "It is easier for a man to grow myriads of olives in Galilee

[38] The NKJV is less helpful, retaining "your sorrow and your conception" in the first part of Gen 3:16a but moving in the second part to "in pain you shall bring forth children."

[39] Hanneke Reuling, *After Eden: Church Fathers and Rabbis on Genesis 3:16–21* (Jewish and Christian Perspective Series; Leiden/Boston: Brill, 2006), 31, 37.

than to rear one child in Eretz Israel."[40] Nor has the interpretive tradition on the near side of the KJV (chronologically) been lacking in dissenters from the Chrysostom 'line.' It was well represented, for example, among medical doctors in the nineteenth century, as they found themselves required to become careful exegetes in order to dispute settled societal convictions about pain in childbirth—convictions that were inhibiting medical intervention to lessen that pain.[41]

## III. 1 Chr 4:9–10 and the Chronicler's Theology of Retribution

If we now possess a reading of Gen 3:16–17 (as I think we do) which both allows us to read all the vocabulary in a way that is consonant with its normal usage elsewhere in the Old Testament and to read the whole coherently as a unit, it is also the case that we have also now further grounded our understanding of the relationship between the pain of Jabez's mother and the pain of Jabez in 1 Chr 4:9–10. We are not reading of the mother's birthpangs here. We are reading of her challenging familial, including economic, circumstances—the circumstances in which her son grew up and of which his name speaks. The fact that he is "called" by this "name" (קראה שמו, v. 9) might well have suggested to him and to others that he was fated to continue to experience this pain; but in fact he found himself part of a people Israel who were called by a different name, and who were given an important promise as such, when they faced economic and other adversity (2 Chr 7:13–14): "if my people, who are called by my name (נקרא־שמי), will humble themselves and pray and seek my face and turn from their wicked ways, then will I hear from heaven and will forgive their sin and will heal their land."[42] So "Jabez cried out (ויקרא) to the God of Israel" (1 Chr 4:10) and God answered him. The story speaks of an actual reversal of fortune, not merely of the avoidance of future trouble hinted at in his name, in an ancient Israelite context in which many likely believed still that "the fathers eat sour grapes, and the children's teeth are set on

[40] Reuling, *After Eden*, 61, 235.

[41] Linda S. Schearing, "Parturition (Childbirth), Pain, and Piety: Physicians and Genesis 3:16a," in *Mother Goose, Mother Jones and Mommie Dearest: Biblical Mothers and Their Children* (ed. Cheryl Kirk-Duggan and Tina Pippin; SBLSymS 61. Atlanta: Society of Biblical Literature, 2009), 85–96.

[42] See Boda, (*1–2 Chronicles*, 273) who writes of 2 Chr 7:14: "In this ancient context the 'name' is intimately associated with the very essence of the one who bears it; so here to be 'called by my name' is to be intricately associated with this deity, that is, to be the people of Yahweh in covenant relationship."

edge" (Ezek 18:2)—that the present generation might still be "heir to the judgments on their predecessors."[43] It is over against such views that the Chronicler develops his well-known "theology of immediate retribution" of which "there is no better statement than God's speech to Solomon in [2 Chr] 7:13–15."[44] The story of Jabez illustrates, specifically, *this* important theme; that no-one's present and future, in this story of Israel, is determined by the past, and specifically by the circumstances in which their ancestors found themselves, and by the actions that they took back then. The future is open; no-one is fated to *continue* under God's judgement; the forgiveness of sin and the healing of the land are possible, if God's people will only pray. Jabez prays and he receives his reward, which reflects the characteristic rewards received by the faithful elsewhere in Chronicles.[45] It is not "the *first* [my italics] reference to the doctrine of retribution in the book"[46]—the first is assuredly the reference to Er in 2:3, which is closely followed by the reference to Achan/Achar in 2:7.[47] Both characters serve as negative foils for the positive character of Jabez and indeed it is arguable that other elements in 1 Chr 2:3–35 also serve such a preparatory, contrastive function,[48] while certain elements in 4:11–43 perform the same function retrospectively.[49] The Jabez pericope is not the first reference to the doctrine of retribution in the book; but it is a *significant* such reference.

It was this doctrine of divine retribution in 1–2 Chronicles that I first set out to explore as my thesis topic when I began working with Hugh in 1982. Ultimately he very tolerantly allowed me to digress into 1–2 Kings. I am delighted to have been able to return to the topic in this essay thirty years later. As he knows too well, I am quite capable of long digressions in pursuit of my goals.

---

43 Williamson, *1 and 2 Chronicles*, 33.

44 Boda, *1–2 Chronicles*, 287.

45 Klein (1 *Chronicles*, 47) lists these rewards as "rest and quiet, building projects, military victories, a large family, wealth, international reputation, and respect from citizens." Jabez explicitly receives wealth and respect.

46 Contra Klein, 1 *Chronicles*, 133.

47 Boda, *1–2 Chronicles*, 48–49.

48 Sparks, *The Chronicler's Genealogies*, 236–40.

49 So Heard ("Echoes of Genesis," 12–13) although his suggestion that it is Jabez's non-violent acquisition of land in contrast to that of Simeon, Reuben, and the Transjordanian tribes that makes him "more honoured than his brothers" has not as yet met with acceptance.

# WAS DAVID A JUDAHITE OR AN EPHRAIMITE? LIGHT FROM THE GENEALOGIES

Sara Japhet

The question presented in the title may seem no more than a provocation: is there any doubt that David *was* a Judahite? David's descent from Judah is presented in biblical sources in two forms: in a vertical genealogy that draws a direct line from Peretz, Judah's son, to David, and in an explicit declaration of David himself in one of his speeches. Thus we learn that:

> This is the line of Peretz: Peretz begot Hezron, Hezron begot Ram, Ram begot Aminadab, Aminadab begot Nahshon, Nahshon begot Salmah, Salmon begot Boaz, Boaz begot Obed, Obed begot Jesse and Jesse begot David. (Ruth 4:18–22)[1]

David presents this line of descent as a theological maxim in his farewell address to the assembly of Israel:

> The Lord God of Israel chose me of all my father's house to be king over Israel forever. For He chose Judah to be ruler, and of the family of Judah, my father's house; and of my father's sons He preferred to make me king over all Israel. (1 Chr 28:4)[2]

---

[1] A more elaborate form of this genealogy, which goes back to Judah and forward to the ramifications of Jesse's family, appears in 1 Chr 2:2–17: "The sons of Judah ... his daughter-in-law Tamar also bore him Peretz and Zerah.... The sons of Peretz: Hezron and Hamul.... The sons of Hezron: Jerahmeel, Ram and Chelubai. Ram begot Aminadab, and Aminadab begot Nahshon.... Nahshon was the father of Salma, Salma of Boaz, Boaz of Obed, Obed of Jesse. Jesse begot Eliab his firstborn ... David the seventh...." Opinions vacillate regarding the priority of these lists: Chronicles as a source for Ruth (thus Martin Noth, *Überlieferungsgeschichtliche Studien* [Tübingen: Max Niemeyer, 1943], 119–20; Wilhelm Rudolph, *Chronikbücher* [HAT 1.21; Tübingen: Mohr (Siebeck), 1955], 16; Roddy Braun, *1 Chronicles*, [WBC 14; Waco, Tex.: Word Books, 1986], 34; and more); Ruth as a source for Chronicles (Edward L. Curtis and Albert A. Madsen, *A Critical and Exegetical Commentary on the Books of Chronicles* [ICC; New York: Scribner, 1910], 87; Ralph Klein, *1 Chronicles* [Hermeneia; Minneapolis: Fortress, 2006], 94 n. 46; Thomas Willi, *Chronik 1–10* [BKAT 24; Neukirchen: Neukirchener Verlag, 2009], 88–89); or a common source to both lists (Jacob M. Myers, *1 Chronicles* [AB 14, Garden City New York, 1965], 14). See also Sara Japhet, *I and II Chronicles: A Commentary* (OTL; London: SCM; Louisville, Ky.: Westminster John Knox, 1993), 71.

[2] On the theological import of this statement and its place in the Chronicler's overall view of David's and Solomon's election see, among others: Sara Japhet, *The Ideology of the Book of Chronicles and its Place in Biblical Thought* (trans. Anna Barber; BEATAJ 9;

These explicit, straightforward statements left no room for doubt regarding David's descent; they themselves became a cornerstone for further theological elaborations.[3]

However, other biblical data do raise doubts regarding this genealogical view and put it under a question mark. Even the very insistence on David's pedigree may be seen as a kind of reassurance concerning, or, if you wish, polemic against, possible different views on the subject, and the matter deserves further investigation.

## I. Three Sources of Doubt

Doubts regarding David's descent arise from three different sources: (a) the nature of the genealogical list in 1 Chr 2:9–12; (b) the story of David in the book of Samuel; (c) various details gleaned from occasional contexts, unrelated to a particular theological framework.

(a) The genealogy of Jesse, David's father, in 1 Chr 2:9–17 is comprised of three different components, of different literary forms: a general introduction, enumerating the sons of Hezron (v. 9); a vertical genealogy of Jesse, leading from Ram to Jesse (vv. 10–12); and a segmented genealogy of the family of Jesse (vv. 13–17). While scholars generally agree that the third part of the passage, which mentions by name Jesse's seven sons, his two daughters and their sons, and the husband of one of the daughters, is an authentic record,[4] this is not the case with the other two parts of the passage. The artificial nature of the genealogy in vv. 10–12 is universally recognized, as well as the Chronicler's own formulation of the introduction in v. 9.[5] The linear genealogy of 1 Chr 2:9–12 is a literary construct, with distinct theological goals.

---

Frankfurt: Peter Lang 1989, 445–52; 3rd printing: Winona Lake: Eisenbrauns, 2009), 347–353; Braun, *1 Chronicles*, 271; Klein, *1 Chronicles*, 520–21; Gary N. Knoppers, *1 Chronicles 1–9, 10–29* (AB 12, 12a; New York: Doubleday, 2004), 2:938–39.

[3] See for example the genealogy of Jesus in Matt 1:1–17, dependent on the family tree of Chronicles, with its calculation of 14 generations from Abraham to David through Judah (for a different genealogy, see Luke 3:23–38). See, among others, Marshall D. Johnson, *The Purpose of Biblical Genealogies* (Cambridge: Cambridge University Press, 1969), 146–208.

[4] See among others H. G. M. Williamson, *1 and 2 Chronicles* (NCB; Grand Rapids: Eerdmans, 1982), 51; Rudolph, *Chronikbücher*, 16–17, Simon J. de Vries, *1 and 2 Chronicles* (FOTL 11; Grand Rapids: Eerdmans, 1989), 40; and more.

[5] See already Julius Wellhausen, *De gentibus et familiis Judaeis* (Göttingen: Dieterich, 1870), 17 (Heb. trans.: Lizah Ulman and Gershon Galil; Jerusalem: Dinur, 1985), 16; followed by Curtis and Madsen, *Critical and Exegetical Commentary*, 87; Abraham Malamat, "King Lists of the Old Babylonian Period and Biblical Genealogies," in idem, *Israel in Biblical*

(b) No genealogical information regarding David's descent is provided in the book of Samuel except for some details concerning his immediate family, that is, the names of his father and three of his brothers (1 Sam 16:1, 18; 17:12, 58). The absence of such information is all the more glaring when compared with the accounts of Samuel and Saul, the other two major protagonists of the book, for whom the book of Samuel provides detailed pedigrees going five generations back and explicitly marking their tribal affiliations (1 Sam 1:1; 9:1–2a respectively). It seems rather obvious that the author of Samuel did not possess a similar genealogy of Jesse, David's father.[6] This absence is supplemented to a certain degree by the note at the end of Ruth, which connects Jesse to Boaz through Obed (Ruth 4:17), and finally by the artificial genealogy of 1 Chr 2:10–12, featuring the full family tree from Ram to Jesse, which is repeated in Ruth 4:18–22.

(c) So far do the negative aspects of the question take us. What then is the positive evidence that may be gleaned from the biblical material regarding David's descent? Two facts are provided by the stories in Samuel: the more insistent fact that the family's residence was the town of Bethlehem, and the-once mentioned fact that Jesse was "an Ephrathite" (1 Sam 17:12). Where do these facts lead us?

## II. The Problematic 'Ephrathite'

Although there were during the biblical period at least two towns by the name of Bethlehem, one in Judah and one in Zebulun (Josh 19:15; also perhaps Judg 12:8, 10), there is no doubt that the 'Bethlehem' connected with Jesse's family is the one in Judah. Not only is it identified once as located in Judah (1 Sam 17:12), but this location makes geographical sense in the context of David's stories; Bethlehem is mentioned in these stories too often to be mistaken.

The title 'Ephrathite' (אפרתי) is a gentilic form, presented in biblical dictionaries as deriving from two different names: "of the tribe of

*Times* (Jerusalem: Mosad Bialik, 1983), 24–45, 41–42 (in Hebrew); Japhet, *I and II Chronicles*, 20–21; H. G. M. Williamson, "Sources and Redaction in the Chronicler's Genealogy of Judah," *JBL* 98 (1979): 351–59 (357–58); Willi, *Chronik 1–10*, 78; Braun, *1 Chronicles*, 34; and more.

[6] Zakovitch regards the absence of David's genealogy as an intentional literary device: "The book of Samuel refrains intentionally from presenting a broad family background for David and is content with mentioning the name of his father." Yair Zakovitch, *Inner-biblical and Extra-biblical Midrash and the Relationship between Them* (Tel-Aviv: Am Oved, 2009), 193 (in Hebrew).

Ephraim," and "of Ephrath/ah."[7] The first usage is attested in the references to Samuel and Jeroboam, as well as to any member of the tribe of Ephraim.[8] Indeed, this meaning of the title is so self-evident that some of the translations actually present the Hebrew אפרתי as 'Ephraimite'—see, for example, the NRSV and the NJPS for Judg 12:5; 1 Sam 1:1; 1 Kgs 11:26.[9]

The second usage is illustrated by two verses: in the introduction of Jesse, David's father (1 Sam 17:12), and in the description of the family of Elimelech, the protagonists of Ruth (Ruth 1:2). In these cases the translations present them as 'Ephrathites' rather than 'Ephraimites' (see NJPS and NRSV). The different derivation is not indicated by anything in the word itself or by its usage in the biblical texts, and is determined solely by exegetical considerations. Since these people come from Bethlehem—a well known Judahite town—and since Bethlehem itself is sometimes identified as 'Ephrath/ah,'[10] the appellative is seen as deriving from the name of the town rather than from the name of the tribe.

Although the distinction between these two derivations of אפרתי, and the specific origin of the gentilic form, are almost universally accepted, my contention is that this distinction should nevertheless be called into question: are these indeed two different designations? Can we say more about Ephrath than just identifying it as a different name for Bethlehem? And, what are the implications of such an investigation for the question set at the title of our article? The answer to these questions is to be found in what may seem at first an unexpected place—the genealogies of the first chapters of Chronicles—to which we now turn.

## III. How the Genealogies of 1 Chronicles Help

The name 'Ephrath,' or its more common prolonged form 'Ephrathah,' appears four times in the genealogies of the tribe of Judah (1 Chr 2:19, 24, 50; 4:4).[11] Ephrath/ah is presented there as a woman, the second wife of

---

[7] See, among others, BDB, 68; *HALOT*, 81.

[8] "There was a certain man of Ramathaim, a Zuphite from the hill country of Ephraim, whose name was Elkanah ... an Ephraimite" (אפרתי; 1 Sam 1:1); "Jeroboam son of Nebat, an Ephraimite (אפרתי) of Zeredah" (1 Kgs 11:26); "Whenever one of the fugitives of Ephraim said, 'Let me go over,' the men of Gilead would say to him, 'Are you an Ephraimite (אפרתי)?'" (Judg 12:5–6a).

[9] The AV reads "Ephraimite" only in Judg 12:5.

[10] "So Rachel died and she was buried on the way to Ephrath, that is Bethlehem" (Gen 35:19, rephrased in Gen 48:7).

[11] The two forms had originally different functions—the one being the absolute form of the name and the other, with the locative ending ה, denoting direction: 'to Ephrath' (see

Caleb (1 Chr 2:19, 24, 50; 4:4), the mother of Hur (2:19) and perhaps also of Ashhur (2:24).[12] Hur is actually called: "the first-born of Ephrathah" (2:50; 4:4). The lists of her descendents are cited in 1 Chr 2:50–53+4:2–4 and 4:5–8.[13]

According to the terminological code of the genealogical lists, individuals stand for ethnic units, be these families, clans or tribes.[14] The use of this code makes it possible for a locality to be the 'son' of a person, for a person to be a 'father' of a locality, or even to be a father of 'half a town.'[15] Within the framework of this code, 'marriage' signifies the amalgamation of two groups, of different origins, the 'wife' most often, and certainly the 'concubine,' signifying an ethnic element of a secondary, sometimes foreign, origin in respect to the major, dominant group. Thus in the genealogies of Judah we hear that his wife, "the daughter of a certain Canaanite, whose name was Shua, bore him three sons" (Gen 38:2–5; somewhat rephrased in 1 Chr 2:3). "Eiphah, Caleb's concubine," bore him several sons, as did his concubine Ma'achah (v. 49), Eiphah representing the Midianite element within the clan of Caleb (see Gen 25:4; 1 Chr 1:33; Isa 60:6), while Ma'achah represented the Aramean element (Gen 22:24; Josh 13:13, and more).

This is the context in which the identity of 'Ephrath' should be looked for: she is the 'wife' of two dominant components of the tribe of Judah,

---

Gen 35:16, 19; 48:7). As in other similar cases, the original locative ending eventually lost its accusative/locative meaning, and the two forms came to represent the absolute state of the name. The same process is apparent in other names such as Timnah/Timnathah, Hamath/Hamathah, Abel/Abelah and more (Timnah: Josh 15:10, 57; Timnathah as locative: Gen 38:12, 13, 14; Judg 14:1, 5; Timnathah as an absolute name: Josh 19:43; Judg 14:1, 2. Hamath: 2 Sam 8:9 and passim; Hamathah: 1 Chr 18:3. Abel: 1 Kgs 15:20, 22; Abelah: 2 Sam 20:15 (perhaps also 14), etc. On the weakening of the final -ה as part of a general loss of the original accusative ending, see GKC §90f–g,250–51 and n. 1 on p. 251. The different forms in Chronicles are merely equivalent alternatives, with no additional function.

[12] The text of 2:24 is certainly corrupt; according to a common restoration (suggested by Wellhausen and followed by many) it should read: "After the death of Hezron, Caleb came to Ephrath, the wife of his father Hezron." If this restoration is adopted, Ashhur would be the son of Caleb rather than of Hezron. See Wellhausen, *De gentibus*, 14 n. 1; Heb. trans. 14 n. 12; Curtis and Madsen, *Critical and Exegetical Commentary*, 92; Rudolph, *Chronikbücher*, 16; Japhet, *I and II Chronicles*, 81–82; and more.

[13] For an analysis of the literary structure of these texts, in their original form and in their secondary incorporation into Chronicles, see Japhet, *I and II Chronicles*, 69, 78–82.

[14] This code or, in Wellhausen's definition, "ethnological language," has been discussed by whoever has dealt with the genealogies, and I refer to this discussion only briefly here, as necessary. See Abraham Malamat, "The early beginnings" in *A History of the Jewish People* (ed. Haim H. Ben-Sasson; trans. George Weidenfeld and Nicolson Ltd.; Cambridge: Harvard University Press, 1976), 63–66; Robert R. Wilson, *Genealogy and History in the Biblical World* (New Haven, Yale University Press, 1977), 137–98.

[15] There are ample examples in the genealogies, especially for the tribe of Judah. See 1 Chr 2:42, 44, 45 and more. See, among others, de Vries, *1 and 2 Chronicles*, 38.

Caleb and perhaps also Hezron. This makes her an eponymic name for an ethnic group which, in the context of the tribe of Judah, is of a different, non-Judahite origin. Being a 'wife' rather than a 'concubine' confers upon her a status similar to that of her 'husbands,' the Judean clans; but she is Caleb's second, younger wife, and if also the wife of Hezron, she is but one among his other wives.

What is the origin of the name Ephrath and what does she represent? Ephrath is the constructed feminine form of the gentilic אפרתי, which means that she represents the Ephraimite families who lived within the territory of Judah.[16] These Ephraimites spread from the mountains of Ephraim southward, settled in the "hills of Judah," and eventually mixed with the Judahite population of the region. Their three major localities were Kiriath-Jearim, Bethlehem and Beth-Gader (1 Chr 2:51), and it seems that the entire area of their settlement was eventually named after their eponymic name: Ephrath/ah. Eventually the name was regarded as an appellative of Bethlehem, as illustrated by the glosses of Gen 35:19 and 48:7. It was probably also a poetic designation of the other major towns inhabited by the sons of Hur; so indicates Ps 132:6, where Ephrathah is paralleled to שדה יער, probably an allusion to Kiriath-Jearim.[17]

We have no explicit textual clue to the time of the Ephraimite settlement in the Judean hills. Na'aman suggests—taking into consideration the archeological surveys of the region—that this settlement had taken place as early as the eleventh century BCE, at the same time as the Judean expansion from the south to the southern and central parts of the Judean hills to form the kernel of what was to become "great Judah."[18] According to the

[16] As far as I know, only Na'aman saw the connection between Ephrath and Ephraim, and used this insight as a basis for reconstructing the process of settlement in the northern part of the Judean hills. See Nadav Na'aman, "Ephraim, Ephrath and the Settlement in the Judean Hill Country," *Zion* 49 (1984): 325–31 (in Hebrew). Haran pointed to the contacts between the people settled in the hills of Ephraim and the town of Bethlehem, and saw in the title 'Ephrathite' a possible expression of this affinity, but did not clarify what this affinity was. Regarding the origin of Elkanah, Samuel's father, Haran suggested that he was a Bethlehemite, rather than an Ephraimite (Menahem Haran, *Ages and Institutions in the Bible* (Tel Aviv: Am Oved, 1972), 95–96 (in Hebrew).

[17] This connection was suggested by Franz Delitzsch, *Biblical Commentary on the Psalms* (trans. Francis Bolton, from the second German ed.; 3 vols.; Edinburgh: T&T Clark, 1892–1894), 3:*ad loc*; quoted by Na'aman, "Ephraim, Ephrath," 329 and n. 14.

[18] Na'aman, "Ephraim, Ephrath," 329. For the development of the tribe of Judah, see Roland de Vaux, "The Settlement of the Israelites in Southern Palestine and the Origins of the Tribe of Judah," in Harry T. Frank, ed., *Translating and Understanding the Old Testament, Essays in Honor of Herbert Gordon May* (Nashville: Abingdon, 1970), 108–34.

textual evidence of Chronicles, however, and seen from the perspectives of the tribe of Judah, of the geographical region called Judah, and of the political entity of the kingdom of Judah, the Ephraimites are regarded as a 'wife,' a secondary, foreign element in respect to the dominant component of the region.

## IV. 'Ephrathite' as Ethnic Label

Taking this meaning of Ephrath as our starting point, how should we interpret or translate the two occurrences of the gentilic form אפרתי when the reading "Ephraimite" is not self-evident from the context? The question applies to the use of this appellative in the references to Jesse (1 Sam 17:12) and the family of Elimelech (Ruth 1:2). As I have shown above, scholarly literature, including dictionaries, handbooks, commentaries and translations, renders the term 'Ephrathite' and derives it from the name Ephrathah, as referring to the town of Bethlehem. However, although such a derivation is linguistically possible, it is not supported by the texts themselves.

First Samuel 17:12 reads: "Now David was the son of an Ephrathite of Bethlehem of Judah, named Jesse." Since Bethlehem and its location in Judah are explicitly mentioned, the title 'Ephrathite' could hardly be a second reference to Jesse's place of residence, namely "of Bethlehem," as suggested by the dictionaries; it surely points to an additional element in Jesse's identity. The same is true of Ruth 1:1–2: "a certain man of Bethlehem of Judah went to . . . Moab, he and his wife and his two sons . . . Ephrathites from Bethlehem in Judah." The definition 'Ephrathites' is not a third reference to Bethlehem, but an additional element of the family's identity. In both cases 'Ephrathite/s' refers to these people's tribal or familial affiliation, which could be explained in two different—though connected—ways. The one is to regard the gentilic form אפרתי as having throughout one meaning, that is, 'Ephraimite.' According to this view, both Jesse (and of course his whole household), and the family of Elimelech were identified as Ephraimites, living in the town of Bethlehem in Judah.[19]

The other option is to regard the gentilic form as deriving from the name 'Ephrath,' and see it as a name of a clan, the families of which lived

[19] This is the view of Na'aman, who says in a cursory fashion, that the origin of David was from Ephraim ("Ephraim, Ephrath," 331).

in the northern region of Judah.[20] If we adopt this possibility we would have to suppose that the name 'Ephrath'—originally an artificial term, the purpose of which was to illustrate in genealogical terms the ethnic developments within the tribe of Judah—was also used as a definition of an actual ethnic reality. This view would mean that there existed in Israel at some point an ethnic entity called 'Ephrath,' which comprised families of Bethlehem and their relatives, the descendents of the "woman" Ephrath. Since in any case the name Ephrath is a derivative of Ephraim, we would have to assume that these people—Ephraimites who settled in Judah and eventually mixed with the local Judahite population—defined themselves as one component of the tribe of Judah, and connected themselves to the Calebites; they nevertheless preserved their unique origins by affiliating themselves with their "mother."

The advantage of the first interpretation is the fact that it is based on a strong linguistic foundation, illustrated in the biblical usage. By contrast, the second interpretation has no apparent support from the biblical sources; there is apparently no explicit allusion to a clan called 'Ephrath' and to its whereabouts. However, there is in fact one verse, found in an unexpected text, which does confirm this view of the appellative Ephrath. I refer to Micah 5:1: "But you, O Bethlehem of Ephrathah, who are one of the little clans of Judah" (ואתה בית לחם אפרתה צעיר להיות באלפי יהודה). The common renderings of צעיר in this verse are "little," "small," "least," and the like—as illustrated by the quotation above.[21] While these meanings are possible, no explanation is provided for the fact that such an important town in Judah as Bethlehem would be described as "little,"

20 This is the view of Aaron Demsky, expressed already in the title of his article: "The Clans of Ephrath: Their Territory and History," *TA* 13–14 (1986–1987): 46–59. Demsky regards Ephrath as a name of a "family league" but does not discuss the origin of the name or its connection to the other occurences of the gentilic form. According to him "The Ephrathites stemmed from Hezron... through the former's son Ram.... The Ephrathites.... maintained their independent origin through the matronymic Ephrath" (57). De Vaux too regards Ephrathah as a name of clan, but according to him it was the most authentic Judahite clan: "The only pure clan is that of Ephrathah settled in Bethlehem" ("The Settlement of the Israelites in Southern Palestine," 134). An inconclusive view is presented by Gershon Galil, "The Genealogies of the Tribe of Judah" (Ph.D.diss., The Hebrew University of Jerusalem, 1983), 82 (in Hebrew).

21 BDB: "little with the idea of insignificant," (859; thus NRSV); *HALOT*: "the smaller one, the smallest" (1041, thus NEB); NJPS: "least." See also the commentaries; e.g., "The least among the thousands of Judah" (John M. Powis Smith, *A Critical and Exegetical Commentary on Micah, Zephaniah, Nahum, Habakkuk, Obadiah and Joel* [ICC; Edinburgh: T&T Clark, 1911], 103).

"small," "insignificant," or "least."[22] It is my contention that the meaning of צעיר in this verse is no different than its more common meaning, that is, 'young,' and that the verse should read: "you are the young one among the clans/families of Judah." This description of Bethlehem/Ephrathah preserves the memory that 'the Ephraimites of Bethlehem' do not belong to the old, original, families of Judah but are a new, young, component of the tribe. The message of this passsage, like that of many other similar instances in the Bible, would be that the future savior will come not from the old, established families of the tribe, but from the youngest one.

## V. David as Judahite and Ephraimite

Whether we interpret the title אפרתי as simply 'Ephraimite,' or whether we preserve the use of 'Ephrathite' and derive the title from an ethnic group by that name, the conclusion regarding David's origin is similar: David belonged to one of the Ephraimite families who settled in the northern part of the Judean hills, which eventually amalgamated with the Judean population and affiliated themselves with the tribe of Judah. From a distant vantage point David could be identified as either or both, Judahite and Ephraimite. This understanding of David's origin may illuminate some aspects of his history and reign. It may explain the antagonistic attitude of some of the older and more established elements of the tribe of Judah such as Nabal the Calebite (1 Sam 25:19) or the inhabitants of Ziph (1 Sam 26:1), and it provides another context for his anointing by Samuel, the Ephraimite prophet. It may also explain David's appeal to the northern tribes, the relatively smooth transfer of loyalty from Saul's house to him (2 Sam 5:1–4), and his success in establishing the united kingdom.

After the defection of the northern tribes and the establishment of northern Israel as a kingdom of its own, and after the anointing of the Ephraimite Jeroboam as king over northern Israel, the separation of Judah from the other tribes of Israel was emphasized and idealized. Within the kingdom of Judah the theological concept gradually developed that it was Judah who was chosen from among the tribes of Israel and destined to rule. This idea is implied in Gen 49:8–10 and explicitly stated in Ps 78:67–68 and 1 Chr 5:2: "Judah became more powerful and . . . a leader came from him." The absolute legitimacy of the Davidic dynasty now demanded that

[22] See Zekharyah Kallai, "Bethlehem," *Encyclopedia Biblica* (Jerusalem: Mosad Bialik, 1954), 2:86–88 (in Hebrew).

the election of David was not merely a choice of the person David himself to be king of Israel "for ever," as established by Nathan's prophecy (2 Sam 7:5–16), but that his Judahite origin be made absolutely clear. This mission was willingly undertaken by the biblical genealogists, and found its eloquent expression in the Chronicler's history.

# THE TWO AHABS OF THE SOUTH: JOASH AND JOSIAH

John Jarick

Within the book of Chronicles there are often to be found plays-on-words or ironic twists to the names of the kings of Judah, such that the designation of a monarch turns out to be related to a specific aspect of his reign. This literary device is considerably more prominent in Chronicles than it is in the parallel stories to be found in the book of Kings, to the extent that it appears to have been a deliberate feature of the telling of the tales in Chronicles, an indication of the systematization of accounts and the tying up of loose ends that characterizes the work of the editors of the book.[1]

In order to see something of this feature, the present study scrutinizes the intriguing cases of two specific monarchs who share a crucial element in their regal names and who also share a crucial element in their fates within the story-world of Chronicles. The kings to be investigated here are Joash and Josiah, whose stories are told in 2 Chr 22–24 and 34–35 respectively (with parallel accounts in 2 Kgs 11–12 and 22–23).[2]

## I. The Regal Names

The English forms of the names of these two kings, 'Joash' and 'Josiah,' might lead a casual reader to think that the common element is the initial syllable 'Jo,' but that is somewhat coincidental. In Hebrew they are יואש (normally so spelt in Chronicles, though on one occasion as יאש)[3]

---

[1] I have attempted to trace aspects of this feature in my commentaries on *1 Chronicles* (Sheffield: Sheffield Academic Press, 2002) and *2 Chronicles* (Sheffield: Sheffield Phoenix Press, 2007), particularly in the latter volume in the "Survey of Judah's Kings," 63–87, but the present study seeks to develop the notion more thoroughly in the cases of the two kings Joash and Josiah.

[2] This essay is a modified version of a paper delivered to the 19th Congress of the International Organization for the Study of the Old Testament at the University of Ljubljana in July 2007, in the Chronicles session chaired by Hugh Williamson. It is a pleasure to present it in this volume as a tribute to Hugh, whose scholarship I have much admired and whose collegiality I have much appreciated over the years.

[3] Of the eight occurrences of the name of this Judahite king in Chronicles, the spelling יואש appears seven times (1 Chr 3:11; 2 Chr 22:11; 24:2, 4, 22, 24; 25:25) and the spelling יאש appears once (2 Chr 24:1). There are also six occurrences of יואש as the name of a

and יאשיהו,[4] with the common denominator being the verbal element of אש. The English versions of the names mask this common element by having no equivalent to the Hebrew letter א and by transliterating the Hebrew letter ש as 'sh' in the case of Joash but as 's' in the case of Josiah. But matters are already difficult enough in Hebrew, since one of the three root-letters of the verb is not evident in the form utilized for the names, and also because the name יואש is often spelt with a ו following the initial י, which makes it look like the divine element 'Yo,' an abbreviation of 'YAHWEH.' Indeed on several occasions in the book of Kings (though never in the book of Chronicles) the name is given in the form יהואש,[5] which indisputably opens with the divine designation 'Yeho.' If the fullest spelling is accepted as the proper form of the name of Joash or Jehoash, that is יהואש, then the name would appear to be making the proclamation or expressing the hope that 'Yeho' does whatever action is denoted by the verb אש. This would be the same expression, in reverse order, as that set forth in the name of יאשיהו, which similarly is saying that 'Yahu' does whatever action is denoted by the verb אש, there in the imperfect or forward-looking formation. The other possibility for יואש is that it too is the imperfect formation of אש rather than being the divine element plus אש, and that the shorter spelling of י (for the imperfect) and then א and ש is to be accepted. In this case, the name Joash is simply stating that 'he אש-es' or 'may he אש' without specifying whether it is the deity or the monarch who does the activity designated by אש.

Well, then, what does it mean to speak of someone being called upon to אש or being known for such an activity? The form אש could derive from a hollow verbal root אוש (or איש) or from an initial-ו root ואש (or such a root transmogrified into an initial-י stem יאש) or from a final-ה root אשה). Unfortunately none of these possible roots is commonly used in Biblical Hebrew, and so we moderns cannot say for certain what

northern Israelite monarch (2 Chr 25:17, 18, 21, 23 [2x], 25) and three further occurrences of the same form for the name of other individuals (1 Chr 4:22; 12:3; 2 Chr 18:25). For the spellings in Kings, see below (n. 5).

[4] The name יאשיהו appears nineteen times in Chronicles (1 Chr 3:14, 15; 2 Chr 33:25; 34:1, 33; 35:1, 7, 16, 18, 19, 20 [2x], 22, 23, 24, 25 [2x], 26; 36:1) and fourteen times in Kings (1 Kgs 13:2; 2 Kgs 21:24, 26; 22:1, 3; 23:16, 19, 23, 24, 28, 29, 30, 34 [2x]).

[5] Of the seventeen occurrences of the name of Joash king of Judah in the book of Kings, the spelling יואש appears nine times (2 Kgs 11:2; 12:20, 21; 13:1, 10; 14:1, 3, 17, 23) and the spelling יהואש eight times (2 Kgs 12:1, 2, 3, 5, 7, 8, 19; 14:13). Of the eighteen occurrences of the name of Joash king of Israel, nine are in the form יואש (2 Kgs 13:9, 12, 13 [2x], 14, 25; 14:1, 23, 27) and nine in the form יהואש (2 Kgs 13:10, 25; 14:8, 9, 11, 13, 15, 16, 17). The form יואש also occurs in 1 Kgs 22:26 as a son of King Ahab.

resonance there may have been in ancient Hebrew ears when they heard the names יואש and יאשיהו. Of the possibilities just listed, only the verb יאש is to be found explicitly in the biblical literature, five times in a *niphal* or reflexive form and once in a *piel* or intensive form,[6] neither of which gives us the *qal* or simple active meaning that we might seek for the usage in these royal names; if nonetheless we were to accept as relevant here the presumed basic meaning of that particular root and apply it to the designations of the monarchs in question, we would have something like 'YAHWEH despairs,'[7] a most unlikely name for royal parents to have bestowed upon the heir to the throne. More plausible as a royal name would be the lexicographical postulations of a hollow root אוש (or איש), which is said to mean either 'to be strong' or 'to give.'[8] If indeed a name like Josiah means 'YAHWEH is strong' or 'YAHWEH strengthens,' then it would be analogous to the royal names Amaziah and Hezekiah, which yield such meanings through their verbal elements of אמץ and חזק respectively. Or if indeed Josiah is a proclamation that 'YAHWEH gives,' then it is a similar kind of name to that of his son Johanan, whose name proclaims that 'YAHWEH is gracious' through its verbal element of חנן.

But I am attracted to the suggestion of Wilhelm Gesenius and Martin Noth that we are to reckon with a verbal root אשה, which has not come down to us in Biblical Hebrew but which the lexicographers relate to a

---

[6] The *niphal* occurrences are 1 Sam 27:1; Isa 57:10; Jer 2:25; 18:12; Job 6:26; and the *piel* occurrence is Eccl 2:20.

[7] The lexica give the basic meaning of the root as 'to despair' or 'to be cast down in spirit' (BDB, 384; *DCH*, 72; Samuel P. Tregelles, *Gesenius' Hebrew and Chaldee Lexicon to the Old Testament Scriptures* [London: Samuel Bagster and Sons, 1846], cccxxvi).

[8] BDB postulate such an unattested verb, איש or אוש, supposedly meaning 'to be strong,' and accordingly they present the name יואש as meaning 'YAHWEH is strong' (BDB, 35, 219), while Gesenius similarly postulates a root אוש, but with the meaning 'to give,' and accordingly he presents the name יואש as meaning 'YAHWEH gives' (Tregelles, *Gesenius' Hebrew and Chaldee Lexicon*, lxxxiii, cccxxxvi, cccxxxix); both lexicons postulate a different underlying root for 'Josiah' (see n. 9 below). KBL[3] also see אוש, 'to give' (*schenken*), as underlying יואש (KBL[3], 376, 380), and possibly also as underlying יאשיהו (365), though for the latter name they present other possibilities as well (also see n. 9 below). The meaning of 'YAHWEH gives' is accepted for both of these regal names by H. B. MacLean ("Joash," *IDB* 2:909; and "Josiah," *IDB* 2:996), citing the Arabic *ʾwš*, 'to give,' though in the latter case ("Josiah," 996) he notes that an alternative possibility is that the root is the Arabic *ʾasā*, 'to nurse, cure.' 'YAHWEH gives' is accepted as the meaning of Joash's name by D. Matthew Stith ("Joash," *NIDB* 3:317) and by William S. Caldecott and David F. Payne ("Joash"; *ISBE* 2:1062 ['YAHWEH has bestowed']), as well as by Hayim Tadmor ("Joash," *EncJud* 10:110; so also 2nd ed. 11:341). William Johnstone (*1 and 2 Chronicles, Volume 2: 2 Chronicles 10–36: Guilt and Atonement* [JSOTSup 254; Sheffield: Sheffield Academic Press, 1997], 121, 233) presents 'the LORD has provided' as the certain meaning of 'Joash' and 'may the LORD provide' as the most likely meaning of 'Josiah.'

cognate Arabic root meaning 'to heal.'[9] In fact another form of this root is clearly at work in the telling of the tale of another king of Judah in the book of Chronicles, for we read that "in the thirty-ninth year of his reign Asa was diseased in his feet, and his disease became severe; yet even in his disease he did not seek YAHWEH, but sought help from physicians" (2 Chr 16:12). The storyteller does not spell out that the name 'Asa' (אסא) is a term for 'healer' or 'physician' in the Aramaic language,[10] though the story does bring this disease upon the king as a consequence of his having made an alliance with the king of Aram. One imagines that the early readers of the tale, presumably knowing the Aramaic language reasonably well and perhaps having consulted an אסא from time to time themselves, would have chuckled at this pun that juxtaposes the Aramaic word for 'physician' (the king's name אסא) with the Hebrew word for 'physicians' (רפאים), and they would hardly have missed the irony of a so-called physician who cannot heal himself and cannot even find healing from others who are termed physicians, but instead sinks to an ignominious death.

## II. A Shared Fate

That an ironic resonance of 'YAHWEH heals' is at work in Chronicles' telling of the tales of the two kings Joash and Josiah does seem to be borne

---

[9] Gesenius postulates a root אשה with the meaning 'to sustain' or 'to heal,' and accordingly presents the name יאשיהו as meaning 'YAHWEH heals' (Tregelles, *Gesenius' Hebrew and Chaldee Lexicon*, lxxxiii, cccxxvi). As mentioned in n. 8 above, H. B. MacLean notes the possibility of the Arabic *'asā*, 'to nurse, cure,' lying behind at least one of the two names (*IDB* 2:996). Robert Althann similarly notes regarding 'Josiah' (*ABD* 3:1015) that the root might be Arabic *'asā*, 'to heal,' citing Martin Noth, *Die israelitischen Personennamen in Rahmen der gemeinsemitischen Namengebung* (BWANT, 3:10; Stuttgart: W. Kohlhammer, 1928), 212. KBL[3] offer אשה, 'to heal' (*heilen*), as one of three possible etymologies for יאשיהו, the other two being ישה, 'to bring forth' (*hervorbringen*), and אוש, 'to give' (*geben*) (KBL[3], 365). Meanwhile BDB also postulates אשה, but supposedly meaning 'to support,' and accordingly presents the name יאשיהו as meaning 'YAHWEH supports' (BDB, 78); this meaning is accepted for Josiah's name by Samuel J. Schultz ("Josiah," *ISBE* 2:1138) and by Uriah Y. Kim ("Josiah," *NIDB* 3:413 ['may YAHWEH support']), but no proposal is accepted by Moshe Weinfeld ("Josiah," *EncJud* 10:288; so also 2nd ed. 11:457).

[10] See Marcus Jastrow, *A Dictionary of the Targumim, the Talmud Babli and Yerushalmi, and the Midrashic Literature* (New York: G. P. Putnam's Sons, 1903), 88. This case, and the case of Jehoshaphat appointing judges in 2 Chr 19, are dealt with by Moshe Garsiel (*Biblical Names: A Literary Study of Midrashic Derivations and Puns* [trans. Phyllis Hackett; Ramat Gan: Bar-Ilan University Press, 1987], 264–265) as prime examples of a midrashic name derivation being a factor in story creation. Raymond B. Dillard (*2 Chronicles* [WBC 15; Waco: Word Books, 1987], 129–130) notes that "the Chronicler may be using a paronomasia on the name of both kings," and cites Avigdor Shinan and Yair Zakowitch, "Midrash on Scripture and Midrash within Scripture," *ScrHier* 31 (1986): 255–77 (272).

out in the shared fate that is created for them in that telling, for there is a striking parallel in the way in which Chronicles brings the reigns of both of those monarchs to an end.

Concerning Joash, readers are told of him abandoning Yahwistic religion, whereupon:

> The spirit of God took possession of Zechariah the son of the priest Jehoiada, and he stood above the people and said to them, "Thus says God: 'Why do you transgress YAHWEH's commandments, so that you cannot prosper? Because you have forsaken YAHWEH, he has also forsaken you.'" But they conspired against him, and by command of the king they stoned him to death in the court of YAHWEH's house. (2 Chr 24:20–21)

YAHWEH's vengeance is swift, with Joash suffering a catastrophic defeat at the hands of "the army of Aram," all because the people of Judah

> had abandoned YAHWEH, the God of their ancestors; thus [the army of Aram] executed judgment on Joash. When they had withdrawn, leaving him severely wounded, his servants conspired against him because of the blood of the son of the priest Jehoiada, and they killed him on his bed. (2 Chr 24:24–25)

This version of events can certainly be interpreted as developing an ironic spin on the king's name, if indeed the name 'Joash' were understood by ancient Hebrew listeners as carrying the meaning 'he heals' (that is, 'the deity heals,' or in its longer form 'Jehoash' as 'YAHWEH heals'), for evidently the deity does not heal the king after he is left severely wounded by the foreign forces, on account of his not having listened to the divine word that had been preached to him by the son of his former mentor.

Concerning Josiah, eight generations later, readers are told of him embarking on the disastrous policy of confronting Pharaoh Neco of Egypt, whereupon the pharaoh

> sent envoys to him, saying, "What have I to do with you, king of Judah? I am not coming against you today, but against the house with which I am at war; and God has commanded me to hurry. Cease opposing God, who is with me, so that he will not destroy you." But Josiah would not turn away from him, but disguised himself in order to fight with him. He did not listen to the words of Neco from the mouth of God, but joined battle in the plain of Megiddo. The archers shot King Josiah; and the king said to his servants, "Take me away, for I am badly wounded." So his servants... brought him to Jerusalem, and there he died. (2 Chr 35:21–24)

Once again the story appears to contain an ironic spin on the king's name, if indeed 'Josiah' means 'YAHWEH heals,' for the deity does not heal the king after he is left severely wounded by the archers, on account of his not having listened to the divine word that had been proclaimed to him by the pharaoh.

The parallels between the fates of the ancestor Joash and the descendant Josiah are too marked to be entirely coincidental in this story-world. In Chronicles' telling, both Joash and Josiah ignore a clear word from YAHWEH and are thereupon wounded in battle and are manifestly not healed of those wounds by YAHWEH. The book of Kings makes no such connections between these two monarchs: neither of them receives and ignores any word from YAHWEH that would make their respective fates deserved under a scheme of divine retribution, and the details of their deaths are dissimilar to the Chronicles accounts.

In the case of Joash, the Kings account reads as follows:

> At that time King Hazael of Aram went up, fought against Gath, and took it. But when Hazael set his face to go up against Jerusalem, King Jehoash [*sic*] of Judah took all the votive gifts that Jehoshaphat, Jehoram, and Ahaziah, his ancestors, the kings of Judah, had dedicated, as well as his own votive gifts, all the gold that was found in the treasuries of YAHWEH's house and of the king's house, and sent these to King Hazael of Aram. Then Hazael withdrew from Jerusalem. Now the rest of the acts of Joash, and all that he did, are they not written in the Book of the Annals of the Kings of Judah? His servants arose, devised a conspiracy, and killed Joash in the house of Millo, on the way that goes down to Silla. It was Jozacar son of Shimeath and Jehozabad son of Shomer, his servants, who struck him down, so that he died. (2 Kgs 12:18–22)

It is clear that in the telling of the tale in the book of Kings, Joash is not wounded in battle at all, but is the victim of a nefarious conspiracy within the royal household, taking place considerably later than the threat from the army of Aram and presumably unconnected to those earlier events. This makes for a much different scenario than Chronicles' depiction of certain opportunists with foreign connections merely finishing off the king after the army of Aram has left him lying severely wounded.

In the case of Josiah, the Kings account tells us:

> In his days Pharaoh Neco king of Egypt went up to the king of Assyria to the River Euphrates. King Josiah went to meet him; but when Pharaoh Neco met him at Megiddo, he killed him. His servants carried him dead in a chariot from Megiddo, brought him to Jerusalem, and buried him in his own tomb. (2 Kgs 23:29–30)

Thus in the book of Kings there is no battle scene for Josiah either. That Josiah 'went to meet' Neco, and that Neco 'met' him at Megiddo might be construed as a meeting in battle, but it is not necessarily so; it can be interpreted as an encounter of the two monarchs and their representatives without any battle taking place between their troops. In any case there is no explicit battle scene in the Kings account, and certainly no carrying of a wounded Josiah back to Jerusalem; rather the picture is of the king of Judah being put to sudden death by the Egyptian pharaoh when the two rulers meet at Megiddo.

It seems that Chronicles has conformed the dénouements of Joash and Josiah to parallel each other on the basis of their names having the same essential meaning. Indeed it is interesting to note that an incidental similarity that the book of Kings has between the deaths of King Josiah and King Ahaziah, namely that both those monarchs received a fatal blow at Megiddo and were then carried back to Jerusalem in their chariot, is not to be found in Chronicles.[11] Ahaziah's name is quite distinct from Josiah's name, and so Ahaziah is not in Megiddo and he does not have a chariot-journey back to Jerusalem, as far as the book of Chronicles is concerned. Ahaziah shares the key element of his name—אחז, 'he grasps' or 'he seizes'—with two other kings of Judah, namely Ahaz and Jehoahaz, and so it is with those two that he is to be compared in Chronicles. Accordingly, we find that a crucial expression in the Chronicles version of the tale of Ahaziah, making it clear that the capture and execution of the king bearing the name 'YAHWEH Seizes' was from the hand of God himself rather than simply by the hand of the multiple-king-slayer Jehu, is unique to Chronicles.[12] So too a crucial expression in the Chronicles version of the tale of Ahaz, making it clear that the devastating defeat of the king bearing the name 'He Seizes' (that is, 'The Deity Seizes') was the work of God himself in giving Judah over into the hand of the king of Aram and the hand of the king of Israel, is only to be seen in Chronicles.[13] And in the case of Jehoahaz, only in Chronicles had that king's father (none other than Josiah) been told by Pharaoh Neco that the pharaoh was under

---

[11] Compare 2 Chr 22:8–9 with 2 Kgs 9:27–28.

[12] "But it was ordained by God that the downfall of Ahaziah should come about through his going to visit Joram, for when he came there he went out with Jehoram [*sic*] to meet Jehu son of Nimshi, whom YAHWEH had anointed to destroy the house of Ahab" (2 Chr 22:7).

[13] "Therefore YAHWEH his God gave him into the hand of the king of Aram, who defeated him and took captive a great number of his people and brought them to Damascus; and he was also given into the hand of the king of Israel, who defeated him with great slaughter: Pekah son of Remaliah killed one hundred and twenty thousand in Judah in one day, all of them valiant warriors, because they had abandoned YAHWEH, the God of their ancestors" (2 Chr 28:5–6).

the command of God, and so the Jehoahaz story's context in that telling provides an indication that Neco's removal of the king bearing the name 'YAHWEH Seizes' is also to be seen as the workings of God.[14]

Accordingly, in the Chronicles scheme of fashioning the stories of Judah's kings around the meanings of their names, Joash and Josiah are made to replicate each other's destiny. Each of these monarchs is severely wounded in battle but takes some time to die of his wounds; their names appear to proclaim that their God is a God of healing, and yet in both cases that God refrains from performing such an act, since both men are being justly recompensed for their rejection of a clear word from God prior to the commencement of battle. Meanwhile it is noticeable that no other king of Judah is depicted in Chronicles as being fatally wounded in battle. Yet one notorious king of Israel is so depicted, namely the arch-villain King Ahab.

## III. Echoes of Ahab

The story of Ahab's end in Chronicles, paralleled in Kings, runs as follows:

> The king of Israel said to Jehoshaphat [king of Judah], "I will disguise myself and go into battle, but you wear your robes." So the king of Israel disguised himself, and they went into battle... And a certain man drew his bow and unknowingly struck the king of Israel between the scale-armour and the breastplate; so he said to the driver of his chariot, "Turn around, and carry me out of the battle, for I am wounded." The battle grew hot that day, and the king of Israel propped himself up in his chariot facing the Arameans until evening; then at sunset he died. (2 Chr 18:29, 33–34; cf. 1 Kgs 22:30, 34–35)

The connections between that depiction and the end of Josiah later in Chronicles are striking, for in the scene there that is not paralleled in the book of Kings we read that Josiah

> disguised himself in order to fight with him [i.e. Neco]... And the archers shot King Josiah; so the king said to his servants, "Take me away, for I am badly wounded." So his servants took him out of the chariot and carried

[14] Just nine verses after Neco's message to Josiah that "God has commanded me to hurry; cease opposing God, who is with me" (2 Chr 35:21), we read that "the king of Egypt deposed him [i.e. Jehoahaz] in Jerusalem... The king of Egypt made his brother Eliakim king over Judah and Jerusalem and changed his name to Jehoiakim; but Neco took his brother Jehoahaz and carried him to Egypt" (36:3–4).

him in his second chariot and brought him to Jerusalem; there he died. (2 Chr 35:22–24)

Note the evident key features with which Josiah's battle strategy and outcome replicate Ahab's battle strategy and outcome: entering the battle in disguise but being struck nonetheless, instructing the charioteer to take him out of the battle on account of his wounded state but eventually dying nonetheless. There are of course some incidental differences of detail, but the basic similarities are clear, all the more so because of the stark differences over against the account of Josiah's end in the book of Kings, where we read simply that "when Pharaoh Neco met him at Megiddo, he killed him; and his servants carried him dead in a chariot from Megiddo" (2 Kgs 23:29–30). The book of Kings sees no analogies whatsoever between good King Josiah of Judah and wicked King Ahab of Israel, but the book of Chronicles has clear echoes of Ahab's fate in the fate of Josiah.[15] The echoes in the fate of Joash are somewhat fainter, in that there is no depiction of a disguise-on-the-battlefield strategy nor is the king quoted as giving instructions to his charioteers to carry him from the heat of the battle after he has been wounded, but the same essential outcome of being left severely wounded by the battle yet only dying some time later is brought out by the Chronicles account in contradistinction to the version of events in the book of Kings.

But why is it that Chronicles presents the fates of Joash and Josiah in terms so clearly reminiscent of the fate of Ahab? At first sight this seems a bizarre choice on the part of the storytellers, since these two southern rulers were both renowned for being repairers of the Jerusalem Temple,[16] while the northern monarch was equally renowned in the received traditions for the depths of his wickedness.[17]

---

[15] That there are similarities between the death of Ahab and the death of Josiah in Chronicles' presentation has been noted by a number of commentators, not least our honorand: H. G. M. Williamson, *1 and 2 Chronicles* (NCB; London: Marshall, Morgan & Scott, 1982), 409, 411. See also Edward Curtis and Albert Madsen, *A Critical and Exegetical Commentary on the Books of Chronicles* (ICC; Edinburgh: T&T Clark, 1910), 517; Raymond B. Dillard, *2 Chronicles* (WBC 15; Waco: Word Books, 1987), 292; Steven S. Tuell, *First and Second Chronicles* (IBC; Louisville: John Knox, 2001), 241; and Isaac Kalimi, *The Reshaping of Ancient Israelite History in Chronicles* (Winona Lake: Eisenbrauns, 2005), 23.

[16] The story of Joash restoring the house of YAHWEH is told in 2 Chr 24:4–14 (cf. 2 Kgs 11:4–16), while the story of Josiah's restoration programme is told in 2 Chr 34:8–13 (cf. 2 Kgs 22:3–7).

[17] The book of Kings tells many stories concerning Ahab's wickedness in 1 Kgs 16–22. Chronicles has much less to say about northern kings, but nonetheless does tell the story of YAHWEH seeking to "entice King Ahab of Israel, so that he may go up and fall

The compilers of Chronicles evidently feel that they must provide a theological explanation for the ignominious deaths of the temple restorers. Accordingly, they create parallel scenarios in which their heroes possess a fatal flaw: the two kings apparently grow so confident about their own blessedness that they ignore the divine counsel given to them, thus riding foolishly into an identical fate that is inevitable within the strict story-telling conventions of Chronicles. Their horrid end is their own doing in this story-world, and they have no-one to blame but themselves.

The black-and-white ideology of Chronicles is clear: you might have cleansed and repaired the temple, you might even have renewed the covenant and celebrated the greatest Passover of any of the kings of Judah,[18] but if after all that you feel so headstrong as to ignore a word from the LORD, then you have sunk to the depths of notorious King Ahab of Israel, and you deserve to die his death. Your names may proclaim 'YAHWEH heals,' but your stories will be made to proclaim that YAHWEH ruthlessly destroys those who disobey him. Such is the systematic scheme set out in the book of Chronicles, at work here in the tales of Joash and Josiah, the two Ahabs of the south.

at Ramoth-gilead" (2 Chr 18:19) and also in later stories deploys such expressions as "the house of Ahab led Israel into unfaithfulness" (21:13) and "he did what was evil in YAHWEH's sight, as the house of Ahab had done" (22:4).

[18] The tradition said of Josiah's Passover celebration that "no Passover like it had been kept in Israel since the days of the prophet Samuel; none of the kings of Israel had kept such a Passover as was kept by Josiah" (2 Chr 35:18; cf. 2 Kgs 23:22).

# THE CITATION AND INTERPRETATION OF THE LAW IN CHRONICLES: THE CHRONICLER'S DISTRIBUTION OF EXEGETICAL DEVICES IN THE NARRATIVES OF SOLOMON AND HEZEKIAH

Kevin L. Spawn

In the last ca. 25 years, the Chr's handling of the Law has received renewed scholarly attention.[1] One aspect of his use of the pentateuchal traditions is the introduction of exegetical tools to cite the Law (e.g., "as it is written in the Law of the LORD" ככתוב בתורת יהוה, 2 Chr 31:3). These citation formulae are distributed in three discrete parts of Chronicles widely recognized for their importance to the Chr's message of restoration for his community. The greatest concentrations of these exegetical devices[2] occur in the narratives of Solomon (2 Chr 4:7, 20; 8:13), Hezekiah (30:5, 16, 18; 31:3) and Josiah (34:21, 24; 35:12, 13, 26).[3] In Chronicles, the distribution of these hermeneutical tools was not only part of the Chr's answer to the division of "all Israel," but it also promoted the interpretation and observance of the Law in his community. After examining the use of citation formulae in the narratives of the first two of these monarchs, the aforementioned literary effects of the Chr's distribution of exegetical devices will be summarized. Accordingly, this essay also serves as a basis for the future examination of the hermeneutical tools employed in the Josianic account.

## I. The Law in Recent Research in Chronicles

In his essay "History," H. G. M. Williamson responded to selected examinations of the interpretation of the Law in the postexilic historiography in

[1] In the 1980s, a debate about the reading of selected postexilic citation formulae surfaced in biblical studies between Michael Fishbane, *Biblical Interpretation in Ancient Israel* (Oxford: Clarendon Press, 1985), and H. G. M. Williamson, "History," in *It Is Written: Scripture Citing Scripture: Essays in Honour of Barnabas Lindars, SSF* (ed. Don A. Carson and H. G. M. Williamson; Cambridge: Cambridge University Press, 1988), 25–38.

[2] The citation formulae addressed in this study as exegetical devices will be defined immediately below.

[3] For Hezekiah as a Second Solomon, see H. G. M. Williamson, *Israel in the Book of Chronicles* (Cambridge: Cambridge University Press, 1977), 119–25. For the view that Hezekiah and Josiah parallel features of both David and Solomon in Chronicles (e.g., "Hezekiah: New David and New Solomon"), see Mark A. Throntveit, *When Kings Speak: Royal Speech and Royal Prayer in Chronicles* (SBLDS 93; Atlanta, Ga.: Scholars Press, 1987), 121–25.

contemporary scholarship.[4] Based on his extensive research of the books of Chronicles and Ezra-Nehemiah, Williamson suggested that selected exegetical devices in this literature (e.g., כמשפט 35:13; ככתוב v. 26) should be read more narrowly than Michael Fishbane proposed in his *Biblical Interpretation in Ancient Israel.* Since these hermeneutical tools had been read in a number of conflicting ways for more than a century,[5] this persistent lack of a scholarly consensus was an impetus for my syntactical examination of citation formulae in the Old Testament.[6] Two results of this research relate to the exegetical devices addressed in this essay. First, while Fishbane's monograph obviously deserves continued study, a syntactical examination of the adverbial and relative constructions in this debate has, in my estimation, confirmed the more circumscribed, less unwieldy readings of the exegetical devices in the non-synoptic portions of the postexilic historiography advocated by Williamson and other scholars dating back more than a century.[7]

Second, even though biblical historiographers attribute various topics (e.g., cultic regulations, legal stipulations, the deeds of kings, laments, genealogies, poetic fragments) to a range of sources (e.g., Torah, the Book of the Upright, the Annals of the Kings of Judah and Israel), selected postexilic exegetical devices used to interpret the Law are distinguishable from all other citation formulae in the Old Testament. The forms and functions characteristic of these *developed exegetical devices* in the non-synoptic postexilic historiography concern the following features: the

[4] Williamson, "History," 25–38. His essay responded primarily to the analysis of selected exegetical devices in Chronicles and Ezra-Nehemiah in Michael Fishbane, *Biblical Interpretation.* For Fishbane's subsequent scholarship on biblical interpretation, see idem, *The Garments of Torah: Essays in Biblical Hermeneutics* (Bloomington, Ind.: Indiana University Press, 1989); idem., "Inner-Biblical Exegesis," in *Hebrew Bible/Old Testament, the History of its Interpretation. Vol. I: From the Beginnings to the Middle Ages (Until 1300). Part 1: Antiquity* (ed. Magne Sæbø; Göttingen: Vandenhoeck & Ruprecht, 1996), 33–48.

[5] For an example of the debated reading of the postexilic exegetical devices in biblical scholarship of the 19th century, see Kevin L. Spawn, *"As It Is Written" and Other Citation Formulae in the Old Testament: Their Use, Development, Syntax and Significance* (BZAW 311; Berlin: de Gruyter, 2002), 10.

[6] For the conclusions of this study as it relates to exegetical devices, see Spawn, *Citation Formulae*, 241–58. For a brief overview of this investigation, see idem, "Sources, References to," in *Dictionary of Old Testament—Historical Books* (ed. Bill T. Arnold and H. G. M. Williamson; Downers Grove, Ill.: IVP Academic, 2005), 935–41.

[7] E.g., for the six different readings of the citation formula ככתוב בתורה in Neh. 10:35 (34 ET) by scholars since Carl F. Keil, *Chronik, Esra, Nehemia und Esther* (Leipzig: Dörffling und Franke, 1870), 569, see Spawn, *Citation Formulae*, 2–12.

increased use of abbreviated forms (e.g., ככתוב);[8] the decreased use of compound constructions;[9] the consistent positioning of a citation device beside its antecedent (or referent);[10] the marking of two hermeneutical horizons (i.e., a reference to the Law is distinguished from its interpretation in the same immediate literary context); and the use of the syntactical features of ancient Hebrew (e.g., disjunctive clauses, *waw*-explicativa, suffixes) to distinguish these horizons or to otherwise clarify the referent of a citation formula.[11] The distribution of exegetical devices exhibiting one or more of these features in the narratives of Solomon, Hezekiah, and Josiah has an observable literary and theological effect in the book of Chronicles.[12]

## II. Exegetical Devices in the Narratives of Solomon and Hezekiah in Chronicles

The Chr interprets the Law with hermeneutical tools in a distinguishable way in each of the narratives of these three monarchs. Their use in the narrative of Hezekiah depends upon those introduced by the Chr in the account of the temple (2 Chr 2:1–8:16).

---

[8] The abbreviation of the postexilic citation formulae with ככתוב (ככתוב בתורת יהוה e.g., 2 Chr 31:3; ככתוב בספר משה e.g., 35:12; ככתוב בתורה e.g., Neh. 10:37; and ככתוב e.g., 2 Chr 30:5) continues later into the Second Temple Period with ככ (e.g., CD 19:1). For two significant factors in the development of these ככתוב formulae in the postbiblical period, see Spawn, *Citation Formulae*, 122–23 n. 259.

[9] In contrast to the non-synoptic postexilic exegetical devices, compound constructions are characteristically employed in the deuteronomistic literature (for his categorization of relevant deuteronomistic phraseology, see Moshe Weinfeld, *Deuteronomy and the Deuteronomistic School* [Oxford: Clarendon, 1972], 336–38). For a five-part compound citation device in this literature, see the formulation "according to their statutes, according to their ordinance, according to the law and according to the commandment that the LORD commanded the sons of Jacob" (כחקתם וכמשפטם וכתורה וכמצוה אשר צוה יהוה) in 2 Kgs 17:34b (see idem, *Deuteronomistic School*, 338, 21g cf. 21c, f, h and j).

[10] Outside of the postexilic historiography, a clause, for example, may intrude between a citation device and its referent (e.g., "The dogs licked up his [Ahab's] blood, *where the prostitutes washed themselves,* according to the word of the LORD that he [the prophet Elijah] had spoken" 1 Kgs 22:38b). In v. 38b, a disjunctive clause (italics) interrupts the placement of the citation formula ("according to the word of the LORD that he had spoken") beside its referent ("the dogs licked up his blood"). For the prophetic judgment cited in v. 38b, see 21:19b (" 'Thus says the LORD: In the place where dogs licked up the blood of Naboth, dogs will also lick up your blood' ").

[11] E.g., *contra* the disjunctive clause interrupting the relation between the citation formula and its referent in 1 Kgs 22:38b (see the comments on 1 Kgs 21–22 in n. 10 above).

[12] This investigation also led to the identification of other relevant hermeneutical tools (e.g., כתורה, כמצות משה, אשר צוה יהוה).

## 1. *The 'Golden' Age and the Splendor of the Temple in the Solomon Narrative*

### a. *2 Chronicles 4:7*

In the temple construction narrative (2 Chr 3:1–5:1), the Chr abridged the details of the structure and furnishings of the temple to feature the splendor of the central sanctuary of YAHWEH. The Chr added a comprehensive list of the golden vessels in 4:7–10 to an existing inventory of such objects in vv. 19–22 from 1 Kgs 7:47–50. Consequently, his account features more than his deuteronomistic source (1 Kgs 7) the gold that overlaid the beams, doors, cherubim, porch, and rafters of the temple.[13] Since the magnificence of Solomon's temple symbolized, above all else, the majesty of YAHWEH,[14] according to the Chr, the production of the ten golden lampstands for the nave in 2 Chr 4:7 also promoted the structure as a sign of the surpassing greatness of the God of Israel. The insertion of an exegetical device in v. 7a also manifests the Chr's skill as an exegete.

> He [Solomon] made *ten* golden lampstands according to their ordinance (ויעש את מנרות הזהב עשר כְּמִשְׁפָּטָם), and placed them in the sanctuary, *five on the south side and five on the north* (2 Chr 4:7).

The citation formula כְּמִשְׁפָּטָם marks the provision in the pentateuchal legislation for lighting the tabernacle by the lamps of the golden lampstand (Exod 25:31–37; 37:17–24). By affixing a suffix to the phrase כְּמִשְׁפָּטָם in 2 Chr 4:7a, the Chr made מנרות the grammatical antecedent of the pronoun (3mp) of כְּמִשְׁפָּטָם.[15] Without attributing either the number or the arrangement of the ten lampstands (italics) in 2 Chr 4:7 to the pentateuchal traditions, the Chr appears to have used the resumptive pronoun of כְּמִשְׁפָּטָם to link the production of golden lampstands of the first temple in v. 7a to the pentateuchal regulations for illuminating the tabernacle. Consequently, the two rows of lampstands in the Solomonic

13 "Although the themes of wealth and wisdom are evident in the Chronicler's Vorlage, the Chronicler links them more explicitly and exclusively to Solomon's temple project, rather than his royal rule" (Mark J. Boda, "Legitimizing the Temple: The Chronicler's Temple Building Account," in *From the Foundations to the Crenellations: Essays on Temple Building in the Ancient Near East and Hebrew Bible* [ed. Mark J. Boda and Jamie Novotny; AOAT 366; Münster: Ugarit-Verlag, 2010], 303–318 [305]).

14 Steven L. McKenzie, *1–2 Chronicles* (AOTC; Nashville, Tenn.: Abingdon Press, 2004), 242.

15 In Late Biblical Hebrew, masculine suffixes are frequently employed for feminine antecedents (GKC §135o), especially in Chronicles (Joüon §149b).

Temple are an interpretation of the pentateuchal tradition of the lighting the tabernacle.[16]

According to Carol Meyers, instead of possessing a symbolic meaning alone, the most significant attribute of these ten lampstands was their "light-giving property."[17] Solomon's production of several lampstands for the main room (היכל) of the temple was an adaptation of the tabernacle legislation (vv. 7–8).[18] This interpretation of the Law apparently met the need of the priests for more lighting, since the nave (היכל) of the temple was significantly larger than the sanctuary (הקדש) of the tabernacle (Exod. 26:15–20 cf. 1 Kgs 6:2–36).

The Chr's insertion of the ten golden lampstands into the temple narrative (2 Chr 3:1–5:1) of the 'Golden' Age of biblical Israel is consistent with his observable interest in the bronze and gold contents of the temple. In v. 7, the Chr's citation and interpretation of the Law is linked to his historiographical purpose to magnify God. The implication of the increased lighting of these ten מנרות in v. 7 becomes explicit in v. 20.

b. *2 Chronicles 4:20*

Complementing the interpretation of the tabernacle legislation in v. 7, the similar citation formula "according to the ordinance [כמשפט]" in v. 20 marks the positioning of the lampstands with *burning lamps* before the inner sanctuary (הדביר) in the days of the reforms of Hezekiah (cf. Exod 25:31–37; 27:20–21):

> the lampstands of pure gold with their lamps to burn them [the lamps on their lampstands] according to the ordinance [כמשפט] in front of the inner sanctuary (2 Chr 4:20).

As with the provision for the lighting of the sanctuary in v. 7, the burning of the lamps in v. 20 is also based upon the Law.

---

16 According to William M. Schniedewind ("The Chronicler as an Interpreter of Scripture," in *The Chronicler as an Author: Studies in Text and Texture* [ed. M. Patrick Graham and Steven L. McKenzie; JSOTSup 263; Sheffield: Sheffield Academic, 1999], 158–80 [175]) the ten lampstands in v. 7 were an "extrapolation" from the tabernacle prescriptions, noting that they consisted of gold as prescribed. "Extrapolation" may be another way of accounting for a reference to the Law and its interpretation in v. 7.

17 Carol Meyers, "Lampstand," *ABD* 4:141–43 (143).

18 For the view that this citation formula in v. 7 does not refer to the Torah, while כמשפט later in this same chapter does (see כמשפט in 2 Chr 4:20), see Leslie C. Allen, "The First and Second Books of Chronicles," in *The New Interpreter's Bible* (ed. Leander E. Keck; vol. 3; Nashville, Tenn.: Abingdon, 1999), 297–659 (485).

The sublime effect of the burning of all the lamps on the ten lampstands in the ornate nave further underscores the Chr's interest in 2 Chr 3:1–5:1 in portraying the temple as a symbol of the majestic God of Israel. The excellence of the main hall may possibly have prompted the priests to recall the extraordinary nature of their ministrations. According to the Chr, the citation and interpretation of the tabernacle legislation in ch. 4 made a distinctive contribution to his history of the 'Golden' Era of biblical Israel. Based upon the Chr's underscoring of the golden features of the temple discussed above, the interpretation of the pentateuchal regulations for lighting the sanctuary in 2 Chr 4 enhanced the role of the temple in the Solomonic narrative as a sign of the majesty of God. Even though Zerubbabel's temple paled in comparison to the first one,[19] the archetype established by the Chr in ch. 4 may have prompted his community both to recover the symbolic nature of their smaller temple and to develop their interpretation of the Law.[20]

### c. *2 Chronicles 8:12–14*

To conclude the accounts of the temple construction and dedication (2 Chr 2–8), the Chr expanded 1 Kgs 9:25 to 2 Chr 8:12–16 ("all the work of Solomon from the day the foundation of the House of YAHWEH was laid until it was finished" v. 16). In addition to marking the fulfillment of the legal traditions in v. 13, the Chr adds that the cultic traditions of David had also been accomplished by the completion of the first temple (v. 14).

> Then Solomon offered up burnt offerings to YAHWEH on the altar of YAHWEH that he had built in front of the vestibule, as the duty of each day required, *offering* according to the commandment of Moses [כמצות משה] *for the sabbaths, the new moons, and the three annual festivals—the festival of unleavened bread, the festival of weeks, and the festival of booths.* According to the ordinance of his father David [כמשפט דויד אביו], he appointed the divisions of the priests for their service, and the Levites for their offices of

[19] E.g., the foundation of the Zerubbabel temple (Ezra 3:10–13) and its memorial crown(s) of silver and gold (Zech 6:9–15).

[20] In addition to the Chr's literary technique in 2 Chr 4, M. J. Boda has demonstrated that the Chr also legitimated the postexilic temple for his community by linking the detailed construction narrative of "the earlier temple of David-Solomon to the ideal premonarchial ages of Abraham and Moses, whose worship sites (Moriah altar and wilderness tabernacle) possessed impeccable credentials" (Boda, "Legitimizing the Temple," 318, cf. 315–18). The Chr's use of the details of the early stages of temple construction to legitimize his cultic site appears to be attributable to the broad tradition of temple building in the ancient Near East. See further Boda, "Legitimizing the Temple," 310–12.

> praise and ministry alongside the priests as the duty of each day required, and the gatekeepers in their divisions for the several gates; for so David the man of God had commanded (2 Chr 8:12–14).

Regarding the exegetical device כמצות משה, the Chr's rewriting of his source results in a more detailed account of Solomon's extensive support of the sacrificial offerings for the cult (italics) according to legal traditions. This fulfillment of both the legal and cultic traditions in 2 Chr 8:12–14 advances further the Chr's depiction of the 'Golden' Age as a paradigm for his community.[21]

The climax of the centralization of the worship of all the tribes under Solomon, which builds in Chronicles from at least 1 Chr 10, reaches its apex with the appearance of YAHWEH (2 Chr 7:11–22) at the conclusion of the temple dedication (5:2–8:16).[22] These three exegetical devices (4:7, 20; 8:14) are an important part of the fulfillment of the Law in the Chronistic 'Golden' Age. Not only do they underscore the glorious temple as a symbol of God's majesty but they also mark the fulfillments of the legal and cultic traditions of this paradigmatic era. This citation and interpretation of the Law also established a model for the exegetical tools in the Hezekiah and Josiah narratives.

### 2. *The Hezekiah Narrative*

After the narration of two centuries of Judean history across twenty chapters (2 Chr.10–29), the Chr reintroduces four exegetical devices in 2 Chr 30:5–31:3 (30:5, 16, 18; 31:3). Before his significant abridgement of both 2 Kgs 18–20 and Isa 36–39 in 2 Chr 32, the Chr expanded the portrait of Hezekiah as the great cultic reformer of 'all Israel' in 2 Chr 29–31. According to the Chr's account, Hezekiah's reformation consisted of the purification of the temple and its personnel (29:3–36), the celebration of Passover (30:1–27), and the arrangements for the perpetual support of the cultic worship of YAHWEH (31:1–21). Even though some of the parallels between

---

[21] For his view of a Mosaic redaction of Chronicles in the second century BCE to correct the idealized portrayal of the Davidic kingdom and cult in Jerusalem, see Ernst Michael Dörrfuß, *Mose in den Chronikbüchern: Garant theokratischer Zukunftserwartung* (BZAW 219; Berlin: de Gruyter, 1994). For his classification of these devices into "Authorization Formulas" and "Regulation Formulas" to account for the Chr's use of the authority of Moses and David, see Simon J. De Vries, "Moses and David as Cult Founders in Chronicles," *JBL* 107 (1988): 619–39; idem, *1 and 2 Chronicles* (FOTL; Grand Rapids, Mich.: Eerdmans, 1989). For an assessment of De Vries' classifications, see Spawn, *Citation Formulae*, 252–55.

[22] See 2 Chr 8:16 above.

the accounts of Solomon and Hezekiah in Chronicles concern the use of these exegetical devices,[23] the Chr employed hermeneutical tools in the latter narrative in an observably different way than those in the 'Golden' Age.

### a. *2 Chronicles 30:5*

A decree was drawn up to gather 'all Israel' to Jerusalem and to purify the temple personnel and the people (30:2–3; cf. 29:12–36; 30:15–18). The Chr used a negative formulation of ככתוב ("for they had not kept it in large numbers[24] as it was written" כי לא לרב עשו ככתוב 2 Chr 30:5) to stress how a Passover celebration of 'all Israel'—to whom Deut. 16:1–7 was directed—would reverse the longstanding practice of the disobedience of this law.

> For the king and his officials and all the assembly in Jerusalem had taken counsel to keep the Passover in the second month (for they could not keep it at its proper time because the priests had not sanctified themselves in sufficient number, nor had the people assembled in Jerusalem). So they decreed to make a proclamation throughout all Israel... that the people should come and keep the Passover to Yahweh the God of Israel, at Jerusalem; for they had not kept it in great numbers as it was written [כי לא לרב עשו ככתוב] (2 Chr 30:2–3, 5).

In v. 5, this exegetical device emphasizes the centuries of Israel's disregard for this pilgrim festival.

### b. *2 Chronicles 30:16*

After being shamed by the ritually unclean worshippers slaughtering the Passover lambs (vv. 15–16a), the priests and certain Levites sanctified themselves for their duties.

> They [the worshippers from the north] slaughtered the Passover lambs on the fourteenth day of the second month. After being put to shame, the priests and Levites sanctified themselves and brought burnt offerings to the House of Yahweh. After *they took their accustomed posts* according to the Law of Moses the man of God (כתורת משה איש־האלהים), the priests

---

23 Williamson, *Israel*, 119–25.

24 The rendering of לרב is generally understood to mark the extensive participation in the Passover celebration of Hezekiah ("in large numbers" see MT, LXX, cf. v. 13), while Sara Japhet (*I & II Chronicles*, [Louisville, Ky.: Westminster John Knox, 1993], 940–41) translates this phrase according to the frequency of observance "often / many times."

dashed the blood that they received from the hands of the Levites (והכהנים זרקים את־הדם מיד הלוים)[25] (2 Chr 30:15–16).

The adverbial phrase כתורת משה איש־האלהים, which is followed by a disjunctive participial clause in v. 16b, qualifies the remainder of v. 16a (italics). This exegetical device marks that the priests and the Levites took their respective positions in the cult according to the Law (e.g., Lev 8:1–36 cf. Num 3:5–4:49). Based on these pentateuchal traditions, the Levites as support staff assisted the Aaronite priests.[26] During the exceptional event of the Passover of Hezekiah, the Levites passed the blood to the priests after they slaughtered the *paschal* sacrifice on behalf of the ritually impure worshippers (vv. 16b–17).[27]

c. *2 Chronicles 30:18*

A second negative exegetical device in 2 Chr 30 is employed in v. 18a. Despite the extension of the Passover celebration to a second month (vv. 1–12), this formulation ("otherwise than as it is written" בלא ככתוב, v. 18a) marks the cultic impurity of many northern worshippers eating the *paschal* sacrifice in the second month.

---

25 For the reconstructed ו and its significance, see Spawn, *Citation Formulae,* 219 n. 4, 223, 250–55.

26 For the subordinate role of the Levites as support staff to the Aaronite priests, see Duane A. Garrett, "Levi, Levites," in *The Dictionary of the Old Testament: Pentateuch* (ed. T. Desmond Alexander and David W. Baker; Downers Grove, Ill.: IVP Academic, 2003), 519–22. For his reconstruction of the Chr's account of the Davidic realignment of Levitical duties in the cult, see John Kleinig, *The LORD's Song: the Basis, Function and Significance of Choral Music in Chronicles* (JSOTSup 156; Sheffield: Sheffield Academic, 1991), 39–42, 70.

27 See Allen, "Chronicles", 618. In v. 16, according to Schniedewind, "A clever blending of the Torah of Moses and the cultic ritual tradition is then reflected by the apposition of כמשפט [sic] 'according to custom' and כתורת משה 'according to the Law of Moses'" (Schniedewind, "Interpreter," 176; see also idem, "Innerbiblical Exegesis," in *Dictionary of Old Testament—Historical Books* (ed. Bill T. Arnold and H. G. M. Williamson; Downers Grove: IVP Academic, 2005), 502–9 [508]). However, the phrase employed by the Chr in v. 16 is, in fact, כמשפטם. Due to the semantic breadth of משפט (see *HALOT* 2:651–52; *DCH* 5:563–64), כמשפטם does not always function as an exegetical tool or citation device (see Spawn, *Citation Formulae*, 200).

According to Sara Japhet (*The Ideology of the Book of Chronicles and its Place in Biblical Thought* [rev. ed.; BEATAJ 9; Frankfurt: Lang, 1997], 240–41) כתורת משה איש־האלהים in v. 16 sanctions the Levites sprinkling the blood of the Passover lamb. According to her broad reading of this adverbial expression, the contents of vv. 15a and 16 but not v. 15b are attributed to the pentateuchal tradition (idem, *Ideology*, 240). Consequently, Japhet contends that the Chr in 2 Chr 30:16 departs from the pentateuchal law. However, the Chr's use of a disjunctive clause in v. 16b restricts, in my opinion, the qualification of כתורה to v. 16a, resulting in an interpretation of the Law in v. 16b.

> For a multitude of the people, many of them from Ephraim, Manasseh, Issachar, and Zebulun, had not cleansed themselves, yet they ate the Passover otherwise than as it is written [בלא ככתוב] (2 Chr 30:18a).

The Chr used a negative form of ככתוב to single out the state of ritual uncleanness of many worshippers attending Hezekiah's Passover in the second month. Even though the Law is not his chief concern, both its citation and appropriation in 'all Israel' are observably part of his interests in 2 Chr 30 (vv. 5, 16, 18). Based on the hermeneutical tools distributed in this chapter, the Chr's use of exegetical devices—one regular citation and two negative formulations—is noteworthy.

d. *2 Chronicles 31:3*

An exegetical device is used in 2 Chr 31:3 to draw a distinctive parallel between Hezekiah and the Chronistic Solomon of the 'Golden' Age.

> The contribution of the king from his own possessions was for the burnt offerings: the burnt offerings of the morning and evening, and the burnt offerings for the Sabbaths, the new moons, and the appointed festivals, as it is written in the Law of YAHWEH (ככתוב בתורת יהוה) (2 Chr 31:3).

First, in their respective celebrations, both Solomon and Hezekiah made extravagant provisions for the burnt offerings prescribed in the Law. In addition to David's elaborate preparations for the temple (1 Chr 29:1–5), Hezekiah's provision for the temple in 2 Chr 31:2–3 is modeled after Solomon's fulfillment of "the ordinance of David his father [כמשפט דויד אביו]" in 8:14.[28] The Chr also used exegetical devices to cite the Law in both 8:13 and 31:3, linking Hezekiah and Solomon as kings of exceptional eras of the implementation of the legal and cultic traditions.[29] Even though it is not his chief concern, the Chr's interests in the observance of the Law by both the king (31:21) and the people (v. 4) are not to be minimized.

> Every work that he undertook in the service of the House of God, and in accordance with the Law and the commandments, to seek his God, he [Hezekiah] did with all his heart; and he prospered. (2 Chr 31:21)
>
> He [Hezekiah] commanded the people who lived in Jerusalem to give the portion due to the priests and the Levites, so that they may be strong [יחזקו] in the Law of YAHWEH. (2 Chr 31:4)

---

[28] Williamson, *Israel*, 122.

[29] See our analysis of 2 Chr 8:12–14 above.

This reading of the exegetical device in v. 3 fits well with a normal rendering of יחזקו in the last clause of v. 4. According to Sara Japhet, "the purpose clause refers not to the 'priests and Levites' but to 'the people', to whom the king's command was delivered. The king's motivation is presented as directing the people to be strong in the law, in fulfilling its ordinances."[30] As the examination of exegetical devices in 2 Chr 30 suggests, the longed-awaited recovery of the observance of the Law in the Hezekiah narrative was led by the king himself.

e. *Conclusion to Hezekiah Narrative*

In 2 Chr 30–31, the Chr employed exegetical devices both to make parallels and to draw contrasts with those used in the Solomon narrative. By gathering 'all Israel' for a momentous celebration (30:5) at the temple richly supplied with sacrifices from the monarch (31:3), the Chr modeled part of his portrait of Hezekiah upon his account of Solomon. The punctuation of these topics with exegetical tools assists the Chr's concern for the handling of the Law in his community. The negative formulation in 30:5 not only emphasizes the great achievement of Hezekiah but it also indicates that disregard for the festival would likely have otherwise continued. This latter situation is suggested by the two remaining uses of these hermeneutical tools in the Hezekiah narrative. First, even though they eventually sanctify themselves, several of the temple personnel are initially unprepared to assume their duties in the cult (30:16). Second, despite this delay of the celebration to the second month, many worshippers were still not ready to participate in the celebration one month later. Employing a citation formula to mark transgressions of the Law, the Chr's interest in the proper handling of the Law is once again underscored. Consequently, the use of these hermeneutical tools in 2 Chr 30–31 marks a partial modeling of the paradigm of citation and interpretation in the Solomon narrative.

As the cultic reformer and spiritual leader of his people, according to the Chr, Hezekiah exhibited a nuanced approach to the interpretation of the Law. In addition to encouraging the temple personnel to rededicate themselves (2 Chr 30:22, 24b), the spiritual leadership of Hezekiah is highlighted by the way he led the northerners to seek YAHWEH despite their cultic impurity (vv. 17–18a). Rather than becoming distraught with their disobedience to the Law, according to the Chr, Hezekiah stressed

30 Japhet, *I & II Chronicles*, 964.

to the lawbreakers a profound theological principle (vv. 18b–19). Due to the spiritual acuity of the king, YAHWEH heard and healed the people (v. 20). After extending the celebration another seven days (v. 23), the Chr emphasizes that the great joy of Hezekiah's Passover had not been experienced in Jerusalem since "the time of Solomon" (v. 26).

## III. Conclusion

The Chr placed exegetical devices in the temple narrative (2 Chr 2:1–8:16), in part, to offer a paradigm for the citation and interpretation of the Law in his community. This model connected the handling of the Law with the splendor of the temple, the majesty of YAHWEH and the 'Golden' Age of the fulfillment of the legal and cultic traditions (3:1–5:1). The Chr employs exegetical devices in 2 Chr 30–31 to draw both parallels and contrasts with this paradigm established in the Solomon narrative. Consequently, the Hezekiah narrative marks an important but imperfect recurrence of the citation and interpretation of the Law in Chronicles. Although outside the scope of this essay, the account of Josiah (2 Chr 34–35), under whose reign the book of the Law was discovered, completes the Chr's distribution of exegetical devices to promote the citation and interpretation of the Law. In Chronicles, the further the combined reigns of David and Solomon recede into the past (1 Chr 10–2 Chr 9), and the nearer the narrative gets to the exile (2 Chr 36), the more the Chr introduces exegetical devices into his history to model the citation and interpretation of the 'Golden' Era.[31] Even though the pentateuchal traditions are not his chief interest, the Chr has successfully punctuated strategic narratives in Chronicles with exegetical devices to develop the observance and handling of the Law in his community. The meticulous reading of exegetical devices in the postexilic historiography remains one of the many enduring contributions of H. G. M. Williamson to the scholarship of the Hebrew Bible.

[31] Spawn, *Citation Formulae*, 257–58.

# PART V

# MISCELLANY

# GENESIS 1 AS HOLINESS PREAMBLE

Bill T. Arnold

Of his many notable contributions, H. G. M. Williamson's *The Book Called Isaiah*, stands as a magisterial example of careful scholarship and makes a contribution not only to Isaianic studies but to redaction-critical theory itself.[1] In what follows, I offer a study of Genesis 1 that in some respects proposes a role for a Holiness author not unlike Professor Williamson's understanding of Deutero-Isaiah.[2] It is a pleasure to offer these ideas here in his honor.

In a recent commentary, I proposed the view that Genesis was compiled by a Holiness redactor using P and non-P materials, whose purpose was to bring together all of Israel's traditions on the primeval and ancestral ages in a unified whole.[3] In that venue, I could do little more than stake out a position, noting that the nature and provenance of the priestly materials in Genesis have been much discussed since the mid 1990s. Currently there is broad consensus on the existence of P and H, although much debate surrounds questions on the limits of each and the relative dating of each.[4] This last issue is especially pertinent to the research question I am addressing here; that is, to what extent was the earlier of these priestly sources redacted by the later? To put this another way, to what extent has a scholar of the Holiness school redacted P, assuming as I do that recent work emphasizing the sequential priority of P to H is correct? Here I return to this topic in order to offer a few details specific to Gen 1 as it relates to Gen 2, taking the first chapter as a preamble for the rest of Genesis composed by an author of the Holiness legislation.[5] While my

---

[1] H. G. M. Williamson, *The Book Called Isaiah: Deutero-Isaiah's Role in Composition and Redaction* (Oxford: Clarendon/Oxford University Press, 1994).

[2] Ibid., 240–41.

[3] Bill T. Arnold, *Genesis* (NCBC; Cambridge and New York: Cambridge University Press, 2009), 12–18.

[4] This is illustrated recently by the diverse views in the studies collected in Sarah Shectman and Joel S. Baden, eds., *The Strata of the Priestly Writings: Contemporary Debate and Future Directions* (ATANT 95; Zürich: Theologischer Verlag Zürich, 2009).

[5] For the sake of convenience, I will refer to Gen 1:1–2:3 simply as Gen 1, and to Gen 2:4–25 simply as Gen 2. For my use of "Holiness legislation" rather than Holiness Code, see Baruch J. Schwartz, "The Strata of the Priestly Writings and the Revised Relative Dating of

proposal is that an H redactor is responsible for Genesis essentially as we have it now, his role for Gen 1 specifically was more that of an author creating an entirely new composition. I will close with a few observations on the consequences of this conclusion for investigations of the Pentateuch generally.

## I. Genesis 1 in Recent Investigation

The identification of Gen 1 as a priestly text found wide acceptance during the nineteenth century and became an established datum of source criticism after Wellhausen's configuration.[6] Renewed investigation of Gen 1 is needed today in light of a new approach emerging in recent decades, beginning with the significant contributions of Israel Knohl, in which the sequential priority of H to P has been challenged.[7] This work has led further to reinvestigation of the nature and extent of both H and P. In addition to Knohl, Jacob Milgrom identified numerous similarities between texts traditionally thought of as P materials but with themes and phraseology of the so-called Holiness Code (Lev 17–26).[8] With regard specifically to Gen 1, Knohl concluded that the chapter is entirely P material, including the Sabbath etiology (2:2–3),[9] whereas Milgrom demurred. He argued initially that the Sabbath etiology was a Holiness insertion in an older P composition but eventually concluded that the entire chapter is to be

---

P and H," in Shectman and Baden (eds.), *The Strata of the Priestly Writings*, 1–12, esp. 6–7; and Jeffrey Stackert, *Rewriting the Torah: Literary Revision in Deuteronomy and the Holiness Legislation* (FAT 52; Tübingen: Mohr Siebeck, 2007), 2.

[6] Julius Wellhausen, *Prolegomena to the History of Israel* (Atlanta, Ga.: Scholars Press, 1994), 297–308 and 385–91; repr. of *Prolegomena to the History of Israel* (trans. J. Sutherland Black and Allan Menzies, with preface by W. Robertson Smith; Edinburgh: Adam & Charles Black, 1885); trans. of *Prolegomena zur Geschichte Israels* (2nd ed.; Berlin: G. Reimer, 1883).

[7] Israel Knohl, *The Sanctuary of Silence: The Priestly Torah and the Holiness School* (Minneapolis: Fortress, 1995). An early version of chapter 1 of this book detailed his views in English as early as 1987: Israel Knohl, "The Priestly Torah Versus the Holiness School: Sabbath and the Festivals," *HUCA* 58 (1987): 65–117. The priority of P to H is indeed a dramatic *volte-face*, the consequences of which are only now beginning to be explored; cf. Schwartz, "Strata of the Priestly Writings," esp. 5–10.

[8] For Milgrom's contributions to the discussion, see among others Jacob Milgrom, *Leviticus 17–22: A New Translation with Introduction and Commentary* (AB 3A; New York: Doubleday, 2000), 1319–64, and Jacob Milgrom, "The Antiquity of the Priestly Source: A Reply to Joseph Blenkinsopp," *ZAW* 111 (1999): 10–22.

[9] Knohl, *Sanctuary of Silence*, 104 and 163.

attributed to a Holiness redactor.[10] In this brief paper, I offer observations that I believe buttress this approach and support Milgrom's later views, although his arguments were left undeveloped.

The author of Gen 1 set out intentionally to compose an entirely new creation account for ancient Israel, intended precisely to supplement, nuance, and to some degree, correct the older and greatly venerated account of Gen 2. In making such a claim at the outset, I am in substantial agreement with the recent study of Mark S. Smith, who uses 'commentary' as a way to describe the relationship between Gen 1 and the creation account of Gen 2.[11] While some would go further and argue that Gen 1 was intended to 'replace' Gen 2,[12] I think this unlikely. The account of 2:4–3:24 would presumably have been unassailable in authority for his readership; he accepted the older venerated creation account because he had no choice. But in Gen 1 the author has turned the creation of the cosmos into an etiology for the Sabbath as the chief concern among other priestly topics. This author is aware that his is not the first word on creation. Other Israelites had spoken of the origins of the cosmos, as had others in Mesopotamia and Egypt. The author of Gen 1 sets out intentionally to fill certain missing gaps in these earlier accounts, especially Gen 2. By supplementing and framing the older account while still retaining it as authoritative, the Holiness author/redactor has provided a tapestry of creation theology.

This investigation of three familiar themes of Gen 1 starts at the denouement of the chapter, the institution of the Sabbath (2:2–3), and works in reverse order. The author was dissatisfied with Gen 2 as a suitable beginning for the following reasons, in order of themes most important to

---

10 Milgrom himself did not investigate the possibility beyond passing references; Jacob Milgrom, "The Case for the Pre-Exilic and Exilic Provenance of the Books of Exodus, Leviticus and Numbers," in *Reading the Law: Studies in Honour of Gordon J. Wenham* (LHBOTS 461; ed. J. Gordon McConville and Karl Möller; New York & London: T&T Clark, 2007), 48–56, esp. 56. Earlier, Yairah Amit had proposed something similar for Gen 1, as had Edwin Firmage; Yairah Amit, "Creation and the Calendar of Holiness," in *Tehillah le-Moshe: Biblical and Judaic Studies in Honor of Moshe Greenberg* (ed. Mordechai Cogan, Barry L. Eichler and Jeffrey H. Tigay; Winona Lake, Ind.: Eisenbrauns, 1997), 13–29 (Heb., with English summary, pp. 315–16) and Edwin Firmage, "Genesis 1 and the Priestly Agenda," *JSOT* 82 (1999): 97–114. Cooper and Goldstein largely followed Amit and Firmage; Alan Cooper and Bernard R. Goldstein, "The Development of the Priestly Calendars (I): The Daily Sacrifice and the Sabbath," *HUCA* 74 (2003): 1–20, esp. 5 and 13–14.

11 Mark S. Smith, *The Priestly Vision of Genesis 1* (Minneapolis, Minn.: Augsburg Fortress, 2009), 129–38.

12 David M. Carr, *Reading the Fractures of Genesis: Historical and Literary Approaches* (Louisville, Ky: Westminster John Knox, 1996), 74–75 and 317.

him. First, Gen 2 did not adequately provide a background for Sabbath-keeping. Second, Gen 2 did not adequately establish Israel's animal taxonomy, especially as such is needed to understand and appreciate the dietary restrictions of Lev 11. Third, Gen 2 did not properly establish the times and seasons central to Israel's festival system. Fourth, Gen 2 failed to refute the *Weltanschauungen* of Mesopotamia and Egypt, because it was more narrowly focused on the Canaanite world-view.[13] This last item is the only one not specifically related to a trajectory into other portions of the Pentateuch, as I hope to show, and will not therefore be included in the remarks below. Genesis 1, then, has filled these gaps and has provided a preamble for a larger project than that envisioned in Gen 2. Yet by linking the new composition to Gen 2 with the תולדות catch phrase (2:4a) borrowed from 5:1, which I believe is the original opening line of an older priestly source, the Holiness author/redactor has intentionally retained Gen 2 as an authoritative yet now nuanced text. This author is also responsible for extending the תולדות phrase over the entire Genesis narrative creating a new macro-structure.

## II. The Sabbath

We start at the conclusion of Gen 1 because the Sabbath is the most important theme for this author. Such a bold assertion is deduced by the simple fact that the Sabbath etiology of 2:2–3 is the source of the seven-part structure for the whole chapter rather than an afterthought added later.[14] The Sabbath theme was the organizing principle from the start, and the sanctification of the seventh day was reserved for the conclusion for rhetorical effect. This author considered Gen 2 wholly inadequate as a beginning because it did not provide a foundation for Sabbath-keeping. On the contrary, the infinitives construct of purpose at 2:15—"to till it and keep it"—outline the *raison d'être* for humanity's existence but with no foundation for cessation of work. The newly created אדם has been placed in the garden as a representative of Yhwh God in order to cultivate (עבד) the earth and as the one responsible for keeping or protecting it (שׁמר).

[13] The first three of these topics were taken up in a similar vein as a "new priestly vision of reality" in Mark S. Smith, *The Origins of Biblical Monotheism: Israel's Polytheistic Background and the Ugaritic Texts* (New York: Oxford University Press, 2001), 169.

[14] Milgrom eventually concluded this; Jacob Milgrom, "$H_R$ in Leviticus and Elsewhere in the Torah," in *The Book of Leviticus: Composition and Reception* (VTSup 93; ed. Rolf Rendtorff, Robert A. Kugler, and Sarah Smith Bartel; Leiden/Boston: Brill, 2003), 34.

The only restrictions in the garden are stated immediately in the next verse, a prohibition against eating the fruit of the tree of the knowledge of good and evil (2:16). After the Great Transgression, the human is further condemned to work the soil and earn his bread "by the sweat of [his] face" (3:17–19), focusing only on the necessity of physical labor to provide one's sustenance. This was not deemed adequate to prepare the reader for the important role of Sabbath in subsequent texts, especially Exod 31:12–17 and 35:2–3, both of which have been identified as originating from the Holiness School.[15] Thus a new introduction was necessary, portraying God himself as resting from all the work of creation, and offering a model for subsequent texts mandating cessation of work on a seven-day pattern.[16]

The institution of the Sabbath itself (2:2–3) is about divine rest or cessation from work (וישבת, "and [God] rested") and holiness (ויקדש, "and [God] hallowed it"). The lexeme קדש (*HALOT* 1072–78), famously so central to the Holiness legislation (Lev 17–26), does not occur elsewhere in Genesis, and in fact, does not occur again until the burning-bush revelation to Moses ("the place on which you are standing is holy ground," Exod 3:5).[17] With regard to Sabbath-observance, it seems surprising to some that humans are not specifically prohibited in Gen 2:2–3 from working on the seventh day, and yet these two verses clearly prepare for that important prohibition (Exod 31:12–17 and 35:2–3). In general, the Sabbath law is intended to teach that God is sovereign both over time and over Israel, and that therefore every seventh day, Israelites must renounce their autonomy and affirm God's dominion. "Keeping the sabbath is acceptance of the sovereignty of God."[18] Thus the purpose of Gen 1 was establishing that sovereignty first; the prohibition against work would come later. Moreover, Knohl has shown that P and H have different perspectives on the Sabbath.[19] He has identified the prohibition of Sabbath-work

---

15 Knohl, *Sanctuary of Silence*, 14–19; and for H's distinctive phraseology on Sabbath, see Lev 25:1–7, ibid., 122; contra Saul M. Olyan, "Exodus 31:12–17: The Sabbath according to H, or the Sabbath according to P and H?" *JBL* 124 (2005): 201–09.

16 Knohl argues that the lack of a specific prohibition against work in 2:2–3 means Gen 1 is P and not H, on which see below; Israel Knohl, *The Divine Symphony: The Bible's Many Voices* (Philadelphia: The Jewish Publication Society, 2003), 163–64.

17 This excludes, of course, the geographical name Kadesh (קדש) at Gen 14:7; 16:14; and 20:1, and the cult prostitute (קדשה) at Gen 38:21–22.

18 Matitiahu Tsevat, "The Basic Meaning of the Biblical Sabbath," in *The Meaning of the Book of Job and Other Biblical Studies: Essays on the Literature and Religion of the Hebrew Bible* (New York: Ktav Publishing House, 1980), 39–52, esp. 49; repr. from *ZAW* 84 (1972): 447–59.

19 Knohl, *Sanctuary of Silence*, 14–19 and 162–63; Knohl, "The Priestly Torah," 72–77.

specifically as a Holiness theme (as at Exod 20:11 and 31:17). By contrast, P contains no explicit prohibition against Sabbath work, and in fact, the only clear mention of the Sabbath in P (assuming Gen 2:2–3 is H) is concerned only with proper sacrifices to be offered on this day (Num 28:9–10). Indeed, any mention of Sabbath in a P creation account, especially one connecting Sabbath to the concept of God's 'resting,' would be surprising given P's focus on the cultic sphere and the essential numinous dimension of God, along with its aversion for anthropomorphic and anthropopathic descriptions of God. This leaves Knohl with the unusual move of suggesting that Gen 2:2–3 is actually P's compromise with popular religion, a concession to a lesser position, by accepting and portraying the Sabbath in the pre-Mosaic period narrated in Genesis. Thus it is possible to propose that H developed its prohibition against Sabbath work elsewhere based on P's reluctant concession in Gen 2:2–3.[20] As with most such theories, the simplest explanation is usually the most likely, and it seems simpler in my opinion to assume, with Amit, Firmage, and Milgrom, that Gen 2:2–3 is itself from the hand of a Holiness author. If so, then for reasons noted above, so too must the entire chapter be from the hand of the Holiness author/redactor.

## III. The Animals

Another topic that the author of Gen 1 found to be inadequately treated in Gen 2 is that of Israel's animal taxonomy. The author of Gen 1 felt a particular need to prepare the reader for the dietary restrictions of Lev 11, which the older creation account of Gen 2 had not properly done. That account, which I believe the author of Gen 1 had before him as an authoritative text, assumed a vegetarian diet for the first human couple (2:16), while animals were created for the sole purpose of human companionship (2:18–19). Although this would be modified further after the flood account,[21] the author of Gen 1 was not satisfied with what he perceived as

[20] Thomas J. King, *The Realignment of the Priestly Literature: The Priestly Narrative in Genesis and Its Relation to Priestly Legislation and the Holiness School* (Princeton Theological Monograph Series 102; Eugene: Wipf & Stock Publishers, 2009), 145–47. Similarly, it is possible to argue that the prohibition itself is avoided because of P's position that no law was given prior to the Israelites' arrival at Sinai; Joel S. Baden, "Identifying the Original Stratum of P: Theoretical and Practical Considerations," in Shectman and Baden (eds.), *The Strata of the Priestly Writings*, 13–29, esp. 21–22.

[21] Gen 9:2–3. Although Gen 9:1–17 is typically assigned to P, the presence of themes from Gen 1 ("be fruitful and multiply," 9:1) and "covenant" (ברית), instead of "testimony"

a failure in Gen 2 to distinguish properly among the various sorts of animals, which would of course provide for the proper distinctions between acceptable and unacceptable animals for consumption. Central to this discussion, and often commented upon by scholars, is the role of the lexeme בדל (Hiphil, הבדיל). Simply put, "the making of distinctions ... is the essence of the priestly function."[22] It has a cultic sense of separating clean from unclean, or the holy from the common (Lev 10:10; cf. Lev 20:25), and yet H also uses it for separation between peoples (Num 16:21; Lev 20:24, 26).[23] Indeed, this verb is central to H's doctrine of holiness, modeled after YHWH himself who brings order from chaos, so that the whole world, the nations of the world, and animals of nature must all be so distinguished in Israel's pursuit of holiness.[24] Central to our focus here, the use of בדל in Lev 11:47 in the culminating statement distinguishing clean from unclean foods has often been compared to its use in Gen 1 (verses 4, 6, 7, 14, 18). Although none of these uses in Gen 1 is specifically about animals or the dietary laws, they reflect an interest in the chapter in the separation of items not belonging together, which is also a separation of items for specific tasks (light vs. darkness, waters above vs. waters below, and day vs. night). Accordingly, the precise spelling of this term for distinguishing between clean and unclean animals in Lev 11:47 is found also in Gen 1:14a: "Let there be lights in the dome of the sky *to separate* (להבדיל) the day from the night." The author of Gen 1 had other lexical options for drawing such distinctions (e.g., פרד, "separate," *DCH* 6:754–55; *HALOT* 3:962–63), but he chose this particular term, making an intentional link between Gen 1 and Lev 11 entirely plausible.[25] In general, Gen 1 explains that God separates and sorts out the various components of the new cosmos according to function, just as later Israelites must separate and sort animals for consumption—clean from the unclean.

(עדות), lead me to assume a Holiness composition for it as well. In this case, the Holiness School would be responsible for the progression from vegetarianism to meat-eating to the dietary laws.

[22] Jacob Milgrom, *Leviticus 1–16: A New Translation with Introduction and Commentary* (AB 3; New York: Doubleday, 1991), 615.

[23] For discussion of the role of H in the redaction of the final form of the book of Numbers, and especially as it relates to Num 16:21, see Knohl, *Sanctuary of Silence*, 78–85 and 88, n. 89.

[24] Milgrom, *Leviticus 17–22*, 1411–12.

[25] Many scholars assume a mixture of P and H in Lev 11, accepting at least H interpolations at 11:39–40 and 43–45, and assuming H is responsible for the final form; Milgrom, *Leviticus 1–16*, 691–98; Knohl, *Sanctuary of Silence*, 69–70.

The primary level taxa in Gen 1 and Lev 11 are highly complex.[26] In particular, two separate fourfold schema have been conflated in Lev 11 to form a fivefold schema: (1) high carriage land animals, (2) low carriage land animals, (3) two-legged aerial animals, (4) six-legged aerial animals, and (5) aquatic animals.[27] The author of Gen 1 employed a simpler threefold schema (land animals, aerial animals, and aquatic animals; Gen 1:20–25, 28), although at times this was a truncated fourfold schema (1:30) or even a fivefold taxonomic schema (1:26).[28] The zoological specifics are quite complex, but Richard Whitekettle has shown that the ancient Israelites tolerated a great deal of latitude in the way they categorized animals. They allowed fluidity between a large number of schema, as the examples in Gen 1 and Lev 11 show, and there was no formal taxonomic system although all worked with the basic categories of land animals, aerial animals, and aquatic animals. Yet this last observation—the preponderance of three basic categories, land, aerial, and aquatic—brings us to an exception in Gen 2:19–20. The first mention of animals in the older creation account uses a truncated threefold schema resulting in only two categories: land and aerial animals (2:19). The next verse relies on a fourfold schema, which is however also truncated, this time yielding three categories: domesticated land animals, wild land animals, and aerial animals (2:20).[29] The creation account in Gen 2 omits aquatic animals altogether, which is a rarity in the Hebrew Bible. The references to the animals in Gen 2:19–20 may simply reflect the older and less developed taxonomic categories when compared to Gen 1 or Lev 11.[30] In any case, it is at least suggestive that the author of Gen 1 thought these truncated references to the animals in Gen 2, omitting as they do any mention of the aquatic category, needed supplementation. Thus the fuller lists of Gen 1:20–28 were slightly correcting the older creation account of Gen 2, and preparing the reader for the dietary laws of Lev 11.[31]

---

[26] For more on how the Israelites gave conceptual order to their inventory of animals, see Richard Whitekettle, "Where the Wild Things Are: Primary Level Taxa in Israelite Zoological Thought," *JSOT* 93 (2001): 17–37.

[27] Ibid., 31–33.

[28] Ibid., 19–20, 24–27, and 29–31.

[29] For details and discussion, see ibid., 19–20 and 27–28.

[30] Indeed, Whitekettle (ibid., 33–34) has shown that the texts support a basic development from simpler to more complex classification schemata.

[31] For similar conclusions on different grounds, see Firmage, "Genesis 1," esp. 104–10.

## IV. The Festivals

A third topic central to the composition of Gen 1 is the apparent lack of knowledge in Gen 2 of Israel's national festivals, or at least a failure to prepare for and appreciate them fully. The absence of any references to the creation of time and especially the markers of time (sun, moon, and stars) was an inadequacy of Gen 2 that Gen 1 intentionally sets out to rectify. In the older account, after the initial assertion that "YHWH God made the earth and the heavens" (2:4b), there is no further mention of the heavens, and there is no mention of celestial bodies at all. It is my contention that the author of Gen 1 sets out to prepare the reader for the "appointed festivals" of YHWH (מועדי יהוה) of Lev 23,[32] by addressing generally the creation of time in 1:3–5, which is more important for this author than the creation of space.[33] Even this is preparatory to the author's creation of the sun, moon, and stars "for signs and for seasons and for days and years" at 1:14b, which sets up a specific trajectory for Lev 23. Indeed, the rest of the paragraph describes in detail the creation of the lights in the dome to separate light from darkness, day from night, to rule the day and nighttime, and to give light to the earth (1:14–19), all while carefully side-stepping the Hebrew words for sun and moon, of course, in order to avoid association with the names for the deities, Shemesh and Yarikh, and in order to objectify the celestial bodies as much as possible.[34] Specifically it is the redundant purpose clause of v. 14b that comes to the author's central concern: time itself and the time-markers of the dome are created for the express purpose of notifying the Israelites when they must observe their sacred festivals, especially Passover and Unleavened Bread (Lev 23:5–8), Firstfruits (Lev 23:9–22), Feast of Trumpets (Lev 23:23–25), Yom Kippur (Lev 23:26–32), and Succoth (Lev 23:33–43).[35] Together these

---

[32] Cf. Lev 23:3, 4, 37, 44. N.B.: the occurrence in v. 44 is written defectively: מעדי יהוה. We also find here reference to "my [YHWH's] appointed festivals" (מועדי, 23:2) and to convocations to be celebrated "at the time appointed for them" (במועדם, 23:4). Cf. also Num 29:39; Ps 104:19. On the technical sense of מועד as festival, (time of) appointed feast for Israel's national festivals, see *DCH* 5:179–82, esp. 181–82, and Klaus Koch, "מוֹעֵד," *TDOT* 8:167–73, esp. 169–71.

[33] Walter Vogels, "The Cultic and Civil Calendars of the Fourth Day of Creation (Gen 1,14b)," *SJOT* 11 (1997): 163–80, esp. 178–79.

[34] Arnold, *Genesis*, 42–43.

[35] For the argument that Sabbath-observance (Lev 23:2b–3) is an interpolation of the exilic Holiness redactor, cf. Jacob Milgrom, *Leviticus 23–27: A New Translation with Introduction and Commentary* (AB 3B; New York: Doubleday, 2001), 1954–55.

are the "appointed festivals" of YHWH (מועדי יהוה) as is emphasized at the beginning and conclusion of the list (Lev 23:2, 4 and 44, and cf. v. 37).

This functional use of heavenly bodies is similar to that of Mesopotamian cosmogony, in which the creating deities placed them in the skies as signs of the course of time intentionally so humans would observe them and measure time by them, and to direct their lives according to the divine will revealed in them.[36] One also finds references in Babylonian texts to "heavenly writings" (*šiṭir šamāmī*, or *šiṭir burūmê*) as a metaphor, in which the sun, moon, and stars are heavenly script with the capacity to be read and interpreted.[37] We have numerous Mesopotamian texts, including the *Enuma Elish*, which portray the gods as producers of celestial signs (*ittu or ṣaddu*) at the time of creation.[38] The account of Marduk's creation of heaven in the *Enuma Elish* includes the fixing of heaven itself, the position of the constellations, and the position specifically of Jupiter (i.e., *Neberu*, *Enuma Elish* v:6),[39] as well as the stars and the moon, establishing a twelve-month year and a thirty-day month.[40] While the Babylonian scholars were most interested in observing these phenomena for divinatory purposes, the intent of highlighting them in Gen 1:14 as "signs" and "seasons" is more narrowly focused.[41] In fact, in light of the fascination with celestial signs

[36] Richard J. Clifford, *Creation Accounts in the Ancient Near East and the Bible* (CBQMS 26; Washington, D.C.: Catholic Biblical Association, 1994), 67–73.

[37] Francesca Rochberg, *The Heavenly Writing: Divination, Horoscopy, and Astronomy in Mesopotamian Culture* (Cambridge & New York: Cambridge University Press, 2004), 1–3. For the calendric interests of the most important Babylonian astronomical texts, cf. pp. 6–8.

[38] GISKIM *ittu* A, "sign, omen, ominous sign," which may or may not be related etymologically to Hebrew אות (Gen 1:14b; *CAD* I/J 304–310; *AHw* 406). Alternatively, *ṣaddu*, "sign, signal" (*CAD* Ṣ 56–57; *AHw* 1073), and at times these two terms occur in parallelism (*CAD* I/J 307–8). We have numerous texts illustrating the perception of such signs, although most are not specifically related to creation of the cosmos; e.g., a Neo-Assyrian letter-writer reports "the signs—whether of heaven or earth or [of the divinatory series] *šumma izbu*, as many as there were—I wrote them down," *ABL* 223:6–7; cf. Simo Parpola, *Letters from Assyrian and Babylonian Scholars* (SAA 10; Helsinki, Finland: Helsinki University Press, 1993), 4, text #2.

[39] Cf. *AHw* 773–74; *CAD* N, 147.

[40] *Enuma Elish* iv:138–v:49; Benjamin R. Foster, "Epic of Creation," *COS* 1.111:390–402, esp. 398–99, Stephanie Dalley, *Myths from Mesopotamia: Creation, the Flood, Gilgamesh, and Others* (2nd ed.; Oxford: Oxford University Press, 2000), 254–56. Marduk specifically makes mention of these as "celestial signs" at v:23 to be observed in the sky for direction. Unfortunately, the text is broken at the point of his creation of the sun at v:23–48; Philippe Talon, *Enūma Eliš: The Standard Babylonian Creation Myth* (SAACT 4; Helsinki: The Neo-Assyrian Text Corpus Project, 2005), 57.

[41] For more on the celestial bodies as communicative signs and the conceptual framework behind lunar, planetary, meteorological, and stellar phenomena as divine writ, see Rochberg, *Heavenly Writing*, 165–202 and 259–86.

in Mesopotamian texts, it seems likely the author of Gen 1 has set out intentionally to distinguish Israel's use of these phenomena as marks of sacred festivals from the Babylonian focus on divinatory readings of the signs. In Gen 1, the signs of heaven have been transformed from divinatory guidelines to be read by the well-informed into a sacred calendar in the sky on display for all Israelites to follow.

Genesis 1:14b is a consecutive clause following a jussive in the previous clause (1:14a), and here expressing purpose; God calls the celestial bodies into existence in order for them to serve as something specific.[42] The three successive prepositional phrases introduced by ל have a utilitarian goal, denoting the specific purpose for the lights of the dome: they are to be used "for signs and for seasons and for days and years."[43] "Signs" (אתת) is ambiguous, denoting concepts as diverse as memorials, tokens of proof, portents of the future, miraculous events, as well as the occasional use for sacred festivals (e.g., Exod 13:9; 31:13).[44] Because of this ambiguity, "signs" is modified by the two additional prepositional phrases in epexegetical fashion: "for seasons and for days and years." The English translation of ולמועדים as "and for seasons" (NRSV, and passim) is especially indelicate in this context because it gives the impression the author has in view the yearly four seasons, whereas it has been shown convincingly that in this context the term is referring to the festivals and religious feast days of Israel's liturgical calendar.[45] As we have seen, this term is a *leitwort* in Lev 23, and is central to Israel's understanding of the various sacred days as holy convocations (מקרא־קדש, Lev 23:3, 7, 8, 21, etc.).[46] To remove any remaining ambiguity, the author has further modified this purpose clause in v. 14b with one final prepositional phrase: ולימים ושנים, "and for days and years." The lights in the dome are not only marking the passage of time but their specific *raison d'être* is for marking Israel's religious calendar, as is routinely done in Lev 23 to determine when to celebrate the festival; e.g., "in the first month, on the fourteenth day of the month..." (Lev 23:5). By progressively narrowing the focus—from signs, to appointed festivals, to days and years—the author of Gen 1:14 has shown that the sun, moon,

---

42 Joüon, 119k; Bill T. Arnold and John H. Choi, *A Guide to Biblical Hebrew Syntax* (Cambridge and New York: Cambridge University Press, 2003), 89.

43 For the preposition ל to denote "for the purpose of, to be used for" see *DCH* 4:481–82.

44 Cf. *DCH* 1:165–67.

45 Vogels, "Cultic and Civil Calendars," 163–66. I find the hendiadyc proposal of Speiser highly unlikely: "let them mark the fixed times," Ephraim A. Speiser, *Genesis: Introduction, Translation, and Notes* (AB 1; Garden City, N.Y.: Doubleday, 1964), LXVII.

46 And cf. Num 10:10; 15:3; 28:2; 29:39 and Deut 31:10.

and stars were given for the purpose of calendrical calculations related to Israel's festivals, and has therefore prepared the reader for subsequent texts, especially Lev 23.

## V. Concluding Remarks

The three foci surveyed here—Sabbath-observance, animal taxonomy, and sacred festivals—are distinctive concerns of H, and permeate all of Gen 1. H's phraseology and theology are not limited to Gen 2:2–3 but permeate the whole chapter. Indeed, it is possible that the creation of the human in 1:26–27 in the *imago Dei* is also H's critique of, and supplement to, the older account's placement of the human in Eden "to till it and keep it" (2:15b). But the specific way in which Gen 1:26–27 might be connected to subsequent Holiness texts of the Pentateuch is not as clear as it is in the case of the three topics presented above, and at any rate, the issues surrounding 1:26–27 are too complex for brief treatment.[47] In sum, we should consider it a strong possibility, perhaps becoming a probability, that Gen 1 was composed by a scholar of the Holiness school.[48] We may speculate about sources he had before him but primary among them was the creation account of Gen 2, which he viewed as authoritative to the point of being unassailable. He simply could not dismiss it, or contravene its propositions. Nevertheless, he considered Gen 2 inadequate as *the* creation account for ancient Israel, and was compelled to counterbalance it in at least these three important ways. He composed Gen 1 as a new creation account, intentionally with other Holiness texts or Holiness redactions in view; especially those related to Sabbath-observance (Exod 31:12–17 and 35:2–3), dietary law (Lev 11), and religious festivals (Lev 23).

In these brief reflections, I have investigated the relationship between Gen 1 and Gen 2. But this naturally raises questions about Gen 1 and the Eden Narrative (so, including Gen 3), the Scroll of Adam's Descendants (Gen 5), the Flood Narrative (Gen 6:9–9:29), and the ancestral narratives of Genesis. Similar observations and results may be possible for this author's relationship with other texts in Genesis and the Pentateuch. How extensive was the Holiness redaction of Genesis?...of the Pentateuch? These are questions currently being addressed by a number of scholars

[47] But see Firmage, "Genesis 1," 101–3.

[48] And so we would support the suggestions of Amit, Firmage, and the later speculations of Milgrom, although he was unable to develop this further.

reconsidering the relationship of H to P. What I am proposing is that Gen 1 is more akin to an ancient theogony than cosmogony,[49] and as such it functions as a prologue for J's account of creation and other materials in the book of Genesis, and does so intentionally.

"All beginnings are difficult."[50] In Mesopotamia, it seems likely the older Atra-hasis epic was considered inadequate as a beginning, and so it was replaced by the *Enuma Elish*.[51] The latter intentionally began with a temporal clause, *enūma elish* "when on high…," perhaps in order to supplant the older Atra-hasis epic's beginning line, *inūma ilu awīlum* "when the gods like men…".[52] The new creation story was thus written to supplement or supplant an older but well-known account. Similarly, the author of Gen 1 was not satisfied with Gen 2 as a beginning. As in the Mesopotamian texts, our author has produced a new text, beginning with an entirely new temporal clause in order to supplement and nuance the older account beginning with its own temporal clause: "In the day that the LORD God made…" (2:4b).[53] Perhaps the author of Gen 1 accepted Gen 2 as a theologoumenon, or theological conversation partner, one he considered inherently authoritative. And so he produced a new beginning intended to complement and slightly correct the perspectives of Gen 2. How much he also reworked and supplemented other P and non-P texts of Genesis and the rest of the Pentateuch is a topic for further research.

---

49 For this generic distinction, see Frank Moore Cross, "The 'Olden Gods' in Ancient Near Eastern Creation Myths and in Israel," in *From Epic to Canon: History and Literature in Ancient Israel* (ed. Frank Moore Cross; Baltimore: Johns Hopkins University Press, 1998), 73–83, and for my discussion on how this relates to Gen 1, see Arnold, *Genesis*, 45–47.

50 כל התחלות קשות; *Mek. Jethro* 19,5.

51 This is particularly so since Atra-hasis does not actually recount a creation of the cosmos but of humanity only; Wilfred G. Lambert, Alan R. Millard and Miguel Civil, *Atra-hasis: The Babylonian Story of The Flood* (Winona Lake, Ind.: Eisenbrauns, 1999).

52 Bernard F. Batto, *Slaying the Dragon: Mythmaking in the Biblical Tradition* (Louisville, Ky.: Westminster/John Knox, 1992), 38–39.

53 I have argued that the syntax of 1:1–3 was, in fact, modeled after that of 2:4b–7: (1) dependent, temporal clause, 1:1 and 2:4b; (2) parenthetical circumstantial clause, 1:2 and 2:5–6; and (3) main clause, 1:3 and 2:7; Arnold, *Genesis*, 35 and 56. It seems likely the temporal clause of Gen 5:1b was also in view; ibid., 85.

# WHO DESTROYED ASHKELON?
# ON SOME PROBLEMS IN RELATING TEXT TO ARCHAEOLOGY

Hans M. Barstad

The destruction of Ashkelon by Nebuchadnezzar in 604 BCE appears to belong among the better-known facts of scholarship.[1] At least this is what we may learn when presented with the secondary literature in the area. Since publications are numerous, however, I can only mention a couple of the more recent studies in the present context.

Quite representative, and particularly influential, of course, are some of the more prestigious encyclopaedias of our subject. According to David Schloen, the Philistine period ended with Nebuchadnezzar's destruction of the city in 604 BCE. Schloen also claims that:

> Evidence has also been found for the final fiery destruction of Philistine Ashkelon in 604 BCE, including the complete skeleton of one of the victims of the disaster lying amid the burnt debris.[2]

And Lawrence Stager writes: "In 604 BCE, Nebuchadnezzar destroyed Ashkelon and led Aga', the last king of Philistine Ashkelon, into exile in Babylon."[3]

---

[1] The Jubilar and the present author have spent much time in the Isaiah scroll. I am very grateful that I can offer these few lines on another common interest.

[2] See David Schloen, "Ashkelon," in *OEANE* 1:222.

[3] See Lawrence E. Stager, "Ashkelon," in *NEAEHL* 1:104. Since this article provides a fine survey of prevalent views concerning the destruction of Ashkelon, I will comment and quote from it in some detail. In Stager's *NEAEHL* essay, there is very little documentation for Iron II (p. 107) whereas the Persian period is the richest on the site (pp. 107–108). There is no mention of the Babylonian period under 'excavation results,' which indicates that little relevant to the Neo-Babylonian period has been found. Under 'history' (p. 104), Stager writes: "In the seventh century BCE Ashkelon was ruled by Mitinti II, son of Sidqa, a vassal of Esarhaddon and of Ashurbanipal. After the decline of the Assyrian empire in the West, first the Egyptians (in the time of Psamtik I) and then the Babylonians gained ascendancy. In 604 BCE, Nebuchadnezzar destroyed Ashkelon and led Aga', the last king of Philistine Ashkelon, into exile in Babylon. The sons of Aga', sailors, and various nobles received rations from Nebuchadnezzar. Herodotus (I, 103–106) reports that Scythian soldiers sacked the temple of Aphrodite Ouriana (the Celestial Aphrodite) at Ashkelon, which was considered by the Greeks to be the 'oldest temple consecrated to this deity.' Because Scythians served in Nebuchadnezzar's army, it is possible that Herodotus singled out this episode to epitomize the general destruction of Ashkelon by the Babylonians in 604 BCE Mopsus, seer and hero of the Trojan war, reached Ashkelon and died there (according to

Quite characteristic is also the following quotation taken from Donald Redford:

> Meanwhile, in the same month, Nebuchadnezzar invested Ashkelon. Before the end of December it had been captured and utterly destroyed. Antimenidas, a Greek mercenary and brother of the poet Alcaeus, was serving with the Babylonian army on this occasion; and a fragment of Alcaeus in honor of his brother's homecoming describes the awful fate of the city, many of whose inhabitants had been sent to the House of Hades. The remaining population together with Aga the king was deported to Babylonia, where an expatriate community calling itself 'Ashkelon' was to be found in the following century. The uninhabited ruins were to stand a haunt for the wild beasts for over a hundred years, a mute witness to the Babylonian fury.[4]

Ephraim Stern writes laconically that Nebuchadnezzar conquered Ashkelon in 604 BCE, and "took its king captive, destroyed the city, and deported all its inhabitants."[5] Daniel M. Master also considers the destruction of Ashkelon during the Neo-Babylonian period to be an historical fact:

> ... when Nebuchadnezzar destroyed Ashkelon in 604 BCE. Nebuchadnezzar claims to have made the site a 'tell,' and recent archaeological excavations have shown that he accomplished his goal.[6]

We notice from the few, but fairly representative, quotations above, how Schloen refers to evidence for the final fiery destruction of Philistine Ashkelon; Stager writes that the city was destroyed; Redford that it was utterly destroyed, and that all inhabitants were deported to Babylon; Stern that all inhabitants were deported; Master that the destruction made the city

---

the fifth-century BCE Lydian historian Xanthos). Under the Persians, Ashkelon became a 'city of the Tyrians' and the headquarters of a Tyrian governor (Pseudo-Scylax, Periplus I, 78, late fourth century BCE). The Phoenicians curried favors from their Persian overlords by providing naval power and maritime wealth. Coastal cities as far south as Ashkelon grew rich from Phoenician commerce ..." (p. 104).

[4] Donald B. Redford, *Egypt, Canaan, and Israel in Ancient Times* (Princeton, NJ: Princeton University Press, 1992), 455–56.

[5] Ephraim Stern, *Archaeology of the Land of the Bible*. Vol. 2. *The Assyrian, Babylonian, and Persian Periods 732–332 BCE* (ABRL; New York: Doubleday, 2001), 304.

[6] Daniel M. Master, "Trade and Politics: Ashkelon's Balancing Act in the Seventh Century BCE," *BASOR* 330 (2003): 47–64, 61. Master, in another essay, dates a market place at Ashkelon in the following way: "The date of this market is secure because fills beneath it contain East Greek Wild Goat II pottery, creating a *terminus post quem* for the foundation of the market of at least 625 BCE Moreover, the end of the Ashkelon market is marked by the comprehensive destruction wrought by Nebuchadnezzar in 604 BCE" Daniel M. Master, "From the Buqêʿah to Ashkelon," in *Exploring the* Longue Durée. *Essays in Honor of Lawrence E. Stager* (ed. J. David Schloen; Winona Lake, IN: Eisenbrauns, 2009), 305–17, 312.

into a tell. All scholars blame Nebuchadnezzar for the destruction, and date it exactly to the year 604 BCE.

## I. Some Questions about the Destruction of Ashkelon

What is particularly striking to an outsider (a non-archaeologist) is the exact dating of the destruction of Ashkelon to the year 604 BCE.[7] Since this date is assumed beforehand to be the time of the event, there appears never to be any real discussion on this point. When Schloen, for instance, refers to details of mass destruction—burnt debris from the latter part of the Iron Age—Ashkelon is automatically connected to 604 BCE because this is already an aspect of scholarly convention.[8] It has become a scientific truth. That the destruction of the city in 604 BCE has become axiomatic in this way is clearly indicated also by the following quotation from Stager:

> Archaeology cannot be so precise as to date the destruction of Ashkelon to 604 BCE, but the Babylonian Chronicle leaves little doubt that the late 7th-century destruction we found all over the site, followed by a 75–80-year gap in occupation until the Persian Period, was the work of Nebuchadrezzar in 604 BCE.[9]

Directly or indirectly, this scholarly consensus concerning the destruction of Ashkelon is strongly influenced by Wiseman's edition of the Neo-Babylonian chronicle texts found in the British Museum, published in 1956.[10] We shall return to Wiseman later. However, in order to facilitate

---

[7] In reality, works that refer to Nebuchadnezzar's destruction of Ashkelon in the year 604 BCE are overwhelming, and not many of them can be referred to here. The scholarly literature varies from fairly comprehensive paraphrasing of the historical event to a few short sentences and minor footnotes. In other words, there can be little doubt that we are dealing with what appears to be an established scholarly fact. For two representative recent examples, see Nadav Na'aman, "When and How Did Jerusalem Become a Great City? The Rise of Jerusalem as Judah's Premier City in the Eighth–Seventh Centuries BCE," *BASOR* 347 (2007): 21–56, n. 4, and David Lipovitch, "A Reconstruction of Achaemenid-Period Ashkelon Based on the Faunal Evidence," in *Exploring the* Longue Durée. *Essays in Honor of Lawrence E. Stager* (ed. J. David Schloen; Winona Lake, IN: Eisenbrauns, 2009), 263–72, 265–66.

[8] Schloen, "Ashkelon," 222.

[9] Lawrence E. Stager, "Ashkelon and the Archaeology of Destruction: Kislev 604 BCE," in *Joseph Aviram Volume* (ed. Abraham Biran, Amnon Ben-Tor, Gideon Foerster, Abraham Malamat, David Ussishkin; Eretz-Israel 25; Jerusalem: The Israel Exploration Society, 1996), 61*–74*, 71*.

[10] Donald J. Wiseman, *Chronicles of Chaldean Kings (626–556 BC) in the British Museum* (repr. of 1956 ed.; London: The British Museum, 1961). I discuss Wiseman's edition below in some detail.

the later discussion it may be useful to present here the text that "leaves little doubt" that Nebuchadnezzar destroyed Ashkelon in 604 BCE. I refer to BM 21946 from Grayson's edition (originally published in 1975).

This tablet is in poor condition due to many breaks on the surface. Also, the bottom part of the tablet has been completely lost. Grayson regards the text as part of his "Chronicle 5, Chronicle Concerning the Early Years of Nebuchadnezzar."[11] The historical context is the battle of Carchemish in 605 BCE. Apparently, according to Grayson Chronicle 5, Nebuchadnezzar massacred the Egyptians. This is the time of Pharaoh Necho II (610–595 BCE) but unfortunately there are no surviving Egyptian sources.[12] Grayson's translation for Nebuchadnezzar's first year is as follows:

> 15 The first year of Nebuchadnezzar (II): In the month Sivan he mustered his army and 16 marched to Hattu. Until the month Kislev he marched about victoriously in Hattu. 17 All the kings of Hattu came into his presence and he received their vast tribute. 18 He marched to *Ashkelon* and in the month Kislev he captured it, 19 seized its king, plundered [and sac]ked it. 20 He turned the city into a ruin heap. In the month Shebat he marched away and [returned] to Bab[ylon].[13]

Grayson himself comments on the occurrence of the name 'Ashkelon' in this text that nothing can be read with certainty.[14] Assuming for the moment, however, that 'Ashkelon' is the correct reading, it still appears to me that certain questions arise about how the text has been correlated with the event in question.

It is unfortunate, for example, that so many (including Master, cited above)[15] have taken at face value the claim made by Nebuchadnezzar in line 20 of the chronicle that he made the city in question into a "ruin heap." Self-glorification and overstatements are after all common in ancient Near Eastern chronicles and annals, not least in relation to campaigns

---

[11] A. Kirk Grayson, *Assyrian and Babylonian Chronicles* (repr. of 1975 ed.; TCS 5; Locust Valley, New York: J. J. Augustin; Winona Lake, IN: Eisenbrauns, 2000), 99.

[12] Roberto B. Gozzoli, *The Writing of History in Ancient Egypt during the First Millennium* BC *(ca. 1070–180* BC*). Trends and Perspectives* (Egyptology 5; London: Golden House Publications, 2006), 101. In the same place, Gozzoli also refers to the Neo-Babylonian attack on Egypt very much later in Nebuchadnezzar's career.

[13] Grayson, *Assyrian and Babylonian Chronicles*, 100.

[14] I quote Grayson's comment in full: "18 uru x-x-(x)-*il-lu-nu*: Nothing can be read with certainty. Wiseman read: uru *Iš*(?)-*qi*(?)-*il-lu-nu*. Cf. Wiseman, Chron. p. 28 and p. 58." (Grayson, *Assyrian and Babylonian Chronicles*, 100).

[15] Master, "Trade and Politics," 61.

and battles.[16] Also, the demolition of whole cities was not feasible in this time-period, either from a military logistics perspective or from the point of view of Neo-Babylonian economy and imperial policy in general (cf. also below). Some scholars (including Master)[17] argue that the interests of Assyria in relation to Ashkelon were purely political and military, and that there was no economic interest. This is unlikely from what we now know about how empires were run in the first millennium.[18] Trade, tribute and military operations abroad cannot be separated.

Similarly, the idea expressed by not a few scholars that a city's entire population might have been deported is also impossible for various, but above all for logistical reasons. Here, the information in line 19 of our text ("seized its king...") probably describes what actually happened. Nebuchadnezzar had inherited this practice, a way of controlling and running the empire, from the Assyrians. When a king conspired against the Assyrian or Babylonian kings, he was replaced, and taken to Babylon or Assyria as an "honorary captive."

A different kind of problem is represented by Stager's use of mostly classical sources in his survey of the history of Ashkelon (Herodotus, Xanthus, Pseudo-Scylax).[19] However, this may occasionally cause problems. In earlier times, classical authors were considered among the most important sources for our knowledge of the history of the ancient Near East. Today, as a result of the fast growing corpus of contemporary Mesopotamian documents, this is regarded as more problematic.[20] Clearly, this does not imply that classical texts should not be used. Occasionally, they may

---

16 On the very partial view of the fall of Babylon in Assyrian sources, see John A. Brinkman, "Through a Glass Darkly. Esarhaddon's Retrospects on the Downfall of Babylon," *JAOS* 103 (1983): 35–42. On the Babylonian Chronicle as a historical source, see John A. Brinkman, "The Babylonian Chronicle Revisited," in *Lingering Over Words. Studies in Ancient Near Eastern Literature in Honor of William L. Moran* (ed. Tzvi Abusch, John Huehnergard, and Piotr Steinkeller; HSS 37; Atlanta, Georgia: Harvard Semitic Museum, 1990), 73–104.

17 Master, "Trade and Politics," *passim*.

18 A growing number of studies deals with Neo-Babylonian imperial economy in particular. See, for instance, Bernd Funck, "Studien zur sozialökonomischen Situation Babyloniens im 7. und 6. Jahrhundert v. u. Z.", in *Gesellschaft und Kultur im Alten Vorderasien* (ed. Horst Klengel; SGKAO 15; Berlin: Akademie-Verlag, 1982), 47–67. See also below under heading II.

19 See footnote 3 above.

20 Amélie Kuhrt, "Assyrian and Babylonian Traditions in Classical Authors. A Critical Synthesis," in *Mesopotamien und seine Nachbarn. Politische und kulturelle Wechselbeziehungen im alten Vorderasien vom 4. bis. 1. Jahrtausend.* XXV Rencontre assyriologique internationale Berlin 3. bis 7. Juli 1978 (ed. Hans J. Nissen and J. Renger; Berliner Beiträge zum Vorderen Orient I:2; Berlin: Reimer, 1982), 539–53.

even be regarded as very useful. However, no text should be taken at face value. It is imperative that each and every case is looked into separately and accurately. In my view, the sources used by Stager are not sufficient, nor adequately discussed.

When we do turn to the Mesopotamian documents, they press upon us the question as to *which* events should be correlated with the archaeological evidence of mass destructions in the region—specifically, whether we should be thinking of events in the earlier Neo-Assyrian history, prior to the Neo-Babylonian period and to the 604 BCE in particular. From Neo-Assyrian sources we learn that Ashkelon, similar to other powerful city-states of this period, took part on more than one occasion in political and military alliances in order to throw off the Assyrian oppression. Moreover, Ashkelon was possibly more inflexible and rebelled even more than other city states of the Neo-Assyrian Empire. The consequence of this, of course, would be a string of punitive campaigns. From the series of rebellious kings in Ashkelon during the Neo-Assyrian period, I will mention two here. The confrontations occurred under the reigns of Tiglath-pileser III (744–727 BCE) and Sennacherib (704–681 BCE).

Tiglath-pileser III's difficulties with Ashkelon in the campaign of 733–732 BCE are well known.[21] Metinti of Ashkelon paid tribute, but revolted later in an anti-Assyrian alliance. Following this event, Metinti was replaced by Rukinti.[22] Destruction levels have been found in Philistia following these campaigns.[23] My question is: Why are not the campaigns of 733–732 BCE at least discussed in connection with the burnt debris found at Ashkelon?

From Sennacherib's annals, we learn how the third campaign of 701 was directed against Syria. Ashkelon (king Sidqa) and Sidon were taken by force, but other states like Ammon, Arvad, Ashdod, Byblos, Edom, Moab,

---

[21] See A. Kirk Grayson, "Assyria," in *CAH* 3,2:71–102, 78; Roland Lamprichs, *Die Westexpansion des neuassyrischen Reiches. Eine Strukturanalyse* (AOAT 239; Neukirchen-Vluyn: Neukirchener Verlag, 1995), 122, 136, 148; Walter Mayer, *Politik und Kriegskunst der Assyrer* (ALASP 9; Münster: Ugarit Verlag, 1995), 308–09.

[22] For a reference to the rebellion of Metinti of Ashkelon under Tiglath-pileser in the Calah annals, see Hayim Tadmor, *The Inscriptions of Tiglath-pileser III King of Assyrian. Critical Edition, with Introductions, Translations and Commentary* (2nd printing of 1994 ed., with *addenda et corrigenda*; Jerusalem: The Israel Academy of Sciences and Humanities, 2007), 82–83. The same Mitinti, a son of Sidqa, appears to have grown up and to have been educated at the Assyrian court (Lamprichs, *Die Westexpansion*, 161, n. 13, 256).

[23] Terence C. Mitchell, "Israel and Judah From the Coming of Assyrian Domination Until the Fall of Samaria, and the Struggle for Independence in Judah (c. 750–700 BC)," in *CAH* 3,2: 335.

and Samsimurum paid tribute without resistance.[24] The latter was the normal procedure. Again, one could ask: Are there any reasons why Sennacherib's campaign against Ashkelon should not be connected with the massive destruction remains found at Ashkelon?

These questions gain further force when we consider the innate difficulties concerning the identification of the destruction layers at Ashkelon itself. In his *NEAEHL* article on the city, Stager asserts that the tell was not occupied during the Neo-Babylonian period, and indeed he does not refer to any Neo-Babylonian evidence.[25] The Persian period, he claims, is by far the richest on the site. However, from Near Eastern archaeology and history in general we know that it has always been a problem to distinguish clearly between Achaemenid material culture and local cultures. Because of the way "the Persian Empire" was run for over 200 years, it left few distinct material traces (it is "the invisible empire"). It is, for instance, difficult to distinguish between Mesopotamian and Achaemenid[26] and between Phoenician and Achaemenid cultures.[27] My question would be: how then is it possible to distinguish so clearly between Philistine and Persian cultures in the way it has been done by Stager and others? How can one be sure that the destructions in question are from the Neo-Babylonian period? How can one distinguish between destructions made during late Neo-Assyrian and early Neo-Babylonian times, or during late Neo-Babylonian and early Achaemenid periods? This is, I believe, a problem.

## II. Mesopotamian Imperial Policy and the Philistines

First millennium Mesopotamia has, typically, been referred to as "The Age of the Empires."[28] In reality, the Neo-Babylonian Empire of the 6th century

---

[24] For Sennacherib's 701 campaign, see Grayson, *CAH* 3,2: 110; Lamprichs, *Die Westexpansion*, 148–49; Mayer, *Politik und Kriegskunst*, 100, n. 3, 356–57.

[25] See footnote 3 above.

[26] Ernie Haerinck, "Babylonia under Achaemenid Rule," in *Mesopotamia and Iran in the Persian Period: Conquest and Imperialism 539–331. Proceedings of a Seminar in Memory of Vladimir G. Lukonin* (ed. John Curtis; London: British Museum Press, 1997), 26–34.

[27] Josette Elayi, "La domination perse sur les cités phéniciennes," in *Atti del II Congresso internazionale di studi fenici e punici. Roma, 9–14 Novembre 1987 1* (CSF 30; Roma: Istituto per la civiltà fenicia e punica. Consiglio nazionale della ricerche, 1991), 77–85.

[28] See, for instance, Francis Joannès, *The Age of Empires. Mesopotamia in the First Millennium* (transl. Antonia Nevill; Edinburgh: Edinburgh University Press, 2004). One advantage of this volume is that it is short, but succinct and recent, and written by an Assyriologist who also works with historical issues. The presentation is definitely based on a *longue*

was only the fifth in line of successful empires in Mesopotamia. The earlier ones were those of Sargon of Akkad (23rd century), the Third Dynasty of Ur (21st century), Hammurabi of Babylon (18th century), and the Neo-Assyrian Empire (8th–7th centuries BCE).[29]

A major concern in the history of Mesopotamia in the first millennium is continuation and consolidation. The story of the Neo-Assyrian, Neo-Babylonian ("Chaldean"), and Achaemenid ("Persian") empires is also the story of how empires "inherit" their predecessors. The respective founders of these empires, Tiglath-pileser III (c. 744–727),[30] Nebuchadnezzar II (c. 604–562), and Cyrus II (c. 559–530), were not really innovative. Following the initial takeover and strengthening of positions, the control of the vast empires was kept up above all through more or less annual military campaigns throughout the empire. These campaigns were combined with a rich variety of financial and diplomatic arrangement.

Here, Nebuchadnezzar II is not different from any of his predecessors (or successors). This is seen clearly by Weippert. He comments on the destruction of Ashkelon in the following way:

> In this year and the next [605–604 BCE], after his accession to the throne, Nebuchadnezzar subjugated all of Syria up to the border with Egypt. In general it seems that all that was necessary was the demonstration of Babylonian military might. Only of the Philistine city of Ascalon is it reported that she barred her gates against Nebuchadnezzar, who subsequently conquered and destroyed her at the close of 604.[31]

Nebuchadnezzar inherited the Neo-Assyrian trade empire, and he expanded it. During the Neo-Babylonian period trade flourished as never

*durée* perspective, and Joannès shows how imperial macro-economy and international politics go hand in hand. Cf. also Mogens Trolle Larsen, "The Tradition of Empire in Mesopotamia," in *Power and Propaganda. A Symposium on Ancient Empires* (ed. Mogens Trolle Larsen; Mesopotamia. CSA 7; Copenhagen: Akademisk Forlag, 1979), 75–103.

29 William Hallo and William Kelly Simpson, *The Ancient Near East. A History* (New York: Harcourt Brace Jovanovich, 1971), 173–74.

30 Tiglath-pileser III, regarded as the founder of the Neo-Assyrian Empire, divided his growing territory into provinces. These administrative units made it possible to keep the huge empire together. However, Tiglath-pileser, too, appears to have followed the practice of his predecessors. See Paul Garelli, "The Achievement of Tiglath-pileser III. Novelty or Continuity?" in *AH, ASSYRIA... Studies in Assyrian History and Ancient Near Eastern Historiography Presented to Hayim Tadmor* (ed. Mordechai Cogan and Israel Eph'al; *ScrHier* 33; Jerusalem: Magnes, 1991), 46–51, 46.

31 Manfred Weippert, "The Relations of the States East of the Jordan with the Mesopotamian Powers during the First Millennium BC," *Studies in the History and Archaeology of Jordan* 3 (1987): 97–105, 101.

before.[32] Yet again, we notice how continuity represents a key word in imperial policy. When Nebuchadnezzar took over the highly successful Neo-Assyrian infrastructure, his goal was to consolidate and expand.

For this reason we learn with interest that some scholars have now begun to look for continuity also within the various parts that made up the enormous empire, including Philistia. Whereas scholars earlier believed that the Philistines were primarily an Iron Age I phenomenon, more and more is now known about the continued existence of the Philistines also through the following periods.[33] As noted in a substantial study by Bryan Stone, the Philistines suffered a similar fate to Judah during the Neo-Babylonian period.[34] Thus, the Babylonian conquest may not have completely wiped out the Philistines and their culture. After the destruction of Ekron and Ashdod, there is some evidence of continued Philistine occupation. Also similarly to the fate of Judah, kings from Ashdod, Ashkelon and Gaza received an allowance from the Babylonian king. People from Ashkelon lived in Babylon and near Nippur in settlements named after Gaza and Ashkelon.[35]

Oded and Zadok have written on the topics of foreigners in Babylon on several occasions.[36] Important observations concerning foreigners in Babylon were made by Zadok already a long time ago. One valuable piece of information to be learnt from Zadok is that the number of Phoenicians, Philistines and Moabites in first millennium Mesopotamia was very small.[37] This again fits the situation that only the kings and their extended families,

---

[32] Muhammad A. Dandamaev, "Neo-Babylonian Society and Economy", in *CAH* 3,2: 253–75, in particular 273–75. Cf. also Amihai Mazar, *Archaeology of the Land of the Bible. 10,000–586 BCE* (ABRL; New York: Doubleday, 1990), 549.

[33] A recent survey is found in Seymour Gitin, "Philistia in Transition: The Tenth Century BCE and Beyond," in *Mediterranean Peoples in Transition. Thirteenth to Early Tenth Centuries BCE. In Honor of Professor Trude Dothan* (ed. Seymour Gitin, Amihai Mazar, and Ephraim Stern; Jerusalem: Israel Exploration Society, 1998), 162–183.

[34] Bryan J. Stone, "The Philistines and Acculturation: Culture Change and Ethnic Continuity in the Iron Age," *BASOR* 298 (1995): 7–32, with further literature.

[35] Stone, "The Philistines and Acculturation," 25.

[36] See, for instance, Bustenay Oded, "The Settlements of the Israelite and the Judean Exiles in Mesopotamia in the 8th–6th Centuries BCE," in *Studies in Historical Geography and Biblical Historiography Presented to Zecharia Kallai* (ed. Gershon Galil and Moshe Weinfeld; VTSup 81; Leiden: Brill, 2000), 91–103; Ran Zadok, "Foreigners and Foreign Linguistic Material in Mesopotamia and Egypt," in *Immigration and Emigration Within the Ancient Near East. Festschrift E. Lipiński* (ed. Karel van Lerberghe and Antoon Schoors; OLA 65; Leuven: Peeters, 1995), 431–47.

[37] Ran Zadok, "Phoenicians, Philistines, and Moabites in Mesopotamia," *BASOR* 230 (1978): 57–65, 62.

as well as other key figures necessary for the control of the empire, were "invited" to stay in Babylon.

## III. Wiseman's Chronicles of the Chaldean Kings (1956)

One very important publication in relation to the debate on the fall of Ashkelon is Donald Wiseman's Chronicles of Chaldean Kings, originally published in 1956.[38] The influence is not least reflected in the way in which the book has been used by non-Assyriologists.[39]

Wiseman's transliteration and translation of the relevant part of BM 21946 obv. 18 reads: *a-na (āl)iš?-qi?-il-lu-nu illik-ma*... ("he marched to the city of Askelon..."). [40] Wiseman comments on the toponym Ashkelon in three different places in his book. In addition to the text that I have already quoted, he also writes in the introduction: "The reading of this name is doubtful because of an erasure in the text (see p. 85)."[41] Finally, in "Additional Notes" Wiseman comments on the very conjecture *(āl)iš?-qi?-il-lu-nu*. Here, he writes: "The first two signs are doubtful, being written over an erasure."[42] In the same place, Wiseman explains that he has made the reconstruction "Ashkelon" in BM 21946 because of the occurrence of the name in the contemporary Weidner Chronicle ([*amēl*] *iš-qil-lu-na-a*).[43]

---

[38] I am grateful to my friend Ebbe Egede Knudsen for considerable help with Late Babylonian palaeography. Needless to say, since I am a pure amateur, he should not be blamed for the mistakes I make all the time in this area.

[39] One scholar who was vital in introducing Wiseman's important publication to a wider audience was Abraham Malamat. See Abraham Malamat, "A New Record of Nebuchadrezzar's Palestinian Campaign," *IEJ* 6 (1956): 246–56. The following quotation (from p. 251, n. 15) touches on the text under discussion here: "Although the first two signs of the name are mutilated, Wiseman would appear to be correct in completing: Is[!]-qi-il-lu-nu. These words strike a note reminiscent of the biblical prophecies of wrath directed at this city (Jer. xlvii, 5–7; Zeph. ii, 4–7)."

[40] Wiseman, *Chronicles*, 68–69. Footnote 1 (p. 68) of the quotation refers to the problem with the name Ashkelon. The footnote reads: "Over erasure, see note 85."

[41] Wiseman, *Chronicles*, 28, n. 3. We should also note his comments on p. 28 in support of the conjecture. He discusses mainly two issues, the Aramaic "Adon" letter and the Weidner Chronicle. None of these arguments are acceptable today as support for reading "Ashkelon" into BM 21946 (see below).

[42] Wiseman, *Chronicles*, 85.

[43] See also Donald J. Wiseman, *Nebuchadrezzar and Babylon* (The Schweich Lectures of the British Academy 1983; Oxford: Oxford University Press, 1985), 23 n. 158. In this note, Wiseman's statement that "the reading remains however uncertain" shows clearly that he has not changed his mind from the *editio princeps*. His reference to Grayson in the same footnote implies simply that this view is now supported also by Grayson.

Wiseman also provides his readers with a handwritten copy of BM 21946. Here the erasure with the text over it is clearly indicated.[44] Plate XV also shows that the text ends abruptly after line 18, and that there is no context from which to make any conjectures. In addition, the surface of the text is not at all well preserved.

As Wiseman himself makes quite clear, the toponym Ashkelon does not occur in BM 21946; it is *put into* the texts. This leads to two conclusive observations. The first one is that there is not really much difference between Grayson's "Nothing can be read with certainty" and Wiseman's "The reading of this text is doubtful because of an erasure in the text."[45]

Some have misunderstood this and appear to think that Wiseman may have been persuaded by Grayson to change his original meaning.[46] In reality, what Wiseman does is to sustain his original view. In his Schweich lectures, indeed, he adds further arguments *against* the possibility that Ashkelon is referred to.[47]

---

44 Wiseman, *Chronicles*, Pl. XV.

45 Incidentally, the same view is held by Zadok who also translates "Ashkelon" but transliterates $^{\mathrm{uru}}$x-x-(x)-*il-lu-nu*. Ran Zadok, *Geographical Names According to New and Late-Babylonian Texts* (TAVO 7; Répertoire géographique des textes cunéiformes 8; Wiesbaden: Otto Harrassowitz, 1985), 183.

46 So Stager, "Ashkelon and the Archaeology of Destruction," 72* n. 1: "In the *editio princeps* of the *Chronicle*, D. J. Wiseman (1956:68, 85) restored Ashkelon (*iŝ?-qi?-*[erasure]-*il-lu-nu*) as the name of the captured city in BM 21946, obverse line 18. Later, W. F. Albright, accompanied by Wiseman and A. Sachs, re-examined the tablet in the British Museum and concluded that Wiseman's reading was correct. More recently A. K. Grayson (1980) declared the reading of the name Ashkelon to be "very uncertain." He apparently convinced Wiseman that his earlier reading was 'uncertain' (Wiseman 1991:23, n. 158). In 1992 my colleague P. Machinist asked I. Finkel, curator of cuneiform in the Department of Western Asiatic Antiquities in the British Museum, to check the tablet once again for the name of the captured city. In a letter dated November 11, 1992, Finkel responded with this reading of the text in question: *ana URU iŝ-qi-*[erasure]-*il-lu-nu*, noting that the first syllable *iŝ* is 'quite clear'; the second is probably *qi* (the doubled *Winkelhaken* made with a trembling stylus); the third is 'almost certainly an erasure in which the scribe possibly wrote and then erased *aleph*; and the last three syllables *-il-lu-nu* have never been in doubt. This fresh assessment reconfirms the reading Ashkelon as the city which Nebuchadrezzar captured and destroyed in Kislev 604 BCE." One could comment on the above that the argument that *-il-lu-nu* is secure, and that it supports the conjecture, is problematic. Place names ending with *-nu* are not infrequent in Late Babylonian. One name among others mentioned by Schaudig is $^{\mathrm{uru}}$*da-da-nu* (Hanspeter Schaudig, *Die Inschriften Nabonids von Babylon und Kyros' des Grossen* [AOAT 256; Münster: Ugarit-Verlag, 2001], 712).

47 "Several scholars have followed the suggestion made in my first edition of this Babylonian Chronicle that it could be linked with the siege of Ashkelon 12 miles north of Gaza in 604 BC. This is, I now think, unlikely, since Aga' king of Ashkelon was held in Babylon about the time of Nebuchadrezzar" (Wiseman, *Nebuchadrezzar and Babylon*, 25). Since Ashkelon is not an option any longer, Wiseman suggests both Sidon and Tyre as possible alternatives (pp. 26–27).

The second observation concerns the validity of the conjecture. A conjecture is in reality mere guesswork, and can only be regarded as valid (that is, possible) if the arguments supporting it can be said to be sound. Wiseman presents basically two different grounds for restoring *(āl)iš?-qi?-il-lu-nu* in BM 21946. The first is that Ashkelon is mentioned in the so-called Weidner Chronicle.[48] However, from the wider context of the Weidner Chronicle we learn how a large number of kings from various important cities in Nebuchadnezzar's empire (including Jerusalem) lived in Babylon. This custom of keeping "honorary captives" was a way of controlling the empire. What is said about Ashkelon in the Weidner Chronicle could be said also about Ashdod, Byblos, Sidon or Tyre (just to mention a few examples!). But there is no argument for bringing any of these cities into BM 21946 obv. 18 if there are no text internal palaeographical reasons to do so.[49]

The second argument for Wiseman's conjecture is the so-called "Adon Letter."[50] This text, written in Aramaic, on papyrus, was discovered at Saqqara in 1942. In the letter, an alleged "king Adon" sends a message, apparently from Syria-Palestine, to the Egyptian Pharaoh for help. The text has been dated, tentatively, to the end of the 7th century BCE.[51]

Several cities have been suggested as Adon's city: Ammon, Aphek, Ashdod, Ashkelon, Byblos, Edom, Ekron, Gath, Gaza, Lachish, Moab, Tyre, and Sidon.[52] When reviewing the comprehensive 'Adon' literature it appears that we have no way of identifying the king and city in question. For this reason it goes without saying that this text cannot be used any longer for an attempt to reconstruct 'Ashkelon' in BM 21946.

Summing up, we may conclude that none of the arguments used by Wiseman in 1956 support the conjecture 'Ashkelon.' As I found this quite frustrating, I asked Professor Wilfred Lambert if he could collate the text in question for me.[53] "I looked at the tablet in the British Museum last Thursday with the following result," he wrote to me subsequently:

---

48 Wiseman, *Chronicles*, 28 n. 4, 85.

49 Examples of unproblematic conjectures in our text are Ha[ma]th (obv. 8) and Bab[ylon] (obv. 20). See Grayson, *Assyrian and Babylonian Chronicles*, 99 and 100.

50 "An Aramaic letter addressed to a Pharaoh requesting help against the approaching Babylonian king may have come from Askelon at this time" (Wiseman, *Chronicles*, 28).

51 For bibliography, see Joseph A. Fitzmyer and Stephen A. Kaufman, *An Aramaic Bibliography*. Part I. *Old, Official, and Biblical Aramaic* (Publications of the Comprehensive Aramaic Lexicon Project; Baltimore, MD: The Johns Hopkins University Press, 1992), 54.

52 For a discussion of several of these suggestions, see Wiseman, *Nebuchadrezzar and Babylon*, 25–26.

53 The quotation, drawing, and other information are all from Professor Lambert's letter to me, dated June 2, 2004. I am extremely grateful to Professor Lambert for collating the

BM 21946 obv. 18:

a-na $^{uru}$iš-k[i]??-x-il-lu-nu

To my eyes (aided by those of another scholar in the Study Room on last Thursday) the IŠ is complete and certain. The following sign might be K[I] (if so to be rendered q[í]), but the following space has traces which due to damage or ancient erasure (I cannot be sure which) do not add up to any sign, certainly not QI. So the best I could do would be to render:

$^{uru}$iś-q[í]?-(ras.?)-il-lu-nu

As we see, Professor Lambert, too, ends up with two question marks. However, he informs me in his letter that this is of little importance. According to Lambert, there is no other place name known which could fit save for ancient Ashkelon, so the remaining problems do not have great general consequence.

## IV. Conclusion

In the present paper I have discussed briefly the archaeological, historical and palaeographical evidence that have been used to prove that Nebuchadnezzar destroyed Ashkelon in the year 604 BCE In my view this view can no longer be supported. There are various reasons for this. However, the main argument of the present essay is that the Akkadian text that has been used in support of Nebuchadnezzar's sack of Ashkelon (BM 21946 obv. 18) simply does not give sufficient support for making such a claim. "Ashkelon" in BM 21946 is a textual emendation, and should therefore be evaluated as one. We should test the conjecture 'Ashkelon' along a scale possessing rankings like 'very likely,' 'likely,' 'less likely,' 'not likely,' and 'not at all likely.' In view of the evidence that I have presented above, there is no doubt in my mind that the conjecture 'Ashkelon' shall have to be classified as 'not at all likely.'

---

text for me, and for giving me permission to reproduce his drawing here. I was very sorry to learn that Professor W. G. Lambert died 9th November 2011. He was always very kind to me, and helped me on numerous occasions. Professor Lambert was a very fine person, and he will be missed by many. Likewise, I am very thankful to Mrs. Felicity Smail, New College office, Edinburgh, who scanned the drawing for me.

# WHERE WAS TARSHISH?

John Day

Much of the early career of Hugh Williamson, in whose honour this essay is dedicated, was devoted to the study of the books of Chronicles, while in more recent years his attention has been focused primarily on the book of Isaiah. It is a curious fact that these are the two Old Testament works having the largest number of references to the place name Tarshish (1 Chr 1:7; 7:10; 2 Chr 9:21; 20:36–37; Isa 2:16; 23:1, 6, 10, 14; 60:9; 66:19).[1] Although a number of locations have been proposed, for a long time the consensus has been that Tarshish was located at Tartessos at the mouth of the Guadalquivir in southern Spain,[2] but in recent years a number of scholars, including Arie van der Kooij and André Lemaire, have reargued the older view (first attested in Josephus, *War*, 7.23; *Antiquities*, 1.127; 9.208) that it should be equated with Tarsus in Cilicia.[3] Hugh Williamson himself, whilst referring to Tarshish as being "across the Mediterranean" in his Chronicles commentary, which possibly indicates that he had Tartessos in mind, has been persuaded that it was Tarsus in his more recent Isaiah commentary.[4] The purpose of the present essay is to reinvestigate this matter.

---

[1] The other allusions are in Gen 10:4; 1 Kgs 10:22; 22:49 (Eng. 48); Ps 48:8 (Eng. 7); 72:10; Jer 10:9; Ezek 27:12, 25; 38:13; Jonah 1:3; 4:2.

[2] See, e.g., Hans Wildberger, *Jesaja Kapitel 13–27* (BKAT 10/2; Neukirchen-Vluyn: Neukirchener Verlag, 1978), 869–70, Eng. trans. *Isaiah 13–27* (trans. Thomas H. Trapp; Continental Commentary; Minneapolis: Fortress, 1997), 422; Michael Koch, *Tarschisch und Hispanien* (Madrider Forschungen 14; Berlin: W. de Gruyter, 1984); Moshe Elat, "Tarshish and the Problem of Phoenician Colonisation in the Western Mediterranean," *OLP* 13 (1989): 55–69; Edward Lipiński, *Itineraria Phoenicia* (OLA 127, Studia Phoenicia 18; Leuven: Peeters, 2004), 225–65. Although Samuel Bochart is often said to have been the first to equate Tarshish with Tartessus, this actually goes back much earlier to Hippolytus and others; see Lipiński, *Itineraria Phoenicia*, 233–34.

[3] Arie van der Kooij, *The Oracle of Tyre: The Septuagint of Isaiah XXIII as Version and Vision* (VTSup 71; Leiden: Brill, 1998), 40–47; André Lemaire, "Tarshish-*Tarsisi*: problème de topographie historique biblique et assyrienne," in *Studies in Historical Geography and Biblical Historiography Presented to Zecharia Kallai* (ed. Gershon Galil and Moshe Weinfeld; VTSup 81; Leiden: Brill, 2000), 44–62. Cf. too Andrew Das, "Paul of Tarsus: Isaiah 66.19 and the Spanish Mission of Romans 15.24, 28," *NTS* 54 (2008): 60–73.

[4] H. G. M. Williamson, *1 and 2 Chronicles* (NCB; Grand Rapids, Mich.: Eerdmans; London: Marshall, Morgan & Scott, 1982), 235; idem, *A Critical and Exegetical Commentary on Isaiah 1–27* (ICC; London: T&T Clark, 2006), 1: 226–27, n. 109.

## I. Tartessos or Tarsus?

First I shall consider Ps 72, a psalm whose implication that Tarshish was in the far west has often been overlooked. Speaking of the universal extent of the king's reign, as ideally conceived, v. 8 declares: "May he have dominion from sea to sea, and from the river to the ends of the earth." This is further explicated in vv. 10–11: "May the kings of Tarshish and the isles render him tribute, may the kings of Sheba and Seba bring gifts. May all kings fall before him, all nations give him service." Quite clearly Tarshish and the isles on the one hand and Sheba and Seba on the other represent the furthest known parts of the world ("the ends of the earth"). Sheba is Saba in southern Arabia (the modern Yemen) and Seba is in east Africa; these certainly represent the most remote places in a southerly direction. Tarshish and the isles must correspondingly be located in the furthest known western part of the Mediterranean sea, seeing that the Old Testament regularly depicts Tarshish as being in the west (with the exception of the late Chronicler). This simply does not fit Tarsus, which was more or less due north from Joppa! However, it does fit Tartessos, which was similarly regarded as the furthermost known place in the west by other ancient writers (cf. Strabo, *Geography*, 3.2.12). A number of places further west than Tarsus are cited elsewhere in the Old Testament, e.g. Crete (Caphtor), Rhodes (Rodanim), Ionia (Javan), Libya (Lubim, Lehabim, Put) and Lydia (Lud), most of which are mentioned in passages that also refer to Tarshish, so we should certainly expect Tarshish to be further west than all of those. Similarly in the book of Jonah we read that in order to avoid his divine call to preach to the Ninevites, the prophet boarded a ship at Joppa going to Tarshish, away from the presence of the Lord. Nineveh, the capital of Assyria, was of course to the north-east of Israel, and if Jonah were heading for Tarsus he would actually have been going nearer to Nineveh than if he had stayed in Joppa! A voyage to the furthest known place in the Mediterranean, as indicated by Ps 72, would have been far more appropriate for Jonah's purpose. Curiously, the discussions by both van der Kooij and Lemaire of the location of Tarshish fail to discuss these implications of Ps 72 and Jonah.

The next piece of evidence bearing on the location of Tarshish which I shall consider is an inscription of King Esarhaddon of Assyria, ca. 671 BCE,[5]

[5] Cf. Riekele Borger, *Die Inschriften Asarhaddons, Königs von Assyrien* (AfO 9; Graz: Im Selbstverlage des Herausgebers, 1956), 86. The translation by A. Leo Oppenheim in *ANET*,

which states that "all the kings from amidst the sea—from Cyprus, Ionia, as far as Tarsisi—bowed to my feet and I received heavy tribute from them." It is clear from this that Tarsisi (universally agreed to be Tarshish) must be the most distant place named, and west of Ionia, just as Ionia is west of Cyprus. Consequently it is impossible to equate it with Tarsus, which would rather have been the nearest of these places from Assyria's point of view. Van der Kooij's denial that this is the case is inadmissible, while Lemaire does not adequately discuss the implications of Esarhaddon's statement.[6] Moreover, we know that Tarsus was spelled תרז (Tarz) in Aramaic on fifth century BCE coins from Tarsus[7] and Tarzi or Tarzu in Neo-Assyrian inscriptions,[8] which further distinguishes it from Tarsisi. Furthermore, Tarzi/Tarzu is designated a city and Tarsisi a country in Akkadian. Van der Kooij and Lemaire point out that the Hittite spelling was Tarsha,[9] but this is a non-Semitic spelling dating from the pre-biblical period. Moreover, the Aramaic and Akkadian names (like the Hittite) confirm that *-s* at the end of the Greek form Tarsos (whence we get the form Tarsus) is simply a Greek ending, thus further heightening the difference from Tarshish. It might be thought that Tartessos in Spain was outside the Assyrian sphere of influence.[10] However, reference to tribute being brought from Tartessos becomes intelligible when we recall that Esarhaddon mentions this in the context of his conquest of Tyre: Tartessos was a Phoenician colony, so in conquering Tyre Esarhaddon could lay claim to her dependent colonies as well, even if this was true only in a nominal sense.

It is interesting to observe that in Isa 23, which very likely refers to the same fall of Tyre as Esarhaddon's inscription,[11] not only are the ships of Tarshish told to lament (vv. 1, 14), but Tarshish itself is somehow affected by the event (v. 10). Moreover, the inhabitants of Tyre are encouraged

290 reads, "All the kings from (the islands) amidst the sea—from the country Iadnana (Cyprus), as far as Tarsisi, bowed to my feet and I received heavy tribute from them," omitting the reference to Ionia, but this is clearly a slip.

[6] Van der Kooij, *The Oracle of Tyre*, 43; Lemaire, "Tarshish-*Tarsisi*," 49–50, 53.

[7] Ernest Babelon, *Catalogue des monnaies grecques de la Bibliothèque nationale: Les Perses achéménides* (Paris: Rollin & Feuardent, 1893), xxvi, 17–18.

[8] Simo Parpola, *Neo-Assyrian Toponyms* (AOAT 6; Neukirchen-Vluyn: Neukirchener Verlag; Kevelaer: Butzon & Bercker, 1970), 349.

[9] Van der Kooij, *The Oracle of Tyre*, 44–45; Lemaire, "Tarshish-*Tarsisi*," 54.

[10] Van der Kooij, *The Oracle of Tyre*, 43; Lemaire, "Tarshish-*Tarsisi*," 52.

[11] So Wildberger, *Jesaja Kapitel 13–27*, 864–66, Eng. trans. *Isaiah 13–27*, 417–19; Ronald E. Clements, *Isaiah 1–39* (NCB; Grand Rapids and London: Eerdmans and Marshall, Morgan & Scott, 1980), 191–92.

to escape to Tarshish (v. 6), just as they are told to flee to Kittim (v. 12). Since Kition, whence the name Kittim derives, was a Phoenician (indeed Tyrian) colony, it makes excellent sense if Tarshish was so too. This was indeed the case with Tartessos, as both classical sources and archaeology attest,[12] but not so with Tarsus, even though the Phoenicians had dealings with it.

It is sometimes claimed that an identification of Tarshish with Tarsus fits better with the references to the places mentioned alongside it in Ezek 27:12–14, Isa 66:19 and Gen 10:4.[13] However, with regard to Ezek 27, it should be noted that Tarshish is mentioned alongside Ionia (v. 12), and Rhodes is mentioned shortly afterwards in v. 15, as is Libya (Put) shortly before (in v. 10). In the light of Tarshish's reputation as the furthest known western place (Ps 72:10), Tarshish must be further west than all of these, which simply does not fit Tarsus. Furthermore, we should note that Ezek 27:12–24 is a distinct unit listing Tyre's trading partners, moving broadly from west to east. It is therefore significant that Tarshish is the very first place mentioned, suggesting it was indeed the furthest west. However, this pattern would be broken if we were to locate Tarshish at Tarsus rather than Tartessos. Moreover, as classical sources attest, the Phoenicians were famous for their trade with Tartessos, so it would be surprising for this place not to be mentioned in Ezek 27. As for Isa 66:19, Tarshish is mentioned alongside Libya (Put)[14] and Lydia (Lud), so Tarshish ought to be to the west of both of those, which again does not fit Tarsus but would cohere with Tartessos.

Finally, with regard to Gen 10:4, we would argue that Tarshish—as the furthest known place in the west—must be to the west of Ionia, Rhodes and Cyprus, which are also mentioned in this verse. Interestingly, the names of the sons of Javan (Ionia) come in two pairs here, "Elishah and Tarshish, Kittim and Rodanim."[15] Since it is widely agreed that Elishah and

---

[12] Cf. Adolf Schulten, *Tartessos* (Hamburg: Cram, de Gruyter, 1950); Maria E. Aubet, *The Phoenicians and the West* (trans. Mary Turton; 2nd ed.; Cambridge: Cambridge University Press, 2001); Ann Neville, *Mountains of Silver & Rivers of Gold: The Phoenicians in Iberia* (Oxford: Oxbow Books, 2007); Michael Dietler and Carolina López-Ruiz, eds., *Colonial Encounters in Ancient Iberia* (Chicago: University of Chicago Press, 2009).

[13] E.g. van der Kooij, *The Oracle of Tyre*, 41–43; Lemaire, "Tarshish-*Tarsisi*," 48–49; Williamson, *Isaiah 1–27*, I: 227, n. 109.

[14] The MT has "Pul," which is otherwise unknown. It is widely accepted that we should follow the LXX in reading "Put," which is several other times mentioned alongside Lydia (Lud or Ludim, Jer 46:9; Ezek 27:10; 30:5), as in Isa 66:19.

[15] The MT has Dodanim, but it is generally accepted that we should read Rodanim with the LXX, the Samaritan version and the parallel text in 1 Chr 1:7.

Kittim refer to two different parts of Cyprus,[16] it is clear that the list is not in strict geographical order, since Tarshish intervenes between them. Rather, P has divided the names into two groups on the basis of their being singular or plural. With regard to these pairings, Paul-Eugène Dion suggested that Kittim and Rodanim are modernizing terms added by P to explain the preceding names Elishah and Tarshish.[17] In this way he tries to account for there being two references to Cyprus here, but it also follows that he believes Rodanim (Rhodes) is a modernizing term for Tarshish.[18] However, the argument is weak. Not only are there no grounds for believing that Tarshish was regarded as an archaic term—it continued to be used in the post-exilic period in Jonah as well as in different parts of Third Isaiah (in addition to Chronicles)—but it clearly cannot be equated with Rhodes. This is not only because nowhere else in Gen 10 does P provide

---

[16] Jonas C. Greenfield ("Elishah," *IDB* 2: 92) was perhaps right in conjecturing that Kittim and Elishah designated respectively the Phoenician and Greek parts of Cyprus. The name Kittim certainly derives from Kition, a Cypriot city of Phoenician foundation, and denotes Cyprus or a part of it in Old Testament passages, though it was subsequently used for Macedonia (1 Macc 1:1; 8:5) and the Romans (Dan 11:30; Qumran), doubtless through later reinterpretations of Num 24:24. That Elishah reflects an older name for Cyprus, Alashiya, seems very likely. After many years in which it had been suspected that Alashiya was Cyprus, or a part of Cyprus, because of its abundance of copper (cf. El-Amarna letters 33–36, 40, especially 35, and Papyrus Anastasi IV), this has been decisively proved by a petrographic analysis of the clay of the El-Amarna and Ugaritic tablets sent from Alashiya. See Yuval Goren, Israel Finkelstein and Nadav Na'aman, "The Location of Alashiya. Petrographic Analysis of the Tablets," *AJA* 107 (2003): 233–55. That the name Alashiya was still used in the first millennium is shown by a fourth century BCE Cypriot inscription from Tamassos referring to Apollo Alasiotas. However, Edouard Lipiński, "Les Japhétites selon Gen 10,1–4 et 1 Chr 1,5–7," *ZAH* 3 (1990): 40–53 (50–51) has suggested that Elishah reflects the name Ulysses, thereby denoting the island of Ithaca whence he came, but we have no evidence that Ithaca was ever called Ulysses. Older views now rejected include that of Eduard Meyer, *Geschichte des Alterthums* I (Stuttgart: J. G. Cotta, 1884), 341, who believed Elishah denoted Carthage, and that this was reflected in Dido's alternative name Elissa. However, we likewise have no evidence that Carthage was called Elissa and it is difficult to see why it should be attributed to the Greeks (Gen 10:4), since it was originally a Phoenician colony and subsequently an independent state till 146 BCE. Again, Friedrich Schmidtke (*Die Japhetiten der biblischen Völkertafel* [BSHT 7; Breslau: Müller & Seiffert, 1926], 69–70) equated Elishah with Elaiussa, a site on the coast of Cilicia, but this is not attested before the 2nd century BCE (Schmidtke identified it with Wilusa, a place attested in Hittite texts, but this is now equated with Ilios, i.e. Troy.) There is also nothing to be said for Josephus's equation of Elishah with the Aeolians (*Ant.* 1.127) or the view of Paul-Richard Berger, "Ellasar, Tarschich und Jawan, Gn 14 und Gn 10," *WO* 13 (1982): 50–78 (57–60), that it was Lissa in Crete.

[17] Paul-Eugène Dion, "Les *KTYM* de Tel Arad: Grecs ou Phéniciens?," *RB* 99 (1992): 70–97 (84–85).

[18] However, on p. 84, n. 84, Dion identifies Tarshish with Tarsus, at any rate probably for Isa 23; regarding this latter, see my arguments in favour of Tartessos above.

two names for the same place—as Dion himself concedes[19]—but also because in Ezek 27 the prophet (who is similar in date and outlook to P) refers to Kittim and Elishah as two distinct places (vv. 6, 7), as he also does with regard to Tarshish and Rhodes (vv. 12, 15).[20] On the other hand, Giovanni Garbini has argued that Tarshish in Gen 10:4 is to be equated with Tarsus, even though he admits that Tarshish was elsewhere equivalent to Tartessos (though he does not discuss in which passages this is so).[21] Garbini regards both Elishah and Kittim as representing Cyprus and holds that it would be appropriate for Tarsus in nearby Cilicia to be mentioned alongside them. Dodanim, usually emended to Rodanim (Rhodes; see above n. 15), Garbini prefers to read as Donanim, supposing this likewise to be in Cilicia (cf. *dnnym* in the Karatepe inscription, *KAI* 26). However, this emendation is entirely conjectural, without supporting evidence. Moreover, we have already seen above that the Semitic forms of the name of Tarsus do not cohere with Tarshish. It is more natural to suppose that Tarshish in Gen 10:4 is the same Tarshish mentioned elsewhere in the Old Testament.

It is to be noted that in Gen 10:4 Tarshish is listed under the sons of Javan (Ionia), whereas in Isa 23 it is closely aligned with Tyre. This is to be explained by the fact that between the mid-seventh century and the time of the Priestly source Tartessos had come under Greek influence, as archaeology attests (cf. Herodotus, *History*, 1.163; 4.152).[22] Similarly Kittim is listed as a son of Javan in Gen 10:4, although its centre, Kition, was originally a Phoenician colony. Contrary to Gordon J. Wenham,[23] therefore, there is no problem in Tartessos being attributed to the Greeks in Gen 10:4.

Although we have repeatedly noted above that Tarsus is much too far to the east to accommodate the Old Testament's references to Tarshish, since so many other places further west are also referred to (Libya, Crete, Rhodes, Lydia, Ionia), we still need to provide an answer to Lemaire's question why, if Tarshish is Tartessos, the Old Testament has no refer-

---

19 Dion, "Les *KTYM* de Tel Arad," 85.

20 In Ezek 27:15 it is generally agreed that we should read "Rhodians" (בני רדן) with the LXX rather than MT's "Dedanites" (בני דדן). Dedan is mentioned a few verses later in Ezek 27:20 alongside other Arabian locations. It is therefore out of place in v. 15, where it is immediately followed by a reference to "many coastlands/islands," phraseology associated elsewhere with the Mediterranean.

21 Cf. Giovanni Garbini, "Tarsis e Gen. 10,4," *BeO* 7 (1965): 13–19.

22 See Yuli B. Tsirkin, "The Greeks and Tartessos," *Oikumene* 5 (1986): 163–71.

23 Gordon J. Wenham, *Genesis 1–15* (WBC 1; Waco, Tex.: Word Books, 1987), 202.

ences to other western places like Malta, Sicily, Sardinia and Carthage.[24] The answer is, I think, fairly simple. It was only quite late that Carthage came to prominence, and Malta, Sicily, and Sardinia were not well known to the Israelites. On the other hand, Tartessos was well known to the Israelites because of its important sources of silver and other metals procured by the Phoenicians. Interestingly, the metals referred to as being extracted from Tarshish agree perfectly with its identification as Tartessos. The Old Testament states that Tarshish was the source of silver, iron, tin, and lead (Ezek 27:12), and Jer 10:9 singles out especially silver. It should also be noted that a pre-exilic Hebrew ostracon (variously dated to ca. 800 or ca. 620 BCE) refers to "silver of Tarshish for the temple of YAHWEH: 3 sh(ekels)."[25] Probably Isa 60:9 also associates silver (as well as gold) with Tarshish. Similarly, ancient classical sources highlight Tartessos's wealth of silver in particular (Strabo, *Geography*, 3.2.11; Diodorus Siculus, *Universal History*, 5.35) but also other metals. In addition to silver, Pliny (*Natural History*, 3.3), mentions lead, iron, copper and gold, while Avienus (*Ora Maritima*, 293), cites it as a source of tin. However, Lemaire points out that these same metals were also associated with the Taurus mountains north of Tarsus.[26] Against this, however, it may be noted that whilst the Phoenicians were familiar with Tarsus, ancient classical sources nowhere single it out as a special trading place for metals used by the Phoenicians in the way they do with Tartessos.

Interestingly, the phrase "ships of Tarshish" (1 Kgs 10:22; 22:49 [Eng. 48]; Isa 2:16; 23:1, 14; 60:9; Ezek 27:25; Ps 48:8 [Eng. 7]) is a further indication that Tarshish was a very remote place. The implication of these references that the ships of Tarshish were particularly impressive, going to Ophir and other exotic places, is that they were large boats capable of going long distances. Since they are named "ships of Tarshish" this suggests that Tarshish was a similarly remote place, which fits Tartessos admirably but does not cohere very well with Tarsus. Strikingly, Herodotus (*History*, 1.163) informs us that the Phocaeans, "the pioneer navigators of the Greeks," used special ships to go to Tartessos. He states: "They used to sail not in deep, broad-beamed merchant vessels but in fifty-oared galleys." Such special ships

24 Lemaire, "Tarshish-*Tarsisi*," 52.

25 Pierre Bordreuil, Felice Israel and Dennis Pardee, "Deux ostraca paléo-hébreux de la collection Sh. Moussaieff," *Sem* 46 (1996): 49–76 (49–61); Hershel Shanks, "Three Shekels for the LORD: Ancient Inscriptions Record Gift to Solomon's Temple," *BAR* 23/6 (1997): 28–32.

26 See Lemaire, "Tarshish-*Tarsisi*," 55–57.

would not have been needed for a journey from Israel to Tarsus, which could be reached by coastal shipping.[27]

It has been widely accepted that the Semitic and Greek names Tarshish and Tartessos[28] are perfectly compatible philologically, though without spelling out why, Lemaire claims they are not. However, *-os* is readily understood as a Greek ending, and of course Greek does not have the letter *sh*, naturally rendering this by *s* or *ss*. With regard to the *t* in the middle of Tartessos in place of *sh*, this can be explained if the name is indigenous in origin, with this sound being variously reproduced in Semitic and Greek renderings.

## II. Other Minority Views

We have concluded that throughout the Old Testament Tarshish is Tartessos in Spain, not Tarsus in Cilicia. However, before we consider the variant location found in the Chronicler, we need briefly to note our objections to various minority viewpoints that have been suggested. Thus, Cyrus H. Gordon proposed that Tarshish is not a place at all but a name for the sea.[29] However, the contexts in which the word occurs clearly indicate a definite location, as real as the other places mentioned alongside it. It has also very occasionally been suggested that Tarshish was in India[30] or Ethiopia,[31] but both views conflict with the evidence of the Old Testament and Esarhaddon's inscription that it was somewhere in the west. One minority view that does locate it in the west is that of Paul-Richard Berger,[32] who thought it was Carthage, as did the LXX on a few occasions.[33] However,

27 Cf. Schmidtke, *Die Japhetiten der biblischen Völkertafel*, 71.

28 Lemaire, "Tarshish-*Tarsisi*," 52.

29 Cyrus H. Gordon, "The Wine-Dark Sea," *JNES* 37 (1978): 51–52; similarly Sidney B. Hoenig, "Tarshish," *JQR* 69 (1979): 181–82.

30 José María Blázquez, *Tartessos y los orígenes de la colonización fenicia en occidente* (Acta Salamanticensia, Filosofía y Letras 58; 2nd ed.; Salamanca: Universidad de Salamanca, 1975), 15–21.

31 Origen, Psalmus LXXI:9 (= LXXII:10), in PG 12 (1862), 1524, though he says Tarshish in Jonah is Tarsus.

32 Berger, "Ellasar, Tarschisch und Jawan, Gn 14 und Gn 10," 61–65.

33 Generally the LXX transliterates the name, but in Isa 23:1, 6, 10, 14 it renders it as "Carthage" and in Ezek 27:12, 25; 38:13 by "Carthaginians." It is significant that in both Isa 23 and Ezek 27 the allusions are in connection with the Phoenician city-state of Tyre, which had extensive trading connections with the west. Moreover, Carthage had an importance in the second century BCE (up till its destruction in 146 BCE), which it did not have at the time of the original composition of Isa 23 and Ezek 27. It is therefore understandable how the LXX mistook the original meaning of Tarshish here.

quite apart from its relative unimportance during the period of many of the Old Testament's allusions to Tarshish, it is difficult to understand why Gen 10:4 should represent Carthage as a son of Javan (Ionia), since it was in no sense Greek and maintained Phoenician culture for many centuries; furthermore, it was never noted for its silver. Another view, proposed by August Knobel, identified Tarshish in Gen 10:4 and probably Isa 66:19 with the habitation of the Etruscans in Italy,[34] though elsewhere he saw Tarshish as Tartessos. However, apart from the fact that there is insufficient evidence to justify distinguishing more than one Tarshish, the name of the Etruscans (Greek Tursenoi), which seems to derive from that of the Tursha, one of the Sea peoples, lacks a final *s* or *sh*, unlike Tarshish. Guy Bunnens supposes that the name Tarshish was applied to various places in the far west.[35] However, though the general location is correct, once again there is insufficient evidence to distinguish more than one Tarshish. William F. Albright, whilst accepting that the biblical Tarshish and Assyrian Tarsisi are probably Tartessos, believed that the root meaning was "refinery" and that the name could be applied to various places, including Tarshish in the Nora stone, which he believed was Nora itself, in southern Sardinia.[36] The Nora stone contains a Phoenician inscription dated palaeographically to the ninth or early eighth century BCE Although the precise translation of the text as a whole is disputed, it is widely agreed that it contains a reference to both "in Tarshish" and "in Sardinia." It appears to refer to someone who was in Tarshish being banished to Sardinia,[37] in which case Tarshish is being contrasted rather than equated with Sardinia. Incidentally, we

34 August Knobel, *Die Völkertafel der Genesis* (Giessen: J. Ricker, 1850), 86–94; idem, *Die Genesis erklärt* (KEAHT; 2nd ed.; Leipzig: S. Hirzel, 1860), 111–12.

35 Guy Bunnens, *L'expansion phénicienne en Méditerranée* (Brussels and Rome: Institut historique belge de Rome, 1979), 347–48.

36 William F. Albright, "The Role of the Canaanites in the History of Civilization," in *The Bible in the Ancient Near East: Essays in Honor of William Foxwell Albright* (ed. G. Ernest Wright; Garden City, N.Y.: Doubleday, 1961), 328–62 (346–47); idem, "New Light on the Early History of Phoenician Colonization," *BASOR* 83 (1941): 14–22 (21). Albright's view that Tarshish means "refinery," appealing to Akkadian *rašāšu*, "to melt," has gained little following.

37 On the Nora stone see, e.g., Brian Peckham, "The Nora Inscription," *Or* 41 (1972): 457–68; Frank M. Cross, "An Interpretation of the Nora Stone," *BASOR* 208 (1972): 13–19; Gösta W. Ahlström, "The Nora Inscription and Tarshish," *Maarav* 7 (1991): 41–49; William H. Shea, "The Dedication on the Nora Stone," *VT* 41 (1991): 241–45; Anthony J. Frendo, "The Particles *beth* and *waw* and the Periodic Structure of the Nora Stone Inscription," *PEQ* 128 (1996): 8–11.

have other evidence linking Tartessos with Sardinia,[38] which might favour Tarshish being Tartessos here.

## III. The Divergent View of the Chronicler

However, an alternative location is presupposed in the Chronicler, who wrongly supposed that Tarshish was to be reached by going south along the Red Sea. This is clear from both 2 Chr 9:21 and 20:36–37, where he misunderstood the references to ships of Tarshish in his *Vorlage* in 1 Kings to mean ships going to Tarshish. Thus, in 2 Chr 20:36–37 King Jehoshaphat of Judah joined King Ahaziah of Israel in building ships to go to Tarshish at Ezion-geber (on the Red Sea), but the ships were wrecked and so were unable to go to Tarshish. The underlying *Vorlage* in 1 Kgs 22:49 (Eng. 48), however, states explicitly that the ships of Tarshish destroyed at Ezion-geber were intended to go to Ophir, which was located somewhere on the coast of the Arabian peninsula (cf. Gen 10:29).[39] Similarly, 2 Chr 9:21 speaks of Solomon's ships going with the servants of Huram (*sic*) every three years to Tarshish, bringing back gold, silver, ivory, apes and peacocks. The nature of some of these objects again indicates a destination reached along the Red Sea, not the Mediterranean (probably Ophir; cf. 1 Kgs 9:26–28 = 2 Chr 8:17–19), but the Chronicler has again misunderstood a reference in his underlying source in 1 Kgs 10:22 to ships of Tarshish, taking it to mean ships going to Tarshish. This is rightly recognized in both cases by commentators such as Hugh Williamson,[40] but whereas Sara Japhet rightly considers the Chronicler to have mislocated Tarshish along the shore of the Red Sea in 2 Chr 20:36–37, she inconsistently assumes that he places it in the western Mediterranean in 2 Chr 9:21.[41] Raymond Dillard is worse in that he fails to comment on the location of Tarshish in 2 Chr 20:36–37, merely referring the reader to his comment on 2 Chr 9:21, where he states that "It is not necessary to conclude that the author was

---

38 Juli B. Tsirkin, "The Phoenicians and Tartessos," *Gerión* 15 (1997): 243–51 (247).

39 This is widely accepted and supported by the context of the reference to Ophir in Gen 10:29 and coheres with 1 Kgs 9:26–28 and 22:49 (Eng. 48), which indicate that it was reached via the Red Sea. I am unconvinced by Edward Lipińksi (*Itineraria Phoenicia*, 189–223), who dismisses these biblical allusions as unreliable and locates Ophir on the Mediterranean coast of North Africa. Since gold is not actually found there, he proposes that this North African Ophir was merely a distribution point for gold which had been brought overland from West Africa.

40 Williamson, *1 and 2 Chronicles*, 235, 303.

41 Sara Japhet, *I & II Chronicles* (OTL; London: SCM, 1993), 641, 802.

ignorant either of the type of the vessel or of the geography."[42] Dillard does not properly explain how this can be the case, but his comment in the Introduction that "the Bible does not lie... It is without error in all that it teaches"[43] shows where he is coming from. Anyway, what we have seen in the Chronicler demonstrates that by ca. 300 BCE the location of Tarshish was being forgotten.

It is a delight to dedicate this essay to my good friend Hugh Williamson, whom I have been privileged to know for over forty years, first when we were students together at Cambridge and more recently at Oxford, where we have been colleagues for twenty years. I have always been impressed by the amazing energy he puts into everything he does, and I take this opportunity to salute his many outstanding contributions to scholarship.

[42] Raymond B. Dillard, 2 *Chronicles* (WBC 15; Waco, Tex: Word Books), 73, 160.
[43] Dillard, 2 *Chronicles*, xviii.

# THE *SOTAH*: WHY IS THIS CASE DIFFERENT FROM ALL OTHER CASES?

Richard Elliott Friedman

It is an honor to dedicate this essay to Hugh Williamson, who, in the three decades I have known him, has always epitomized what it means to be both a scholar and a gentleman.

If one has any doubt that the law of the suspected adulteress, the *sotah* (Num 5:11–31), is a particularly perplexing case in biblical law, he or she has only to look at the variety of the scholarly literature. The remarkable range of utterly different explanations of what is going on in the procedure is striking even in our field, which is not exactly known for consensus. Also remarkable is how certain scholars, from ancient to contemporary times, have each been that their understanding was correct. A woman whose husband suspects her of adultery drinks a potion, and if certain physical conditions materialize, she is guilty and cursed. Shlomo Eidelberg wrote that "its sole purpose *could only have been* to force a confession from her as an alternative to the bitter potion."[1] Dennis Pardee, with no less certainty, wrote that "*there can be no doubt* that a form of illness—whatever it may have been medically speaking—was thought to follow the drinking of the water by a guilty woman."[2] Alice Bach, likewise writing with finality, said, "It reflects the patriarchal attempt to assure a husband that his honor could be restored if he had so much as a suspicion that his wife had been fooling around. Female erotic desire, then, was understood as erratic, a threat to the social order. By drowning such desire, the traditional order was assured of continuing dominance over women's bodies."[3]

Other scholars have been more circumspect in their explanations but no less diverse. Tikva Frymer-Kensky wrote of a particular medical

---

[1] Shlomo Eidelberg, "Trial by Ordeal in Medieval Jewish History: Laws, Customs and Attitudes," *PAAJR* 46/47, Jubilee Volume (1928–29/1978–79) [Part 1] (1979–1980): 105–20 (110). So Maimonides, *Hilkot Sotah*, III.

[2] Dennis Pardee, "*MĀRÎM* in Numbers V," *VT* 35 (1985): 112–15 (113).

[3] Alice Bach, "Good to the Last Drop: Viewing the Sotah (Numbers 5.11–31) as the Glass Half Empty and Wondering How to View It Half Full," in *Women in the Hebrew Bible* (ed. A. Bach; New York: Routledge, 1999), 503–22.

condition that might be involved: a prolapsed uterus.[4] Josephus wrote that it could be edema.[5]

One challenge for all of these explanations is that, in order to work, they require something that could not be counted on to happen. Drinking a potion (of 'holy' water, dust from the Tabernacle floor, and ink from words on a parchment) cannot be guaranteed to produce prolapsed uteri or any other particular condition in all guilty adulteresses. Nor can it be relied upon to produce their confessions. Jacob Milgrom, doubting that the potion that is described in this law could produce any sure symptoms, therefore proposed that the law's effect was precisely to find all women not guilty and thus to prevent "lynchings."[6] The advantage of his explanation over most others was that it did not depend on something that could not be counted upon to occur. Rather it was based precisely on the fact that nothing would occur. But, like many other explanations, it still does not account for why this procedure is applied solely to adultery and not to any other crimes. Should not arsonists, thieves, and everybody else who is suspected of anything be protected from lynchings as well? Likewise for any explanation that sees this law as a trial by ordeal, the question remains: why use the ordeal only for adultery out of all the laws in the Bible and not for any other offence? Compare the law code of Hammurabi, which uses the river ordeal for a case similar to this one, but it uses it for a case of sorcery as well.[7]

What this situation of interpretive תהו ובהו reflects is that there is something in the wording and structure of this law that has been stymying us for centuries (for millennia, actually). It is filled with unusual wordings, unique procedures, and unprecedented components. We need to account for them, not in a one-by-one manner, but, if possible, in an explanation that addresses all of them consistently.

---

[4] Tikva Frymer-Kensky, "The Strange Case of the Suspected Sotah (Numbers V 11–31)," *VT* 34 (1984): 11–26; and in Bach, "Last Drop," 463–74.

[5] Josephus, *Ant.* III:vi:6.

[6] Jacob Milgrom, "The Case of the Suspected Adulteress," in *The Creation of Sacred Literature* (ed. Richard Elliott Friedman; Berkeley: University of California Press, 1981), 69–75 (74); cf. Herbert C. Brichto, "The Case of the sotah and a Reconsideration of Biblical Law," *HUCA* 46 (1975): 55–70. On the unity of the inscription, as seen in scholarship of recent decades, see Milgrom and Brichto above, and also Michael Fishbane, "Accusations of Adultery: A Study of Law and Scribal Practice in Numbers 5:11–31," reprinted in Bach, *Women in the Hebrew Bible*, 487–502.

[7] Laws 2 (accusation of sorcery) and 132 (suspected adultery).

The law states that it is about a situation in which a husband suspects that his wife has had an "intercourse of seed" with another man. She has not been caught, and there are no witnesses. He takes her to a priest and brings an offering of a tenth of an ephah of barley flour. The priest makes a potion of holy water and dust from the Tabernacle's floor, and he rubs the words of curses from a scroll into the water. The priest loosens the woman's hair and has her swear that if she has not gone astray with someone "in place of" her husband then she will be cleared by the "bitter cursing water" but that, if she has been with someone in place of her husband, then YHWH will make her a curse among her people when He sets her "thigh sagging and womb swelling." If she has not been thus made impure, "she shall be cleared and will conceive seed." As for the man, the law concludes that he shall be clear of a crime, while the woman shall bear her crime.

## I. An Enigmatic Text

There are other biblical laws that contain ambiguities, enigmas, and elements that are open to a variety of understandings. This one, however, may very well be the law that offers the most.

First, the entire context appears to be ritual rather than judicial. Why is its procedure performed in front of a priest, not a judge? Why is it at the Tabernacle, not at a court or city gate? Why does the law require that the husband bring an offering? Why does it require an ingredient called 'holy water,' which is something that appears nowhere else in the Pentateuch?

Second, there are multiple questions of wording. Why does the law specify an intercourse of *seed*? That is not usual in other biblical laws concerning adultery. Would not any sexual acts between a man and a married woman be considered adultery? The law against adultery in Lev 20:10 does not mention seed. The law concerning sex with a betrothed woman in Deut 22:23, 25 likewise has just שׁכב without reference to seed. Nor does the decalogue commandment "you shall not commit adultery" specify seed. Only the law against adultery in Lev 18:20 explicitly forbids having an intercourse of seed with a man's wife, but that is in a section that deals with impurity (which is also mentioned here in the *sotah* law), which necessarily must involve a fluid: blood or semen. That is, seed is not just a euphemism. It is not a non-specific term. It is mentioned only when it *matters*. So the question is: why does it matter in the case of the *sotah*?

Further, why does the law say 'in place of' (תחת) her husband rather than some wording that would convey 'in addition to' her husband or 'as well as' her husband? Indeed, why have this phrase at all? The sentence would make perfectly good sense without it. Interpreters and translators have usually taken תחת here to mean 'under' her husband, and then they have suggested that this probably means 'under her husband's authority.' But תחת never has this meaning anywhere else in the Torah, whereas it means 'in place of' twenty-four times. When referring to relations between people, תחת means 'in place of' in every occurrence in narrative or law in the Torah (frequently with the sense of 'instead of').[8] When referring to being under a person's power or authority, the Biblical Hebrew way of expressing this is rather the phrase תחת יד.[9]

Again, why does the law add that 'the man' will be clear of a crime? In the first place: which man? There are two men referred to in the very first verses of this law, which outline the situation: the husband and the adulterer. Why does it not specify which of these two men is meant in the closing verses? We might have thought that this is because it is obvious that only one man, the adulterer, is in a situation of perhaps being responsible for a crime. But in fact interpreters have more often taken this verse to refer to the husband, not the adulterer. And when we ask: of what crime does the husband need to be cleared, the common answer is that he needs to be cleared of libel, of being a מוציא שם רע against his wife. But that seems to be groundless. In this text the husband has not accused his wife of anything. He suspects her, and so he does what the law prescribes. He takes her for the procedure that deals with the thing that he suspects. He makes no claim, and there is no libel.

Finally on questions of wording: why is the law formulated like no other? It has multiple plays on words. Paronomasia is common in Biblical Hebrew prose and poetry, but it is not common in law.[10] In this law

[8] Gen 4:25; 22:13; 36:33–39; 44:33; Exod 21:23; 29:30; Lev 6:15; 16:32; Num 3:12, 41, 45; 8:18; 32:14; Deut 2:12, 21, 22, 23; 10:6; see also Gen 30:2; 50:19.

[9] Gen 16:9; Exod 18:10; 21:20; see also Judg 3:30. Baruch Levine cites Ezek 23:5, "Aholah whored תחת me," as proof of תחת meaning under someone's jurisdiction; Baruch Levine, *Numbers 1–20* (AB; New York: Doubleday, 1993), 197. On the contrary, it is at least as likely that the verse means that Aholah whored with someone *in place of* God rather than under God's authority. Levine says that תחת there may be an "abbreviation" of תחת יד, but that is groundless. It rather emphasizes the point that תחת and תחת יד mean two different things.

[10] See, for example, Jack Sasson, "Wordplay in the OT," *IDB*: *Supplementary Volume*, 968–70; Baruch Halpern and Richard E. Friedman, "Composition and Paronomasia in the Book of Jonah," *HAR* 4 (1980): 77–92.

there is the patent alliterative pun on the bitter cursing water: מי המרים המאררים. There is the use of the term נעלם ('hidden') in the case of a woman who has מעלה מעל ('made a breach'). There is a similar metathesis of root letters in the term פרע ('loosening' her hair) followed by the use of עפר ('dust'). And there is yet another metathesis of root letters in the term עשׂירת ('a tenth') followed by the use of שׂערים ('barley flour'). Intriguingly, all of the puns occur in passages that involve some unprecedented element of the procedure. In the case of מי המרים המאררים, this is the only use of 'holy water' in the Hebrew Bible. In the case of נעלם and מעל, the woman's making a breach is the only use of this word מעל for a breach against a man; elsewhere it refers only to breaches against God. In the case of the עפר and פרע, the dust in this law is the only use of dust from the Tabernacle in biblical law. And as for the עשׂירת and the שׂערים, the barley flour here is the only use of barley flour for a grain offering. What is the significance of using plays in language in connection with four different unique, enigmatic aspects of this procedure?

Third, there are puzzling aspects of the facts of the law. Why is it used only for suspicion of adultery but not for any other offence? Why is it used only on a woman but not on a man who is suspected of adultery? If it is a trial by ordeal, why is it the only case of ordeal in biblical law? And why is it that the woman is not executed even if the procedure reveals her guilt? Adultery is a capital crime in the Bible.

All of these enigmas are pieces of the overarching question of why this one case requires such a different resolution from other cases of adultery and in fact from all other legal cases in the Pentateuch.

## II. The Enigmas as Signs

Let us address first the crux of the procedure, namely the specific physical developments that reveal whether the woman is guilty of having had an intercourse of seed with a man in place of her husband. These physical signs are the swelling of her womb and the sagging of her thigh. Now, what if a man were to tell an audience: "I have some news. Pretty soon you're going to see my wife's womb swell and her thigh sag." What would a hundred out of a hundred people understand him to be saying? He is saying that his wife is pregnant (though she should not forgive him for the 'sagging thigh' comment). Likewise, if a woman were to initiate gossip, starting a rumor about another woman by saying, "Soon you'll be seeing her womb swelling and her thigh sagging," absolutely everyone who hears it would understand the implication: she is pregnant.

What are the implications for our understanding of this law if the text means just what this phrase appears most naturally to mean: that it is a case about a woman's being pregnant? How does this fit with the text? The situation would be as follows:

A man suspects that his wife has had intercourse with another man instead of him, but there is no proof, no witness, and she has not been caught in the act. There is only one thing that would prove that she has had this intercourse with another man rather than with her husband, and the proof would be one hundred percent certain: if she is pregnant. The husband takes her to the priest—not to establish that she is pregnant. That will be established in due time anyway, revealed by the changes in her figure. The purpose of the priest's procedure is to administer a potion that, if she is pregnant, will produce a curse. The water's function is not to make her womb swell. Its function is just what the text says: to be מאררים—viz. to cause a curse.[11] She becomes a curse among her community, and she will bear her sin, which is to say it is between her and God; there is no punishment from humans. If, however, she is not pregnant, then she can conceive seed in the future. And either way, whether she is pregnant or not, the man (i.e. the suspected adulterer, not the husband) is cleared. Nothing has established his guilt or innocence, and nothing has caused a curse on him.

This scenario accounts for the law's specifically mentioning an intercourse of seed. No other sexual act can be tested by the *sotah* procedure. Only an act that can produce pregnancy is the subject of this law. It also accounts for why this law is used only for suspicion of adultery but for no other offence; and for the law's repeated concern with impurity. The terms for purity and impurity are used nine times in the text of the law. As we noted above, impurity is explicitly associated with adultery elsewhere in the Torah only in the one case that specifies an intercourse of seed (Lev 18:20).

This reading of the law accounts for its specifying that it has to be a case of a woman's having had intercourse with a man *in place of*—instead of—her husband. It has to be a situation in which she has had recent intercourse with the other man but not with her husband. That is the only way that her pregnancy would prove that she has committed adultery. This is precisely the situation in the narrative of David and Bathsheba. Her

---

[11] Jack Sasson proposes a reading of "waters that bless" and "waters that curse" in "Numbers 5 and the 'Waters of Judgment,'" in Bach, *Women in the Hebrew Bible*, 483–86.

husband Uriah is away in the army, and David has impregnated her. David brings Uriah back and tries (and fails) to get him to go home. Uriah rather swears that he will not "lie with my wife" (2 Sam 11:11). So David arranges Uriah's death, and he takes Bathsheba as his own wife as soon as her mourning period is over (11:27). That way, when her pregnancy becomes visible, it will not be proof of adultery. Similarly in the New Testament, in the Gospel of Matthew (1:18–19) Joseph initially takes Mary's pregnancy to indicate adultery on her part during the period of their betrothal.

The scenario of pregnancy also accounts for why the law applies only to women and not to men suspected of adultery, and it accounts for the law's notation that the man is clear of guilt. It is a law that is strictly for women. Only pregnancy can establish guilt, and the *sotah* potion works to produce a curse only in tandem with pregnancy.

This also explains why the woman is not executed. None of the usual legal standards for guilt and execution are present. Elsewhere two or more witnesses are required for capital punishment (Num 35:30; Deut 17:6). Here, however, the text emphasizes in four different ways that there is nothing that meets the standard of proof of guilt in any other criminal matter: the 'offence' has been hidden from her husband's eyes; she has remained undetected; there is no witness against her; she has not been caught. Her pregnancy leaves no doubt that she has done it, but it is an *ex post facto*, non-specific revelation of an act (or acts) that took place at an unknown time in the recent past. It does not reveal when, where, with whom, how many times, or under what circumstances the act took place. It does not reveal whether a woman's intercourse of seed was rape or consensual, which elsewhere is required to establish a woman's guilt (Deut 22:23–27).

This then accounts for why the law is a matter for the Tabernacle and not for the courts. The law prescribes a ritual that, in the case of guilt, brings about a curse. If she is pregnant, then the bitter cursing waters do what a court cannot do. That is, her punishment is out of human hands. It is turned over to God. Thus the entire matter is a ritual procedure rather than a judicial one. Holy water, ink from words of curses, and Tabernacle dust are tools of magic and not of law. The text's paronomasia, too, is more naturally associated with the language of magic than is the wording of legal texts.[12] Magical language more commonly involves rhyme and/or

---

[12] Shawna Dolansky, *Now You See It, Now You Don't: Biblical Perspectives on the Relationship between Magic and Religion* (Winona Lake, IN: Eisenbrauns, 2008), esp. p. 80. For other magical aspects of the procedure, see Fishbane, "Accusations," 501, n. 45.

alliteration ('abracadabra') and playful language formulas ('Now you see it, now you don't.') than does legal phrasing.

What is attractive about this solution to the *sotah* case, then, is precisely that it presents a single consistent explanation for every one of the law's numerous conundrums. Aside from its appeal in terms of Occam's Razor, though, it is in fact the solution to which all of the conundrums point. We have long treated them as enigmas, but they were more properly signs, items of evidence, which pointed to the meaning of the case.

## III. Why the Signs have not been Read Accurately

Now scholars have frequently understood that pregnancy figures in *some* way in this matter. In Gray's commentary on Numbers, he cited a colleague who had proposed that this law had developed from an "original rite administered in cases of suspicion aroused by pregnancy."[13] But still no one went the next step to say that this was what was happening here in the biblical law itself. Driver wrote, "The woman is suspected by her husband of infidelity but is not known to be pregnant." This appears to be close to the scenario we have pictured, but then he wrote that since swelling is normal in a pregnant woman, it would prove nothing. Rather, he said, the swelling and the sagging are themselves the punishment rather than the proof: if she has committed adultery but is not pregnant, then she will become sterile; if she has committed adultery and is pregnant, then "she will lose the unborn child in her womb by miscarriage." And if she is innocent, then she "will bear seed."[14] But this explanation is still subject to the same criticism as many other proposals: it requires an outcome that cannot be counted upon to occur. Frymer-Kensky eschewed such views because, she said, "There is no reason to suppose that the woman was pregnant at the time of the trial," even though she acknowledged on the next page that "A swelling belly seems to be a description of pregnancy rather than of unfortunate events."[15] Baruch Levine seems to have come the closest to our understanding of the text. He wrote:

---

[13] George Buchanan Gray, *A Critical and Exegetical Commentary on Numbers* (ICC; Edinburgh: T&T Clark, 1903), 49.

[14] G. R. Driver, "Two Problems in the Old Testament Examined in the Light of Assyriology," *Syria* 33 (1956): 73–77. Driver further said that, since the procedure would not in fact produce these results biologically, they were rather psychologically-induced effects.

[15] Frymer-Kensky, "Strange Case," 467–68.

> In the case projected here, the husband in question had cause to suspect his wife, most likely because she had become pregnant. The husband had reason to conclude that the pregnancy was not attributable to him.[16]

Levine here seemed to have captured the situation, but then he wrote:

> If the woman was truthful in denying the charge, she would retain her conception and carry to term. If, however, she was lying, the liquid mixture would produce deleterious somatic effects, causing the woman's belly to distend and her thighs to sag. This is probably a way to describe a miscarriage.[17]

He thus turned his explanation into one that, again, required an outcome that could not be counted upon to occur. Not understanding תחת to mean *in place of* her husband, he still imagined that there would be uncertainty over whether the pregnancy was caused by the husband or by the other man.[18] He therefore needed the mixture to produce biological effects miraculously. But water with dust and ink in it does not cause miscarriages; a distended 'belly' and sagging thighs are not a description of miscarriage even metaphorically; and an innocent woman who was unlucky enough to have a miscarriage would be regarded as proven to be an adulteress in this view.

Levine, further, saw the husband as following this procedure so as to strengthen the husband's case for divorcing his wife. There is, however, no basis for this view. There is no mention of divorce or the husband's motives in this law, and, in any case, we know nothing at all about what the standards or requirements of divorce are in the Priestly law because divorce is never mentioned at all in the Priestly source (other than that a priest cannot marry a divorcée). Levine asserts: "The Priestly view of divorce followed the Deuteronomic interpretation that the only basis for divorce was adultery or serious sexual misconduct (Deut 24:1)."[19] But there are no grounds for this claim at all. We do not know that the Deuteronomic law saw illicit sex and adultery as the only grounds for divorce; that appears to be a rabbinic derivation from the case of remarriage in Deut 24, which is far from certain; and we do not know that the Priestly law followed the Deuteronomic law on this point or, for that matter, on anything.

---

[16] Levine, *Numbers 1–20*, 181.
[17] Levine, *Numbers 1–20*, 182.
[18] See above, n. 9.
[19] Levine, *Numbers 1–20*, 193.

Most scholars thus sensed that pregnancy fit somewhere in this picture, but none concluded that this law—in which a woman's swelling womb and sagging thigh establish that she has had sex with a man—was thus about this woman's being pregnant.

Why did we never understand the law this way? First, there was a matter of the timing. Readers imagined that the swelling and sagging take place immediately, right there at the ceremony. But there is no reason to think this at all. The text does not say or imply it. The timing of the physical signs is simply not mentioned in the law.

Second, the law's wording implied to many interpreters that the potion is what causes the physical effects: "this cursing water will come in your insides, to swell the womb and make the thigh sag." This, however, is not clear in the text. Just before this, the text says that it is God who causes the physical effects. (That is, God brings about pregnancies.)[20] In that context, the clause in question may mean "this cursing water will come in your insides *at the swelling of the womb and the sagging (or causing to sag) of the thigh.*" The potion, in this case, is, at most, part of the divine agency, not something that can, in itself, magically cause bodily effects.

Third, the word בטן is commonly misunderstood to mean 'belly' rather than 'womb' even though it means 'womb' in every other occurrence in the Torah. God tells Rebekah, "There are two nations in your בטן" (Gen 25:23). Jacob tells Rachel, "Am I in place of God,[21] who has held back the fruit of the בטן from you?!" (30:2). The narrator says about both Rebekah and Tamar, "And here were twins in her בטן" (25:24; 38:27). And Deuteronomy refers to offspring as "fruit of the בטן" five times (Deut 7:13; 28:4, 11, 18, 53). English versions commonly translate all of the occurrences of בטן in Genesis as 'womb.' But when these very same translations get to Num 5, they change it to 'belly.' Even though the word refers to pregnancy everywhere else in the Pentateuch, and even though it refers to bodily evidence of a woman's intercourse of seed here in Num 5, interpreters and translators resisted seeing the plain sense of the word here. And this opened the door for a variety of alternate biological explanations of the law. Why did they resist seeing the plain, consistent sense of בטן here? The probable reason was that they had already made one or both of the two leaps that are described above. That is, once they assumed that the swelling and sagging take place right there at the ceremony, and/or once

[20] Elsewhere God enables pregnancies and withholds them.

[21] This text, incidentally, uses תחת to mean "in place of."

they assumed that the potion was the thing that caused these physical effects, the idea of pregnancy no longer occurred to them, and the womb did not seem to be the point.

Fourth, it may be that, even if there was once a period in which this ceremony had actually been performed, it had not been performed for many centuries before its earliest interpreters—Josephus and the rabbis of the early centuries of the Christian Era—began to try to understand it. The law in Numbers specifically requires that dirt/dust from the floor of the Tabernacle is a necessary ingredient of the potion. We have argued elsewhere that a Tabernacle was present only in the first Jerusalem Temple.[22] If that is correct, then this law had not been practiced for some six centuries before our earliest interpreters. Indeed, the rabbinic sources assert that Rabbi Yohanan ben Zakkai abolished the *sotah* practice,[23] but that makes no sense. At most, such an act would have been a formal abolition of something that had ceased to be practiced by his time anyway. Eidelberg says as much, and cites Saul Lieberman.[24] Did ben Zakkai even have the authority to abolish it while the (second Jerusalem) Temple was still standing? Would that not have been up to the priests? And after the Temple was destroyed, what was the point of abolishing it? That is: whatever the status of the Tabernacle in the first Temple, the rabbis' (and Josephus') recent acquaintance was only with a (second) Temple that surely contained no Tabernacle, and so they had no way of knowing what this already ancient, moot law was about. In any case, whether or not one is persuaded by the evidence that there was an actual Tabernacle located in the first Temple, the questionable rabbinic claim about ben Zakkai, as well as Josephus' questionable claim that the procedure produced edema, are further indications that the law of the *sotah* was not current in memory by the first century CE The gap in time between the practice and the interpretation has meant that all of us who have tried to explain it in the last two millennia have started from scratch on an exceptionally enigmatic legal text.

Why then does this text stand out among enigmatic laws, and what has made it so difficult to interpret? The reason may be related to the

---

[22] Richard Friedman, "The Tabernacle in the Temple, *BA* 43 (1980): 241–48; *The Exile and Biblical Narrative* (HSM 22; Atlanta: Scholars Press, 1981): 48–61; "Tabernacle," *ABD* 6:292–300.

[23] *m. Sotah* 9:9.

[24] Eidelberg, "Trial by Ordeal," 111 n.; Saul Lieberman, *Tosefta Ki-Fshutah*, VIII: Nashim (New York: Jewish Theological Seminary, 1973).

fact that it concerns pregnancy. Law is constructed upon precedent. It is on the basis of precedent that it is understood and applied. But there is no precedent in human experience for pregnancy, no other situation in which two lives are so utterly intertwined (except, remotely, the case of conjoined twins). Thus, the other best known biblical law relating to pregnancy has been similarly perplexing and has produced a comparable range of readings. It is the case of the fighters who impact a pregnant woman (Exod 21:22–25). Its wording, "and her children go out, and there will not be an injury," has been understood in two, nearly opposite ways: (1) the woman has a miscarriage, and there is no further injury to her, or (2) the woman gives birth, and there is no injury to the child. Besides this central point, there is a plethora of questions of detail and wording in the law.[25] In both the case of the fighters and the case of the *sotah*, we have little recourse to other laws for precedents. Pregnancy is as unique legally as it is biologically and socially.

This, we believe, is what has made the case of the *sotah* so challenging. It is almost entirely self-contained, without parallel or precedent elsewhere in the laws. In the end, it is the law's uniqueness—and all the idiosyncratic elements and terms that this uniqueness generates—that points to its meaning.

---

[25] See the treatment of these multiple questions in William Propp, *Exodus 19–40* (AB; New York: Doubleday, 2006), 221–30.

# ENTERING AND LEAVING THE PSALTER: PSALMS 1 AND 150 AND THE TWO POLARITIES OF FAITH

Susan Gillingham

> What we call the beginning is often the end
> And to make an end is to make a beginning.
> The end is where we start from...
> Every phrase and every sentence is an end and a
> beginning,
> Every poem an epitaph...[1]

Beginnings and endings hold a continuous fascination in poetry and fiction, both ancient and modern: the linear intersects with the cyclical, evoking both time and eternity, as much of Eliot's *Four Quartets* seeks to convey. Within Scripture, from the beginning of Genesis to the end of Revelation, there is an integral relationship between *Urzeit* and *Endzeit*, which Hermann Gunkel's work on the mythical *Chaoskampf* at the beginning and ending of these two books argued over a century ago.[2]

The relatively recent interest in the canonical shaping of the Hebrew Bible has similarly resulted in a new focus on the beginnings and endings of particular scrolls. An obvious example, in a text which has preoccupied Hugh Williamson for several years, is Isaiah: scholars such as Christopher Seitz, Paul Smith, Marvin Sweeney, David Carr and Anthony Tomasino have each demonstrated in different ways that parts of the first and last chapters of Isaiah deliberately echo one another. They refer to examples such as the play on "heaven and earth" (1:2/66:1); the anti-cultic polemic (1:10–20/66:1–6); the personification of Zion (1:21–26/66:7–13) and her judgment and redemption (1:27–31/66:14–17); and the consummation of the wicked by fire (1:31/66:24). The vocabulary in particular verses suggests that, in 1:29–31 at least, there may be some deliberate connections: examples include מהגנות and אל־הגנות in 1:29–30 and 66:17; בחרתם in 1:29 and בחרו in 66:4; and יבשו in 1:29 and יבשו in 66:5. Whoever was responsible for the final stages of the scroll of Isaiah seems to have been

[1] T. S. Eliot, "Little Gidding," Part V, lines 6–8 and 16–17, in *T. S. Eliot Collected Poems 1909–1962* (London: Faber and Faber, 2002), 208.

[2] Hermann Gunkel, *Schöpfung und Chaos in Urzeit und Endzeit: eine religionsgeschichtliche Untersuchung über Gen 1 und Ap Joh 12* (Göttingen: Vandenhoeck & Ruprecht, 1895).

concerned to end with the beginning and begin with the ending.[3] Hugh Williamson's commitment to the *ICC* series ends at Isa 27 and so will never reach the last chapter, but he has written at length on Isa 1, and here he makes the same point.[4]

However, Pss 1 and 150 do not conform to this pattern. The disparity is to some extent modified if we take a larger introductory unit (i.e. reading Pss 1 and 2 as one, given that neither has a superscription and both have several examples of corresponding language), and similarly presume a longer conclusion to the Psalter (taking as one unit the Hallel in Pss 146–150), but the differences between the very first and very last psalms are still rather marked. Psalm 1 is about the welfare of an individual Jew and his place within the 'congregation of the righteous' (בעדת צדיקים). In Ps 1 the insularity is reflected in the references to the wicked and the righteous (vv. 4, 5 and 6) revealing that the psalmist belongs to an inner community of law-abiding pious Jews—if not the Hasidim, then a party quite like them who separated themselves from other members of their community. The vision of Ps 150 by contrast could not be more universal, illustrated by the very last verse which calls on 'all those who have breath' to 'praise Yah' (כל הנשמה תהלל יה). Israel's identity no longer seems to be demarcated by the community of faith; rather, its raison d'être takes its starting point from the whole of the created order and from the God who infuses it with his presence.

Yet the extent of the difference between the first and last psalms does depend on where the 'bookends' of the Psalter really are. If we assume the beginning and ending really comprise Pss 1–2 and Pss 146–150, or Pss 1–2 and Pss 149–150, and not Pss 1 and 150 on their own, that contrast is modified.

---

3 See Christopher Seitz, "Isaiah 1–66: Making Sense of the Whole," in Christopher Seitz, *Reading and Preaching the Book of Isaiah* (Philadelphia: Fortress Press, 1988), 107; Paul A. Smith, *Rhetoric and Redaction in Trito-Isaiah: The Structure, Growth and Authorship of Isaiah 56–66* (VTSup 62; Leiden: Brill, 1995), 154; Marvin Sweeney, *Isaiah 1–4 and the Post-Exilic Understanding of the Isaianic Tradition* (BZAW 171, Berlin: de Gruyter, 1988), 97–98; David Carr, "Reaching for Unity in Isaiah," *JSOT* 57 (1993): 61–80; and Anthony Tomasino, "Isaiah 1.1–2.4 and 63–66, and the Composition of the Isaianic Corpus," *JSOT* 57 (1993): 81–93.

4 See H. G. M. Williamson, *A Critical and Exegetical Commentary on Isaiah 1–27, Volume 1, Commentary on Isaiah 1–5* (ICC; London: T&T Clark, 2006), 11: "The most impressive [correspondences]... are confined to vv. 29–31 and possibly 2–3." Other similarities are due to "author(s) of the latter [i.e. chs. 65–66] rounding off the work as a whole with a sense of closure." This was probably the work of a redactor, "framing his assemblage with conscious reference to the ending of the book which he was thus introducing."

## I. Psalms 1–2 and Psalms 146–150[5]

Psalms 1–2 are often taken as a unit because neither has a superscription and so both stand outside Book I of the Psalter, and because each offers several linguistic correspondences. The most convincing include: the use of אשרי at the beginning of Ps 1 and at the end of Ps 2; the use of ישב to depict the seat of the scoffers in Ps 1:2 (twice), echoed in Ps 2:4 which describes God sitting 'enthroned'; the use of הגה to describe the reflective murmuring on God's Law in Ps 1:2 and to depict the sinister growlings of the nations in Ps 2:1; and the reference to the way (דרך) of the wicked which will perish (אבד) at the very end of Ps 1, echoing the reference to the rulers who will perish (אבד) in the way (דרך) at the end of Ps 2. Furthermore, each is preoccupied, to different degrees, with the belief that the righteous and the wicked will have two different destinies. In Ps 1, the individual who meditates by day and night on the Torah of the Lord (בתורת יהוה) will be rewarded over and against his wicked fellow men; whilst in Ps 2, the king who trusts in the decree of God (הק יהוה) will ultimately show the shallowness of the hubris of the Gentile nations. So Ps 1 ends with the judgment of the wicked, and Ps 2, with the judgment on the hostile nations, and in each psalm, the fate of the godless is described in eschatological terms. Psalm 1 uses the image of the chaff, with its associations with harvesting at the Day of Judgment, and Ps 2 depicts God, seated on his heavenly throne, pouring out his anger on the nations. So for stylistic and theological reasons, Pss 1 and 2 could be read as one unit.[6]

Psalms 146–150, part of the final five-fold Hallel at the end of the Psalter, could also be seen as a self-contained work. Just as Pss 1:1 and 2:12 are conjoined by the 'inclusio' אשרי so Pss 146–150 are conjoined by the repeated הללו־יה at the beginning of Ps 146 and the end of Ps 150. Like Pss 1 and 2, the collection has several linguistic correspondences with neighbouring psalms. One example is the reference to the 'snow and frost' in Pss 147:16

[5] A seminal comparison of Pss 1–2 and 146–150 is by Erich Zenger, "Der Psalter als Buch," in *Der Psalter in Judentum und Christentum* (Herders Biblische Studien 18; Freiburg: Herder, 1998), 1–57 (esp. 39–48). See also Nancy L. deClaissé–Walford, *Reading from the Beginning. The Shaping of the Hebrew Psalter* (Macon GA: Mercer University Press, 1997), 37–48 and 99–103.

[6] This is the way they have sometimes been read in Jewish and Christian tradition: the most quoted examples are *4QFlorilegium,* where Pss 1 and 2 are referred to together; some manuscripts of Acts 13:33, where Ps 2 is called the "first psalm"; and the Babylonian Talmud Tractate *Berakoth 9b–10a,* which refers to the two psalms as one, beginning and ending with אשרי.

("He gives snow like wool; he scatters frost like ashes") and 148:8 ("fire and hail, snow and frost, stormy wind fulfilling his command!"). Another is in the call of praise where Israel is explicitly mentioned in Pss 148:14 ("He has raised up a horn for his people, praise for all his faithful, for the people of Israel who are close to him. Praise the LORD!") and 149:2 ("Let Israel be glad in its Maker; let the children of Zion rejoice in their King!"). A final example is in the references to the tambourine and dance in Pss 149:3 ("Let them praise his name with dancing, making melody to him with tambourine and lyre") and 150:4 ("Praise him with tambourine and dance; praise him with strings and pipe!").

There are several correspondences between Pss 146–150 and Pss 1–2. Although Pss 1–2 are more aware of the power of evil over the individual (Ps 1) and the community (Ps 2), and Pss 146–150, of the greater might of God over the entire cosmos, each collection has clear references to God's coming judgment, whether on individual sinners (Ps 1:5), other nations (Ps 2:8–9) or on the created order in all its diversity (Pss 146:7; 149:7–9). Whether this is a theme more influenced by the wisdom psalms, as Erich Zenger has suggested, or is more indicative of the eschatological thrust of the Psalter, as David Mitchell has argued, it is clear that both the first two psalms and last five psalms do have a clear forward look.[7] Furthermore, although the vision at the end of the Psalter is more cosmic and universal, the particularities of Israel *as a people* constantly break through earlier psalms in the collection: there are references here to Zion (Pss 146:10, 147:12; 149:2) and Jerusalem (Ps 147:2, 12), to Israel (Pss 147:2, 19; 148:12; 149:2) and Jacob (Pss 146:5;147:19) and even to חסידיו in Ps 149:9, alongside calls of praise to all peoples and rulers of the earth (Pss 146:5–7; 148:11–12; 149:7) and to all the beasts of the earth and the created order (Pss 146:5–7; 147:9–11; 148:11–12). So although the dominant theme in Pss 146–150 is more universalistic, and the tone more open to God's created order beyond Israel alone, there are a number of theological themes spread throughout which also occur in the first two psalms.

[7] See Zenger, "Das Psalter als Buch," 45–46, which discusses the way in which Pss 1–2 and 146–150 are developed in ben Sirach, which combines the two themes of praise of God as giver of the Law (Ps 1) and praise of God the Creator. See also David C. Mitchell, *The Message of the Psalter: An Eschatological Programme in the Book of Psalms* (JSOTSup 252; Sheffield: Sheffield Academic Press, 1997), 296–303.

## II. Psalms 1–2 and Psalms 149–150[8]

The correspondence between the beginning and the ending of the Psalter is particularly evident when we compare just Pss 2 and 149, where the national and political concerns are more pronounced. In Ps 2:9 the promise to the king is that he will break the power of the nations with a 'rod of iron' (בשבט ברזל) whilst in Ps 149:8, the nobles of the nations are to be bound in 'chains of iron' (בכבלי ברזל). And just as Ps 149:2 begins with a call to the children of Zion 'to rejoice' in God who is their King (בני־ציון יגילו במלכם) so Ps 2 ends with a call to the people to 'rejoice with fear' (וגילו ברעדה), also using גיל. God's judgement is over all the nations of the world (Pss 2:1–3 and 149:7, 9) and they are warned that it will come upon them (Pss 2:10 and 149:8). In each psalm, by contrast, Zion is explicitly referred to as inheriting God's promises (Pss 2:6 and 149:2).

So it is really Ps 2 which reduces the contrast between the beginning and ending of the Psalter, particularly as it stands in relation to Ps 149. The *differences* are most apparent, therefore, in just Pss 1 and 150.

## III. Psalm 1 and Psalm 150

Despite their correspondences with their neighbours, Pss 1 and 150 are actually best understood as independent units. Psalm 1, for example, as we have already noted, has a different orientation from the national and political concerns in Ps 2. It defines unbelievers in general terms such as the 'wicked' (רשעים), the 'sinners' (חטאים), and the 'scoffers' (לצים) whilst Ps 2 sees those who oppose God as 'the nations' (גוים) 'the peoples' (ולאמים), 'the kings of the earth' (מלכי־ארץ), and 'the princes' (ורוזנים). Psalm 1 is clearly a didactic psalm: it has just one speaker and one audience. In Ps 2 the interest in the king suggests it is a royal psalm, and its several liturgical elements result in it having at least three different voices, addressing at

[8] A comparison of these two pairs of psalms is found in Gianni Barbiero, *Das erste Psalmenbuch als Einheit* (ÖBS 16; Frankfurt: Peter Lang, 1999), 50–51. Barbiero quotes Notker Füglister in "Ein garstig Lied—Ps 149," in *Freude an der Weisung des Herrn. Beiträge zur Theologie der Psalmen, Festschrift H. Groß* (ed. Ernst Haag and Frank Lothar Hossfeld; Stuttgart: Verlag Katholisches Bibelwerk, 1986), 104: "Damit ist Ps 149 thematisch nicht nur auf Ps 2, sondern auch auf Ps 1 bezogen … Damit bilden Ps 1–2 einerseits und Ps 149–50 (bzw. 148–149) andererseits eine redaktionelle Klammer." See also Frank Lothar Hossfeld and Erich Zenger, *Die Psalmen I. Psalm 1–50* (NEchtB 29; Würzburg: Echter Verlag, 1993), 51–2.

least three audiences—the Gentile nations, the nation of Israel, and the king. The correspondences between Pss 2 and 89 at the end of Book III and between Pss 2 and 41 at the end of Book I suggest that Ps 2 was included an introduction to Books I–III *before* the addition of Ps 1. Psalm 1, by contrast, is a carefully constructed and self-contained composition (it has three quatrains with two bicola in each) and the use of א as the first letter of the first word and ת as the first letter of the last word may well have been deliberate, to signify completeness. Its dualism and its concern with God's judgement on the wicked were probably the reason for connecting it to Ps 2, which in turn may well have been adapted in order to create a closer link with its neighbour (the didactic elements in verses 5 and 10–12 being the best examples). So if Ps 2 introduces Books I–III, Ps 1, added somewhat later, introduces the entire Psalter.

Psalm 150 is similarly an independent unit, of almost equal length to Ps 1, and could be divided, as Ps 1, into three quatrains with two bicola in each. Its identical beginning and ending ('Praise Yah!') create an important unit, akin to use of letters א and ת in Ps 1. Because the calls to praise in Ps 150 create correspondences with the Hallel before it, it is easy to see why it was added here.[9] Nevertheless, its repeated brief calls to praise mark it out as a final expanded doxology, rounding off not only Book V but the Psalter as a whole, reminiscent of the earlier doxologies at the end of Books I to IV in Pss 41, 72, 89 and 106.

Taken as independent psalms, 1 and 150 could not be more different. The first psalm is not only personal and reflective, but it has a didactic concern—teaching the congregation about keeping the Torah—whereas the last psalm is a hymn of praise addressed not to the community but to God. The subject of Ps 1 is 'the blessed man,' the subject of Ps 150 is 'Yah' or 'El.' Furthermore, the quiet murmuring of the law in Ps 1:2 could not contrast more with the jubilant sounds of the music in Ps 150:3–5. Psalm 1 suggests a more private setting, away from the song and dance of public worship. Psalm 150 reverberates with a joyful liturgical setting, whereas

[9] These include the call in 145:21b to all creatures to praise God's name for ever, echoed in Ps 150:6; also the reference to God's mighty deeds (וגבורתיך) in 145:4, 11–12 and 150:2. The emphasis on the instruments of praise in Ps 150 is also found in Pss 147:7 and 149:9. Psalm 148 offers a lengthy list of those who should praise God which anticipates the calls to praise in Ps 150. These are developed in an as-yet unpublished paper by D. Human, offered at SBL at Rome 2009, entitled "'Praise Beyond Words': Psalm 150 as *Grand Finale* of the Crescendo in the Psalter."

Ps 1 seems to shun it.[10] Psalm 1 has clear dualistic concerns, focused on the different destinies of the righteous and the wicked; the means of finding God is by way of an obedient will, and the suppliant sees the life of faith defined by 'enemies' who are in fact within his own congregation. Psalm 150 has no such dualism; if one omits the first and last 'praise Yah' and the jussive call to praise in v. 6, there are ten calls of praise which bring the community of faith and the whole created order into the orbit of the worship of God—rather like the tenfold fiats of God in Gen 1.[11] Far from finding enemies within the congregation, those participating are bound together in their praise of their Creator. Just as Ps 1 is focused on the importance of meditating on the words of the law, through the discipline of the will, Ps 150 is about the way in which music takes a congregation beyond the medium of words, through a spontaneous and uninhibited spirit of praise.

The private meditation of the blessed man in Ps 1 keeps him as safe as a tree by running waters (v. 3), which suggests an allusion to the trees within the Temple courts, as is evidenced in Pss 52:8 and 92:12.[12] Psalm 150 gives us a virtual orchestra of praise echoing from the Temple outwards: the call of the shofar (v. 3) suggests the summons to praise comes from the inner Temple; the music of the harp and lyre, usually attributed to the priests and Levites, suggest a summons from the outer temple, and the dancing and tambourines, suggest roles played by women and laypeople worshiping in the outer courts.[13] So if the metaphor of the tree in Ps 1 does have allusions to the Temple courts, where the suppliant believes

---

[10] John Eaton, who has written so much about the music of the Psalms, reflects in *The Psalms: A Historical and Spiritual Commentary with an Introduction and New Translation* (London & New York: T&T Clark International, 2003), 486: "As horns are blown, frame drums tapped, strings swept and plucked, pipes breathed and cymbals shivered, the sounds of nature come together—the praise of the waters and the winds, grasses and leaves, lions and birds, goats and oxen, mothers and children, and the circling turning dancers represent the movement of the world around God, from him and to him again."

[11] Later Jewish tradition, still emphasizing the creation theme, maintains there are thirteen calls of praise and compares these with the thirteen attributes with which God governs the world: see for example Abraham Cohen, תהלים: *The Psalms with Introduction and Commentary* (Rev. ed.; ed. Ephraim Oratz and R. Shalom Shahar; London, Jerusalem, New York: Soncino Press, 1992), 479.

[12] The point, though controversial, is to my mind convincingly argued by Jerome F. D. Creach, in "Like a Tree Planted by the Temple Stream: The Portrait of the Righteous in Psalm 1.3," *CBQ* 61 (1999): 34–46, who, citing Ezek 47:12 as well as Pss 52:8 and 92:12–13, argues that this verse provides a picture of the righteous individual in the Temple.

[13] This is developed by Human, "Praise Beyond Words," referring also to an article by Friedhelm Hartenstein, "'Wach auf, Harfe und Leier, ich will wecken das Morgenrote (Ps 57,9)'—Musikinstrumente als Medien des Gotteskontakts im alten Orient und im Alten

he is most safe and secure, the contrasting movement in Ps 150 is from the heart of the Temple *outwards*. Furthermore, Ps 150 suggests not only an earthly Temple where such music would take place, but also alludes to a heavenly Temple: the use of the term 'El' for God is important for it has allusions not only to El's rule on earth but also to his kingship in his heavenly court.[14] The blessed man in Ps 1, by contrast, has his eyes fixed on the earthly congregation, where both the wicked and the righteous live together and where the different destinies are worked out. So Ps 150, departing more radically from the emphasis on Israel and the Hasidim in Ps 149 (and by implication from the psalmist in the first psalm) moves the people out of Zion into the wider world; Ps 1, meanwhile, seeks security in Zion and away from the world at large, anticipating in an individual way the more national concerns echoed in Ps 2:6.

These contrasts may best be understood by comparing the names used of God in each psalm. Psalm 1 refers twice to God, who in both cases is Yahweh (v. 2, "the law of the LORD" [תורת יהוו]; and v. 6, "for the LORD knows..." [כי־יודע יהוה]). Psalm 150 praises God as 'Yah' (יה) at the beginning and end. This shortened form, used especially in the Egyptian Hallel and Creation Hallel, suggests it was a particular liturgical term.[15] The praise in the heart of the psalm is, however, given to El.[16] This is not only El as the overall Creator and King, and El whose sanctuary is both in heaven and on earth, but also here it is El who has performed "mighty deeds" (גבורתיך), i.e. here taking on the attributes of Yahweh, the protector and guide of the people's history. The two abbreviated terms for God, the one distinct to Israel and the other more universal, fit ideally with the tone of the psalm, as the use of the God only as 'Yahweh' fits the tenor of the first psalm.

---

Testament," in *Musik, Tanz und Gott. Tonspuren durch das Alte Testament* (ed. Michaela Geiger and Rainer Kessler; Stuttgart: Katholisches Bibelwerk Verlag, 2007), 101–28.

[14] This point is also made by Human, "Praise Beyond Words."

[15] 'Yah' occurs, with three exceptions, in the last two books of the Psalter (and only five other times outside it), almost always within a call to praise (Pss 94:7, 12; 102:19; 104:35, 45; 106:48; 111:1; 112:1; 113:1, 9; 115:17, 18 [*2]; 116:19; 117:2; 118:5[*2], 14, 17, 18, 19; 122:4; 130:3; 135:3, 4, 21; 146:1, 10; 147:1, 20; 148:1, 14; 149:1, 9; 150:1, 6 [*2]). Its occurrence in the old cultic song of deliverance from Egypt, Exod 15:2, and in the ancient cultic war-cry in Exod 17:16, suggests not only its liturgical origins but that these were also quite ancient.

[16] El, a general NW Semitic term for 'god,' found in theophoric names, sanctuary names, pithoi and other cultic objects throughout Syro-Palestine, is known as a wise and kindly Creator deity, sitting above the primordial waters on his holy mountain, from where he presides over a heavenly council. It is not surprising that he is often found in creation Psalms (such as 19:2, "The heavens are telling the glory of El," and 29:3, "El of Glory thunders"). El is never used on its own in any one psalm; it is usually interchangeable with Yah, as here, or with Elohim.

Walter Brueggemann explains the differences between Pss 1 and 150 as an intentional focus initially on 'obedience' then ultimately on 'praise.'[17] Psalm 1, he argues, stands for a more works-orientated faith and Ps 150, a more trust-orientated attitude of praise. The rest of the Psalter moves in one direction or another between these polarities of faith, until the final resolution is of trust over works. This offers an interesting paradigm, but it seems that the comparison above has shown that the more obvious theological contrast is between a faith which starts with a meditation which focuses on Jewish community marked and constrained by the Torah of Yahweh and ends with a celebration which challenges that community to embrace a faith which is open to all.

Both psalms offer not only a visual image of reflection and praise but an auditory experience as well. The reception history of these two psalms illustrates further just how differently they have been developed both in art and in music. In the many illuminated manuscripts portraying the 'blessed man' (often assumed to be David) in Ps 1, the figure is usually alone, often beset with enemies. The Utrecht Psalter and the Stuttgart Psalter are amongst the earliest Christian examples, whilst more recent Jewish illustrations by Marc Chagall and Irv Davis make the same point.[18] By contrast, representations of Ps 150 are usually bursting with lively details of people singing, playing and dancing in worship. The Utrecht and Stuttgart Psalters again provide this contrast (as well as giving extraordinary insights into the music of the ninth century). Similarly, Marc Chagall's window on Ps 150 in Chichester Cathedral, with its reds and blues, evokes a very different world from his representation of Ps 1.[19]

[17] See Walter Brueggemann, "Bounded by Obedience and Praise: The Psalms as Canon," *JSOT* 50 (1991): 63–92.

[18] For the Utrecht Psalter and Psalm 1, with an explanation of the illustration, see http://psalter.library.uu.nl (Digital facsimile of Ms. 32 kept by Koert van der Horst, Keeper of Manuscripts, Daaf Samson, Automation Department). For the Stuttgart Psalter, see http://medieval.library.nd.edu/facsimiles/litfacs/stutpsal/2r.html (Manuscript Facsimiles of the Medieval Institute of the University of Notre Dame). For Marc Chagall, see http://www.biblical=art.com/artwork.asp?id_artwork=22817&showmode=Full#artwork (web version hosted by Rolf E. Staerk). For Irv Davis, see http://judaism.about.com/library/2_artlit/bl_artpsalms_a.htm (web version About.Com/ReligionandSpirituality/Judaism), which also has a contrasting representation of Psalm 150.

[19] For the Utrecht Psalter and Ps 150, with an explanation of the illustration, see n. 18 above. For an image of Ps 150 in the Stuttgart Psalter, see *The Utrecht Psalter in Medieval Art* (ed. Koert van der Horst, William Noel, and Wilhelmina C. M. Wüstefeld (London: Harvey Miller Publishers, 1996), 6, Fig. 6. For an image of Chagall's window of Ps 150, see http://www.flickr.com/photos/dspender/3438549233/in/set-72157603996844452/. Flickr is

In terms of contrasting musical representations, the settings by Thomas Tallis from the late sixteenth century and from Edward Elgar from the late nineteenth century evoke the simple, quiet, controlled and reflective nature of Ps 1.[20] This again contrasts starkly with Anton Bruckner's composition of Ps 150 in the nineteenth century and Igor Stravinsky's in the twentieth which both demonstrate the vitality and vibrancy of the psalm, to the extent that the music is the more important medium than the words themselves.[21]

Two most evocative representations are of Ps 150. One is in sculpture, the other in music, and both depict the praises of children.[22] Perhaps the finest example in a visual representation of Ps 150 is in the Museo dell' Opera del Duomo, Florence, by Luca della Robbia. Dating from 1428–31, simply entitled 'Cantoria,' his first documented commission, it was originally one of two marble 'organ pulpits' (the other was designed later by Donatello) over the sacristy doors. Although not a singing gallery, della Robbia's ten reliefs—four on two levels on a wider front panel, two on the narrower side panels—are of children, young and old, wearing the garb of actual children in Florence. They are playing, singing and dancing Ps 150, which is inscribed on the three levels of the reliefs.[23] The different cameos, taken as a piece, are most moving, suggesting children's praise as

hosted by Yahoo, and the particular image of Ps 150 here was taken by David Spender in 2009.

[20] A performance of Tallis's version of Psalm 1 can be found at http://www.classicalarchives.com/work/134341.html (main domain classicalarchives.com); see also *Music for a Reformed Church Vol 6*, no. 25 ("Tunes for Archbishop Parker's Psalter: *Man blest no doubt*") by Alistair Dixon and the Chapelle du Roi (SIGCD022). Elgar's version can be found at http://www.amazon.com/gp/recsradio/radio/B00002ZE0/ref=pd_krex_listen_dp_img?ie=UTF8&refTagSuffix=dp_img (main domain Amazon.com music sampler); see also *Psalms from St Pauls Vol 1: Psalms 1-17, no. 1* ("Beatus vir, qui non abiit") by St Paul's Cathedral Choir with Andrew Lucas (organ) and John Scott (conductor) (Hyperion CDP11001).

[21] A performance of Bruckner's composition of Psalm 150 can be found at http://www.youtube.com/watch?v=MnHtj7JXCuc. This is from the First Night of the Proms (2009) with Jiří Bělohlávek conducting Ailish Tynan, the BBC Symphony Chorus and BBC Symphony Orchestra. Stravinsky's version can be found at http://www.amazon.com/gp/recsradio/radio/B00031X7Y/ref=pd_krex_listen_dp_img?ie=UTF8&refTagSuffix=dp_img (main domain Amazon.com music sampler).

[22] Hugh Williamson, with his wealth of experience of Sunday School teaching in Suffolk, might appreciate these two examples, especially the final (more local) one.

[23] Both reliefs were dismounted in 1688, finally being brought to the Duomo Museum. See John T. Paoletti and Gary M. Radke, *Art in Renaissance Italy* (3rd ed.; London: Laurence King, 2005), 245.

spontaneous and jubilant, unconstrained and without any judgement of others, as the composer of Ps 150 would also affirm.[24]

A comparable musical medium for Ps 150, also given entirely to children's praise, is Benjamin Britten's *Psalm 150,* written in 1960 for the centenary celebrations of Britten's preparatory school in Aldeburgh. It lasts just five minutes; yet as a performance, its structure, content and style are unforgettable. Starting with a lively dance, based upon the praise of God to the sound of the trumpet, it merges into an animated round in A major, inspired by 'let everything that hath breath,' and moves into a forceful march with the words 'O Praise God.' The finale—for the context is Christian—is the *Gloria,* which recapitulates much that has gone before. In all this the choice of instruments is left to the conductor, but the children can both improvise and be guided, thus imitating both the spontaneity and form inherent of the psalm itself.[25]

The first and last psalms of the Psalter undoubtedly stand in stark contrast with one another, but these very differences complete what is lacking in the other. Torah meditation is taken up into Temple worship which in turn is marked by an acknowledgement of Torah. An inward-looking faith has to encounter one which looks outwards, but the awareness of God's presence throughout the cosmos is given a focus by remembering the community of faith. Our examples from reception history have shown how images of personal piety can be viewed alongside images of praise accessible to everyone; and when it comes to listening to each psalm as a performance, words of prayer and teaching have to be heard in the context of music and unselfconscious praise. Ultimately the simplicity of a childlike faith confounds the best of our efforts to hold together these theological conundrums, as someone once said to those who, perhaps more in the spirit of Ps 1 than Ps 150, held too protectively to both Torah and Temple.[26]

---

[24] To view these images, see http://www.operaduomo.firenze.it/english/luoghi/museo_3.asp. For other images of Robbia's work see Mary Ann Sullivan at http://www.bluffton.edu/~sullivanm/italy/florence/duomomuseo/cantoriadellarobbia.html (Bluffton University Ohio).

[25] For a performance of Britten's Psalm 150, see http://www.classicalarchives.com/work/164277.html (main domain classicalarchives.com). See also "Psalm 150, for children's chorus and instruments, Op 67", conductor Steuart Bedford with New London Children's Choir; English Choral Music: NAXOS 2003.

[26] Matt 21:14–16, quoting from Ps 8:2–3.

A REFERENCE TO THE COVENANT CODE IN 2 KINGS 17:24–41?

André Lemaire

Second Kings 17 is now famous as a chapter heavily influenced by the Deuteronomistic tradition,[1] more precisely by a theological interpretation of the fall of the kingdom of Israel in 2 Kgs 17:7–41. However, most commentators have also emphasized the composite character of this chapter, over against the hypothesis of Martin Noth of a single Deuteronomistic composition during the exile, around 560 BCE. We do not intend to discuss here all the details of the composite character of this chapter, but will try to show that the end of the chapter may contain an early reference to the first corpus of Israelite laws. To this end, we shall, first, analyze the composition of 2 Kgs 17:24–41, trying to distinguish early and later levels; and, second, compare the indications of the early level with the earliest Israelite corpus in the Pentateuch.

## I. Composition of 2 Kings 17:24–41

As already clearly stated by C. F. Burney about 17:24–41: "The narrative is certainly composite."[2] Actually there is an obvious contradiction between vv. 32, 33, 41 which say that the new immigrants "feared Yahweh" and v. 34 which emphasizes that "they feared not Yahweh"![3] Clearly, we have,

[1] See, for instance, Steven L. McKenzie, *The Trouble with Kings. The Composition of the Books of Kings in the Deuteronomistic History* (VTSup 42; Leiden: Brill, 1991), 140–42; Jerome T. Walsh, "2 Kings 17: The Deuteronomist and the Samaritans," in *Past, Present, Future. The Deuteronomistic History and the Prophets* (ed. Johannes Cornelis de Moor and Harry F. van Rooy; OtSt 44; Leiden: Brill, 2000), 315–23.

[2] Charles F. Burney, *Notes on the Hebrew Text of the Books of Kings: With an Introduction and Appendix* (Oxford: Clarendon, 1903), 333. See also, for instance, Ernst Würthwein (*Die Bücher der Könige. 1 Kön. 17–2. Kön. 25* [ATD 11/2, Göttingen: Vandenhoeck & Ruprecht, 1984], 398) who writes "Der in sich komplexe Abschnitt 17,24–41…"; Jules F. Gomes, *The Sanctuary of Bethel and the Configuration of Israelite Identity* (BZAW 368; Berlin: de Gruyter, 2006), 49.

[3] *Ibid.*; Shawn Z. Aster, "'They Feared God'/'They Did Not Fear God': On the Use of *yĕrēʾ* YHWH and *yārēʾ ʾet* YHWH in 2 Kings 17:24–41," in *Birkat Shalom: Studies in the Bible, Ancient Near Eastern Literature, and Postbiblical Judaism Presented to Shalom M. Paul on the Occasion of his Seventieth Birthday* (ed. Chaim Cohen; Winona Lake, Ind.: Eisenbrauns, 2008), 134–41, tried to understand this opposition as a difference in meaning of ירא but this explanation seems to be forced.

at least, two levels: an earlier one that was rather positive about the issue of the story of sending an Israelite priest to Bethel, and a later one that was very negative about the issue of this story.

Now, let us look more carefully at the detailed verses. According to Burney, "Verses 24–34[a], 41 ... form, in part at least, an ancient narrative embodied by R[D]."[4] The beginning of this narrative is clearly indicated in v. 24: "The king of Assyria brought people from Babylon, Cuthah, Avva, Hamath, and Sepharvaim ...". Although the precise original location of these immigrants and the precise dating of their arrival in the ancient territory of Israel during Sargon's reign (721–705 BCE) is somewhat debated,[5] a similar transference of population is also indicated in royal Neo-Assyrian texts[6] and supposed by a few Neo-Assyrian tablets found in Gezer, Hadid, and Samaria:[7] its historicity is now generally recognized.

In the general context of this transference of population by Sargon II, vv. 25–28 tell a more specific story about Bethel, apparently to be dated at the beginning of this immigration (25a). The new immigrants were confronted by a plague (lions attacking men) and it was interpreted as the indication of the wrath of the local god.[8] The phrase אלהי הארץ (vv. 26–27), clearly means here "god of the country" and not "god of the world." This means that YHWH was viewed as a god tied to the country of Israel, at the most as a national god but not yet as a universal god. As in the Khirbet Beit Lei inscription dating from around 701 BCE,[9] we are still in the context of monolatry not of monotheism.

---

[4] Burney, *Notes on the Hebrew Text*, 33.

[5] See, for instance, Nadav Na'aman, "Population Changes in Palestine Following Assyrian Deportation," *TA* 20 (1993): 104–25; Gary N. Knoppers, "Cutheans or Children of Jacob? The Issue of Samaritan Origins in 2 Kings 17," in *Reflection and Refraction: Studies in Biblical Historiography in Honour of A. Graeme Auld* (ed. Robert Rezetko, Timothy H. Lim, W. Brian Aucker; VTSup 113; Leiden: Brill, 2007), 223–39 (231).

[6] Cf., for instance, "The Annals (Sargon II)," translated by K. Lawson Younger Jr. (*COS* 2.118A: 293): "The Tamudi ... I settled them in Samaria/Samerina"; and "Nimrud Prisms D & E (Sargon II)," translated by K. Lawson Younger Jr. (*COS* 2.118D:295–96): "I repopulated Samerina more than before. I brought into it people from countries conquered by my hands. I appointed my eunuch as governor over them."

[7] Cf. Nadav Na'aman and Ran Zadok, "Assyrian Deportations to the Province of Samerina in the Light of Two Cuneiform Tablets from Tel Hadid," *TA* 27 (2000): 159–88; see the various documents translated by K. Lawson Younger Jr. (*COS* 3.115–18: 262–65; *COS* 3.122: 270–71).

[8] For lions used as instruments of the divine wrath, see 1 Kgs 13:24; 20:36; see also Mordechai Cogan and Hayim Tadmor, *II Kings: A New Translation with Introduction and Commentary* (AB 11; Garden City, N.Y.; Doubleday, 1988), 210: "All the incidents involving lions in Kings are staged in northern Israel, and so it would seem that local northern tradition underlies them."

[9] See recently André Lemaire, "Le 'Dieu de Jérusalem' à la lumière de l'épigraphie," in *Jérusalem antique et médiévale. Mélanges en l'honneur d'Ernest-Marie Laperrousaz*

Now the practical problem was apparently not the identity of the "god of the country," clearly supposed to be YHWH, but the way to pay him homage (verb ירא), to respect his usages, his rules, his laws. It was about the משפט אלהי הארץ (vv. 26–27), "the custom of the god of the country." This phrase seems to be one of the keys of the story and to suppose that there was a known special manner to pay homage to YHWH, that there were specific Israelite customs. Actually, the immigrants recognize that "they do not know the custom of the god of the country" (v. 26) and the "king of Assyria" sends a deportee priest "to teach them the custom of the god of the country" (v. 27), which was effectively done (v. 28).

At first look, this king's decision looks surprising and commentators have discussed whether it is likely that a king of Assyria gave such an order. Actually there are a few sentences in Sargon's inscriptions that are more or less similar and it seems that Sargon could commission authoritative personnel to teach new settlers "correct instruction in serving the gods and king (*palah ili ù šarri*)."[10] These somewhat parallel sentences do not prove the detailed story of vv. 25–28 but reveal that it is not unlikely,[11] especially if one thinks the Assyrian governor in Samaria, explicitly mentioned in the royal inscription, could act in the name of Sargon. It is all the more possible that the Bethel sanctuary was known as a royal sanctuary toward the middle of the 8th century BCE (Amos 7:13) and, after the fall of the kingdom, was probably directly under the authority of the Assyrian governor in Samaria. So, in one way or another, during the Assyrian period, the priest in charge of the Bethel sanctuary was probably a kind of official of the Assyrian administration and nominated by it.[12]

One may note that this Bethel priest is apparently given one function alone: he must teach (ירה) "the custom of the god of the country (משפט

(ed. Caroline Arnould-Béhar and André Lemaire; Collection de la Revue des Études Juives 52, Leuven/Paris: Peeters, 2010), 49–58. For the change from monolatry to monotheism, see André Lemaire, *The Birth of Monotheism: The Rise and Disappearance of Yahwism* (Washington, D.C.: Biblical Archaeology Society, 2007).

[10] See Shalom M. Paul, "Sargon's Administrative Diction in II Kings 17:27," *JBL* 88 (1969): 73–74; Cogan and Tadmor, *II Kings*, 210; Andreas Fuchs, *Die Inschriften Sargons II. aus Khorsabad* (Göttingen: Cuvillier, 1993), 44, line 74; K. Lawson Younger Jr., "The Fall of Samaria in Light of Recent Research," *CBQ* 61 (1999): 461–82 (469); Gomes, *The Sanctuary of Bethel*, 53.

[11] See already David P. Wright, "The Laws of Hammurabi as a Source for the Covenant Collections (Exodus 20:23–23:19)," *Maarav* 10 (2003): 11–87 (66): "This story may have a kernel of historical truth when it claims that the king of Assyria (who would be Sargon II) sent back a deported priest to teach the people Israelite religious customs (2 Kgs 17:27–28)."

[12] *Pace* Jean-Daniel Macchi ("Les controverses théologiques dans le judaïsme de l'époque postexilique. L'exemple de 2 Rois 17,24–41," *Transeu* 5 [1992]: 85–93 [88]) who interprets these verses as polemical while they may be simply telling a historical fact.

אלהי הארץ)" (v. 27b), i.e., "how they should revere YHWH (איך ייראו את־ יהוה)" (v. 28b). And this teaching was apparently successful[13] since it is repeated three times that "they revered YHWH" (vv. 32a, 33a, 41a). We shall come back below to the content of this teaching. For now, it is enough to emphasize that this function of teaching attributed to a priest is not new since it is clearly mentioned in other biblical texts,[14] for example:

> They teach your precepts (יורו משפטיך) to Jacob
> and your instruction (ותורתך) to Israel. (Deut 33:10)
>
> Her priests teach for money. (Mic 3:11)
>
> Teaching (תורה) will not disappear from the priest. (Jer 18:18)

The following verses, vv. 29–31, are very surprising since, after v. 28, they seem to contradict it. They describe the religious attitude of the groups of immigrants who keep, each one, their own original religion, with the cult of his previous main deity. The identification of some of these deities is still discussed but the main problem is the place of this list. One might expect this list just after v. 24. Actually v. 29b seems to be a reference to v. 24b. So, a transference of vv. 29–31 just after v. 24 might be a solution. These verses, however, repeatedly use the verb עשׂה 'to make,' with a god as complement, which seems characteristic of the anti-idolatry polemic. Furthermore, the mention of שמרנים in v. 29b could be an allusion to the post-exilic anti-Samaritan polemics. If that is the case, the best solution is probably to consider vv. 29–31 as a well informed[15] "post-Exilic addition to the book"[16] of Kings, a kind of scholarly commentary.

As we have already mentioned, v. 32a ("and they were revering YHWH") is probably the positive primitive conclusion of vv. 24–28. This positive conclusion is nuanced by the addition of v. 32b, where the double mention

---

[13] We do not see why vv. 25–28 is called a "sarkastisch" midrash by Würthwein, *Die Bücher der Könige,* 401; or "satirische Beispielerzählung" by Christian Frevel, "Vom Schreiben Gottes. Literarkritik, Komposition und Auslegung von 2 Kön 17,34–40," *Bib* 72 (1991): 23–48 (23).

[14] See, for instance, Roland de Vaux, *Les institutions de l'Ancien Testament II* (Paris: Cerf, 1967), 206–8.

[15] See, for instance, K. Lawson Younger Jr., "The Repopulation of Samaria (2 Kgs 17:24, 27–31) in Light of Recent Study," in *The Future of Biblical Archaeology: Reassessing Methodologies and Assumptions: The Proceedings of a Symposium August 12-14, 2001 at Trinity International University* (ed. James K. Hoffmeier and Alan Millard; Grand Rapids: Eerdmans, 2004), 254–80.

[16] See already Harold H. Rowley, "The Samaritan Schism in Legend and History," in *Israel's Prophetic Heritage: Essays in Honor of James Muilenburg* (ed. Bernhard W. Anderson and Walter J. Harrelson; New York/London: Harper, 1962), 208–22 (212).

of במות seems to be a hint that this is typical of a redactor at the time of Hezekiah (cf. 2 Kgs 18:4 הוא הסיר את־הבמות). If we put aside v. 33 where v. 33a repeats v. 32a and v. 33b is probably an addition by the same scribe as vv. 29–31, the conclusion of the Hezekian redactor is probably given in v. 34a: "Until this day, they act according to the first/previous customs (כמשׁפטים הראשׁנים)."

In the general context of 2 Kgs 17:24–41, the phrase כמשׁפטים הראשׁנים seems to refer to the idolatrous cult of the new settlers who went on revering their previous deities. However, if vv. 29–31 is a late, post-exilic addition, the phrase "the first customs" may originally have had another meaning for the Hezekian scribe: the teaching of the priest of Bethel could be recognized as truly Israelite, teaching authentic ancient Israelite traditions and customs. However, these ancient customs were no longer conforming to the current Yahwistic tradition as promoted by Hezekiah's reform, especially with the suppression of the במות.[17] In a way, the משׁפטים ראשׁנים were outdated and had now to be updated by the משׁפטים אחרנים of the cultic reform of Hezekiah. The Bethel priest could go on teaching the ancient Israelite tradition but, now, he had to give up his role as a non-Levite sacrificer in the בית הבמות of Bethel.

With most of the commentators, the following vv. 34b–40 contain many characteristic Deuteronomistic phrases.[18] The insertion of this homiletic judgment[19]/Deuteronomistic commentary is clearly indicated by the resumption (with a small difference) of v. 34aβ in 40b: כמשׁפטים הראשׁנים, "according to their previous custom,"[20] which, in this context,

---

[17] For the historicity of the religious reform of Hezekiah, see Lemaire, *The Birth of Monotheism*, 87–94; Ze'ev Herzog, "Is There Evidence for the Intentional Abolishment of Cult in the Arad and Tel Beersheba Excavations?," *ErIsr* 29 (2009): 125–36; Israel Finkelstein and Neil Asher Silberman, "Temple and Dynasty: Hezekiah, the Reformation of Judah and the Emergence of the Pan-Israelite Ideology," *ErIsr* 29 (2009): 348–57.

[18] See Moshe Weinfeld, *Deuteronomy and the Deuteronomic School* (Clarendon: Oxford, 1972), 320–51; Cogan and Tadmor, *II Kings*, 212–13: "Deuteronomistic throughout." See also Macchi, "Les controverses théologiques," 91–92 (but why consider it "post-deutéronomiste"?); F. Blanco Wissmann, *"Er tat das Rechte..." Beurteilungeskriterien und Deuteronomismus in 1 Kön 12–2 Kön 25* (ATANT 93; Zurich: Theologischer Verlag, 2008), 160–61: "nachträgliche Korrektur"; Mark Zvi Brettler, *The Creation of History in Ancient Israel* (London: Routledge, 1995), 130. For an essay to distinguish different levels in 2 Kgs 17:34–40, see Frevel, "Vom Schreiben Gottes," 23–48.

[19] James A. Montgomery and Henry S. Gehman, *A Critical and Exegetical Commentary on the Books of Kings* (ICC; New York: Scribner, 1951), 471, 477.

[20] See already Burney, *Notes on the Hebrew Text*, 333: "Verse 40[b] rounds off the interpolation by the repetition of v. 34[a]"; see also Frevel, "Vom Schreiben Gottes," 25: "Denn in vv 34–40 ist nicht mehr von den Kolonisten die Rede"; Walsh, "2 Kings 17," 318; Gary N. Knoppers, "Cutheans or Children of Jacob?," 231–32. *Pace* M. Z. Brettler, *The Creation of History*

clearly refers to customs of Israelites.[21] The polemic tone of this redaction is clearly indicated at the beginning: "They do not revere YHWH" (v. 34b)! It is difficult to date this Deuteronomistic redaction but a dating during Josiah's reign is all the more tempting since this king apparently profaned the Bethel sanctuary (2 Kgs 25:15–20; cf. 1 Kgs 13:1–5).

Verse 41a takes up again, for the third time, the positive primitive conclusion of the story in vv. 25–28, while v. 41b with the verb עבד as in v. 33b, is again a small anti-idolatrous addition in the same line as vv. 29–31, 33b.

So, a detailed literary analysis of 2 Kgs 17:24–41 seems to reveal three main strata:

1. A first/earlier stratum:[22] vv. 24–28, 32–33a, 34a, 41a.[α] It tells how the priest of the sanctuary of Bethel went on teaching how to revere YHWH, even though this was done in the context of a בית במות and by non-Levite priests (v. 32b).[23] These verses probably belong to a "proto-deuteronomistic" redaction during Hezekiah's reign.[24] For this redactor, the teaching of the Bethel priest was good but he was only teaching "according to the first/previous customs (כמשפטים הראשנים)" and not according to the new rules of the reform of Hezekiah who suppressed the במות (2 Kgs 18:4a). One may note that this story seems to recognize that

*in Ancient Israel*, 1995, 130–33; Marvin A. Sweeney, *I and II Kings. A Commentary* (OTL, Louisville: Westminster John Knox, 2007), 392: with an inversed relative chronology: "vv 34–40 represent an earlier text and ... vv 24–34 ... a later redaction from the Josianic reform."

21 See Würthwein, *Die Bücher der Könige*, 401; McKenzie, *The Trouble with Kings*, 142; Walsh, "2 Kings 17," 318.

22 See Bernhard Stade, "Miscellen 16. Anmerkungen zu 2 Kö. 15–21," *ZAW* 6 (1886): 156–89 (167–70); Montgomery and Gehman, *A Critical and Exegetical Commentary*, 471.

23 See already Montgomery and Gehman (*A Critical and Exegetical Commentary*, 473) about the "good priest": "We may presume that his party had the benevolent assistance of Hezekiah."

24 For such a redaction, see Helga Weippert, "Die 'deuteronomistischen' Beurteilungen der Könige von Israel und Juda und das Problem der Redaktion der Königsbücher," *Bib* 53 (1972): 301–39; W. Boyd Barrick, "On the 'Removal of the 'High Places' in 1–2 Kings," *Bib* 55 (1974): 257–59; Helga Weippert, "'Der Ort, den Jahwe erwählen wird, um dort seinen Namen wohnen zu lassen.' Die Geschichte einer alttestamentlichen Formel," *BZ* 24 (1980): 76–94 (86–87); André Lemaire, "Vers l'histoire de la rédaction des livres des Rois," *ZAW* 98 (1986): 221–36 (224–27, 232); idem, "Toward a Redactional History of the Book of Kings," in *Reconsidering Israel and Judah Recent Studies on the Deuteronomistic History* (ed. Gary N. Knoppers and J. Gordon McConville; Sources for Biblical and Theological Study 8; Winona Lake: Eisenbrauns, 2000), 446–61 (450–53, 458); Erik Eynikel, *The Reform of King Josiah and the Composition of the Deuteronomistic History* (OtSt 33; Leiden: Brill, 1996); Baruch Halpern and André Lemaire, "The Composition of Kings," in *The Books of Kings. Sources, Composition, Historiography and Reception* (ed. Baruch Halpern and André Lemaire; VTSup 129; Leiden: Brill, 2010), 123–53 (132–34).

Bethel played a religious role with, probably, some scribal activity, during the 8th century BCE, even after the fall of Samaria.[25] The new analysis of the Bethel excavations by I. Finkelstein and L. Singer-Avitz would fit such an interpretation.[26] Actually E. A. Knauf[27] already made a proposal which places in Bethel the writing of the Exodus tradition, of the core book of Hosea, and of the "Book of Saviours," during the 8th century BCE. However such a location is still largely conjectural.

2. About a century later, a Josian redactor added vv. 34b–40 with a condemnation of the teaching of the Bethel priest, that, according to him, was a total failure, and a condemnation of the Samaritans. For this Josian redactor, the מִשְׁפָּטִים רִאשֹׁנִים are completely outdated and should be replaced by the collection of the new מִשְׁפָּטִים: the core of Deuteronomy. So the audience of this Bethel priest "does not revere YHWH" at all (v. 34b). This appreciation seems to be in line with Josiah's profanation of Bethel (2 Kgs 23:15–18; cf. 1 Kgs 13:2).
3. Again about a century later, probably at the beginning of the Persian period, a new Deuteronomistic monotheistic redaction condemned the cult of the Samaritans as idolatrous: vv. 29–31, 33b, 41a$^{\beta}$–b.

## II. Historical Interpretation of the Earliest Stratum

Now it is clear enough that, for historical appreciation, the historian should essentially take into consideration the first/earlier stratum. In this source, the priest of Bethel is presented as a teacher (מורה) and the content of his teaching is indicated by two synonymous phrases:[28]

the custom of the god of the country (משפט אלהי הארץ; v. 27b)
how they should revere YHWH (איך ייראו את־יהוה; v. 28b).

Furthermore, this teaching seems to correspond to the first/previous customs (כמִשְׁפָּטִים הָרִאשֹׁנִים), i.e., the customs anterior to Hezekiah's

[25] See already Gomes, *The Sanctuary of Bethel*, 53: "Bethel escaped destruction and continued to function as a sanctuary during the Assyrian period."

[26] Israel Finkelstein and Lily Singer-Avitz, "Reevaluating Bethel," *ZDPV* 125 (2009): 33–48. For the previous interpretation, see Jean-Marie van Cangh, "Béthel: archéologie et histoire," in *Les sources judaïques du Nouveau Testament: Recueil d'essais* (BETL 204; Leuven: Peeters, 2008), 441–49.

[27] Ernst A. Knauf, "Bethel: The Israelite Impact on Judean Language and Literature," in *Judah and the Judeans in the Persian Period* (ed. Oded Lipschits and Manfred Oeming; Winona Lake, Ind.: Eisenbrauns, 2006), 291–349 (320–21).

[28] See already Aster, "They Feared God," 139.

reform suppressing the במות. Apparently the Bethel priest was teaching the Israelite customs such as they were known during the 8th century BCE. Although not explicitly stated, the phrases suggest a complete set of these customs, eventually written as a collection, a code[29] of laws and customs.[30]

Since the 19th century, most commentators on the Pentateuch have distinguished at least three ancient Israelite "codes": the Covenant Code (CC), the Deuteronomic Code (D) and the Holiness Code (H). Although there was and is still some dispute, especially about the succession of H after D and D after CC, these three codes are generally considered to have been written in the chronological order: first CC, second D, and finally, after the exile, H. The detailed analysis of B. M. Levinson[31] seems to have conclusively shown that the author(s) of H knew and used the text of D and that the author(s) of D knew and used the text of the CC.[32]

Actually the CC (Exod 20:22–23:33) is generally considered to be one of the most ancient Israelite codes.[33] Its precise *Sitz im Leben* has been and is still discussed,[34] especially because it is difficult to be certain whether some parts of this CC suppose a historical context anterior to kingship or not.[35]

---

[29] Although not to be understood as a code of the late Roman period and later, the word "code" is traditionally used for collections of laws and customs in the ancient Near East.

[30] Actually משפט was translated נמוס (*nomos*) in Targum Jonathan: see Daniel J. Harrington and Anthony J. Saldarini, *Targum Jonathan of the Former Prophets* (ArBib 10; Wilmington, Del./Edinburgh: Michael Glazier, 1987), 298.

[31] See, for instance, Bernard M. Levinson, *Deuteronomy and the Hermeneutics of Legal Innovation* (New York: Oxford University Press, 1997), esp. 149–50; idem, "Is the Covenant Code an Exilic Composition? A Response to John Van Seters," in *In Search of Pre-Exilic Israel. Proceedings of the Oxford Old Testament Seminar*, (ed. John Day; JSOTSup 406; London and New York, 2004), 272–325; *idem*, "The Manumission of Hermeneutics: The Slave Laws of the Pentateuch as a Challenge to Contemporary Pentateuchal Theory," in *Congress Volume Leiden* 2004 (ed. André. Lemaire; VTSup 109; Leiden: Brill, 2006), 281–324. *Pace* John Van Seters, *A Law Book for the Diaspora: Revision in the Study of the Covenant Code*, New York: Oxford University Press, 2003); *idem*, "Revision in the Study of the Covenant Code and a Response to my Critics," *SJOT* 21 ( 2007): 5–28.

[32] See, for instance, Norbert Lohfink, "Fortschreibung? Zur Technik vom Rechtsrevisionen im deuteronomischen Bereich, erörtert an Deuteronomium 12, Ex 21,2–11 und Dtn 15,12–18," in *Das Deuteronomium und seine Querbeziehungen* (ed. Timo Veijola; Schriften der Finnischen Gesellschaft 62; Göttingen: Vandenhoeck & Ruprecht, 1996), 133–61.

[33] See lately Thomas B. Dozeman, *Commentary on Exodus* (Eerdmans Critical Commentary; Grand Rapids: Eerdmans, 2009), 497–500.

[34] See, for instance, Guy Lasserre, "Quelques études récentes sur le Code de l'Alliance," *RTP* 125 (1993): 267–76.

[35] That is the reason why some commentators dated it, or, at least, its earlier stratum, in pre-monarchic period. See Brevard S. Childs, *The Book of Exodus* (OTL; Philadelphia: Westminster, 1974), 457; Martin Noth, *Das zweite Buch Mose: Exodus* (ATD 5; Göttingen: Vandenhoeck & Ruprecht, 1978), 141: "Da im Bundesbuch kein Bezug auf staatliche Einrichtungen genommen wird, kann damit gerechnet werden, dass es noch in vorstaatli-

However most of the commentators tend now to think that the redaction of CC is to be dated in the 8th century BCE. Some of them connect it with the social situation of the kingdom of Israel[36] and others with the beginning of the Neo-Assyrian period.[37] This last dating seems to be partly connected with the appreciation of the influence of the Laws of Hammurabi on the Covenant collection. It is still an object of debate, however, since it is difficult to be certain whether the laws of Hammurabi were a direct source of the CC or whether this influence was more pervasive in the Levant since the second millennium BCE.[38] In one way or another, it seems clear that this influence had to take into account original Israelite traditions. In this context, the royal sanctuary of Bethel toward the end of the 8th century BCE[39] appears as a likely place where the CC could have been taught and eventually written. Actually D. P. Wright already noted,

cher Zeit zusammengestellt worden ist. Aber ein Beweis dafür lässt sich nicht erbringen"; Ludger Schwienhost-Schönberger, *Das Bundesbuch (Ex 20,22–23,33)* (BZAW 188; Berlin/New York: de Gruyter, 1990), 271–76 (for the "Grundbestand"); Jay W. Marshall, *Israel and the Book of the Covenant. An Anthropological Approach to Biblical Law* (Atlanta: Scholars Press, 1993); T. Desmond Alexander, "The Composition of the Sinai Narrative in Exodus xix,1–xxiv 11," *VT* 49 (1999): 2–20; John S. Bergma, *The Jubilee from Leviticus to Qumran* (VTSup 115; Leiden: Brill, 2007), 140–41.

[36] Frank Crüsemann, "Das Bundesbuch—historischer Ort und institutioneller Hintergrund," in *Congress Volume Jerusalem 1986* (ed. John A. Emerton; VTSup 40; Leiden: Brill, 1988), 27–41; Schwienhorst-Schönberger, *Das Bundesbuch*, 271; Frank Crüsemann, *Die Tora: Theologie und Sozialgeschichte des alttestamentlichen Gesetzes* (München: Guetersloher Verlagshaus, 1992), 229 (partly).

[37] Yuichi Osumi, *Die Kompositionsgeschichte des Bundesbuches Exodus 20,22b–23,33* (OBO 105; Freiburg: Universitätsverlag; Göttingen: Vandenhoeck & Ruprecht, 1991), 220; Crüsemann, *Die Tora*, 215, 230; Rainer Albertz, *A History of Israelite Religion in the Old Testament Period. Volume I: From the Beginnings to the End of the Monarchy* (OTL; Louisville: SCM, 1994), 182–86; Ralf Rothenbusch, *Die kasuistische Rechtsammlung im 'Bundesbuch' (Ex 21,2–11.18–22,16) und ihr literarischer Kontext im Licht altorientalischer Parallelen* (AOAT 259; Münster: Ugarit-Verlag, 2000), 481; Levinson, "Is the Covenant Code an Exilic Composition," 294–97, 316–17; Jan Christian Gertz, *Grundinformation Altes Testament: Eine Einführung in Literatur, Religion und Geschichte des Alten Testaments* (Göttingen: Vandenhoeck & Ruprecht, 2007), 223–24.

[38] For this debate, see Wright, "The Laws of Hammurabi," 11–87; Bruce Wells, "The Covenant Code and Near Eastern Legal traditions," *Maarav* 13 (2006): 85–118; David P. Wright, "The Laws of Hammurabi and the Covenant Code: A Response to Bruce Wells," *Maarav* 13 (2006): 211–60; idem, *Inventing God's Law: How the Covenant Code of the Bible Used and Revised the Laws of Hammurabi* (New York: Oxford University Press, 2009); Frank H. Polak, "Review of D. P. Wright, *Inventing God's Law: How the Covenant Code of the Bible Used and Revised the Laws of Hammurabi*," *RBL* [http://www.bookreviews.org] (2010). A pervasive influence was already proposed by Shalom M. Paul (*Studies in the Book of the Covenant in the Light of Cuneiform and Biblical Law* [VTSup 18; Leiden: Brill, 1970], 99–105) and the discovery of a juridical tablet in Hazor (summer 2010) reveals that, at least, it is not unlikely.

[39] This would be a *terminus ad quem* and CC could have existed before or integrated earlier Israelite traditions.

in reference to 2 Kgs 17:27–28: "A deported priest would be an attractive candidate for the author of CC."[40]

## III. Conclusion

This tentative identification would give a perfect *Sitz im Leben* for the story of a priest teaching "the custom of the god of the country (משפט אלהי הארץ)" (v. 27b). More precisely, the first/previous customs (משפטים ראשנים) (v. 34a) could be compared to the משפטים that should be placed in front of the Israelites in Exod 21:1 (cf. also 21:9b, 31b) and that Moses told them in Exod 24:3. This identification is all the more tempting since the word משפטים seems to have been the title of the CC,[41] or, at least, of the civil laws in casuistic form of Exod 21:1–22:16.[42] As is well known, the rule concerning the altar in CC presupposes the existence of several sanctuaries (Exod 20:24) and is probably anterior to the reform of Hezekiah (or outside its territory of application). If the teaching of the Bethel priest was CC, one can understand that a Hezekian redaction could, at the same time, recognize that, on one hand, this teaching was a legitimate Israelite teaching, emphasizing the only cult of YHWH according to the ancient Israelite religious tradition, and, on the other hand, that it was not up to date since it did not take into account the drastic reform of Hezekiah suppressing the במות.[43]

---

[40] Wright, "The Laws of Hammurabi," 66.

[41] Cf. Bernard S. Jackson, "Some Literary Features of the Mishpatim," in *Wünschet Jerusalem Frieden: Collected Communications to the XIIth Congress of the IOSOT Jerusalem 1986* (ed. Matthias Augustin and Klaus-Dietrich Schunk; BEATAJ 13; Frankfurt am Main: Peter Lang, 1988), 235–42; Joe M. Sprinkle, *'The Book of the Covenant': A Literary Approach* (JSOTSup 174; Sheffield: JSOT Press, 1994), 204: "There is insufficient reason to end the משפטים at 22.16 as some critics suggest"; Levinson, "Is the Covenant Code an Exilic Composition?" 281–83; Jean-Louis Ska, "From History Writing to Library Building: The End of History and the Birth of the Book," in *The Pentateuch as Torah. New Models for Understanding Its Promulgation and Acceptance* (ed. Gary N. Knoppers and Bernard M. Levinson; Winona Lake: Eisenbrauns, 2007), 145–69 (166–67); Bernard S. Jackson, *Wisdom-Laws: A Study of the Mishpatim of Exodus 21:1–22:16* (Oxford: Oxford University Press, 2006), 453–54, 461–62.

[42] Cf. Osumi, *Die Kompositionsgeschichte des Bundesbuches*, 87–147, 219; Cornelius Houtman, *Exodus Vol. 3: Chapters 20–40* (Historical Commentary on the Old Testament; Leuven: Peeters, 2000), 81, 84–90; Dozeman, *Commentary on Exodus*, 496.

[43] The appreciation of Gomes (*The Sanctuary of Bethel*, 50) of "the benign attitude to the Bethel cult reflected in vv. 24–28" should be nuanced: these verses are positive about the *teaching* of the Bethel priest, not about his cult. See also the remarks against the hypothesis of CC as a Hezekian Code by Crüsemann, *Die Tora*, 230.

It is a great pleasure to dedicate this modest essay identifying the משפט אלהי הארץ and the משפטים ראשנים of 2 Kgs 17:26–27, 34a, 40b to H. G. M. Williamson whom I have known for thirty years, during which time I have had many opportunities to appreciate him as a scholar and an excellent colleague always ready to help, especially as a critical reader of the Supplements to *Vetus Testamentum* manuscripts.

# SHIPS AND OTHER SEAFARING VESSELS IN THE OLD TESTAMENT

Jill Middlemas

It is widely held that the ancient Israelites regarded ships and activities that took place on the sea with a measure of scepticism. For example, Joseph Blenkinsopp relates this attitude to "... the typical Israelite allergy to the sea, seafaring, and international trade"[1] and Hugh Williamson writes more generally that "By and large, the Israelites were not a nautical people, and indeed they seem to have been deeply suspicious of most things to do with the sea."[2] Nevertheless, trade via cargo vessels was one facet of the economy of the ancient world and the term for ships appears not infrequently within the Old Testament (roughly 50 times).[3] A re-examination of the role of ships can shed new light on how they function within the rhetoric of the Old Testament and provide a topic of interest for Professor Williamson, who constructs, sails, and races model yachts off the Suffolk coastline in Great Britain.[4]

## I. Where are Ships and Shipping Found?

Ships are referred to in a variety of ways in the Old Testament, but the main terms share the consonants of the root אנה from which we have אני (7 times), אניה (5 times), and אוניות.[5] Also attested are צי, ציים, and תבה as well as the *hapax legomena* כלי, and שכיות.[6] As a collective term for ships or more accurately a fleet of ships the singular אֳנִי is found primarily

[1] Joseph Blenkinsopp, *Isaiah 1–39* (AB 19; New York: Doubleday, 2000), 343.

[2] H. G. M. Williamson, *Isaiah 1–5* (vol. 1; London: T&T Clark, 2006), 226.

[3] If I were to include all 26 times the ark appears in Gen 6–9, this number would be just under 75.

[4] For an older study on shipping more generally in the ANE, see Richard D. Barnett, "Early Shipping in the Near East," *Antiquity* 32 (1958): 220–30.

[5] There is no implicit claim here that the nouns are derived from the verbal root. See the concerns about the "root fallacy" expressed by James Barr, *The Semantics of Biblical Language* (1961; repr., London: SCM, 1996), 100–106.

[6] A possible third *hapax legomenon* would be the root *bar* understood as some type of shipping/freighting vessel in Isa. 43:14. This would require a slight emendation to the text. It has not been included here as it remains fairly controversial, but there is a discussion of the translation in conjunction with a discussion of the verse.

in the chronicles about kings within the books of Kings (1 Kgs 9:26–27; 1 Kgs 10:11; 3x in 1 Kgs 10:22), although one time it appears in the prophecy of Isaiah (Isa 33:21, parallel to צִי). As might be expected the references to ships in the monarchical literature appear in conjunction with rulers. King Solomon of the united kingdom of ancient Israel and King Hiram of Tyre (Phoenicia) are said to have had fleets of ships. Solomon's fleet was stationed at Ezion-Geber on the Red Sea in Edom (1 Kgs 9:26 // 2 Chr 20:36). Both kings used their fleets for trade (1 Kgs 10:11, 22). In addition, references to ships reinforce the impression of a strong relationship between the two kings by speaking of Hiram sending ships with his own sailors together with those of Solomon (1 Kgs 9:27). Moreover, Solomon had stationed his Tarshish ships[7] alongside those of Hiram (1 Kgs 10:22 // 2 Chr 9:21). Tarshish here is generally agreed to refer to the type of ship—capable of long distance travel replete with cargo—rather than a place.[8] The final reference to אני in the singular occurs in a late prophecy within the book of Isaiah, which speaks of a divine age of peace, described at one point as "a place of broad rivers and streams, where no rowing boat (אני־שיט)[9] with oars can go" (Isa 33:21).

The feminine אניה, a seeming derivative of אנה, appears strikingly less. It is found confined to proverbial or allegorical uses as in Prov 30:19 and in the prophecy of Jonah (Jonah 1:3, 4, 5 twice), which itself is arguably an allegory. In Proverbs a ship sailing on the high seas is part of an example of those things beyond the comprehension of the human mind. In the book of Jonah, the ship functions as part of the setting for the book and becomes personified in order to heighten the tension in the narrative (Jonah 1:4). Again, we find a sea-going vessel related to Tarshish. In this instance, Tarshish represents the geographical location to which the boat travels and which is Jonah's intended destination (Jonah 1:3).

The plural form אוניות appears the most frequently of the nouns related to אנה. Its use overlaps that found already, but it conveys new ranges of meaning as well. It appears in a wide range of passages in the Hebrew Bible including, alongside kings (1 Kgs 9:27; twice in 22:49–50 [Eng. 48–49]; 2 Chr 8:18; 9:21; 20:36–37), within prophecy (Deut 28:68;

[7] References to Tarshish occur ten times in biblical literature with references to ships, see 1 Kgs 10:22 (twice); 22:49; 2 Chr 20:36; Ps 48:8; Isa 2:16; 23:1, 14; 60:9; Ezek 27:25. See the overview by David W. Baker, "Tarshish," in *ABD* 6:331–33.

[8] See the discussion in Williamson, *Isaiah 1–5*, 199.

[9] שיט 'oar' is a *hapax legomenon*, but has been related to the root שוט 'to lash or whip,' conveying the sense of lashing the sea.

Isa 2:16; 23:1, 14 cf. v. 10;[10] 43:14; 60:9; Ezek 27:9, 25, 29; Dan 11:40), in conjunction with references to the tribes of ancient Israel (Gen 49:13; Judg 5:17), in allegorical allusions (Job 9:26; Prov 31:14), and in the psalms (Pss 48:7 [Eng. 8]; 104:26; 107:24). In conjunction with kings, the ships of Solomon and Hiram are again paired (2 Chr 8:18; 9:21), but a specialized use of the term occurs in the phrase, "the men of ships, who knew the sea" (1 Kgs 9:27). Like Solomon, Jehoshaphat had built ships. Unlike Solomon, his ships were not referred to as a fleet (אֳנִי) and they were shipwrecked (twice in 1 Kgs 22:49 [Eng. 48], 50 [Eng. 49] // 2 Chr 20:36–37).

By far the greatest number of occurrences of the term אוניות is in prophecy, but the plural appears within other biblical literature as well. With the exception of a positive role ascribed to ships in Isa 60:9, prophecies including sea craft are used repeatedly in prophetic oracles to indicate divine punishment (Deut 28:68; Isa 2:16; 23:1, 14; 43:14; Ezek 27; Dan 11:40). The referent also serves an etiological function when it is used along with the inheritance of Zebulun, the son of Jacob (Gen 49:13) and the territory of Dan during the time of the Judges (Judg 5:17). A proverbial/allegorical sense is found in the book of Job as a way of representing Job's life (9:26) and in the book of Proverbs, where merchant ships provide another exemplary role for the strong woman at the close of the book (Prov 31:14). In the Psalms, ships appear in passages that highlight the deity's power and might (Pss 48:7 [Eng. 8]; 104:26) and examples of noteworthy human response (Ps 107:23).

There are three terms that appear in conjunction with smaller sea craft and watertight, sea-going vessels that appear rarely. The term צי refers to a river-going boat and it appears four times. All uses occur in prophecy, with the plural being attested in conjunction with destruction (of Asshur and Eber in Num 24:24; of Egypt in Ezek 30:9; of Antiochus IV Ephiphanes in Dan 11:30). As mentioned previously the singular צי appears in a late prophetic text about the implementation of divine rule likened to broad rivers and streams where no "majestic ship can pass" (Isa 33:21). Although not exactly a ship, the term תבה connotes a vessel able to traverse water. Although it occurs just under 30 times, it is found in only two stories in the Old Testament: of Noah's ark (26 times in Gen 6:14–9:18) and of the reed basket that carried baby Moses (Exod 2:3, 5).

[10] Verse 10 is difficult and usually emended on the basis of the LXX to refer once again to the ships of Tarshish. See the commentaries.

Even more rarely, two *hapax legomena* found scattered within the prophecies of the book of Isaiah (all prophecies of doom) denote water-going vessels. The more general term 'vessel' in the plural (כלי) appears once in conjunction with the material of its construction (גמא) as a water-tight boat capable of traversing the Nile (and perhaps beyond)—the reed skiffs of Isa 18:2 (see also Job 9:26). Also, the plural שכיות derived from שכה occurs in one of the Isaianic prophecies of judgement parallel to אוניות that summarizes main themes appearing in the collection at the beginning of the book (Isa 2:16).

## II. Synthesis

An examination of the terms for ships reveals that they can be organized into seven different categories: etiological or historical detail, mythological use, references to construction, the privilege of kings, prophetic judgement and salvation, proverbial or allegorical use, and as illustrative of shipping business or trade.

### 1. *Etiological or Historical Use*

The terminology for ships occurs in conjunction with etiological or historical information. It is found in an etiology related to the territory bequeathed to Zebulun, one of Jacob's sons in Gen 49:13, and also in the story of the heroes Deborah and Barak in Judg 5:17. In Genesis it is said that Zebulun's territory borders on the sea, "Zebulun shall dwell at the shore of the sea; he shall become a haven for ships" (Gen 49:13). In the Judges account, Deborah lists a series of the ancient Israelite tribes that failed to come to the aid of the confederation in Judg 5:15b–17. She includes among them the tribe of Dan, which is described as abiding with the ships (Judg 5:17).

Two verses from the book of Daniel in which the term 'ships' appears can also be included within this section. The concluding chapters of Daniel (10–12) contain a type of quasi-prophecy that is more historical in nature. In 11:30–39 the writer draws on events in the life of Antiochus IV Epiphanes to create a portrait of the king before his downfall and relates those details in a more imaginative way in vv. 40–45.[11] The biblical writer

[11] See the commentaries, especially John E. Goldingay, *Daniel* (WBC 30; Dallas: Word Books, 1989), 269–319 (301–5).

indicates that the Romans employed ships to repel the attempt of Antiochus to subjugate Egypt in v. 30. The imaginative construal of the end of Antiochus, based less on actual historical facts and more on past experiences of his actions, includes a scenario in which he again sets out to conquer Egypt (11:40). The biblical writer appears to draw on the knowledge that Antiochus possessed a navy, which was particularly successful in his second campaign against Egypt in 169 BCE, and likens a final Egyptian invasion to a whirlwind that included land and sea forces: chariots, horsemen, and many ships.

### 2. *Mythological Use*

Twice in the Psalms the poet employs the terminology of ships in the midst of mythological information that bolsters the portrait of an impressively powerful Yahweh. In one of the Psalms of Zion, a subsection of Hymns of Praise, the poet fashions a scenario in which Jerusalem looks on while Yahweh smashes the ships of Tarshish with the east wind (Ps 48:7 [Eng. 8]). Another mythological scene appears in Ps 104, a hymn of creation, in which the poet portrays creation as an expression of the majesty and rulership of Yahweh. In Ps 104, the poet celebrates various aspects of the created order, including sea creatures (vv. 25–26) and maritime activity (lit. 'the going of ships'). The ships appear in the same verse as the mythical sea creature Leviathan (v. 26) and thus deserve mention as a type of mythological use.

### 3. *Construction*

One of the areas of overlap that joins some of the examples of ships and other water-going vessels in the Old Testament has to do with descriptions of construction. Although Kings Solomon and Jehoshaphat 'built' ships, there is no information on what the construction entailed. When the agents of construction are not royal, as with the case of Noah and the mother of Moses, some details are given. Noah made his ark according to a divine blueprint of the sturdiest of woods and covered it inside and out with pitch (Gen 6:14–9:18). Like Noah, the mother of Moses also built a floating device (תבה), but unlike Noah she acted on her own initiative: "And when she could hide him no longer she took for him a basket made of bulrushes, and daubed it with bitumen and pitch" (Exod 2:3, 5). Like other women in the Exodus tradition who are portrayed as acting against the orders of Pharaoh in order to save the male children (the midwives come readily to mind), the mother of Moses acted on her own initiative to save her child. The floating ark that she constructed was made from items to which she had access—the basket, bitumen, and pitch. She is the only woman said to have built a watertight sailing vessel in the Old Testament. The תבה she constructs is distinguished from Noah's in that it is made of reed or papyrus (גמא, cf. Isa 18:2). Although linked through the rare word תבה, Noah and Moses' mother contrast each other. Noah's actions in response to divine initiative led to the saving of creation, while the maternal instincts of Moses' mother led ultimately to the saving of a people.

## 4. *Privilege of Kings*

Ships and ship-building are by and large portrayed as the prerogative of kings. Solomon has sea-going vessels that far exceed the description of a mere boat. In 1 Kgs 10:22 it is said that Solomon has a Tarshish fleet and it is generally agreed that the descriptor Tarshish has less to do with location than with size. The debate has transpired partly because the Chronicler's rendition describes the ships of Solomon and Jehoshaphat as those intended to travel to Tarshish (2 Chr 9:22; 20:36–37), but the Chronicler's view in this instance is widely regarded as a misunderstanding of his sources. Moreover, the exotic and rare cargo found in Solomon's ships of ivory, apes, and peacocks does not suggest a Mediterranean destination as would be implied if Tarshish were taken literally. 'Tarshish fleet,' then, indicates sea-going vessels able to cross great waters—perhaps ocean going ships.[12] The shipping activities of King Solomon were examples of his great wealth and power (cf. 1 Kgs 10:23) and contribute, therefore, to exhibiting how incredible he was perceived to be.[13]

The only other king in the Old Testament attested to have had ships was Jehoshaphat, and the reference is very short (as it is to his reign generally; 1 Kgs 22:49–50). Jehoshaphat is said to have tried to renew maritime activities at the port of Ezion-Geber, but the attempt failed when the ships were destroyed. The Kings account reports also that King Ahaziah's entreaty to share in the maritime activities was rejected by Jehoshaphat.

---

[12] See the commentaries, especially Mordechai Cogan, *1 Kings* (AB 10; New York: Doubleday, 2001), 319; and Marvin A. Sweeney, *I and II Kings* (OTL; Louisville: Westminster John Knox, 2007), 151.

[13] Gary N. Knoppers, *Two Nations Under God: The Deuteronomistic History of Solomon and the Dual Monarchies* (vol. 1; HSM 52; Atlanta: Scholars Press, 1993), 130–31.

Hints about maritime trade appear in conjunction with the account of kings and ship building/sailing. That Hiram, representative of the Phoenicians and king of Tyre, is said to have mariners familiar with the sea (1 Kgs 9:27; 2 Chr 8:18) reinforces the impression of Phoenicians as the sea traders in the First Temple period. Ancient Israel participates in maritime trade, but only through its alliance with the Phoenicians.

### 5. *Prophecy*

Ships appear in prophecies outside of the prophetic material as well as within those found in the books named after prophets. In literature outside of the biblical prophetic books ships function either as instruments of Yahweh's wrath, as in Balaam's prophecy in Num 24:24, or as the means by which the deity accomplishes punishment: "And Yahweh will bring you back in ships to Egypt, a journey which I promised that you should never make again" (Deut 28:68). Ships are also the object of the deity's wrath as in the Chronicler's account of the judgement of Jehoshaphat for his alliance with Ahaziah of the northern kingdom: "The ships were wrecked and were not able to go to Tarshish" (2 Chr 20:37b). What is perhaps more interesting about the story of Jehoshaphat is how the Chronicles account conveys the information found also in Kings (1 Kgs 22) in an ideologically motivated way. In the Chronicles account Jehoshaphat's pursuit of an alliance with Ahaziah results in the prophetic condemnation of Eliezer son of Dadavahu, and the destruction of the ships stationed in the harbor of Ezion-Geber is attributed to the deity's wrath. Through this interpretation the Chronicler constructs the events according to a sin/prophetic condemnation/divine punishment theological pattern found elsewhere in Chronicles.[14]

Within the prophetic literature the term 'ships' appears in conjunction mainly with prophecies of judgement. In the summary of various Isaianic themes found in the second chapter of the book of Isaiah, the deity's actions against all things lifted up in pride or hubris will be made low on the Day of Yahweh.[15] Included in the prophetic imagination are the ships of Tarshish and beautiful boats (a *hapax legomenon* linked to the Egyptian loan word *śkty*; Isa 2:16).[16] Because shipping was so closely associated

[14] Sara Japhet, *I and II Chronicles* (OTL; Philadelphia: Fortress, 1993), 801–2.

[15] For more on this passage, see Blenkinsopp, *Isaiah 1–39*, 192–96; and Williamson, *Isaiah 1–5*, 189–230.

[16] On the translation, see Williamson, *Isaiah 1–5*, 199–200.

with the Phoenicians, several oracles in the prophetic literature predict the destruction of Tyre using the motif of ships (Isa 23; Ezek 27). In Isa 23 merchant ships ('ships of Tarshish') returning to Tyre after an excursion to Cyprus are commanded to lament the destruction of Tyre twice, in vv. 1 and 14 (cf. v. 10): "Wail, O ships of Tarshish for your harbor is destroyed." The command forms an inclusio around the oracle against Tyre, which is subject to Yahweh's judgement because of its pride (vv. 8–9).

In a most imaginative take on an Oracle Against the Nations (OAN), the book of Ezekiel depicts the city of Tyre as a ship that is sunk in the heart of the high seas. Sandwiched in the middle of a series of oracles against Tyre (Ezek 26–28), the prophet creates an extended metaphor of the city as a well-equipped and well-stocked merchant vessel (ch. 27). Tyre as a ship (vv. 5–9) actually alternates with Tyre as a city (vv. 9b–11) in the poem.[17] In the opening verses of the chapter, Ezekiel is commanded by Yahweh to announce to Tyre its downfall using the language of the funeral dirge. In the prophetic speech the city is related to a beautiful ship that is crafted from the most sturdy and appropriate woods (vv. 4b–5–6), replete with the finest linen as a sail (v. 7), and manned by wise and noble men (vv. 8–9). When the metaphor shifts to the city, its imagery of warriors hanging their shields, helmets, and arrows on the city walls (vv. 10–11) actually functions to suggest the heavy defences of the cargo ship. The amount of detail given to the ship and the city of Tyre as well as its trading partners and goods is not matched in the account of the destruction of the ship (vv. 25b–27). As Carol Newsom rightly notes, Ezekiel destroys the ship he carefully and slowly built up in one fell swoop; literally, he sinks it in one verse (v. 26): "Ezekiel simply takes the ship to sea and sinks it in a single, sudden verse."[18] Heavily laden with cargo the Tyre ship cannot withstand the driving east wind (cf. Ps 48:7 [Eng. 8]) and sinks into the heart of the sea. The ignoble end of the Tyre ship is witnessed by all seafaring men who descend from their ships (v. 29) to stand on the shore and lament along with many others (vv. 28–36). The elaborate metaphor of Tyre the city as a ship would certainly have resonated with ancient

---

[17] See the commentaries, especially Margaret Odell, *Ezekiel* (Smyth & Helwys Bible Commentary; Macon: Smyth & Helwys, 2005), 343–55. Cf. Hubert J. van Dijk, *Ezekiel's Prophecy on Tyre* (BibOr 29; Rome: Pontifical Biblical Institute, 1968).

[18] Carol A. Newsom, "A Maker of Metaphors: Ezekiel's Oracles Against Tyre," *Int* 38 (1984): 151–64 (157), reprinted in *"This Place is Too Small for Us": The Israelite Prophets in Recent Scholarship* (ed. Robert P. Gordon; Sources for Biblical and Theological Study 5; Winona Lake, Ind.: Eisenbrauns, 1995), 191–204 (197).

audiences and its sudden destruction reinforces the impression of the power of the deity Yahweh and the authority of the prophet Ezekiel by confirming, confronting, and shattering perceptions.[19]

Although less well known for their seafaring prowess, the Babylonians traded on the waters in antiquity (travelling along the Euphrates) and are even known to have sailed to the Persian Gulf (Herodotus, I, 194).[20] One of the prophecies found in the collection of material known as Deutero-Isaiah reflects an awareness of their activity and predicts the destruction of their boats and the lamentation that will take place at the time of the deity's wrath: "For your sakes I have sent to Babylon and I will bring down all of them as fugitives and the Chaldeans in the ships of their lamentation/rejoicing"[21] (Isa 43:14).[22]

Included among Ezekiel's OAN is a series against Egypt (Ezek 29:1–32:32). In the midst of the third oracle (30:1–19) it is related that the news of the systematic destruction of Egypt carried out by Yahweh will be brought to the Ethiopians (Nubians) via messengers who sail up the Nile (30:9). Joseph Blenkinsopp has argued that the prose comment should be regarded as an addition that provides an interpretation of the poetic recital of Egypt's downfall in the light of a prophecy in Isaiah (ch. 18) in which Ethiopians (biblical Kush) also feature.[23] In other words Ezekiel 30:9 is an example of Fortschreibung, or the ongoing process of the reappropriation and reinterpretation of biblical literature. In Isaiah's prophecy the oracle was about dissuading an alliance with Egypt (Isa 18:1–7), but the Ethiopians are portrayed at the beginning of the prophecy sending envoys in papyrus vessels (כלי־גמא) over the water (18:2), possibly to Judah (vv. 1–2). After

---

19 For a sensitive analysis of the rhetorical strategy of the metaphor of Tyre as a ship, see Newsom, "A Maker of Metaphors," 156–58; and in the reprinted essay, 196–98.

20 Knowledge of activity on the Euphrates was noted already by Franz Delitzsch, *Biblical Commentary on the Prophecies of Isaiah*, II (4th ed.; trans. James S. Banks; Edinburgh: T&T Clark, 1890), 183–84.

21 The root here can either be understood as a cry of lamentation (as Jer 14:12; Ps 106:44) or as one of pride or joy. It does not matter for the point being made here. See Delitzsch, *Isaiah*, 184; and the commentaries.

22 'The translation is difficult and br has sometimes been emended to 'boats' (making a nice parallel with 43:14b as well as being consistent with the Targum translation, Ugaritic *br* and Greek Βαρις). Nevertheless, the term probably represents a rare form of ברח (cf. Isa 27:1; Job 26:13) and is better translated with reference to fugitives. On the translation, see Joseph Blenkinsopp, *Isaiah 40–55: A New Translation with Introduction and Commentary* (AB 19A; New York: Doubleday, 2000), 226 and John Goldingay and David Payne, *Isaiah 40–55*, vol. 1. (ICC; London: T&T Clark, 2007), 293–96.

23 Joseph Blenkinsopp, *Ezekiel* (IBC; Louisville: John Knox, 1990), 134. Walther Eichrodt (*Ezekiel* [trans. Cosslett Quinn; OTL; London: SCM, 1970], 414) maintains a similar view.

closer scrutiny it is questionable that this represents an example of an interpretation of the prophecy of Isaiah. The text is most obviously related to 30:4, which speaks of the 'anguish' that will be in Ethiopia, a powerful nation in its own right and often in an alliance with Egypt. Except for the term 'messengers,' there are no words in common in the prophecies of Ezekiel and Isaiah—even the biblical terms for the river boats are different (כְּלֵי־גֹמֶא in Isa 18:2; צִים in Ezek 30:9). What they seem to share is the idea of Ethiopian messengers relaying information of disaster (of Egypt in Ezekiel, of the Assyrians in Isaiah). Nevertheless, except for travel by boats on the Nile, there is little to link the two prophecies and it is difficult to see how one illuminates the other. Instead of offering an example of inner-biblical allusion, the imagery seems to reflect that the sea travel of the Ethiopians as well as their close ties to Egypt was a known occurrence in the ancient world. In this respect the biblical imagery captures some details of ancient maritime activity, even as it had of the Babylonians in the Isaianic prophecy in Isa 43:14.

Finally, there are also prophecies of salvation which use terminology for ships. In Isaiah, the prediction of the future period of peace to be instituted by Yahweh is said to be a watery haven "where no rowing boat can go, nor stately ship can pass" (Isa 33:21). The two types of vessels provide the opposite limits of the range of small to large sea craft and likely function as a hendiadys: no ships of any sort can traverse Yahweh's peaceful waters. An odd play on the nature of ships to bring cargo is found in a prophecy of salvation in Trito-Isaiah among the kernel of prophecies that are exclusively positive. Chapter 60 is addressed to Zion with proclamations of Yahweh's overturning the disaster that had befallen the city. In Isa 60:8–9 the deity addresses the city with the promise of the repatriation of diaspora Judahites. Foreign nations will flood to Zion bringing the exiles and refugees along with offerings and tribute, "the ships of Tarshish … bring your sons from afar, their silver and gold with them." The prophecy seemingly rebuts the threat in Deuteronomy (28:68) that ships will convey the Israelites back to Egypt to be enslaved.[24] This, then, provides a clear example of the type of inner biblical negotiation that appears in biblical material being rethought and reworked within a religious community.

24 Other Deuteronomic prophecies have been overturned in Trito-Isaiah, e.g., Deut. 23 by Isa 56:3–7.

### 6. *Proverbial/Allegorical Use*

The referent 'ships' appears in passages of a more proverbial or allegorical nature as well. In the book of Proverbs, for example, it comes in a particular wisdom expression of the step pattern '3 and 4', suggesting the exhaustion of a topic. In Prov 30:18–19, the sage uses this formula to speak of four mysterious or wondrous things beyond the understanding of human beings.[25] These include "the way of a ship in the heart of the sea." The passage of the ship on the waves is perceived and portrayed as wondrous and mysterious to behold, so ships were viewed with admiration in at least some of the biblical literature. Again in Proverbs the referent is used to augment what is portrayed as laudable, in this instance, the strong woman, sometimes understood as the good wife in the closing chapter of Proverbs (Prov 31:14). Likened to the ships of the merchant, this idealized woman brings food from afar to feed her family and household. It remains a matter for debate, but a good case can be made that the idealized woman in Prov 31 represents Wisdom Woman, who is found personified in chs. 1–9.[26] Like the use of ships in conjunction with King Solomon in the biblical historiographical material, the simile functions to make the character of the woman even more impressive.

In the book of Job the referent ships is found as one of three images employed in an allegorical sense to convey the speed with which the days of a human life (Job's) pass. The passage motivates the transition to Job's direct accusation of the deity that takes place in 9:25–10:22.[27] The stricken man focuses at the beginning of his reproach on how his miserable condition remains unalleviated and the river-boats of reed provide an analogy for the passing of his life (cf. Isa 18:1–2, where this type of Egyptian reed boat appears also).

A special allegory is established in the story of Jonah. The ship provides the means for Jonah's flight from Yahweh that establishes the tension between the deity and the prophet at the beginning of the book (Jonah 1:3). Like many ships in the Old Testament more generally, the ship is mentioned in conjunction with Tarshish (emphasized three times in 1:3), but in Jonah the actual location of Tarshish is meant rather than the

[25] See the commentaries, e.g. Crawford H. Toy, *The Book of Proverbs* (1899; repr., ICC; Edinburgh: T&T Clark, 1970), 530–32.

[26] E.g., Thomas P. McCreesh, "Wisdom as Wife: Proverbs 31:10–31," *RB* 92 (1985): 25–46.

[27] See the commentaries, e.g. David J. A. Clines, *Job 1–20* (WBC 17; Dallas: Word Books, 1989), 213–52 (224–25, 239–40).

type of boat exclusively. Although the geographical location of Tarshish remains under debate, it is most often linked with Tartessos in southern Spain, suggesting that Jonah sought to flee to the farthest point in the known world—a place where it was estimated that Yahweh's presence did not extend.[28] In addition to providing the means for flight, the ship provides an instructive analogy about faith. After Yahweh had hurled a great wind upon the sea, the ship thought itself to break up (Jonah 1:4) and the mariners grew frightened. In direct contrast to Jonah who was in the innermost part of the ship fast asleep, the mariners were on deck, actively throwing the ship's cargo into the sea in a desperate attempt to lighten the boat and save it from certain disaster (Jonah 1:5). The ship appears as the location for the contrast drawn between the unfaithful and disobedient Jonah and the god-fearing mariners.

## 7. *Business on the Sea*

Biblical literature provides one means of assessing societies and economies in the ancient world, and an investigation of seafaring is a convenient entry point. Ships made possible the exchange of goods and ideas in the ancient world. They can, therefore, contribute valuable information regarding how the biblical writers understood this type of business and those who participated in it.

The Phoenicians are depicted most frequently as trading on the seas. They were the middle-men of the ancient world. However, the Phoenicians are not the only ones portrayed in the Old Testament as having an occupation on the sea. Psalm 107:23 relates that part of the world's population were mariners. The poem goes on to express how those who "went down to the sea in ships, doing business on the great waters" had faith in Yahweh because they could see the dramatic actions of the deity in the wind and the waves of the sea. It was exactly their faith that saved them when the sea became a tumult of waves and gales that threatened destruction (vv. 26–30) and which led the psalmist to use them as an example of those who can give thanks in the midst of the congregation (vv. 31–32).[29] In this respect, mariners, more probably fishermen, represent

[28] Williamson (*Isaiah 1–5*, 226–27) informs that Josephus' locating Tarshish in Tarsus in Asia Minor as the referent for Tarshish has been gaining ground in recent years and seems to fit the biblical context of Gen 10:4; Isa 66:19; Ezek 27:12–14 better.

[29] See the commentaries and John Day, *Psalms* (OTG; Sheffield: JSOT Press, 1990), 47–48.

the only occupation included among the illustrations of faithful responses to Yahweh in Ps 107. On another occasion trading on the seas is used as an example of the type of occupation in which the strong woman ('wife' or Wisdom Woman) of Prov 31 engages.

It is possible to gather some information about trade more generally, especially when considering references to ships (and Tyre, in fact) in the monarchical and the prophetic literature. The list of goods available in the monarchical literature—Ophir gold,[30] gold, silver, ivory, apes, and peacocks, can be supplemented from a list of trading partners and wares inserted into Ezekiel's prophecy against Tyre (27:12–25a) that includes iron, tin, wood, precious stones, ebony, dyed and embroidered clothing, and horses and their paraphernalia, foodstuffs and wine, ingredients for perfume, wheat, and even human beings. Tyre in Ezek 27 is portrayed as the center of trade, where raw materials come in and finished products exit—all carried by Phoenician Tarshish ships. Trade partners included parts of Africa, the coastal cities of the Mediterranean, and the Levantine region. It is difficult to completely understand the intricacies of trade in ancient times and in antiquity, but a reconstruction is possible given the trade list in Ezek 27. Lines of discussion include whether it represents the emergence of free trade generated and sustained by a merchant class[31] instead of state sponsored and controlled trade like that appearing in conjunction with Hiram and Solomon in the Kings account, as well as if Tyre's trade in goods represented a type of exploitative trade in which precious materials and goods were sent to the harbour city only to result in the distribution of manufactured cheap, luxury goods.[32]

It is worthwhile mentioning in this context that in the almost complete absence of surviving native epigraphical evidence that might enable reconstructions of the Phoenician kingdoms, the Old Testament material about Phoenicia becomes a valuable resource for reconstructive purposes (especially when assessed in conjunction with other sources—the Amarna letters, Assyrian records and reliefs, documents from Ugarit, Josephus, Greek histories, etc), although clearly it must be used with caution.

---

[30] Variously understood as a geographical location (Job 28:16; Ps 45:19) and as a special type of refined or high quality gold (Isa 13:12; Job 22:24).

[31] Mario Liverani, "The Trade Network of Tyre According to Ezek. 27," in *Ah, Assyria…Studies in Assyrian History and Ancient Near Eastern Literature Presented to Hayim Tadmor* (ed. Mordechai Cogan and Israel Eph'al; ScrHier 33; Jerusalem: Magnes, 1991), 75–79.

[32] Odell (*Ezekiel*, 347–50) builds on the work of Maria E. Aubet, *Phoenicians and the West: Politics, Colonies and Trade* (trans. Mary Turton; Cambridge: Cambridge University Press, 1993), 241, 247–47.

The texts themselves alert us to be cautious in gleaning the Old Testament for historical details, as the list of cargo in the analogy of Tyre as a ship indicates (Ezek 27:12–25). The goods are luxury goods that provide a helpful list of wares that might have been traded by the Phoenicians, but there remains a question of how much the list is meant to contribute to augmenting the status and reputation of Tyre (as a nation under Yahweh's judgement) and how much it actually represents actual products carried to and fro. In addition, the list also fails to include certain details that might have been expected. The Phoenicians were known for crafting the luxury item of carved ivory, but this product is not mentioned. This lack of detail begs the question of how much the biblical writer actually knew of the wares traded and how much was an imaginative construal to supplement the prophecy. In this respect, it helps to be cognizant of the type of literature in which details are embedded when there is an interest in using the Old Testament to shed light on the ancient world.

The references to ships also provide some information about political alliances. The key example here is well known, but worth mentioning in this context. King Solomon of Judah and King Hiram of Tyre are portrayed as being in a close alliance. Solomon's ships accompanied those of Hiram, and Hiram appeared to have bolstered Solomon's reign with wares necessary for his building projects as well as other luxury goods. Fleets of cargo vessels appearing in conjunction with Solomon reinforce the impression of Solomon as a king adroit at international diplomacy and involved in alliances with foreign nations (the opposite impression being given for Jehoshaphat). The business of shipping was also a means of furthering political ties, thus signalling a way of assessing the link between economics and politics in the ancient world.

## III. Conclusions

A consideration of ships in the Old Testament opens up a wealth of different discussion topics. One important insight afforded by such a lexical study is that ships are not just found conceptualized in the Old Testament only as a historical reality—as a feature of the economic situation of the ancient world, for example. Ships function in a great many different ways and even become loosed of concrete historical moorings to function ideologically. Examples of this type of usage are found in the list of trade wares in Ezekiel (Ezek 27:12–25a); in the imaginative metaphor of Tyre as a ship in Ezekiel (also Ezek 27); in Tarshish ships as conveying legendary grandiose size (Isa 2:16); and in how the ships of Jehoshaphat indicate something more about the Chronicler's view of kingship and of the importance of prophecy and repentance (2 Chr 20:37). Also, the survey of the lexical stock related to ships contributes to adding details about the ancient world that have been less well known or less well reflected in the historical reconstructions of biblical scholars. Babylon, in addition to being the great empire typically associated with powerful kings and lowly vassals and an ideology of power,[33] was also known (albeit probably not renowned) for its use of water for trade (Isa 43:14). Moreover, the biblical writers made use of their knowledge of the Nile activities of Ethiopian messengers (Ezek 30:9, cf. Isa 18:2).

So, it is profitable to study biblical terms, such as those related to ships, to glean the contexts in which they are found, but I would like to return to where this examination started—the scepticism of the ancient Israelites towards ships. The biblical writers also admired seafaring vessels—they were wondrous to behold, mysterious in their ways of travel, finely crafted in their details, expertly sailed, and beautiful to watch as they rode the waves of the seas. They were even used to augment the reputation of various individuals. It is important, therefore, to expand our conception of ancient Israelite attitudes towards ships to take into account the positive ways that they were perceived and portrayed in the biblical literature.

[33] For a careful and illuminating analysis of the symbols of Neo-Babylonian power and reflections of it in biblical material, see David S. Vanderhooft, *The Neo-Babylonian Empire and Babylon in the Latter Prophets* (HSM 59; Atlanta: Scholars Press, 1999).

# WHO ARE THE BAD GUYS IN THE PSALMS?

Patrick D. Miller

In another context, I have sought to identify elements of the anthropology of the Psalter.[1] Drawing on such Psalms as 8, 62, and 51, I dealt with the human creature as sinner, but beyond that generally ignored all the words about evil-doers and the wicked, who come in many forms and often in the Psalter.[2] That, however, leaves a conspicuous hole in the effort to look at how the human creature acts and lives as we see it in the Psalms. So I am going to take another shot at the question, specifically with regard to what I am calling colloquially "the bad guys."

Along with others I have argued that Ps 1, often memorized and treasured for its substance, has a special place as an introduction both to the first book of the Psalter (Pss 3–41) as well as to the Psalter as a whole. As it introduces all that is to follow, it does so by setting out two ways that one may go in the human journey and what their outcomes are. One is the way of the righteous and the other the way of the wicked. In the process, the reader of the Psalter is introduced here at the beginning to the bad guys. And as one reads through the Psalter, one finds them present again and again and, not surprisingly, with a variety of designations. Some of the labels are quite broad and general, for example, "doers of evil" (פעלי און; Pss 5:6 [Eng. 5]; 6:9 [Eng. 8]; 14:4; etc.); "oppressors" (עשקים; Pss 72:4; 119:121–122); "transgressors" (פשעים; Pss 37:38; 51:15 [Eng. 13]); "evildoers" (מרעים; 26:5; 27:2); "men of blood" (אנשי דמים; 26:9). Others are more specific, e.g., "speakers of lies" (דברי כזב; 5:7); "man of blood and deceit" (איש־דמים ומרמה; 5:7), and other references to false witnesses and liars (27:12; 50:19–20). And, of course, the bad guys are often simply identified

[1] For over thirty years, Hugh Williamson has been a dear friend and greatly respected and trusted colleague. From the time we first came to know each other in the Old Testament seminar in Cambridge, it was clear that here was one of the sharpest and most thoughtful of contemporary interpreters of Scripture. That awareness has only grown through the years. When it is joined with Hugh's many modes of hospitality, one can only be grateful for an opportunity such as this both to pay tribute and to say thank you.

[2] Patrick D. Miller, "What is a Human Being? The Anthropology of the Psalter I," in *The Way of the Lord: Essays in Old Testament Theology* (FAT 39; Tübingen: Mohr Siebeck, 2004; Grand Rapids: Eerdmans, 2007), 226–36; and idem, "The Sinful and Trusting Creature: The Anthropology of the Psalter II," in *The Way of the Lord: Essays in Old Testament Theology* (FAT 39; Tübingen: Mohr Siebeck, 2004; Grand Rapids: Eerdmans, 2007), 237–49.

as enemies of the one who is praying (איבים; שוררים; צוררים 3:8; 5:9; 6:11; 7:7; etc.) or "my pursuers" (רדפים; Ps 7:2).

## I. The Wicked

The most common term for the bad guys in Ps 1 occurs in the first line of the Psalter and then appears three more times in this brief Psalm: "(the) wicked" (רשעים). The category "wicked" is then paralleled by the term "sinners" (חטאים) both in the first verse and a second time in v. 5. In the first verse, however, there is a third group, the לצים, translated variously as "the scornful," the insolent," "scoffers," and the like. While these three groups by no means exhaust the various designations of bad guys in the Psalms, as I have indicated above, the important function of Ps 1 as an introduction to the Psalter suggests that a closer look at the three groups may help us understand more about those who are the opposite of or opposed to the righteous, the God-fearers, those who trust in the Lord and so live and act.

As far as I can tell, רשעים, "the wicked" are not only the primary category of bad guys in Ps 1 but also the most frequent designation in the Psalter as a whole. There are over eighty references to רשעים in the Psalms. As in Ps 1, the wicked are frequently in parallel with or set over against "the righteous" (צדיק; Ps 7:10 [Eng. 9]; 11:5; 34:22 [Eng. 21]; 37:28–29, 39–40; 58:4–12 [Eng. 3–11]; 68:3–4; 75:11[Eng. 10]; 97:10–12; 112:6, 10). While they are often referred to without further elaboration, in a number of psalms their behavior is spelled out in some detail. In Ps 50 with its recital of several violations of the commandments, the general category into which such people fall is "the wicked":

> 16But to the wicked God says:
> "What right have you to recite my statutes,
> or take my covenant on your lips?
> 17For you hate discipline,
> and you cast my words behind you.
> 18You make friends with a thief when you see one,
> and you keep company with adulterers.
> 19You give your mouth free rein for evil,
> and your tongue frames deceit.
> 20You sit and speak against your kin;
> you slander your own mother's child.[3]

[3] Translation here and elsewhere from NRSV.

Specific commandment violations are in view, specifically theft, adultery, and false witness, but the words that are "cast behind you" are an implicit allusion to the whole of the Decalogue.

In Ps 82 all the gods are condemned to death for their neglect of the poor and their partiality toward the wicked. In other words, deity is in a sense defined by how the gods respond to the activities of the wicked, in this case with particular regard to their oppression of the weak and the poor. The corollary of this is illustrated in Ps 146:9:

> The LORD watches over the strangers;
> he upholds the orphan and the widow,
> but the way of the wicked he brings to ruin.

Richly illustrative of the ways of the wicked, Ps 10 begins with the same point we have just identified: "In arrogance the wicked persecute the poor" (v. 2). They are greedy and self-focused. One of the primary problems with the wicked in this psalm is their assumption that they can do whatever they want to get what they want and God will never notice. They do not see God as involved in any way: "In the pride of their countenance the wicked say, 'God will not seek it out'; all their thoughts are 'There is no God' " (v. 4). Their mouths are full of lies, deceit, and profanity (v. 7) and they murder the innocent (v. 8) and seize the poor (v. 9).

All of these characteristics of the way of the wicked are heard again and again in the Psalms. For example, the wicked are often identified as lying and deceitful (Pss 31:18–19 [Eng. 17–18];[4] 58:4 [Eng. 3]; 109:2; 139:19–20).[5] They kill and murder (37:14), the righteous as much as the poor (37:32); and they borrow but do not pay back (37:21). They are loaded with wealth—ill-gotten gains—and assume because of that a kind of arrogance and ease (see Ps 73).

Consistent with Ps 1, much of the reference to the wicked is about their final fate and the certainty of their destruction, whether by God's hand (Pss 3:8 [Eng. 7]; 9:6 [Eng. 5]; 11:6; 68:3; 75:11 [Eng. 10]; 91:8; 139:19; 145:20; 146:9; 147:6), as a result of actions of the ruler (101:8), or as the outcome of their wicked ways (Pss 1:6; 34:22 [Eng. 21]; 140:9; 141:10).

---

[4] Note in this instance that the lying lips are ones that speak with arrogance (גאוה) and contempt (בוז), on which see below.

[5] Elsewhere I have noted how often lying and deceit is the form of oppression against the righteous and innocent and poor in the Psalter. The commandment against false witness and lying seems to be the commandment in the second table of the Decalogue that is most often violated by the wicked in their oppressive acts. See Patrick D. Miller, *They Cried to the LORD: The Form and Theology of Biblical Prayer* (Minneapolis: Fortress, 1994), 82.

## II. The Sinners

Alongside the wicked in Ps 1 are "sinners" (חטאים; vv. 1, 5). In both cases, the parallel association seems to equate the terms, and to some degree that is to be assumed. There are differences, however, as one looks at the role of sinners in the psalms that follow. For one thing, the term "sinners" is a relatively rare term in the Old Testament generally and occurs only a few times elsewhere in the Psalms (Pss 25:8; 26:9; 51:15 [Eng. 13]; 104:35). Only one other time does the category of "sinners" occur in parallel with "the wicked": "Let sinners be consumed from the earth, and let the wicked be no more" (Ps 104:35). Once again, as in Ps 1, there seems to be no real distinction in their way of acting or their end. Similarly, Ps 26:9–10 describes the way of sinners in a manner that compares closely with the many representations of the wicked:

> 9Do not sweep me away with sinners,
> nor my life with the blood thirsty,
> 10those in whose hands are evil devices,
> and whose right hands are full of bribes.

A somewhat different feel to the character of this category is given in the other Psalms where the term "sinners" appears. There is no question of the negative character of the designation and its applicability to all sorts of bad actions. But the term "sinner" can apply to the one who prays and not only to those who seek to oppress or destroy the one who cries out for help. Note in this regard Ps 25:8–9:

> 8Good and upright is the Lord;
> therefore he instructs sinners in the way.
> 9He leads the humble in what is right,
> and teaches the humble his way.

In contrast to what we hear in Ps 104:35 about the sinners and the wicked generally, sinners are not here destroyed but *instructed in the way*, which, as one sees from the next verse, is "his way," that is, the Lord's way. This is underscored by the earlier petition of the psalmist: "Do not remember the sins of my youth or my transgressions" (v. 7). Over against God's remembering his youthful sins, the psalmist pleads for God's remembering his mercy (רחמים) and steadfast love (חסד, v. 6). God's חסד brought to mind can overcome the psalmist's sins being brought to mind. So the psalmist prays: "Forgive all my sins" (v. 17 [Eng. 18]). The sinners are not always the objects of divine wrath and to be destroyed. Rather they are there among the psalmists and capable of being taught how to live a different way.

Confirmation of that is given in Ps 51. No psalm more directly addresses the reality of sin and identifies it as much or more with the psalmist who prays as with others. While several terms for bad actions are used in the psalm, for example, "transgressions" (פשעים) and "iniquities" (עונות), most noticeable is the absence of any reference to the wicked (רשעים) or wickedness (רשע) and the frequency of references to sins and sinners. Five different words from the root חטא occur in the psalm and the root itself appears seven times. The primary function of the psalm is confession of the psalmist's sin and plea for forgiveness. While that sin may merit punishment (v. 6 [Eng. 4]), like Ps 25 calling for God not to remember the sins of the sinner the hope here is for God to look away from the sins and blot them out (v. 11 [Eng. 9]). Sinners can be taught a different way (12, 15 [Eng. 10, 13]).

The absence of any reference to wickedness or the wicked in the face of such frequent references to sin and guilt, transgressions and iniquity suggests the possibility that there is some distinction between the wicked and sinners, the latter being characteristic, as Ps 51 suggests (e.g., v. 5 [Eng. 7]), while the wicked are an unredeemable group. The confessing psalmist may and does associate himself with bad actions and bad actors, but not with the wicked. They seem to be a separate group.[6]

## III. The Arrogant

In its delineation of those with whom the righteous should not associate, Ps 1 adds a third category, the לצים, translated in different ways, as indicated above, because there is no clear single meaning to the term. It seems to have to do with a kind of arrogance, and the fact that nearly all the uses of לץ or לצים occur in Proverbs gives some clues. In some cases, the word לץ or לצים is parallel to or associated with "the wicked" (e.g., Prov 9:7; 21:10–12) as in Ps 1:1. More commonly the לץ or לצים—or the verbal forms underlying the category term—are parallel to and thus contrasted with the wise (e.g., Prov 9:8, 12; 13:1; 19:25; 20:1; 21:11) or spoken

[6] If that is the case, the parallelism between wicked and sinners in Ps 1 may not be as simple as appears at first glance. While the two cola of v. 5 can be read in fairly precise parallel to each other, it may be that in the case of the wicked we have the kind of injustice and subsequent judgment that the Lord sets as the way and outcome of all the gods in Ps 82, while the עדה or "assembly" in which the sinners may or will not stand or enter is the community of the people, which can and does have a legal role but only as a part of its responsibilities. See in this regard, D. Levy and Jacob Milgrom, "*'ēdâ*," *TDOT*, 10:468–80.

of as those who are uninterested in or opposed to wisdom and the wise (e.g., Prov 15:12). Confirming this contrast are instances where the לץ is associated with the fool (כסיל or אויל; e.g., Prov 1:22; 14:6–7; 24:9).[7] Such usage does not give precision for definition, because so many categories of bad guys and bad actions are contrasted with the wise and wisdom, but it does tend to support the kind of definition that Christoph Barth gives: "The *lyṣ* is a typical manifestation of what it means to be 'unwise' in one's plans, words, and actions—presumptuous, arrogant, and conceited."[8]

In light of the place that the לצים have in the introductory Ps 1 and their frequency in the counsel of Proverbs, it is surprising to discover that they do not appear again in the Psalter except in one important context where the noun or participle form is absent but the verb occurs in the Hiphil. The subject of the verb in this instance is זדים: "The זדים deride/scorn me utterly" (Ps 119:51). An association of the לצים and the זדים occurs in one other place: "The insolent/arrogant (זד), haughty (יהיר) person, named 'Scoffer' (לץ), acts with arrogant (זדון) pride" (Prov 21:24). This is set over against those who watch mouth and tongue to keep out of trouble (v. 23).

The זדים, who seem to be a version of the לצים, appear in the Psalter only in three places. One is Ps 86:14 (cf. 54:6 [Eng. 3]).[9] Here it is in the context of a petition or prayer with the psalmist's account as "the זדים rise up against me, a band of the ruthless seeks my life." Then there is added a third clause: "and they do not set you (i.e., the LORD) before them." So here is a critical explanatory note about the זדים: They do not pay attention to God. That may be as in Ps 10 where the wicked say "God will not seek it out," and "There is no God." Or it may be in contrast to what precedes Ps 86:14, where the psalmist has proclaimed his devotion to the LORD and the LORD's ways and his conviction that "you alone are God" (Ps 86:8–13).[10]

The other two places where the זדים appear in the Psalter are in Pss 19 and 119, the psalms that most acutely take up the focus of Ps 1 on the Torah or law. In Ps 19, the psalmist prays that God will keep him away from the זדים, who are not so much the wicked as the presumptuous and arrogant, who do not set God before them and so do not keep his law. The

[7] For further examples and discussion, see Christoph Barth, "*lyṣ*," *TDOT*, 7:547–52.
[8] Barth, "*lyṣ*," 550.
[9] The word זרים in Ps 54:5[Eng. 6] is probably to be read as זדים.
[10] Frank-Lothar Hossfeld and Erich Zenger, *Psalms 2: A Commentary on Psalms 51-100* (Hermeneia; Minneapolis: Fortress, 2005), 375.

association of the positive description of the law and the benefits of keeping it that precedes this prayer is similar to the positive view of the one who meditates on the torah that immediately follows the warning not to sit in the assembly of the לצים in Ps 1:1–3. Involvement and contact with the לצים or זדים is not so much with the generally wicked as it is with those who are so self-oriented and arrogant that they disdain the law and the one who gives it as a way for the righteous to go.

That such is the case is confirmed by the occurrences of זדים in Ps 119. It is not so much that the זדים are the only ones who do not set God and the law before them. Indeed the wicked appear in the Psalm also as those who do not keep the law (e.g., vv. 53 and 61), as is implied in Ps 1. In Ps 119, however, unlike anywhere else in the Psalter except Ps 19, the זדים appear as often as the wicked to describe the bad guys. In vv. 21–22, they are those "who wander from your commandments" and heap scorn (חרפה) and contempt (בוז) on the one praying. Mention has already been made of the description of the זדים acting presumptuously and arrogantly (v. 51) in this case, the verb being the root from which the noun לצים is derived. Then in v. 69, the זדים appear again, this time as those who smear the righteous with lies. Their appearance is in the middle of an elaborated claim of the psalmist about the goodness of God and of God's commandments. By their spreading of lies they demonstrate their arrogance and rejection of the commandments. Exactly the same thing happens in the next segment of the psalm (vv. 73–80; cf. v. 78), and in the following stanza (vv. 81–88) the זדים once more are those who "flout your law" or do not act in accordance with God's teaching (v. 85). The final mention of the זדים refers to their oppression (עשק, v. 122). The wicked then are referred to three times, seeking to trap the psalmist (vv. 95, 110), but known to be done away with by the Lord (v. 119).

That arrogance and presumptuousness, manifest in disregard for divine instruction and direction, are what is at stake in the appearance of the זדים shows itself clearly in a number of narrative or other contexts where nominal or verbal forms of the root זיד appear. In Deut 1:42–43, after the Lord has told Moses to tell the people, who are wandering in the wilderness, that they are not to go up into the land, Moses reports: "Although I told you, you would not listen. You rebelled against the command of the Lord and, acting presumptuously (ותזדו), went up into the hill country." Similarly in Neh 9:16 and 29, we are told the people "acted presumptuously (הזידו) and did not obey your commandments." Finally, one notes in Isa 13:11 that the wicked appear alongside the זדים in a manner that shows their association and similarity while marking some distinction:

I will punish the world for its evil,
and the wicked (רשעים) for their iniquity;
I will put an end to the pride of the arrogant (זדים)
and lay low the insolence of tyrants.

## IV. Conclusion

In sum, 'the wicked' is an all-encompassing characterization of the bad guys of the psalms-the easiest, quickest, and most common identification. These are sinners also, and as such not to be associated with. 'The sinners,' however, are a category that is more general and one from which persons may separate themselves and seek God's forgiveness. The wicked are sinners, but there are sinners whose voice is heard in the psalms as they seek forgiveness and a new way (e.g., Pss 32 and 51). From Ps 1 and elsewhere, especially the two psalms that also focus especially on God's law (Pss 19, 119), we learn that there is also a group, who may be an element among the wicked but who are recognized especially as those who claim to be able to make it on their own, who do not take account of God, and who especially do not attend to the Lord's instruction about the way to go in life.

# DAVID'S STRONGHOLD AND SAMSON'S ROCK OF ETAM

Nadav Na'aman

The episode of David's wars with the Philistines opens as follows: "When the Philistines heard that David had been anointed king over Israel, all the Philistines went up to search of David; but David heard (of it) and went down to the מצודה" (2 Sam 5:17). The Philistines "spread out (וינטשו)[1] in the hilly plain (עמק)[2] of Rephaim" (v. 18), near a toponym called Baal Perazim. A second text describes an episode that took place in the course of the Philistine campaign, when their troops encamped in the hilly plain of Rephaim and their avant-garde (מצב) was stationed at Bethlehem (2 Sam 23:13–17; see 1 Chr 11:15–19). The two texts make it clear that the first target of the Philistine campaign was Bethlehem, David's home town. In this situation, David organized his troops, conducted a surprise frontal attack on the Philistine forces and won a decisive victory (2 Sam 5:17–21; 1 Chr 14:8–12). So decisive was his victory that the Philistines ran away leaving behind their statues of gods, and David carried them off as booty (2 Sam 5:21; see 1 Chr 14:12).[3]

Where was the מצודה referred to in 2 Sam 5:17b located? Ostensibly, the answer is clarified by the text of 2 Sam 23:13 (and 1 Chr 11:15), which states that when the Philistines encamped near Bethlehem, David was in the cave of Adullam. However, David's retreat to Adullam, a site located in the Shephelah near Philistine territory, out of the highlands of Judah and far away from the battlefield, is highly unlikely. Either the author of 2 Sam 23:13 or a late redactor must have borrowed the cave of Adullam

---

[1] For discussion of the Niphal form of the verb נטש, see N. L. Tidwell, "The Philistine Incursions into the Valley of Rephaim (2 Sam. v 17ff.)," in *Studies in the Historical Books of the Old Testament* (ed. John A. Emerton; VTSup 30; Leiden: Brill, 1979), 190–212 (195–98); P. Kyle McCarter, *II Samuel* (AB 9; Garden City: Doubleday, 1984), 153.

[2] For the interpretation of biblical עמק in the sense of 'hilly plain,' see Yoel Elitzur, " 'So He sent Him Out to the Vale of Hebron.' On the Hilly *'Emeq* in the Hebrew Bible," *Beit Mikra* 54/2 (2009): 5–20 (Hebrew). The Rephaim hilly plain extended from the end of the Valley of Hinnom, near Jerusalem (see Josh 15:8; 18:16), up to Bethlehem.

[3] For the battle near Baal Perazim, see Tidwell, "Philistine Incursions," 205–12. However, I very much doubt his conclusion (p. 206) that v. 17 "is not properly part of the first battle-report." On the contrary, the two episodes in vv. 17–27 are a coherent literary unit, which v. 17 forms an integral part of.

from the story of David's flight from Saul and the formation of his band (1 Sam 22:1), and mistakenly inserted its name into the story of the three warriors who fought against the Philistine outpost at Bethlehem.

Many scholars have recognized that the two episodes of David's war with the Philistines (2 Sam 5:17–25; 1 Chr 14:8–16) originally formed an independent unit[4] that the author of the history of David extracted from an old written source.[5] McCarter suggested that the episode should be dated to an early stage of David's career, when David still maintained a base of operations in Adullam.[6] However, according to the cycle of David stories, the cave was his headquarters only during the initial phase of his wanderings, whereas the breach with the Philistines took place only after he began gaining power in the highlands. Only at this stage did the Philistines realize that David, their former loyal vassal, might endanger their hegemonic status and therefore attacked him. Since the cave of Adullam does not fit the story of the Philistine attack on Bethlehem, another place should be sought for the מצודה mentioned in 2 Sam 5:17.

In what follows, I will try to clarify the meaning of the term מצד/מצודה in the cycle of David stories, investigate its function and suggest a location for the מצודה mentioned in 2 Sam 5:17. The article is written in honour of Prof. Hugh Williamson, an old friend and an outstanding biblical scholar. As Biblical Hebrew and intertextuality are both part of Hugh's legacy, I hope that he will enjoy this small contribution that tries to combine the two approaches in an effort better to understand an episode of the David cycle stories.

## I. Mountain Strongholds in Edom and the Ancient Near East

Diodorus Siculus, who lived in the second half of the first century BCE, described the Nabataeans' rock as follows:

> There is also in the land of the Nabataeans a rock, which is exceedingly strong since it has but one approach, and using this ascent they mount it a

[4] This was already recognized by Julius Wellhausen, *Die Composition des Hexateuchs und der historischen Bücher des Alten Testament* (2nd ed.; Berlin: de Gruyter, 1889), 256.

[5] See Nadav Na'aman, "Sources and Composition in the History of David," in *The Origins of the Ancient Israelite States* (ed. Volkmar Fritz and Philip R. Davies; JSOTSup 228; Sheffield: Sheffield Academic, 1996), 170–86 (173–79).

[6] McCarter, *II Samuel*, 153, 495.

> few at a time and thus store their possessions in safety. (Diodorus Siculus, *Diodorus of Sicily*, II.48.6 [Oldfather, LCL])

> But when the time draws near for the national gathering at which those who dwell round about are accustomed to meet ... they travel to the meeting, leaving on a certain rock their possession and their old men, also their women and their children. This place is exceedingly strong but unwalled, and it is distant two days journey from the settled country. (Diodorus Siculus, *Diodorus of Sicily*, IX.95.1–2 [Oldfather, LCL])

Diodorus describes how Athenaeus, an officer of Antigonus, seized the rock by surprise attack at midnight and took prisoners as well as rich booty (frankincense, myrrh, and about five hundred talents of silver). Diodorus continues to describe another campaign that took place after the disastrous end of Athenaeus' campaign—that of Demetrius, son of Antigonus. Whereas Athenaeus reached the 'rock' by surprise, the Nabataeans discovered Demetrius' advancing troops:

> The barbarians, having thus learned at once that the Greeks had come, sent their property to the rock and posted there a garrison that was strong enough since there was a single artificial approach. (Diodorus Siculus, *Diodorus of Sicily*, IX, 97, 1 [Oldfather, LCL])

Diodorus lived more than 250 years after the events he described and drew upon the writings of earlier historians. The place name Petra means 'rock' (in Greek), and the Nabataean 'rock' has usually been identified as Umm el-Biyara, near Petra. But it is not clear whether Diodorus referred to only one specific stronghold, or to several 'rocks' rising around Petra that were able to supply secure shelter in time of danger.[7]

In recent years, it has become clear that the Nabataeans were not the first nation who built strongholds ('rocks') in the eastern Wādi Arabah mountainous area. Scholars discovered a series of strongholds located throughout the rocky area, all dated to the late Iron Age. The best known site is as-Sela', a remarkable mountain stronghold in whose vicinity a relief of Nabonidus was recently discovered.[8] Five strongholds were discovered

---

[7] For the Hasmonaeans' adoption of the Nabataean strategy of preparing strongholds for a time of emergency, see Ze'ev Meshel, "The Nabataean 'Rock' and the Judean Desert Fortresses," *IEJ* 50 (2000): 109–15.

[8] Stephen Hart, "Sela': The Rock of Edom?" *PEQ* 118 (1986): 91–95; Manfred Lindner, Ulrich Hübner and Elisabeth Gunsam, "*Es-Sela'*—2500 Jahre Fliehburg und Bergfestung in Edom, Südjordanien," *Das Altertum* 46 (2001): 243–78, with earlier literature. For the relief of Nabonidus, see Stephanie M. Dalley and Anne Goguel, "The *Sela'* Sculpture: A Neo-Babylonian Rock Relief in Southern Jordan," *ADAJ* 41 (1997): 169–76; Fawzi Zayadine, "Le relief néo-babylonien à Sela' près de Tafileh: Interpretation historique," *Syria* 76 (1999):

in the area south and north of Petra, indicating that Umm el-Biyara, the most widely known stronghold in this region, is only representative of a much larger phenomenon.[9] Other mountain strongholds were discovered in the more northern mountainous area between Petra and Buseirah,[10] and new sites are due to be discovered when more surveys take place in this difficult to approach mountainous area.[11]

Lindner and Knauf have examined the system of strongholds and have suggested that they formed part of the Edomite economic and social landscape. They were built in inaccessible places, in locations that can be accessed only through a steep single track, and were intended for temporary dwellings. They interpret these mountain strongholds as 'central places' for a predominantly non-sedentary population, hence forming part of the regional economy. They also emphasize their role as places where commodities might have been stored safely under minimal guard and the local population could find shelter in time of danger.[12]

As textual evidence for the refuge function of 'rocks' we may cite the words of Jer 48:28: "Leave the cities, and dwell in the rock (סלע). O inhabitants of Moab! Be like the dove that nests in the side of the mouth of a gorge." According to the legendary story of 'the outrage of Gibeah,' the defeated Benjaminites "fled toward the wilderness to the rock (סלע) of Rimmon" (Judg 20:45). Most of the running Benjaminites did not escape, but "six hundred men turned and fled toward the wilderness to the rock

83–90; Paolo Gentili and Claudio Saporetti, "Nabonedo a Sela'," *Geo-Archeologia* 21/1 (2001): 39–58; Bradley L. Crowell, "Nabonidus, as-Sila', and the Beginning of the End of Edom," *BASOR* 348 (2007): 75–88.

[9] Manfred Lindner and Ernst A. Knauf, "Between the Plateau and the Rocks: Edomite Economic and Social Structure," *Studies in the History and Archaeology of Jordan* 6 (1997): 261–64, with earlier literature; Manfred Lindner, Ernst A. Knauf, Johannes Hübl and John P. Zeitler, "An Iron Age (Edomite) Occupation of Jabal al-Khubtha (Petra) and Other Discoveries on the 'Mountain of Treachery and Deceit,'" *ADAJ* 41 (1997): 177–88; Manfred Lindner and Jürgen Zangenberg, "'Die ihr Nest zwischen den Sternen Bauen…' Zu den edomitischen Bergfestungen im Süden Jordaniens," in *Vielseitigkeit des Alten Testaments. Festschrift für Georg Sauer zum 70. Geburtstag* (ed. James A. Loader and Hans Volker Kieweler; Frankfurt: Lang, 1999), 281–316.

[10] Manfred Lindner, Ernst A. Knauf, Ulrich Hübner and Johannes Hübl, "From Edomite to Late Islamic: Jabal as-Suffaha North of Petra," *ADAJ* 42 (1990): 225–40; Ulrich Hübner and Manfred Lindner, "Archaeological Check-Up on Jabal ash-Sharāh: Edomite Khirbat al-Kūr," *ADAJ* 47 (2003): 225–33.

[11] Chaim Ben David, "Mountain Strongholds of Edom," *Cathedra* 101 (2002): 7–18 (Hebrew).

[12] Lindner and Knauf, "Between the Plateau and the Rocks," 261–64.

of Rimmon, and abode at the rock of Rimmon four months" (v. 47). The story's author was well aware of the role of a desert 'rock' as a safe place for runaways and describes how the defeated Benjaminites desperately tried to reach there. Once a group of the refugees found shelter in the rock, they were relieved of the fear of their pursuing enemies.[13]

The escape in time of danger to shelters located on craggy mountains is amply attested in the Assyrian royal inscriptions and I will suggest a few examples. Nūr-Adad of Dagara, a district of Zamua, rebelled against Ashurnaṣirpal II, was defeated, and "climbed up a rugged mountain" to save his life.[14] Ameka of Zamua rebelled against Ashurnaṣirpal. After he was defeated and his country conquered, he escaped "to a rugged mountain (*šadê marṣi*)."[15] Shalmaneser III conquered most of the territory of Ahuni of Bīt-Adini and the latter escaped to his west-Euphrates territory and there "he had made as his stronghold Mount Šītamrat, a mountain peak on the banks of the Euphrates, which is suspended from heaven like a cloud."[16] In his twelfth regnal year, Shalmaneser III crossed the Euphrates and marched to the land of Paqarhubuni, "and the people became frightened and took to a rugged mountain (*šadû marṣu*)."[17] Finally, in his thirty-first regnal year, Shalmaneser conducted a campaign to the land of Namri. Overwhelmed by fear, the inhabitants abandoned their cities "and ascended a rugged mountain."[18] These and other texts illustrate the strategy of people who lived near rugged mountains of finding shelter in mountain strongholds until the enemy retreated and the danger terminated. These sheltering places were probably prepared in advance, but such details are not related in the Assyrian inscriptions.

---

13 For the location of the Rock of Rimmon, see Hardwicke Rawnsley, "The Rock of Pomegranate," *PEFQS* 11 (1879): 118–26; William F. Birch, "The Rock of the Pomegranate," *PEFQS* 11 (1879): 127–29; idem, "The Rock of Rimmon or the Pomegranate," *PEFQS* 12 (1880): 106–7; idem, "The Rock Rimmon," *PEFQS* 14 (1882): 50–55; Charles F. Burney, *The Book of Judges with Introduction and Notes* (London: Rivingtons, 1918 [Reprint: New York: KTAV Publishing House, 1970], xxi, 486.

14 Albert K. Grayson, *Assyrian Rulers of the Early First Millennium* BC *I* (*1114–859* BC) (RIMA 2; Toronto: University of Toronto Press, 1991), 244, lines 98–99.

15 Grayson, *Assyrian Rulers II*, 247, lines 59–61.

16 Albert K. Grayson, *Assyrian Rulers of the Early First Millennium* BC *II* (*858–745* BC) (RIMA 3; Toronto: University of Toronto Press, 1996), 21–22, lines 69–70.

17 Grayson, *Assyrian Rulers II*, 38, line 17–18; 47, line 42; 53, lines 7–8.

18 Grayson, *Assyrian Rulers II*, 71, lines 188–189. For further examples, see e.g., Grayson, *Assyrian Rulers II*, 104, lines 40, 43; *AHw* 613b, no. 6a.

## II. Biblical Strongholds and the Stronghold of Zion

The reality behind the term מצודה in the cycle stories of David needs clarification. For example, the term appears in combination with Zion in the story of David's conquest of Jerusalem (2 Sam 5:7, 9; 1 Chr 11:5), but interchanges with the cave (מערה) of Adullam in the story of David's flight from Saul (1 Sam 22:1, 4–5). Schunck pointed out that although מצודה and מערה are not synonyms (see Judg 6:2; Ezek 33:27), in some cases there is a close connection between the two terms, as מערה might have been a hole in a cliff.[19] In his opinion, all references to מצודה and מצדות/מצד (1 Sam 22:4–5; 23:14, 19; 24:1 [MT 23:29], 22; 2 Sam 23:14; 1 Chr 11:16; 12:8, 16) should be translated as "hiding place" (*Schlupfwinkel*), except for the references to the מצודה/מצד of Zion (2 Sam 5:7, 9; 1 Chr 11:5, 7), which should be rendered "stronghold." Schunck proposed that the basic form מצד* has the meaning of "a difficult to approach place," from which the meanings of "hiding place" and "stronghold" developed.[20]

Did the מצודה of Zion differ from all other sites called either מצודה or מצדות/מצד in the cycle of David stories? The story of Jerusalem's conquest ends with the statement, "David dwelt in the מצודה and called it the City of David. And David built round about from the Millo inward" (2 Sam 5:9). He also built a palace in the place (v. 11). Thus, the shift from a stronghold (מצודה) to a city ("City of David") is the outcome of David's extensive building operations in the site. Indeed, biblical narrators do not use the term מצודה to describe the post-David city of Jerusalem. In other words, before David's building operations, the narrator regarded Zion as a mountain stronghold (מצודה), and in this sense it is similar to all other places that were called by this and the closely related noun מצד.[21]

We may conclude that the definition "mountain stronghold" fits well all references to מצודה in the Bible.[22] Like the Edomite mountain strongholds, whose configurations differ from each other but were joined by the function they fulfilled in time of war and danger, so were the mountain strongholds also referred to in the cycle of David stories, all sharing the

---

[19] Klaus-Dietrich Schunck, "Davids 'Schlupfwinkel' in Juda," *VT* 33 (1983): 110–13.

[20] Ibid., 112.

[21] The recent excavations in the area near the spring of Gihon demonstrated that Iron I Jerusalem was indeed a mountain stronghold. See Ronny Reich and Eli Shukron, "The Recent Discovery of a Middle Bronze II Fortification in the City of David, Jerusalem," in *City of David Studies of Ancient Jerusalem. The 10th Annual Conference* (ed. Eyal Meiron; Jerusalem: Megalim, 2009), 13*–33*.

[22] HALOT, 622.

role of shelter and refuge from external danger. Schunck's definition, "hiding places," refers to their function, but misses their fundamental character as mountain strongholds. Their 'rocky' appearance is also evident from the interchange of מצודה and שן־סלע ("rocky crag") in Job 39:28, and מצודה and סלע ("rock") in 2 Sam 22:2; Pss 18:3; 31:4; and 71:3. Mountain strongholds have many different forms, sharing only the function of refuge in time of danger. In this light we may assume that the cave of Adullam was located in a steep rocky place, and hence might be called either a "cave" or a "stronghold" (1 Sam 22:1, 4–5).

## III. David's Stronghold and Samson's Rock

Where was the stronghold (מצודה) to which David "went down" while facing the Philistine onslaught (2 Sam 5:17) and in which he organized his troops for battle? As noted above, the cave of Adullam (2 Sam 23:13) does not fit the topographical context of the story. The place must be sought not far away from the Valley of Rephaim, where the battle was waged. Unfortunately, David's stories do not convey details of its location.[23]

However, there is another source, not yet examined in this context, that might shed light on this problem: the story of Samson at the Rock of Etam (Judg 15:8b–19). It follows the episode of the burning of the grain fields and the smiting of the Philistines in the Timnah area (Judg 15:1–8a). After the slaughter, Samson "went down and stayed in the cleft of the rock of Etam," and the Philistines "came up and encamped in Judah and spread out (וינטשו) in Lehi" (vv. 8b–9). The men of Judah, subjugated then to the Philistines, negotiated with the invading troops and sent three thousand men to persuade Samson to surrender to the Philistines. He agreed to be bound and delivered, provided that the men of Judah would not fall upon him (vv. 11–13). When delivered to the Philistines in Lehi, Samson broke the bonds and killed a thousand Philistines with an ass's bone (vv. 14–17). The story closes with the episode of Samson's thirst and the miraculous outburst of water from the rock (vv. 17–19).

Where was the Rock of Etam, the place in which Samson sought refuge from the Philistines? Two suggestions were put forth by scholars. Etam (עיטם) appears in the list of cities fortified by Rehoboam (2 Chr 11:6)

---

[23] Mazar argued that the stronghold was probably located at el-Ḥaḍr, about 5 km southwest of Bethlehem, where five inscribed bronze arrowheads have been discovered. See Benjamin Mazar, "The Military Elite of King David," *VT* 13 (1963): 310–20 (315 n. 4).

and in the list of towns of the Bethlehem district, missing in the MT but preserved in the LXX of Josh 15:59a.[24] From the early stage of modern research, it was identified as Kh. el-Ḫôḫ, south of Bethlehem, near ʿAin ʿAṭān, which preserved the town's ancient name.[25] In 1838, Robinson already suggested identifying the cleft of the Rock of Etam in the cliffs of the nearby Wādi Urṭās.[26]

Some scholars criticized this identification on the ground that the Bethlehem area is remote from the arena in which Samson's cycle stories takes place. Moreover, the verb ירד, which the narrator used to describe Samson's and the men of Judah's arrival to the Rock of Etam (Judg 15:8, 11), does not fit a place in the highlands of Judah. Instead of a rocky cliff in the highlands of Judah, they suggested identifying the Rock of Etam as ʿIrāq Ismaʿīn, a steep rock located in Wādi Ismaʿīn, about four kilometers east-southeast of Zorah.[27] A monastery was built there in the Byzantine period, which Gass and Zissu identified as the Monastery of Samson ("a monastery Sampso") that Johannes Moschos mentioned in his book "partum Spirtuale."[28] According to this identification, Samson found shelter in a rocky place located not far away from Zorah, his birth place.

Several arguments might be raised against this identification. First, according to Judg 16:3, Samson carried the Gaza gates "to the top of the hill that is in front of Hebron." Thus, his refuge in the Rock of Etam, in the highlands of Judah, is not the only instance in which he climbed up into the highlands. Second and more important, ʿIrāq Ismaʿīn is located outside the highlands of Judah and does not fit the role of the men of Judah in the plot. This is indicated by 1 Sam 22:5, according to which the

---

[24] George A. Cooke, *The Book of Joshua* (The Cambridge Bible for Schools and Colleges; Cambridge: Cambridge University Press, 1918), 151–152; Martin Noth, *Das Buch Josua* (2nd ed.; HAT I/7; Tübingen: Mohr Siebeck, 1953), 92, 99. See *BHS* on Josh 15:59a.

[25] Hans-Joachim Kraus, "Chirbet el-chōch," *ZDPV* 72 (1956): 152–62, with earlier literature. Guerin mentions a site called Kh. ʿAin el-Lehi located about nine km northwest of Kh. el-Khôkh and identified it with Biblical Lehi. See Victor Guérin, *Description géographique, historique et archéologique de la Palestine*, II: *Judée* (Paris: Imprimerie imperiale, 1869; reprint Amsterdam: Oriental Press, 1969), 396–400.

[26] Edward Robinson and Eli Smith, *Biblical Researches in Palestine, Mount Sinai and Arabia Petraea: A Journal of Travels in the Year 1838* (Boston: Crocker and Brewster, 1841), 477; idem, *Later Biblical Researches in Palestine, and in the Adjacent Regions: A Journal of Travels in the Year 1852* (Boston: Crocker and Brewster, 1856), 273–74.

[27] The identification was first made by James E. Hanauer, "Khurbet 'Orma," *PEFQS* 18 (1886): 25. For detailed discussions, see Conrad Schick, "Artuf und seine Umgebung," *ZDPV* 10 (1887): 143–46; James E. Hanauer, "The Rock of Etam and the Cave of Adullam," *PEFQS* 28 (1896): 162–64; Erasmus Gass, "Simson und die Philister. Historische und archäologische Rückfragen," *RB* 114 (2007): 377–80, with earlier literature.

[28] Erasmus Gass and Boaz Zissu, "The Monastery of Samson up the Rock of Etham in the Byzantine Period," *ZDPV* 121 (2005): 168–83.

prophet Gad ordered David, who stayed then in the cave of Adullam, to depart "and go to the land of Judah." Moreover, in the story of 1 Sam 23:3, David's men explicitly described Keilah as a town located outside of Judah. Zorah, like Adullam and Keilah, was located in the eastern margins of the Shephelah, outside the confines of the Judahite highlands. The prominent role of the men of Judah in the story does not make sense in the context of Wādi Isma'īn and the nearby Zorah. Third, the identification of 'Irāq Isma'īn with the "Sampso Monastery" is quite uncertain and there is no clear evidence that the place was a monastery. But even if we assume for the moment that the identification is correct, the site does not differ from other Byzantine sites identified as the loci of Samson's heroic deeds.[29] At the most, it indicates how the Samson story was geographically interpreted in the Byzantine period. Thus, we may conclude that the identification of the Rock of Etam at 'Irāq Isma'īn is unlikely. It should best be identified near the town carrying this name in the southern part of the Bethlehem region.

Missing in all the discussions conducted so far is the textual evidence indicating the dependence of the Samson story on the cycle of David stories and his warriors' wars with the Philistines. Let me present the evidence for this claim in detail.

First, in the two stories, the Philistines are the stronger side who invaded the highlands of Judah but were ultimately severely defeated. Second, David and Samson "went down" (וירד) to the stronghold/the cleft of the Rock of Etam (2 Sam 5:17b; Judg 15:9) and the Philistines "came up" (ויעלו) to arrest them. Moreover, in both episodes, the Philistine army "spread out" for battle; the verbal form is known in the biblical textual corpus only in 2 Sam 5:18, 22 and Judg 15:9. Whereas the verbal forms "went down" and "spread out" fit the context of David's war with the Philistines, they do not fit the Samson story and hence seem to have been borrowed from the story of David. Third, Shamma, son of Agee, one of David's Three, fought single-handedly against the Philistines at Lehi (2 Sam 23:11), similar to Samson who fought the Philistines single-handed in this place (Judg 15:9, 14). Moreover, the episode of Shamma closes with the words "YHWH brought about a great victory" (2 Sam 23:12b), and Samson explicitly attributes his victory to YHWH (Judg 15:18). Fourth, the motif of thirst and the seeking of water is common to the episode of David and the Three at Bethlehem (2 Sam 23:15–17) and that of Samson after his victory at Lehi (Judg 15:18). The element of thirst appears abruptly in

[29] Ibid., 171–72.

the Samson story and is likely to have actually been a borrowing from the story of David and the Three. Fifth, the Three "broke (ויבקעו) through the Philistine camp" and drew water from the well in the gate of Bethlehem (2 Sam 23:16), and God "broke (ויבקע)" the מכתש[30] so that water came from it (Judg 15:19). Sixth, following his victory at Baal-perazim, David declares that "YHWH has burst through my enemies before me like an outburst water" (2 Sam 5:20). The motif of YHWH bringing an outburst of water, as a metaphor or in reality, is common to the David and Samson stories. No wonder that the two episodes are closed by the renaming of the two locations of the divine intervention, Baal-perazim in the first and En-hakkore in the second.

Some other elements in the Samson story are also borrowed from the cycle of David stories. Examples of these can include the motif of the men of Judah who sought to deliver the hero to the pursuing enemy (Saul and the Philistines), and the number of three thousand men who participate in the pursuit (1 Sam 24:2; 26:2; Judg 15:11). It is clear that the story of Samson in the Rock of Etam was shaped in conjunction with the stories of David's wars with the Philistines and that its author systematically borrowed elements from the stories of David and his warriors.

Did the author of the Samson story also borrow the location of the Rock of Etam from the story of David's war with the Philistines? At the very least, Etam's location fits very well the arena of the war waged in the hilly plain of Rephaim. The rocky stronghold is located about three kilometers southwest of Bethlehem, the town where the Philistines' avant garde was posted, and is an ideal place for hiding and for making preparations for war held in the north of Bethlehem area.

The question of whether the author of the Samson story borrowed the name of the site from either a written source or verbal tradition, or selected it because it fitted so well the arena of David's wars with the Philistines, must remain open. One may speculate that the place name Adullam (עדלם) (2 Sam 23:13; 1 Chr 11:15) is a mis-copy of Etam (עיטם) because the former was better known as a hiding place of David (1 Sam 22:1) and was also called מצודה (1 Sam 22:4–5). But there is no textual support for this assumption. We should best leave the exact location of David's stronghold open, and yet assume that the Rock of Etam is a reasonable candidate for its location.

[30] For the meaning of the noun מכתש, see Walter Gross, *Richter, übersetzt und ausgelegt* (HTKAT; Freiburg: Herder, 2009), 709–10.

# BIBLIOGRAPHY


Abusch, I. Tzvi. *Mesopotamian Witchcraft: Toward a History and Understanding of Babylonian Witchcraft Beliefs and Literature.* Ancient Magic and Divination 5. Leiden: Brill, 2002.

Ackroyd, Peter R. *Exile and Restoration: A Study of Hebrew Thought of the Sixth Century* BC OTL. Philadelphia: Westminster, 1968.

Adair, James. "A Methodology for using the Versions in the Textual Criticism of the Old Testament." *JNSL* 20/2 (1994): 111–42.

Aejmelaeus, Anneli. *On the Trail of the Septuagint Translators: Collected Essays.* rev. ed. Leuven: Peeters, 2007.

Aharoni, Yohanan. *The Land of the Bible: A Historical Geography.* Philadelphia: Westminster, 1979.

Aḥituv, Shmuel. *Handbook of Ancient Hebrew Inscriptions: from the Period of the First Commonwealth and the Beginning of the Second Commonwealth.* Jerusalem: Musad Bialek, 1992. (Hebrew).

Ahlström, Gösta W. "Isaiah VI. 13." *JSS* 19 (1974): 169–72.

——. *Who Were the Israelites?* Winona Lake, Ind.: Eisenbrauns, 1986.

——. "The Nora Inscription and Tarshish." *Maarav* 7 (1991): 41–49.

Ahuvya, Avraham. "והנה 'ישב' ו'שוב' כמו 'יטב' ו'טוב'" *Lešonenu* 39 (1975): 21–36.

Albertz, Rainer. *A History of Israelite Religion in the Old Testament Period: Volume I: From the Beginnings to the End of the Monarchy.* OTL. Louisville: SCM, 1994.

——. "Darius in Place of Cyrus: The First Edition of Deutero-Isaiah (Isaiah 40.1–52.12) in 521 BCE." *JSOT* 27 (2003): 371–88.

Albrecht, Karl. "את vor dem Nominativ und beim Passiv." *ZAW* 47 (1929): 274–83.

Albright, William F. "The Egyptian Correspondence of Abimilki, Prince of Tyre." *JEA* 23 (1937): 190–203.

——. "New Light on the Early History of Phoenician Colonization." *BASOR* 83 (1941): 14–22.

——. "The Nebuchadnezzar and Neriglissar Chronicles." *BASOR* 143 (1956): 28–33.

——. "The Role of the Canaanites in the History of Civilization." Pages 328–62 in *The Bible in the Ancient Near East: Essays in Honor of William Foxwell Albright.* Edited by G. Ernest Wright. Garden City, N.Y.: Doubleday, 1961.

Alexander, T. Desmond. "The Composition of the Sinai Narrative in Exodus xix, 1–xxiv 11." *VT* 49 (1999): 2–20.

Allen, Leslie C. *Ezekiel 1–19, 20–48.* WBC 28, 29. Waco: Word Books, 1990.

——. "The First and Second Books of Chronicles." Pages 297–659 in vol. 3 of *The New Interpreter's Bible.* Edited by Leander E. Keck. 12 vols. Nashville, Tenn.: Abingdon, 1999.

Alster, Bendt and Takayoshi Oshima. "Sargonic Dinner at Kaneš: The Old Assyrian Sargon Legend." *Iraq* 69 (2007): 1–20.

Alter, Robert. *Genesis.* New York: W. W. Norton, 1996.

Althann, Robert. "Josiah." Pages 1015–1018 in vol. 3 of *ABD.* Edited by David Noel Freedman. 6 vols. New York: Doubleday, 1992.

Amiran, Ruth. "The Water Supply of Israelite Jerusalem." Pages 75–78 in*Jerusalem Revealed: Archaeology in the Holy City 1968–1974.* Edited by Yigael Yadin. New Haven: Yale University Press, 1976.

Amit, Yairah. "Creation and the Calendar of Holiness." Pages 13–29 in *Tehillah le-Moshe: Biblical and Judaic Studies in Honor of Moshe Greenberg.* Edited by Mordechai Cogan, Barry L. Eichler and Jeffrey H. Tigay. Winona Lake, Ind.: Eisenbrauns, 1997.

Anbar, Moshe. "La 'Reprise'." *VT* 38 (1988): 384–98.

Andersen, Francis I. and David Noel Freedman. *Hosea.* AB 24. New York: Doubleday, 1980.

Anteby-Yemini, Lisa. "Israël et la Méditerranée; des relations ambiguës." Pages 247–268 in *La Méditerranée des anthropologues. Fractures, filiations, contiguïtiés, L'atelier méditerranéen*. Edited by Diogini Albera and Mohamed Tozy. Paris: Maisonneuve & Larose, 2005.

Apóstolo, Silvio Sergio Scatolini. "On the Elusiveness and Malleability of 'Israel.'" *Journal of Hebrew Scriptures* 6 (2006): Article 7.

Arnold, Bill T. and John H. Choi. *A Guide to Biblical Hebrew Syntax*. Cambridge and New York: Cambridge University Press, 2003.

Arnold, Bill T. *Genesis*. NCBC. Cambridge and New York: Cambridge University Press, 2009.

Aster, Shawn Z. "'They Feared God'/'They Did Not Fear God': On the Use of *yĕrē' Yhwh* and *yārē' 'et Yhwh* in 2 Kings 17:24–41." Pages 134–41 in *Birkat Shalom: Studies in the Bible, Ancient Near Eastern Literature, and Postbiblical Judaism Presented to Shalom M. Paul on the Occasion of his Seventieth Birthday*. Edited by Chaim Cohen. Winona Lake, Ind.: Eisenbrauns, 2008.

Astour, Michael C. "Maḫādu, the Harbor of Ugarit." *JESHO* 13 (1970): 113–27.

Aubet, María E. *The Phoenicians and the West: Politics, Colonies and Trade*. Translated by Mary Turton. Cambridge: Cambridge University Press, 1993.

——. *The Phoenicians and the West: Politics, Colonies and Trade*. 2nd ed. Translated by Mary Turton. Cambridge: Cambridge University Press, 2001.

Auld, Graeme. *Kings Without Privileges: David and Moses in the Story of the Bible's Kings*. Edinburgh: T&T Clark, 1984.

Avioz, Michael. "A Rhetorical Analysis of Jeremiah 7:1–15." *TynBul* 57 (2006): 173–89.

Avishur, Yitshak. *Stylistic Studies of Word-Pairs in Biblical and Ancient Semitic Literatures*. AOAT 210. Kevelaer: Butzon & Bercker; Neukirchen-Vluyn: Neukirchener, 1984.

Babelon, Ernest. *Catalogue des monnaies grecques de la Bibliothèque nationale: Les Perses achéménides*. Paris: Rollin & Feuardent, 1893.

Bach, Alice. "Good to the Last Drop: Viewing the Sotah (Numbers 5.11–31) as the Glass Half Empty and Wondering How to View It Half Full." Pages 503–22 in *Women in the Hebrew Bible*. Edited by Alice Bach. New York: Routledge, 1999.

Baden, Joel S. "Identifying the Original Stratum of P: Theoretical and Practical Considerations." Pages 13–29 in *The Strata of the Priestly Writings: Contemporary Debate and Future Directions*. Edited by Sarah Shectman and Joel S. Baden. ATANT 95. Zürich: Theologischer Verlag Zürich, 2009.

Baer, David A. "It's All about Us": Nationalistic Exegesis in the Greek Isaiah (Chapters 1–12)." Pages 29–48 in *"As Those who are Taught." The Interpretation of Isaiah from the LXX to the SBL*. Edited by Claire Mathews McGinnis and Patricia K. Tull. SBLSymS 27. Atlanta: SBL, 2006.

Bailey, John. "Usage of Post Restoration Period Terms Descriptive of Priest and High Priest." *JBL* 70 (1951): 217–25.

Baker, David W. "Tarshish." Pages 331–33 in vol. 6 of *ABD*. Edited by David Noel Freedman. 6 vols. New York: Doubleday, 1992.

Baltzer, Klaus. *Deutero-Isaiah: A Commentary on Isaiah 40–55*. Hermeneia: A Critical and Historical Commentary on the Bible. Minneapolis: Fortress, 2001.

Bandstra, Barry L. "Word Order and Emphasis in Biblical Hebrew Narrative: Syntactic observations on Genesis 22 from a Discourse Perspective." Pages 109–23 in *Linguistics and Biblical Hebrew*. Edited by Walter R. Bodine. Winona Lake, Ind.: Eisenbrauns, 1992.

Barbiero, Gianni. *Das erste Psalmenbuch als Einheit*. ÖBS 16. Frankfurt: Peter Lang, 1999.

Bar-Efrat, Shimeon. *Narrative Art in the Bible*. JSOTSup 70. Sheffield: Almond, 1989.

Barnett, Richard D. "Early Shipping in the Near East." *Antiquity* 32 (1958): 220–30.

Barr, James. *Comparative Philology and the Text of the Old Testament*. Oxford: Clarendon, 1968.

——. *Comparative Philology and the Text of the Old Testament*. Oxford: Oxford University Press, 1968.

——. "The Symbolism of Names in the OT." *BJRL* 52 (1969): 11–29.
——. *The Semantics of Biblical Language*. Oxford: Clarendon, 1961; repr., London: SCM, 1996.
Barré, Michael L. "A Rhetorical-Critical Study of Isaiah 2:12–17." *CBQ* 65 (2003): 522–34.
Barrick, W. Boyd. "On the 'Removal of the High Places' in 1–2 Kings." *Bib* 55 (1974): 257–59.
Barth, Christoph. "ליץ, *lyṣ*." Pages 547–52 in vol. 7 of *TDOT*. Edited by G. Johannes Botterweck, Helmer Ringgren, and Heinz-Josef Fabry. Translated by David E. Green. 15 vols. Grand Rapids: Eerdmans, 1997.
Barth, Hermann. *Die Jesaja-Worte in der Josiazeit: Israel und Assur als Thema einer produktiven Neuinterpretation der Jesajaüberlieferung*. WMANT 48. Neukirchen-Vluyn: Neukirchener Verlag, 1977.
Barthel, Jörg. *Prophetenwort und Geschichte: Die Jesajaüberlieferung in Jes 6–8 und 28–31*. FAT 19. Tübingen: Mohr Siebeck, 1997.
Barthélemy, Dominique. *Les devanciers d'Aquila: première publication intégrale du texte des fragments du Dodécaprophéton*. VTSup 10. Leiden: Brill, 1963.
——. *Critique textuelle de l'Ancien Testament*. Tome 2. *Isaïe, Jérémie, Lamentations*. OBO 50/2. Fribourg: Éditions universitaires; Göttingen: Vandenhoeck & Ruprecht, 1986.
Bartlett, John R. *Edom and the Edomites*. JSOTSup 77. Sheffield: JSOT, 1989.
Batto, Bernard F. *Slaying the Dragon: Mythmaking in the Biblical Tradition*. Louisville, Ky.: Westminster/John Knox, 1992.
Becker, Joachim. *Messiaserwartung im Alten Testament*. SBS 83. Stuttgart: Katholisches Bibelwerk, 1977.
Becker, Uwe. *Jesaja—Von der Botschaft zum Buch*. FRLANT 178. Göttingen: Vandenhoeck & Ruprecht, 1997.
Beckingham, Charles F. "Appendix: The Society of Biblical Archaeology 1870–1919." Pages 155–58 in *The Royal Asiatic Society: Its History and Treasures*. Edited by Stuart Simmonds and Simon Digby. Leiden: E. J. Brill, 1979.
Ben David, Chaim. "Mountain Strongholds of Edom." *Cathedra* 101 (2002): 7–18 [Hebrew].
Ben Yehudah, Eli'ezer. *Thesaurus totius Hebraitatis*. Jerusalem: Talpioth; Berlin: Langenscheidt, 1908–59.
Ben Zvi, Ehud. "Inclusion and Exclusion from Israel as Conveyed by the Use of the Term Israel in Post-Monarchic Biblical Texts." Pages 95–149 in *The Pitcher is Broken: Memorial Essays for Gösta W. Ahlström*. Edited by Steven W. Holloway and Lowell K. Handy. JSOTSup 190. Sheffield: Sheffield Academic, 1995.
——. *Hosea*. FOTL 21A/1. Grand Rapids: Eerdmans, 2005.
——. "Are There any Bridges out There? How Wide was the Conceptual Gap between the Deuteronomistic History and Chronicles?" Pages 59–86 in *Community Identity in Judean Historiography: Biblical and Comparative Perspectives*. Edited by Gary N. Knoppers and Kenneth A. Ristau. Winona Lake, Ind.: Eisenbrauns, 2009.
Berger, Paul-Richard. "Ellasar, Tarschich und Jawan, Gn 14 und Gn 10." *WO* 13 (1982): 50–78.
Berges, Ulrich. *Das Buch Jesaja. Komposition und Endgestalt*. Herders Biblische Studien 16. Freiburg: Herder, 1998.
Bergma, John S. *The Jubilee from Leviticus to Qumran*. VTSup 115. Leiden: Brill, 2007.
Berlin, Adele and Marc Zvi Brettler, eds. *The Jewish Study Bible*. New York: OUP, 2004.
——. *The Dynamics of Biblical Parallelism*. Bloomington: Indiana University Press, 1985.
Berliner, Abraham. "Marx." *Literarisches Centralblatt für Deutschland* 38/27 (1887): 727.
Bernhardt, Karl-Heinz. "Dalman, Gustaf." Pages 322–3 in *TRE* 8. Edited by Gerhard Müller. Berlin: de Gruyter 1981.
Beuken, Willem A. M. "Isa. 56:9–57:13—An Example of the Isaianic Legacy of Trito-Isaiah." Pages 48–64 in *Tradition and Reinterpretation in Jewish and Early Christian Literature*. Edited by Jan Willem van Henten et al. StPB 36. Leiden: Brill, 1986.

——. "*Servant and Herald* of Good Tidings: Isaiah 61 as an Interpretation of Isaiah 40–55." Pages 411–42 in *The Book of Isaiah—Le Livre d'Isaie: Les oracles et leurs relecteurs: unité et complexité de l'ouvrage*. Edited by Jacques Vermeylen. BETL 81. Leuven: Leuven University Press, 1989.

——. "The Main Theme of Trito-Isaiah 'The Servants of Yhwh.'" *JSOT* 47 (1990): 67–87.

——. "Isaiah Chapters LXV–LXVI: Trito-Isaiah and the Closure of the Book of Isaiah." Pages 204–21 in *Congress Volume: Leuven, 1989*. Edited by John A. Emerton. VTSup 43. Leiden: Brill, 1991.

——. *Jesaja 1–12: Unter Mitwirkung und in Übersetzung aus dem Niederländischen von Ulrich Berges*. HTKAT. Freiburg: Herder, 2003.

——. *Jesaja 13–27*. HTKAT. Freiburg: Herder, 2007.

Beyse, Karl-Martin. "שָׁלֹשׁ [*sic*] *šālōš*." Pages 119–28 in vol. 15 of *TDOT*. Edited by G. Johannes Botterweck, Helmer Ringgren, and Heinz-Josef Fabry. Translated by David E. Green. 15 vols. Grand Rapids: Eerdmans, 2006.

Birch, Samuel. "The Progress of Biblical Archaeology." *TSBA* 1 (1872): 1–12.

——. ed. *Records of the Past*. 12 volumes. London: Samuel Bagster, 1873–81.

——. "Four Fragments of Papyrus belonging to the Edinburgh Museum of Science and Art." *PSBA* 7 (1884–1885): 79–89.

Birch, William F. "The Rock of the Pomegranate." *PEFQS* 11 (1879): 127–29.

——. "The Rock of Rimmon or the Pomegranate." *PEFQS* 12 (1880): 106–7.

——. "The Rock Rimmon." *PEFQS* 14 (1882): 50–55.

Blake, Barry J. *Case*. Cambridge Textbooks in Linguistics. Cambridge: Cambridge University Press, 1994.

Blázquez, José María. *Tartessos y los orígenes de la colonización fenicia en occidente*. Acta Salamanticensia, Filosofía y Letras 58. 2nd ed. Salamanca: Universidad de Salamanca, 1975.

Blenkinsopp, Joseph. *Ezra-Nehemiah: A Commentary*. OTL. Philadelphia: Westminster, 1988.

——. "A Jewish Sect of the Persian Period." *CBQ* 52 (1990): 5–20.

——. *Ezekiel*. IBC. Louisville: John Knox, 1990.

——. *Isaiah 1–39: A New Translation with Introduction and Commentary*. AB 19. New York: Doubleday 2000.

——. *Isaiah 40–55: A New Translation with Introduction and Commentary*. AB 19A. New York: Doubleday, 2002.

——. *Isaiah 56–66: A New Translation with Introduction and Commentary*. AB 19B. New York: Doubleday, 2003.

Block, Daniel I. *The Book of Ezekiel: Chapters 1–24*. NICOT. Grand Rapids: Eerdmans, 1997.

——. "My Servant David: Ancient Israel's Vision of the Messiah." Pages 17–56 in *Israel's Messiah in the Bible and the Dead Sea Scrolls*. Edited by Richard S. Hess and M. Daniel Carroll R. Grand Rapids: Baker, 2003.

Blum, Erhard. "Jesajas prophetisches Testament: Beobachtungen zu Jes 1–11 (Teil II)." *ZAW* 109 (1997): 12–29.

——. "Israels Prophetie im altorientalischen Kontext. Anmerkungen zu neueren religionsgeschichtlichen Thesen." Pages 81–115 in *"From Ebla to Stellenbosch": Syro-Palestinian Religions and the Hebrew Bible*. Edited by Izak Cornelius and Louis Jonker. Abhandlungen des deutschen Palästina-Vereins 37. Wiesbaden: Harrassowitz, 2008.

Boda, Mark J. "Terrifying the Horns: Persia and Babylon in Zechariah 1:7–6:15." *CBQ* 67 (2005): 22–41.

——. "From Dystopia to Myopia: Utopian (re)visions in Haggai and Zechariah 1–8." Pages 211–49 in *Utopia and Dystopia in Prophetic Literature*. Edited by Ehud Ben Zvi. Publications of the Finnish Exegetical Society 92. Helsinki/Göttingen: Finnish Exegetical Society/Vandenhoeck & Ruprecht, 2006.

——. "Figuring the Future: The Prophets and Messiah." Pages 35–74 in *The Messiah in the Old and New Testaments*. Edited by Stanley E. Porter. McMaster New Testament Studies. Grand Rapids; Cambridge: Eerdmans, 2007.

——. "Redaction in the Book of Nehemiah: A Fresh Proposal." Pages 25–54 in *Unity and Disunity of Ezra-Nehemiah: Redaction, Rhetoric, Reader*. Edited by Mark J. Boda and Paul Redditt. Hebrew Bible Monographs. Sheffield: Sheffield Phoenix, 2008.

——. "Identity and Empire, Reality and Hope in the Chronicler's Perspective." Pages 249–72 in *Community Identity in Judean Historiography: Biblical and Comparative Perspectives*. Edited by Gary N. Knoppers and Kenneth A. Ristau. Winona Lake, Ind.: Eisenbrauns, 2009.

——. "Legitimizing the Temple: The Chronicler's Temple Building Account." Pages 303–18 in *From the Foundations to the Crenellations: Essays on Temple Building in the Ancient Near East and Hebrew Bible*. AOAT 366. Edited by Mark J. Boda and Jamie Novotny. Münster: Ugarit-Verlag, 2010.

——. *1–2 Chronicles*. Cornerstone Biblical Commentary. Carol Stream, IL: Tyndale House, 2010.

Boda, Mark J. and Jamie R. Novotny, eds. *From the Foundations to the Crenellations: Essays on Temple Building in the Ancient Near East and Hebrew Bible.* AOAT 366. Münster: Ugarit-Verlag, 2010.

Bonnard, Pierre E. *Le second Isaïe, son disciple et leurs éditeurs Isaïe 40–66*. EBib. Paris: J. Gabalda, 1972.

Bordreuil, Pierre and Dennis Pardee. "Le combat de Ba'lu avec Yammu d'après les textes ougaritiques." *MARI* 7 (1993): 63–70.

Bordreuil, Pierre, Felice Israel and Dennis Pardee. "Deux ostraca paléo-hébreux de la collection Sh. Moussaieff." *Sem* 46 (1996): 49–76.

Borger, Riekele. *Die Inschriften Asarhaddons, Königs von Assyrien. AfO* 9. Graz: Im Selbstverlage des Herausgebers, 1956.

Bosshard-Nepustil, Erich. *Rezeptionen von Jesaja 1–39 im Zwölfprophetenbuch: Untersuchungen zur literarischen Verbindung von Prophetenbüchern in babylonischer und persischer Zeit*. OBO 156. Göttingen: Vandenhoeck & Ruprecht, 1997.

Botterweck, G. Johannes and Helmer Ringgren eds. *TDOT*. 15 vols. Translated by John T. Willis, Geoffrey W. Bromiley and David E. Green. Grand Rapids: Eerdmans, 1974–2006.

Braudel, Fernand. "Mediterrane Welt." Pages 7–10 in *Die Welt des Mittelmeeres: Zur Geschichte und Geographie kultureller Lebensformen*. Edited by Fernand Braudel, Georges Duby and Maurice Aymard. Frankfurt am Main: Fischer, 1986.

——. *Les Mémoires de la Méditerranée: Préhistoire et Antiquité*. Paris: Éditions de Fallois, 1998.

Braun, Roddy L. "Chronicles Ezra Nehemiah: Theology and Literary History." Pages 52–64 in *Studies in the Historical Books of the Old Testament*. Edited by John A. Emerton. VTSup 30. Leiden: Brill, 1979.

——. *1 Chronicles*. WBC 14. Waco, Tex.: Word Books, 1986.

Brayford, Susan. *Genesis*. SCS. Leiden: Brill, 2007.

Brettler, Mark Z. *The Creation of History in Ancient Israel*. London: Routledge, 1995.

Brichto, Herbert C. "The Case of the sotah and a Reconsideration of Biblical Law." *HUCA* 46 (1975): 55–70.

Brinkman, John A. "Through a Glass Darkly. Esarhaddon's Retrospects on the Downfall of Babylon." *JAOS* 103 (1983): 35–42.

——. "The Babylonian Chronicle Revisited." Pages 73–104 in *Lingering Over Words. Studies in Ancient Near Eastern Literature in Honor of William L. Moran*. Edited by Tzvi Abusch, John Huehnergard, and Piotr Steinkeller. HSS 37. Atlanta, Ga.: Harvard Semitic Museum, 1990.

Briquel-Chatonnet, Françoise. *Les relations entre les cites de la côte phénicienne et les royaumes d'Israël et de Juda*. Studia Phoenicia 12. OLA 46. Leuven: Peeters, 1992.

Britten, Benjamin. *Psalm 150, for children's chorus and instruments, Op 67*. by Steuart Bedford. New London Children's Choir; English Choral Music: NAXOS. 2003. http://www.classicalarchives.com/work/164277.html. [accessed June 30, 2011].

Brooke, Alan E., Norman McLean and Henry St. John Thackeray. *The Old Testament in Greek: According to the text of Codex Vaticanus, Vol. 2: The Later Historical Books. Part 1: I and II Samuel*. Cambridge: Cambridge University Press, 1927.

Broyles, Craig C. and Craig A. Evans. *Writing and Reading the Scroll of Isaiah: Studies of an Interpretive Tradition*. 2 vols. Leiden: Brill, 1997.

Bruckner, Anton. *Ps 150*. Part 1. by Jiří Bělohlávek, Ailish Tynan. BBC Symphony Chorus and BBC Symphony Orchestra.youtube. http://www.youtube.com/watch?v=MnHtj7JXCuc [accessed June 30, 2011].

Brueggemann, Walter. "Bounded by Obedience and Praise: The Psalms as Canon." *JSOT* 50 (1991): 63–92.

Budge, Ernest A. Wallis. "Memoir of Samuel Birch, LL.D., D.C.L., F.S.A., &c." *TSBA* 9/1 (1886): 1–41.

——. *The Rise and Progress of Assyriology*. London: Martin Hopkinson, 1925.

Budwig, Nancy. "The Linguistic Marking of Agentivity and Control in Child Language." *Journal of Child Language* 16 (1989): 263–84.

Buhl, Frants, and Heinrich Zimmern. *Wilhelm Gesenius' Hebräisches und Aramäisches Handwörterbuch über das Alte Testament*. 16th ed. Leipzig: Vogel, 1915.

Bunnens, Guy. *L'expansion phénicienne en Méditerranée*. Brussels and Rome: Institut historique belge de Rome, 1979.

Burkitt, Francis C. *Fragments of the Books of Kings according to the Translation of Aquila*. Cambridge: University Press, 1897.

Burney, Charles F. *Notes on the Hebrew Text of the Books of Kings: With an Introduction and Appendix*. Oxford: Clarendon, 1903.

——. *The Book of Judges with Introduction and Notes*. London: Rivingtons, 1918. Repr. New York: KTAV Publishing House, 1970.

Cahill, Jane. "A Rejoinder to 'Was the Siloam Tunnel Built by Hezekiah?' " *BA* 60/3 (1997): 184–85.

Caldecott, William S. and David F. Payne. "Joash." Pages 1062–64 in vol. 2 of *ISBE*. Edited by Geoffrey W. Bromily. 4 vols. Grand Rapids: Eerdmans, 1979–1988.

Calvin, John. *Genesis*. Wheaton/Nottingham: Crossway, 2001.

Cangh, Jean-Marie van. "Béthel: archéologie et histoire." Pages 441–49 in *Les sources judaïques du Nouveau Testament*. Edited by Jean-Marie van Cangh. BETL 204. Leuven: Peeters, 2008.

Carmignac, Jean. "Comparaison entre les manuscrits 'A' et 'B' du Document de Damas." *Revue de Qumrân* (1959): 53–67.

Carr, David M. "Reaching for Unity in Isaiah." *JSOT* 57 (1993): 61–80.

——. *Reading the Fractures of Genesis: Historical and Literary Approaches*. Louisville, Ky: Westminster John Knox, 1996.

Carroll, Robert P. *Jeremiah: A Commentary*. OTL. London: SCM, 1986.

Cassuto, Umberto. *A Commentary on the Book of Genesis, Part I: From Adam to Noah*. Translated by Israel Abrahams. 2nd ed. Magnes: Jerusalem, 1973.

*Catalogue of the Library of the Society of Biblical Archaeology*. London: Harrison and Sons, 1876.

Cates, Arthur. *Secretary's Report for the Year 1878*. London: Society of Biblical Archaeology, 1879.

Cathcart, Kevin J. and Robert P. Gordon. *Targum of the Minor Prophets*. ArBib 14. Wilmington, Del.: Michael Glazier, 1989.

Cathcart, Kevin J., ed. *The Letters of Peter le Page Renouf*. 4 vols. Dublin: University College Dublin, 2002–04.

——, ed. *The Correspondence of Edward Hincks*. 3 vols. Dublin: University College Dublin Press, 2007–2009.

Ceulemans, Reinhart. "A Critical Edition of the Hexaplaric Fragments of the Book of Canticles, with Emphasis on their Reception in Greek Christian Exegesis." Ph.D. diss., Katholieke Universiteit Leuven, 2009. In preparation as monograph (Leuven: Peeters).

Chagall, Marc. Illustrations. Biblical Art on the WWW hosted by Rolf E. Staerk. http://www.biblicalart.com/artwork.asp?id_artwork=22817&showmode=Full#artwork. [accessed June 30, 2011]

Chalmers, Scott. *The Struggle of Yahweh and El for Hosea's Israel.* Hebrew Bible Monographs 11. Sheffield: Sheffield Phoenix, 2008.

Chambers, Iain. *Mediterranean Crossings: The Politics of an Interrupted Modernity.* Durham and London: Duke University Press, 2008.

Childs, Brevard S. *The Book of Exodus.* OTL. Philadelphia: Westminster, 1974.

——. *Isaiah.* OTL. Louisville: Westminster John Knox, 2001.

Chilton, Bruce D. *The Isaiah Targum.* ArBib 11. Edinburgh/Wilmington, Del.: T&T Clark/Michael Glazier, 1987.

Clements, Ronald E. *Isaiah 1–39.* NCB. Grand Rapids and London: Eerdmans and Marshall, Morgan & Scott, 1980.

——. "Zion as Symbol and Political Reality: A Central Isaianic Quest." Pages 3–17 in *Studies in the Book of Isaiah: Festschrift Willem A. M. Beuken.* Edited by Jacques T. A. G. M. Van Ruiten and Marc Vervenne. BETL 132. Leuven: Peeters, 1997.

Clifford, Richard J. *Creation Accounts in the Ancient Near East and the Bible.* CBQMS 26. Washington, D.C.: Catholic Biblical Association, 1994.

Clines, David J. A. *Job 1–20.* WBC 17. Dallas: Word Books, 1989.

——, ed. *DCH.* 7 vols. Sheffield: Sheffield Academic, 1993–.

Cogan, Mordechai. *Imperialism and Religion: Assyria, Judah, and Israel in the Eighth and Seventh Centuries BCE.* Missoula, Mont.: Scholars, 1974.

——. *1 Kings.* AB 10. New York: Doubleday, 2001.

Cogen, Mordechai and Hayim Tadmor. *II Kings.* AB 11. New York: Doubleday, 1988.

Cohen, Abraham. תהלים*: The Psalms with Introduction and Commentary.* Rev. ed. Edited by E. Oratz and R. Shalom Shahar. London-Jerusalem-New York: Soncino, 1992.

Collins, John J. "Isaiah 8:23–9:6 in its Greek Translation." Pages 205–22 in *Scripture in Transition. Essays on Septuagint, Hebrew Bible, and Dead Sea Scrolls in Honour of Raija Sollamo.* Edited by Anssi Voitila and Jutta Jokiranta. JSJSup 126. Leiden: Brill, 2008.

Collins, Terry. "The Literary Contexts of Zechariah 9:9." Pages 29–40 in *The Book of Zechariah and Its Influence.* Edited by Christopher Tuckett. Aldershot: Ashgate, 2003.

Conrad, Joseph. *Lord Jim: A Tale.* Edinburgh and London: William Blackwood & Sons, 1900.

Cooke, George A. *The Book of Joshua.* The Cambridge Bible for Schools and Colleges. Cambridge: Cambridge University Press, 1918.

Cook, Stanley A. "A Pre-Massoretic Biblical Papyrus." *PSBA* 25 (1903): 34–56.

Cooper, Alan and Bernard R. Goldstein. "The Development of the Priestly Calendars (I): The Daily Sacrifice and the Sabbath." *HUCA* 74 (2003): 1–20.

Cooper, William R. "Introduction." *TSBA* 1 (1872): i–iv.

——. *Serpent Myths of Ancient Egypt.* London: Robert Hardwicke, 1873.

Corré, Alan D. "*'ēlle, hēmma = sic.*" *Bib* 54 (1973): 263–64.

Craigie, Peter C., Page H. Kelley and Joel F. Drinkard, Jr. *Jeremiah 1–25.* WBC 26. Dallas: Word Books, 1991.

Crawford, Sidnie White. *Rewriting Scripture in Second Temple Times.* Studies in the Dead Sea Scrolls and Related Literature. Grand Rapids: Eerdmans, 2008.

Creach, Jerome F. D. "Like a Tree Planted by the Temple Stream: The Portrait of the Righteous in Psalm 1.3." *CBQ* 61 (1999): 34–46.

Cross, Frank M. "An Interpretation of the Nora Stone." *BASOR* 208 (1972): 13–19.

——. "The 'Olden Gods' in Ancient Near Eastern Creation Myths and in Israel." Pages 73–83 in *From Epic to Canon: History and Literature in Ancient Israel.* Edited by Frank Moore Cross. Baltimore: Johns Hopkins University Press, 1998.

Crowell, Bradley L. "Nabonidus, as-Sila', and the Beginning of the End of Edom." *BASOR* 348 (2007): 75–88.

Crüsemann, Frank. *Studien zur Formgeschichte von Hymnus und Danklied in Israel.* WMANT 32. Neukirchen-Vluyn: Neukirchener, 1969.

——. "Das Bundesbuch—historischer Ort und institutioneller Hintergrund." Pages 27–41 in *Congress Volume Jerusalem 1986*. Edited by John A. Emerton. VTSup 40. Leiden: Brill, 1988.
——. *Die Tora: Theologie und Sozialgeschichte des alttestamentlichen Gesetzes*. München: Gütersloher Verlagshaus, 1992.
Curtis, Edward and Albert Madsen. *A Critical and Exegetical Commentary on the Books of Chronicles*. ICC. Edinburgh/New York: T&T Clark/Scribner, 1910.
Curtiss, Samuel I. *Franz Delitzsch: A Memorial Tribute*. Edinburgh: T&T Clark, 1891.
Dahood, Mitchell J. "Some Ambiguous Texts in Isaias." *CBQ* 20 (1958): 41–49.
——. *Proverbs and Northwest Semitic Philology*. Rome: Pontificium Institutum Biblicum, 1963.
——. *Psalms I: 1–50*. AB 16. Garden City, N.Y.: Doubleday, 1966.
Dalley, Stephanie M. and Anne Goguel. "The Sela' Sculpture: A Neo-Babylonian Rock Relief in Southern Jordan." *ADAJ* 41 (1997): 169–76.
Dalley, Stephanie M. *Myths from Mesopotamia: Creation, the Flood, Gilgamesh, and Others*. 2nd ed. Oxford: Oxford University Press, 2000.
Dalman, Gustaf H. "Der leidende Messias nach der Lehre der Synagoge im ersten nachchristlichen Jahrtausend." Ph.D. diss., Leipzig University (Karlsruhe: Reiff), 1887.
——. *Der leidende und der sterbende Messias der Synagoge im ersten nachchristlichen Jahrtausend*. Schriften des Institum Judaicum in Berlin 4. Berlin: Reuther, 1888.
——. *Der Gottesname Adonaj und seine Geschichte*. Berlin: Reuther, 1889.
——. *Jesaja 53: Das Prophetenwort vom Sühneleiden des Heilsmittlers, mit besonderer Berücksichtigung der synagogalen Litteratur*. Schriften des Institutum Judaicum in Leipzig 25. Leipzig: Faber, 1890; 2nd ed., Schriften des Institutum Judaicum in Berlin 13. Berlin: Evangelische Vereins-Buchhandlung, 1891.
——. *GJPA*. Leipzig: Hinrichs, [1]1894, [2]amplified 1905 = 1960, 1978, 1981, 1989.
——. *Aramäischen Dialektproben*. Leipzig: Hinrichs, [1]1896, [2]amplified 1927 = 1960, 1978, 1981, 1989.
——. *Die richterliche Gerechtigkeit im Alten Testament*. Studien zur biblische Theologie 2. Kartell-Zeitung akademisch theologischer Vereine auf deutschen Hochschulen. Berlin: Nauck, 1897.
——. *Aramäisch-neuhebräisches [Hand-] Wörterbuch zu Targum, Talmud und Midrasch, mit Vokalisation der targumischen Wörter nach südarabischen Handschriften und besonderer Bezeichnung des Wortschatzes des Onkelostargums, Teil I–II*. Frankfurt: Kauffmann, [1]1897–1901, [2]corr. and amp. 1922, [3]1938 = 1967, 1987, 1997 ... 2007.
——. *Christentum und Judentum*. Schriften des Institutum Judaicum zu Berlin 24. Leipzig: Faber, 1898.
——. *Die Worte Jesu I*. Leipzig: Hinrichs, 1898.
——. "Das hebräische Neue Testament von Franz Delitzsch." *Saat auf Hoffnung* 39 (1902): 150–57.
——. "Die Juden im heutigen Palästina, was sie wollen und sollen." *Saat auf Hoffnung* 54 (1917): 30–31
——. *Jesus-Jeschua*. Leipzig: Hinrichs, 1922.
——. "Gustaf Hermann Dalman." Pages 1–29 in vol. 4 of *Die Religionswissenschaft der Gegenwart in Selbstdarstellungen*. Edited by D. Erich Stange. 5 vols. Leipzig: Meiner, 1928.
Dandamaev, Muhammad A. "Neo-Babylonian Society and Economy." Pages 253–75 in vol. 3:2 of CAH. Edited by John Boardman et al. 2nd ed. Cambridge: Cambridge University Press, 2000.
Danell, Gustaf A. *Studies in the Name Israel in the Old Testament*. Uppsala: Appelbergs Boktryckeriaktiebolag, 1946.
Das, Andrew. "Paul of Tarsus: Isaiah 66.19 and the Spanish Mission of Romans 15.24, 28." *NTS* 54 (2008): 60–73.
Davidson, Andrew B. *Hebrew Syntax*. 3rd ed. Edinburgh: T&T Clark, 1902.

Davies, Graham I. *The Schweich Lectures and Biblical Archaeology*. Oxford: Oxford University Press for the British Academy, 2011.
Davies, Philip. R. *The Damascus Covenant: An Interpretation of the "Damascus Document."* JSOTSup 25. Sheffield: JSOT, 1983.
Davis, Irv. Illustrations. About.Com/ Religion and Spirituality / Judaism [accessed June 30, 2011].
——. http://judaism.about.com/library/2_artlit/bl_artpsalms_a.htm [accessed June 30, 2011].
Day, John. *God's Conflict with the Dragon and the Sea: Echoes of a Canaanite Myth in the Old Testament*. University of Cambridge Oriental Publications 35. Cambridge: Cambridge University Press, 1985.
——. *Psalms*. OTG. Sheffield: JSOT, 1990.
De Sousa, Rodrigo. "Problems and Perspectives on the Study of Messianism in LXX Isaiah." Pages 135–52 in *The Old Greek of Isaiah: Issues and Perspectives*. Edited by Arie van der Kooij and Michaël N. van der Meer. CBET 55. Leuven: Peeters, 2010.
De Vries, Simon J. "Moses and David as Cult Founders in Chronicles." *JBL* 107 (1988): 619–39.
——. *1 and 2 Chronicles*. FOTL 11. Grand Rapids: Eerdmans, 1989.
DeClaissé-Walford, Nancy L. *Reading from the Beginning. The Shaping of the Hebrew Psalter*. Macon, Ga.: Mercer University Press, 1997.
Delitzsch, Franz. "Christentum und jüdische Presse." *Saat auf Hoffnung* 19 (1882): 83–146.
——. *Christentum und jüdische Presse. Selbsterlebtes*. Erlangen: Andreas Deichert, 1882.
——. *Commentar über das Buch Jesaja*. BKAT 3/1. 4th ed. Leipzig: Dörffling & Franke, 1889.
——. *Biblical Commentary on the Prophecies of Isaiah*, II. 4th edition. Translated by James S. Banks. Edinburgh: T&T Clark, 1890.
——. *Biblical Commentary on the Psalms*. Translated by Francis Bolton. 2nd ed. 3 vols. Edinburgh: T&T Clark, 1892–1894.
Delling, Gerhard. "τρεῖς, τρίς, τρίτος." Pages 216–17 in vol. 8 of *TDNT*. Edited by Gerhard Kittel and Gerhard Friedrich. Translated by Geoffrey W. Bromiley. 10 vols. Grand Rapids: Eerdmans, 1997.
Demsky, Aaron. "The Clans of Ephrath: Their Territory and History." *TA* 13–14 (1986–1987): 46–59.
Dequeker, Luc. "Darius the Persian and the Reconstruction of the Jewish Temple in Jerusalem (Ezra 4, 23)." Pages 67–92 in *Ritual and Sacrifice in the Ancient Near East*. Edited by Jan Quaegebeur. OLA 55. Leuven: Peeters, 1993.
——. "Nehemiah and the Restoration of the Temple After Exile." Pages 547–67 in *Deuteronomy and Deuteronomic Literature: Festschrift C. H. W. Brekelmans*. Edited by Marc Vervenne and Johan Lust. BETL 133. Leuven: Peeters/Leuven University, 1997.
Dever, William G. "Biblical Archaeology Today: Death and Rebirth." Pages 706–22 in *Biblical Archaeology Today, 1990*. Edited by Avraham Biran and Joseph Aviram. Jerusalem: Israel Exploration Society, 1993.
Dhorme, Edouard. *A Commentary on the Book of Job*. Translated by Harold Knight. London: Nelson, 1967.
Dicou, Bert. *Edom, Israel's Brother and Antagonist: The Role of Edom in Biblical Prophecy and Story*. JSOTSup 169. Sheffield: Sheffield Academic, 1994.
Dietler, Michael and Carolina López-Ruiz eds. *Colonial Encounters in Ancient Iberia*. Chicago: University of Chicago Press, 2009.
Dietrich, Walter. *Jesaia und die Politik*. BEvT 74. Munich: Chr. Kaiser Verlag, 1976.
Diewert, David A. "Job 7:12: *Yam, Tannin* and the Surveillance of Job." *JBL* 106 (1987): 203–15.
Dillard, Raymond B. *2 Chronicles*. WBC 15. Waco: Word Books, 1987.
Dillmann, August. *Der Prophet Jesaja*. 5th ed. KEHAT 5. Leipzig: S. Hirzel, 1890.
——. *Genesis Critically and Exegetically Expounded*. Translated from the 4th German edition by William B. Stevenson. Edinburgh: T&T Clark, 1897.

Dines, Jennifer M. *The Septuagint*. London: T&T Clark, 2004.

Dion, Paul-Eugène. "Les KTYM de Tel Arad: Grecs ou Phéniciens?" *RB* 99 (1992): 70–97.

Dixon, Robert M. W. *Ergativity*. Cambridge Studies in Linguistics. Cambridge and Melbourne: Cambridge University Press, 1994.

Dobbs-Allsopp, F. W. et al. *Hebrew Inscriptions: Texts from the Biblical Period of the Monarchy with Concordance*. New Haven: Yale University Press, 2005.

Dörrfuß, Ernst Michael. *Mose in den Chronikbüchern: Garant theokratischer Zukunftserwartung*. BZAW 219. Berlin: de Gruyter, 1994.

Dogniez, Cécile. "L'indépendance du traducteur grec d'Isaïe par rapport au Dodekapropheton." Pages 229–46 in *Isaiah in Context. Studies in honour of Arie van der Kooij on the Occasion of his Sixty-Fifth Birthday*. Edited by Michael N. van der Meer, Percy van Keulen, Willem Th. van Peursen, and Bas Ter Haar Romney. VTSup 38. Leiden: Brill, 2010.

Dolansky, Shawna. *Now You See It, Now You Don't: Biblical Perspectives on the Relationship between Magic and Religion*. Winona Lake, Ind.: Eisenbrauns, 2008.

Dozeman, Thomas B. *Commentary on Exodus*. Eerdmans Critical Commentary. Grand Rapids: Eerdmans, 2009.

Dozy, Reinhard. *Supplément aux dictionnaires Arabes*. 2 vols. Leiden: Brill, 1881; repr. Beirut: Liban, 1968.

Driver, Godfrey R. "Two Misunderstood Passages of the Old Testament." *JTS* 6 (1955): 82–87.

——. "Two Problems in the Old Testament Examined in the Light of Assyriology." *Syria* 33 (1956): 73–77.

Drower, Margaret S. "The Early Years." *Excavating in Egypt: The Egypt Exploration Society 1882–1982*. Edited by T. G. H. James. London: British Museum Publications, 1982.

Duguid, Iain. "Messianic Themes in Zechariah 9–14." Pages 265–80 in *The Lord's Anointed. Interpretation of Old Testament Messianic Texts*. Edited by Philip E. Satterthwaite, Richard S. Hess, and Gordon J. Wenham. Tyndale House Studies. Carlisle, UK: Paternoster; Grand Rapids: Baker, 1995.

——. "But Did They Live Happily Ever After? The Eschatology of the book of Esther." *WTJ* 68 (2006): 85–98.

Duhm, Bernhard. *Das Buch Jesaia übersetzt und erklärt*. HKAT 3/1. Göttingen: Vandenhoeck & Ruprecht, 1892.

——. *Das Buch Jesaja*. HKAT 3/1. 4th ed. Göttingen: Vandenhoeck & Ruprecht, 1922.

Durand, Jean-Marie. "Le mythologème du combat entre le dieu de l'orage et la mer en Mésopotamie." *MARI* 7 (1993): 41–61.

Eaton, John. *The Psalms: A Historical and Spiritual Commentary with an Introduction and New Translation*. London & New York: T&T Clark International, 2003.

Edelman, Diana V. "Ezra 1–6 as Idealized Past." Pages 47–59 in *A Palimpsest: Rhetoric, Ideology, Stylistics, and Language Relating to Persian Israel*. Edited by Ehud Ben Zvi, Diana V. Edelman, and Frank Polak. Piscataway, N.J.: Gorgias Press, 2009.

Ehring, Christina. *Die Rückkehr JHWHs: Traditions- und religionsgeschichtliche Untersuchungen zu Jesaja 40,1–11, Jesaja 52,7–10 und verwandten Texten*. WMANT 116. Neukirchen-Vluyn: Neukirchener, 2007.

Ehrlich, Arnold B. *Randglossen zur hebräischen Bibel*. 7 vols. Leipzig: J. C. Hinrich, 1908–1914.

——. *Jesaia, Jeremia*. Randglossen zur Hebräischen Bibel: Textkritisches, Sprachliches und Sachliches 5. Leipzig: Hinrichs, 1912.

Eichrodt, Walther. *Ezekiel*. OTL. Translated by Cosslett Quinn. London: SCM, 1970.

Eidelberg, Shlomoh. "Trial by Ordeal in Medieval Jewish History: Laws, Customs and Attitudes." *PAAJR* 46/47, Jubilee Volume (1928–29/1978–79) [Part 1] (1979–1980): 105–120.

Eidevall, Göran. *Grapes in the Desert: Metaphors, Models and Themes in Hosea 4–14*. ConBOT 43. Stockholm: Almqvist & Wiksell, 1996.

Eisenbeiss, Sonja, Bhuvana Harasimhan, and Maria Voeikova. "The Acquisition of Case." Pages 369–83 in *The Oxford Handbook of Case*. Edited by Andrej Malchukov and Andrew Spencer. Oxford: Oxford University Press, 2009.

Eisenlohr, August. "On the Political Condition of Egypt before the reign of Ramses III; probably in connection with the Establishment of the Jewish Religion. From the Great Harris Papyrus." *TSBA* 1 (1872): 355–84.

Eissfeldt, Otto. "*nûaḥ* 'sich vertragen.'" Pages 124–28 in vol. 3 of *Kleine Schriften*. Edited by Rudolph Sellheim and Fritz Maass. 6 vols. Tübingen: J.C.B. Mohr, 1962–1979.

Elat, Moshe. "Tarshish and the Problem of Phoenician Colonisation in the Western Mediterranean." *OLP* 13 (1989): 55–69.

Elayi, Josette. "La domination perse sur les cités phéniciennes." Pages 77–85 in *Atti del II Congresso internazionale di studi fenici e punici. Roma, 9–14 Novembre 1987 1*. Collezione di studi fenici 30. Roma: Istituto per la civiltà fenicia e punica. Consiglio nazionale della ricerche, 1991.

Elgar, Edward. "*Beatus vir, qui non abiit.*" in *Psalms from St Pauls, Vol 1: Psalms 1–17* by St Paul's Cathedral Choir with Andrew Lucas (organ) and John Scott (conductor). Hyperion CDP11001. http://www.amazon.com/gp/recsradio/radio/B000002ZE0/ref=pd_krex_listen_dp_img?ie=UTF8&refTagSuffix=dp_img. [accessed June 30, 2011]

Eliot, T. S. "Little Gidding." Part V lines 6–8 and 16–17 in *T. S. Eliot Collected Poems 1909–1962*. London: Faber and Faber, 2002.

Elitzur, Yoel. "'So He sent Him Out to the Vale of Hebron.' On the Hilly *'Emeq* in the Hebrew Bible." *Beit Mikra* 54.2 (2009): 5–20 [Hebrew].

Elliger, Karl. *Die Einheit des Tritojesaia (Jesaia 56–66)*. Stuttgart: W. Kohhammer, 1928.

Emerton, John A. "The Translation and Interpretation of Isaiah vi.13." Pages 85–118 in *Interpreting the Hebrew Bible: Essays in honour of E.I.J. Rosenthal*. Edited by John A. Emerton and Stefan C. Reif. University of Cambridge Oriental Publications 32. Cambridge: Cambridge University Press, 1982.

Engelken, Karen. "Kanaan als nicht-territorialer Terminus." *BN* 52 (1990): 47–63.

Engels, Johannes. "Syrien, Phönikien und Judäa in den *Geographika* Strabos von Amaseia' (Strab. Geog. 16,2,1–46)." Pages 85–98 in *Die Septuaginta—Texte, Theologien, Einflüsse: 2. Internationale Fachtagung veranstaltet von Septuaginta Deutsch (LXX.D), Wuppertal 23.–27.7.2008*. Edited by W. Kraus and M. Karrer. WUNT 252. Tübingen: Mohr Siebeck, 2010.

Enger, Philipp A. *Die Adoptivkinder Abrahams: Eine exegetische Spurensuche zur Vorgeschichte des Proselytentums*. BEATAJ 53. Frankfurt am Main: Lang, 2006.

Eskenazi, Tamara C. *In an Age of Prose: A Literary Approach to Ezra-Nehemiah*. SBLMS 36. Atlanta: Scholars, 1988.

Evans, Craig A. *To See and Not Perceive: Isaiah 6.9–10 in Early Jewish and Christian Interpretation*. JSNTSup 64. Sheffield: JSOT, 1989.

Ewald, Heinrich. *Ausführliches Lehrbuch der hebräischen Sprache des Alten Bundes*. 8th ed. Göttingen: Dieterich, 1870.

Eynikel, Erik. *The Reform of King Josiah and the Composition of the Deuteronomistic History*. *OtSt* 33. Leiden: Brill, 1996.

Fabre, Thierry and Robert Ilbert. *Les représentations de la Méditerranée*. Paris: Maisonneuve et Larose, 2000.

Fauconnier, Gilles. *Mental Spaces: Aspects of Meaning Construction in Natural Language*. Cambridge: Cambridge University Press, 1994.

—— and Eve Sweetser. *Spaces, Worlds, and Grammar*. Chicago: University of Chicago Press, 1996.

—— and Mark Turner. "Blending as a Central Process of Grammar." Pages 113–29 in *Conceptual Structure, Discourse and Language*. Edited by Adele E. Goldberg. Stanford: CSLI, 1996.

——. *Mappings in Thought and Language*. Cambridge: Cambridge University Press, 1997.

——. *The Way We Think: Conceptual Blending and the Mind's Hidden Complexities*. New York: Basic Books, 2002.

Fensham, Frank C. *The Books of Ezra and Nehemiah*. NICOT. Grand Rapids: Eerdmans, 1983.

Fiddes, Paul. "The Cross of Hosea Revisited." *RevExp* 90 (1993): 175–90.

Field, Frederick. *Origenis Hexaplorum quae supersunt sive Veterum interpretum Graecorum in totum Vetus Testamentum fragmenta*. 2 vols. Oxford: Clarendon, 1875.

Finkelstein, Israel and Lily Singer-Avitz. "Reevaluating Bethel." *ZDPV* 125 (2009): 33–48.

Finkelstein, Israel and Neil A. Silberman. "Temple and Dynasty: Hezekiah, the Reformation of Judah and the Emergence of the Pan-Israelite Ideology." *ErIsr* 29 (2009): 348–57.

Firmage, Edwin. "Genesis 1 and the Priestly Agenda." *JSOT* 82 (1999): 97–114.

Fischer, Bonifatius, ed. *Genesis*. VL 2. Freiburg: Herder, 1951.

Fischer, Thomas and Udo Rüterswörden. "Aufruf zur Volksklage in Kanaan (Jesaja 23)." *WO* 12 (1981): 36–49.

Fishbane, Michael A. *Biblical Interpretation in Ancient Israel*. Oxford: Clarendon, 1985.

——. *The Garments of Torah: Essays in Biblical Hermeneutics*. Bloomington, Ind.: Indiana University Press, 1989.

——. "Inner-Biblical Exegesis." Pages 33–47 in *Hebrew Bible/Old Testament I: The History of its Interpretation. From the Beginnings to the Middle Ages (Until 1300). Part 1: Antiquity*. Edited by Magne Sæbø. Göttingen: Vandenhoeck & Ruprecht, 1996.

——. "Accusations of Adultery: A Study of Law and Scribal Practice in Numbers 5:11–31." Pages 487–502 in *Women in the Hebrew Bible*. Edited by Alice Bach. New York: Routledge, 1999.

Fitzmyer, Joseph A. and Stephen A. Kaufman. *An Aramaic Bibliography*. Part I. *Old, Official, and Biblical Aramaic*. Publications of the Comprehensive Aramaic Lexicon Project. Baltimore, Md.: The Johns Hopkins University Press, 1992.

Flint, Peter W. "The Septuagint Version of Isaiah 23:1–14 and the Masoretic Text." *BIOSCS* 21 (1988): 35–54.

Foh, Susan. "What is the Woman's Desire?" *WTJ* 37 (1974): 376–83.

Fohrer, Georg. *Das Buch Jesaja*. 2 vols. ZBK 19. 2nd ed. Zurich: Zwingli, 1966–1967.

Foster, Benjamin R. "Epic of Creation." Pages 390–402 in *COS*. 3 vols. Edited by William W. Hallo. New York: Brill, 1996.

——. *Before the Muses. An Anthology of Akkadian Literature*. 3rd ed. Bethesda: CDL, 2005.

Fraade, Steven D. *Enosh and His Generation: Pre-Israelite Hero and History in Postbiblical Interpretation*. SBLMS 30. Chico: Scholars, 1984.

Fraine, Jean de. *Esdras en Nehemias*. Roermond: J. J. Romen & Zonen, 1961.

France, R. T. "Servant of YAHWEH." Pages 744–47 in *Dictionary of Jesus and the Gospels*. Edited by Joel B. Green, Scot McKnight, and I. Howard Marshall. Downers Grove: InterVarsity, 1992.

Frankenburg, Wilhelm. *Die Sprüche*. HKAT 2.3. Göttingen: Vandenhoeck, 1898.

Fredriksen Landes, Paula. *Augustine on Romans: Propositions from the Epistle to the Romans. Unfinished Commentary on the Epistle to the Romans*. SBL Text and Translation 23. Chico: Scholars, 1982.

Frendo, Anthony J. "The Particles *beth* and *waw* and the Periodic Structure of the Nora Stone Inscription." *PEQ* 128 (1996): 8–11.

Fretheim, Terrence E. *The Suffering of God: An Old Testament Perspective*. OBT. Philadelphia: Fortress, 1984.

Frevel, Christian. "Vom Schreiben Gottes. Literarkritik, Komposition und Auslegung von 2 Kön 17,34–40." *Bib* 72 (1991): 23–48.

Fried, Lisbeth S. "The Land Lay Desolate: Conquest and Restoration in the Ancient Near East." Pages 21–54 in *Judah and Judeans in the Neo-Babylonian Period*. Edited by Oded Lipschits and Joseph Blenkinsopp. Winona Lake: Eisenbrauns, 2003.

——. *The Priest and the Great King: Temple-Palace Relations in the Persian Empire*. Winona Lake, Ind.: Eisenbrauns, 2004.

——. "Temple Building in Ezra 1–6." Pages 319–38 in *From the Foundations to the Crenellations: Essays on Temple Building in the Ancient Near East and Hebrew Bible*. Edited by Mark J. Boda and Jamie R. Novotny. AOAT 366. Münster: Ugarit-Verlag, 2010.

——. "*Deux ex Machina* and Plot Construction in Ezra 1–6." Forthcoming in *Prophets and Prophecy in Ancient Israelite Historiography*. Edited by Mark J. Boda and Lissa Wray Beal. Winona Lake: Eisenbrauns.

Friedman, Richard. "The Tabernacle in the Temple." *BA* 43 (1980): 241–48.

——. *The Exile and Biblical Narrative*. HSM. Atlanta: Scholars, 1981.

——. "Tabernacle." Pages 292–300 in vol. 6 of the *ABD*. Edited by David Noel Freedman. 6 vols. New York: Doubleday, 1992.

Frymer-Kensky, Tikva. "The Strange Case of the Suspected Sotah (Numbers V 11–31)." *VT* 34 (1984): 11–26.

Fuchs, Andreas. *Die Annalen des Jahres 711 v. Chr. nach Prismenfragmenten aus Ninive und Assur*. SAAS 8. Helsinki: The Neo-Assyrian Text Corpus Project, University of Helsinki, 1998.

——. *Die Inschriften Sargons II. aus Khorsabad*. Göttingen: Cuvillier, 1993.

Fürst, Julius. *Hebräisches und chaldäisches Handwörterbuch über das Alte Testament*. 3rd ed. Leipzig: B. Tauchnitz, 1876.

Füglister, Notker. "Ein garstig Lied—Ps 149." Pages 81–105 in *Freude an der Weisung des Herrn. Beiträge zur Theologie der Psalmen, Festschrift H. Groß*. Edited by Ernst Haag and Frank Lothar Hossfeld. Stuttgart: Verlag Katholisches Bibelwerk, 1986.

Funck, Bernd. "Studien zur sozialökonomischen Situation Babyloniens im 7. und 6. Jahrhundert v. u. Z." Pages 47–67 in *Gesellschaft und Kultur im Alten Vorderasien*. Edited by Horst Klengel. SGKAO 15. Berlin: Akademie–Verlag, 1982.

Galil, Gershon. "The Genealogies of the Tribe of Judah." Ph.D. diss., The Hebrew University of Jerusalem, 1983. (Hebrew)

Gall, August F. von. *Der Hebräische Pentateuch der Samaritaner*. Giessen: Töpelmann, 1918.

Galling, Kurt. "The 'Gōlā-List' According to Ezra 2//Nehemiah 7." *JBL* 70 (1951): 149–58.

——. "Die Liste der aus dem Exil Heimgekehrten." Pages 89–108 in *Studien zur Geschichte Israels im persischen Zeitalter*. Tübingen: Mohr Siebeck, 1964.

Garbini, Giovanni. "Tarsis e Gen. 10,4." *BeO* 7 (1965): 13–19.

Garelli, Paul. "The Achievement of Tiglath–pileser III. Novelty or Continuity?" Pages 46–51 in *AH, ASSYRIA... Studies in Assyrian History and Ancient Near Eastern Historiography Presented to Hayim Tadmor*. Edited by Mordechai Cogan and Israel Eph'al. *ScrHier* 33. Jerusalem: Magnes, 1991.

Garrett, Duane A. "Levi, Levites." Pages 519–22 in *The Dictionary of the Old Testament: Pentateuch*. Edited by T. Desmond Alexander and David W. Baker. Downers Grove: IVP Academic, 2003.

Garsiel, Moshe. *Biblical Names: A Literary Study of Midrashic Derivations and Puns*. Translated by Phyllis Hackett. Ramat Gan: Bar-Ilan University Press, 1987.

Gass, Erasmus and Boaz Zissu. "The Monastery of Samson up the Rock of Etham in the Byzantine Period." *ZDPV* 121 (2005): 168–183.

Gass, Erasmus. "Simson und die Philister. Historische und archäologische Rückfragen." *RB* 114 (2007): 372–402.

Gelb, Ignace J. "A New Clay-Nail of Hammurabi." *JNES* 7 (1948): 267–71.

Gentili, Paolo and Claudio Saporetti. "Nabonedo a Sela'." *Geo-Archeologia* 21.1 (2001): 39–58.

George, Andrew. *The Babylonian Gilgamesh Epic: Introduction, Critical Edition and Cuneiform Texts*. 2 vols. Oxford: Oxford University Press, 2003.

Gerleman, Gillis. "Der Nicht-Mensch: Erwägungen zur hebräischen Wurzel *NBL*." *VT* 24 (1974): 147–58.

Gertz, Jan Christian. *Grundinformation Altes Testament: Eine Einführung in Literatur, Religion und Geschichte des Alten Testaments*. Göttingen: Vandenhoeck & Ruprecht, 2007.

Gesenius, Wilhelm. *Commentar über den Jesaja: Ersten Theiles erste Abteilung enthaltend die Einleitung und Auslegung von Kapitel 1–12*. Leipzig: F. C. W. Vogel, 1821.
——. *Thesaurus philologicus criticus linguae hebraeae et chaldaeae Veteris Testamenti*. 3 vols. Leipzig: F. C. W. Vogel, 1835–1853.
Gibson, John C. L. *Textbook of Syrian Semitic Inscriptions. Volume 1: Hebrew and Moabite Inscriptions*. Oxford: Clarendon, 1971.
——. *Davidson's Introductory Hebrew Grammar: Syntax*. Edinburgh: T&T Clark, 1994.
Gill, Dan. "The Geology of the City of David and its Ancient Subterranean Water-works." Pages 1–28 in *Excavations at the City of David 1978–1985: Directed by Yigal Shiloh IV*. Edited by Donald T. Ariel and Alon de Groot. Qedem 35. Jerusalem: Institute of Archaeology of the Hebrew University of Jerusalem, 1996.
Gitin, Seymour. "Philistia in Transition: The Tenth Century BCE and Beyond." Pages 162–83 in *Mediterranean Peoples in Transition. Thirteenth to Early Tenth Centuries BCE. In Honor of Professor Trude Dothan*. Edited by Seymour Gitin, Amihai Mazar, and Ephraim Stern. Jerusalem: Israel Exploration Society, 1998.
Glassner, Jean-Jacques. *Mesopotamian Chronicles*. Writings from the Ancient World 19. Atlanta: Society of Biblical Literature, 2004.
Goldingay, John. *Daniel*. WBC 30. Dallas: Word Books, 1989.
——. *Isaiah*. 3rd ed. NIBCOT 13. Peabody, Mass.: Hendrickson, 2001.
—— and David Payne. *Isaiah 40–55*. 2 vols. ICC. London: T&T Clark, 2007.
Gomes, Jules F. *The Sanctuary of Bethel and the Configuration of Israelite Identity*. BZAW 368. Berlin: de Gruyter, 2006.
Gonçalves, Francolino J. *L'Expédition de Sennachérib en Palestine dans la littérature hébraïque ancienne*. EBib 7. Paris: J. Gabalda, 1986.
Gooding, David W. *The Account of the Tabernacle: Translation and Textual Problems of the Greek Exodus*. TS 6. Cambridge: Cambridge University Press, 1959.
——. "Two Possible Examples of Midrashic Interpretation in the Septuagint Exodus." Pages 45–48 in *Wort, Lied und Gottesspruch: Festschrift für Joseph Ziegler*. Vol. 1. Edited by Josef Schreiner. Würzburg: Echter Verlag, 1972.
Gordon, Cyrus H. "The Wine-Dark Sea." *JNES* 37 (1978): 51–52.
Gordon, Robert P. "Dialogue and Disputation in the Targum to the Prophets." *JSS* 39 (1994): 7–17.
——. "Terra Sancta and the Territorial Doctrine of the Targum to the Prophets." Pages 119–31 in *Interpreting the Hebrew Bible: Essays in Honour of E. I. J. Rosenthal*. Edited by John A. Emerton and Stefan C. Reif. Cambridge: Cambridge University Press, 1982. Repr. Pages 317–26 in *Hebrew Bible and Ancient Versions*. Aldershot: Ashgate, 2006.
——. "'Couch' or 'Crouch'?: Genesis 4:7 and the Temptation of Cain." Pages 195–209 in *On Stone and Scroll: Essays in Honour of Graham Ivor Davies*. Edited by James K. Aitken, Katharine J. Dell, and Brian A. Mastin. BZAW 420. Berlin: de Gruyter, 2011.
Goren, Yuval, Israel Finkelstein and Nadav Na'aman, "The Location of Alashiya. Petrographic Analysis of the Tablets." *AJA* 107 (2003): 233–55.
Görg, Manfred. "Ophir, Tarschisch und Atlantis: Einige Gedanken zur symbolischen Geographie." *BN* 15 (1981): 76–86.
Goshen-Gottstein, Moshe H. *The Hebrew University Bible: The Book of Isaiah*. Jerusalem: Magnes Press/Hebrew University, 1995.
Gosse, Bernard. "Detournement de la vengeance du Seigneur contre Edom et les nations en Isa 63,1–6." *ZAW* 102 (1990): 105–10.
Goulder, Michael D. *Isaiah as Liturgy*. SOTSMS. Aldershot, England: Ashgate, 2004.
Gozzoli, Robert B. *The Writing of History in Ancient Egypt during the First Millennium BC (ca. 1070–180 BC)*. Trends and Perspectives, Egyptology 5. London: Golden House Publications, 2006.
Grabbe, Lester. *Ezra-Nehemiah*. Old Testament Readings. London/New York: Routledge, 1998.
——. *Judaism from Cyrus to Hadrian: Volume 1–The Persian and Greek Periods*. Philadelphia: Fortress, 1992.

Grainger, John D. *Hellenistic Phoenicia*. Oxford: Oxford University Press, 1991.
Gray, George B. *A Critical and Exegetical Commentary on Numbers*. Edinburgh: T&T Clark, 1903.
——. *A Critical and Exegetical Commentary of the Book of Isaiah I–XXXIX.* ICC. Edinburgh: T&T Clark, 1912.
Grayson, A. Kirk and Wilfred G. Lambert. "Akkadian Prophecies." *JCS* 18 (1964): 7–30.
——. Kirk. *Babylonian Historical-Literary Texts*. Toronto Semitic Texts and Studies 3. Toronto: University of Toronto Press, 1975.
——. Kirk. *Assyrian Rulers of the Early First Millennium BC I (1114–859 BC)*. RIMA, Vol. 2. Toronto: University of Toronto Press, 1991.
——. Kirk. *Assyrian Rulers of the Early First Millennium BC II (858–745 BC)*. RIMA, Vol. 3. Toronto: University of Toronto Press, 1996.
——. Kirk. "Assyria." Pages 71–102 in vol. 3:2 in CAH. Edited by John Boardman et al. 2nd ed. Cambridge: Cambridge University Press, 2000.
——. Kirk. *Assyrian and Babylonian Chronicles*. TCS 5. Locust Valley, New York: J. J. Augustin, 1975. Repr., Winona Lake, Ind.: Eisenbrauns, 2000.
Greenfield, Jonas C. "Elishah." Page 92 in vol. 2 of *IDB*. Edited by G.A. Buttrick. 4 vols. Nashville, Abingdon, 1962.
Gressmann, Hugo. "Foreign Influences in Hebrew Prophecy." *JTS* 27 (1926): 241–54.
Grogan, Geoffrey W. "Isaiah." Pages 433–863 in *Proverbs–Isaiah.* Vol. 6 of *The Expositor's Bible Commentary*. Edited by Tremper Longman III and David E. Garland. Rev. ed. Grand Rapids: Zondervan, 2008.
Gross, Walter. *Richter, übersetzt und ausgelegt*. HTKAT. Freiburg: Herder, 2009.
Guérin, Victor. *Description géographique, historique et archéologique de la Palestine,* II: *Judée*, Paris : Imprimerie imperiale, 1869. Repr. Amsterdam: Oriental Press, 1969.
Guillaume, Alfred. *Hebrew and Arabic Lexicography: A Comparative Study.* Leiden: Brill, 1965.
Gunkel, Hermann. *Schöpfung und Chaos in Urzeit und Endzeit: eine religionsgeschichtliche Untersuchung über Gen 1 und Ap Joh 12*. Göttingen: Vandenhoeck & Ruprecht, 1895.
——. *Creation and Chaos in the Primeval Era and the Eschaton: A Religio-Historical Study of Genesis 1 and Revelation 12.* Translated by K. William Whitney, Jr. The Biblical Resource Series. Grand Rapids: Eerdmans, 2006.
Güterbock, Hans G. "Die historische Tradition und ihre literarische Gestaltung bei Babyloniern und Hethitern bis 1200, I." *ZA* 42 (1934): 1–91.
——. "Die historische Tradition und ihre literarische Gestaltung bei Babyloniern und Hethitern II. *ZA* 44 (1938): 45–145.
Hadley, Judith M. "Hebrew Inscriptions." Pages 366–80 in *Dictionary of the Old Testament Historical Books.* Edited by Bill T. Arnold and H. G. M. Williamson. Downers Grove, Ill.: InterVarsity, 2005.
Haerinck, Ernie. "Babylonia under Achaemenid Rule." Pages 26–34 in *Mesopotamia and Iran in the Persian Period: Conquest and Imperialism 539–331. Proceedings of a Seminar in Memory of Vladimir G. Lukonin.* Edited by John Curtis. London: British Museum Press, 1997.
Hagedorn, Anselm C. *Between Moses and Plato: Individual and Society in Deuteronomy and Ancient Greek Law*. FRLANT 204. Göttingen: Vandenhoeck & Ruprecht, 2004.
Hagner, Donald Alfred. *Matthew 1–13.* WBC 33a. Dallas, Tex.: Word Books, 1993.
Hallo, William W. "From Qarqar to Carchemish: Assyria and Israel in the Light of New Discoveries." *BA* 23.2 (1960): 33–61.
Hallo, William W. and K. Lawson Younger Jr., eds. *COS*. 3 vols. Leiden: Brill, 1997–2002.
Hallo, William W. and William Kelly Simpson. *The Ancient Near East: A History*. New York: Harcourt Brace Jovanovich, 1971.
——. *The Ancient Near East: A History*. 2nd ed. Fort Worth, Tex.: Harcourt Brace, 1998.
Halpern, Baruch, and Richard E. Friedman. "Composition and Paronomasia in the Book of Jonah." *HAR* 4 (1980): 77–92.
Halpern, Baruch. "A Historiographic Commentary on Ezra 1–6: Achronological Narrative and Dual Chronology in Israelite Historiography." Pages 81–142 in *The Hebrew Bible and*

*Its Interpreters*. Edited by William H. Propp, Baruch Halpern, and David Noel Freedman. Winona Lake: Eisenbrauns, 1990.

Halpern, Baruch and André Lemaire. "The Composition of Kings." Pages 123–53 in *The Books of Kings. Sources, Composition, Historiography and Reception*. Edited by André Lemaire and Baruch Halpern. VTSup 129. Leiden: Brill, 2010.

Hamilton, Victor P. *Genesis 1–17*. NICOT. Grand Rapids: Eerdmans, 1990.

Hanauer, James E. "Khurbet 'Orma." *PEFQS* 18 (1886): 24–26.

——. "The Rock of Etam and the Cave of Adullam." *PEFQS* 28 (1896): 162–64.

Hanhart, Robert. *Sacharja 1,1–8,23*. BKAT 14/1. Neukirchen-Vluyn: Neukirchener Verlag, 1998.

Hanson, Paul D. *The Dawn of Apocalyptic*. Philadelphia: Fortress, 1975.

——. *The Dawn of Apocalyptic: The Historical and Sociological Roots of Jewish Apocalyptic Eschatology*. Rev. ed. Philadelphia: Fortress, 1979.

Haran, Menahem. *Ages and Institutions in the Bible*. Tel Aviv: Am Oved, 1972. (Hebrew)

Harl, Marguerite. *La Genèse*. La Bible d'Alexandrie. Paris: Cerf, 1986.

Harrington, Daniel J. and Anthony J. Saldarini. *The Targum Jonathan of the Former Prophets*. ArBib 10. Wilmington, Del.: Michael Glazier, 1987.

Hart, Stephen. "Sela': The Rock of Edom?" *PEQ* 118 (1986): 91–95.

Hartenstein, Friedhelm. " 'Wach auf, Harfe und Leier, ich will wecken das Morgenrote (Ps 57,9)'—Musikinstrumente als Medien des Gotteskontakts im alten Orient und im Alten Testament." Pages 101–28 in *Musik, Tanz und Gott. Tonspuren durch das Alte Testament*. Edited by Michaela Geiger and Rainer Kessler. Stuttgart: Katholisches Bibelwerk Verlag, 2007.

Hayes, Elizabeth R. *The Pragmatics of Perception and Cognition in MT Jeremiah 1.1–6.30: A Cognitive Linguistics Approach*. BZAW. Berlin; New York: Walter de Gruyter, 2008.

Heard, R. Christopher. "Echoes of Genesis in 1 Chronicles 4:9–10: An Intertextual and Contextual Reading of Jabez's Prayer." *Journal of Hebrew Scriptures* 4 (2002): 1–28.

Heidel, Alexander. *The Babylonian Genesis. The Story of Creation*. 2nd ed. Chicago: Chicago University Press, 1951.

Hendel, Ronald S. "The Date of the Siloam Inscription: A Rejoinder to Rogerson and Davies." *BA* 59/4 (1996): 233–37.

——. *The Text of Genesis I–II: Textual Studies and Critical Edition*. New York: Oxford University Press, 1998.

——. "The Oxford Hebrew Bible: Prologue to a New Critical Edition." *VT* 58 (2008): 324–51.

Herdner, Andrée. *CTA*. Mission de Ras Shamra 10. Paris: Imprimerie Nationale, Geuthner, 1963.

Herrmann, Johannes. "Zu Gen $41_{43}$, Jer $22_{29}$, $7_{4}$." *ZAW* 62 (1950): 321–22.

Herzfeld, Michael. "Practical Mediterraneanism: Excuses for Everything, from Epistemology to Eating." Pages 45–63 in *Rethinking the Mediterranean*. Edited by W. V. Harris. Oxford: Oxford University Press, 2005.

Herzog, Zeev. "Is There Evidence for the Intentional Abolishment of Cult in the Arad and Tel Beersheba Excavations?" *ErIsr* 29 (2009): 125–36.

Hill, Andrew E. *1 & 2 Chronicles*. NIVAC. Grand Rapids: Zondervan, 2003.

Hincks, Edward, Jules Oppert, Henry C. Rawlinson and W. H. F. Talbot. "Comparative Translations of the Inscription of Tiglath Pileser I." *JRAS* 18 (1861): 150–219.

Hoenig, Sidney B. "Tarshish." *JQR* 69 (1979): 181–82.

Höffken, Peter. *Das Buch Jesaja: Kapitel 1–39*. Neuer Stuttgarter Kommentar: Altes Testament 18.1. Stuttgart: Katholisches Bibelwerk, 1993.

Høgenhaven, Jesper. *Gott und Volk bei Jesaja: Eine Untersuchung zur biblischen Theologie*. ATDan 24. Leiden: Brill, 1988.

Holladay, John S. "Judeans (and Phoenicians) in Egypt in the Late Seventh to Sixth Centuries." Pages 405–37 in *Egypt, Israel, and the Ancient Mediterranean World: Studies in Honour of Donald B. Redford*. Edited by Gary N. Knoppers and Antoine Hirsch. Probleme der Ägyptologie 20. Leiden: Brill, 2004.

Holladay, William L. *Jeremiah 2: A Commentary on the Book of the Prophet Jeremiah Chapters 26–52*. Hermeneia: A Critical and Historical Commentary on the Bible. Philadelphia: Fortress, 1989.
Holmgren, Fredrich. "Yahweh the Avenger: Isaiah 63:1–6." Pages 133–48 in *Rhetorical Criticism: Essays in Honor of James Muilenburg*. Edited by Jared J. Jackson and Martin Kessler. PTMS 1. Eugene: Pickwick, 1974.
Hoop, Raymond de. "The Interpretation of Isaiah 56:1–9: Comfort or Criticism?" *JBL* 127 (2008): 671–95.
Horden, Peregrine and Nicolas Purcell. *The Corrupting Sea. A Study of Mediterranean History*. Oxford: Blackwell, 2000.
Horden, Peregrine. "Mediterranean Excuses: Historical Writing on the Mediterranean since Braudel." *History and Anthropology* 16 (2005): 25–30.
Horst, Friedrich. *Hiob 1–19*. BKAT 16/1. Neukirchen-Vluyn: Neukirchener, 1968.
Horst, Koert van der, William Noel and Wilhelmia C. M. Wüstefeld, eds. *The Utrecht Psalter in Medieval Art*. London: Harvey Miller Publishers, 1996.
Horst, Koert van der. "Utrecht Psalter and Ps 1, ms. 32." Utrecht University Library. http://psalter.library.uu.nl/ [accessed June 30, 2011].
Hossfeld, Frank Lothar and Erich Zenger. *Die Psalmen I. Psalm 1–50*. NEchtB 29. Würzburg: Echter Verlag, 1993.
Hossfeld, Frank-Lothar, Erich Zenger, Klaus Baltzer, and Linda Maloney. *Psalms 2: A Commentary on Psalms 51–100*. Hermeneia: A Critical and Historical Commentary on the Bible. Minneapolis: Fortress, 2005.
Houtman, Cornelis. *Exodus Vol. 3: Chapters 20–40*. Historical Commentary on the Old Testament. Leuven: Peeters, 2000.
Hübner, Ulrich and Manfred Lindner. "Archaeological Check-Up on Jabal ash-Sharāh: Edomite Khirbat al-Kūr." *ADAJ* 47 (2003): 225–33.
Hultgren, Stephen. *From the Damascus Covenant to the Covenant of the Community: Literary, Historical, and Theological Studies in the Dead Sea Scrolls*. STDJ 66. Leiden: Brill, 2007.
Human, D. "'Praise Beyond Words': Psalm 150 as Grand Finale of the Crescendo in the Psalter." Paper presented at the SBL International Congress. Rome, 2009.
Hunger, Hermann. *Astrological Reports to Assyrian Kings*. SAA 8. Helsinki: Helsinki University Press, 1992.
Ibn Ezra, R. Abraham. In vol. 11 of מקראות גדולות. Edited by Akivah Frenkel [פרענקעל]. Warsaw: Lebensohn, 1860–69.
Ibn Janaḥ, Abu 'l-Walîd Marwân. *Book of the Hebrew Roots*. Edited by Adolf Neubauer. Oxford: Clarendon, 1875.
Jackson, Bernard S. "Some Literary Features of the Mishpatim." Pages 235–42 in *Wünschet Jerusalem Frieden: Collected Communications to the XIIth Congress of the IOSOT. Jerusalem 1986*. Edited by Matthias Augustin and Klaus-Dietrich Schunk. BEATAJ 13. Frankfurt: Peter Lang, 1988.
——. *Wisdom-Laws. A Study of the Mishpatim of Exodus 21:1–22:16*. Oxford: Oxford University Press, 2006.
Janzen, J. Gerald. "Metaphor and Reality in Hosea 11." *Semeia* 24 (1982): 7–44.
Japhet, Sara. "Sheshbazzar and Zerubabbel against the Background of the Historical and Religious Tendencies of Ezra Nehemiah." *ZAW* 94 (1982): 66–98.
——. *I & II Chronicles*. OTL. Philadelphia: Fortress, 1993.
——. *I & II Chronicles: A Commentary*. OTL. London/Louisville, Ky.: SCM/Westminster/John Knox, 1993.
——. "Composition and Chronology in the Book of Ezra-Nehemiah." Pages 189–216 in *Second Temple Studies: 2. Temple and Community in the Persian Period*. Edited by Tamara C. Eskenazi and Kent H. Richards. JSOTSup 175. Sheffield: JSOT, 1994.
——. *The Ideology of the Book of Chronicles and its Place in Biblical Thought*. BEATAJ 9. Frankfurt: Lang, 1997.

——. *The Ideology of the Book of Chronicles and its Place in Biblical Thought.* Translated by Anna Barber. BEATAJ 9. Frankfurt: Peter Lang, 1989. 3rd printing: Winona Lake: Eisenbrauns, 2009.
Jarick, John. *1 Chronicles.* Readings: A New Biblical Commentary. Sheffield: Sheffield Academic, 2002.
——. *2 Chronicles.* Sheffield: Sheffield Phoenix, 2007.
Jastrow, Marcus. *A Dictionary of the Targumim, the Talmud Babli and Yerushalmi, and the Midrashic Literature.* New York: G. P. Putnam's Sons, 1903.
Jauhiainen, Marko. "Turban and Crown Lost and Regained: Ezekiel 21: 29–32 and Zechariah's Zemah." *JBL* 127 (2008): 501–11.
Jigoulov, Vadim S. *The Social History of Achaemenid Phoenicia. Being a Phoenician, Negotiating Empires.* Bible World. London: Equinox, 2010.
Joannès, Francis. *The Age of Empires. Mesopotamia in the First Millennium.* Translated by Antonia Nevill. Edinburgh: Edinburgh University Press, 2004.
Johnson, Marshall D. *The Purpose of Biblical Genealogies.* Cambridge: Cambridge University Press, 1969.
Johnstone, William. *1 and 2 Chronicles, Volume 2: 2 Chronicles 10–36: Guilt and Atonement.* JSOTSup 254. Sheffield: Sheffield Academic, 1997.
Jong, Matthijs J. de. *Isaiah Among the Ancient Near Eastern Prophets: A Comparative Study of the Earliest Stages of the Isaiah Tradition and the Neo-Assyrian Prophecies.* VTSup 117. Leiden: Brill, 2007.
Joüon, Paul and Takamitsu Muraoka. *A Grammar of Biblical Hebrew.* Subsidia Biblica 27. Rome: Editrice Pontificio Istituto Biblico, 2006.
——. *Grammaire de l'hébreu biblique.* 2nd ed. Rome: Pontifical Biblical Institute, 1947.
Kaiser, Otto. *Das Buch des Propheten Jesaja: Kapitel 1–12.* 5th ed. Das Alte Testament Deutsch 17. Göttingen: Vandenhoeck & Ruprecht, 1981.
——. *Der Prophet Jesaja: Kapitel 13–39.* ATD 18. Göttingen: Vandenhoeck & Ruprecht, 1983.
——. *Isaiah 1–12: A Commentary.* 2nd ed. OTL. Translated by John Bowden. London: SCM, 1983.
Kakkanattu, Joy Philip. *God's Enduring Love in the Book of Hosea.* FAT 2. *Reihe*, 14. Tübingen: Mohr Siebeck, 2006.
Kalimi, Isaac. *Zur Geschichtsschreibung des Chronisten.* BZAW 226. Berlin/New York: de Gruyter, 1995.
——. *An Ancient Israelite Historian: Studies in the Chronicler, His Time, Place and Writing.* Assen: van Gorcum, 2005.
——. *The Reshaping of Ancient Israelite History in Chronicles.* Winona Lake: Eisenbrauns, 2005.
Kallai, Zecharia. *Historical Geography of the Bible: The Tribal Territories of Israel.* Jerusalem: Magnes, 1986.
——. "Bethlehem." Pages 86–88 in vol. 2 of *Encyclopedia Biblica.* 9 vols. Jerusalem: Mosad Bialik, 1954. (Hebrew)
Katzenstein, H. Jacob. *The History of Tyre. From the Beginning of the Second Millennium BCE until the Fall of the Neo-Babylonian Empire in 538 BCE.* Jerusalem: Schocken Institute for Jewish Research, 1973.
Keefe, Alice. *Woman's Body and Social Body in Hosea.* JSOTSup 338. London: Sheffield Academic, 2001.
Keil, Carl F. and Franz Delitzsch. *Isaiah.* Vol. 7 of *Commentary on the Old Testament.* Translated by James Martin. Edinburgh: T&T Clark, 1866–1891. Repr., Peabody, Mass.: Hendrickson, 2001.
Keil, Carl F. *Chronik, Esra, Nehemia und Esther.* Leipzig: Dörffling und Franke, 1870.
Kellermann, Ulrich. *Nehemia: Quellen, Überlieferung und Geschichte.* BZAW 102. Berlin: Töpelmann, 1967.
Kelly, Brian. "Retribution Revisited: Covenant, Grace and Restoration." Pages 206–27 in *The Chronicler as Theologian: Essays in Honor of Ralph W. Klein.* Edited by M. Patrick

Graham, Steven McKenzie, and Gary N. Knoppers JSOTSup 371. Sheffield: Sheffield Academic, 2003.
Kidner, Derek. *Ezra and Nehemiah: An Introduction and Commentary*. Downers Grove, Ill.: Inter-Varsity, 1979.
Kiesow, Klaus. *Exodustexte im Jesajabuch: literarkritische und motivgeschichtliche Analysen*. OBO 24. Fribourg: Editions Universitaires, 1979.
Kim, Uriah Y. "Josiah." Pages 413–15 in vol. 3 of *New Interpreter's Dictionary of the Bible*. Edited by Katherine D. Sakenfeld. 5 vols. Nashville: Abingdon, 2006–2010.
Kimchi. In vol. 7 of מקראות גדולות. Edited by Akivah Frenkel [פרענקעל]. Warsaw: J. Lebensohn, 1862.
King, Leonard W. *The Seven Tablets of Creation*. London: Luzac, 1909.
King, Thomas J. *The Realignment of the Priestly Literature: The Priestly Narrative in Genesis and Its Relation to Priestly Legislation and the Holiness School*. Princeton Theological Monograph Series 102. Eugene: Wipf & Stock Publishers, 2009.
Kister, Menahem. "Biblical Phrases and Hidden Biblical Interpretations and Pesharim." Pages 27–39 in *The Dead Sea Scrolls: Forty Years of Research*. Edited by Devorah Dimant and Uriel Rappaport. STDJ 10. Jerusalem: Magnes; Leiden: Brill, 1992.
——. "The Development of the Early Recensions of the Damascus Document." *DSD* 14 (2007): 61–76.
Klein, Michael L. *The Fragment-Targums of the Pentateuch According to their Extant Sources*. Vol. 1. AnBib 76. Rome: Biblical Institute, 1980.
Klein, Ralph W. *1 Chronicles*. Hermeneia: A Critical and Historical Commentary on the Bible. Minneapolis: Fortress, 2006.
Kleinig, John. *The LORD's Song: the Basis, Function and Significance of Choral Music in Chronicles*. JSOTSup 156. Sheffield: Sheffield Academic, 1991.
Knauf, Ernst A. "Bethel: The Israelite Impact on Judean Language and Literature." Pages 291–349 in *Judah and the Judeans in the Persian Period*. Edited by Oded Lipschits and Manfred Oeming. Winona Lake, Ind.: Eisenbrauns, 2006.
Knobel, August. *Die Völkertafel der Genesis*. Giessen: J. Ricker, 1850.
——. *Die Genesis erklärt*. KEHAT. 2nd ed. Leipzig: S. Hirzel, 1860.
Knobel, Ludwig. *Der Prophet Jesaja*. 4th ed. KEHAT 5. Leipzig: Hirzel, 1872.
Knohl, Israel. "The Priestly Torah Versus the Holiness School: Sabbath and the Festivals." *HUCA* 58 (1987): 65–117.
——. *The Sanctuary of Silence: The Priestly Torah and the Holiness School*. Minneapolis: Fortress, 1995.
——. *The Divine Symphony: The Bible's Many Voices*. Philadelphia: The Jewish Publication Society, 2003.
Knoppers, Gary N. *Two Nations Under God: The Deuteronomistic History of Solomon and the Dual Monarchies*. HSM 52. Atlanta: Scholars, 1993.
——. "History and Historiography: The Royal Reforms." Pages 178–203 in *The Chronicler as Historian*. Edited by M. Patrick Graham, Kenneth G. Hoglund, and Steven L. McKenzie. JSOTSup 238. Sheffield: Sheffield Academic, 1997.
——. "In Search of Postexilic Israel: Samaria after the Fall of the Northern Kingdom." Pages 150–80 in *In Search of Preexilic Israel*. Edited by John Day. JSOTSup 406. Edinburgh: T&T Clark, 2004.
——. *1 Chronicles 1–9*. AB 12. New York: Doubleday, 2004.
——. *1 Chronicles 10–29*. AB 12a. New York: Doubleday, 2004.
——. "What has Mt. Zion to do with Mt. Gerizim? A Study in the Early Relations between the Jews and the Samaritans in the Persian Period." *SR* 34 (2005): 307–36.
——. "Revisiting the Samarian Question in the Persian Period." Pages 265–89 in *Judah and the Judeans in the Persian Period*. Edited by Oded Lipschits and Manfred Oeming. Winona Lake, Ind.: Eisenbrauns, 2006.
——. "Cutheans or Children of Jacob? The Issue of Samaritan Origins in 2 Kings 17." Pages 223–39 in *Reflection and Refraction: Studies in Biblical Historiography in Honour of*

*A. Graeme Auld*. Edited by Robert Rezetko, Timothy H. Lim, and W. Brian Aucker. VTSup 113. Leiden: Brill, 2007.
——. "Did Jacob become Judah?: Assessing Israel's Reconstitution in Deutero-Isaiah." Pages 39–67 in *Studies on Bible, History and Linguistics—Proceedings of the Sixth International meeting of the Société d'Études Samaritaines, Pápa, Hungary, 20–25 July 2008*. Edited by József Zsengellér. Studia Samaritana 6. Berlin: de Gruyter, 2011.
Knowles, Melody D. "Pilgrimage imagery in the returns in Ezra." *JBL* 123 (2004): 57–74.
Koch, Michael. *Tarschisch und Hispanien*. Madrider Forschungen 14. Berlin: W. de Gruyter, 1984.
Koch, Ulla S. *Babylonian Liver Omens*. Copenhagen: Carsten Niebuhr Institute of Near Eastern Studies. Museum Tusculanum, 2000.
——. *Secrets of Extispicy: The Chapter Multābiltu of the Babylonian Extispicy Series and Niṣirti bārûti Texts mainly from Aššurbanipal's Library*. AOAT 326. Münster: Ugarit-Verlag, 2005.
Koenen, Klaus. *Ethik und Eschatologie im Tritojesajabuch*. WMANT 62. Neukirchen-Vluyn: Neukirchener, 1990.
Köhler, Ludwig, Walter Baumgartner, and Johann Jakob Stamm. *HALOT*. Leiden: Brill 1994.
Kooij, Arie van der. *Die alten Textzeugen des Jesajabuches. Ein Beitrag zur Textgeschichte des Alten Testaments*. OBO 35. Freiburg: Universitätsverlag; Göttingen: Vandenhoeck & Ruprecht, 1981.
——. " 'The Servant of the Lord': A Particular Group of Jews in Egypt according to the Old Greek of Isaiah. Some Comments on LXX Isa 49,1–6 and Related Passages." Pages 383–96 in *Studies in the Book of Isaiah: Festschrift Willem A.M. Beuken*. Edited by Jacques van Ruiten and Marc Vervenne. BETL 132. Leuven: Peeters, 1997.
——. "Isaiah in the Septuagint." Pages 513–529 in vol. 2 of *Writing and Reading the Scroll of Isaiah: Studies of an Interpretive Tradition*. Edited by Craig C. Broyles and Craig A. Evans. 2 vols. Leiden: Brill, 1997.
——. *The Oracle of Tyre: The Septuagint of Isaiah XXIII as Version and Vision*. VTSup 71. Leiden: Brill, 1998.
——. "Wie heisst der Messias. Zu Jes 9,5 in den alten griechischen Versionen." Pages 156–69 in *Vergegenwärtigung des Alten Testaments. Beiträge zur biblischen Hermeneutik. Festschrift für Rudolf Smend zom 70. Geburtstag*. Edited by Christoph Bultmann, Walter Dietrich, and Christoph Levin. Göttingen: Vandenhoeck & Ruprecht, 2002.
——. "The Septuagint of Isaiah and the Mode of Reading Prophecies in Early Judaism. Some Comments on LXX Isaiah 8–9." Pages 597–611 in *Die Septuaginta–Texte, Kontexte, Lebenswelten. Internationale Fachtagung veranstaltet von Septuaginta Deutsch (LXX.D), Wuppertal 20.–23. Juli 2006*. Edited by Martin Karrer und Wolfgang Kraus. WUNT 219. Tübingen: Mohr Siebeck, 2008.
Koole, Jan L. *Isaiah III, Volume 1: Isaiah 40–48*. Translated Anthony P. Runia. Historical Commentary on the Old Testament. Kampen: Kok Pharos, 1997.
——. *Isaiah III, Volume 3: Isaiah 56–66*. Translated by Anthony P. Runia. Historical Commentary on the Old Testament. Leuven: Peeters, 2001.
Kratz, Reinhard G. *Kyros im Deuterojesaja-Buch: redaktionsgeschichtliche Untersuchungen zu Entstehung und Theologie von Jes 40–55*. FAT 1. Tübingen: Mohr Siebeck, 1991.
——. "Der Anfang des Zweiten Jesaja in Jes 40,1f. und seine literarischen Horizonte." *ZAW* 105 (1993): 400–419.
——. "Der Anfang des Zweiten Jesaja in Jes 40,1f. und das Jeremiabuch." *ZAW* 106 (1994): 243–61.
——. *Die Komposition der erzählenden Bücher des Alten Testaments: Grundwissen der Bibelkritik*. UTB 2157. Göttingen: Vandenhoeck & Ruprecht, 2000.
——. "Das Neue in der Prophetie des Alten Testaments." Pages 1–22 in *Prophetie in Israel: Beiträge des Symposiums "Das Alte Testament und die Kultur der Moderne" anlässlich*

*des 100. Geburtstags Gerhard von Rads (1901–1971) Heidelberg, 18–21 Oktober* 2001. Edited by Irmtraud Fischer, Konrad Schmid, and H. G. M. Williamson. Altes Testament und Moderne 11. Münster: LIT, 2003.
——. "Israel in the Book of Isaiah." *JSOT* 31 (2006): 103–28.
——. "Rewriting Isaiah: The Case of Isaiah 28–31." Pages 245–66 in *Prophecy and Prophets in Ancient Israel*. Edited by John Day. LHBOTS 531. New York & London: T&T Clark International, 2010.
——. "Der Pescher Nahum und seine biblische Vorlage." Pages 99–145 in *Prophetenstudien: Kleine Schriften II*. FAT 74. Tübingen: Mohr Siebeck, 2011.
——. "Jesaja in den Texten vom Toten Meer." Pages 243–71 in *Prophetenstudien: Kleine Schriften II*. FAT 74. Tübingen: Mohr Siebeck, 2011.
Kraus, Hans-Joachim. "Chirbet el-chōch." *ZDPV* 72 (1956): 152–62.
Kugel, James L. *The Idea of Biblical Poetry: Parallelism and Its History*. New Haven: Yale University Press, 1981.
Kugler, Robert A. *From Patriarch to Priest. The Levi-Priestly Tradition from Aramaic Levi to Testament of Levi*. SBLEJL 9. Atlanta: Scholars, 1996.
Kuhl, Curt. "Die 'Wiederaufnahme'—ein literarkritische Prinzip?" *ZAW* 64 (1952): 1–11.
Kuhrt, Amélie. "Assyrian and Babylonian Traditions in Classical Authors. A Critical Synthesis." Pages 539–53 in *Mesopotamien und seine Nachbarn. Politische und kulturelle Wechselbeziehungen im alten Vorderasien vom 4. bis. 1. Jahrtausend*. XXV Rencontre assyriologique internationale Berlin 3. bis 7. Juli 1978. Edited by Hans J. Nissen and Johannes Renger. Berliner Beiträge zum Vorderen Orient I:2. Berlin: Reimer, 1982.
Kutscher, Raphael. *The Brockmon Tablets: Royal Inscriptions*. Haifa: Haifa University Press, 1989.
Laberge, Léo. *La Septante d'Isaïe 28–33. Étude de tradition textuelle*. Ottawa: Chez Auteur, 1978.
Lambert, Wilfred G. *The Background of Jewish Apocalyptic*. London: The Athlone, 1978.
——. "A New Look at the Babylonian Background of Genesis." *JTS* 16 (1965) 287–300. Repr. pages 96–113 in *I Studied Inscriptions from Before the Flood*. Edited by Richard S. Hess and David T. Tsumura. Winona Lake, Ind.: Eisenbrauns, 1994.
——, Alan R. Millard and Miguel Civil. *Atra-hasis: The Babylonian Story of The Flood*. Winona Lake, Ind.: Eisenbrauns, 1999.
——. "Mesopotamian Creation Stories." Pages 15–59 in *Imagining Creation*. Edited by Markham J. Geller and Mineke Schipper. Leiden: Brill, 2008.
Lamprichs, Roland. *Die Westexpansion des neuassyrischen Reiches. Eine Strukturanalyse*. AOAT 239. Neukirchen–Vluyn: Neukirchener Verlag, 1995.
Lancaster, Steven P. and Gary A. Long. "Where They Met: Separations in the Rock Mass Near the Siloam Tunnel's Meeting Point." *BASOR* 315 (1999): 15–26.
Landy, Francis. *Hosea*. Sheffield: Sheffield Academic, 1995.
——. "The Oracle against Tyre (Isa 23)." Pages 239–51 in *Berührungspunkte: Studien zur Sozial- und Religionsgeschichte Israels und seiner Umwelt. Festschrift für Rainer Albertz zu seinem 65. Geburtstag*. Edited by I. Kottsieper, Rüdiger Schmitt, and Jakob Wöhrle. AOAT 350. Münster: Ugarit-Verlag, 2008.
Lane, Edward W. *An Arabic-English Lexicon*. 8 vols. London: Williams and Norgate, 1893.
Larsen, Mogens Trolle. "The Tradition of Empire in Mesopotamia." Pages 75–103 in *Power and Propaganda. A Symposium on Ancient Empires*. Edited by Mogens Trolle Larsen. Mesopotamia. CSA 7. Copenhagen: Akademisk Forlag, 1979.
Lasserre, Guy. "Quelques études récentes sur le Code de l'Alliance." *RTP* 125 (1993): 267–76.
Law, T. Michael. "A History of Research on Origen's Hexapla." *BIOSCS* 40 (2007): 30–48.
——. "Aquila *Kaige*, and Jewish Revision." Forthcoming in *The Greek Bible and the Rabbis*. Edited by T. Michael Law and Alison G. Salvesen. CBET. Leuven: Peeters.

——. "Do 'the Three' reveal anything about the textual history of the Books of Kings? The Hebrew Text behind the Later Greek Jewish Versions in 1 Kings." Forthcoming in *After Qumran: Old and New Editions of Biblical Texts. The Historical Books*. Edited by Hans Ausloos, Bénédicte Lemmelijn and Julio Trebolle Barrera. BETL. Leuven: Peeters.
Legge, Francis. "The Society of Biblical Archaeology." *JRAS* (1919): 25–36.
Leichty, Erle. *The Omen Series Šumma Izbu*. TCS 4. Locust Valley, N.Y.: J. J. Augustin, 1970.
Lemaire, André. "Vers l'histoire de la rédaction des livres des Rois." *ZAW* 98 (1986): 221–36.
——. "Tarshish-Tarsisi: problème de topographie historique biblique et assyrienne." Pages 44–62 in *Studies in Historical Geography and Biblical Historiography Presented to Zecharia Kallai*. Edited by Gershon Galil and Moshe Weinfeld. VTSup 81. Leiden: Brill, 2000.
——. "Toward a Redactional History of the Book of Kings." Pages 446–61 in *Reconsidering Israel and Judah. Recent Studies on the Deuteronomistic History*. Edited by Gary N. Knoppers and J. Gordon McConville. Sources for Biblical and Theological Study 8. Winona Lake, Ind.: Eisenbrauns, 2000.
——. *The Birth of Monotheism. The Rise and Disappearance of Yahwism*. Washington: Biblical Archaeological Society, 2007.
——. "Le 'dieu de Jérusalem' à la lumière de l'épigraphie." Pages 49–58 in *Jérusalem antique et medieval. Mélanges en l'honneur d'Ernest-Marie Laperrousaz*. Edited by Caroline Arnould-Béhar and André Lemaire. Collection de la Revue des Études Juives 52. Leuven/Paris: Peeters, 2010.
Leske, Adrian M. "Context and meaning of Zechariah 9:9." *CBQ* 62 (2000): 663–78.
Lessing, Reed. "Satire in Isaiah's Tyre Oracle." *JSOT* 28 (2003): 89–112.
——. *Interpreting Discontinuity: Isaiah's Tyre Oracle*. Winona Lake: Eisenbrauns, 2004.
Levin, Christoph. "*Gustaf Dalman und die Brüdergemeine*." Pages 10–26 in *Festakt Prof. Gustaf Dalman "Zum 150. Geburtstag."* Edited by Christfried Böttrich. Greifswalder Universitätsreden (N.F.) 117. Greifswald: Ernst-Moritz-Arndt-Universität Greifswald, 2005.
Levine, Baruch. *Numbers 1–20*. AB. New York: Doubleday, 1993.
——. "The Language of Holiness: Perceptions of the Sacred in the Hebrew Bible." Pages 241–55 in *Backgrounds for the Bible*. Edited by Michael P. O'Connor and David Noel Freedman. Winona Lake, Ind: Eisenbrauns, 1997.
Levinson, Bernard M. *Deuteronomy and the Hermeneutics of Legal Innovation*. Oxford: Oxford University Press, 1997.
——. "Is the Covenant Code an Exilic Composition? A Response to John Van Seters." Pages 272–325 in *In Search of Pre-Exilic Israel. Proceedings of the Oxford Old Testament Seminar*. Edited by John Day. JSOTSup 406. London: T&T Clark, 2004.
——. "The Manumission of Hermeneutics: The Slave Laws of the Pentateuch as a Challenge to Contemporary Pentateuchal Theory." Pages 281–324 in *Congress Volume Leiden 2004*. VTSup 109. Leiden: Brill, 2006.
Levy, D. and Jacob Milgrom, "עֵדָה, *'ēdâ*." Pages 268–80 in vol. 10 of *TDOT*. Edited by G. Johannes Botterweck, Helmer Ringgren, and Heinz-Josef Fabry. Translated by David E. Green. 15 vols. Grand Rapids: Eerdmans, 1999.
Levy, Thomas E., et al. "Reassessing the Chronology of Biblical Edom: New Excavations and $^{14}$C Dates from Khirbet en-Nahas (Jordan)." *Antiquity* 78 (2004): 865–79.
Lieberman, Saul. *Tosefta ki-Fshutah*. New York: Jewish Theological Seminary, 1973.
Lindner, Manfred, Ernst Axel Knauf, Ulrich Hübner and Johannes Hübl. "From Edomite to Late Islamic: Jabal as-Suffaha North of Petra." *ADAJ* 42 (1990): 225–40.
Lindner, Manfred and Ernst Axel Knauf. "Between the Plateau and the Rocks: Edomite Economic and Social Structure." *Studies in the History and Archaeology of Jordan* 6 (1997): 261–64.
Lindner, Manfred, Ernst Axel Knauf, Johannes Hübl and John P. Zeitler. "An Iron Age (Edomite) Occupation of Jabal al-Khubtha (Petra) and Other Discoveries on the 'Mountain of Treachery and Deceit.'" *ADAJ* 41 (1997): 177–88.

Lindner, Manfred and Jürgen Zangenberg. "'Die ihr Nest zwischen den Sternen Bauen...' Zu den edomitischen Bergfestungen im Süden Jordaniens." Pages 281–316 in *Vielseitigkeit des Alten Testaments. Festschrift für Georg Sauer zum 70. Geburtstag*. Edited by James A. Loader and Hans Volker Kieweler. Frankfurt: P. Lang, 1999.

Lindner, Manfred, Ulrich Hübner, and Elisabeth Gunsam. "Es-Sela'—2500 Jahre Fliehburg und Bergfestung in Edom, Südjordanien." *Das Altertum* 46 (2001): 243–78.

Lipiński, Edward. "The Elegy on the Fall of Sidon in Isaiah 23." *ErIsr* 14 (1978): 79*–88*.

——. "Les Japhétites selon Gen 10,1–4 et 1 Chr 1,5–7." *ZAH* 3 (1990): 40–53.

——. *Itineraria Phoenicia*. OLA 127. Studia Phoenicia 18. Leuven: Peeters, 2004.

Lipovitch, David. "A Reconstruction of Achaemenid–Period Ashkelon Based on the Faunal Evidence." Pages 263–72 in *Exploring the* Longue Durée. *Essays in Honor of Lawrence E. Stager*. Edited by J. David Schloen. Winona Lake, Ind.: Eisenbrauns, 2009.

Liverani, Mario. "The Trade Network of Tyre According to Ezek. 27." Pages 75–79 in *Ah, Assyria... Studies in Assyrian History and Ancient Near Eastern Literature Presented to Hayim Tadmor*. Edited by Mordechai Cogan and Israel Eph'al. *ScrHier* 33. Jerusalem: Magnes, 1991.

Loewenstamm, Samuel E. "ספר חדש של גורדון בחקר האוגריתית: Review article of Cyrus H. Gordon, *Ugaritic Manual*." *Tarbiz* 25 (1956): 468–72.

Lohfink, Norbert. "Isaias 8,12–14." *BZ* 7 (1963): 98–104.

——. "Fortschreibung? Zur Technik vom Rechtsrevisionen im deuteronomischen Bereich, erörtert an Deuteronomium 12, Ex 21,2–11 und Dtn 15,12–18." Pages 133–61 in *Das Deuteronomium und seine Querbeziehungen*. Edited by Timo Veijola. Schriften der Finnischen Gesellschaft 62. Göttingen: Vandenhoeck & Ruprecht, 1996.

Long, Burke O. "Framing Repetitions in Biblical Historiography." *JBL* 106 (1987): 390–92.

Louth, Andrew, ed. *Genesis 1–11*. Ancient Christian Commentary on Scripture. Downers Grove: InterVarsity, 2001.

Luckenbill, Daniel D. *The Annals of Sennacherib*. Chicago: University of Chicago Press, 1924.

Lundbom, Jack R. *Jeremiah 1–20*. AB 21A. New York: Doubleday: 1999.

Lust, Johan. "The Identification of Zerubbabel with Sheshbassar." *ETL* 63 (1987): 90–95.

Luz, Ulrich. *Matthew 8–20*. Translated by James E. Crouch. Hermeneia, Edited by Helmut Koester. Minneapolis: Fortress, 2001.

Luzzatto, David. *Elementi grammaticali del caldeo biblico e del dialetto talmudico babilonese*. Padova: Bianchi, 1865.

Macchi, Jean-Daniel. "Les controverses théologiques dans le judaïsme de l'époque postexilique. L'exemple de 2 Rois 17,24–41." *Transeu* 5 (1992): 85–93.

MacDonald, John. "The Particle את in Classical Hebrew: Some New Data on its Use with the Nominative." *VT* 14 (1964): 264–75.

Machinist, Peter. "Hosea and the Ambiguity of Kingship in Ancient Israel." Pages 153–81 in *Constituting the Community: Studies on the Polity of Ancient Israel in Honor of S. Dean McBride, Jr.* Edited by John T. Strong and Steven S. Tuell. Winona Lake, Ind.: Eisenbrauns, 2005.

Macintosh, Andrew A. *Isaiah xxi: A Palimpsest*. Cambridge: Cambridge University Press, 1980.

——. *Hosea*. ICC. Edinburgh: T&T Clark, 1997.

——. "Light on ליץ." Pages 479–492 in *On Stone and Scroll: Essays in Honour of Graham Ivor Davies*. Edited by James K. Aitken, Katharine J. Dell, and Brian A. Mastin. BZAW 420. Berlin: de Gruyter, 2011.

MacLean, Hugh B. "Joash." Pages 909–11 in vol. 2 of *IDB*. Edited by George A. Buttrick. 4 vols. Nashville: Abingdon, 1962.

——. "Josiah." Pages 996–99 in vol. 2 of *IDB*. Edited by George A. Buttrick. 4 vols. Nashville: Abingdon, 1962.

Mafico, T. M. "Just, Justice." Pages 1127–29 in vol. 2 of *ABD*. Edited by David Noel Freedman. 6 vols. New York: Doubleday, 1992.

Malamat, Abraham. "The Historical Setting of Two Biblical Prophecies on the Nations." *IEJ* 1 (1950–1951): 149–59.
——. "A New Record of Nebuchadrezzar's Palestinian Campaign." *IEJ* 6 (1956): 246–56.
——. "The Early Beginnings." Pages 63–66 in *A History of the Jewish People*. Edited by Haim H. Ben-Sasson. Translated by George Weidenfeld and Nicolson Ltd. Cambridge, Mass.: Harvard University Press, 1976.
——. "King Lists of the Old Babylonian Period and Biblical Genealogies." Pages 24–45, 41–42 in *Israel in Biblical Times*. Edited by Abraham Malamat. Jerusalem: Mosad Bialik, 1983. (Hebrew)
——. *History of Biblical Israel*. Culture and History of the Ancient Near East 7. Leiden: Brill, 2001.
Mankowski, Paul V. *Akkadian Loanwords in Biblical Hebrew*. HSS 47. Winona Lake, Ind.: Eisenbrauns, 2000.
Männchen, Julia. *Gustaf Dalmans Leben und Wirken in der Brüdergemeine, für die Judenmission und an der Universität Leipzig 1855–1902*. Abhandlungen des Deutschen Palästinavereins 9/1. Wiesbaden: Harassowitz, 1987.
——. *Gustaf Dalman als Palästinawissenschaftler in Jerusalem und Greifswald: 1902–1941*. Abhandlungen des Deutschen Palästinavereins 9/2. Wiesbaden: Harassowitz, 1993.
——. *Das Herz zieht nach Jerusalem. Gustaf Dalman zum 150. Geburtstag*. Greifswald/Putbus: Rügendruck, 2005.
——. "*Gustaf Dalman—auf der Grenze: Leben und Forschen zwischen Kirche und Wissenschaft*." Pages 109–26 in *Greifswalder theologische Profile*. Edited by Tilman Beyrich, Irmfried Garbe, and Thomas Willi. Greifswalder theologische Forschungen 12. Frankfurt: Peter Lang, 2006.
Manuscript Facsimiles of the University of Notre Dame. "Stuttgart Psalter." Medieval Institute of the University of Notre Dame. http://medieval.library.nd.edu/facsimiles/litfacs/stutpsal/2r.html [accessed June 30, 2011].
Marcos, N. Fernández. *The Septuagint in Context. Introduction to the Greek Versions of the Bible*. Leiden: Brill, 2000.
Marshall, Jay W. *Israel and the Book of the Covenant: An Anthropological Approach to Biblical Law*. Atlanta: Scholars, 1993.
Marti, Karl. *Das Buch Jesaja*. KHC 10. Tübingen: Paul Siebeck, 1900.
Mason, Rex. "Some Chronistic Themes in the Speeches of Ezra-Nehemiah." *ExpTim* 101 (1989): 72–76.
——. *Preaching the Tradition: Homily and Hermeneutics After the Exile*. Cambridge: Cambridge University Press, 1990.
——. "The Use of Earlier Biblical Material in Zechariah 9–14: A Study in Inner Biblical Exegesis." Pages 1–208 in *Bringing Out the Treasure: Inner Biblical Allusion and Zechariah 9–14*. Edited by Mark J. Boda and Michael H. Floyd. JSOTSup 304. Sheffield: Sheffield Academic, 2003.
Master, Daniel M. "Trade and Politics: Ashkelon's Balancing Act in the Seventh Century BCE." *BASOR* 330 (2003): 47–64.
——. "From the Buqêʿah to Ashkelon." Pages 305–17 in *Exploring the* Longue Durée. *Essays in Honor of Lawrence E. Stager*. Edited by J. David Schloen. Winona Lake, Ind.: Eisenbrauns, 2009.
Mathews, Claire R. *Defending Zion: Edom's Desolation and Jacob's Restoration (Isaiah 34–35) in Context*. BZAW 236. Berlin: de Gruyter, 1995.
Mathews, Kenneth A. *Genesis 1–11:26*. NAC Ia. Nashville: Broadman and Holman, 1996.
Mauser, Ulrich. *Gottesbild und Menschwerdung*. Tübingen: Mohr Siebeck, 1971.
Mayer, Walter. *Politik und Kriegskunst der Assyrer*. ALASP 9. Münster: Ugarit Verlag, 1995.
Mays, James L. *Hosea*. OTL. London: SCM, 1969.
——. *Psalms*. IBC. Louisville: John Knox, 1994.
Mazar, Amihai. *Archaeology of the Land of the Bible. 10.000–586 BCE*. ABRL. New York: Doubleday, 1990.

Mazar, Benjamin. "The Military Elite of King David." *VT* 13 (1963): 310–20.
McCarter, P. Kyle. *II Samuel.* AB 9. Garden City: Doubleday, 1984.
McCarter, P. Kyle, Jr. *Ancient Inscriptions: Voices from the Biblical World.* Washington, D.C.: Biblical Archaeology Society, 1996.
McCarthy, Carmel. *Deuteronomy. BHQ* 5. Stuttgart: Deutsche Bibelgesellschaft, 2007.
McCarthy, Dennis J. "Covenant and Law in Chronicles-Nehemiah." *CBQ* 44 (1982): 25–44.
McConville, J. Gordon. "Ezra-Nehemiah and the Fulfilment of Prophecy." *VT* 36 (1986): 205–24.
McCreesh, Thomas P. "Wisdom as Wife: Proverbs 31:10–31." *RB* 92 (1985): 25–46.
McKane, William. *Proverbs: A New Approach.* OTL. London: SCM, 1970.
——. *Jeremiah.* ICC. Edinburgh: T&T Clark, 1986.
McKenzie, Steven L. *The Chronicler's Use of the Deuteronomistic History.* HSM 33. Atlanta: Scholars, 1985.
——. *The Trouble with Kings. The Composition of the Books of Kings in the Deuteronomistic History.* VTSup 42. Leiden: Brill, 1991.
——. *1–2 Chronicles.* Abingdon Old Testament Commentary. Nashville, Tenn.: Abingdon, 2004.
Mercati, Giovanni. *Psalterii Hexapli Reliquiae. Pars prima. Codex rescriptus Bybliothecae Ambrosianae O 39 sup. Phototypice Expressus et Transcriptus.* Bibliotheca Apostolica Vaticana. Città del Vaticano: Bybliotheca Vaticana, 1958.
Meshel, Zeev. "The Nabataean 'Rock' and the Judean Desert Fortresses." *IEJ* 50 (2000): 109–15.
Metzenthin, Christian. *Jesaja-Auslegung in Qumran.* ATANT 98. Zürich: Theologischer Verlag Zürich, 2010.
Meyer, Eduard. *Geschichte des Alterthums I.* Stuttgart: J. G. Cotta, 1884.
Meyer, Rudolph and Herbert Donner. *Wilhelm Gesenius' Hebräisches und Aramäisches Handwörterbuch über das Alte Testament.* 18th ed. Berlin: Springer, 2007.
Meyers, Carol. *Discovering Eve: Ancient Israelite Women in Context.* Oxford: Oxford University Press, 1988.
——. "Lampstand." Pages 141–43 in vol. 4 of *ABD*. Edited by David Noel Freedman. 6 vols. London: Doubleday, 1992.
Meyers, Eric M. "Messianism in First and Second Zechariah and the 'End' of Biblical Prophecy." Pages 127–42 in *"Go to the Land I Will Show You": Studies in Honor of Dwight W. Young*. Edited by Joseph E. Coleson and Victor H. Matthews. Winona Lake, Ind.: Eisenbrauns, 1996.
Middlemas, Jill. "Trito-Isaiah's Intra- and Inter-nationalization: Identity Markers in the Second Temple Period." Pages 105–23 in *Judah and the Judeans: Negotiating Identity in an International Context*. Edited by Oded Lipschits, Gary N. Knoppers, and Manfred Oeming. Winona Lake, Ind.: Eisenbrauns, 2011.
Milgrom, Jacob. "The Case of the Suspected Adulteress." Pages 69–75 in *The Creation of Sacred Literature*. Edited by Richard Elliott Friedman. Berkeley: University of California Press, 1981.
——. *Leviticus 1–16: A New Translation with Introduction and Commentary.* AB 3. New York: Doubleday, 1991.
——. "The Antiquity of the Priestly Source: A Reply to Joseph Blenkinsopp." *ZAW* 111 (1999): 10–22.
——. *Leviticus 17–22: A New Translation with Introduction and Commentary.* AB 3A. New York: Doubleday, 2000.
——. *Leviticus 23–27: A New Translation with Introduction and Commentary.* AB 3B. New York: Doubleday, 2001.
——. "$H_R$ in Leviticus and Elsewhere in the Torah." Pages 24–40 in *The Book of Leviticus: Composition and Reception*. Edited by Rolf Rendtorff, Robert A. Kugler, and Sarah Smith Bartel. Leiden/Boston: Brill, 2003.
——. "The Case for the Pre-Exilic and Exilic Provenance of the Books of Exodus, Leviticus and Numbers." Pages 48–56 in *Reading the Law: Studies in Honour of Gordon J.*

*Wenham*. Edited by J. Gordon McConville and Karl Möller. New York & London: T&T Clark, 2007.
Miller, James Maxwell and John H. Hayes. *A History of Ancient Israel and Judah*. 2nd ed. Louisville, Ky.: Westminster John Knox, 2006.
Miller, Patrick D. *They Cried to the Lord: The Form and Theology of Biblical Prayer*. Minneapolis: Fortress, 1994.
——. "The Sinful and Trusting Creature: The Anthropology of the Psalter II." Pages 237–49 in *The Way of the Lord: Essays in Old Testament Theology*. FAT 39. Tübingen: Mohr Siebeck, 2004; Grand Rapids: Eerdmans, 2007.
——. "What is a Human Being? The Anthropology of the Psalter I." Pages 226–36 in *The Way of the Lord: Essays in Old Testament Theology*. Tübingen: Mohr Siebeck, 2004; Grand Rapids: Eerdmans, 2007.
Min, Kyung-Jin. *The Levitical Authorship of Ezra-Nehemiah*. JSOTSup 409. London & New York: T&T Clark, 2004.
Mitchell, David C. *The Message of the Psalter: An Eschatological Programme in the Book of Psalms*. JSOTSup 252. Sheffield: Sheffield Academic, 1997.
Mitchell, Terence C. "Israel and Judah From the Coming of Assyrian Domination Until the Fall of Samaria, and the Struggle for Independence in Judah (c. 750–700 BCE)." Pages 322–70 in vol. 3:2 of CAH. Edited by John Boardman et al. 2nd ed. Cambridge: Cambridge University Press, 2000.
Moberly, R. W. L. "'In God We Trust'? The Challenge of the Prophets." *ExAud* 24 (2008): 18–33.
Montgomery, James A. and Henry S. Gehman. *A Critical and Exegetical Commentary on the Books of Kings*. ICC. New York: T&T Clark, 1951.
Moorey, P. R. S. *A Century of Biblical Archaeology*. Cambridge: Lutterworth, 1991.
Moran, William L. "Gen 49,10 and Its Use in Ez 21,32." *Bib* 39 (1958): 405–25.
——. Review of Richard Hentschke, *Die Stellung der vorexilischen Schriftpropheten zum Kultus*. *Bib* 41 (1960): 420–21.
Morris, Gerald. *Prophecy, Poetry and Hosea*. JSOTSup 219. Sheffield: Sheffield Academic, 1996.
Moughtin-Mumby, Sharon. *Sexual and Marital Metaphors in Hosea, Jeremiah, Isaiah, Ezekiel*. Oxford: Oxford University Press, 2008.
Muilenburg, James. "The Book of Isaiah Chapters 40–66." Pages 381–773 in vol. 5 of *IB*. Edited by George A. Buttrick et al. 12 vols. Nashville: Abingdon, 1956.
——. "Holiness." Pages 616–25 in vol. 2 of *The IDB*. Edited by George A. Buttrick. 4 vols. Nashville: Abingdon, 1962.
Müller, Hans-Peter. "Ergativelemente im akkadischen und althebräischen Verbalsystem." *Bib* 66 (1985): 385–417.
Muraoka, Takamitsu. *Emphatic Words and Structures in Biblical Hebrew*. Jerusalem/Leiden: Magnes/ Brill, 1985.
——. *A Greek-English Lexicon of the Septuagint*. Leuven: Peeters, 2009.
Murphy-O'Connor, Jerome. "The Damascus Document Revisited." *RB* 92 (1985): 223–46.
Myers, Jacob M. *1 Chronicles*. AB 14. New York: Doubleday, 1965.
——. *Ezra, Nehemiah*. AB 14. Garden City, N.Y.: Doubleday, 1965.
Na'aman, Nadav. "Ephraim, Ephrath and the Settlement in the Judean Hill Country." *Zion* 49 (1984): 325–31. (Hebrew)
——. "Population Changes in Palestine Following Assyrian Deportation." *TA* 20 (1993): 104–25.
——. "Sources and Composition in the History of David." Pages 170–86 in *The Origins of the Ancient Israelite States*. Edited by Volkmar Fritz and Philip R. Davies. JSOTSup 228. Sheffield: Sheffield Academic, 1996.
Na'aman, Nadav and Ran Zadok. "Assyrian Deportations to the Province of Samerina in the Light of Two Cuneiform Tablets from Tel Hadid." *TA* 27 (2000): 159–88.

——. "When and How Did Jerusalem Become a Great City? The Rise of Jerusalem as Judah's Premier City in the Eight–Seventh Centuries BCE." *BASOR* 347 (2007): 21–56.

Neville, Ann. *Mountains of Silver & Rivers of Gold: The Phoenicians in Iberia.* Oxford: Oxbow Books, 2007.

Newsom, Carol A. "A Maker of Metaphors: Ezekiel's Oracles Against Tyre." *Int* 38 (1984): 151–64 (157), reprinted as Pages 191–204 in *"This Place is Too Small for Us": The Israelite Prophets in Recent Scholarship.* Edited by Robert P. Gordon. Sources for Biblical and Theological Study 5. Winona Lake, Ind.: Eisenbrauns, 1995.

Nielsen, Kirsten. " 'I am like a lion to Ephraim': Observations on Animal Imagery and Old Testament Theology." *ST* 61 (2007): 184–97.

Nihan, Christophe. "Trois cultes en Ésaïe 57,3–13 et leur signification dans le contexte religieux de la Judée à l'époque perse." *Transeu* 22 (2001): 143–67.

——. "Ethnicity and Identity in Isaiah 56–66." Pages 67–104 in *Judah and the Judeans: Negotiating Identity in an International Context.* Edited by Oded Lipschits, Gary N. Knoppers, and Manfred Oeming. Winona Lake, Ind.: Eisenbrauns, 2011.

Nöldeke, Theodor. *Berichte über die Verhandlungen der königl. Akademie der Wissenschaften zu Berlin.* Berlin: Verlag der königlichen Akademie der Wissenschaften, 1879.

——. *Neue Beiträge zur semitischen Sprachwissenschaft.* Strassburg: K. J. Trübner, 1910.

Norin, Stig. "The Age of the Siloam Inscription and Hezekiah's Tunnel." *VT* 48 (1998): 37–48.

Norris, Edwin. *Assyrian Dictionary.* 3 vols. London: Williams and Norgate, 1868–1872.

North, Christopher R. *Isaiah 40–55: The Suffering Servant of God.* 2nd ed. London: SCM, 1956.

North, Robert. "Does Archeology Prove Chronicles Sources?" Pages 375–401 in *A Light Unto My Path: Old Testament Studies in Honor of Jacob M. Myers.* Edited by Howard M. Bream, Ralph D. Heim, and Carey A. Moore. Philadelphia: Temple University Press, 1974.

Norton, Gerard J. "Collecting Data for a New Edition of the Fragments of the Hexapla." Pages 251–62 in *IX Congress of the International Organization for Septuagint and Cognate Studies, Cambridge 1995.* Edited by Bernard A. Taylor. SBLSCS 45. Atlanta: Scholars, 1997.

Noth, Martin. *Die israelitischen Personennamen in Rahmen der gemeinsemitischen Namengebung.* BWANT 3:10. Stuttgart: W. Kohlhammer, 1928.

——. *Überlieferungsgeschichtliche Studien.* Tübingen: Max Niemeyer, 1943.

——. *Das Buch Josua.* 2nd ed. HAT I/7. Tübingen: Mohr Siebeck: 1953.

——. *The History of Israel.* Translated by Stanley Godman. London: Black, 1958.

——. *Das zweite Buch Mose: Exodus.* ATD. Göttingen: Vandenhoeck & Ruprecht, 1978.

——. *The Chronicler's History.* Translated by H. G. M. Williamson. JSOTSup 50. Sheffield: JSOT, 1987.

Novick, Tzvi. "Pain and Production in Eden: Some Philological Reflections on Genesis iii 16." *VT* 58 (2008): 235–44.

Odeberg, Hugo. *Trito-Isaiah.* UUA 1. Uppsala: A.-B. Lundequistska Bokhandeln, 1931.

Oded, Bustenay. *War, Peace and Empire: Justifications for War in Assyrian Royal Inscriptions.* Wiesbaden: Ludwig Reichert Verlag, 1992.

——. "ונתתי שלום בארץ' (ויקרא כ"ו 6): נוסח אשורי פרק באידיאולוגיה המלכותית האשורית'" *ErIsr* 24 (1993): 148–57.

——. "The Settlements of the Israelite and the Judean Exiles in Mesopotamia in the 8th–6th Centuries BCE." Pages 91–103 in *Studies in Historical Geography and Biblical Historiography Presented to Zecharia Kallai.* Edited by Gershon Galil and Moshe Weinfeld. VTSup 81. Leiden: Brill, 2000.

Odell, Margaret. *Ezekiel.* Smyth & Helwys Bible Commentary. Macon: Smyth & Helwys, 2005.

Oestreich, Bernhard. *Metaphors and Similes for Yahweh in Hosea 14:2–9(1–8): A Study of Hoseanic Pictorial Language.* Friedensauer Schriftenreihe: Theologie 1. Frankfurt: Peter Lang, 1998.

Olyan, Saul M. "Exodus 31:12–17: The Sabbath according to H, or the Sabbath according to P and H?" *JBL* 124 (2005): 201–09.

——. *Disability in the Hebrew Bible: Interpreting Mental and Physical Differences*. Cambridge: Cambridge University Press, 2008.

Oorschot, Jürgen van. *Von Babel zum Zion: Eine literarkritische und redaktionsgeschichtliche Untersuchung*. BZAW 206. Berlin: de Gruyter, 1993.

Osumi, Yuichi. *Die Kompositionsgeschichte des Bundesbuches Exodus 20,22b–23,33*. OBO 105. Freiburg: Universitätsverlag; Göttingen: Vandenhoeck & Ruprecht, 1991.

Oswalt, John N. *The Book of Isaiah. Chapters 1–39*. NICOT. Grand Rapids: Eerdmans, 1986.

Ottley, Richard R. *The Book of Isaiah according to the Septuagint (Codex Alexandrinus)*. Vol. 1. London: Cambridge University Press, 1904.

Paoletti, J.T. and Gary M. Radke. *Art in Renaissance Italy*. 3rd ed. London: Laurence King, 2005.

Pardee, Dennis. "*MĀRÎM* in Numbers V." *VT* 35 (1985): 112–15.

——. "The 'Aqhatu Legend." Pages 343–58 in vol. 1 of *COS*. Edited by William W. Hallo and K. Lawson Younger. 3 vols. Leiden: Brill, 1997–2002.

——. "The Baʿlu Myth." Pages 241–74 in vol. 1 of *COS*. Edited by William W. Hallo and K. Lawson Younger. 3 vols. Leiden: Brill, 1997–2002.

Parker, Simon B. *Stories in Scripture and Inscriptions: Comparative Studies on Narratives in Northwest Semitic Inscriptions and the Hebrew Bible*. New York and Oxford: Oxford University Press, 1997.

Parpola, Simo. *Neo-Assyrian Toponyms*. AOAT 6. Neukirchen-Vluyn: Neukirchener Verlag; Kevelaer: Butzon & Bercker, 1970.

—— and Kazuko Watanabe. *Neo-Assyrian Treaties and Loyalty Oaths*. SAA II. Helsinki: Helsinki University Press, 1988.

——. *Letters from Assyrian and Babylonian Scholars*. SAA 10. Helsinki: Helsinki University Press, 1993.

Parunak, Henry Van Dyke. "Oral Typesetting: Some Uses of Biblical Structure." *Bib* 62 (1981): 153–69.

Patai, Raphael. *The Children of Noah: Jewish Seafaring in Ancient Times*. Princeton: Princeton University Press, 1998.

Paul, Shalom M. "Sargon's Administrative Diction in II Kings 17:27." *JBL* 88 (1969): 73–74.

——. *Studies in the Book of the Covenant in the Light of Cuneiform and Biblical Law*. VTSup 18. Leiden: Brill, 1970.

Peckham, Brian. "The Nora Inscription." *Or* 41 (1972): 457–68.

Petit, Françoise. *La chaîne sur la Genèse*. TEG 3. Leuven: Peeters, 1995.

Petterson, Anthony R. *Behold Your King: The Hope for the House of David in the Book of Zechariah*. LHBOTS 513. New York; London: T&T Clark, 2009.

Pfeiffer, Henrik. *Jahwes Kommen von Süden: Jdc 5; Hab 3; Dtn 33 und Ps 68 in ihrem literatur- und theologiegeschichtlichen Umfeld*. FRLANT 211. Göttingen: Vandenhoeck & Ruprecht, 2005.

Pleins, J. David. *The Social Visions of the Hebrew Bible: A Theological Introduction*. Louisville, Ky.: Westminster John Knox, 2001.

Plöger, Otto. "Reden und Gebete im deuteronomistischen und chronistischen Geschichtswerk." Pages 35–49 in *Festschrift für Günther Dehn*. Edited by Wilhelm Schneemelcher. Neukirchen-Vluyn: Neukirchener Verlag, 1957.

Polak, Frank H. "Review of D. P. Wright, *Inventing God's Law: How the Covenant Code of the Bible Used and Revised the Laws of Hammurabi*." *RBL* [http://www.bookreviews.org] (2010).

Porten, Bezalel. *Archives from Elephantine: The Life of an Ancient Jewish Military Colony*. Berkeley: University of California Press, 1968.

——. "Theme and Structure of Ezra 1–6: From Literature to History." *Transeu* 23 (2002): 27–44.

Prijs, Joseph, and Bernhard Prijs. *Die Basler hebräischen Drucke.* Olten: Urs Graf, 1964.
Procksch, Otto. *Jesaja.* KAT 9/1. Leipzig: Deichert, 1930.
Propp, William. *Exodus 19–40.* AB. New York: Doubleday, 2006.
Provan, Iain W. *Ecclesiastes/Song of Songs.* NIVAC. Grand Rapids: Zondervan, 2001.
Rad, Gerhard von. *Genesis.* OTL. Rev. ed. Philadelphia: Westminster, 1972.
Rainey, Anson F. *Canaanite in the Amarna Tablets: A Linguistic Analysis of the Mixed Dialect Used by the Scribes from Canaan.* 4 vols. HO. Leiden: Brill, 1996.
Rainey, Anson F. and R. Steven Notley. *The Sacred Bridge: Carta's Atlas of the Biblical World.* Jerusalem: Carta, 2006.
Rashi, R. Solomon ben Isaac. In vol. 11 of מקראות גדולות. Edited by Akivah Frenkel [פרענקעל]. Warsaw: J. Lebensohn, 1864.
Rawnsley, Hardwicke. "The Rock of Pomegranate." PEFQS 11 (1879): 118–26.
Redford, Donald B. *Egypt, Canaan, and Israel in Ancient Times.* Princeton, N.J.: Princeton University Press, 1992.
Reich, Ronny. "Reconsidering the Karstic Theory as an Explanation to the Cutting of Hezekiah's Tunnel in Jerusalem." *BASOR* 325 (2002): 75–80.
Reich, Ronny and Eli Shukron. "Jerusalem: 2. The Gihon Spring and Eastern Slope of the City of David." Pages 1801–7 in NEAEHL 5. Edited by Ephraim Stern. Jerusalem: Israel Exploration Society, 2008.
——. "The Recent Discovery of a Middle Bronze II Fortification in the City of David, Jerusalem." Pages 13–33 in *City of David: The Story of Ancient Jerusalem. The 10th Annual Conference.* Edited by Eyal Meiron. Jerusalem: Megalim, 2009.
Renaud, Bernard. "La 'Grande mer' dans l'Ancien Testament: de la géographie au symbole." Pages 75–101 in *La Bíblia i el Mediterrani: Actes del Congrés de Barcelona 18–22 de setembre de 1995.* Edited by Agustí Borrell, Alfonso de la Fuente, and Armand Puig. Scripta Biblica I. Abadia de Monserrat: Associació Bíblica de Catalunya, 1997.
Rengstorf, Karl H. "Gustaf Dalmans Bedeutung für die Wissenschaft vom Judentum." *Wissenschaftlich Zeitschrift der Ernst Moritz Arndt-Universität Greifwald: Gesellschafts- und sprachwissenschaftliche Reihe* 4.4/5 (1954/55): 373–77.
Renouf, Edith. "Biography." Pages v–cxxxiii of vol. 4 of *The Life-Work of Sir Peter le Page Renouf.* Edited by Gaston Maspero et al. 4 vols. Paris: Ernest Leroux, 1902–1907.
Renz, Thomas. "Proclaiming the Future: History and Theology in Prophecies against Tyre." *TynBul* 51 (2000): 17–58.
Reuling, Hanneke. *After Eden: Church Fathers and Rabbis on Genesis 3:16–21.* Jewish and Christian Perspective Series. Leiden: Brill, 2006.
Revell, Ernest J. "The Battle with Benjamin (Judges XX 29–48) and Hebrew Narrative Techniques." *VT* 35 (1985): 417–33.
——. "The Repetition of Introductions to Speech as a Feature of Biblical Hebrew." *VT* 47 (1997): 91–110.
Reventlow, Henning Graf. "Gattung und Überlieferung in der 'Tempelrede Jeremias', Jer 7 und 26." *ZAW* 81 (1969): 315–52.
Reynier, Chantal. *La Bible et la mer.* Lire la Bible 133. Paris: Cerf, 2003.
Robbia, Lucia della. Various works. Bluffton University, Ohio. http://www.bluffton.edu/~sullivanm/italy/florence/duomomuseo/cantoriadellarobbia.html. [accessed June 30, 2011].
——. Various works. Museo dell'Opera del Duomo. http://www.operaduomo.firenze.it/english/luoghi/museo_3.asp. [accessed June 30, 2011].
Robinson, Edward and Eli Smith. *Biblical Researches in Palestine, Mount Sinai and Arabia Petraea: A Journal of Travels in the Year 1838.* Boston: Crocker and Brewster, 1841.
Robinson, Edward, Eli Smith et al. *Later Biblical Researches in Palestine, and in the Adjacent Regions: A Journal of Travels in the Year 1852.* Boston: Crocker and Brewster, 1856.
Rochberg, Francesca. *The Heavenly Writing: Divination, Horoscopy, and Astronomy in Mesopotamian Culture.* Cambridge & New York: Cambridge University Press, 2004.

Rofé, Alexander. "Isaiah 66:1–4: Judean Sects in the Persian Period as Viewed by Trito-Isaiah." Pages 205–17 in *Biblical and Related Studies Presented to Samuel Iwry*. Edited by Ann Kort and Scott Morschauer. Winona Lake, Ind.: Eisenbrauns, 1985.

——. "The Onset of Sects in Postexilic Judaism: Neglected Evidence from the Septuagint, Trito-Isaiah, Ben Sira, and Malachi." Pages 39–49 in *The Social World of Formative Christianity and Judaism: Essays in Tribute to Howard Clark Kee*. Edited by Jacob Neusner et al. Philadelphia: Fortress, 1988.

——. *Introduction to the Literature of the Hebrew Bible*. Jerusalem Biblical Studies 9. Jerusalem: Simor, 2009.

Rogerson, John and Philip R. Davies. "Was the Siloam Tunnel Built By Hezekiah?" *BA* 59/3 (1996): 138–49.

Rooke, Deborah. *Zadok's Heirs: The Role and Development of the High Priesthood in Ancient Israel*. Oxford: Oxford University Press, 2000.

Rose, Wolter H. *Zemah and Zerubbabel: Messianic Expectations in the Early Postexilic period*. JSOTSup 304. Sheffield: Sheffield Academic, 2000.

——. "Messianic Expectations in the Early Postexilic Period." Pages 168–85 in *Yahwism After the Exile: Perspectives on Israelite Religion in the Persian Era*. Edited by Rainer Albertz and Bob Becking. Studies in Theology and Religion 5. Assen: Van Gorcum, 2003.

——. "Zacharia." Pages 247–329 in *Daniël—Ezra—Haggai—Zacharia—Esther—Nehemia—Maleachi: Zeven bijbelboeken uit de Perzische periode*. Geert W. Lorein and Wolter H. Rose. Commentaarreeks op het Oude Testament De Brug 11. Heerenveen: Groen, 2010.

Rosenberg, Stephen G. "The Siloam Tunnel Revisited." *TA* 25 (1998): 116–30.

——. "The Parker Mission and Hezekiah's Tunnel." *Strata* 27 (2009): 79–87.

Rosenthal, Franz, *Die Aramaistische Forschung seit Th. Nöldekes Veröffentlichungen*. Leiden: Brill, 1939.

Rost, Leonhard. *Israel bei den Propheten*. BWANT 19. Stuttgart: Kohlhammer, 1937.

Rothenbusch, Ralf. *Die kasuistische Rechtsammlung im 'Bundesbuch' (Ex 21,2–11.18–22,16) und ihr literarischer Kontext im Licht altorientalischer Parallelen*. AOAT 259. Münster: Ugarit-Verlag, 2000.

Rothstein, Johann Wilhelm. *Juden und Samaritaner: die grundlegende Scheidung von Judentum und Heidentum: eine kritische Studie zum Buche Haggai und zur jüdischen Geschichte im ersten nachexilischen Jahrhundert*. BWANT 3. Leipzig: Hinrichs, 1908.

Rowley, Harold H. "The Samaritan Schism in Legend and History." Pages 208–22 in *Israel's Prophetic Heritage: Essays in Honor of James Muilenburg*. Edited by Bernhard W. Anderson and Walter J. Harrelson. New York/London: Harper, 1962.

Rudolph, Wilhelm. *Esra und Nehemia samt 3 Esra*. HAT 1/20. Tübingen: J. C. B. Mohr (Paul Siebeck), 1949.

——. *Chronikbücher*. HAT 1.21. Tübingen: Mohr (Siebeck), 1955.

——. "Jesaja 23,1–14." Pages 166–74 in *Festschrift Friedrich Baumgärtel zum 70. Geburtstag 14. Januar 1958 gewidmet von den Mitarbeitern am Kommentar zum Alten Testament (KAT)*. Edited by J. Herrmann. Erlanger Forschungen 10. Erlangen: Universitätsbund Erlangen, 1959.

——. *Jeremia*. 3rd ed. HAT 12. Tübingen: Mohr Siebeck, 1968.

Rylands, W. H. "Secretary's Report for the Year 1886." *PSBA* 9 (1886–1887): 56–61.

Salvesen, Alison. "עֲטָרָה." Pages 6–13 in *Semantics of Ancient Hebrew*. Edited by Takamitsu Muraoka. Abr-Nahrain Supplement Series 6. Leuven: Peeters, 1998.

Sandmel, Samuel. "Genesis 4:26b." *HUCA* 32 (1961): 19–29.

Sasson, Jack M. "Canaanite Maritime Involvement in the Second Millennium BC." *Journal of American Oriental Studies* 86 (1966): 126–38.

——. "Wordplay in the OT." Pages 968–70 in *Interpreter's Dictionary of the Bible: Supplementary Volume*. Nashville: Abingdon, 1976.

——. "Numbers 5 and the 'Waters of Judgment'." Pages 483–86 in *Women in the Hebrew Bible*. Edited by Alice Bach. New York: Routledge, 1999.

Sasson, Victor. "The Siloam Tunnel Inscription." *PEQ* 114 (1982): 111–17.

Sauer, Georg. "Die Umkehrforderung in der Verkündigung Jesajas." Pages 277–95 in *Wort, Gebot, Glaube: Beiträge zur Theologie des Alten Testaments. Walther Eichrodt zum 80. Geburtstag*. Edited by Hans J. Stoebe, Johann J. Stamm, and Ernst Jenni. Zürich: Zwingli Verlag, 1970.

——. "Ernst Sellin in Wien." *Jahrbuch für die Geschichte des Protestantismus in Österreich* (FS für Wilhelm Kühnert) 96 (1980): 138–46.

Saur, Markus. *Der Tyroszyklus des Ezechielbuches*. BZAW 386. Berlin/New York: de Gruyter, 2008.

Sayce, Archibald H. *Records of the Past*. Second series. 6 vols. London: Samuel Bagster, 1888–92.

——. *Reminiscences*. London: Macmillan, 1923.

Saydon, Paul P. "Meanings and uses of the particle את." *VT* 14 (1964): 192–210.

Schäfer, Rolf. "Lamentations." Pages 17*–20*, 30*–34, 43*–46*, 113*–136*, 54–72 in *Megilloth. BHQ* 18. Stuttgart: Deutsche Bibelgesellschaft, 2004.

Schaper, Joachim. "Rereading the Law: Inner-Biblical Exegesis of Divine Oracles in Ezekiel 44 and Isaiah 56." Pages 125–44 in *Recht und Ethik im Alten Testament: Beiträge des Symposiums 'Das Alte Testament und die Kultur der Moderne' anlässlich des 100. Geburtstags Gerhard von Rads (1901–1971) Heidelberg, 18.–21. Oktober 2001*. Edited by Bernard M. Levinson and Eckart Otto. Altes Testament und Moderne 13. Münster: LIT Verlag, 2004.

Schaudig, Hanspeter. *Die Inschriften Nabonids von Babylon und Kyros' des Großen*. AOAT 256. Münster: Ugarit-Verlag, 2001.

Schearing, Linda S. "Parturition (Childbirth), Pain, and Piety: Physicians and Genesis 3:16a." Pages 85–86 in *Mother Goose, Mother Jones and Mommie Dearest: Biblical Mothers and Their Children*. Edited by Cheryl Kirk-Duggan and Tina Pippin. SBL SemeiaSt 61. Atlanta: SBL, 2009.

Schick, Conrad. "Artuf und seine Umgebung." *ZDPV* 10 (1887): 131–146.

Schloen, David. "Ashkelon." Page 222 in vol. I of *OEANE*. Edited by Eric M. Meyers. New York: Oxford University Press, 1997.

Schmid, Konrad. *Buchgestalten des Jeremiabuches: Untersuchungen zur Redaktions- und Rezeptionsgeschichte von Jer 30–33 im Kontext des Buches*. WMANT 72. Neukirchen-Vluyn: Neukirchener Verlag, 1996.

Schmid, Konrad and Odil Hannes Steck. "Restoration Expectations in the Prophetic Tradition of the Old Testament." Pages 41–81 in *Restoration: Old Testament, Jewish, and Christian Perspectives*. Edited by James M. Scott. JSJSup 72. Leiden: Brill, 2001.

Schmidt, Werner H. *Exodus 1.1–6.30*. BKAT 2/1. Neukirchen-Vluyn: Neukirchener Verlag, 1988.

Schmidtke, Friedrich. *Die Japhetiten der biblischen Völkertafel*. BSHT 7; Breslau: Müller & Seiffert, 1926.

Schniedewind, William M. "The Chronicler as an Interpreter of Scripture." Pages 158–80 in *The Chronicler as Author: Studies in Text and Texture*. Edited by M. Patrick Graham and Steven L. McKenzie. JSOTSup 263. Sheffield: Sheffield Academic, 1999.

——. "Innerbiblical Exegesis." Pages 502–9 in *Dictionary of Old Testament—Historical Books*. Edited by Bill T. Arnold and H. G. M. Williamson. Downers Grove: IVP Academic, 2005.

Schoors, Antoon. *Jesaja*. BOT 9. Roermond: J. J. Romen & Zonen, 1972.

Schulten, Adolf. *Tartessos*. Hamburg: Cram, de Gruyter, 1950.

Schultz, Samuel J. "Josiah." Pages 1138–39 in vol. 2 of *ISBE*. Edited by Geoffrey W. Bromily. 4 vols. Grand Rapids: Eerdmans, 1979–1988.

Schunck, Klaus-Dietrich. "Davids 'Schlupfwinkel' in Juda." *VT* 33 (1983): 110–13.

Schwartz, Baruch J. "The Strata of the Priestly Writings and the Revised Relative Dating of P and H." Pages 1–12 in *The Strata of the Priestly Writings: Contemporary Debate and Future Directions*. Edited by Sarah Shectman and Joel S. Baden. ATANT 95. Zürich: Theologischer Verlag Zürich, 2009.

Schwienhorst-Schönberger, Ludger. *Das Bundesbuch (Ex 20,22–23,33)*. BZAW 188. Berlin: de Gruyter, 1990.

Scullion, John J. *Isaiah 40–66*. OTM 12. Wilmington: Michael Glazier, 1982.

Seeligmann, Isaac L. *The Septuagint Version of Isaiah. A Discussion of its Problems*. Mededelingen en verhandelingen Ex Oriente Lux 9. Leiden: Brill, 1948.

——. "Hebräische Erzählung und biblische Geschichtsschreibung." *Theologische Zeitschrift* 18 (1962): 314–24.

——. *The Septuagint Version of Isaiah and Cognate Studies*. Edited by R. Hanhart and H. Spieckermann. FAT 40. Tübingen: Mohr Siebeck, 2004.

Segal, Moses H. *A Grammar of Mishnaic Hebrew*. Oxford: Clarendon, 1927.

Seifert, Brigitte. *Metaphorisches Reden von Gott im Hoseabuch*. FRLANT 166. Göttingen: Vandenhoeck & Ruprecht, 1996.

Seitz, Christopher. "Isaiah 1–66: Making Sense of the Whole." Pages 105–26 in *Reading and Preaching the Book of Isaiah*. Edited by Christopher Seitz. Philadelphia: Fortress, 1988.

——. *Isaiah 1–39*. IBC. Louisville: John Knox, 1993.

Shaheen, Naseeb. "Siloam End of Hezekiah's Tunnel." *PEQ* 109 (1977): 107–12.

——. "The Sinuous Shape of Hezekiah's Tunnel." *PEQ* 146 (1979): 103–8.

Shanks, Hershel. "Three Shekels for the Lord: Ancient Inscriptions Record Gift to Solomon's Temple." *BAR* 23/6 (1997): 28–32.

Sharp, Carolyn J. *Prophecy and Ideology in Jeremiah: Struggles for Authority in the Deutero-Jeremianic Corpus*. Old Testament Studies. London: T&T Clark, 2003.

Shea, William H. "The Dedication on the Nora Stone." *VT* 41 (1991): 241–45.

Shectman, Sarah and Joel S. Baden, eds. *The Strata of the Priestly Writings: Contemporary Debate and Future Directions*. ATANT 95. Zürich: Theologischer Verlag Zürich, 2009.

Sherwood, Yvonne. *The Prostitute and the Prophet: Hosea's Marriage in Literary-Theoretical Perspective*. JSOTSup 212. Sheffield: Sheffield Academic, 1996.

Shiloh, Yigal. "City of David: Excavation 1978." *BA* 42 (1979): 165–71.

——. *Excavations at the City of David I: 1978–1982*. Qedem 19. Jerusalem: Institute of Archaeology of the Hebrew University of Jerusalem, 1984.

Shinan, Avigdor and Yair Zakowitch. "Midrash on Scripture and Midrash within Scripture." *ScrHier* 31 (1986): 255–77.

Shorrock, Robert. *The Challenge of Epic. Allusive Engagement in the Dionysiaca of Nonnus*. MnS 210. Leiden: Brill, 2001.

Siculus, Diodorus. *Diodorus of Sicily*. Translated by Charles Henry Oldfather. LCL 279. Cambridge, Mass.: LCL, 1933.

Simons, Jan. *Jerusalem in the Old Testament: Researches and Theories*. Leiden: Brill, 1952.

Ska, Jean-Louis. "From History Writing to Library Building: The End of History and the Birth of the Book." Pages 145–69 in *The Pentateuch as Torah. New Models for Understanding Its Promulgation and Acceptance*. Edited by Gary N. Knoppers and Bernard M. Levinson. Winona Lake, Ind.: Eisenbrauns, 2007.

Skinner, John. *A Critical and Exegetical Commentary on Genesis*. ICC. 2nd ed. Edinburgh: T&T Clark, 1930.

Smith, George. "The Chaldean Account of the Deluge." *TSBA* 2 (1873): 213–34.

Smith, John M. Powis. *A Critical and Exegetical Commentary on Micah, Zephaniah, Nahum, Habakkuk, Obadiah and Joel*. ICC. Edinburgh: T&T Clark, 1911.

Smith, Mark S. *The Origins of Biblical Monotheism: Israel's Polytheistic Background and the Ugaritic Texts*. New York: Oxford University Press, 2001.

——. *The Priestly Vision of Genesis 1*. Minneapolis, Minn.: Augsburg Fortress, 2009.

Smith, Paul A. *Rhetoric and Redaction in Trito-Isaiah: The Structure, Growth and Authorship of Isaiah 56–66*. VTSup 62. Leiden: Brill, 1995.

Soisalon-Soininen, Ilmari. "Die Wiedergabe des Hebräischen, als Subjekt Stehenden Personalpronomens im Griechischen Pentateuch." Pages 115–28 in *De Septuaginta: Studies in Honour of John William Wevers on his Sixty-Fifth Birthday*. Edited by Albert Pietersma and Claude Cox. Mississauga, Ont.: Benben Publications, 1984.

Sommer, Benjamin D. "Allusions and Illusions: The Unity of the Book of Isaiah in Light of Deutero-Isaiah's Use of Prophetic Tradition." Pages 156–86 in *New Visions of Isaiah*. Edited by Roy F. Melugin and Marvin A. Sweeney. JSOTSup 214. Sheffield: Sheffield Academic, 1996.

——. *A Prophet Reads Scripture: Allusion in Isaiah 40–66*. Stanford: Stanford University Press, 1998.

Sparks, James T. *The Chronicler's Genealogies: Towards an Understanding of 1 Chronicles 1–9*. Academia Biblica 28. Atlanta: Society of Biblical Literature, 2008.

Spawn, Kevin L. *"As It Is Written" and Other Citation Formulae in the Old Testament: Their Use, Development, Syntax and Significance*. BZAW 311. Berlin: de Gruyter, 2002.

——. "Sources, References to." Pages 935–41 in *Dictionary of Old Testament—Historical Books*. Edited by Bill T. Arnold and H. G. M. Williamson. Downers Grove: IVP Academic, 2005.

Speiser, Ephraim A. *Genesis: Introduction, Translation, and Notes*. AB 1. Garden City, N.Y.: Doubleday, 1964.

Spender, David. "Marc Chagall's window on Ps 150 in Chichester Cathedral." Ca. 2009. Flicker. http://www.flickr.com/photos/dspender/3438549233/in/set-72157603996844452/. [accessed June 30, 2011].

Sprinkle, Joe M. *'The Book of the Covenant'. A Literary Approach*. JSOTSup 174. Sheffield: JSOT, 1994.

Spurrell, G. J. *Notes on the Text of the Book of Genesis*. 2nd ed. Oxford: Clarendon, 1896.

Stackert, Jeffrey. *Rewriting the Torah: Literary Revision in Deuteronomy and the Holiness Legislation*. FAT 52. Tübingen: Mohr Siebeck, 2007.

Stade, Bernhard. "Miscellen 16. Anmerkungen zu 2 Kö. 15–21." *ZAW* 6 (1886): 156–89.

——. "Die Dreizahl im Alten Testament." *ZAW* 26 (1906): 124–41.

Stager, Lawrence E. "Ashkelon." Page 104 in vol. 1 of NEAEHL. Edited by Ephraim Stern. New York: Carta, 1993.

——. "Ashkelon and the Archaeology of Destruction: Kislev 604 BCE." Pages 61*–74* in *Joseph Aviram Volume*. Edited by Abraham Biran, Amnon Ben–Tor, Gideon Foerster, Abraham Malamat, and David Ussishkin. *ErIsr* 25. Jerusalem: The Israel Exploration Society, 1996.

Stamm, Johann Jacob. "Der name Nabal." Pages 205–13 in *Beiträge zur Hebräischen und altorientalischen Namenkunde*. Edited by Johann Jacob Stamm, Ernst Jenni, and Martin A. Klopfenstein. OBO 30. Freiburg: Universitätsverlag, 1980.

Steck, Odil Hannes. *Bereitete Heimkehr: Jesaja 35 als redaktionelle Brücke zwischen dem Ersten und dem Zweiten Jesaja*. SBS 121. Stuttgart: Katholisches Bibelwerk, 1985.

——. "Tritojesaja im Jesajabuch." Pages 403–6 in *The Book of Isaiah/Le livre d'Isaïe: les oracles et leurs relectures unité et complexité de l'ouvrage*. Edited by Jacques Vermeylen. BETL 81. Leuven: Peeters, 1989.

——. *Der Abschluß der Prophetie im Alten Testament. Ein Versuch zur Frage der Vorgeschichte des Kanons*. BThSt 17. Neukirchen-Vluyn: Neukirchener Verlag, 1991.

——. *Gottesknecht und Zion: Gesammelte Aufsätze zu Deuterojesaja*. FAT 4. Tübingen: Mohr (Siebeck), 1992.

——. *Studien zu Tritojesaja*. BZAW 203. Berlin: de Gruyter, 1991.

Stern, Ephraim. *Archaeology of the Land of the Bible*. Vol. 2 *The Assyrian, Babylonian, and Persian Periods 732–332 BCE*. ABRL. New York: Doubleday, 2001.

Stern, Menahem, ed. *Greek and Latin Authors on Jews and Judeans, Vol. I: From Herodotus to Plutarch*. Jerusalem: Israel Academy of Sciences and Humanities, 1974.

Stith, D. Matthew. "Joash." Pages 317–19 in vol. 3 of *New Interpreter's Dictionary of the Bible*. Edited by Katherine D. Sakenfeld. 5 vols. Nashville: Abingdon, 2006–2010.

Stoebe, Hans Joachim. *Das zweite Buch Samuelis*. KAT VIII.2. Gütersloh: Gütersloher Verlag, 1994.

Stone, Bryan J. "The Philistines and Acculturation: Culture Change and Ethnic Continuity in the Iron Age." *BASOR* 298 (1995): 7–32.

Strauss, Hans. *Hiob 19.1–42.17*. BKAT 16/2. Neukirchen-Vluyn: Neukirchener Verlag, 2000.

Stravinsky, Igor. *Performance I.* by Pierre Boulez. the Berlin Philharmonic Orchestra. Deutsche Grammophon, ASIN: B000031X7Y. amazon. http://www.amazon.com/gp/recsradio/radio/B000031X7Y/ref=pd_krex_listen_dp_img?ie=UTF8&refTagSuffix=dp_img. [accessed June 30, 2011].

Sutcliffe, Edmund F. "A Gloss in Jeremiah VII 4." *VT* 5 (1955): 313–14.

Sweeney, Marvin. *Isaiah 1–4 and the Post-Exilic Understanding of the Isaianic Tradition.* BZAW 171. Berlin: de Gruyter, 1988.

——. *Isaiah 1–39 with an Introduction to Prophetic Literature.* FOTL 16. Grand Rapids: Eerdmans, 1996.

——. *I & II Kings. A Commentary.* OTL. Louisville: Westminster John Knox, 2007.

Tadmor, Hayim. "Joash." Columns 110–11 in vol. 10 of *EncJud.* Edited by Cecil Roth and Geoffrey Wigoder. 16 vols. Jerusalem: Keter Publishing House, 1972. (Page 341 in vol. 11 of *EncJud.* 2nd ed. Edited by Fred Skolnik. 22 vols. Macmillan Reference USA, 2006).

——. *The Inscriptions of Tiglath–pileser III King of Assyrian. Critical Edition, with Introductions, Translations and Commentary.* Jerusalem: The Israel Academy of Sciences and Humanities, 1994. 2nd printing with *addenda et corrigenda.* Jerusalem: The Israel Academy of Sciences and Humanities, 2007.

Tal, Abraham. *The Samaritan Targum of the Pentateuch: A Critical Edition, I.* Tel-Aviv: Tel-Aviv University, 1980.

——. "The Role of Targum Onqelos in Literary Activity During the Middle Ages." Pages 159–71 in *Aramaic in its Historical and Linguistic Setting.* Edited by Holger Gzella and Margaretha L. Folmer. Wiesbaden: Harassowitz, 2008.

Tallis, Thomas. "Tunes for Archbishop Parker's Psalter: *Man blest no doubt*" in *Music for a Reformed Church.* vol. 6. no. 25 by Alistair Dixon. Chapelle du Roi. SIGCD022. http://www.classicalarchives.com/work/134341.html. [accessed June 30, 2011]

Talmon, Shemaryahu. "Ezra and Nehemiah (Books and Men)." Page 322 in *Interpreter's Dictionary of the Bible Supplementary Volume.* Edited by Keith Crim. Nashville: Abingdon, 1976.

——. "The Presentation of Synchroneity and Simultaneity in Biblical Narrative." *ScrHier* 27 (1978): 9–26.

Talon, Philippe. *Enūma Eliš: The Standard Babylonian Creation Myth.* SAACT 4. Helsinki: The Neo-Assyrian Text Corpus Project, 2005.

Talshir, Zipora. *The Alternative Story of the Division of the Kingdom: 3 Kingdoms 12:24a–z.* Jerusalem Biblical Studies 6. Jerusalem: Simor, 1993.

Talstra, Eep. "The Discourse of Praying: Reading Nehemiah 1." Pages 219–36 in *Psalms and Prayers.* Edited by Bob Becking and Eric Peels. Leiden: Brill, 2007.

Tarler, David and Jane M. Cahill. "David, City of." Pages 52–67 in *ABD* 2. Edited by David Noel Freedman. New York: Doubleday, 1992.

Tawil, Hayim. *An Akkadian Lexical Companion for Biblical Hebrew.* Jersey City, N.J.: Ktav, 2009.

Taylor, Charles. *Hebrew-Greek Cairo Genizah Palimpsests from the Taylor-Schechter Collection including a Fragment of the Twenty-Second Psalm according to Origen's Hexapla.* Cambridge: Cambridge University Press, 1900.

Ter Haar Romeny, R. Bas and Peter J. Gentry. "Towards a New Collection of Hexaplaric Material for the Book of Genesis." Pages 285–99 in *X Congress of the International Organization for Septuagint and Cognate Studies, Oslo 1998.* Edited by Bernard A. Taylor. SBLSCS 51. Atlanta: Scholars, 2001.

Thompson, John A. *1, 2 Chronicles.* NAC 9. Nashville: Broadman & Holman Publishers, 1994.

Throntveit, Mark A. *When Kings Speak: Royal Speech and Royal Prayer in Chronicles.* SBLDS 93. Atlanta: Scholars, 1987.

——. *Ezra-Nehemiah.* IBC. Louisville, Ky.: John Knox, 1992.

Tidwell, N. L. "The Philistine Incursions into the Valley of Rephaim (2 Sam. v 17ff.)." Pages 190–212 in *Studies in the Historical Books of the Old Testament*. Edited by John A. Emerton. VTSup 30. Leiden: Brill, 1979.

Tiemeyer, Lena-Sofia. "The Watchman Metaphor in Isaiah lvi–lxvi." *VT* 55 (2005): 378–400.

——. *For the Comfort of Zion: The Geographical and Theological Location of Isaiah 40–55*. VTSup 139. Leiden: Brill, 2011.

Tomasino, Anthony. "Isaiah 1.1–2.4 and 63–66, and the Composition of the Isaianic Corpus." *JSOT* 57 (1993): 81–93.

Torczyner, Harry. "Dunkle Bibelstellen." Pages 274–80 in *Vom Alten Testament: Karl Marti zum siebzigsten Geburtstage gewidmet von Freunden, Fachgenossen und Schülern*. Edited by Karl Budde. BZAW 41. Giessen: Töpelmann, 1925.

Toy, Crawford H. *The Book of Proverbs*. ICC. California: C. Scribner's Sons, 1899; Repr., Edinburgh: T&T Clark, 1970.

Tregelles, Samuel P. *Gesenius' Hebrew and Chaldee Lexicon to the Old Testament Scriptures*. London: Samuel Bagster and Sons, 1846.

Troxel, Ronald L. "Economic Plunder as a Leitmotif in LXX-Isaiah." *Bib* 83 (2002): 375–91.

——. *LXX-Isaiah as Translation and Interpretation. The Strategies of the Translator of the Septuagint of Isaiah*. JSJSup 124. Leiden: Brill, 2008.

Tsevat, Matitiahu. "The Basic Meaning of the Biblical Sabbath." Pages 39–52 in *The Meaning of the Book of Job and Other Biblical Studies: Essays on the Literature and Religion of the Hebrew Bible*. New York: Ktav Publishing House, 1980.

Tsirkin, Juli B. "The Greeks and Tartessos." *Oikumene* 5 (1986): 163–71.

——. "The Phoenicians and Tartessos." *Gerión* 15 (1997): 243–51.

Tsumura, David T. *Creation and Destruction. A Reappraisal of the* Chaoskampf *Theory in the Old Testament*. Winona Lake, Ind.: Eisenbrauns, 2005.

Tuell, Steven S. *First and Second Chronicles*. IBC. Louisville: John Knox, 2001.

——. "The Priesthood of the "Foreigner": Evidence of Competing Polities in Ezekiel 44:1–14 and Isaiah 56:1–8." Pages 183–204 in *Constituting the Community: Studies on the Polity of Ancient Israel in Honor of S. Dean McBride, Jr.* Edited by John T. Strong and Steven S. Tuell. Winona Lake, Ind.: Eisenbrauns, 2005.

Tur-Sinai, Naftali H. (H. Torczyner). *Pešuṭo šel miqra'*. Vol 1. Jerusalem: Kiryath Sepher, 1962.

Van der Merwe, Christo H. J., Jackie A. Naudé, and Jan H. Kroeze. *A Biblical Hebrew Reference Grammar*. Sheffield: Sheffield Academic, 1999.

Van Dijk, Hubert J. *Ezekiel's Prophecy on Tyre*. BibOr 29. Rome: Pontifical Biblical Institute, 1968.

Van Seters, John. *A Law Book for the Diaspora: Revision in the Study of the Covenant Code*. Oxford: Oxford University Press, 2003.

——. "Revision in the Study of the Covenant Code and a Response to My Critics." *SJOT* 21 (2007): 5–28.

Van Wijk-Bos, Johanna W. H. *Ezra, Nehemiah, and Esther*. Westminster Bible Companion. Louisville, Ky.: Westminster John Knox, 1998.

Vanderhooft, David S. *The Neo-Babylonian Empire and Babylon in the Latter Prophets*. HSM 59. Atlanta: Scholars, 1999.

Vaughn, Andrew G. *Theology, History, and Archaeology in the Chronicler's Account of Hezekiah*. Atlanta: Scholars, 1999.

Vaux, Roland de. *Les Institutions de l'Ancien Testament II*. Paris: Cerf, 1967.

——. "The Settlement of the Israelites in Southern Palestine and the Origins of the Tribe of Judah." Pages 108–34 in *Translating and Understanding the Old Testament, Essays in Honor of Herbert Gordon May*. Edited by Harry T. Frank. Nashville: Abingdon, 1970.

——. *Ancient Israel: Its Life and Institutions*. Translated by John McHugh. London: Darton, Longham, and Todd, 1973.

Verkinderen, F. "Les cités phéniciennes dans l'Empire d'Alexandre le Grand." Pages 287–308 in *Studia Phoenicia V. Phoenicia and the East Mediterranean in the First Millennium BC* Edited by Edward Lipiński. OLA 22. Leuven: Peeters, 1987.

Vermeylen, Jacques. *Du prophète Isaïe à l'apocalyptique: Isaïe, I–XXXV, miroir d'un demi-millénaire d'expérience religieuse en Israël.* Vol. 1. EBib. Paris: Gabalda, 1977.

——. *Du prophète Isaïe à l'apocalyptique: Isaïe, I–XXXV, miroir d'un demi-millénaire d'expérience religieuse en Israël.* Vol. 2. EBib. Paris: Gabalda, 1978.

Vincent, Louis-Hugues. *Underground Jerusalem: Discoveries on the Hill of Ophel (1909–11).* Translated from the French. London: Horace Cox, 1911.

Vitringa, Campegius. *Commentarius in librum prophetarum Jesaiae. Pars Prior et Pars Posterior. Editio Nova.* Basel, 1732.

Vogels, Walter. "The Cultic and Civil Calendars of the Fourth Day of Creation (Gen 1,14b)." *SJOT* 11/2 (1997): 163–80.

Volz, Paul. *Jesaja*, II. KAT 9.2. Leipzig: Deichertsche, 1932.

Vööbus, Arthur. *The Pentateuch in the Version of the Syro-Hexapla: A Facsimile Edition of a Midyat Manuscript discovered 1964.* CSCO 369; Subsidia 45. Leuven: Peeters, 1976.

Waard, Jan de. "Ruth." Pages *5–*7, *25–26, *37–38*, *51–56*, 3–10 in *Megilloth. BHQ* 18. Stuttgart: Deutsche Bibelgesellschaft, 2004.

Wade, Martha L. *Consistency of Translation Techniques in the Tabernacle Accounts of Exodus in the Old Greek.* SBLSCS 49. Leiden: Brill, 2003.

Wagner, Siegfried. *Franz Delitzsch: Leben und Werk.* TVG Monografien. Giessen: Brunnen, 1978.

Wagner, Thomas. *Gottes Herrschaft: Eine Analyse der Denkschrift (Jes 6,1–9,6).* VTSup 108. Leiden: Brill, 2006.

Walsh, Jerome T. "2 Kings 17: The Deuteronomist and the Samaritans." Pages 315–23 in *Past, Present, Future: The Deuteronomistic History and the Prophets.* Edited by Johannes Cornelis de Moor and Harry F. van Rooy. *OtSt* 44. Leiden: Brill, 2000.

Waltke, Bruce K. and Michael O'Connor. *An Introduction to Biblical Hebrew Syntax.* Winona Lake, Ind.: Eisenbrauns, 1990.

Waltke, Bruce K. *Genesis.* Grand Rapids: Zondervan, 2001.

Walton, John. *Genesis.* NIVAC. Grand Rapids: Zondervan, 2001.

Watson, Wilfred G. E. *Classical Hebrew Poetry: A Guide to Its Techniques.* JSOTSup 26. Sheffield: JSOT, 1984.

Watts, John D. W. *Isaiah 1–33.* WBC 24. Rev. ed. Nashville: Thomas Nelson, 2005.

Wechter, Pinchas. *Ibn Barūn's Arabic works on Hebrew Grammar and Lexicography.* Philadelphia: Dropsie College, 1964.

Wehr, Hans. *A Dictionary of Modern Written Arabic.* Edited by J. Milton Cowan. Ithaca, N.Y.: Spoken Language Services, 1994.

Weinfeld, Moshe. *Deuteronomy and the Deuteronomistic School.* Oxford: Clarendon, 1972.

——. "Josiah." Page 288 in vol. 10 of *EncJud.* Edited by Cecil Roth and Geoffrey Wigoder. 16 vols. Jerusalem: Keter Publishing House, 1972. (Page 457 in vol. 11 *EncJud.* 2nd ed. Edited by Fred Skolnik. 22 vols. Macmillan Reference U.S.A., 2006.)

Weippert, Helga. "Die 'deuteronomistischen' Beurteilungen der Könige von Israel und Juda und das Problem der Redaktion der Königsbücher." *Bib* 53 (1972): 301–39.

——. " 'Der Ort, den Jahwe erwählen wird, um dort seinen Namen wohnen zu lassen': Die Geschichte einer alttestamentlichen Formel." *BZ* 24 (1980): 76–94.

Weippert, Manfred. "The Relations of the States East of the Jordan with the Mesopotamian Powers during the First Millennium BC." *Studies in the History and Archaeology of Jordan* 3 (1987): 97–105.

Weissert, David. "Alexandrian Analogical Word-analysis and Septuagint Translation Techniques. A case study of חול–חיל–חלל." *Textus* 8 (1973): 31–44.

Weitzman, Michael P. "The Reliability of Retroversions of the Three from the Syrohexapla: A Pilot Study in Hosea." Pages 317–59 in *Origen's Hexapla and Fragments: Papers presented at the Rich Seminar on the Hexapla, Oxford Centre for Hebrew and Jewish Studies,*

*25th July–3rd August 1994*. Edited by Alison Salvesen. TSAJ 58. Tubingen: Mohr Siebeck, 1998.
——. *The Syriac Version of the Old Testament: An Introduction*. University of Cambridge Oriental Publications 56. Cambridge: Cambridge University Press, 1999.
Wellhausen, Julius. *De gentibus et familiis Judaeis*. Göttingen: Dieterich, 1870. Translated by Lizah Ulman and Gershon Galil. Jerusalem: Dinur, 1985. (Hebrew)
——. *Die Composition des Hexateuchs und der historischen Bücher des Alten Testament*. 2nd ed. Berlin: de Gruyter, 1889.
——. *Die kleinen Propheten übersetzt und erklärt*. 3rd ed. Berlin: G. Reiner, 1898.
——. *Einleitung in die drei ersten Evangelien*. Berlin: Reimer, 1905.
——. *Einleitung in die drei ersten Evangelien*. 2nd ed. Berlin: Reimer, 1911.
——. *Prolegomena to the History of Israel*. Atlanta, Ga.: Scholars, 1994. Reprint of *Prolegomena to the History of Israel*. Translated by. J. Sutherland Black and Allan Menzies, with preface by W. Robertson Smith. Edinburgh: Adam & Charles Black, 1885. Translation of *Prolegomena zur Geschichte Israels*. 2nd ed. Berlin: G. Reimer, 1883.
Wells, Bruce. "The Covenant Code and Near Eastern Legal Traditions." *Maarav* 13 (2006): 85–118.
Wells, Roy D. " 'Isaiah' as an Exponent of Torah: Isaiah 56.1–8." Pages 140–55 in *New Visions of Isaiah*. Edited by Roy F. Melugin and Marvin A. Sweeney. JSOTSup 214. Sheffield: Sheffield Academic, 1996.
Wenham, Gordon J. *Genesis 1–15*. WBC 1. Waco, Tex.: Word Books, 1987.
Werner, Wolfgang. "Vom Prophetenwort zur Prophetentheologie. Ein redaktionsgeschichtlicher Versuch zu Jes 6,1–8,16." *BZ* 29 (1985): 1–30.
Wessely, Charles. "Un nouveau fragment de la version grecque du Vieux Testament par Aquila." Pages 224–29 in *Mélanges offerts à M. Émile Chatelain*. Edited by Émile Chatelain. Paris: A. Champion, 1910.
Westenholz, Joan Goodnick. *Legends of the Kings of Akkade*. Mesopotamian Civilizations 7. Winona Lake, Ind.: Eisenbrauns, 1997.
Westermann, Claus. *Das Buch Jesaja: Kapitel 40–66*. ATD 19. Göttingen: Vandenhoeck & Ruprecht, 1966.
——. *Isaiah 40–66*. Translated by David M. G. Stalker. Philadelphia: Westminster, 1969.
——. *Genesis 1–11*. Translated by John J. Scullion. Minneapolis: Augsburg, 1984.
Wevers, John W. *Notes on the Greek Text of Genesis*. SBLSCS 35. Atlanta: Scholars, 1993.
——. *Notes on the Greek Text of Exodus*. SBLSCS 30. Atlanta: Scholars, 1993.
White, Sidnie A. "A Comparison of the 'A' and 'B' Manuscripts of the Damascus Document." *Revue de Qumrân* 48 (1987): 537–53.
Whitekettle, Richard. "Where the Wild Things Are: Primary Level Taxa in Israelite Zoological Thought." *JSOT* 93 (2001): 17–37.
Whitelam, Keith. *The Just King*. JSOTSup 12. Sheffield: Sheffield Academic, 1979.
Whitney Jr., K. William. *Creation and Chaos in the Primeval Era and the Eschaton*. Grand Rapids: Eerdmans, 2006.
Whybray, R. Norman. *Isaiah 40–66*. NCB. London: Marshall, Morgan & Scott, 1975.
Wiese, Christian. *Wissenschaft des Judentums und protestantische Theologie im wilhelminischen Deutschland—Ein Schrei ins Leere?* Schriftenreihe des Leo Baeck-Instituts 61. Tübingen: Mohr Siebeck, 1999.
Wildberger, Hans. *Jesaja*. BKAT 10. Neukirchen-Vluyn: Neukirchener Verlag, 1971.
——. *Jesaja*. 2nd ed. BKAT X/1. Neukirchen-Vluyn: Neukirchener Verlag, 1980.
——. *Isaiah 1–12: A Continental Commentary*. Translated by Thomas H. Trapp. Minneapolis: Fortress, 1991.
——. *Jesaja Kapitel 13–27*. BKAT 10/2. Neukirchen-Vluyn: Neukirchener Verlag, 1978.
——. *Isaiah 13–27*. Translated by Thomas H. Trapp. CC. Minneapolis: Fortress, 1997.
——. *Isaiah 28–39*. Translated by Thomas H. Trapp. Minneapolis: Fortress, 2002.
Wilkinson, Bruce. *The Prayer of Jabez: Breaking Through To The Blessed Life*. Sisters, OR: Multnomah, 2000.

Willi, Thomas. *Chronik 1–10*. BKAT 24. Neukirchen: Neukirchener Verlag, 2009.

Williams, Ronald J. *Williams' Hebrew Syntax*. Rev. and enl. 3rd ed. by John C. Beckman. Toronto: University of Toronto Press, 2007.

Williamson, H. G. M. *Israel in the Books of Chronicles*. Cambridge: Cambridge University Press, 1977.

——. "Sources and Redaction in the Chronicler's Genealogy of Judah." *JBL* 98 (1979): 351–59.

——. "The Origins of the Twenty-Four Priestly Courses: A Study of 1 Chronicles 23–27." Pages 251–68 in *Studies in the Historical Books of the Old Testament*. Edited by John A. Emerton. VTSup 30. Leiden: Brill, 1979.

——. *1 and 2 Chronicles*. NCB. London/Grand Rapids: Marshall, Morgan & Scott/Eerdmans, 1982.

——. "The Composition of Ezra i–vi." *JTS* 34 (1983): 1–30.

——. *Ezra, Nehemiah*. WBC 16. Waco: Word Books, 1985.

——. *Ezra and Nehemiah*. OTG. Sheffield: JSOT, 1987.

——. "History." Pages 25–38 in *It Is Written: Scripture Citing Scripture: Essays in Honour of Barnabas Lindars, SSF*. Edited by Don A. Carson and H. G. M. Williamson. Cambridge: Cambridge University Press, 1988.

——. "The Concept of Israel in Transition." Pages 141–61 in *The World of Ancient Israel*. Edited by Ronald E. Clements. Cambridge: Cambridge University Press, 1989.

——. *The Book Called Isaiah: Deutero-Isaiah's Role in Composition and Redaction*. Oxford: Clarendon, 1994.

——. "Isaiah 6,13 and 1,29–31." Pages 119–28 in *Studies in the Book of Isaiah. Festschrift Willem A. M. Beuken*. Edited by Jacques van Ruiten and Marc Vervenne. BETL 132. Leuven: Peeters, 1997.

——. *Variations on a Theme: King, Messiah and Servant in the Book of Isaiah*. Carlisle: Paternoster, 1998. (Didsbury Lectures, 1997).

——. "Isaiah and the Holy One of Israel." Pages 22–38 in *Biblical Hebrew, Biblical Texts: Essays in Memory of Michael P. Weitzman*. Edited by Ada Rapoport-Albert and Gillian Greenberg. JSOTSup 333. Sheffield: Sheffield Academic, 2001.

——. "Temple and Worship in Isaiah 6." Pages 123–44 in *Temple and Worship in Biblical Israel*. Edited by John Day. London: T&T Clark, 2005.

——. *Commentary on Isaiah 1–5*. Vol. 1 of *A Critical and Exegetical Commentary on Isaiah 1–27*. ICC. London: T&T Clark, 2006.

——. "On Getting Carried Away with the Infinitive Construct of נשא." Pages 357*–367* in *Shai le-Sara Japhet: Studies in the Bible, its Exegesis and its Language*. Edited by Moshe Bar-Asher, Dalit Rom-Shiloni, Emanuel Tov, and Nili Wazana; Jerusalem: Bialik Institute, 2007. (Hebrew)

——. *Holy, Holy, Holy: The Story of a Liturgical Formula*. Julius-Wellhausen-Vorlesung 1. Berlin: de Gruyter, 2008.

——. "The Waters of Shiloah (Isaiah 8:5–8)." Pages 331–43 in *The Fire Signals of Lachish: Studies in the Archaeology and History of Israel in the Late Bronze Age, Iron Age, and Persian Period in Honor of David Ussishkin*. Edited by Israel Finkelstein and Nadav Na'aman. Winona Lake, Ind.: Eisenbrauns, 2011.

Wilson, Alfred M. "The Particle את in Hebrew." *Hebraica* 6/2–3 (1889–1890): 139–50, 212–24.

Wilson, Robert R. *Genealogy and History in the Biblical World*. New Haven, Yale University Press, 1977.

Wiseman, Donald J. *Chronicles of Chaldean Kings (626–556 BC) in the British Museum*. London: The British Museum, 1956. Repr., London: The British Museum, 1961.

——. *Nebuchadrezzar and Babylon*. The Schweich Lectures of the British Academy, 1983. Oxford: Oxford University Press, 1985.

Wissmann, F. Blanco. *"Er tat das Rechte…" Beurteilungskriterien und Deuteronomismus in 1 Kön 12–2 Kön 25*. ATANT 93. Zürich: Theologischer Verlag Zürich, 2008.

Wolff, Hans W. *Hosea*. Hermeneia: A Critical and Historical Commentary on the Bible. Philadelphia: Augsburg Fortress, 1974.

Wong, Gordon C. I. "Faith and Works in Isaiah XXX 15." *VT* 47 (1997): 236–46.

Wright, David P. "The Laws of Hammurabi as a Source for the Covenant Collections (Exodus 20:23–23:19)." *Maarav* 10 (2003): 11–87.

——. "The Laws of Hammurabi and the Covenant Code: A Response to Bruce Wells." *Maarav* 13 (2006): 211–60.

——. *Inventing God's Law: How the Covenant Code of the Bible Used and Revised the Laws of Hammurabi*. Oxford: Oxford University Press, 2009.

Wright, Jacob L. *Rebuilding Identity: The Nehemiah Memoir and its Earliest Readers*. BZAW. Berlin: de Gruyter, 2004.

——. "Ezra." Pages 263–70 in *The New Interpreter's Bible: One Volume Commentary*. Edited by Beverly Roberts Gaventa and David Petersen. Nashville: Abingdon, 2010.

Würthwein, Ernst. "Amos-Studien." *ZAW* 62 (1950): 10–52.

——. *Die Bücher der Könige. 1 Kön. 17–2 Kön. 25*. ATD 11,2. Göttingen: Vandenhoeck & Ruprecht, 1984.

Young, Ian, Robert Rezetko and Martin Ehrensvärd. *Linguistic Dating of Biblical Texts. Volume 1: An Introduction to Approaches and Problems.* London & Oakville: Equinox Publishing Ltd., 2008.

Younger, K. Lawson. "The Siloam Tunnel Inscription: An Integrated Reading." *UF* 26 (1994): 543–56.

——. "The Fall of Samaria in Light of Recent Research." *CBQ* 61 (1999): 461–82.

——. "The Repopulation of Samaria (2 Kgs 17:24, 27–31) in Light of Recent Study." Pages 254–80 in *The Future of Biblical Archaeology*. Edited by James K. Hoffmeier and Alan Millard. Grand Rapids, Eerdmans, 2004.

Zadok, Ran. "Phoenicians, Philistines, and Moabites in Mesopotamia." *BASOR* 230 (1978): 57–65.

——. *Geographical Names According to New and Late-Babylonian Texts*. TAVO 7. Répertoire géographique des textes cunéiformes 8. Wiesbaden: Otto Harrassowitz, 1985.

——. "Foreigners and Foreign Linguistic Material in Mesopotamia and Egypt." Pages 431–47 in *Immigration and Emigration Within the Ancient Near East. Festschrift E. Lipiński*. Edited by Karel van Lerberghe and Antoon Schoors. OLA 65. Leuven: Peeters, 1995.

Zakovitch, Yair. *Inner-biblical and Extra-biblical Midrash and the Relationship between Them*. Tel-Aviv: Am Oved, 2009.

Zayadine, Fawzi. "Le relief néo-babylonien à Sela' près de Tafileh: Interpretation historique." *Syria* 76 (1999): 83–90.

Zenger, Erich. "Der Psalter als Buch." Pages 1–57 in *Der Psalter in Judentum und Christentum*. Herders Biblische Studien 18. Freiburg: Herder, 1998.

Ziegler, Joseph. *Untersuchungen zur Septuaginta des Buches Isaias*. ATA 12/3. Münster: Aschendorff, 1934.

——. *Beiträge zum griechischen Dodekapropheton*. Göttingen: Vandenhoeck & Ruprecht, 1943.

——. *Septuaginta; Vetus Testamentum Graecum, auctoritate Societatis Litterarum Gottingensis editum, Vol. 13 Duodecim prophetae*. Göttingen: Vandenhoeck & Ruprecht, 1943.

——. *Eusebius Werke, Vol. 9. Der Jesajakommentar*. GCS. Berlin: Akademie Verlag, 1975.

Zimmerli, Walther. *Ezekiel*. 2 vols. Hermeneia: A Critical and Historical Commentary on the Bible. Philadelphia: Fortress, 1979; 1983.

Zobel, Hans-Jürgen. "יִשְׂרָאֵל; *yiśrā'ēl*." Pages 397–420 in vol. 6 of *Theological Dictionary of the Old Testament*. Edited by G. Johannes Botterweck, Helmer Ringgren, and Heinz-Josef Fabry. Translated by David E. Green and Douglas W. Stott. 8 vols. Grand Rapids: Eerdmans, 1990.

Zorell, Franz. *Lexicon hebraicum et aramaicum Veteris Testamenti*. Rome: Pontificium Institutum Biblicum, 1957.

# AUTHOR INDEX

# INDEX OF REFERENCES